THE DIARY OF

John Evelyn

By the same editor

The Writings of John Evelyn

THE DIARY OF
John Evelyn

Edited by
Guy de la Bédoyère

THE BOYDELL PRESS

First published 1995
The Boydell Press, Woodbridge

ISBN 0 85115 639 8

The Boydell Press is an imprint of Boydell & Brewer Ltd
PO Box 9, Woodbridge, Suffolk IP12 3DF, UK
and of Boydell & Brewer Inc.
PO Box 41026, Rochester, NY 14604–4126, USA

British Library Cataloguing-in-Publication Data
A catalogue record for this book is available
from the British Library

Library of Congress Cataloging-in-Publication Data applied for

The paper used in this publication meets the minimum requirements
of American National Standard for Information Sciences –
Permanence of Paper for Printed Library Materials, ANSI Z39.48–1984

Printed in Great Britain by
St Edmundsbury Press Ltd, Bury St Edmunds, Suffolk

CONTENTS

FOREWORD AND ACKNOWLEDGEMENTS

When John Evelyn (1620-1706) wrote his *Diary* he intended to record his life for the benefit of his descendants. The manuscript remained stored at his home, Wotton House in Surrey, amongst the vast heap of papers which this remarkably industrious man left at his death. It was not until 1813 that its importance was recognised when one William Upcott noticed it during a social call. He immediately alerted a Surrey antiquarian called William Bray and within five years a selection had been transcribed and published. It led directly to the first edition of Pepys's *Diary* in 1825.

Evelyn's *Diary* was extremly popular during the nineteenth century and Bray's text was adapted for numerous editions. However, restricted access to the manuscript concealed the fact that Bray's transcription was filled with errors, excisions and even additions. It was not until 1955 that a definitive version appeared after years of work by Dr Esmond de Beer, with an Oxford Standard Authors edition following in 1959. Sadly, both these editions have been out of print for some time and only a selection by John Bowle has subsequently been available, though this too is also out of print.

Ironically copies of the unsatisfactory nineteenth century *Diary* text are far more readily found in secondhand bookshops than de Beer's text in any form. In the interests of making at least some of de Beer's text available this edition has been prepared in order to issue the greater part of those sections of the *Diary* which are likely to be most of use to students of Evelyn's life, and the literature and the history of the period. Naturally there have been substantial excisions in order to reduce the massive length of the original to manageable proportions. However so far as possible these have been restricted to the diarist's lengthy accounts of his travels abroad, sermons and his brief notices which are of little value. The appearance of this edition has turned out to be particularly apposite as in February 1995 the manuscript, and all of Evelyn's other papers, were acquired by the British Library thereby ensuring their conservation and security for all time.

The selection, transcription, and typesetting have been carried out by myself using both Dr de Beer's definitive text and the original manuscript of the *Diary*. Any inadequacies and errors are therefore entirely my responsibility. Thanks are due to the Trustees of the respective estates of Major Peter Evelyn and Dr E.S. de Beer for permission to use those copyright parts of the text and editorial notes, and to Mr H.J.R. Wing, Assistant Librarian at Christ Church for making the manuscript (prior to transfer to the British Library) and other facilities available. I am also grateful to Professor John Miller for his comments, and to Richard Barber of Boydell and Brewer for his help in making this paperback edition of my selection possible.

Guy de la Bédoyère

INTRODUCTION

EVELYN'S LIFE AND CHARACTER

The *Diary* of John Evelyn is one of our principal literary sources for life and manners in the English seventeenth century. Written by a cultivated man of property and means it forms a comprehensive account of a life spent during a period of exceptional change. Evelyn lived through the Civil War, the Commonwealth, the Restoration, the reigns of Charles II and James II, the Glorious Revolution of 1688, the reigns of William III and Mary II, and the first part of the reign of Anne. He saw his country move from being one of the lesser, and least influential, states in Europe into a nation on the brink of becoming a major world power. He witnessed and participated in the growth of a reasoned and critical approach to science which paved the way for the coming of the Industrial Revolution in the century after his death.

From a human point of view Evelyn's *Diary* is a fascinating and moving record of a long life and all its experiences. Evelyn, unlike Pepys, whose *Diary* covers barely a decade, takes us from his childhood right up to a few weeks before his death. We see the transition from enthusiastic youth through marriage and family to an infirm old age when, with so many of his friends and family dead, he sensed his time had passed.

In his own time John Evelyn had a considerable personal reputation, both as a friend and associate of royalty and the famous, and also as a learned man. He was the author of a number of books on many different subjects, and translated others in Latin or French into English. He was a founding member of the Royal Society and his friends included Samuel Pepys, Robert Boyle and Christopher Wren. He was also a celebrated gardener and authority on trees. In short he was one of a vitally important and influential group of men at the centre of seventeenth century English society and learning.

Evelyn's grandfather, George Evelyn, had manufactured gunpowder during the latter part of the reign of Elizabeth I and had even enjoyed the grant of a royal monopoly. He grew extremely wealthy on the proceeds and married twice, fathering twenty four children. He was able to buy several estates in Surrey and one of these, Wotton, was inherited by Richard Evelyn, the only son of his second marriage when he died in 1603. Richard Evelyn married Elianor Standsfield and they had five children who grew to maturity, a large number by the expectations of the day. George, the eldest son, was groomed and educated to inherit the estate which he dutifully did on his father's death in 1640. Thereafter he lived a long life as a respected landowner and sat in Parliament under Charles II, and William and Mary.

The diarist was the second son, born in 1620, and in this position was able to escape much of the pressure and duty imposed on his elder brother. He spent most of his childhood with his maternal step-grandmother in Lewes. He found this a secure environment and evaded his father's plans to send him to

Eton, 'unreasonably terrified with the report of the severe discipline there'. His relaxed education only took a firmer direction when, in 1637, he was admitted into the Middle Temple in London to study law. In 1638 he went up to Balliol College at Oxford. Some of his almanacs survive in the college and they show that at this time he was, by our standards, barely literate.

As a second son Evelyn had means but no obligation to the family estate. His mother had died several years before his father and this, coupled with the gradual decline of political stability in England in the years leading up the Civil War, left Evelyn with no particular need or wish to stay at home. He seized his opportunity and embarked on what turned out to be a long, active and creative life. It began with a period of travelling on the continent, Evelyn having decided to 'absent my selfe from this ill face of things at home', preferring 'the pursute of Vanity'. He has been criticised for this, especially in view of the fact that he was, by conviction, a staunch Royalist.

But it is clear that he was not, on the whole, a man given to the active pursuit of passionate causes of any kind; at least not if doing so would involve him in taking unnecessary risks. This does not mean that he was in any sense a coward – he stayed at his post as a Commissioner for Sick and Wounded Seamen during the Plague Year without hesitation – but rather that he could see all too easily the folly of going through life driven by emotion. His most profound feelings were instead reserved for his devotion to the Protestant Church and God who, he believed, hounded sinners with an unforgiving vengeance. But even this he dealt with in a practical manner, recording sermons and his sins to appease the Almighty.

Evelyn was not then what he or his contemporaries would have described as a 'Gallant', or what we would call a 'romantic'. He had difficulty balancing his respect for Charles II along with his outrage at the decadence of the Restoration court. The drinking, gaming, and parading of mistresses were 'all dissolution' to Evelyn. When news came in January 1686 that Charles's most famous former concubine Nell Gwyn had been seen attending Catholic services, well, that was 'no greate losse to the Church.' This slightly repressed image was largely his own creation and reflected his need to present himself as a man aware of the morally correct and Christian way to behave. But Pepys recorded a social evening at Evelyn's Deptford house:

> Mr Evelyn's repeating of some verses made up of nothing but the
> various acceptations of may and can, and doing it so aptly upon
> occasion of something of that nature, and so fast, did make us all die
> almost with laughing ...[1]

So the serious side of his personality was undoubtedly balanced by a sense of humour which also occasionally reveals itself in the *Diary*.

---

[1] *Diary*, 10 September 1665.

Evelyn was fascinated by his world but he always viewed it with a sense of detachment. Although he was in many senses a man typical of the best of his age, he never identified himself irrevocably with any political group or movement. While Pepys for example refused to continue in office after the arrival of William and Mary in 1688, Evelyn was more inclined to accept the situation and viewed the tide of change with interest.

This detachment makes him all the more accessible to anyone taking an interest in his life for he seems somehow timeless. There is no doubt that Evelyn has tended to captivate the minds of those who study him. It is particularly interesting that he appears to have had exactly the same effect on some of his contemporaries. Pepys, who occasionally found him a little conceited and some of his books more than slightly boring, also made one of the most revealing observations ever made of Evelyn by one of his friends, 'he being a very ingenious man, and the more I know him, the more I love him.'[1] Much later, in 1701, Ralph Thoresby found him, 'above measure civil and courteous.'[2]

Evelyn was undoubtedly a caring and considerate man and his *Diary* shows that he loved his wife and children, and was concerned for the welfare of his servants. But he was very aware of his status, and that of others. He was invariably respectful, if not obsequious, to those whom he knew to be his betters and patronised his inferiors. The introductory sections of the various editions of his most famous book, *Sylva*, illustrate this very well. Part of the dedication to Charles II includes the passage:

> You are our Θεὸς ὑλιχὸς, *Nemorensis Rex* [God of the forest-trees,
> King of the grove], as having once your Temple, and Court too under
> that Holy Oak which you Consecrated with your Presence, and We
> celebrate with just Acknowledgement to God for your Preservation.[3]

In later editions, for example the fourth (1706), a glossary of terms was attached but with the proviso:

> let it be remember'd that I did not altogether compile this Work for the
> sake of our ordinary Rustics (meer Foresters and Wood-men) but for the
> more Ingenious; the Benefit, and Diversion of Gentlemen, and Persons
> of Quality.[4]

However so as not to disadvantage those of 'meaner Capacities' an explanation of technical terms followed. Evelyn's élitism, intellectual and social, would be regarded as unacceptable today – but such a comparison is inappropriate. By the standards of his age Evelyn stood out as a man of dignity, philanthropy and loyalty. After all it was Pepys, usually regarded as so

---

[1] *Diary*, 29 April 1666.
[2] De Beer, I, 39.
[3] *Sylva*, 1664, *Dedication*.
[4] *Silva* (E changed the spelling), 1706, *Advertisement*.

much more a man for all ages, who received bribes, deceived his wife and hit his servants.

Evelyn was intensely conscious of his own need for self-expression and he also clearly had an aversion to anonymity. This does not mean that he was characterised by an overbearing egocentricity, but it did lead to his literary outpourings and also contributed to the writing of the *Diary*. Unlike Pepys who wrote only for himself and recorded everything which happened, however sordid his part may have been, Evelyn wrote a more formal diary which avoided such revelations. Instead he reported events in a much more bald and factual manner, only occasionally revealing his deeper feelings. He seems to have felt an obligation to act as a conscientious reporter of events, personal or public. Evelyn also wished to present himself as a pious, God-fearing man (which of course he was) and therefore made copious notes of sermons, abbreviated details of which appear in increasing numbers towards the end of the *Diary*. When he recorded family tragedies he tended to describe only his personal feelings, while references to his wife's reactions are rare and brief. This is especiallly the case with the descriptions of the deaths of his eldest son and daughter in 1658 and 1685 respectively. Evelyn was therefore, if not self-obsessed, certainly self-absorbed.

After a visit to Holland and the Spanish Netherlands in 1641 a lingering, and well-timed, sense of duty propelled him to turn up at the Battle of Brentford in November 1642 just in time to witness the Royalist retreat. Rather than participate in this ignominious withdrawal Evelyn saw a much more sensible alternative. To have become involved in the fighting, he argued, would simply have been to help expose the Wotton estate to Parliamentary depradations 'without any advantage to his Majestie'. Equally it would not have fitted in with his plans to satisfy further his curiosity for new sights and impressions abroad which, we may be sure, he would have indulged whether there had been a civil war or not. After a few months making preparations, and exercising his tastes for landscaping at Wotton, he left England in late 1643 and spent the next few years exploring France, Italy and Switzerland. In 1646 he contracted smallpox in Switzerland but after a period of recuperation, returned to France later that year and came into contact with the exiled court of Charles II, meeting the king's ambassador to France, Sir Richard Browne. In 1647 he married Browne's daughter Mary.

Browne had no son living and Evelyn easily filled the vacant place. Their libraries were combined and many of their books were bound in a uniform style carrying their personal monograms, arms and mottos. In 1649 Evelyn returned to England without his wife in order to see about finding somewhere to live, having decided to accept the practical reality of the Commonwealth and to live with it. Eventually he accepted Browne's offer to sell Evelyn his estate at Sayes Court, Deptford. At the time the house was a run-down Elizabethan manor-house adjacent to the naval dockyards. He decided that this unsalubrious location was compensated for by the available land and its convenient, but not excessive, proximity to London. He bought the estate and returned to France in July 1649. Apart from a brief visit to England in the summer of 1650 this was his last journey abroad and he came back to England for good in early 1652.

In the summer of 1652 he was followed by his wife, pregnant with their first son and the Evelyns became firmly settled at Sayes Court where they lived until 1694. Evelyn himself entered his most productive phase of writing while at the same time laying out the gardens of Sayes Court, and virtually rebuilding the whole house, at considerable expense. He seems always to have been close to great events of the time, moving nearer to the centre stage once Charles II was restored to the throne in 1660. But by then he and Mary had already suffered the loss of their eldest son, Richard. By the age of five he had turned out to be a gifted and captivating child but a series of fits and a fever in the midst of an appalling winter carried him off in January 1658. Evelyn and his wife were reduced to despair. He wrote to Browne on 14 February describing it as 'an accident that has made so great a breach in all my contentments, as I do never hope to see repaired'. The following morning their fourth son George, born the previous June, died too. Their second son had died as an infant some years before and only the third, John, survived to adulthood. The empassioned account of Richard's life and death belies our belief that parents in an age of chronic infant mortality were better equipped to cope with such a loss and serves as a rare instance of Evelyn revealing his inner feelings.

Evelyn found solace both in writing and in the excitement of the collapse of the Commonwealth. His most celebrated works were produced in the early years of the reign of Charles II. He was best known in his own lifetime, and during the eighteenth century, for his book *Sylva, or a Discourse of Forest Trees*, a work produced in 1664 at the request of the Royal Society following his delivery of a paper on the subject in 1662. The idea was to draw attention to the damage done to England's wooded estates during the Interregnum and to encourage reforestation. *Sylva* was one of his most substantial works and he prepared three further editions in his lifetime. In the same year he produced a lavish translation of Fréart's *The Parallel of the Antient Architecture*, easily his most attractive book. Others produced in the 1650s and 60s included various tracts on fashion and manners (*Tyrannus, A Character of England*), pollution (*Fumifugium*), art (*Sculptura*), and gardening (*Kalendarium Hortense*), and various translations.

Evelyn's choice of themes reflect the age. Like many educated men of his time he was intrigued by the new developments which were taking place in the fields of scientific learning and academic study. Unencumbered by our modern obsession with exclusive disciplines, he had no hesitation in participating in or writing about anything which interested him. In 1661, for example, he produced a report on Tenerife despite never having been there. Although the presentation of experiments and novelties, and Evelyn's catholic choice of subjects, seem haphazard to us, this was a time when many classifications which we take for granted were being built up. It was only by exploring everything that a more rational way of understanding science and nature could be developed.

In his *Diary* Evelyn recorded details of freaks on display at fairs, whales washed up on the Greenwich foreshore and blood-curdling tales of surgical operations. He was thought perfectly suitable to take part in a survey of old St Paul's in 1666, alongside Christopher Wren. He discovered the wood-carver Grinling Gibbons and presented him to Charles II. His garden at Sayes Court was a celebrated sight of the road to Kent. He served as a Commissioner for sick and wounded seamen during the Dutch Wars and was instrumental in founding Greenwich Hospital. He attended meetings of the Royal Society and watched experiments which might be concerned with anything from astronomy to a microscopic examination of worms.

By the 1670s Evelyn's literary output began to wane. His work as a Commissioner for the sick seamen was time-consuming, while he was now over fifty. Moreover he, like many of his enlightened friends, had been demoralised by the disappointed hopes of the Restoration. Charles II was an engaging man but Evelyn found him ineffectual and far too interested in enjoying himself to be concerned with real problems. For example, the opportunities afforded by the Great Fire of London in 1666 had been wasted almost as soon as they appeared. Evelyn had been one of the first to present the King with a plan to rebuild the City as a better place in which to live. His tracts *Fumifugium*, and *A Character of England* had already pleaded the cause of removing the pollutive industries to more distant locations. Like the plan for the new London, *Fumifugium* had been received with enthusiasm but was quietly forgotten, though it is almost the only one of Evelyn's works which has been frequently reproduced in modern times. In 1674 he produced *Navigation and Commerce* which was concerned with the causes and consequences of the three Dutch Wars. It was intended to act as a preface to a full history of the conflict. However the Third Dutch War had ended that year and in the interests of peace the plan for the full history was abandoned, and unsold copies of the preface were recalled.

Around the same time Evelyn became involved in a curious relationship. It has been seen as the most controversial phase of his whole life. Whatever the truth it is clear that it was the only time that Evelyn may have been distracted from common sense by emotion. The relationship concerned a young woman called Margaret Blagge, born in 1652. Evelyn first met her in 1669 when she was a maid of honour at court. However it was not until 1672 that they entered into a pact of 'inviolable' friendship whereby Evelyn was to become her spiritual guide and to act as a guardian of her interests. They met regularly to eat and pray together. It was an emphatically platonic relationship but Margaret Blagge's intense pursuit of devotional activities might now be considered possible evidence of a slightly unbalanced mind. Evelyn appears to have had honourable intentions but it is equally possible that he expressed in his power over her religious life, sexual feelings that another might have expressed in a more physical way. Although he discouraged her relationship with Sidney Godolphin, whom she secretly married in 1675, Evelyn certainly convinced himself that he had Margaret's best interests at heart as he described in his *Life of Mrs Godolphin*, not published until 1847, 'Freindshipp is beyond all relationships of flesh and blood, because it is less materiall.'[1]

The most revealing facet of the whole episode is that Margaret married Sidney Godolphin without telling Evelyn. Evelyn, not unnaturally, felt his trust had been betrayed but it is very interesting that she avoided telling him her plans. It is difficult not to form the conclusion that she somehow feared his power over her. Margaret had been born at the same time as his eldest son Richard and this somehow seems to have contributed to the attachment – Evelyn refers to the connection in his *Life of Mrs. Godolphin*. It is also interesting that Evelyn's second daughter, Elizabeth, did exactly the same as Margaret, ten years later, in 1685. She eloped with the nephew of a Surveyor of the Navy and married him. Her appalled father disowned and disinherited her. When Elizabeth contracted smallpox a few weeks later he wrote to his wife making it clear he thought the illness God's judgement.[2]

Elizabeth died on 29 August 1685. Both she and Margaret Godolphin may have found Evelyn an overpowering and possessive figure whom they felt it necessary to deceive, knowing they would never have convinced him that they had needs beyond him. If this was true Evelyn would have been mortified, had he known. Margaret Blagge's marriage was short for she died in 1678 following the birth of her son. Her husband was so distraught that Evelyn was left to sort out her affairs and even the arrangements to transport her body to the Godolphin church in Cornwall. What Mary Evelyn's feelings were can only be guessed at but it is difficult to believe that the esteemed Mr Evelyn's behaviour did not provoke at least a little gossip behind closed doors.

During the reign of James II (1685-88) Evelyn reached his highest official post as a Commissioner of the Privy Seal, despite his reservations about the new king's attitude to the Protestant church. Evelyn avoided having to apply the privy seal to documents that troubled his conscience by not turning up but James's reign was over sufficiently quickly for this not to become ever a major personal issue. The new regime of William and Mary of Orange was preferable to Evelyn simply because there was less abuse of royal privilege and Protestantism was once more in the ascendant.

In the latter part of his life Evelyn became much more preoccupied with ensuring the stability and security of the family, though he found time to be involved in the building of Greenwich Hospital. In the *Diary* historical events are recorded more often as paraphrases of public notices rather than the eyewitness accounts of the 1660s and 1670s. Sermons, the estate at Wotton

---

[1] *Life of Mrs Godolphin*, 1847, 37.
[2] See below, 22 August 1685.

and his grandchildren become dominant themes. Mary had borne altogether eight children, as well as suffering several miscarriages. But only the youngest, Susanna, outlived them. In fact all their three daughters survived childhood but the elder two, Mary, and Elizabeth, had died within months of each other in 1685 of smallpox at the ages of 19 and 17 respectively. Susanna married one William Draper in 1693 and produced several children. In 1694 John and Mary moved to Wotton to live with his brother George at the latter's request. The situation was not entirely satisfactory for Evelyn preferred to be closer to the centre of affairs, and as a result used his son's house in Dover Street in London while he was away in Ireland acting as a commissioner for the Irish revenue from 1692. Sayes Court was let to a series of tenants, one of whom was Peter the Great of Russia, in England to study ship-building. The 'Tsar of Muscovy's' only achievement as far as Evelyn was concerned was the destruction of the garden he had spent decades nurturing and cultivating.

Evelyn's son John had never been a healthy individual and he came back to England in 1696, eventually dying in 1699 at the age of 44. Evelyn does not record the illness in detail but it seems evident that his son was profoundly depressed and had been for some time. This may have been a clinical condition expressed in physical deterioration and susceptibility to infection. Fortunately for the diarist he left a son, also called John but usually known as Jack. He became the most important person in John Evelyn's later life as the only living descendant by the direct male line. George's son had died in 1691 leaving George with only a daughter and grand-daughters. This became the occasion of a family dispute when the husband of one of George's grand-daughters sought to force a revised settlement of the Wotton estate. A new agreement was reached increasing the amount of the estate available to settle on George's female offspring. George himself died in late 1699 and the Wotton estate accordingly passed to Evelyn who now concentrated his efforts on making sure his grandson was married and employed. The solution lay through the auspices of Sidney, now Baron, Godolphin, for some years now Evelyn's patron. Godolphin, as Lord Treasurer, found a position for young Jack as a Treasurer for the Revenue and subsequently promoted him to act as a Commissioner of the Prizes. In the meantime a marriage settlement was arranged with Godolphin's niece Ann Boscawen, financed with the assistance of William Draper who provided funds for a mortgage on the Wotton estate.

Evelyn's writings in later years were very limited, the principal work being a study of coins and medals called *Numismata* published in 1697. However it was not received with great enthusiasm largely because of the many typographical errors it contained and its rambling prose. Evelyn also prepared new editions of *Sylva* and the *Parallel of the Antient Architecture*.

In his closing years Evelyn became more and more subjected to bouts of ill-health characterised by constipation and kidney trouble. However he found time to begin his revision of the *Diary* in 1700 and also to compose a short book of advice on running an estate for his grandson. Jack was safely married by late 1705 so that when he died in 1706 at his house in Dover Street, London, Evelyn must have felt confident about the future of his family and estate. Mary Evelyn died three years later. Both were buried at Wotton church.

THE TEXT OF THE DIARY

Evelyn called his *Diary* the *Kalendarium, My Journal &c.* It survives today with the rest of his papers in the British Library. Evelyn wrote in a scrawling longhand which became progressively cramped, and filled more of the paper, eventually crossing the margins. While this is occasionally difficult to read there is usually no need to restore style or tense which has had to be done by all those responsible for transcribing Samuel Pepys's shorthand *Diary*. Problems arise from Evelyn's abbreviations, haphazard spellings (typical for the period), and his occasional errors or inconsistencies.

Evelyn used a blank almanac evidently acquired for the express purpose of containing his *Diary*. There are more than 730 pages measuring 23.1 by 15.5cm. The last nine years are covered on single sheets contained in a separate paper cover. De Beer observed that it is clear both from the content, and the style of writing that this was not a diary which was written up on a daily or even weekly basis. Instead it is essentially a chronological series of memoirs written up in hindsight at various different times of the diarist's life. Various amendments appear throughout the document, either adding passages, or words, or sometimes deleting sections.

Evelyn relied on notes to write up his *Diary*, and even refers to the date on which he started making them (1631). These, with very few exceptions preserved from his student days at Balliol, do not survive. For his travels in Europe he embellished his notes with details derived from contemporary travel books. In his later life he also included information taken from newspapers. It appears that he wrote the opening part of the *Diary*, up to about 1644, somewhere around 1660. Why he should have stopped here is unknown but with the return of his wife's family from France, as well as his own increasingly prolific literary outpourings, he may simply have not had enough time. He did not resume the text for about twenty years, finally catching up with himself about the year 1684. Thereafter the *Diary* became more of a true diary. By 1697 the almanac was full and he continued on loose sheets, eventually beginning to re-write the whole work in 1700 in a new volume called the *De Vita Propria*, literally 'concerning one's own life'. This seems to have been written more or less about the same time but only covers his early life up to 1644. It provides valuable additional detail for certain passages in the *Kalendarium*.

THE PUBLICATION OF THE DIARY AND EVELYN'S REPUTATION

In 1818 the *Kalendarium* was published in edited form by a Surrey antiquarian called William Bray with the assistance of an associate called William Upcott.

Upcott had discovered the manuscript on a social call to the widow of Sir Frederick Evelyn, the diarist's great-great-grandson, Mary, Lady Evelyn, at the Wotton family seat in 1813. Upcott was then serving as assistant librarian at the London Institution at 8 Old Jewry, the former office of Evelyn's bankers Clayton and Morris. Some letters from Evelyn to the bankers have recently emerged. They were probably found in the building by Upcott, who collected autographs, and almost certainly led to his visit to Wotton.

As a young man Bray had known the diarist's grandson Sir John Evelyn, who died in 1763. The *Diary* was clearly well-known to the family for Lady Evelyn knew exactly what it was, 'Bless me if here isn't old Sylva's Diary...', she is reported to have exclaimed. Sir John Evelyn had also written a brief diary in a series of notebooks now stored amongst the family papers and we can probably assume that he had modelled it on his grandfather's, part of which he had copied out. Lady Evelyn had little respect for the innumerable bundles of letters, notes and papers, using them for dress-patterns and general scrap paper.

The publication of the *Diary* was successful, leading directly to the publication of Pepys's *Diary* a few years later, and was followed in 1825 with a collection of Evelyn's writings edited by William Upcott. The *Diary* went through a number of editions in the nineteenth and early twentieth centuries, despite the fact that Bray's transcription was inaccurate containing mistakes, substitutions, omissions and additions. Bray was not deliberately negligent, rather he was interested in creating an edition which was easily readable, accessible and respectful to Evelyn's popular reputation as a man of unassailable virtue. As such the *Diary*'s publication helped promote Evelyn as a kind of idealised proto-Victorian. Upcott described Evelyn as, 'The amiable, accomplished, and worthy Patriot and Philosopher' and 'the most perfect model of what an English gentleman should be: who living was an example of public and private virtue...'[1]

The appearance of Evelyn's unpublished *Life of Mrs Godolphin* in 1847, which described his relationship with Mrs Godolphin as one based purely on a mutual interest in religion and devotional practices, reinforced this image. Anything which might have diminished Evelyn in the eyes of an admirer was left out of the published *Diary*. His tart comments on the disposability of the Duchess of Norfolk are a case in point (see 9 May 1683), which Bray omitted. Yet the passage reveals Evelyn's sense of humour and gives the text a human quality normally associated exclusively with Pepys.

It was not until 1955 that Evelyn's *Diary* was published in a complete and accurate form. Transcribed and edited by Esmond S. de Beer the *Diary* fills six volumes with text, introduction, notes and index, and includes the full *De Vita Propria*. The reason for such a long delay lay in the fact that William Upcott, out of both a genuine concern for the safety of the papers, and a greed

---

[1] Upcott, W., 1825, *Miscellaneous Writings of John Evelyn*, vii, and xxiii.

for additions to his collection, had helped himself to large quantities of books and manuscripts from Wotton. He always claimed that this was with the family's permission but later members of the Evelyn family believed otherwise, especially as they had to buy some of them back at the sale of Upcott's possessions after his death. In consequence no-one was allowed access to the manuscript of the *Diary* until 1921. Even then problems with publishing and the war meant a delay of thirty four years. Despite the appearance of a single volume version of the de Beer text in 1959 the *Diary* has scarcely been available since. All of these modern versions are currently out of print.

EVELYN'S BOOKS

Austin Dobson, editor of one of the later versions of Bray's text of the *Diary*, described Evelyn's books as 'not seldom, exceedingly wearisome to read'. In them Evelyn continually resorts to embellishing his points with repetition, classical references, and lists in an effort to create a learned and authoritative image. Acceptable by the standards of his day, and even admired, Evelyn's method now seems convoluted and lacking in redeeming points of style. This is a pity because there are many instances in the *Diary* which show him to have been an observant and perceptive writer.

Despite Evelyn's significant posthumous reputation no annotated collection of his works appeared until recently. The 1825 *Miscellaneous Writings of John Evelyn* reproduced his texts more or less as published with very little comment. The preparation for my own selection, published in 1995, revealed that Evelyn was a consummate literary performer who selected and adapted material from almost anywhere. He was sometimes inaccurate and frequently derivative both in idea and content. De Beer showed that Evelyn had exhibited the same practice while writing up his accounts of his travels abroad. His books and tracts show not only what Evelyn had read but also what it was necessary for a seventeenth century virtuoso to show he had read, reflecting his motto *Omnia explorate, meliora retinete*.[1] If he made mistakes while doing so this appears to have been lost on his audience who were simply impressed at his remarkable range and prolific ouput.

Evelyn undoubtedly made a significant literary contribution to his age. His *Fumifugium* is an articulate treatise on the effects of atmospheric pollution. *A Character of England* is a witty condemnation of English society in the 1650s. *Sylva* records many techniques for the cultivation of trees that might otherwise have been lost for ever. *A Parallel of the Antient Architecture* was a translation from the French but nevertheless it made available to English architects details of classical architecture in a form which could be copied or adapted for new buildings.

---

[1] 'Prove all things, hold fast that which is best,' *Thessalonians* V.21.

BOOKS ABOUT JOHN EVELYN

The best overall introduction to John Evelyn's life is contained in Volume I of E.S. de Beer's definitive version of the *Diary*. Other reasonably modern biographies are those by John Bowle, *John Evelyn and His World* (1981); the two books by W.G. Hiscock, *John Evelyn and his Family Circle* (1955), and *John Evelyn and Mrs Godolphin* (1951). Florence Higham's short biography, *John Evelyn Esquire* (1968) is probably the most balanced and perceptive account of the diarist's life though Virginia Woolf's essay in *The Common Reader* (1925) is an interesting critique of his personality. Further details are contained in the the select bibliography. The definitive account of all Evelyn's own books is Geoffrey Keynes, *John Evelyn: a study in bibliophily & a bibliography of his writings* (Cambridge 1937, Oxford 1968). The only current edition of Evelyn's books and tracts is the present editor's *Writings of John Evelyn* (1995) and the only annotated collection ever published.

EPILOGUE

None of John Evelyn's immediate relatives or descendants ever emulated his achievements or shared his interests. Almost without exception conscientious and loyal they were content with the anonymity of family responsibilities and minor offices. However, Evelyn's great-grandson, Sir John Evelyn (1706-67), the second baronet, rose to be Clerk of the Green Cloth under George III. His great-great-grandson, Edward Venables Vernon Harcourt (1757-1847), became Archbishop of York in 1807 but the diarist remained a family phenomenon and was remembered as such.

Sayes Court in Deptford was demolished during the eighteenth century and replaced with an almshouse which was still standing in the early twentieth century. That no longer exists but part of the garden survives as Sayes Court Recreation Ground. Czar Street nearby commemorates Peter the Great's destructive tenancy in 1698. The main road running through Deptford is named Evelyn Street and close to Sayes Court is a public house called the John Evelyn, complete with a portrait of the diarist holding his *Sylva*, an honour he would not have have been flattered by. St Nicholas, Deptford, is still in use and contains a memorial to his son Richard, and his daughter Mary.

Wotton House, near Dorking, still stands and is owned by the Evelyn family though it is no longer occupied by them. On the death of Mary, Lady Evelyn, widow of Sir Frederick Evelyn, in 1817 the estate passed to collateral relatives descended from the children of Evelyn's grandfather's first wife in anticipation of the failure of the direct male line. Nevertheless there are a number of living descendants of the diarist through Susanna Draper, and his grandchildren Sir John Evelyn and Elizabeth Harcourt.

In 1992 for reasons which remain a mystery the graves of John and Mary Evelyn in Wotton church were desecrated and their remains disturbed.

A NOTE ABOUT THE TEXT

Evelyn's *Diary* is a complex document. Evelyn did not make daily entries until old age and much of the earlier part was written up from notes. Entries can vary from extensive accounts of personalities and occasions to the briefest note of dinner guests or of a sermon. The present selection is based on that transcribed by the late Dr E.S. de Beer for his 1955 edition and the reader should be in no doubt that credit is entirely due to him for making the frequently barely legible text available to a wider public. Nineteenth century editions based on William Bray's bowdlerised text are often wildly inaccurate, containing insertions, alterations, and deletions.

In order to reduce the text to manageable proportions the vast bulk of the brief, and uninformative, notices have been cut. De Beer showed that a significant proportion of his European journeys had been written up from contemporary travel books. In later life Evelyn concentrated on including lengthy accounts of sermons or writing up current events from newspapers. Most of these have been excised.

There has not been room to provide extensive notes. However, footnotes are provided at points of particular interest. The text is accompanied by an Evelyn family tree, a chronological list of major personal and public events, a list of principal personalities with biographical details, a glossary and a select index.

The text is essentially unaltered with original spelling and punctuation retained. Evelyn's marginal additions have been incorporated into the text. Unlike Pepys Evelyn wrote in longhand and confined himself to occasional and usually obvious abbreviations such as 'Lon:' for London. He used a five-pointed star, the pentangle ★, to refer to Mrs Godolphin. Translations of Latin phrases are supplied in the footnotes. The only major change is the division of the text clearly into years, months and daily entries. The original manuscript is distinguished by erratic divisions, making an unreconstructed text difficult to follow. Occasional sections have been introduced from his late revision of the first part of the *Kalendarium*, the *De Vita Propria* (see above, p. 13) or his grandson's copy of the *Kalendarium* (see below, p. 52) where they add useful information or make up a section missing from the original.

Note that for his travels abroad Evelyn used the 'New Style' Gregorian calendar, in use on the continent, which was ten days ahead of the 'Old Style' Julian calendar employed in England until 1752. He generally makes it clear when changing from one to the other (see for example 4 October 1647).

Symbols: ...   indicates where text has been cut.
            < >   word supplied/corrected (the present editor and de Beer).
            [ ]   Evelyn's marginal additions.
            { }   text from *De Vita Propria* or Sir John Evelyn's copy.

JOHN EVELYN'S FAMILY TREE

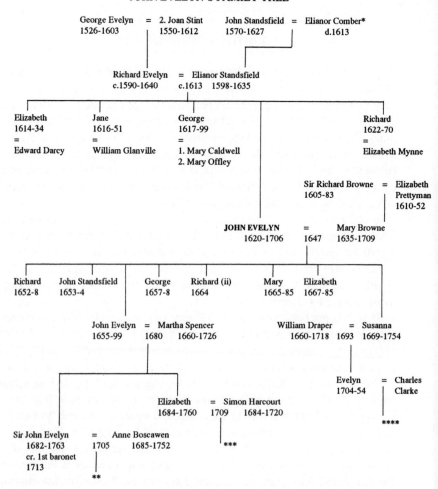

* Note that John Standsfield remarried in 1614. Standsfield's new wife, Jane Michell, despite being Evelyn's step-grandmother, is the 'grandmother' to whom he refers in his entries for 1627, 1629, and 1632 and was responsible for much of the diarist's upbringing. She herself remarried after Standsfield's death, becoming Mrs William Newton (see below, p. 22).

** Sir John Evelyn was succeeded by his son Sir John Evelyn (1706-67), 2nd bart, who was himself succeeded by his own son Sir Frederick Evelyn (1733-1812), 3rd bart. His widow possessed the Evelyn estate in 1813 when Upcott discovered the *Diary* manuscript. There were no children of this marriage and the title passed to male descendants of the first baronet's second son Charles. However the mental instability of the 4th and 5th baronets caused Mary, Lady Evelyn, to bequeath the Evelyn estates at Wotton and Deptford to descendants of the diarist's grandfather's first marriage, to Rose Williams, in spite of the fact that a number of living descendants survived through the female line.

*** There are a number of living descendants of this marriage through Elizabeth and Simon's grandson Edward Venables Vernon Harcourt (see above p. 16).

**** There are a number of living descendants of this marriage (see her epitaph below, p. 356).

My Journal &c:

I was borne about 20 minuts past two in the morning [on Tuesday], being the xxxi, and last of October Anno 1620, after my Father had been married about 7 yeares, and that my Mother had borne him 3 Children viz. Two Daughters and one sonn, about the 33d Yeare of his age, and the 23d of my Mothers.

[My Father was married 27 Jan. 1613 on Thursday, at St. Tho: Southwark. My sist: Eliz: was borne at 9 at night 28 Nov. 1614. Jane: at 4 in the mor: Feb: 16- 1615. My Bro: Geo: at 9 at Night, Wednesday 18 June 1617. My Bro: Richard 7th November 1622].

My Father, named Richard, was of a sanguine complexion, mix'd with a dash of Choler; his haire inclining to light, which (though exceeding thick) became hoary by that time he had attain'd to 30 yeares of age; it was somewhat curled towards the extremes; his beard, (which he ware a little picked, as the mode was,) of a brownish colour and so continu'd to the last, save that it was somewhat mingled with grey haires about his cheekes; which with his countenance was cleare, & fresh colour'd, his eyes extraordinary quick & piercing, an ample fore head, in summ, a very well composed visage and manly aspect: For the rest, he was but low of stature, but very strong: He was for his life so exact and temperat, that I have heard he had never in all his life been surpriz'd by excesse, being ascetic and sparing:

His Wisdome was greate, and judgement most acute; of solid discourse, affable, humble and in nothing affected; of a thriving, neate, silent, and methodical genius; discreetely severe, yet liberall upon on all just occasions both to his Children, strangers, and servants; a lover of hospitality; and in briefe, of a singular & Christian moderation in all his actions; not illiterate, nor obscure; as having continu'd Justice of Peace, and of the Quorum; and served his Country in the Charge of high-Sheriff; being (as I take it) the last dignified with that office for Sussex and Surrey together the same Yeare, before their separation: He was yet a studious decliner of Honors and Titles; being already in that esteeme with his Country, that they could have added little to him, besids their burthen; In fine, a person of that rare conversation, that upon frequent recollection, and calling to memory some Passages of his life, and discourse, I could never charge him with the least passion, or inadvertancy: [His estate esteem'd to be about £4000 per an: well wodded & full of Timber:]

{And here I must not omit to speake somthing in briefe of my Gr:father George Evelyn, the parent of 24 Children, *vzt* 16 Sonns & 8 Daughters, of which 22 were of Rosa his first Wife, and two onely of Joanna his sec<ond,> mother of my Father, Richard, & Katherin, married to Thom: Staughton in Com: Sur: who left no male Issue living: The rest of my Unkles & Aunts, surviving, had considerable Estates left and settl'd upon them, whereof one was John of God-stone, Sole Master of the Powder-Works, of which my Gr: Father had a pattent, deriv'd I think from my Greate Gr-Fa: who first is sayd to be the first who brought that Invention into England out of Flander, from whence & from Genõa we bought powder at excessive rates: And this Manufacture continued in the above-nam'd Family 'till the Civil Wars & late Rebellion; when it was taken from it, & since made a Droug by Severall: [undertakers]}.

My Mother's name was Elianor, sole daughter, & heyresse of John Standsfield Esquire of an antient, and honorable Family (though now extinct) in Shropshire; and Elianor Comber, of a good and well knowne house in Sussex. [She was borne 17. Nov: 1598 in Cliff Sussex, neere Lewes.] She was of proper personage, well timber'd, of a browne complexion; her eyes and haire of a lovely black; of constitution more inclyn'd to a religious Melancholy, or pious sadnesse; of a rare memory, and most exemplary life: for Oeconomiq prudence esteem'd one of the most conspicuous in her Country, which rendr'd her losse universaly deplor'd, both by those who knew, and such as onely heard of her. Thus much in briefe touching my Parents: nor was it reasonable I should speake lesse of them, to whom I owe so much. [oblig'd.]

The Place of my birth was Wotton, in the Parish of Wotton or Black-Heath in the County of Surrey, the then Mansion house of my Father, left him [as above] by my Grandfather, and now [afterwards] my Eldest Brothers. [In the red-Chamber having 2 windows directly towards the N and South respecting the Gardens.] It is situated in the most Sothern part of the Shire, and though in a Vally; yet realy upon a very greate rising, being on part of one of the most eminent hills in England for the prodigious prospect to be seen from its summit, though by few observed. [Lyth-hill, where one may discerne 12 or 13 shires, with part of the Sea, in a serene day.]

The house is large and antient, suitable to those hospitable times {The Building after the antient fashion of our Ancestors (tho' nothing of modish as now the manner is) is not onely very Capacious, but exceedingly Commodious, & almost intirely of Brick}, and so sweetly environ'd with those delicious streames and venerable Woods, as in the judgement of strangers, as well as Englishmen, it may be compared to one of the most tempting and pleasant seats in the Nation [for a great person & a wanton purse to render it Conspicuous:] for it has risings, Woods & Water in aboundance; not destitute of the most most noble and advantagious accommodations; being but [within little more than] 20 miles from Lond: and yet so securely placed, as if it were an hundred; from Darking 3 miles, [6 from Gilford 12 from Kingston] which serves it aboundantly with provisions as well of Land as Sea: I will say nothing of the ayre because the præeminence is universaly given to Surrey; the soile being dry and sandy; but I should speake much of the Gardens, Fountains and Groves that adorne it were they not as generaly knowne to be [amongst] the most natural & [most] magnificent that England afforded [til this later & universal luxury of the whole nation since abounding in such expenses], and which indeede gave one of the first examples to that elegancy since so much in vogue and followd, for the managing of their Waters and other elegancies of that nature: Let me add the contiguity of 5 or 6 Mannors, the Patronage of the Livings about it; and (what Themistocles pronounc'd for none of the least advantages) the good Neighborhod, all which conspire here to render it an honorable and handsom royalty {with a Royalty about it of neere 7000 Akers}, fit for the present Possessor my worthy Brother, and noble Lady, whose constant Liberality give them title both to the place, and the affections of all that know them: Thus with the Poet:

Nescio qua Natale solum dulcedine cunctos
Ducit, et immemores <non> sinit esse sui.[1]

---

[1] 'I do not know in what way the delightfulness of one's birthplace draws all men nor allows them to be forgetful of her.' Ovid, *Ex Ponto* I.iii.35-6.

I had given me the name of my Grandfather, my Mothers Father, who together with a sister of Sir Tho: Evelyns of Long Ditton, and Mr. Comber, a neere relation of my mothers were my susceptors. [I had given me two handsom pieces of very curiously wrought, & gilt plate.] The sollemnity yet (upon what accident I know not, unlesse some indisposition in me) was perform'd in the Dining rome by Parson Higham the present incumbent of the Parish, according to the forme prescribed by the then glorious CHURCH of ENGLAND.

1621-2

I was now (in reguard of my Mothers weaknesse, or rather costome of persons of quality) put to Nurse to one Peter, a neighbours wife, and tennant; of a good comely, brown & wholsome-complexion, and in a most sweete place towards the hills, flanked with wood, and refreshed with streames, the affection to which kind of solitude, I succked in with my very milke. It appears by a note of my Father that I succked till 17: Jan: 1622, or at least I came not home before.

1622-3

The very first thing that I can call to memory, and from which time forward, I began to observe, was, this yeare my Youngest Brother, being in his Nurses armes, who being then two Yeares and 9 dayes younger then my selfe, was the last child of my deare Parents: [My Bro: Richard was borne at 10 at Night: 9: Nov: Saturday: 1622.]

1624

I was not initiated into any rudiments till neere 4 yeares of age; and then one Frier taught us at the Church-porch of Wotton; and I do perfectly remember the greate talke and stirr about il Conde Gundamar, now Ambassador from Spaine; for neere about this time was the match of our Prince with the Infanta propos'd, and the Effects of that Comet 1618 still working in the prodigious revolutions now beginning in Europ, especialy in Germany, whose sad commotions sprung from the Bohemians defection from the Emperor Mathias, upon which quarell the Sweds brake in, giving umbrage to the rest of the Princes, and the whole Christian world, cause to deplore it [as never since Injoyning any perfect tranquility.]

1625

I was this yeare (being the first of the reigne of King Charles) sent by my Father to Lewes in Sussex, to be with my Grandfather, with whom I pass'd my Child-hood: This was that yeare in which the Pestilence was so Epidemical, that there dy'd in Lond. 5000 a Weeke; & I well remember the strict Watches, and examinations upon the Ways as we pass'd: and I was shortly afterwards so dangerously sick of a Feavor, that (as I have heard), the Physitians despair'd of me.

1626

My Picture was drawne in Oyle by one Chanterell, no ill Painter {& is now in Mr. Newtons Parlor at his house neere Lewes}.[1]

1627

My Grandfather Standsfield dyed this Yeare on the 5. of Feb: and I remember perfectly the solemnity at his funerall; he was buried in the Parish [Church] of All-Soules, where my Grandmother (his second Wife) erected him a pious Monument.

About this time was the Consecration of the Church of South Malling neere Lewes; [Consecrated by Bp: Field Bp: of Oxon: One Mr. Coxhall preached on ... who was afterward minister:] the building whereof was chiefely procur'd by my Grandfather, to which he left a rent Charge of £20 per annum: which likewise I pay'd, til I sold the Impropriation, and that onely because it was so: I lay'd one of the first stones at the building of that Church: [I have often wish'd, I had kept it: til I had ben able to restore it all to the Church:]

1628

It was not till the yeare 1628 that I was put to learne my Latine Rudiments, and to Write, of one Citolin, a Frenchman in Lewes.

1629

I very well remember that generall Muster, prævious to the Ile de Rès expedition; and that I was one day awaken'd in the Morning with the newes of the Duke of Buckinghams being slaine by that wretch Felton, after our disgrace before La Rochelle.

And now I tooke so extraordinary a fansy to drawing, and designing, that I could never after weane my inclinations from it, to the expense of much precious tyme which might have been more advantagiously employd:

1630

For I was now put to schoole to one Mr. Potts in the Cliff; from whom on the 7th of Jan: (being the day after Epiphany) I went to the Free-schole at Southover neere the Towne, of which one Agnes Morley had been the Foundresse, and now Edw: Snatt the Master, under whom I remain'd till I was sent to the University. [This yeare my Grandmother (with whom I sojourn'd) being married to one Mr. Newton a learned and most religious Gent: We went from the Cliff, to dwell at his house in Southover.] I do most perfectly remember the jubilie which was universaly express'd for the happy birth of the

---

[1] William Newton (c.1564-1648), E's step-grandmother's second husband. The portrait is lost.

Prince of Wales 29: May: now CHARLES THE 2D, our most gracious Sovraigne.

1631

There happen'd now an extraordinary dirth in Engl: corne bearing an excessive price: and in imitation of what I had seene my Father do, I began to observe matters more punctualy, which I did use to set downe in a blanke Almanac.

The Lord of Castelhavens arraignement for many shamefull exorbitances was now all the talke; and the birth of the Princesse Mary, afterward Princess of Orange.

1632-33

October 21 my Eldest sister was married to Edw: Darcy Esquire: who little deserved so excellent a person, a woman of so rare vertue: I was not present at the Nuptials; but I was soone after sent for into Surrey, and my Father would very willingly have weaned me from my fondnesse of my too indulgent Grand-mother, intending to have sent me to Eaton; but being neither so provident for my owne benefit, unreasonably terrified with the report of the severe discipline there; I was sent back againe to Lewes, which perversenesse of mine, I have since a thousand times deplor'd.

This was the first time, that ever my Parents had seene all their Children together in prosperity.

Whiles I was now trifling at home I saw London, where I lay one night onely, the next day dined at Bedington {the famous seate of Carie once of the Throcknortons, who first brought Orange Tres out of Spaine} much delighted with the Gardens & curiosities there, as they then appear'd to me:[1] Thence we return'd to the Lady Darcys at Sutton, thence to Wotton, and the 16 of Aug: following 1633 back to Lewes.

Nov: 3: this yeare was my Father made sherif the last (as I thinke) who served in that honorable office for Surrey & Sussex befor they were disjoyned: he had 116 Servants in Liverys, every one liveryd in greene sattin doublets; divers Gentlemen and persons of quality besides waited on him in the same garbe & habit, which at that time (when 30 or 40 was the usual retinue of the High-Sherif) was esteem'd a greate matter; nor was this out of the least vanity, that my Father exceeded (who was one of the greatest decliners of it in the World) but because he could not refuse the Civility of his friends and relations who voluntarily came themselves, or sent in their Servants: But my Father was afterwards most unjustly & spitefully molested by that jeering Judge Richardson, for repreeving the execution of a Woman, to gratifie my L: of Lindsey then Admiral; but out of this he emerged with as much honor as trouble.

---

[1] Beddington was the seat of the Carews. Sir Francis Carew (d.1611) may have planted the orange trees. It was visited in 1600 by Baron Waldstein who called it 'a most lovely garden' and was impressed by underwater images of mythical scenes (see *The Diary of Baron Waldstein*, ed. by G.W. Groos, 1981, p. 164-5). E visited the estate again in 1700 when it was decayed, see below, 20 September 1700.

1634

The King made this Yeare his progresse into Scotland, and Duke James was borne.

Decemb: 15: my deare Sister Darcy departed this life, being ariv'd to her 20th yeare of age, in vertue advanc'd beyond her yeares, or the merit of her Husband the worst of men. It was believed that the indisposition caused by her prety infant, which was borne the 2d of June before, contributed much to her destruction; as infallibly both their deaths did to my Mothers, who not long survived her.

The 24 of December I was therefore sent for home the second tyme to celebrate the obsequies of my Sister, who was interr'd in a very honorable manner, in our Dormitory, joyning to the Parish-Church, where her Monument stands.

1635

On Jan: 7th following I returned to Lewes:

July the 16, my Father being (as I understood) extreamely displeased at my Writing so ill a Character, I put my selfe to the Writing Schoole for a Moneth or two, till I had redressed that in some measure:

But my deare Mother, being now dangerously sick, I was the 3d of Sept: following sent for to Wotton; whom I found so far spent, that all human assistance failing, she in a most heavenly manner departed this Life upon the 29 of the same moneth, about 8 in the Evening of Michaelmas-day. It was a malignant feavor which tooke her away, about the 37th of her age, and 22d of her marriage, to our irreparable losse, and the universal regret of all that knew her. Certaine it is, that the visible cause of her indisposition proceeded from griefe, upon the losse of her daughter, and the Infants that follow'd it; and it is as certaine, that when she perceived the perill, whereto its excesse had engaged her, she strove to compose her selfe, and allay it; but it was too late, and she was forc'd to succumb; Therefore summoning all her Children then living (I shall never forget it) she express'd her selfe in a manner so heavenly, with instructions so pious, and Christian, as made us strangely sensible of the extraordinary losse then imminent; after which, embracing every one of us in particular, she gave to each a Ring with her blessing, and dismiss'd us. Then taking my Father by the hand, she recommended us to his care; and because she was extreamely zealous for the education of my Younger Bro: she requested my Father, that he might be sent with me to Lewes; and so having importun'd him that what he design'd to bestow on her Funeral, he would rather dispose among the poore (for that she feared, God had not a little punished her, for the pomp, and expense of my Sisters) she labourd to compose herselfe for the blessed change which She now expected. There was not a Servant in the house, whom she did not expressly send for, advise, and infinitely affect with her counsell; and thus she continu'd to employ her intervalls, either instructing her relations, or preparing of her selfe: for though her Physitians (who were Dr. Meverell, Dr. Clement, & Dr. Rand) had given over all hopes of her recovery, and Sir Sanders Duncomb tried his celebrated & famous powder upon her; yet she was many days impairing, and endur'd the sharpest conflicts of her sicknesse with admirable patience, and a most christian resignation; reteining both her intellectuals, and ardent affections for her dissolution to the very article of her departure; which hapned, as I sayd, on the 29 of September after she had fallen into a Crisis by a profound sweate (the onely change through all her sicknesse) after which lay<i>ng her hand upon every one of her Children, and <having> taken solemn leave of my Father; with elevated heart, & eyes, she quietly expired, and resign'd her Soule to God.

Thus ended that prudent, and pious Woman in the flowre [almost] of her age, to the unconsolable affliction of her husband, irreparable losse of her Children, and universal regret of all that knew her: She was interred as neere as might be, to her Daughter Darcy, the 3d of October, at night; but with no meane Ceremony.

It was the 3d of the ensuing November after my Bro: Geo: was gon back to Oxford, 'ere I return'd to Lewes, where I made way (according to instructions received of my Father) for my Bro: Rich: who was sent the 12th after.

1636

This Yeare 1636, being extreamely dry, the Pestilence much increased in Lond, and divers parts of England.

The 13th of Feb: I was especialy admitted (and as I remember my other Bro:) into the Middle-Temple Lond: though absent, and as yet at Schoole {...as was then the Course of Education of young gentlemen after their studys in the Universitys, to acquaint them with the Municiple Laws of their owne Country...}.

There were now large contributions to the distressed Palatinate.

The 31 of October came my Father himselfe to see us, and returned the 5t of November following.

The 10th of December he sent a Servant to bring us necessaries &c, and the Plague beginning now to cease.

1637

The 3d. of Apr. 1637 I was sent for from Schoole; where till about the last Yeare I had been extreamely remisse in my studies; so as I went to the Universitie, rather out of shame of abiding longer at Schoole, than for any fitnesse, as by sad experience I found, which put me to relearne all that I had neglected, or but perfunctorily gaind.

It was Apr: 5. that I return'd to Wotton (upon what occasion I do not well remember) and the 9th of May after, that I ariv'd at Oxford, where I was admitted Fellow-Communer of Balliol College upon the 10th in the Chapell there, taking an Oath to be conformable to the Statutes, and Orders of that Society.

On the 29 of May I was MATRICULATED in the Vestry at St. Maries: UBI SUBSCRIPSI ARTICULIS FIDEI, ET RELIGIONIS, ET JURAMENTUM SUSCEPI DE AGNOSCENDA SUPREMA REGIÆ MAJESTATIS POTESTATE, ET DE OBSERVANDIS STATUTIS, PRIVILEGIIS, ET CONSUETUDINIBUS UNIVER-SITATIS. Dr. R: Baily head of St. Johns, being then Vice-Chancelor. [afterwards Bishop.]

It appeares by a letter of my Fathers, that he was upon treaty with one Mr. Bathurst of Trinity Coll: (afterwards Doctor [& Præsident]) who should have been my Tutor; but least my Brothers Tutor Dr. Hobbs, (more zelous in his life, then industrious with his Pupils,) should receive it as an affront; and especialy for that Fellow-Communers in Balliol were no more exempted from Exercise than the meanest Scholars there; my Father sent me thither to one Mr. Geo: Bradshaw (*nomen invisum*)[1] yet the sonn of an excellent Father, beneficed in our Country of Surrey. I ever thought my Tutor had parts enough; but as his ambition [& I fear vices] made him very much suspected of the Colledg; so his grudg to the Governor of it Dr. Lawrence [Margaret Professor] (who he afterwards supplanted) tooke up so much of his tyme, that he seldom, or never had any opportunity to discharge his duty to his Scholars; which, I perceiving, associated my selfe with one Jam: Thicknesse (then a Young man of the foundation, afterwards fellow of the house) by whose learned and friendly Conversation I received a great advantage.

At my first arival Dr. Parkhurst was Master, after his discease Dr. Lawrence, a Chaplaine of his Majesties and Margaret Professor succeeded, an accute and Learned Person; nor do I so much reproch his severity, considering that the extraordinary remissenesse of discipline had (til his coming) much detracted from the reputation of that Colledg.

There came in my tyme to the Coll: one Nathaniel Conopios out of Greece, from [Cyrill] the Patriarch of Constantinople, who returning many yeares after, was made (as I understood) Bishop of Smyrna. [He was the first I ever saw drink Coffé {not heard of then in England, nor til many yeares after made a common entertainement all over the nation, as since that the Chineze Thea; Sack & Tabacco being til these came in, the Universal liquour & Drougs, which maintained such a number of taverns [& coffe houses] as remaine to this day, & might well be spared:...}, which custome came not into England til 30 yeares after.] After I was somewhat settled there in my formalities, (for then was the University exceedingly regular under the exact discipline of William Lawd, Archbish: of Canterbury then Chancelor) I added as benefactor to the Library of the Coll: these Bookes following:

> *Ex dono Johannis Evelyni hujus Coll:*[2]
> *Socio-Commensalis, Filij Richardi*
> *Evelyni, è Com: Surriæ, Armigeri*
> Zanchij Opera Voll: j. 2. 3m.
> Granado in Tho: Aquinatem Vol: j. 2. 3m.
> Novarini Electa Sacra, &
> Cresolij Anthologia Sacra.

Authors (it seemes) desired by the students of Divinity there.

Upon the 2d of July, being the first of the Moneth, I first received the B: Sacrament of the Lords Supper in the Colledg Chapell, one Mr. Cooper, a fellow of the house preching; and at this tyme was the Church of England in her greatest splendor, all things decent, and becoming the peace, and the Persons that govern'd.

The most of the following Weeke I spent in visiting the Colledges, and several rarities of the University, which do very much affect young comers; but I do not find any memoranda's of what I saw.

18 July, I accompanyd my Eldest Bro (who then quitted Oxford) into the Country; and the 9 of Aug: went to visite my friends at Lewes, whenc I returned the 12th <to> Wotton.

---

[1] 'Name unseen', i.e. of unknown reputation.
[2] 'By the gift of John Evelyn to this college.'

17 Sept: I received the B: Sacrament at Wotton-Church, and Octob: 23 went back to Oxon.

5: Nov: I received againe the Holy Comm: in our Coll: Chapell: one Prouse, a Fellow (but a mad one) preaching.

December 9, I offerd at my first exercise in the Hall, and answerd myne Opponent: and upon the 11th following declaymed in the Chapell before the Master, Fellows and Scholars according to the Custome: The 15th after, I first of all Oppos'd in the Hall.

The Christmas ensuing, being at a Comedy, which the Gent: of Excester-Coll: presented to the University, and standing (for the better advantage of seeing) upon a table in the Hall, which was neere to another in the darke; being constrain'd by the extraordinary presse to quit my station, in leaping downe to save my selfe I dash'd my right leg with such violence against the sharp edge of the other board, as gave me an hurt which held me in cure till almost Easter, and confined me to my study.

1638

The 22d of Jan, I would needes be admitted into the dauncing, and Vaulting Schole; of which late activity one Stokes (the Master) did afterwards set forth a pretty booke, which was publish'd with many witty Elogies before it.

Apr: 13th my Father order'd that I should begin to manage myne owne Expenses; which ('til then) my Tutor had don, at which I was much satisfied.

Jul 1: I received the B: Sacr: one Evet, preaching.

The 9th following, I went home to visite my friends and the 26t, with my Bro: and Sister to Lewes, where we aboad till the 31, and thence, to one Mr. Michaels of Haughton neere Arundel (where we were very well treated) and the 2d of Aug: to Portsmouth; and thence having surveyed the fortifications (a greate rarity in that blessed Halcyon tyme in England) my bro: Rich. and I passed into the Ile of Wight, to the house of my Lady Richards, in a place call'd Yaverland; but we returned to our Company the next morning whom we overtooke at Chichester, where having viewed the Citty, and faire Cathedrall, we lodg'd that night, and the day following return'd home ...

About the beginning of September I was so afflicted with a quartan Ague, that I could by no meanes get rid of it untill the December following: This was that fatal Yeare, wherein the rebellious Scots oppos'd the King, upon pretence of the introduction of some new Ceremonies, and the Booke of Comm: Prayer; and madly began our Confusions, and their owne destruction too, as it proved in event.

1639

I came back to Oxon (after my tedious indisposition, and to the infinite losse of my tyme) on the 14th of Jan: 1639, and now I began to look upon the rudiments of Musick, in which I afterwards ariv'd to some formal knowledge, though to small perfection of hand because I was so frequently diverted, with inclinations to newer trifles ...

May 20, accompany'd with one Mr. Jo: Crafford (who afterwards, being my fellow-traveller in Italy, there chang'd his Religion) I tooke a journey of pleasure to see our Summerset-shire Bathes, Bristoll, Cirencester,

Malmesbury, Abington, and divers other townes of lesser note; cursorily view'd, and return'd the 25t.

July 9, my Father sent for me home ...

16. Sept: I went to Lewes, returning not till the 26t: so it was the 8th of Octob. e're I went back to Oxon.

December 14 according to injunctions from the heads of Colledges, I went (amongst the rest) to the Confirmation in St. Maryes; where after Sermon, the Bishop of Oxon: lay'd his hands upon us, with the usual forme of benediction prescrib'd: But this receiv'd (I feare) for the more part, out of curiosity, rather then with that due preparation and advise which had been requisite, could not be so effectual, as otherwise that admirable, and usefull institution might have been; and as I have since deplor'd it.

1640

Jan: 21, came my Bro: Richard from Schole, to be my Chamber-fellow at the University: he was admitted the next day, and Matriculated the 31th.

Feb: 16 was a Comm: again in our Coll: and upon March the 25. my Father happning to be sick, sent both for me and my Bro: to come to him.

Apr: 11th I went to Lond, to see the solemnity of his Majesties riding through the Citty in State to the Short Parliament, which began the 13th following; a very glorious and magnificent sight, the King circl'd with his royal diademe, and the affections of his People. But

The day after I return'd to Wotton againe, where I stay'd (my Fathers indisposition suffering greate intervalls) till Apr: 27th when I was sent to London to be first resident at the Middle-Temple: so as my being at the University, in reguard of these avocations, was of very small benefit to me.

Upon May the 5t following, was the Parliament unhappily dissolved: and the 20th I return'd with my Bro: Geor: to Wotton, who was upon 28 of the same Moneth married at Albury, to Mrs Caldwell (an heyresse of an antient Licestershire family) where part of the nuptials were celebrated.

June 10th, I repaired with my Bro: to the Tearme, to goe into our new Lodgings (that were formerly in Essex-Court) being a very handsome appartiment just over against the Hall-Court; but 4 payre of stayres high; which gave us the advantage of the fairer prospect; but did not much contribute to the love of that impolish'd study; to which (I suppose) my Father had design'd me, when he payd £145 to purchasse our present lives, and assignements afterwards.

London, and especialy the Court, were at this period in frequent disorders, and greate insolencies committed by the abus'd and too happy City: in particular the Bish: of Canterburys Palace at Lambeth was assaulted by a rude rabble from Southwark; my Lord Chamberlayne imprison'd, and many Scandalous Libells, & invectives scatter'd about the streetes to the reproch of Government, and the fermentation of our since distractions; so that upon the 25. of June I was sent for to Wotton; and the 27th after, my Fathers indisposition augmenting, by advice of the Physitians, he repaired to the Bathe.

The 31. I went againe to Lond: to visite one Mr. Duncomb, a Relation of my Brothers Lady, who lay mortaly sick there, and the next day return'd: But on the 7th after, my Bro: Geo: and I, understanding the perill my Father was in upon a suddaine attaque of his infirmity; rod post from Guildford towards him, and found him indeede extraordinary weake. Yet, so, as that continuing his course, he held out till the 8th of September, when I returned <with> him home in his Litter; being, as we conceiv'd, something repair'd in his health.

Octob: 15. I went to the Temple, it being Michaelmas Tearme: and Oct: 30, I saw his Majestie (comming from his Northern expedition) ride in pomp, and a kind of Ovation, with all the markes of an happy Peace restor'd to the affections of his People; being conducted through Lond, with a most splendid Cavalcade; and on November following, the third (a day never to be mention'd without a curse) to that long, ungrateful, foolish and fatal Parliament, the beginning of all our sorrows for twenty yeares after, and the period of the most happy Monarch in the World – *quis talia fando*[1] –.

But my Father being by this time enter'd into a Dropsy, which was an indisposition, the most unsuspected, being a person so exemplarly temperate, and of admirable regiment; hastened me back to Wotton December 12. where the 24th following, being Thursday, between 12 and one at noone, departed this life, that excellent man, and indulgent parent; reteining his senses, and his piety to the last; which he most tenderly express'd in blessing us, whom he now left in the World, and the worst of tymes, whilst he was taken from the evill to come.

1641

January - March It was a sad, and lugubr<i>ous beginning of the Yeare, when on the 2d of Jan: 1640/1, we at night follow'd the mourning hearse to the Church at Wotton; where (after a Sermon, and funebral Oration, by the Minister) my Father was interr'd neere his formerly erected Monument, and mingled with the ashes of our Mother, his deare Wife.

But thus we were bereft of both our Parents in a period when we most of all stood in need of their Counsell and assistance; especially my selfe of a raw, vaine, uncertaine and very unwary inclination; but so it pleased God, to make tryall of my Conduct, in a conjuncture of the greatest and most prodigious hazards, that ever the Youth of England saw; and if I did not amidst all this, impeach my Liberty, nor my Vertue, with the rest who made ship-wrack of both; it was more the infinite goodnesse, and mercy of God, then the least providence or discretion of myne owne, who now thought of nothing, but the pursute of Vanity, and the confus'd imaginations of Young men.

Upon the 27th of Jan: I went with my Bro: to London about finding my Fathers Office, in which something that was then left me, was concern'd; there I aboad till the 17th of March when I returnd to Wotton.

April 1: I went with my Bro: Rich: to Lewes to settle matters with some Tennants of mine there, and came back againe the 9th but upon the 15, I repaired to Lond: to heare, and see the famous Tryall of the Earle of Strafford, Lord Deputy of Ireland; who on the 22d of March before had been summoned before both houses of Parliament, and now appear'd in Westminster-Hall, which was prepar'd with Scaffolds for the Lords and Commons, who together with the King, Queene, Prince, and flowre of the Noblesse were Spectators, and auditors of the greatest malice, and the greatest innocency that ever met

---

[1] The meaning of the full quote is 'Who telling such a tale could refrain from tears'. Virgil, *Aeneid*, II.6.

before so illustrious an Assembly. It was Tho: Earle of Arundell & Surrey Earle Martial of England who was made high Stuard upon this occasion, and the Sequell is too well known.

On the 27th came over out of Holland the young Prince of Orange, with a splendid equipage, to make love to his Majesties eldest daughter, the now Princesse-Royall,[1] and that evening were celebrated the pompous funeralls of the Duke of Richmond, who was carried in Effigie in a<n> [open] Charriot through Lond: in greate solemnity.

29, I kissed the Prince of Wales his hand, in the Lobby behind the house of Lords, and return'd to Wotton on the 30th, where I receiv'd the B: Sacr: the next Sonday.

May 7th I went againe to Lond: with my Bro: and on the 12th following beheld on Tower-hill, the fatal Stroake which sever'd the wisest head in England from the Shoulders of the Earle of Strafford, whose crime coming under the cognizance of no human-Law, a new one was made, not to be a precedent, but his destruction, to such exorbitancy were things arived.

The 23d I receiv'd the B: Sac: and the next day returned to Wotton, and went to Lond againe **June** 28 with my sister Jane: The day after I sate to one Vanderborcht[2] for my picture in Oyle, which I presented her, being her request upon my resolutions to absent my selfe from this ill face of things at home, which gave umbrage to wiser <men> then my selfe, that the Medaill was turning, and our calamities but yet in their infancy:

So upon **July** the 15, having procur'd a passe at the Costome-house where I repeated my oath of Allegeance, I went the 16th from Lond: to Graves-end, accompany'd with one Mr. Caryll, and our Servants, where we arived by 6 that Evening, with a purpose to take the first opportunity of a passage for Holland; but the Wind as yet not favourable, we had tyme to view the Blockhouse of that Towne, which answer'd to another over against it at Tilberry (famous for the Rendezvous of Queen Eliz: in the yeare 88:) which we found stor'd with 20 piece of Cannon, and other ammunition proportionable:

The 19th we rod to Rochester, and having seene the Cathedrall, we went to Chatham to see the Sovraigne, a mo<n>strous Vessel so call'd, being for burthen, defense and ornament the richest that ever spread cloth before the Wind; and especially for this remarkable, that her building cost his Majestie the affections of his Subjects, who quarreld with him for a trifle (as it was manag'd by some of his seacret Enemys, who made this an occasion) refusing to contribute either to their own safty, or his glory.[3]

We return'd againe this evening and <on> the 21, nine in the morning, embarqued in a Dutch Fregat bound for Flushing, convoyd and accompanied by five other stoute Vessells, whereoff one was a Man of Warr, whose assistance we might have needed, if the two Saile which we discover'd to make towards us about midnight (and with whom we all prepar'd for an encounter) had proved to be the enemy which we apprehended; but finding them Norrway-Marchands only, as we approch'd, we at 4 in the morning discry'd the coast of Flanders, and by noone, with a fresh Gale (which made it

---

[1] William (1626-50) and Mary of Orange (1631-60), parents of William of Orange(1650-1702), later William III of England (1688-1702).

[2] Henrik van der Borcht (1614-65). Two versions exist, one in the National Gallery.

[3] See below, 2 February 1696.

the most pleasant passage could be wished) we landed safely at Flushing in Zeland.

And now me thought the Seane was infinitely chang'd, to see so prety and neate a towne in the frontier: Here we first went to view the Pr: of Oranges house and garden, the Wales whereof are washed with Neptune continualy; after that the State-house, which are generaly in all the Low countries magnificently built; but being desirous to over-take the Leagure which was then before Genep, 'ere the summer should be too far expir'd, we went this Evening to Midelbrogh, another sweete town in this Iland of Walcheria; and by night to Der-Veere, from whence upon the 23d we embarqued for Dort: I may not forget that being insufferably tormented with the stitch in my side, caus'd through the impetuous motion of the Wagon, which running very swiftly upon the pav'd Cause-ways, give a wonderfull concussion to such as are unacquainted with that manner of travelling; the Fore-man perceiving me ready to drop from my seate, immediately cur'd and easd me of my payne, by unbuttoning my doublet, and applying an handfull of [could] couch-grasse to my side.

We passe from Der-Veere over many Townes, houses and ruines of demolish'd suburbs &c which have formerly ben swallow'd up by the sea; at what time no less then eight of those Ilands had ben irrecoverably lost, which put me in mind of the deluge, and that description of the Poet.

> ———— *culmen tamen altior hujus*
> *Unda tegit, pressæque latent sub gurgite turres.*[1] Met: j.

By reason of an adverse wind, we were this night constrain'd to Lodg in our Vessel; but on the next day we landed at Dort, the onely virgin, and first towne of Holland.

This Citty is commodiously situated on the river of .... by which it is furnish'd <with> all German Commodities, and especialy Rhenish-Wines and Timber: It hath almost at the extreamity a very spacious, and venerable Church; a stately Senat-house wherein was holden that famous Synod against the Arminians 1618; and in that hall hangeth a Picture of the Passion, an exceeding rare, and much esteemed piece.

It was in this Towne that I first observed the Storkes building on their Chimnies, and frequently in the Streetes, without that any dares to molest them.

Being desirous to hasten towards the Army, I tooke Wagon this afternoone to Roterdam, whither we were hurried in lesse than an houre, though it be ten-miles distant; so furiously do these Fore-men drive. I went first to visite the greate Church; the Doole, and the Burse, the publique statue of the learned Erasmus, which of brasse and a goodly piece; as we pass'd, they shew'd us his house; or rather the meane Cottage wherein he was borne, over which there are extant this distic in capital letters.

> *Ædibus his ortus, mundum decoravit Erasmus*
> *Artibus ingenuis, Religione, Fide.*[2]

The 26, I pass'd by a strait, and most commodious River through Delft, to

---

[1] 'The overflowing waves do still cover its roof, and its towers lie hidden beneath the deluge'. Ovid, *Metamorphoses*, I.289-90.

[2] 'Born in this shrine, Erasmus adorned the world with his noble skills, religion, and faith.'

the Hague; in which journey, I observ'd divers Leprous poore Creatures dwelling, and permitted to ask the charity of passengers, which is convey'd them in a floating box that they cast out; they live in solitary huts on the brink of the Water; & I was told, contract their dissease from their too much eating of fish.

Ariv'd at the Hague, I went first to the Queene of Bohemias Court,[1] where I had the honor to kisse her Majesties hand; and severall of the Princesses, her daughters; Prince Mauris was also there, newly come out of Germany: and my Lord Finch, not long before fled out of England from the fury of the Parliament. It was a fasting-day with the Queene, for the unfortunat death of her husband, and therefore the Presence had been hung with black-Velvet, ever since his disscease; after some discourse with her Majestie we went to our Lodging, and spent the next day in contemplating that most divertissant, and noble Village.

The 28, I went, by the like passage to Leyden, and by the 29th to Utricht, being 30 English miles distant (as they reckon by houres). It was now Kermas, or a Faire in this Towne; the streetes swarming with Boores and rudenesse; so that early the next morning (having visited the antient Bishops Court, and the two very famous Churches) I satisfied my curiosity till my returne, and better leasure: The 30th we came to Rynen, where the Queene of Bohemia hath a neate, & well built Palace, or Country house, built after the Italian manner, as I remember; and so crossing the Rhyne, upon which this Villa is situated, lodged that night in a Country-mans house.

August 2d, we ariv'd at the Leagure, where was then the whole Army encamped about Genep, a very strong Castle situated on the River Wahale, and Commanding all Cuke-Land; but being taken now foure <or> 5 days before, we had onely a sight of the demolitions, and upon the next Sunday, was the thankesgivings-Sermonds, perform'd in Coll: Gorings Regiment (eldest sonne of the since Earle of Norwich) by Mr. Goffe, his Chaplaine (now turn'd Roman, and Fa: Confessor to the Q: Mother) ...

Now (according to the complement) I was receiv'd a Voluntéere in the Company of Cap: Apsley, of whose Cap: Lieutennant, Honywood (Apsley being absent) I received many civilities.

Aug: 3 at night we rod about the lines of Circumvallation, the Generall being then in the field: The next day I was accommodated with a very spatious, and commodious Tent for my Lodging, as before I was with an horse, which I had at command, and an Hutt, which during the excessive heates, was a very greate conveniency; for the sun peircing the Canvass of the Tent, it was during the day unsufferable, and at night, not seldome infested by the mists and foggs, which ascended from the river.

Upon the 6t as the turne came about, I watched on a horneworke, neere our quarters; and traild a pike; being the next morning reliev'd by a company of French: This was our continual duty, till the Castle was refortified, and all danger of quitting that station secur'd.

The 7th I went to see a Convent of Franciscan Friars, not far from our Tents, where we found them at their devotions; and both their Chapell, & Refectory full of the goods of such poore people as at the approch of the Army, had fled

---

[1] Elizabeth (1596-1662), sister of Charles I, mother of *inter alia*: Prince Rupert (1619-82); and Sophia (1630-1714), Electress of Hanover, and mother of George I of England (born 1660, reigned 1714-27), see below, 7 July 1700.

with them thither for Sanctuary. On the day following I went to view all the trenches, aproches, and Mines &c of the besiegers; and in particular I tooke speciall notice of the Wheele-bridg, which Engine his Excellency, had made, to run over the moate, when they storm'd the Castle; as it is since described (with all other particulars of his seige) by the Author of that incomparable Worke, *Hollandia illustrata*: the incredible thicknesse of the Walls, and ramparts of Earth, which a mine had broaken, and crumbl'd all to ashes, did much astonish me.

Upon the 8, I din'd in the horse quarters, with Sir Robert Stone, and his Lady; Sir William Stradling and divers Cavaliers; where there was very good cheere, but hot service for a young drinker as I then was: so that being prety well satisfied with the confusion of Armies, & seiges (if such, that of the United Provinces may be call'd, where their quarters, and encampments are so admirably regular, and orders so exactly observed, as few Cittys, the best disciplin'd, do in the Worlde exceede it, for all Conveniences) I took my leave of the Leagure, and Camerades; and on the 12 of Aug. embarked upon the Wahal (where the Prince had made a huge bridge of boates), in the company of three grave divines, who entertaynd us a greate part of our passage with a long dispute concerning the lawfulnesse of Church Musick ...

13 We arived late at Roterdam, where was at that time their annual Mart or Faire, so furnish'd with pictures (especially Landscips, and Drolleries, as they call those clownish representations) as I was amaz'd: some of these I bought and sent into England. The reason of this store of pictures, and their cheapenesse proceede from their want of Land, to employ their Stock; so as 'tis an ordinary thing to find, a common Farmor lay out two, or 3000 pounds in this Commodity, their houses are full of them, and they vend them at their Kermas'es to very greate gaines.

Here I first saw an Eliphant, who was so extreamely well disciplin'd and obedient, that I did never wonder at any thing more: It was a beast of a mo<n>strous size, yet as flexible and nimble in the joynts (contrary to the vulgar tradition) as could be imagin'd from so prodigious a bulke, & strange fabrick; but I most of all admired at the dexterity, and strength of his proboscis, on which he was able to support two, or three men, and by which he tooke, and reached what ever was offer'd him; his teeth were but short being a femal, and not old, as they told us. I was also shew'd a Pelican, or rather (as I conjectur'd) the Onocratulus of Pliny, having a large bill, tip'd with red, and pointing downewards a little reflected; but what is most prodigious, the under part, annex't to a gullet, so wide, and apt to extend; and would easily have swallowd, a little child: The plumage was white, wall-eyd, the legge red and flatt footed; but in nothing resembling the picture, and description of the fabulous Pelican; which when I told the testy old-man who shew'd it; he was very wroth. There was also a Cock with 4 leggs; but what was most strange, with two rumps or vents, one whereof was at his breast; by which he likewise voyded dongue, as they assur'd us; There was with this fowle an hen having two large Spurrs growing out at her sides, and penetrating through the feathers of her wings.

Upon Aug. 17 I passed againe through Delft, visited the Church, where was the monument of Prince William of Nassau, a peace of rare art; There lyeth likewise intombed with him, his sonn & successor Grave Maurice.

The Senat-house of this Citty hath a very stately Portico, supported with very choyce Pillars of black-marble; being, as I remember of one entire stone: and within, there hangs up a certaine weight<y> vessell of Wood (not much unlike to a butter-Churne) which the adventurous Woman that hath two husbands at one time is to weare for a time about the Towne, her head comming out at the hole, & the rest hanging on her shoulders, as a pennance for incontinency: ...

<20> ... that Evening ariv'd at Leyden where I immediately mounted a Wagon, which that night (as late as it was) brought us to Harlaem and almost to the end of my Last Journey; for I tooke such a Cold, as was like to kill me: About 7 in the Morning, I came to Amsterdam, where being provided of a Lodging, I procur'd to be brought to a Synagogue of the Jewes (it being then Saturday) whose Ceremonies, Ornaments, Lamps, Law, and Scholes afforded matter for my wonder and enquiry: The Women were secluded from the men, being seated above in certaine Galleries by themselves, and having their heads mabbl'd with linnen, after a fantasticall & somewhat extraordinary fashion:

From hence I went to a place (without the Towne) called Over-kirk, where they had a spacious field assign'd them for their dead, which was full of Sepulchers, and Hebrew Inscriptions, some of them very stately, of cost: In one of these Monuments, looking through a narrow crevise, wher the stones were disjoynted, I perceived divers bookes to lye, about a Corps (for it seemes <they use> when any learned Rabby dies, to bury some of his Bookes with him, as I afterwards learn'd): of these, by the helpe of a stick that I had in my hand, I raked out divers leaves, which were all writen in Hebrew Characters but much impair'd with age, and lying. As we return'd we stepp'd in to see the Spin-house of Amsterdam, which is a kind of Bride-well, where incorrigible and Lewd Women are kept in Discipline and Labour; but in truth all is so sweete and neate, as there seemes nothing lesse agreable then the persons and the place. Here we were shew'd an Hospital erected for poore Travelors and Pilgrimes (as they told us) by Queene Eliz: of England, and another maintaind by the Citty. The State, or Senat-house of this vast Towne is (if the designe be perfected) one of the most costly, and magnificent pieces of Architecture in Europ; especialy for the materialls, and the Carvings, which exceedes all description ...

I now expressly chang'd my Lodging, out of a desire to converse amongst the Sectaries that swarm'd in this Citty, to which gaine made every new-fangle acceptable. It was at a Brownists house, where we had an extraordinary good Table; There was in pension with us my L:[Keeper] Finch, and one Sir Jo: Fotherbee; here I also found an English Carmelite, that was travelling through Germanie towards Rome with another Irish Gentleman. I went to see the Weesehouse, which is a foundation like our Charter-house in designe, for the education of decay'd Persons, Orphans, and poore Children, where they are taught severall occupations; and, as I learn'd, the Wenches are so well brought up to housewifry, that men of good worth (who seeke that chiefely in a Woman) frequently take their Wifes from this Seminary. Hence we were carried to see the Rasp-house, where the lusty Knaves are compelld to labour, and it is a very hard labour, the rasping of Brasill, & Log-wood for the Diers, appointed them by their Task-masters. Thence to the Dull-house, a place for mad persons & fooles, like our Bethleem: But none did I so much admire as an Hospitall for their lame and decrepid souldiers, it being for state, order & accommodations one of the worthiest things that I thinke the world can shew of that nature: Indeede it is most remarkable, what provisions are here made and maintain'd for publique and charitable purposes, and to protect the poore from misery, and the Country from beggers.

It was on a Sunday morning about 11, that I purposely went to the Bourse (after the sermons were ended) to see their Dog-market, which lasts till two after-noone. I do not looke on the structure of this Exchange to be comparable

to that of Sir Tho: Gresshams in our Citty of Lond: yet in one respect it
exceeds, that ships of considerable burthen ride at the very key contiguous to
it; and realy it is by extraordinary industry, that as well this Citty, as almost
generaly the Townes of Holland, are so accommodated with Grafts, Cutts,
Sluces, Moles, & Rivers, that nothing is more frequent then to see a whole
Navy of Marchands & others environ'd with streetes & houses, every
particular mans Barke, or Vessell at anker before his very doore, and yet the
Streetes so exactly straite, even, & uniforme that nothing can be more
pleasing, especialy, being so frequently planted and shaded with the beautifull
lime trees, which are set in rowes before every mans house, affording a very
ravishing prospect.

The next day we were entertain'd at a kind of Tavern, calld the Briloft,
appertaining to a rich Anabaptist, where in the upper romes of the house were
divers pretty Water workes rising 108 foote from the ground, which seem'd
very rare, till the Engine was discovered: here were many quaint devices,
fountaines, artificiall musique, noyses of beasts & chirping of birds &c: but
what I most admir'd then, was a lamp of brasse, projecting eight soccketts
from the middle stemm, like to those we use in Churches, which having
counterfeit lights or Tapers in them, had streames of Water issuing, as out of
their Wieekes or Snuffs: the whole branch hanging all this while loose upon a
<s>talk in the middst of a beame, and without any other perceptible commerce
with any pipe; so that unlesse it were by compression of the ayre with a
syringe, I could not comprehend how it should be don. There was likewise
shew'd as a rarity, a Chime of Purselan dishes, which fitted to clock-worke,
rung many changes, and tunes without breaking.

At another place of this Citty, we saw divers other Water-workes; but
nothing more surpriz'd me than that stately, and indeede incomparable quarter
of the Towne, called the Keisers-Graft, or Emperors Streete, which appeares to
be a Citty in a Wood, through the goodly ranges of the stately and umbragious
Lime-trees, exactly planted before each-mans doore, and just at the margent of
that goodly Aquæ-duct, or river, so curiously wharfed with Clincar'd, (a kind
of White sun-bak'd brick) of which material the spacious streetes on either
side are paved. This part of Amsterdam is built, and gained upon the maine
Sea, supported by Piles at an immense Charge, but with everlasting
foundations. Prodigious it is to consider those multitudes, and innumerable
Assemblys of Shipps, and Vessels which continualy ride before this Citty,
which is certainely the most busie concourse of mortall men, now upon the
face of the whole Earth and the most addicted to commerce: Nor must I forget
the Ports[1] & Issues of the Towne, which are very noble Pieces of Architecture,
some of them modern; and so are their Churches (though more Gotick) where
in their Turrets or Steeples, (which are adorn'd after a particular manner for
costs, & invention) the Chimes of Bells are so rarely manag'd, and artificialy
rung, that being curious to know whither the motion were from any
extraordinary Engine, I went up into that of St. Nicholas (as I take it) where I
found one who play'd all sorts of Compositions from the tablature before him,
as if he had fingerd an Organ; for so were the hammers fastned with wyers, to
severall keyes, put into a frame 20 foote below the Bells, upon which (by help
of a Wooden instrument not much unlike a Weavers Shuttle that guarded his
hand) he struck on the keys, and playd to admiration; all this while, through
the clattering of the Wyers, dinn of the too neerely sounding bells, and noise
that his wooden-gloves <made>, the confusion was so greate, that it was

---

[1] Gates.

impossible for the Musitian to heare any thing himselfe, or any that stoode neere him; Yet to those, who were at a distance, and especialy in the streetes, the harmony, and the time were most exact & agreable. The South-Church is richly paved with Blak, and White-marble: The West is a new fabric: Generaly, there are in all the Churches in Holland Organs, Lamps, Monuments &c: carefully preserved from the fury, and impiety of popular reformers, whose zeale has foolishly transported them in other places rather to act like madmen, then religious.

Upon St. Bartholomews-day I went to Hundius's shop to buy some Mapps, greately pleasd with the designes of that indefatigable Person: Mr. Bleaw, the setter-forth of the Atlas's & other Workes of that kind is worthy seeing: At another shop I furnish'd my selfe with some shells, & Indian Curiosities; and so towards the end of August quitted the Towne, returning back againe to Harlem by that straite River which runs betweene them; and in earnest it is a most stupendious prospect, to looke back upon Amsterdam at the end of this River cutt 10 miles in length as straite as a line without the least flexure, and of competent breadth to saile by one another: By the way it is not to be omitted we were shew'd a Cottage where they told us dwelt a Woman, who had then been married to her 25th Husband; and being now a Widdow, was prohibited to marry for the future; yet it could not be proved, that she had ever made any of her husbands away, though the suspicion had brought her divers times to trouble.

Harlem is a very delicat Towne, and hath one of the fairest Churches of the Gotique designe, I had ever seene: There hang in the Steeple (which is very high) two Silver-bells, which they report were brought from Damiate in Egypt, by an Earle of Holland, in memory of whose successe, they are rung out every Evening. In the Nave or the body of the Church, hang the goodliest branches of brasse for tapers that ever I had seene, esteemed of greate value for the curiosity of the Workmanship: also a very faire payre of Organs, which I could not find they made any use of in Divine-Service or so much as to assist them in their singing of Psalmes (as I suppos'd) but onely for shew, and to recreate the people before and after their Devotions, whilst the Burgomasters were walking and conferring about their affaires. There likewise hangs up, neere the West-Window (as I remember) two modells of Shipps, compleately equipp'd, in memory of that invention of Saws under their keeles, with which they cut the Chayne before the port of Damiate.

Having visited this Church, the Fishmarket, and made some enquiry about the Printing-house, the Invention whereof is sayd to have been in this towne, I return'd to Leyden, that renowned University of Batavia: Here, the better to take view of the Citty, I was carried up to the Castle or Pyrgus, built on a very steepe mount artificialy cast up, as 'tis reported, by Hengist the Saxon, at his returne out of England; as a place to retyre to when by any unexpected accident, the Inhabitants should be threatned with suddaine inundations...

The 28, I went to see their Colledg, and Schooles, which are nothing extraordinary; and was Matriculated by the then Magnificus Proffessor who first in Latine demanded of me where my Lod<g>ing in the Towne was; my Name, Age, birth; and to what faculty I addicted my selfe; then recording my Answers in a Booke, he administred an Oath to me, that I should observe the Statutes, & Orders of the University, whiles I stay'd, and then deliver'd me a ticket, by virtue whereof I was made Excise-free; for all which worthy Priveleges, and the paines of Writing, he accepted of a Rix-dollar. Here was the famous Dan: Heinsius, whom I so long'd to see; as well as the E<l>zivirian

Printing house & shop, renown'd for the politenesse of the Character, & Editions of what he has publish'd through Europ.

I went also to visite their Garden of Simples, which was indeede well stor'd with exotic Plants, if the Catalogue presented to me by the Gardiner be a faithfull register. But amongst all the rarities of this place I was much pleasd with a sight of their Anatomy Schole, Theater & Repository adjoyning, which is very well furnish'd with Naturall curiosities; especially with all sorts of Skeletons, from the Whale & Eliphant, to the Fly, and the Spider, which last is a very delicat piece of Art, as well as Nature, how the bones, (if so I may name them) of so tender an Insect, could possibly be separated from the mucilaginous parts of that minute animal ... I could not forget that knife which they here shew'd us, newly taken out of a Drunken Dutch-mans gutts, by an incision in his side, after the sottish fellow had swallow'd it, when tempting to make himselfe vomit, by tickling his throat with the handle of it, he let it slip out of his fingers into his stomac, and had it taken out againe by the hands of that dextrous Chyrurgeon, whose Picture is together with his Patients preserv'd in this excellent Collection ...

September 1. I went hence to Delft, thence to Roterdam, the next morning, and two days after back to the Hague againe to bespeake a Suite of Armor which I causd to be made to fit me, with the harnasse of an Horse man ...[1]

10th I tooke Wagon for Dort, to be present at the reception of Queene-Mother Maria de Medices Dowager of France, Widdow of Henry the Greate, and Mother to the French King Lewes xiiith, and Queene of England, whence she newly ariv'd toss'd to and fro by the various fortune of <her> life; From this Citty she design'd for Collin,[2] conducted by the Earle of Arundell, and the Here van Brederod: I saw at this enterview the Princesse of Orange, and the Lady her daughter, afterward married to the house of Brandenbourg: There was little remarkable in this reception befitting the greatnesse of her Person, but an universal discontent, which accompany'd that unlucky Woman whereever she went. The next day I return'd to Roterdam to dispatch a servant of mine with some things into England.

12th, I went towards the Busse [Bosleduke] passing by the Schone of the Grave, a most invincible fort, neere to which is another calld Jack a tra, not far from Ingle: We arrived at Bosleduc on Sep: 16th. at a time when the new Citadell was advancing with innumerable hands, and incomparable inventions for the draining of the Waters out of the Fenns & Moraces about it, being by Bucketts, Mills, Cochleas, Pumps and the like. Here were now 16 companies, and 9 tropes of Horse: They were also cutting of a new River to passe from the towne to a Castle not far from it, and here we split our skiff terribly, falling fowle upon another through negligence of the Master, who was faine to run on ground to our no little hazard: At our arrival a Souldier conveyed us to the Governor, where our names were taken, and our Persons examin'd very strictly.

17th I was permitted to walke the round, and view the Workes; and obtained Licence to visite a prety Convent of Religious Women of the Order of St. Clara, permitted (it seemes) to enjoy their Monastery & maintenance undisturb'd by articles & capitulations at the Surrender of the Towne, now 12

---

[1] A portrait of E wearing the armour was made about now. Unmentioned in the *Diary* it is illustrated in Antonia Fraser (1993), *Charles II – His Life and Times*, 170.

[2] Cologne.

yeares since; Where we had a Collation & a very Civil entertaynement. They had a very neate Chapell, in which the heart of the Duke of Cleve, their Founder lies inhum'd under a plate of Brasse: Within the Cloyster is a Garden, and in the middle of it an over-growne Lime-tree, out of whose stem, neere the roote, issue 5 upright & exceeding tall suckers or boles, the like whereof for evenesse & height I had not observd.

The Chiefe Church of this City is curiously carved within, & without; furnish'd with a paire of Organs, & a magnificent Font, or Baptistery all of Copper. The 18, I went to see that most impregnable Fort & Towne of Hysdune,where I was exceedingly oblig'd to one Coll: Crombe, the Lieutenant-Governor, who would needes make me accept the honor of being Cap: of the Watch, & to give the Word this night. The Fortification is very irregular; but esteem'd one of the most considerable for strength, & situation, not onely of the Neither-Lands, but of the World ...

On the 22d I went to Roterdam againe to receive a Passe, which I expected from the Cardinal Infanta, then Governor for the K: of Spaine his Bro: in Flanders, being desirous to see that Country in my returne for England whither I was now shaping my Course: And within two days after, having obtain'd another from his Highnesse the Pr: of Orange, upon the 24th of September I departed through Dort, attempting to sayle by the Keele, an obscure harbor so call'd, which the winds not permitting, we were constrayn'd to lye that night at Anker: 25th the next morning we made another Essay, but were againe repuls'd as far as Dort:

The 26t we put to sea afresh from the Keele; but a suddaine storme rising, with the Wind, and the Women (passengers) out-cries, we were forc'd to retyre into Harbor, where there lay threescore Vessells expecting fairer Weather. But we, impatient of the tyme, and inhospitablenesse of the Place set out againe the next morning early having the tyde propitious, though a most contrary and impetuous wind, passing so tirrible & overgrowne a Sea, as put us all in very greate jeopardy of our Lives; for we had much ado to keepe our selves above water, the billows breaking so desperately upon our Vessell, 'til it pleased God about noone to drive us in at a Town called William-Stat, a Place garnison'd by the English, where the Governor hath a faire house; the Workes, and especialy the Counterscarp is worthy of note, curiously hedg'd with a quick<set>, and planted with a stately row of Limes on the Ramparts. The Church is of a round structure with a Cupola: Here I encounter'd two Polish noble-men, who were travelling out of Germany, and had beene in Italy, very accomplish'd persons.

It was now the 28 of Sept: when failing of an appointement, I was constrain'd to returne againe to Dort, for a Bill of Exchange; but it was the 1 of Octob: 'ere I could get back, when at the Keele I numberd 141 Vessells, who durst not yet adventure this fowle Passage: but we animated by the Master of a stout Barke, after a small encounter of Weather ariv'd by 4 that Evening at Stenebergen; In which passage we sailed over a Sea call'd the Plaet, which is an exceeding dangerous Water by reason of two contrary tydes which meete very impetuously: Here, because of the many Shelfes we were forc'd to tyde it along the Channell in sight of two pretty Townes call'd Oude Towne, & Sommers Dyke: but 'ere we could gaine the Place the ebb was so far spent, that we were compell'd to foote it at least a league in a most pelting shower of raine. This is an exceeding impregnable fort.

October 2. with a Gent: of the Rhyne-graves, I went in a Cart (for it was no better, nor other accommodation could we procure) of two Wheeles & one horse to Bergen-op-Zome; ...

The next morning imbarked (for I had refus'd a Convoy of Horse which was offered me), and came early to Lillo, landing short of the Fort, by reason the tyde was against us, which constrain'd us to Land on the beach, where we marched halfe-leg-deepe in mudd, ere we could gaine the Dyke, which for being 5 or 6 miles distant from Lillo we were forced to walke on foote very wett, and discompos'd: Then entering a Boate we pass'd the Ferry, and came into the Castle; being first examin'd by the Sentinel, and conducted to the Governor, who demanded my Passe, to which he set his hand, and asked 2 Rixdollars for a fee, which me thought appeared very unhandsome in a Souldier of his quality; I told him, that I had already purchas'd my Passe to the Commissaries at Roterdam, at which, in a greate fury snatching the Paper out of my hand, he flung it scornefully under a table, and bad me try whether I could get to Antwerp without his permission: But when I drew out the mony, he return'd it as scurvily againe; bidding me pay 14 dutch shill: to the Cantore or Searcher for my contempt, which I was also glad to do with a greate deale of Caution & danger, conceiling my Spanish-passe, it being a matter of Imprisonment; for that the States were therein treated by the names of Rebells; Besides all these exactions, I g<a>ve the Commissary 6 shill: more, to the Souldiers something, and 'ere perfectly cleare of this Severe Frontiere 31 stivers to the Man-of-Warr who lay blocking up the River, twixt Lillo, and the opposit Sconce call'd Lifkinshoeek; Two such Fortresses, as for their circuit are hardly to be paralleld in all Europ besides.

Thus on the 4 of Octob: being (as I remember) Sonday, we passed the Forts of Santa Cruce; St. Philippo, Callò, and St. Maria all appertaining to the Spaynard: Out of St. Maria's came some Dons a'board us; and now I made use onely of my other Passe, to which one of them put his hand, receiving 6 guilders as a gratuity; These after they had sufficiently searched our Vessel, left us very courteously: Then we pass'd by another Man-of-Warr to which we Lower'd o<u>r top-saile, and so after many importunate accidents of this nature twixt these two jealous States, we at last ariv'd safe at Antwerp about 11 in the morning.

Here so soone as I had provided me of a Lodging (which are in this Citty very handsome & convenient) I lost little tyme; but with the conduct of one Mr. Lewkner, spent the afternone (being a little refresh'd) in seeing divers Churches, Coledges, Monasteries &c: I exceedingly admir'd that sumptuous and most magnificent Church of the Jesuites, being a very glorious fabrique without; & within wholy incrusted with marble inlayd & polish'd into divers representations of histories, Landskips, Flowers &c ...

I went hence unto the Vrou-kirke or Notre Dame d'Anvers, which is the Cathedrall of this Citty: It is a very venerable fabrique, built after the Gotick manner, and especialy the Tower, which is in truth of an excessive height: This I ascended, that I might the better take a view of the Country about it, which happning on a day when the sunn shone exceedingly hot, and darted the rays without any interruption, afforded so bright a reflection to us who were above, and had a full prospect of both the Land & Water about it, that I was much confirm'd in my opinion of the Moones being of some such substance as this earthly Globe consists of; perceiving all the subjacent Country (at so smale an horizontal distance) to repercusse such a light as I could hardly looke against; save where the River, and other large Water within our View appeard of a more darke & uniforme Colour, resembling those spotts in the Moone, attributed to the seas there &c according to our new Philosophy & the Phænomenas by optical Glasses: I number'd in this Church 30 priveleg'd Altars, whereof that of St. Sebastians was rarely paynted ...

5 ... The Oesters-house, belonging to the East-India Company is a most beautifull Palace, adorn'd with more then 300 Windows: From hence walking into the Gun-garden I was suffer'd to see as much of the Citadell as is easily permitted to strangers: It is doubtlesse the most matchlesse piece of modern Fortification in the World; for all contrivances of force, and resistance; incomparably accommodated with Logiaments for the Souldiers, & magazines of Warr: The Graffs, ramparts, & Platformes are stupendious. Returning hence by the Shop of Plantine, I bought some bookes for the namesake onely of that famous Printer: But there was nothing about this Citty, which more ravished me then those delicious shades and walkes of stately Trees, which render the incomparably fortified Workes of the Towne one of the Sweetest places in Europ; nor did I ever observe a more quiet, cleane, elegantly built, and civil place then this magnificent and famous Citty of Antwerp, which caused me to spent the next day in farther contemplation of it, and reviewing what I had seene before; ...

Evelyn now sailed down the Scheldt to Brussels

... at 9 in the Morning, being Octob: 7th we ariv'd at Bruxelles, where after I had a little dispatch'd some addresses; I went first to visite the State-house neere the Market-Place; being for the carving in free-stone a most laborious, & <strangely> finish'd Piece; well worth the observing.

The flesh shambles is also built of stone: I was infinitely pleas'd with certaine small Engines, and divices by which a silly Girle or Boy was able to draw-up, or let-downe huge Bridges, which in divers parts of the Citty crossed the Channell, for the benefit of Passengers. The Wal<l>s of this Towne are very intyre, and full of Towers at competent distances. The Cathedrall is built upon a very high, & exceeding steepe ascent, to which we mounted by faire stepps of stone: Hence I walked to a Convent of English Nunns, with whom I sate discoursing most part of this afternoone.

8: ... It was now neere eleaven, when I repaird to his Majesties Agent Sir Henry De Vic, who very courteously receivd me and accommodated me with a Coach & six-horses, which carried me from Bruxelles to Gant, where it was to meete my Lord of Arundel, Earle Martial of England, who had requested me when I was at Antwerp to send it for him, if I went not thither my selfe.

Thus taking leave of Bruxelles, and a sad Court, yet full of Gallant Persons (for in this small Cittye the acquaintance being universal, Ladys & Gentlemen I perceiv'd had greate diversions and frequent meetings) I hasted towards Gant: Upon the Way, I met with divers little Wagons, pretily contriv'd and full of pedling Merchandises, which were drawne by Mastive-Dogs, harnass'd compleately like so many Coach-horses; in some 4, in others six, according to the Charge they drew; as in the Towne of Bruxelles it selfe I had observed: In Antwerp I saw (as I remember) 4 dogs draw 5 lusty Children in a Charriot to my greate astonishment; the Master commands them whither he pleases, crying his Wares about the streetes ...

Evelyn reached Ostend by 9 October

10, I went by Wagon (accompany'd with a jovial Commissary) to Dynkirk, the journey was made all on the sea sands: On our arivall we first viewed the

Court of Guards, The Workes, Towne-house and new Church (which is indeede very beautifull within) and another wherein they shew'd us an excellent piece of our B: Saviours bearing the Crosse. The Harbour in two Channells coming up to the Towne was choaked with a multitude of Prizes. From hence I the next day marched 3 English miles towards the Packet-boate being a pretty Fregat of 6 Gunns, which embarked us for England about 3 in the afternoone: At our going off the Sch<ue>rnken fort (against which our Pinnac ankerd) saluted my L:Martial with 13 greate gunns, which we answerd with 3. and so (not having the Wind favourable) after a little motion, ankerd that night before Calis:

About midnight we weigh'd, and at 4 in the morning being not far from Dover, we could not yet make the Peere till 4 that afternoone, the wind proving contrary and driving us Westward; but at the last we got on shore, being the afternoone of Octob: 12th.

From Dover I that night rood Post to Canterbery, where I visited the Cathedrall, now in greatest splendor, those famous Windoes being intire, since demolish'd by the Phanatiques: The next morning by Sitinbourn, I came to Rochester; and thence to Graves-End, where a Light-horse-man (as they call it) taking us in, we spent our tide as far as Greene-Wich, whence after we had a little refresh'd at the Colledge (for by reason of the Contagion then in Lond: we baulked the Inns) we came to London, landing at Arundel Stayers, where I tooke leave of his Lordship, and retyr'd to my Lodgings in the Middle Temple, being about two in the morning the 14th of October.

Octob: 16 I went to see my Bro: at Wotton, being the 31 of this Moneth (unfortunate for the Irish rebellion which brake out the 23) one & twenty Yeares of age.

November 7: I received the B: Sac, at the Church of Wotton; and in the afternoone went to give my L: Martial a Visite at Albury:

8 I went to Lewes to see my friends in Sussex, accompany'd with my two Brothers.

The 13th I return'd, and the 23d to Lond: where on the 25t following I saw his Majestie ride through the Citty, after his comming out of Scotland and a peace proclaym'd, with greate acclamations and joy of the giddy people.

December 15, I was elected one of the Comptrollers of the Middle-Temple-Revellers, as the fashion of the Young Students & Gentlemen was; the Christmas being kept this Yeare with greate Solemnity; but being desirous to passe it in the Country, I got leave to resigne my Staffe of Office, and went with my Bro: Richard to Wotton. [Statues & heads set up in Temple hall:]

1642

January 10th I gave a Visite to my Co: Hatton of Ditton and went the next to London, [13 Christend Mr. Smiths Sonn at Fan-Church for my Bro: George] returning the next day, but not to Wotton till the 18th.

29, I went againe to Lond, where I stayd till 5 March following, studying a little; but dauncing and fooling more:

February [6: Feb: I received the B:S: at the Midle Temp: Church Dr. Littleton preaching: as also on Quadragessim Sunday:]

March The 23d Mar: I tooke a journey with my Brothers to Northampton faire to buy some saddle horses, & returned the 28 by St. Albans, where we visited the Church, and the ruines of old Verulame, where the L:Chancelor Bacons contemplative monument is the sole ornament worth remembring.[1]

The 19 to Lond, where I remayn'd till May: 2d, & thence on the 5 to Lond. againe, tempted to adventure some monyes upon the Irish reduction; but there remaining some Scrupules, it did not succeede: so on the 23 I returnd to Wotton, till the 7th of **June** when I went againe to Lond: whence on the 23d to Lewes in Sussex, returning the 25t.

July 6, I visited my Bro: at Wotton, from whence with both my Bro: & sister we went **Aug:** 2 a journey of pleasure to Lewes, where we left my sister for the rest of the Summer, returning on the 5 ...

Octob: 3d to Chichester, and thence the next day to see the Seige of Portsmouth; for now was that blody difference betweene the King and Parliament broaken out, which ended in the fatal Tragedy so many yeares after: It was on the day of its being render'd to Sir William Waler, which <gave> me opportunity of taking my leave of Coll: Goring the Governor now embarquing for France:
On the 6t I went from Portsmouth to <Southampton>, lay at Winchester, where I visited the Castle, Schole, Church & K:Arthyrs round table; but especialy the Church and its Saxon Kings Monuments, which I esteemed a worthy antiquity: On the 7th I return'd to Wotton by Farne-ham & Guildford.
Octob: <2>3d was fought that signal Battaile at Edgehill:

November 12: was the Battaile of Braineford[2] surprisingly fought, & to the greate consternation of the Citty, had his Majestie (as 'twas beelievd he would) pursu'd his advantage: I came in with my horse and Armes just at the retreate; but was not permitted to stay longer then the 15th by reason of the Armys marching to Glocester, which had left both me and my Brothers expos'd to ruine, without any advantage to his Majestie.
{I came with my Horse & Armes, & with some mony presented to his Majestie by my Bro: was assigned to ride Volunteere, amongst the Gent: in Pr: Ruperts Troop, who was general of the Horse: But the King marching to Glocester, by which the Gentlemen whose Estates were in Surry & Sussex lay in the immediate power of the Rebells, & would certainely have ben seized as delinquents; nothing of my appearing in Armes, being known, I was advis'd, to obtaine of his Majestie, leave to Travell; since my Estate in the County, would have maintained more against his Majestie, than I could, for him: So as having a Passe procur'd me by sir Ed: Nicholas, then Secretary of state, & a friend of our Family, (whence he had his rise in greate measure) under his

---

[1] The Roman city of *Verulamium*. The monument is in the church of St. Michael which stands on the site of the Roman basilica. In E's day only the old city walls would have been visible.

[2] Brentford.

Majesties hand, I began to resolve on my Returne & preparation to passe into France:}

December 7: I went from Wotton to Lond, to see the so much celebrated line of Communication, & on the 10th return'd: [no body knowing of my having ben in his Majesties Army:] ...

1643

March The 11th I went to see my L: of Salisburys Palace at Hatfeild; where the most considerable rarity besides the house, (inferior to few for its Architecture then in England) was the Garden & Vineyard rarely well water'd and planted: They also shewd us the Picture of Secretary Cicil in Mosaique-worke very well don by some Italian hand.

I must not forget what amaz'd us exceedingly on the night before; viz, a shining clowd in the ayre, in shape resembling a sword, the poynt reaching to the North; it was as bright as the Moone, the rest of the skie being very serene; it began about 11 at night, and vanish'd not 'til about one, seene by all the South of England ...

April 15 to Hatfeild, and neere the Towne of Hartford went to se<e> Sir J:Harris his house new built:

19 I return'd to Lond; calling in by the Way to see his Majesties House and Gardens at Theobalds, (since demolish'd by the Rebells) thence on the 21 to Wotton.

May 2d I went to Lond; where I saw the furious & zelous people demolish that stately Crosse in Cheapeside: The 4th I return'd with no little regrett for the Confusion that threaten'd us:

On the 15, to Lond: againe returning the 17th and resolving to possesse my selfe in some quiet if it might be, in a tyme of so greate jealosy, I built (by my Brothers permission,) {the stews & receptacles for Fish, and built a little study over a Cascade, to passe my Malencholy houres shaded there with Trees, & silent Enough: This trifle, however despicable, was the Occasion of my Bro: vast Expence, when some yeares after, he Inlarged the Gardens, built the Portico, & Cutt the Mount into the present shap<e> it now is of, with the fountaines in the Parterr, which were amenitys not frequent in the best Noble mens Gardens in England: This being finished whilst I was abroad, was conducted by a relation of ours, Georg<e> Evelyn[1] who had ben in Italy, but was mistaken in the Architecture of the Portico, which tho' making a magnificent shew, has greate faults in the Colonade, both as to the Order, which should have ben [Doric] Corinthian & the Ornaments, the rest is very tollerable:}, made a fish-pond, Iland and some other solitudes & retirements at Wotton, which gave the first occasion of improving them to those Water-Workes and Gardens, which afterwards succeeded them, and became the most famous of England at that tyme.

---

[1] A grandson of E's grandfather by his first marriage. See also 26 February 1649.

July 2: I received the B:Sac: On the 11th I went with my Bro: to Godstone to see Sir Jo: Evelyn:

The 12th I return'd, and sent my Black- [manage-] horse and furniture with a friend to his Majestie then at Oxford.

23 July, The Covenant being pressed, I absented my selfe; but finding it impossible to evade the doing of very unhandsome things; and which had been a greate Cause of my perpetuall motions hitherto betweene Lond: and Wotton:

October the 2d, I obtayn'd a Lycense of his Majestie dated at Oxford, & sign'd by the King, to travell againe, so as on **November** 6, lying by the way at Sir Ralph Whitfeilds at Bletchinglee, (whither both my Brothers had conducted me) I arived at Lond: on the 7th and two dayes after tooke boate at the Tower-Wharfe, which carryd me as far as Sittinburne, though not without danger, I being onely in a payre of Oares expos'd to an hidious storme; but it pleas'd God, that we got in before the perill was considerable: From thence by Post I went to Dover accompany'd with one Mr. Thicknesse a very deare friend of mine:

On the 11th having a reasonable good Passage, though the Weather were snowy & untoward enough, we came before Calais; where as we went on shore, mistaking the tyde, our shallop struck with no little danger on the sands; but at length we gott off.

Calais is an extraordinary well fortified Place consider'd in the old Castle, & a new Citadell reguarding the Sea: The Haven consists of a long banke of Sand lying opposite to it: The Market-place and Church are very remarkeable things, besides those reliques of our once dominion there, so as I remember there was engraven in stone upon the front of an antient dwelling which was shew'd us, these words God save the King, in English, together with the name of the Architect and date: The Walls of the Towne are likewise very substantial, but the situation towards the Land not Pleasant in the least, by reason of the Marishes and low-grounds about it. The next day (being the 12th) after diner we tooke horse with the Messagere, hoping to have that night ariv'd at Bollogne; but there fell so greate a Snow, accompanied with hayle, raine & suddaine darknesse, as we had much adoe to retrive the next Village; and in this passage being to goe crosse a Vally where a Causeway and a Bridge was built over a small river, the raine that had fallen making it now an impetuous streame for neere a quarter of a mile, my horse slipping his <footing> had almost been the occasion of my perishing: This night we none of us went to bed, for the Souldiers in those parts leaving little in the Villages, we had enough to get ourselves dry by morning, between the fire and the fresh straw:...

Evelyn travelled south to Paris

... We lay at Paris at the Ville de Venize, where after I had something refresh'd, & put my selfe in equipage, I went to visite Sir Rich: Browne, his Majesties Resident with the French King: ...

On the 5 of **December**, came the Earle of Norwich, Extraordinary Ambassador, whom in a Coach & six horses I went to meete, at the Palais of Monsieur de Bassompieres, at Chaliot, where I had the honor to see that gallant Person his Gardens, Tarraces and rare Prospect: My L: was waited on by the Master of the Ceremonies, and a very greate Cavalcade of men of Quality to the Palais Cardinal.

Where on the 23d he had Audience of the Fr: King and the Q:Regent his Mother, in the Golden Chamber of Presence; from thenc I conducted him to his Lodging in the rue St. Denys & so tooke my Leave.

December 24 I went with some company to see some remarkable places about the Citty; as the Isle, and how 'tis encompassed by the Seine and Oyse rivers: The City is divided into thre<e> Parts, whereof the Towne is greatest: The City lyes betwixt it and the University in forme of an Iland; Over the river Seine is built a stately bridg (call'd Pont Neuf,) by Hen 3d 1578, finished by Hen: 4th his Successor: It consists of 12 Arches, in the middst of which ends the poynt of an Iland handsomely built with artificers houses. The Bridg above is very commodiously divided into one large Passage for Coaches, and two for footemen 3 or 4 foote higher, and of convenient breadth for 8, or 10 to goe on brest; all of hewn free-stone the best I thinke in Europ & growing in the very streetes, though more plentifully at Mont-Martyre within a mile of it ... At foote of this Bridge is a water-house, at the front whereof a greate height is the Story of our B:Saviour and the Woman of Samaria powring Water out of a bucket; above a very rare dyal of severall motions with a chime &c: The Water is conveyd with huge Wheeles, pumps & other Engines from the river beneath: But the confluence of the People, multitude of Coaches and severall accidents passing every moment over this Bridge is the greater miracle, and to a new Spectator, a most prodigious, yet agreable diversion: ...

The Suburbs are those of St.Denys, Honoré, St. Marcel, Jaques, St.Michel, St.Victoire, and St.Germaines which last is the largest and where the nobility and Persons of best quality are seated: And truely Paris, comprehending the Suburbs is certainely for the material the houses are built with, and the many noble and magnificent piles, one of the most gallant Cittys in the World, and best built: large in Circuit, of a round forme, infinitly populous; but situat in a botome environd with gentle declivities, which renders some places very durty, and makes it smell as if sulphure were mingled with the mudd: Yet it is pav'd with a kind of freestone of neere a foote square which renders it more easy to walke on then our pibbles of London: ...

1644

Evelyn spent the first part of 1644 in Paris

March 7th I set forwards with some Company, towards Fontaine Bleau, which is a sumptuous Palace of the Kings (like ours of Hampton-Court) about 14 leagues from the Citty: by the Way we passe through a Forest so prodigiously encompassd with hidious rocks of a Certaine whiteish hard stone, congested one upon another in Mountainous heights, that the like I believe is no where to be found more horrid & solitary: It abounds with Staggs, Wolves, Boares & sometimes more savage bea<s>ts, there being not long after, a Lynx or Ownce killd amongst them who had devowrd some passengers: Upon the Summite of one of these gloomy Precipices, intermingled with Trees & Shrubbs & monstrous protuberances of the huge stones which hang over & menace ruine, is built an Hermitage: passing these solitudes, not without howrly expectation of Rogues who frequently lurke about these denns & do mishchiefe (& for whom we were all well appoynted with our Carabines) we arived that Evening at the Village, where we lay at the Horne, going the next morning early to the

Palace: The Fabrique of this house is nothing so stately & uniforme, as Hampton Court: but Fra: the 1st began much to beautifie it; most of all Hen: 4th, and not a little the last King: It abounds with very faire Halls, Chambers & Gallerys ...

Evelyn toured Normandy, before returning to Paris in April[1]

I tooke a turne in St. Inocents Church-yard where the story of the devouring quality of the ground (consuming Bodys in 24 houres), the Vast Charnells of Bones, Tombs, Piramids and sepultures tooke up much of my time, together with the Hieroglypical Characters of Nicolas Flamens Philosophical Worke, who had both founded this Church, & divers other charitable workes, as himselfe testifies in his booke: Here I observd that divers clearks got their livelyhod by inditing letters for poore mayds & other ignorant people, who came to them for advise, and write for them into the Country, both to their Sweete-hearts, Parents & friends, every large grave stone a little Elevated serving them for Table: ...

I was had by a friend to Monsieur Morines Garden; a person who from an ordinary Gardner, is ariv'd to be one of the most skillfull & Curious Persons of France for his rare collection of Shells, Flowers & Insects: His Garden is of an exact Oval figure planted with Cypresse, cutt flat & set as even as a Wall could have form'd it: The Tulips, Anemonies, Ranunculus's, Crocus's &c being of the most exquisite; were held for the rarest in the World, which constantly drew all the Virtuosi of that kind to his house during the season; even Persons of the most illustrious quality: He lived in a kind of Hermitage at one side of his Garden where his Collection of Purselan, of Currall,[2] whereof one is carved into a large Crucifix, is greately esteemed: besids his bookes of Prints, those of Alberts, Van Leydens, Calot, &c. But the very greatest curiosity which I esteemd, for being very ingenious and particular, was his collection of all the Sorts of Insects, especialy of Buter flys, of which he had so greate Variety; that the like I had never seene: These he spreads, & so medicates, that no corruption invading them he keepes in drawers, so plac'd that they present you with a most surprizing & delightfull tapissry: besides he shewd me the remarkes he had made of their propagation, which he promisd to publish: some of these, as also of his best flowers, he had caus'd to be painted in miniature by rare hands, & some in oyle:

The 6t, I sent my sister, my owne Picture, in Water Colours, which she requested of me: ...

Evelyn travelled on to Blois, Ambois, Tours, and St.Gratian

May It was on the 21 I receiv'd the newes of the sicknesse and death of my Sister in Law, Wife to my Bro: Geo: Evelyn ...

27 **July** I heard excellent Musique at the Jesuites, who have here a Schole and Convent; but a meane Chapell: We had now store of those admirable Melons so much celebrated in France for the best, of the whole Kingdome. But I was

---

[1] De Beer noted (I, 73) that the text of the *Diary* from the beginning up to 19 March 1644 was probably written between 1660 and 1666. The text from this point to 2 July 1649 was probably also written up at about this time.

[2] Porcelain, and Coral.

about this tyme so exceedingly tormented with my gumms, by a new tooth which was growing, that I was faine to be lanced two or three times to give it passage, & aswage the paine:

August 1: My Valet de Chambre, One Garro, a Spaynard, borne in Biscay, for some misdemeanors, I was forc'd to discharge; he demanded of me (besides his Wages) no lesse then 100 Crownes to cary him to his Country, which I refusing to pay, as no part of our agreement; he had the impudence to arest me, and serve me with a Processe: so the next day I was call'd on to appeare in full Court, where both our Advocats pleaded before the Lieutennant Civile: But it was so unreasonable a pretence, that the Judge had not patience to heare it out, but immediately acquitting me, was so civil, as after he had extreamely reproch'd the Advocate who tooke part with my servant, he rose from the Bench, and making a courteous excuse to me, that being a stranger I should be so barbarously usd, conducted me through the Court to the very streete dore: This Varlet afterwards threaten'd to Pistol me ...

On the 18 came the Queene of England to Towers newly ariv'd in France, and taking this Citty in her way to Paris; she was very nobly receiv'd both by people and Cleargy, who went to meete her with all the Train'd bands: After the Harangue, the Archbish: entertaind her Majestie at his owne Palac, Where I did my duty to her: The 20th, she set forwards towards Paris.

Evelyn visited Richlieu and moved southwards to Marseilles by October

October Marcelles: This Towne stands on the Sea-Coast upon a sweete rising; tis well wall'd, & has an excellent Port for Ships, & Gallys, securd by an huge Chayne of Yron which draw crosse the harbour at pleasure; & there is a well fortified tower: besides this, there are also three other Forts or small Castles, especialy that cald the If built on a rock: Ratonneau, & that of St. John strongly garnison'd. But the Castle commanding the Citty, is that of Nostre dame de la Guard: In the Chapell hang up divers Crocodile Skinns:

We went then to Visite the Gallys being about 25 in number. The Captaine of the Gally royal gave us most courteous entertainement in his Cabine, the Slaves in the interim playing both on loud & soft musique very rarely: Then he shew'd us how he commanded their motions with a nod, & his Wistle, making them row out; which was to me the newest spectacle I could imagine, beholding so many hundreds of miserab<l>y naked Persons, having their heads shaken cloose, & onely red high bonnets, a payre of Course canvas drawers, their whole backs, & leggs starke naked, doubly chayned about their middle, & leggs, in Cupples, & made fast to their seates: One Turke amongst them he much favour'd, who waited on him in his Cabine, but naked as he was, & in a Chayne lock'd about his leg; but not coupled.

Then his Gally, I never saw any thing more richly carv'd & Guilded (the Sovraigne excepted) and most of the rest were exceeding beautiful: Here, after we had bestow'd something amongst the Slaves, the Cap: sent a band of them to give us musique at dinner where we lodged. I was amaz'd to contemplate how these miserable Catyfs[1] lye in their Gally, considering how they were crowded together; Yet was there hardly one but had some occupation or other: by which as leasure, in Calmes, & other times, permitts, they get some little monye; in so much as some have after many Yeares of cruel Servitude been able to purchase their liberty: Their rising forwards, & falling back at their

---

[1] = Caitiff, a wretched and worthless person.

Oare, is a miserable spactacle, and the noyse of their Chaines with the roaring of the beaten Waters has something of strange & fearfull in it,. to one unaccostom'd. They are ruld, & chastiz'd with a bulls-pizle dry'd upon their backs, & soles of their feete upon the least dissorder, & without the least humanity: Yet for all this they are Cherefull, & full of vile knavery:

We went after dinner to see the church of St.Victoire, where that Saints head is reserv'd in a shrine of silver which weighs 600 lbs: Thence to Nostre Dame, exceedingly well built: This is the Cathedrall: Then the Duke of Guizes Palace; The Palais of Justice; the Maison du Roy.

But there is nothing more strange than the infinite numbers of slaves, working in the Streets, & carying burthens with their confus'd noises, & gingling of their huge Chaynes: The Chiefe negoce of the Town is silkes & drougs out of Africa, Syria and Egypt: Also Barbara-horses which come hither in great numbers: The Towne is governed by 4 Captaines, & has 3 Consuls, and one Assessor: Three Judges royal; The Marchants have also a Judge for ordinary causes: Here we bought Umbrellos against the heate, and consulted of our jorney to Canes by Land, for feare of the Pickaron Turkes who make prize of many small Vessells about these parts, finding never a Gally bound for Genöa whither we were design'd: so on Octob: 9 we tooke our Mules, passing the first night very late in sight of St.Baume, & the solitary Grott, where the<y> affirme Mary Magdalen did their pennance: the next day we lay at <Fréjus>; which is a Citty built on an old foundation, witnesse the ruines of a most stately Amphitheater, which I went out to designe, being about a flight-shoote from the towne: They call it now the Rolsies: ...

On the 11th we lay at Canes, which is a small port on the Mediterranean; here we agree'd with a Sea-man to transport us to Genoa, so having procurd a bill of Health (without which there is no admission at any Towne in Italy) we embarq'd on the 12 of Octob:...

On the 15, forsaking our Gally we encounterd a little foule Weather, which made us creepe *Terra, Terra* as they call it;[1] and so a Vessell that encounter'd us advis'd us to do: But our Patron striving to double the point of Savona, making out into the Wind, put us all into an incredible hazard; for blowing very hard from Land 'twixt those horrid gapps of the Mountaines, it set so violently, as rais'd on the sudaine a<n> over growne Sea, so as we could not then by any meanes recover the Weather shore for many houres, inso much that what with the Water already enterd, & the confusion of fearfull Passengers ... we were almost uterly abandon'd to despaire; Our Pilot himselfe giving us for gon:

But so it pleas'd God on the suddaine (and as now we were almost sinking downe right, wearied with pumping, & laving out the Water) to appease the Wind, that with much adoe & greate perill we recover'd the Shore, which we now kept within lesse then halfe a league, in view & s<c>ent of those pleasant Villas, & fragrant Orchards which are situated on this Coast, full of Princly retirements for the Sumptuousnesse of their buildings & noblenesse of the plantations;...

16 we got to Anker under the Pharos or Watch-towre erected on an high rock, at the mouth of the Mole of Genoa; the weather being yet so fowle, that for two houres at least we dast not stand in to the haven: Towards the evening adventur'd and came on shore by the Prattique-house ...

17 ... The first Palace of note that we went to Visite was that of Hieronymo del Negros, to which we pass'd by boate crosse the harbour; here I could not

---

[1] As close to land as possible.

but observe the suddaine & devlish passion of a sea-man who plying us, was intercepted by another fellow, that interposd his boate before him, & tooke us in; for the teares gushing out of his eyes, he put his finger in his mouth & almost bit it off by the joynt, shewing it to his antagonist, as an assurance to him of some bloudy revenge, if he ever came neere that part of the harbour any more: And indeed this beautifull Citty is more stayn'd with such horrid acts of revenge & murthers, than any one place in Europ, or haply the World besides where there is a political government; which renders it very unsafe to strangers: This makes it a gally matter to carry a knife about one whose poynt is not broken off.

Evelyn sailed on to Livorno and moved inland to Pisa

The Campanile or Settezonio, built by one John Oenipont a German, consists of severall orders of pillars; 30 in a row, designd to be much higher: It stands alone, on the right side of the Domo or Cathedrall, strangely remarkable for this, that the beholder would expect every moment when it should fall; being built exceedingly declining by a rare adresse of the imortal Architect: and realy I take it to be one of the most singular pieces of workmanship in the World; how it is supported from immediately falling would puzzle a good Geometrician.

Returning to Livorno Evelyn travelled inland, reaching Florence about the 24 October - part of the Kalendarium *is missing here and the* De Vita Propria *supplies details*

{ ... On the <27th> I purchased the Pietra Comm<e>ssa Pieces for my Cabinet;[1] bespoke 4. rare small statues of stucci made onely by that rare Artist Vincetio Brocchi: Collecting some Prints & drawings I went to see the renowned Church, Chapell & Library of St. Laurences in which the Medicean Family are buried, with Banners over them: ...

29 We tooke Horse for Sienna, alighting at *Poggio Imperiale* a house of Pleasure of the Duke, little distant from Florence, but having little time to Consider it, we refer'd it for our coming back from Rome:

We lay this night at st. Cassiano, & I think next day at Barbarini, a small Town, whence P. Urbans family: Then at Poggio Bunci famous for Snuff Tabacco, which the Italians of both sexes take excessivly, we dined, & that night arived at Sienna: (Note, that Snuff was not taken in England at this time nor some yeares after:)- this famous Citty stands on several rocky Hills, which makes it uneven, has an old ruin'd Wall about it, over-grown with Caper shrubs: but the Air is incomparable, whence divers passe the heates of Summer there; Provisions cheape, the Inhabitans Courteous, & the Italian purely spoken. The Citty at a little distance presents the Traveller with an incomparable Prospect, occasion'd by the} many playne brick Towers, which (whilst it was a Free state) were erected for defence: ...

Evelyn reached Rome on 4 November

November On the 7th we went into *Campo Vacino* by the ruines of the *Templum Pacis*, built by Titus Vespatianus, and thought to be the biggest &

---

[1] The cabinet is now in the Victoria and Albert Museum, London.

most ample as well as richly furnish'd of all the Roman Dedicated places; It is now an heape, rather then a Temple; yet dos the roofe, & Volto, continue firme, shewing it to have formerly been of incomparable workmanship: This goodly structure was (none knows how) consumed with fire, the very night (by all computation) that our B:Saviour was borne ...[1]

<12> ... we bent towards Dioclesians Bathes againe, never satisfied with contemplating that moles, in which, after an hundred & fifty <Thousand> Christians were destined to burthens, building 14 yeares; he murthered them all; so as there had neede be a Monastery of Carthusians in memory of the cruelty: It is called Santa Maria degli Angeli, the Architecture M:Angelos, & the Cloister incompassing, walls in an ample Garden: ...

On the 19 I went to visite St.Pietro, that most stupendious & incomparable Basilicam, far surpassing any now extant in the World, & perhapps (Solomons Temple excepted) any that was ever built:

The largenesse of the Piazza before the Portico is worth observing, because it affords you a noble prospect of the Church; crowded up, for the most part in other places, where greate Churches are erected: In this is a fountaine out of which gushes a river, rather than a streame, which ascending a good height, breakes upon a upon a round embosse of Marble into millions of pearles, which fall into the subjacent bason: making an horrible noise: I esteeme this, one of the goodliest fountaines that ever I saw ...

November 20 I went to visite that antient See, that Cathedral of St.John de Laterana, and the holy places thereabout: This is a church of extraordinary devotion, though for outward forme not comparable to St. Peters, being of Gotique Ordonance ...

The next sight which drew us was a wonderfull concourse of people at their devotions before a place called Scala Sancta to which is built a most noble frontspiece: Being enter'd the Portico we saw those large stayers of marble, in number 28, which are never ascended but upon the knees, some lip devotion us'd upon every step, upon which you may perceive divers red speccks of blood (under a grate) which they affirme to have ben drops of our B:Saviours what time he was so barbarously missus'd by Herods souldiers; for these stayres are reported to be transferred hither from his palace in Jerusalem; ...

December 12 I went againe to St. Peters to see the Chapells, Churches, & Grott, under ground, viz, under the whole Church (like our St. Faiths under Paules,) in which lye interr'd a world of Saints, Martyrs, & Popes; amongst the rest Hadrian the 4th, our Countryman, in a chest of Porphyrie: St. Jo: Chrysostom,[2] Petronella; the heads of St. Jacobus minor, St. Lukes, St. Sebastians, and our Thomas of Beccket: A shoulder of St. Christopher, an Arme of Joseph of Arimathea: Longinus; besides 134 more Bishops, Souldiers, Princes, Scholars, Cardinals, Kings, Empp: and their wives to<o> long to particularize.

Hence we walked into the Cemitery <called> Campo Santo, the earth consisting of severall ship Loads of mould transported from Jerusalem, which has the vertue to consume a Carcasse in 24 houres: To this joynes that rare

---

[1] Correctly the Basilica of Maxentius (AD 306-12) or Constantine I (307-337); though even if Vespasian (69-79) or Titus (79-81) had been responsible it could hardly have been burnt down in the year of Christ's birth, a point E fails to appreciate.
[2] E translated Chrysostom's *Golden Book* on the education of children to commemorate the life of his son Richard (d. 1658), see below, 16 September 1658.

Hospital, where was once Neros Circus, & next to this the Inquisition house and Prison the inside whereoff, I thanke God, I was not curious to see. To this joynes his Holinesse's Horse-Guards.

On Christmas-Eve at night I went not to bed, by reason that I was desirous to see the many extraordinary Ceremonyes perform'd then in their Churches, as mid-night Masses, & Sermons; so as I did nothing all this night but go from Church to Church in admiration at the multitude of sceanes, & pageantry which the Friers had with all industry & craft set out to catch the devout women & superstitious sort of people with, who never part from them without droping some mony in a vessell set on purpose: But especialy observable was the pupetry in the Church of the Minerva, representing the nativity &c: thenc I went & heard a Sermon at the Apollinare by which time it was morning.

On Christmas day his holynesse sa<y>ing Masse, the Artillery at st.Angelo went off: and all this day was exposd the Cradle of our Lord:

29 We were invited by the English Jesuites to dinner being their greate feast of Tho: of Canturbury: We din'd in their common Refectory, and afterward saw an Italian Comedy Acted by their Alumni before the Cardinals.

1645

January 15 ... I went to the Ghetto, where the Jewes dwell, as in a suburbs by themselves: being invited by a Jew of my acquaintance to see a Circumcision: here I passed by the Piazza Judea (where their Serraglio begins) for being invirond with wales, they are lock'd up every night: in this place remaines yet part of a stately fabric; which my Jew told me had been a Palace of theirs, for the Ambassador of their Nation in former times, when the<i>r Country was Subject to the Romans ...

Being lead through the Synagogue into a privat house, I found a world of people in a Chamber: by & by came an old man who prepar'd & layd in order divers Instruments brought by a little child of about 7 yeares old in a box, These the man layd in a silver bason: The knife was much like a short Razor to shut into the haft: Then they burnt some Insense in a Censor, which perfum'd the rome all the while the ceremony was doing: In the basin was also a little cap made of white paper like a Capuchins-hood, not bigger then my finger, also a paper of a red astringent powder, I suppose of bole: a small Instrument of Silver cleft in the midst, at one end to take up the prepuce withall, clowtes of fine linnen wrap'd up &c: These all in order the Women from out of another Chamber brought the Infant swadl'd, and deliver'd it to the Rabbie, who caried, and presented it before an Altar or Cuppord dress'd up, on which lay the 5 bookes of Moses, and the Commandments a little unrowled: Before this with profound reverence, and mumbling a few Words he waved the Child to & froo a while; then he delivered it to another Rabbie, who sate all this time upon a Table, he taking it in his hands put it betweene his thighs, whilest the other Jew unbound the blankets that were about it to come at the flesh: at this action all the company fell a singing of an hebrew hymn, and in as barbarous a tone, waving themselves to & fro, a ceremony they observe in all their devotions:

The Infant now strip'd from the belly downewards, the Jew tooke the yard of the child and Chaf'd within his fingers till it became a little stiff, then with the silver Instrument before describ'd (which was held to him in the basin) he tooke up as much of the Præputium as he could <possibly> gather, and so with the Razor, did rather Saw, then cutt it off; at which the miserable babe cry'd extreamely, whiles the rest continu'd their odd tone, rather like howling then singing: then the Rabby lifting the belly of the child to his face, & taking the yard all blody into his mouth he suck'd it a pretty while, having before taken a little V<i>negar, all which together with the blood he spit out into a glasse of red-wine of the Colour of french wine: This don he stripp'd downe the remainder of the fore-skin as farr and neere to the belly as he could, so as it appeared to be to be all raw, then he strew'd the read powder on it to stanch the bleeding and coverd it with the paper-hood, & upon all a Clowte, and so swath'd up the Child as before: All this while the<y> continue their Psalme: Then two of the Women, and two men, viz, he who held the Child, and the Rabbin who Circumcis'd it (the rest I suppose were the Witnesses) dranke some of the Wine mingl'd with the Vinegar, blood & spittle: so ended the slovenly ceremony, and the Rabbin cryes out to me in the Italian tongue perceiving me to be a stranger: Ecco Signior mio, Un Miracolo di dio; because the child had immediately left crying: The Jewes do all in Rome we<a>re yellow hatts, and live onely upon brokage & Usury, very poore and despicable beyond what they are in other territories of Princes where they are permitted.

In late January Evelyn left Rome for the south

{**January** 27[1] ... we set out from the Latine Port towards Naples: The firs<t> part of our way was well pav'd & full of Antiquities especially antient Sepulchers, Inscriptions and ruines; for it was <their> manner to bury much by famous high-roads, where they also placed their Statues, thereby inciting the minds of Men to gallant actions by the memory of their examples: In the right hand we saw the <Aquæduct> of Ancq Martius, and those of Claudius, and the new ones of Sixtus Vth, being a stately peice of Arch work for near 20 Miles: Then we enter the Via Appia 'till we came near Frascati which we left on the other hand, riding by the Wood & Lake celebrated for the fiction of Heleon and Diana}, thence to Veletri, a Towne heretofore of the Volsci where is a publique and faire statue of P:Urban the 8 in brasse, and a stately Fountaine in the streete, here we lay, and drank excellent Wine.

28 ... We reposd this night at Piperno in the Post-house without the Towne; and here I was extreamely troubld with a sore hand which I brought from Rome with me by a mischance, which now began to fester, upon my base unlucky stiffne<c>ked trotting carrion Mule, & which are in the world the most wretched beasts.

Evelyn reached Naples on 31 January; on 7 and 8 February he visited
Vesuvius and Baiae

February 7 ... The mountaine consists of a double top; the one pointed very sharp, and commonly appearing above any clowds; the other blunt; here as we approch'd we met many large and gaping clefts & c<h>asm's, out of which issu'd such sulphurous blasts & Smoake, that we durst not stand long neere them: having gaind the very brim of the top, I layd my selfe on my belly to

---

[1]This part of E's MS is missing, made good here by de Beer from E's grandson's (Sir John Evelyn Bart.,) 1737 copy.

looke over & into that most frightfull & terrible Vorago, a stupendious pit (if any there be in the whole Earth) of neere three miles in Circuit, and halfe a mile in depth, by a perpendicular hollow cliffe, like that from the highest part of Dover-Castle, with now & then a craggy prominency jetting out: The area at the bottom is plaine, like a curiously even'd floore, which seemes to be made by the winds circling the ashes by its eddy blasts: in the middle & center, is a <rising>, or hill shaped like a greate browne loafe, appearing to consist of a sulphurous matter, continualy vomiting a foggy exhalation, & ejecting huge stones with an impetuous noise & roaring, like the report of many musquets discharging: ...

On Sunday, we with our Guide goe to visite the so much celebrated Baiæ, and the natural rarities of the Places adjacent: ... we came to a lake of about two miles in circumference, inviron'd with hills: The Water of it, is fresh & swete on the surface, and salt at botome, some mineral-salt conjectur'd to be the cause; and 'tis reported of that profunditude in the middle, as that it has no botome soundable: The People call it Lago di Agano, from the multitude of Serpents, which involv'd together about the Spring fall downe from the cliffy hills into it: & besides these it has no fish, neither will any live in it: The first thing we did here, was, the old experiment on a Dog, which we lead from that so mortal Cave commonly nam'd Grotto del Cane or Charons Cave: It is not above three, or four paces deepe, and about the height of a man, nor is it very broad: In this Cave whatever has life presently expires; of this we made tryal with two Doggs: which we bound with a Cord to a short pole to guide him the more directly into the farther part of the Den, where he was no soner enter'd, but without the least noyse or so much as strugling, except that he panted for breath, lolling out his tongue, his eyes being fixt, we drew him out dead, to all appearance; but then immediately plunging him into the adjoyning lake, within lesse space then halfe an houre, he recoverd againe, and swimming to shore ran away from us: Another Dog, on whom we try'd the former experiment of the Cave, without the application of the Water, we left starke dead upon the shore: It seemes this has also ben try'd on men, as well as beasts, as on that poore Creature which Peter of Toledo caus'd to go in; likewise on some Turkish Slaves, two Souldiers: & other foolehardy persons, who all perished, & could never be recover'd againe by the Water of the Lake, as are doggs, for which many learned reasons have been offer'd; ...

By mid-February Evelyn had returned to Rome

Feb: the 20th: I went (as was my usual <Costome>) & spent an Afternoone in Piazza Navona, as well to see what Antiquities I could purchase among the people, who hold Mercat there for Medaills, Pictures, & such Curiosities, as to heare the Montebanks prate, & debite their Medicines ...

April <17> We therefore now tooke Coache a little out of Towne, to visite the famous *Roma Subterranea*, being much like those of st. Sebastians: here in a Corn field, guided by two torches we crep't on our bellies into a little hole about 20 paces, which deliver'd us into a large entrie that lead us into severall streetes or allies, a good depth in the bowells of the Earth, a strange & fearefull passages for divers miles, as Bossius has describ'd & measur'd them in his book: we ever & anon came into pretty square roomes, that seem'd to be Chapells, with Altars, & some adorn'd with antient painting, very ordinary: That which renders the passages dreadfull is, the Skeletons & bodies, that are placd on the sides, in degrees one above the other like shelves, whereof some are shut up with a Course flat Stone, & *Pro Christo* or <Chi-Rho> & Palmes ingraven on them, which are supposd to have ben Martyrs: Here in all liklyhood were the meetings of the Primitive Christians during the Persecutions, as Plinius Secundus describes them: As I was prying about, I found a glasse phiole as was conjecturd filld with dried blood, as also two lacrymatories: Many of the bodyes, or rather bones, (for there appeard nothing else) lay so intire, as if placed so by the art of the Chirugion, which being but touch'd fell all to dust: Thus after two or 3 miles wandring in this subterranean Meander we return'd to our Coach almost blind when we came into the day light againe, & even choked with smoake: A French bishop & his retinue adventuring it seemes too farr in these denns, their lights going out, were never heard of more.

May Next day, which was May: 4 having seene the Entrie of the Ambassador of Lucca I went to the Vaticane, where by favour of our Cardinal Protector, Fran: Barberini, I was admitted into the Consistorie, heard the Ambassador make his Oration to the Pope[1] in Latine, & sitting on an elevated state, or Throne, & changing two Pontifical Miters: After which I was presented to kisse his Toe, that is his embrodr'd Slipper, two Cardinals holding up his Vest & Surplice, so as sufficiently bless'd with his thumb & two fingers for that day I returnd home to dinner ...

<c. 17> At executions I saw one hang'd (a Gent) in his Cloak & hatt; For Murder: the<y> strock the malefactor with a club that first stun'd him, & then cut his Throat. At Naples as in Hull in a frame...

On 18 May Evelyn left Rome for the north, making for Venice via Florence to Bologna and to Loiano

From this pleasant Citty we went now towards Ferrara, carrying with us a Bulletino or Bill or Certificat of Sanità (costomarie in all these jealous parts of Italy, especialy the state of Venice) & so put our selves in a boat that was tawd with horses, & often interrupted by the sluces (inventions there to raise the Water for the use of mills, & to fill the artific<i>al chanells) at every of which we stayed till passage was made: Here we went by the Castle Benivoglio, & about night arriv'd at an ougly Inn calld Mal Albergo agreable to its name, whence after we had supp'd, we Embarkd, & passe that night through the Fenns where we were so pester'd with those flying Glow-wormes called Luccioli, that one who had never heard of them, would thinke the Country full of sparks of fire, in so much as beating some of them downe & applying them to a book, I could reade in the darke, by the light they afforded; quitting now our Boate, we took Coach, & by morning, got to Ferrara, where before we were admitted entrance, our Gunns & Armes were taken from us, of Costome, the lock being taken of before, as we were advis'd:...

Evelyn arrived in Venice by the beginning of June

June ... finding my-selfe extreamly weary, & beaten with my Journey, I went to one of their Bagnias, which are made, & treate after the Eastern manner, washing one with hot & cold water, with oyles, rubbing with a kind of Strigil, which a naked youth puts on his hand like a glove of seales Skin, or what ever

---

[1] Innocent X (1644-55).

it be, fetching off a world of dirt, & stretching out one<s> limbs, then claps <on> a depilatorie made of a drug or earth they call Resina, that comes out of Turky, which takes off all the haire of the body, as resin dos a piggs. I think there is orpiment & lime in it, for if it lie on to<o> long it burns the flesh: The curiosity of this Bath, did so open my pores that it cost me one of the greatest Colds & rheumes that ever I had in my whole life, by reason of my comming out without that caution necessary of keeping my selfe Warme for some time after: For I immediately began to visite the famous Places of the Citty And Travellers, do nothing else but run up & downe to see sights, that come into Italy: And this Citty, for being one of the most miraculously plac'd of any in the whole World. built on so many hundred Ilands, in the very sea, and at good distance from the Continent, deser<v>'d our admiration: It has neither fresh, nor any other but salt Water, save what is reserved in Cistrens, of the raine, & such as is daily brought them from *Terra firma* in boates: Yet it wa<n>ts nor fresh water, nor aboundance of all sorts of excellent Provisions, very cheape ...

Twas now Ascension Weeke, & the greate Mart or faire of the whole yeare now kept, every body at liberty, & jollie; the Noblemen stalking with their Ladys on Choppines about 10 foote high from the ground. These are high heeld shoos particularly affected by these proude dames, or as some say, invented to keepe them at home, it being so difficult to walke with them, whence one being asked how he liked the Venetian Dames, replyd, they were *Mezzo Carne, Mezzo Legno;*[1] & he would have none of them: The truth is their Garb is very odd, as seeming allways in Masquerade, their other habite also totaly different from all Nations: The<y> weare very long crisped haire of severall strakes and Colours, which they artificially make so, by washing their heads in pisse, & dischevelling them on the brims of a broade hat that has no head, but an hole to put out their head by, drie them in the Sunn, as one may see them above, out of their windos: In their tire they set silk flowers & sparkling stones, their peticoates comming from their very armepetts, so high as that their very breasts flub over the tying place; so as they are neare three quarters & an halfe Aporn: Their Sleeves are made exceeding wide, under which their smock sleeves as wide & commo<n>ly tucked up to the shoulder, & shewing their naked arme, through false Sleeves of Tiffany girt with a bracelet or two: besides this they go very bare of their breasts & back, with knots of poynts richly tagg'd, about their shoulders & other places, of their body, which the<y> usualy cover with a kind of yellow Vaile of Lawn very transparant. Thus attir'd they set their hands on the heads of two Matron-like servants or old women to support them, who are mumbling their beades: Tis very ridiculous to see how these Ladys crawle in & out of their Gundolas by reason of their Choppines & what dwarfes they appeare when taken down from their Wooden scafolds: Of these I saw neere 30 together stalking, halfe as high more, as the rest of the World; ...

There being at the time a ship bound for the Holy Land, I had now resolved to imbarke myselfe, intending to see Jerusalem, & other parts of Syria, Egypt, & Turky: but after I was provided of all necessaries, laied in Snow to coole our drink, bought some Sheepe, Poultry, Bisquit, Spirits & a little Cabinet of Drouggs &c. in case of sicknesse; our Vessell (whereof Cap: Powell was Master) happnd to be press'd for the service of the State, to Carry Provisions to Candia, which was now nuly attacqu'd by the Turkes; which altogether frustrated my designe, to my greate sorrow, it being but two or 3 daies before we hoped to set saile.

---

[1] Half-flesh, half-wood.

Evelyn travelled inland to Padua, returning to Venice by early July

July Our next sally was the Arsenal thought to be one of the best furnish'd in all the World: We entred by a strong port, allways guarded, & ascending a spacious Gallery, saw armes of back, breast & head, for many Thousands, in another were Saddles, & over them divers Ensignes taken from the Turks: Another hall is for the meeting of the Senat: passing a Graft, are the Smiths forges, where they are continualy at work on Ankers & Iron work: Neere it a Well of fresh Water which they impute to two Rhinceros's hornes which they say lie in it, & will preserve it from ever being empoison'd:

Then we came to where the Carpenters were building, their Magazine of Oares, Masts, &c for an hundred Gallys & ships, which have all their apparell, & furniture neere them: Then the fundarie, where they cast Ordinance: The forge is 450 paces long, & one of them has 13 furnaces: There is one Canon weighing 16573 pounds cast whilst Henry the 3d dined, & put into a Gally, built, rigg'd & fitted for launching within that time: They have also Armes for 12 Galeasses, which are Vessells to row of almost 150 foote long, and 30 large: not counting prow or poup, & contain 28 banks each 7. men, & so carry 1300 Men: with 3 masts: In another a Magazin for 50 Gallys, & place for some hundreds more: Here stands the Bucentaur, with a most ample deck, & so contriv'd, that the Slaves are not seene, having on the Poup a Thron for the Dodge to sit, when he gos in tryumph to espouse the Adriatic: here is also a gallery of 200 yards long for Cables, and over that a Magazine of hemp: Over against these their Saltpeter houses & a large row of Cells or houses to thrust their Gallys in, out of all Weather:

Over the Gate, as we go out, is a roome full of greate & small Guns, some of which discharge 6 times at once: Then there is a Court full of Cannon bullets, Chaines, Grapples, Granados, &c: & over that Armes for 800000 men, & by themselves, armes for 400, taken from some that were in a plot against the State; together with weapons of offence & defence for 62 ships, 32 piece of Ordinance on Carriages taken from the Turks, & one prodigious Mortar-piece:

In a word, tis not to be reckon'd up, what this large place containes of this sort: There were now 23 Gallys, & 4 Gally Grossi here of 100 Oares of a side: The whole Arsenal is walld about, & may be in Compasse about 3 miles, with 12 Toures for the Watch, besides that sea invirons it: The Workmen who are ordinarily 500 march out of it in militarie order, and every evening receive their pay thro<ugh> a small hole in the gate, where the Governor lies.

The next day I saw a wretch executed who had murther'd his Master, for which he had his head chop'd off by an Axe that slid down a frame of timber, betweene the two tall Columns in St.Marcs Piazzo at the sea brink; the Executioner striking on the Axe with a bettle, & so the head fell off the block:

Henc by Gudola we went to se<e> Grimanis Palace, the portico whereoff is excellent work: Indeede the whole World cannot certainly shew a Citty of more stately buildings, considering the extent of it, all of Square Stone, & as chargeable in their foundations, as superstructure, as being all built upon Piles, at an immense cost: ...

The day after being Sonday, I went over to St. Georgio to the Ceremonie of the Schismatic Greekes, who are permitted to have their Church, though they are at defiance with Rome: They allow of no Carved Images, but many painted, especialy the storie of their Patron & his dragon: Their rites differ not much from the Latines, save that of communicating in both species, and distribution of the holy bread: We afterward fell into a dispute with a Candiot concerning the procession of the Holy Ghost: The Church is a noble fabric:

The 26 **September** my deare friend, & 'til now Constant fellow Traveller Mr. Thicknesse, being oblig'd to returne into England upon his particular Concerne, & who had served his Majestie in the Warrs; I accompanied him part of his way, & 28, returnd to Venice: ...

1646

In **January** Signor Molino was chosen Dodge, but the extreame snow that fell, & the cold hindred my going to see the solemnity, so as I stirrd not from Padoa til Shrovetide, when all the world repaire to Venice to see the folly & madnesse of the Carnevall; The Women, Men & persons of all Conditions disguising themselves in antique dresses, & extravagant Musique & a thousand gambols, & traversing the streetes from house to house, all places being then accessible, & free to enter: There is abroad nothing but flinging of Eggs fill'd with sweete Waters, & sometimes not over sweete; they also have a barbarous costome of hunting bulls about the Streetes & Piazzas, which is very dangerous, the passages being generally so narrow in that Citty: Likewise do the youth of the severall Wards & parrishes contend in other Masteries or pastimes so as tis altogether impossible to recount the universal madnesse of this place during this time of licence: Now are the greate banks set up for those who will play at Basset, the Comedians have also liberty & the Operas to Exercise: Witty pasquils are likewise thrown about, & the Mountebanks have their stages in every Corner: The diversion which chiefly tooke me up, was three noble Operas which I saw, where was incomparable Voices, & Musique:

Three daies after this, I tooke my leave of Venice, and went to Padoa to be present at the famous Anatomie Lecture, which is here celebrated with extraordinary apparatus, & lasting almost the whole Moneth, during which I saw three, a Woman, a Child, & a Man dissected, with all the manual operations of the Chirurgion upon the humane body: The one performed by Cavaliere Vestlingius, & Dr. Jo. Athelsteinus Leoncenas, of whom I purchased those rare Tables of Veines & Nerves, & causd him to prepare a third of the Lungs, liver, & Nervi sexti par: with the Gastric vaines, which I transported into England, the first of that kind that had ben ever seene in our Country, & for I ought to know, in the World, though afterwards there were others: [Given after to the R:Society:][1]

When the Anatomie Lectures (which was in the Mornings) were ended, I went to see cures don in the Hospitals, and certainly, as there are greatest helps, & skillfullest Physitians, so there are the most miserable & deplorable objects, to exercise upon, both of Men & Women; Whores, & Virgins, Old & Young; nor is there any I should think, so prevalent document, or lecture against the vice reigning in this licentious Country, than to be Spectator of the miserie, which these poore Creatures undergo, by Trepanning, Launcing, Salivating, Sweating, &c: They are indeede very carefully attended, and with extraordinary Charity: but I do not approve of their so freely admitting young Gentlemen Travellers to see their operations upon some of the femal Sex, who

---

[1] See below, 31 October 1667.

even in the midst of their tortures, are not very modest, & when they begin to be well, plainely lew'd: March:

20 I return'd to Venice where I tooke leave of my Friends: ...

March 24 Having pack'd up my purchases, of Books, Pictures, G<l>asses, Treacle, &c (the making and extraordinary ceremonie whereof, I had ben curious to observe, for tis extremely pompous & worth seeing) I departed from Venice, accompanied with Mr. Waller (the celebrated Poet)[1] now newly gotten out of England, after the Parliament had extreamely worried him, for attempting to put in execution the Commission of Aray, & for which the rest of his Collegues were hanged by the Rebells:

The next day, I tooke leave of my Comrades at Padoa, & receiving some directions from Cavallero Salvatico how to govern my selfe, being of late incommoded with a salt defluction from my head (for which I had a little before ben let blood) I prepard for my Journey towards Milan: It was Easter Monday, that I was invited to Breakfast at the Earle of Arundels; I tooke my leave of him in his bed, where I left that greate & excellent Man in teares upon some private discourse of the crosses had befaln his Illustrious family: particularly the undutifullnesse of his Grandson Philips turning Dominican Frier [Since Cardinal of Norfolke], the unkindnesse of his Countesse, now in Holland; The miserie of his Countrie, now embroild in a Civil War &c: after which he caused his Gentleman to give me directions all written with his owne hand, what curiosities I should enquire after in my Journey, & so injoyning me to write sometimes to him, I departed: ...

Evelyn travelled to Vincenza and on towards Brescia

April ... We din'd at an Inn call'd *Cavalli Caschieiri* neere Peschiera a very strong fort of the Venetian Republique, & neere the Lago di Garda, which dissembogues into that of Mantua neere 40 miles in length, & for being so highly celebrated by my Lord Arundel to me, as the most pleasant spot of Italy, I observ'd it with the more diligence, alighting out of the Coach, & going up to a grove of Cypresses growing about a Gentlemans Country house, from whence indeede it presents a most surprizing Prospect: The hills & gentle risings about it, produces Oranges, Citrons, Olives, Figs & other tempting fruits, & the Waters abounding in excellent Fish, especialy Trouts: In the middle of this Lake stands Sermonea on an Iland: Here Cap: Wray bought a pretty Nag of the Master of our Inn where we dined, for 8 Pistoles, which yet his Wife our hostesse was so unwilling to part with, that she did nothing but kisse, & weepe & hang about the horses neck, till the Captaine rid away: so we came this Evening to Bres<c>ia, which next morning (according to our Costome) we traverst in search of Antiquities & new sights: & here I purchased my fine Carabine of [old] Lazarino Cominazzo which cost me 9 pistols, this Citty being famous for these fire Armes, & that workeman, with Jo: Bap: Franco the best esteem'd; ...

Onwards to Milan

Here, at approch of the Citty, some of our Company (in dread of the Inquisition, severer here than in any place of all Spaine) thought of throwing away some Protestant (by them call'd Heretical) books & papers: It was about

---

[1] Edmund Waller (1606-87), banished for his royalist plotting 1644-51.

3 in the Afternoone that we came thither, where the Officers search'd us
th<o>roughly for prohibited goods, but finding we were onely Gentlemen
Travellers dismissd us for a small reward: so we went quietly to our Inn the
3 Kings, where for that day we refreshed ourselves, as we had neede ...

I went into the Gouvernors Palace, who was then the Condestable of Castile:
tempted by the glorious Tapissries & Pictures, I adventurd so far alone, that
peeping into a Chamber where the greate Man was under the barbers hands, he
sent one of his Negros (a slave) to know what I was, I made the best excuse I
could & that I was onely admiring the Pictures, which he returning, & telling
his Lord, I heard the Governor reply, It was some Spie, upon which I retir'd
with all the Speede I could, pass'd the Guard of Swisse, got into the streete,
and in a moment to my Company, who were gon to the Jesuites Church ...

Passing towards our Lodging, & Walking a turne in the Portico before the
Dome a Cavaliero who pass'd by, hearing some of our Companie speaking
English, looked a good while earnestly on us, and by & by sending his servant
towards us, desird that we would honour him the next day at Dinner; This we
looked on as an odd kind of Invitation, he not speaking at all to us himselfe:
We returnd his Civilitie, with thanks, not fully resolv'd what to do, or what
might be the meaning of it, in this jealous place: But on inquirie, 'twas told us
he was a Scots Colonel, that had an honorable Command in the Citty, so we
agreed to go:...

Next morning we went to the Colonels, who had sent his servant againe to
conduct us to his house; which in truth we found a noble Palace, richly
furnish'd. There were also other Guest<s>, all Souldiers, and one of them a
Scotch man, but not one of all their names could we learn: At dinner he excusd
his rudenesse, that he had not himselfe spoken to us, telling us it was his
costome, when he heard of any English Travlors (who but rarely would be
knowne to passe through that Citty, for feare of the Inquisition) to invite them
to his house, where they might be free: And indeede we had a most sumptuous
dinner, with plenty of Excellent provision, & the wine so tempting, that after
some healths had gon about, & we rissen from the Table, the Colonel leade us
into his hall, where there hung up divers Colours, Saddles, bridles, pistols &
other Armes, being Trophies which he had with his owne hands taken from the
Enemy; & amongst them would needes bestow a paire of Pistols on Cap:
Wray, one of our fellow Travelors, & a good drinking Gent: & on me, a
Turkish bridle woven with silk & very Curiously embossd, with other silk
Trappings, to which hung an halfe moone finely wrought, which he had taken
from a Basshaw that he had slaine: With this glorious spoile, I rid the rest of
my Journey as far as Paris & brought it afterwards into England.

Then he shew'd us a stable of brave horses, with his Menage & Cavalerizzo.
Some of the horses he causd to be brought forth, which he mounted, and
perform'd all the motions of an Excellent horse-man: When this was don, &
he alighted, contrary to the advice of his Groome & Pages, (who it seemes
knew the nature of the beast, & that their Master was a little spirited with
Wine) needes he would have out a fiery horse, that had yet ben Menag'd, &
was very ungovernable; but was else a very beautifull Creature: This he
mounting, the horse getting the raines, in a full carriere, <rose> so
de<s>perately, as he fell quite back, crushing the Colonell so forceably against
the Wall of the Manege, that though he sat on him like a Centaure, yet
recovering the Jade on all foure againe, he desir'd to be taken down, & so led
in, where he cast himselfe upon a Pallet, where with infinite lamentation, after
some time, we tooke our leaves of him, being now speechlesse; and the next
morning coming to visite him, we found before the doore, the Canopie, which

they usualy carry over the Host, and some with lighted tapers, which made us suspect he was in very sad condition, & so indeede we found him, an Irish frier standing by his bed side, as Confessing him, or at least disguising a Confession & other Ceremonies, us<e>d *in extremis*; for we afterwards learn'd that the Gent: was a Protestant, and had this Frier his confident; which doubtlesse was a dangerous thing at Milan, had it ben but suspected: At our enterance he sighed grievously and held up his hands, but was not able to speake: After vomiting some bloud, he kindly tooke us all by the hand, & made signes, that he should see us no more, which made us take our leave of him with extreame reluctancy, & affliction for the Accident:

This sad disaster made us Consult that very Evening about our departure from this Towne as soon as we could, not knowing how we might be enquird after, or engag'd, The Inquisition heare being so cruelly formidable, & inevitable on the least suspicion: The very next morning therefore discharging our Lodgings we agreed for a Coach to Carry us to the foote of the Alpes, not a little concernd for the death of the Colonell, which we now heard of, & that had so courteously entertain'd us:

Evelyn moved north across the Alps, and stayed in a village

In this wretched place, I lay on a bed stuff'd with leaves, which made such a Crackling, & did so prick my skin through the tick, that I could not sleepe: The next morning I was furnish'd with an Asse (for we could not get horses) but without stirrops, but we had ropes tied with a loope to put our feete in...

Next morning we mount againe through strange, horrid, & firefull Craggs & tracts abounding in Pine trees, & onely inhabited with Beares, Wolves, & Wild Goates, nor could we any where see above a pistol shoote before us, the horizon being terminated with rocks, & mountaines, whose tops cover'd with Snow, seem'd to touch the Skies, & in many places pierced the Clowdes. Some of these vast mountaines were but one intire stone, 'twixt whose clefts now & then precipitated greate Cataracts of Mealted Snow, and other Waters, which made a tirrible roaring, Echoing from the rocks & Cavities, & these Waters in some places, breaking in the fall, wett us as if we had pas'd through a mist, so as we could neither see, nor heare one another, but trusting to our honest Mules, jog on our Way: The narrow bridges in some places, made onely by felling huge Fir-trees & laying them athwart from mountaine to mountaine, over Cataracts of stupendious depth, are very dangerous, & so are the passages & edges made by cutting away the maine rock: others in steps, & in some places we passe betweene mountaines that have ben broken & falln upon one another, which is very tirrible, & one had neede of a sure foote, & steady head to climb some of these precipices, harbours for the Bears, & Woulv<e>s, who sometimes have assaulted Travellers:

In these straits we frequently alighted, freezing in the Snow, & anon frying by the reverberation of the Sun against the Cliffs as we descend lower, where we meete now & then a few miserable Cottages, built so upon the declining of the rocks, as one would expect their sliding down: Amongst these inhabite a goodly sort of People having monstrous Gullets or Wenns of flesse growing to their throats, some of which I have seene as big as an hundred pound bag of silver hanking under their Chinns; among the Women especialy, & that so ponderous, as that to Ease them, they many of them were <a> linnen cloth, bound about their head & coming under the chin to support it, but *quis*

tumidum guttur miratur in Alpibus?[1] Their drinking so much snow water is
thought to be the Cause of it, the men using more wine, are not so strumous as
the Women; but the very truth is, they are a race of people, & many greate
Water-drinkers here have not those prodigious tumors: It runs as we say in the
bloud, & is a vice in the race, & renders them so ougly, shrivel'd & deform'd,
by its drawing the skin of the face downe, that nothing can be more fritefull; to
which add a strange puffing habit, furrs, & barbarous Language, being a
mixture of corrupt high German, French, & Italian: The people are of gigantic
Stature, extreamely fierce & rude, yet very honest & trustie:

This night, through unaccessible heights, we came in prospect of *Mons
Sempronius*, now Mount Sampion, which has on its summit a few hutts, & a
Chapell: Approching this, Captaine Wrays Water Spaniel, (a huge filthy Curr,
that had follow'd him out of England), hunted an heard of Goates downe the
rockes, into a river made by the dissolutions of the Snow: Ariv'd at our cold
harbour (though the house had in every roome a Stove), supping with Cheeze
& Milke & wretched wine to bed we go in Cupbords, & so high from the
floore, that we climb'd them by a Ladder, & as we lay on feathers, so are
Coverd with them, that is, betweene two tickes stuff'd with feathers, & all
little enough to keepe one warme: The Ceilings of the roomes are strangely
low for those tall people.

The house was now in September, halfe cover'd with Snow, nor is there
ever a tree or bush growing in many miles: from this unhospitable place then
we hasted away early next morning, but as we were getting on our Mules,
comes a huge young fellow, demanding mony for a Goate, Cap: Wrays Dog
(he affirm'd) had kild the other day: expostulating the matter, & impatient of
staying in the Cold, we set spurrs & endeavor'd to ride away, when a
multitude of People, being by this time gotten together about us (it being
Sonday morning & attending for the Priest to say Masse) stop our Mules, beate
us off our saddles & imediately disarming us of our Carbines, drew us into one
of the roomes of our Lodging, & set a guard upon us.

Thus we continu'd Prisoners till Masse was ended, & then came there halfe
a Score grimm Swisse, & taking upon them to be Magistrates, sate downe on
the Table, and condemn'd us to pay the fellow a pistol for his Goate, & ten
more for attempting to ride away: Threatning that if we did not do it speedily
they would send us to another Prison, & keep us to a day of publique Justice,
where, as they perhaps would have exaggerated the Crime, for they pretended
we span'd our Carabines & would have shot some of them (as indeede the
Captaine, was about to do) we might have had our heads cut off, for amongst
these barbarous people, a very small misdemeanor dos often meete that
animadversion: This we were afterwards told; & though the proceeding
appeerd highly unjust, upon Consultation amongst ourselves, we thought it
safer to rid our selves out of their hands, & the trouble we were brought in,
than to expostulate it among such brutes, & therefore we patiently lay'd downe
the mony, & with fierce Countenances had our Mules, & armes deliverd us,
and glad to scape as we did:

This was cold entertainement, but our journey after was colder, the rest of
the Way having (tis sai'd) ben cover'd with Snow since the Creation; for that
never man remember'd it to be without; & because by the frequent Snowing,

---

[1] Juvenal, *Satires* XIII.162, 'Who wonders at a swollen throat in the Alps?'
According to de Beer (II, 510, note) many of E's contemporary travellers in the area
mention the condition.

the tracks are continualy fill'd up, we passe by severall tall Masts, set up, to guide Those who travell, so as for any miles they stand in ken of one another, like to our Beacons: In some places of divided Mountaines, the Snow quite fills up the Cleft, whilst the bottome being thaw'd, leaves it as it were a frozen Arch of Snow, & that so hard, as to beare the greatest weight, for as it snows often so it perpetualy freezes, & of this I was so sensible, as it flaw'd the very skin of my face: Beginning now to descend a little, Cap: Wrays horse, that was our Sumpter, (& carried all our bagage) plunging through a bank of loose Snow, slid downe a firefull precipice, more than thrice the height of St Paules, which so incens'd the Cholerique Cavalier his Master, that he was sending a brace of bullets into the poore beast, least the Swisse, that was our Guide, should recover him & run away with his burden: but just as his hand was lifting up his Carbine, We gave such a Shout, & pelted the horse so with Snow balls, as with all his might plunging thro the Snow, he fell from another steepe place into another bottome neere a path we were to passe:

It was yet a good while 'ere we got to him, but at last we recovered the place, & easing him of his Charge, hal'd him out of the Snow, where he had ben certainely frozen in, if we had not prevented it before night: It was (as we judg'd) almost two miles that he had slid & fall'n, & yet without any other harme, than the benumming of his limbs for the present, which with lusty rubbing & chafing he began to move, & after a little walking perform'd his journey well enough: All this Way (affrited with the dissaster of the Captaines horse) we trudg'd on foote, driving our Mules before us: & sometimes we fell, & sometimes slid thro this ocean of featherd raine, which after October is impassible: Towards night we came into a larger way, thro vast woods of Pines which cloth the middle parts of these rocks: here they were burning some to make Pitch & Rosin, piling the knotty branches, as we do to make Char-Coale, & reserving that which mealts from them, which harden into Pitch &c: & here we passd severall Cascads of dissolv'd Snow, that had made Channels of formidable depth in the Crevices of the Mountaines, & with such a firfull roaring, as for 7 long miles as we could plainely heare it: It is from these Sourses, that the swift & famous Rhodanus, & the Rhyne which passe thro all France, & Germanie, derive their originals.

Late at night then we got to a Towne call'd Briga which is build at the foote of the Alpes in the Valtoline: Every doore almost had nailed on the outside, & next the Streete, a Beares, Wolfes or foxes-head & divers of them all Three, which was a Salvage kind of sight: but as the Alps are full of these beasts, the People often kill them:

The next morning we return'd our Guide, & tooke fresh Mules & another <guide> to conduct us to the Lake of Geneva, passing through as pleasant a Country, as that which before we had traveld, was melancholy & troublesome, & a strange & suddaine change it seem'd, for the reverberation of the Sunbeames darting from the Mountaines & rocks, that like a Wall range it on both sides, not above 2 flight shots in bredth for some hundreds of miles; renders the passage excessively hot: through such extreames we continud our Journey, whilst that goodly river the Rhone glided by us in a narrow & quiet chanell, almost in the middle of this Canton, & fertilizing the Country for Grasse & Corne which growes here in aboundance, for the Snow which waters it from the hills, brings downe with it a fertil liquor that dos wonderfully impregnat.

Evelyn reached Sion, St. Moritz and Le Bouveret by late May, early June

June ... where being extreamely weary, & complaining of my head, & little accommodation in the house, I caus'd one of our Hostesses daughters to be removed out of her bed, & went immediately into it, whilst it was yet warme, being so heavy with paine & drowsinesse, that I would not stay to have the sheetes chang'd; but I shortly after pay'd dearely for my impatience, falling sick of the Small Pox so soone as I came to Geneva; for by the smell of franc Incense, & the tale the good-woman told me, of her daughters having had an Ague, I afterwards concluded she had ben newly recoverd of the Small Pox: The paine of my head & wearinesse making me not consider of any thing, but how to get to bed so soone as ever I alighted, as not able any longer to sit on horseback:

Notwithstanding this, I went with my Company the next day, hiring a bark to carry us over the Lake [*Lacus Lemanus*], & indeede, sick as I was, the Weather was so serene & bright, the Water so Calme, & aire temperate, that, never had Travelers a sweeter passage: Thus we saild the whole length of the Lake, for about 30 miles, The Countries bordering on it, Savoy & Bearne, affording one of the most delightfull prospects in the World, the Alps, cover'd with Snow, though at greate distance, yet shewing their aspiring tops: ... But being now no more able to hold up my head, I was constrain'd to keepe my Chamber, imagining that my very eyes would have droped out, & this night felt such a stinging all about me that I could not sleepe:

In the morning I was very ill: yet for all that, the Doctor (whom I had now consulted, & was a very learned old man, & as he sayd had ben Physition to Gustavus the greate King of Sweden, when he pass'd this way into Italy, under the name of Monsieur Garse, the Initial letters of *Gustavus Adolphus Rex Sueciæ*, & of our famous Duke of Boukingham returning out of Italy) perswaded me to be let bloud, which he accknowledg'd to me he should not have don, had he suspected the Small-Pox, which brake out a <day> after; for he also purg'd me, & likewise applied *Hirudines ad anum*,[1] & God knows what this had produc'd if the spots had not appeard: for he was thinking of blouding me againe: Wherefore now they kept me warme in bed for 16 daies, tended by a vigilant Swisse Matron whose monstrous Throat, when I sometimes awake'd out <of> unquiet slumbers would affright me: After the pimples were come forth, which were not many, I had much ease, as to paine, but infinitly afflicted with the heate & noysomeness; But by Gods mercy, after five weekes keping my Chamber, being purg'd, & visited by severall of the Towne: espec<i>aly Monsieur Saladine & his Lady, who sent me many refreshments, during my sicknesse: Monsieur Le Chat (my Physitian) to excuse his letting me bloud, told me it was so burnt & vitious, as it would have prov'd the Plague or spoted feavor, had he proceeded by any other method:

The next day after my going abroad, I din'd at Mr. Saladines, & in the afternoone, went crosse the Water on the side of the Lake, to take a Lodging that stood exceeding pleasantly, about halfe a mile off the Citty, for better ayring; but I onely stayed one night, having no Company there save my Pipe; so as the next day, I causd them to row me about the Lake, as far as the greate Stone, which they call Neptunes rock, on which they say, Sacrifice was antiently offer'd to him: Thence I landed at certaine Chery-Gardens, & pretty Villas situate on the rivage, & exceedingly pleasant: ...

Evelyn explored Geneva and its environs during July

---

[1] Leeches to the rear passage.

July ... I went to see the young townes men exercise in Mars field, where the Prizes were pewter plates, & dishes: 'Tis said that some have gain'd competent Estates, by what they have thus won: Here I first saw huge Balistæ or Crosse bows (such as they formerly us'd in wars, before Greate guns were known) shot in: They were placed in frames, & had might<y> screws to bend them, doing execution an incredible distance: They are most accurate at the long-bow, and Musquet, very rarely missing the smalest mark; & I was as buisy with the Carbine I brought with me from Bressia as any of them: After every shot, I found them go into the long house & clense their guns before they charg'd againe ...

... My sicknesse and abode here cost me 45 pistols of gold to my Host, & 5 to my honest Doctor, who for 6 Weekes attendance & the Apothecarie, thought it so generous a reward, that at my taking leave, he presented me with his advice for the regiment of my health, written with his own hand in Latine.

Evelyn travelled north into France during the late summer and early autumn via Lyons and Orleans; at Nevers he lost his dog

October ... here <at Nevers> it was I lost my faithfull Spaniel (Piccioli) who had follow'd me from Rome; it seemes he had ben taken up by some of the Governors pages or foote-men, without recovery, which was a greate displeasure to me, because the curr, had many usefull qualities: The next day we ariv'd at Orleans, taking our turn to row through all the former passages & reckoning that my share amounted to little lesse than 20 legues; sometimes footing it through pleasant fields & medows, sometimes we shot at fouls & other birds, nothing came amisse, sometimes we play'd at Cards, whilst other sung, or were composing Verses; for we had the greate Poet Mr. Waller in our Companie, & some other ingenious Persons: At Orleans we abode but one day, the next (leaving our mad Captaine behind us) I arived at Paris, strangely rejoyc'd, after so many dissasters, & accidents, of a tedious Peregrination, that I was gotten so neere home, & therefore resolved to rest myselfe before I set on any further Motion.

It was now October, & the onely time that in my whole life I spent most idly, tempted from my more profitable recesses; but I soone recovered my better resolutions, & fell to my study, & learning of the high-dutch & Spanish tongues, & now & then refreshing my Dauncing, & such exercises as I had long omitted, & which are not in such reputation among the sober Italians.

There are no further entries for 1646

1647

January 28, I chang'd my Lodging in the Place de Monsieur de Metz neere the Abby of St. Germains, & thence on the 12 **Feb**: to another in Rüe Collumbiers, where I had a very faire Appartment, which cost me 4 pistols per Moneth:

The 18 I frequented a Course of Chymistrie, the famous Monsieur Le Febure operating upon most of the Nobler processes:

March 3, Monsieur Mercure began to teach me on the Lute, though to small perfection.

In **May** I fell sick & had very sore Eyes, for which I was 4 times let blood.

The 22d: My Valet de Chambre Hebert robbed me of the value of three-score pounds in Clothes & plate; but through the dilligence of Sir Richard Browne his Majesties Resident at the Court of France & with whose Lady & family I had contracted a greate Friendship (& particularly set my affections on a Daughter)[1] I recoverd most of them againe; obtaining of the Judge (with no small difficulty) that the processe against my Theife, should not concerne his life, being his first fault:

June 10th: We concluded about my Marriage, in order to which on 26: I went to St.Germans, where his Majestie (then Prince of Wales) had his Court, to desire of Dr. Earles, then one of his Chaplaines, and since, Deane of Westminster, Clearke of the Closset & Bishop of Salisburie, to come with me to Paris.

So on Thursday 27 June 1647 the Doctor Married us in Sir Richard Browne Knight & Baronet My Wifes fathers Chapell, twixt the houres of 11 & 12; some few select friends being present: And this being Corpus Christi feast, solemn<l>y observ'd in these Countries, the stretes were sumptuously hung with Tapissry, & strew'd with flowers.

July 13, I went with my Wife, & her Mother, to St. Cloud, where we collation'd, and were serv'd in Plate:

September 10th, being call'd into England to settle my affaires, after about 4 yeares absence (my Wife being yet very Young, and therefore dispensing with a temporarie & kind separation, whilst left under the care of an excellent Lady, & prudent Mother) I tooke leave of the Prince, & Queene:

October 4: I seald & declared my Will; & that morning went from Paris taking my journey thro Rouen, Dieppe, Ville-Dieu, St. Vallerie, where I staied one day, with Mr. Waller, with whom I had some affaires, & for which cause I tooke this Circle to Calice, where I ariv'd on the 11th and that night Imbarking on the Paquet-boate, was by one aclock gott safe to Dover; for which I heartily put up my Thankes to God, who had conducted me safe to my owne Country, & ben mercifull to me through so many aberrations: Hence taking Post, I ariv'd at London the next day at Evening, being the 2d of October New-style.

On the 4th my Bro: George hearing where I was sent me horses & a kind Invitation, so on the 5t I came to Wotton the place of my Birth, where I found his Lady, my Sister, & severall of my friends and relations, amongst whom I refresh'd my selfe & rejoyc'd 'til the 10th, when I went to Hampton Court, where I had the honour to kiss his Majesties Hand, and give him an Account, of severall things I had in charge, he being now in the power of those execrable Villains who not long after mu<r>der'd him: Here I lay at my Co: Serjeant Hattons at Thames Ditton whence on the 13 I went to London, the next day to Sayes-Court (now my house) at Deptford in Kent,[2] where I found

---

[1] Mary Evelyn (c. 1635-1709), the mother of E's children.

[2] The manor of Sayes Court, Deptford, lay close to the south bank of the Thames about three miles south-east of the City of London, and immediately adjacent to the Royal Naval Dockyard. It took its name from Geoffrey de Say who in 1191 acquired the estate through his marriage to Alice de Maminot. By 1604 it was leased from the crown by Christopher Browne (c.1576-1646), father of Sir Richard Browne, E's

Mr. Pretyman my Wifes Unkle, who had charge of it, & the Estate about it during my F in Laws Residence in France: on the 15th I went to lodge in my owne Chambers at the Middle Temple about the dispatch of my particular concernes.

November 7th I return'd againe to Wotton to visite my brother, & on the 9th my Sister, opened to me her Marriage with Mr.Glanvill:

1648

February 5 I saw a Tragie Comedie acted in the Cock-pit, after there had ben none of these diversions for many Yeares during the Warr.

28 I went to Thistleworth (with my noble friend Sir William Ducy, afterwards Lord Downe) where we dined with Sir Clepesby Crew, and afterwards to see the rare Miniatures of Peter Oliver [and rounds of plaster] & then the curious flowers of Mr. Barills garden: Sir Clepesby has fine Indian hangings, and a very good chimny-piece of Water Colours don by Breugle which I bought for him: Mr. Barill has also some good Medails & Pictures.

April 3. I went to Wotton, thence to a place neere Henly cald Boyne, belonging to one Mr. Elmes, which I thought to have purchas'd & settld in; but we did not accord: So on the 5t I return'd, & the 10th to Lond:

26. There was a greate up-rore in Lond, that the Rebell Armie quartering at Whitehall would plunder the Cittie, who publish'd a proclamation for all to stand on their guard:

May 4 Came-up the Essex petitioners for an agreement 'twixt his Majestie & the Rebells.

---

father-in-law. In a survey of 1608 the Elizabethan manor house was said to have two storeys, eighteen rooms, with gardens and orchards. A further survey in 1651 added that the house was built of timber. E, who had been using the house since 1647, took over the lease from from Sir Richard Browne in 1653 (see 22 February 1653) and lived there until 1694 when he moved to Wotton (4 May 1694). During his residence the gardens became a celebrated sight ('a most beautiful place' and 'we walked in his garden, and a lovely noble ground he hath indeed', Pepys's *Diary*, 1 and 5 May 1665).

There are no known pictures of the house apart from a sketch which E made on a map of Deptford which shows it to have been a triple-gabled house. E did however make an elaborate plan of the house and grounds in 1653 (reproduced in W.G. Hiscock, 1955, *John Evelyn and his Family Circle*, between pages 24-25). This shows that the house lay close to the wall separating the estate from the Dockyard and was approached by a tree-lined avenue from Deptford through two gates. It required a great deal of renovation and expensive repairs which E lived to regret (see 17 April 1680, note), and did not survive long after his death. It was demolished by the middle of the eighteenth century and though the land remained in the Evelyn family as gardens, with an almshouse on the site of the old house, until relatively recently, it has now been sold. Most of the land is covered with industrial buildings though a small south-western section survives as Sayes Court Recreation Ground.

16 The Surry men addressd to the Parliament for the same, of which some were slayne & murder'd by Cromwells guards in the new Palace yard.

I now sold, the Impropriation of South Malling neere Lewes in Sussex to Mr. Kemp & Alcock for 3000 pounds: ...

30 ... There was a rising now in Kent, my Lord of Norwich being in the head of them and their first rendezvous in Broome-fild, next my house at Says-Court whence they went to Maidstone, & so to Colchester where there was that memorable siege:

June 27: I purchas'd the Manor of Hurcott in Worcestershire of my Bro: Geo: for 3300 pounds: on the 29 I return'd to Deptford.

July 1. I sate for my picture (the same wherein is a Deaths head) to Mr. Walker that excellent Painter:[1]

The 10th Newes was brought to me of my Lord Francis Villiers being slaine by the rebells neere Kingston: ...

17th I went to hunting at my Lady Lees, where we kill'd a buck ...

August 16 To Woodcoat to the Wedding of my Bro: Richard who married the Daughter & Coheire, of Esquire Minn lately deceased: by which he had a great Estate both in Land & monie, upon the death of a Brother &c: *Memorandum* that the Coach in which the Bride & Bridegroom were, was overturn'd in coming home, but no harme: ...

28 To Lond, & went to see the celebrated follies of Bartholomew faire.

September 16 Came my lately married Bro: Richard & his Wife to visite me:

17 I shewed them Greenewich & Her Majesties Palace, now possessed by the Rebells ...

October 26: To Lewes, in which journey I escaped a strange fall from my horse in the dark, from an high bank & deepe way about Chaylie:

31 I went to see my Mannor of Preston Beckhelvyn, & the Cliff house:[2]

November November we return'd with my Bro: R: & Glanvill by Shoreham, Bramber (where is a ruinous Castle) Billingshurst where we lay that night, & next day at Woodcot, & on the 6 to Says-Court: ...

29 Myselfe, with Mr. Tho: Offley, & Lady Gerrard Christned my Nieece Mary, Eldest daughter of my Bro: Geo: Evelyn by my Lady Cotton his second Wife: I presented my Niepce a piece of Plate which cost me 18 pounds...

December : I lent 1000 pounds to Esquire Hyldiard on a statute: & this day sold my Mannor of <Hurcott> for 3400 pounds to one Mr. Bridges & on the 4th acknowledgd the fine.

4th I lent 1000 pounds to my Lord Vicount Montague, on a <Mortgage> of Horslay, in Surry: ...

---

[1] Robert Walker (-1658). Now in the National Portait Gallery, London. The 'Deaths head' [skull] has been revealed with x-rays to have been an addition and covered a medal or miniature, probably depicting Mary Evelyn (Malcolm Rogers, NPG).

[2] The property of E's maternal grandfather, John Standsfield, where E's mother was born, and where he was brought up by his maternal step-grandmother until she re-married (see above, 1630).

13 to Lond: The Parliament now sat up the whole night, & endeavord to have concluded the Ile of Wight Treaty, but were surprized by the rebell Army, the Members disperssd, & greate confusion every where in expectation what would be next: I now also gave Mr. Christmas a Receipt for 5000 pounds which being deposited in his hands, had ben repay'd me at severall times.

18. I gott privately into the Council of the rebell Army at Whitehall, where I heard horrid villanies: 20: I return'd to Sayes-Court:

28 my Bro: George came & dined with me:

Memorand This was a most exceeding wett yeare, neither frost or snow all the winter for above 6 days in all, & Cattell died of a Murrain every where:

1649

January 1. I went from Sayes Court (my Fa: in Laws howse in Deptford where I had a Lodging, & some books) to Lond, & on the 2d to see my old friend & fellow Traveller Mr. Henshaw, who had two rare pieces of Steenewicks perspectives:

3d I din'd at Sir Cl: Crews, where was old Sir Arthyr Gorge, after dinner I visited my Lord Montague where was the Marquis of Winchester, Sir Jo: Winter & his Lady: 13. I returnd to S. Court:

17: [To Lond:] I heard the rebell Peters incite the rebell powers met in the Painted Chamber, to destroy his Majestie & saw that Arch Traytor Bradshaw, who not long after condemn'd him.

On the 19 I return'd home, passing an extraordinary danger of being drown'd, by our Whirries falling fowle in the night, on another vessell there at Anker, shooting the Bridge at 3 quarter Ebb, for which his mercy, God Almighty be prais'd.

21. was published my Translation of *Liberty & Servitude*, for the Preface of which I was severely threatn'd:[1]

22d I went through a Course of Chymistrie at S. Court & now was the Thames frozen over, & horrid Tempest of Winds, so different was this part of the Winter from the former:

The Villanie of the Rebells proceeding now so far as to Trie, Condemne, & Murder our excellent King, the 30 of this Moneth, struck me with such horror that I kept the day of his Martyrdom a fast, & would not be present, at that execcrable wickednesse; receiving that sad <account> of it from my Bro: Geo: & also by Mr. Owen, who came to Visite this afternoone, recounting to me all Circumstances.

February 16: Paris being now streitly besieged by the Pr: of Condy, my wife being with her Father & Mother shut up, I writ to comfort her ...

26: Came to see me Cap: George Evelyn my kindsman, the greate Travellor, & one who believed himselfe a better Architect than realy he was, witnesse the

---

[1] This was E's first published work. Written in French by the Sieur de la Mothe le Vayer in 1643 the tract celebrated natural liberty and the natural constraints imposed by living in communities. E translated the text but added his own preface which castigated the lack of liberty under parliamentary rule in England and argued that it was preferable to be ruled by a single monarch than a committee of many.

Portico in the Garden at Wotton; yet the greate roome at Alburie is somewhat better understood: he had a large mind, but over built every thing:[1]

27 Came out of France my Wifes Unkle, (Paris still besieg'd): being rob'd by sea of the Dynkirk Pyrats, I lost among other goods my Wifes Picture painted by Monsieur Bourdon:

March 18 Mr. Owen a sequesterd, & learned Minister, preach'd in our Parlor, & gave us the Blessed Sacrament, which was now wholy out of use: in the Parish Churches which the Presbyterians & Fanatics had usurped: ...

21 I receiv'd letters from Paris from my Wife & Sir Richard, with whom I kept a political Correspondence, with no small danger of being discover'd:

April 2. To Lond, & Inventoried my Moveables, that had hitherto ben dispers'd for feare of Plundering: & writ into France touching my suddaine resolutions of coming over to them: ...

My Italian Collection being now ariv'd, came Moulins the greate Chirurgion to see & admire the Tables of Veines & Arteries, which I purchasd, & caused to be drawne out of several humane bodies at Padua ...[2]

17 I fell dangrously ill of my head, was blisterd, & let blood, & behind the Eares and forehead: & 23d began to have Ease, by using the fumes of Cammomile on Embers applied to my Eares, after all the Physitians had don their best: ...

29. I saw in Lond: an huge Oxe bred in Kent of 17 foote in length, & higher by much than I could reach:

May 12 I bought, & seald the Conveyances for Warley Magna in Essex a Mannor; [Payd 2500 pounds.] ...

30 was Un-king-ship, proclaim'd, & his Majesties Statues throwne downe at St. Paules Portico, & Exchange...

June 16 I kept Court at Warley my late Purchas. I receivd of a debt, 320 pounds from my Bro: Ge: Evelyn:

17: I got a Passe from the Rebell Bradshaw then in greate power ...

20 I went to <Puttny> & other places on the Thames to take prospects in Crayon, to carry into France, where I thought to have them Engrav'd ...

30 Riding out my Brothers stonehorse struck me dangerously on the leg: but it soone healed God be blessed:

July 2. I went from Wotton to Godstone, where was also Sir Jo: Ev<e>lyn of Wilton, where I tooke leave of both Sir Johns, & Ladys: *Memorand*, the prodigious memory of Sir Jo: of Wilts's daughter, since married to Mr. W: Pierepoint & mother of the present Earle of Kingston:[3] ...

12 accompanied by my Co: Stephens, & my Sister Glanvill, who there supp'd with me, & return'd: Whence I tooke post immediately to Dover, where I arived by 9 in the morning, & about 11 that night went on board in a bark, Guarded by a Pinnace of 8 gunns, this being the first time the Paquett

---

[1] See above, 15 May 1643.

[2] See above, January 1646, and below, 31 October 1667.

[3] De Beer notes (I, 73) that as this marriage took place on 8 December 1680 it is self-evident from the notice (which is within the main body of the text) that the *Diary* from this point at the latest cannot have been written up prior to that date.

boate had obtain'd a Convoy, having severall times before ben pillag'd: I carried over with me my Servant Ri: Hoare[1] an incomparable writer of severall hands, whom I afterwards preferrd in the Prerogative Office, at returne of his Majestie. We had a good passage, though chased by a Pyrate for some houres, but he Durst not attaque our fregat & so left us: But we then chased them, til they got under the protection of the Castle at Calais:

The vessell was a small Privateere belonging to the Prince of Wales: I was very sick at Sea, till about 5 in the morning that we landed, before the Gates were open: & so <did> my Lady Catherine Scot daughter to the Earle of Norwich, that follow'd us in a Shallop, with one Mr. Arth: Slingsby, who came out of England *Incognito*. At entrance of the Towne, the Lieutennant Governor being on his horse with the Guards let us passe Courteously ... The Citadell seems to be impregnable, & the whole Country about it, to be laied under Water by sluces for many miles ...

On the 18 I went to St. Germains to kisse his Majesties hands; In this Coach ... went Mrs. Barlow, the Kings Mistris & mother to the Duke of Monemoth, a browne, beautifull, bold, but insipid creature ...

September 5 ... my Wife received with me the H: Sacrament the first time:

10 ... went to see Maisons, a noble pile built by a President of that name, 'tis invirond in a dry, but sweete moate, the offices underground, the Gardens very magnificent, with extraordina<r>y long Walkes set with Elmes, & a noble Prospect on the Sienne towards Paris, but above all, what best pleas'd me, the Artificial Harbour cut out of the River: The house is well furnish'd, & it may compare with any Villa about Rome: ...

13 The King invited the Pr: of Condy to supper at St. Clo's: There I kiss'd the duke of Yorks hand in the Tennis Court, where I saw a famous match 'twixt Monsieur Saumeurs & Coll: Cooke, & so return'd to Paris: 'Twas nois'd about I was knighted, a dignity I often declind:[2] ...

October 15 Came newes of Droghedas being taken, by the Rebells & all put to the Sword, which made us very sad, forerunning the losse of all Ireland ...

November 18 ... I went to see the house, built by the late greate Cardinal de Richlieu: The most observable thing is, the Gallerie painted with the portraicts of the most Illustrious Persons, & signal actions in France, with innumerable Emb-lemes twixt every table: In the middle of the Gallery is a neate Chapell, rarely paved in works & devices of severall sorts of marble, besides the Altarpiece, & 2 statues of white marble, one of St. John, the other of the Virgin Mary &c: of Bernini: The rest of the Apartments are rarely Gilded & Carved, with some good modern Paintings: In the Presence hung 3 huge branches of Chrystal: In the French Kings Bed-chamber, was an Alcove like another Chamber, set as it were in a Chamber like a moveable box, with a rich embroidred bed: The fabric of the Palace is not magnificent, being but of 2 stories, but the Garden is so spacious, as to containe a noble basin, & fountaine

---

[1] Richard Hoare was recommended by E to Sir Richard Browne in a letter of 5 April 1649, see various Bray editions of the Diary which include E's correspondence.

[2] E's father declined an offer of a knighthood in 1630 by not turning up and was fined £50. E seems to have been inclined to emulate this but welcomed the opportunity to serve on royal commissions after 1660. However his grandson, despite admiring his grandfather, was happy to be created a baronet in 1713.

continualy playing, & there is a Mall, with an Elbow or turning to protract it:[1] so I left his Majestie on the Terrace buisie in seeing a Bull-baiting, & return'd home ...

1650

January 1 I begun this Jubilie with the Publique Office in our Chapell: Dind at my Lady Herberts, wife of Sir Ed: Herbert, afterwards Ld: Keeper:

February 6 ... After Evening Prayer came Signor Allessandro one of the Card: Mazarinis Musitians, & a person of greate name for his knowledge in that Art, to visite my Wife, & sung before divers persons of qualitie in my Chamber:

20: I went to the Course & Thuilleries with my Wife &c: where there was much Gallantry ...

May 3 of May, at the Hospital of the Charitie, I saw the whole operation of Lithotomie namely 5 cut of the stone: There was one person of 40 years old had a stone taken out of him, bigger than a turkys Egg: The manner thus: The sick creature was strip'd to his shirt, & bound armes & thighs to an high Chaire, 2 men holding his shoulders fast down: then the Chirurgion with a crooked Instrument prob'd til he hit on the stone, then without stirring the probe which had a small chanell in it, for the Edge of the Lancet to run in, without wounding any other part, he made Incision thro the Scrotum about an Inch in length, then he put in his forefingers to get the stone as neere the orifice of the wound as he could, then with another Instrument like a Cranes neck he pull'd it out with incredible torture to the Patient, especially at his after raking so unmercifully up & downe the bladder with a 3d Instrument, to find any other Stones that may possibly be left behind: The effusion of blood is greate. Then was the patient carried to bed, & dress'd with a silver pipe accomodated to the orifice for the urine to passe, when the wound is sowd up: The danger is feavour, & gangreene, some Wounds never closing: & of this they can give shrewd conjecture by the smothnesse or ruggednesse of the stone: The stone pull'd forth is washed in a bason of water, & wiped by an attendant Frier, then put into a paper, & writen on, which is also entred in a booke, with the name of the person, shape, weight &c of the stone, Day of the moneth, & Operator: After this person came a little Child of not above 8 or 9 yeares age, with much cherefullnesse, going through the operation with extraordinary patience, & expressing greate joy, when he saw the stone was drawn: The use I made of it, was to give Almighty God hearty thankes, that I had not ben subject to this Infirmitie, which is indeede deplorable:

7. I went with my Lady Browne, & my Wife, together with the Earle of Chesterfield, Lord Ossorie & his Bro: to Vamber, a place neere the Citty, famous for the butter, when comming homewards (for we were on foote) my Lord Ossorie stepping into a Garden, the doore open; There step'd a rude fellow to it, and thrust my Lord, with uncivil language from entering in: upon this our young Gallants struck the fellow over the pate, & bid him aske

---

[1] The visit helped E make a suggestion for the new coinage of 1662, see 10 January 1662, note.

pardon; which to our thinking he did with much submission, & so we parted: but we were not gon far, but we heare a noise behind us, & saw people coming with gunns, swords, staves & forks, following, & with our Swords, stones & the help of our servants (one of which had a pistol), make our retreate for neere a quarter of a mile, when an house receiv'd us: by this time numbers of the baser people increasing, we got up into a turret, from whence we could discover their attempts, & had some advantage: however my L: Chesterfield was hurt in the face & back with a stone, his servant in the Eye & forehead, & Sir R: Bro: protecting his Lady with his Cloake, on the shoulder, & his Lady with such a blow on the head & side of her neck as had neere fell'd her:

I myselfe was hurt on the shoulder: my servant La Roch (a stoute Youth) much hurt on the reines: 'Twas a greate mercy that though they were so many, they durst not come neere us with their hookes, & that their gunns did no Execution amongst us, tho fir'd: In the Scuffle one of them was thrust through the arme, another wounded, in his elbow, with his owne Gun, with which one of our Company struck him; We discharged one among them with our Pistol, what hurt it did <I> know not, & we had no more ammunition: Being got up into the Turret & battail below over, they beset the house, but durst not attempt to come up, where they knew we had a trap-doore betweene us, whence we could easily repell them: At last, with much adoe, & making them understand the occasion of the quarrell, we came to parlie, and the conclusion was, that we should all be that angry fellows prisoners: This we absolutely refuse'd: upon which they fell to attacque the house; but coming at last to consider that we might be persons of qualitie (for at first they took us for Burgers of Paris) the company began to slink away, & our Enemie to grow so mild, upon intercession of the Master of the house, & that we might come downe into the next chamber:

I obtain'd leave to Visite my Lord Hatton (comptroller of his Majesties Household) who with some others of our Companie, were taken prisoners in the flight, whom I found under 3 locks & as many doores one within another, in this rude fellows Masters house, who pretended to be steward to one Monsieur St. Germains one of the first Presidents of the *grand Chamber de Parliament* & a Canon of Notre Damme: In this Interim one of our Laquais escaping to Paris during the Scuffle; went & caused the Bailife of St. Germains to come with his Guard & rescue us, which he did, accompanied with Sir Rob: Welch, Mr. Percy Church, & others, with Weapons, & immediately after Monsieur St. Germains himselfe, newes being brought him to Paris that his housekeeper was assaulted, upon which he expressd mighty revenge: But when he saw the Kings Officers, the Gentlemen & noblemen, with his Majesties Resident, & better understood the occasion, he was asham'd of the Accident, begging the fellows pardon, & desiring the Ladys to accept of their Submission, & a Supper at his house, whilst we found for all that, it grieved him to the heart, we had not ben some inferior persons, against whom he might have taken some profitable advantage:

The Bailife in the meanetime exaggerated the affront (& indeede it was a greate one upon no manner of occasion offer'd on our part:) & would have fallen on the little towne, striking downe as many as he mett about the streetes & way. It was 10 a clock at night ere we got to Paris, guarded by Prince Griffith (a certaine Welch Hero, going under that name, & well knowne in England, for his extravagances) together with the Scholars of two Academies who came forth to assist & meete us on horseback; & would faine have alarm'd the Towne we received the affront from, which with much ado we prevented ...

12 Complaint being come to the Queene & Court of France of the affront we had receiv'd at Vamber, The President was ordred to aske Sir R: Bro: his Majesties Resident, Pardon, & the fellow to make submission & be dismissd: There came along with him President Thou, the great Thuanus's sonn & so all was composd: But I have often heard, that gallant Gent: my Lord Ossorie, affirme solemnly, that in all the Conflicts he was ever in at sea, or land (in the most desperate of both which he had often ben) he believed he was never in so much danger, as when these people rose against us: He was usd to call it the *Bataill de Vambre*, & remember it with a greate deale of Mirth, as an Adventure *en Cavaliere*.

June 13 I sate to the famous Sculptor Nanteuil [afterwards made a knight by the French King for his Art:] who engraved my Picture in Coper:[1]
21. I went to see the Samaritan or Pumpe at the End of Pont Noeufe, which though to appearance promising no greate matter, is besides the Machine, furnishd with innumerable rarities both of Art & Nature; Especialy the costly Grotto, where are the fairest Corals, gowing out of the very rock, that I have seene, also huge morsels of Chrystals, Ametheists, & Gold in the mine, & other mettals & marcasites, with two huge Conchas, which the owner told us, cost him 200 Crounes at Amsterdam: He shew'd us a world of landscips & prospects very rarely painted in miniature, some with the Pen & Crayon, with divers antiquities & Relievos of Rome, above all that of the inside of the Amphitheater of Titus incomparable drawne by Monsieur <Linclere> himselfe, two boys, & 3 Sceletons moulded by Fiamingo, a Booke of Statues with the pen made for Hen the 4th rarely executed, & by which one may discover many errours in that of Perriere, who has added divers conceits of his owne that are not in the Originals ... He led us into a stately Chamber, furnished to have entertaind a Prince, with Pictures of the greatest masters ... in a <word> all was greate, choice & magnificent, & not to be pass'd by, as I had often don, without the least suspicion that there were such rare things to be seene, in that place: ...
27 I seald my Will in presence of my Lord Stanhop & Mr. Radcliff, &c & taking leave of my Wife & other friends, tooke horse for England, paying the Messager 8 pistols for me & my servant to Calais, seting out with 17 in Company well arm'd, some Portugezes, Swisse & French, whereof 6 were Captaines & Officers ... & proceeding met a Company of foote (being now within the inroades of the Parties, which dangerously infest this days Journey, from St. Omers & the Frontiers) which we drew very neere to, ready, & resolute to Charge through, & accordingly were ordered & led by a Captaine of our traine; but as we were on the speede, they cald out, & prov'd to be Scotch-men, newly landed & raisd men & few arm'd among them ...

E reverts to the English calendar

Jun: 21 we march'd in good order, the passage being now exceeding dangerous, & got to Calais by a little after two: The sun did so scorch my face in this journey, as made all the Skin peele off:
The 22d I din'd with Mr. Booth his Majesties Agent, & about 3 in the afternoone imbark'd in the Packet-boat (hearing there was a Pirate then also

---

[1] Robert Nanteuil (c. 1623-78); the drawing from which the engraving was made survives, the engraving was used for E's *Silva*, 1706.

setting saile, we had security from molestation), & so with a faire S.W. Wind, in 7 houres we lande'd safe at Dover: The buisy Watch-man would have us to the Major to be searched, but the gent being in bed, we were dismiss'd ...

July 7 ... In the afternoone having a mind to see what doings was among the Rebells now in full possession at White-hall, I went thither, & found one at Exercise in the Chapell, after their Way, & thence to St. James's, where another was preaching in the Court abroad: having finish'd my businesse at London I return'd home where I found severall of my Wifes relations.

17th I went to Lond: to Visite my Bro: & Lady & to obtaine a Passe, intending but a very short stay in England: returning, my Bro: & severall friends were to visite me: Received letters from my Wife, in answer to my Bills of Exchange, lately sent:

23d Went to London about my Accompts, & tooke order about my journey:

25. I went to Wotton, & passing by Epsom, saluted Sir Robert Cook, & visited my sister Glanvill: The Country was now much molested by Souldiers, who took away Gentlemens horses for the Service of the State as then call'd ...

30 ... After dinner I went to visite my Lord Vicount Montague, and returning to Wotton bath'd this Evening in the pond, after I had not for many years ben in cold Water:

August 1. I went to see my Bro: Richard at Woodcot, & after dinner at Durdens, meeting my former acquaintance Mr. Pierson [since L. Bishop of Chester], I had good Conversation: Sir Rob: Cooke invited me next day to dinner: Next day, I visited my Sister Glanvill & saw her little Child my Nephew, & so return'd to Says-Court, next day to London: ...

6th I tooke leave of my friends in Towne, & passing by Mr. Walkers a good painters,[1] he shew'd me an excellent Copie of Titians: thence home till the 12th when I set out towards Paris, taking post at Gravesend, & so that night to Canterbury, where being Surpriz'd by the Souldiers, & having onely an antiquated passe, with some fortunate dexterity I got clear of them; though not without extraordinary hazard, having before counterfaited one, with successe, it being so difficult to procure one of the Rebells without entering into oathes, which I never would do, & at Dover Mony to the Searcher & officers was as authentique as the hand & Seale of Bradshaw himselfe.

13 I came to Dover, where I had not so much as my Trunk open'd: so at 6 in the Evening we set saile, the wind not favorable I was very sea-sick, coming to Anker about one a Clock: about 5 in the morning we had a long-boate to carry us to land, though at good distance; this we willingly enter'd, because two Vessels were chasing us: but being now almost at the harbours mouth, through inadvertancy, there brake in upon us two such huge seas, as had almost sunk the boate, I being neere the middle up in Water: our steeres man, it seemes, apprehensive of the danger was preparing to leape into the sea, and trust his swimming: but seeing the vessell emerge, put her into the peere, & so God be thanked we got wet to Calais, where I went immediately to bed, sufficiently discompos'd: here I was visited by Sir Richard Lloyd.

Next day (15: old. 25 New Style) attending Company, (the passages towards Paris, being so infested with Volunteeres from the Spanish frontieres) I visited Collonel Fitz Williams & his Lady, who had ben the day before to see me: Then my Lord Strafford: I was also visited by Monsieur Zanches d Avila an acquaintance of mine.

---

[1] Robert Walker had painted E earlier, see above, 1 July 1648.

Next morning, the regiment of Picardy consisting of about 1400 horse & foote, & among them a Cap: whom I knew, being come to Towne; I tooke horses for myselfe & servant, and march'd under their Protection to Boulogne: 'Twas a miserable spectacle, to see how these tatter'd souldiers, pillag'd the poore people of their Sheepe, poultry, Corne, Catell, & whatever came in their Way: but they had such ill pay, that they were ready themselves to sterve:

27: I din'd at Montreull, & lay at Abb-Ville now past danger, and warning the poore people (infinitely inquisitive & thankfull) how the Souldiers treated their neighbours, & were marching towards them:

The 28 we got to Pois ... & so the 30, to Paris. As we pass'd St. Denis the people were in up-rore, the Guards doubl'd, & every body running with their goods & moveables to Paris; upon an Alarm'e that the Enemy was within 5 leagues of them; so miserably expos'd was even this part of France at this time: I lay this night at my old Hosts, in Rue Dauphine, & next morning went to see my Wife at her Fathers after 2 monethes absence onely ...

November 6 ... This night Sir Tho: Osborn [since Ld: Treasurer of England], supping with us, his groome was set upon in the streete before our house, & received two wounds, but gave the other nine, who was carried off to the Charite hospital.

7: Sir Tho: went for England, & carried divers letters for me to my friends:

8 Monsieur Nanteuils presented me with my owne Picture, don all with a pen, an extraordinary curiosity: ...

2 **December** I heard a Jesuite preach (at their Greate & magnificent Church) on their Patron Xaveriu's day, on: 1. Cor: 9.19: Eloquently shewing, how he became all things to all men, to gaine some; the chief discourse of his whole Sermon, was Elogies on their Saints: representing their owne patron to be one of the most flattering timeservers that ever was: There succeeded excellent Musick ...

14 I went to visite Mr. Ratcliffe in whose Lodging there was an Impostor that had like to have impos'd upon us, a pretended seacret of Multiplying gold: 'Tis certaine he had lived in Paris some time before in extraordinarie Splendor; but I found him to be an egreageous Cheate ...

31 I gave God thanks for his mercys & protection the past yeare, made up Accompts, which came this yeare to 7075 livers french, neere 600 pounds sterling.

1651

January <8> ... After Evening Prayer came Mr. Wainsford to visite me, he had long ben Consul at Aleppo and told me many strange things of those Countries, the Arabs especialy: he affirm'd, that though they allowd common places of sinn; yet if any man of reputation had his daughter corrupted, he cutt her throat with his owne hands: That though the Arabs were poorely arm'd, they were capable of destroying the greatest powers of the Earth; by knowing how to cover, & conceale their Springs in those Sandy Deserts: That when their <Chief> will shew himselfe in State, all his greate men sit on their armour cover'd with a red Cloth: Their safty is their Excellent horses, <they> ride without Stirrops: dwell in long black Tents, made of a wooll like felt, that resists all weather: Their riches is in Catell and Camels: Sometimes <they> threaten the Citties about them: Damascus itselfe pays them Contribution: ...

27: I had letters of my Grandmother in Laws death Mrs. Newton, for which I was very sorry, though by it I was eased of a rent charge of 60 pounds per ann: she had a most tender care of me during my childhood, & was a Woman of Extraordinary charity & piety, spending most of her time in devotion ...

February 21 I went to see the *Bonnes hommes* a Convent that has a fayr Cloister painted with the Lives of the Eremites, a glorious Altar now erecting in the Chapell: The Garden on a rock with divers descents, with a Vyneyard, & a delicate prospect towards the Citty:

24 I went to see a Dromedarie, a very monstrous beast, much like the Camel, but larger, & with tufts of haire on the neck, knees, & thighs; & two bunches on its back about 3 foote one from the other: There was also dauncing on the rope; but above all surprizing (to those who were ignorant of the addresse) was the Water Spouter, a fellow that drinking onely fountaine water, rendred out of his mouth in severall glasses, all sorts of Wine, & sweete Waters &c: This seacret was so strange, that for a piece of mony the Montebanc discover'd it to me: ...

March 11 This morning I went to the Chastlett or prison, where a Malefactor was to have the Question or Torture given to him, which was thus: They first bound his wrists with a strong roope or smalle Cable, & one end of it to an iron ring made fast to the wall about 4 foote from the floore, & then his feete, with another cable, fastned about 6 foote farther than his uttmost length, to another ring on the floore of the roome, thus suspended, & yet lying but a slant; they slid an horse of wood under the rope which bound his feete, which so exceeding stiffned it, as severd the fellows joynts in miserable sort, drawing him out at length in an extraordinary manner, he having onely a paire of linnen drawers on his naked body: Then they question'd him of a robery, (the Lieutennant Criminal being present, & a clearke that wrot) which not Confessing, they put an higher horse under the rope, to increase the torture & extension: In this Agonie, confessing nothing, the Executioner with a horne (such as they drench horses with) struck the end of it into his mouth, and pour'd the quantity of 2 boaketts of Water downe his throat, which so prodigiously swell'd him, faces, Eyes ready to start, brest & all his limbs, as would have pittied & almost affrited one to see it; for all this he denied all was charged to him: Then they let him downe, & carried him before a warme fire to bring him to himselfe, being now to all appearance dead with paine. What became of him I know not, but the Gent: whom he robbd, constantly averrd him to be the man; & the fellows suspicious, pale lookes, before he knew he should be rack'd, betraid some guilt: The Lieutennant was also of that opinion, & told us at first sight (for he was a leane dry black young man) he would conquer the Torture & so it seemes they could not hang him; but did use in such cases, where the evidence is very presumptuous, to send them to the Gallies, which is as bad as death. There was another fat Malefactor to succeede, wh<o> he said, he was confident would never endure the Question; This his often being at these Trials, had it seemes given him experience of, but the spectacle was so uncomfortable, that I was not able to stay the sight of another: It represented yet to me, the intollerable suffering which our B: S: must needes undergo, when his blessed body was hanging with all its weight upon the nailes on the Crosse ...

May 2 My Wife miscarried, of which she was extreamely ill, proceeding from some Physick prescribd, not believing she was with Child:

23. I went to take leave of the Ambassadors for Spaine, which were my L. Treasurer Cottington & Hide Sir Edw: & as I return'd visited Monsieur Morines Garden, & other rarities, especialy Coralls, Minerals, Stones, & other natural Curiosities: particularly Crabs of the red-sea, the body no bigger than a small birds egg, but flatter, & the 2 leggs or claws a foote in length: he had aboundance of incomparable shells, at least 1000 sorts which furnish'd a Cabinet of greate price, & a very curious collection of Scarabies & Insects, of which he was compiling a natural historie; also the pictures of his Choice flowers & plants in miniature: he told me there were 10000 sorts of Tulips onely: he had also *Tallie douces sans nombre*: he had also the head of the Rynoceros bird, which was indeede very extravagant; & one butterflie resembling a perfect bird: ...

July 11 I let bloud, for my often infirmitie of the Eemeroides ...

August 2 I went with my Wife to Conflance, where were aboundance of Ladys & others bathing in the River: The Ladys had their Tents spread on the Water for privacy: it being exceeding hot weather, we also bathed, & return'd next day by boate to Paris: ...

20 ... I this day received safe, divers books & other things I had sent for out of England, which were reported to have ben taken by the Pyrates: but God be thanked it was otherwise: ...

September 6 I went with my Wife to St. Germaines, to Condoule Mr. Wallers losse: I carried with me, & treated at dinner, that excellent & pious person, The Deane of Pauls Dr. Steward, & Sir Lowes Dives, halfe brother to the Earle of Bristol, who entertain'd us with his wonderfull Escape out of Prison in White-hall, the very evening before he was to have ben put to death, leaping out of a jakes 2 stories high into the Thames at high-Water, in the coldest of Winter, & at night: so as by swiming he got to a boate that attended for him: tho' he was guarded with six musqueteeres: That after this he went about in Womens habits, & then in a Small-Coalemans; Then travell'd 200 miles on foote, Embark'd for Scotland, with some men he had raised, who coming on shore were all surpriz'd & imprison'd on the Marq: of Montrosses score, he not knowing any thing of their barbarous murder of that Hero: This he told us was his 5 Escape, & none lesse miraculous, with this note, That the charging through 1000 men arm'd, or whatever danger could possibly befall a man in his whole life, he believed could not more confound, and distract a mans thoughts, than the execution of a premeditated Escape, The passions of hope & feare being so strong: This Knight was indeede a valiant Gent: but not a little given to romance, when he spake of himselfe. I return'd to Paris the same Evening:

The 7th of September I went to Visite Mr. Hobbs the famous Philosopher of Malmesbury, with whom I had long acquaintance: from whose Window, we <saw> the whole equipage & glorious Cavalcade of the Young French Monarch Lewis the XIVth passing to Parliament, when first he tooke the Kingly Government on him, as now out of Minority & the Queene regents pupilage: First came the <Captain> of the King's Aydes, at the head of 50 richly liveried: Next the Queene Mothers light horse an hundred: The Lieutennant being all over cover'd with Embroiderie & ribbans, having before him 4 Trumpets habited in black velvet, full of Lace, & Casques of the same:

Then the Kings light horse 200: richly habited, with 4 Trumpets in blew velvet embrodred with Gold, before whom rid the Count d'Olonne Coronet, whose belt <was all> set with Pearle: next went the grand Prevosts Company on foot, with the Prevost on horseback, after them, the Swisse in black Velvet toques led by 2 gallant Cavalieres habited in scarlet colour'd Sattin after their Country fashion, which is very fantastick: he had in his cap a pennach of heron, with a band of Diamonds, & about him 12 little Swisse boyes with halebards, which was very pretty: Then came the *Ayde de Ceremonies*; next the grandees of Court, & Governors of Places, Lieutenants Gen: of Provinces magnificently habited & mounted, among <them> one, I must not forget, the Chevalier Paul famous for many Sea-fights & signal exploits there, because 'tis said, he had never ben an Academist, & yet govern'd a very un-rully horse, & beside his rich suite, & Malta Crosse esteem'd at 10 thousand Crownes: These were headed with 2 Trumpets, & indeede the whole Troup cover'd with Gold and Jewells, & rich Caparisons were follow'd by 6 Trumpets in blew Velvet also, præceeding as many Heraulds in blew Velvet Semé'd with *floeur de lys*, and Caduces in their Hands, velvet caps: Behind them came one of the Masters of the Ceremonies, then divers Marishalls, & of the Nobility exceedingly splendid, behind them *Count d'Harcourt Grand Escuyr* alone carrying the Kings Sword in a Scarf, which he held-up in a blew sheath studded with *flor de lyss*; his horse, had for reines two Scarfs of black Taffata:

Then came The foote-men & Pages of the King aboundance of them, new liveried, & with white & red feathers: Next the *Guard de Corps* & other officers, & lastly appear<d> the King himselfe upon an Isabella Barb, on which a housse seméd with Crosses of the Order of the H.G. & *floure de lyces*: The King himselfe like a young Apollo was in a sute so coverd with rich embrodry, that one could perceive nothing of the stuff under it, going almost the whole way with his hat in hand saluting the Ladys & Acclamators who had fill'd the Windos with their beauty, & the aire with *Vive Le Roy*. Indeede he seem'd a Prince of a grave, yet sweete Countenance, now but in the 14th yeare of his Age: After the king followd divers Greate persons of the Court exceeding splendid, also his Esquire, Masters of horse on foote, Then the Company *d'Exempts des Gards*, & six Guards of Scotch, 'twixt their files divers Princes of the bloud, Dukes & Lords: After all these the Queenes guard of Swisse, Pages & foote-men, Then Queene Mother herselfe in a rich Coach, with Monsieur the Kings brother, The Duke of Orleans & some other Lords and Ladys of honour: about the Coach march'd her *Exempts de gards*, Then the Company of the Kings *Gens d'Armes* well mounted 150 with 4 Trumpets and as many of the Queenes, Lastly an innumerable many Coaches full of Ladys and Gallants, & in this Equipage passed this Monarch to the Parliament, henceforth exercising his Kingly Government ...

15 I accompanied Sir R: Bro: my F. in Law to the French-Court, who had a favourable Audience of the French King & Queene [his] Mother, congratulating the one his coming to the exercise of his royal charge, & the others prudent, and happy Administration during her late Regency ... Afterwards I tooke a walk in the Kings Gardens, where I observ'd that the Mall gos the whole Square thereof next the Wall, & bends with an angle so made as to gla<n>ce the ball, which angle is of stone: Ther's a basin at the end of the Garden fed by a noble fountaine & high jetto very plentifully: There were in it two or three boates in which the K. now & then rowes about: In another part is a Compleate fort, made with Bastions, Graft, halfe moones, ravelins & furnishd with greate Gunns, cast up on purpose to in<s>truct the K. in Fortification: ...

22 Arived the newes of the fatal Battail at Worcester, which exceedingly mortified our expectations[1] ...

October 29 ... This morning came newes & Letters to the Queene, & Sir Richard Bro: (who was the first had intelligence of it) of his Majesties miraculous Escape after the fight at Worcester, which exceedingly rejoic'd us ...

1 **December** I receiv'd a Bill of Exchange being now resolv'd to returne into England.
3 ... <Sir> Lew: Dives din'd with us, who amongst other his Adventures, shew'd me divers pieces of broad Gold, which being in his pocket in a fight, preserv'd his life, by receiving a Musket bullet upon them, deaded the violence of it, so as it went no farther, but made such a stroake on the Gold, as fix't the Impressions upon one another, battering & bending severall of them, the bullet it selfe flatted, & retaining on it the colour of the Gold; and assurd us that of an hundred of them which he then it seemes had in his pocket, not one of them scaped without some blemish ...
12 ... My Sister Glanvill sent to desire I would substitute my Proxie, to stand Godfather to her Child, but my intended journey home-ward was so soone to follow, that there was no neede of it:[2] ...
21 Came to Visite my Wife Mrs. Lane, the Lady who conveied the King at his Escape from Worcester to the sea-side.[3]
22 Mr Jo: Cosin (sonn to the Deane) debauch'd by the Priests, writ a letter to me, to mediate for him to his father &c: ...
26 Newes came of the Death of that Rebell Ireton:[4]
31 Preached Dr. Wolly - after which was celebrated the H: Communion, which I receivd also preparatorie to my Journey, & to returne God Almight<y> thanks for his gracious Protection of me this past yeare:

1652

1 **January**: After publique prayers in the Chapell, making up all Accompts, I prepard for my last Journey, being now resolvd to leave France <for> alltogether.
2 ... Came to me this Evening the newes of my Sister Glanvills death in Child-bed, which exceedingly afflicted me: ...
14 I was so hindred by providing & putting up my things, to part with the Carriages to Calais, that I could not be present at Morning Sermon:
16 I sent away my Goods for England by the Way of Rouen: ...
29 Came aboundance of my French & English Acquaintance, & some

---

[1] The battle took place on 3 September. It was Charles II's last attempt to recover his crowm by force and he fled to France.
[2] She died in childbirth about this time and was buried on 19 December; the fate of the child is unknown. The news did not reach E until 2 January 1652 (see below).
[3] Jane Lane (d. 1689).
[4] Henry Ireton (1611-51), a signatory to Charles I's execution and a major player in the military events of the Civil War.

Germans to take leave of me, & conducted me to the Coach & Horses; So about 12 a Clock (in an extraordinary hard Frost, that had continued a good while before,) we set forth & got that night to B<e>aumont ...

31 we found the wayes very deepe with Snow, & exceeding cold; din'd at Pois, lay at Berneè, a miserable Cottage, of miserable people in a Wood, & wholy unfurnish'd, but in a little time, we had sorry beds & some provision, which they told me they hid in the wood, for fear of the frontier Enemy, the Garisons neere them continualy plundering what they had: They told us they were often infested with Wolves: I cannot remember that I ever saw more miserable Creatures: ...

1 **February** 2 din'd at Montreuill, lay at Bollogne 3 & came next day to Calis by 11 in the Morning; so I thought to have embarq'd in the Evening, but feare of Pyrates plying neere the Coast, I durst not trust our small Vessel, 'til Moneday following, when 2 or 3 lusty vessels were to depart: ...

5. It continud so ill weather as no Vessels put to sea; This Evening therefore I met Mr. Heath, Sir Rich: Lloyd, Cap: Paine, & divers of our banish'd Company &c: of whom understanding that the Count de la Strade, Governor of Dynkirk, was in the Towne, who before at Paris, my Lord of Norwich had inform'd me, bought my Wifes Picture of certaine Pyrates, that had plunder'd it at Sea, the yeare before, that she sent it me into England: I made my addresse to him, who frankly told me that indeede he had such a Picture in his owne bed-chamber, amongst other Ladys, & how he came by it; seeming well pleas'd that it was his fortune to preserve it for me, & so generously promising to sende it to any friend I had at Dover, I mentiond a French Merchand there, & so tooke my leave:

6 I Embark'd early in the Packet-boat, but put my goods in a Stouter Vessell: 'twas dark, but exceeding Calme weather, so as we got not to Dover till 8 at night; The other vessell out sailing us an houre & more:...

Evelyn reverts to the English calendar

<Jan> 29: English style (having desir'd Mr. De la Valle to convey a letter to Monsieur Le Compt de Strade, to put him in mind of his promise, & that he would consigne the Picture to him) I tooke horse for Canterbury, thence to Sittenburne, thence, lying at Rochester,

30th to Gravesend, thence, in a pair of Oares, & so landed at Says-Court about 2 in the Afternoone, where I stayed Friday, Sat: & Sonday, to refresh, & looke after my packetts, & goods I brought: ...

February 5: My Bro: Glanvill came to see me, with whom I condold the death of my deare sister, a most ingenious & virtuous woman, & whom I exceedingly loved: Next day he sent me Mourning: & this day I saw the Magnificent Funeral of that arch-Rebell Ireton, carried in pomp from Somerset house to Westminster, accompanied with divers regiments of Souldiers horse & foote; then marched the Mourners, Generall Cromewell (his father in Law) his Mock-Parliament men: Officers, & 40 poore-men in gownes, 3 led horses in housses of black-Cloth: 2 horses led in black-Velvet, & his Charging horse all coverd over with embrodery & gold on crimson Velvet: Then the Guidons, Ensignes, 4 Heraulds, carrying the armes of the State (as they cald it) namely the red Crosse, & Ireland, with the Casque, Wreath, Sword, Spurrs &c: next a <Charriot> Canopied, all of black Velvet, & 6 horses, in this the Corps, the Pall held up by the Mourners on foote: The

Mace & Sword with other marks of his Charge in Ireland (where he died of the Plague) carried before in black Scarfs; Thus in a grave pace, drums coverd with cloth, souldiers reversing their armes, they proceeded thro the streetes in a very solemn manner. This Ireton was a stout rebell, & had ben very bloudy to the Kings party, witnesse his severity at Colchester; when in cold blood he put those gallant gent: Sir Charles Lucas & G. Lisle to death: ...

10 I went to Deptford; where having pretty well settld my buisinesse in Lond: I made preparation for my settlement, no more intending to go out of England, but endeavor a settled life, either in this place, or some other, there being now so little appearance of any change for the better, all being intirely in the rebells hands, and this particular habitation, & the Estate contiguous to it (belonging to my F in Law, actualy in his Majesties service) very much suffering, for want of some friend, to rescue it out of the power of the Usurpers; so as to preserve our Interest, & to take some care of my other Concernes, by the advise, & favour of my Friends, I was advis'd to reside in it, and compound with the Souldiers; being besides, authoriz'd by his Majesty so to do, & encourag'd with a promise, that what was in Lease from the Crowne (if ever it pleas'd God to restore him), he would secure to us in Fee-ferme:[1] I had also addresses, & Cyfers, to Correspond with his Majestie & Ministers abroad; upon all which inducements, I was persuaded to settle hence forth in England, having now run about the World, most part out of my owne Country neere 10 yeares: I therefore now likewise meditated of sending over for my Wife, whom as yet I had left at Paris:

<15> I went to Leusham[2] where I heard an honest sermon ... This was the first Sonday I had ben at Church since my returne, it being now a very rare thing to find a Priest of the Church of England in a Parish pulpet, most of them fill'd with Independents & Phanatics:

15 I saw the *Diamond* & *Rubie* Launch'd, in the Dock at Deptford, carrying 48 Brasse Cannon Each: <Cromwell> & his Grandees present, with greate acclamations: ...

22 I went with my Bro: Evelyn to Wotton, to give him what directions I was able about his Garden, which he was now desirous to put into some forme: but for which he was to remove a mountaine, that <was> over-growne with huge trees, & thickett, with a moate, within 10 yards of the very house: This my Brother immediately attempted, & that without greate Cost for more than an hundred yards South, by digging downe the Mountaine, & flinging it into a rapid streame, which not onely carried the Land &c away, but filled up the moate, & leveld that noble area where now the Garden & fountaine is: The first occasion of my Bro: making this alteration, was my building of a litle retiring place betweene the great wood East ward, next the Meadow, where some time after my Fathers death I made a triangular Pond, or little stew, with an artificial rock, after my coming out of Flanders[3] ...

March 15 This night was an Ecclipse of the Moon, I writ Letters to my Wife &c: concerning my resolution of settling; also to the Deane touching my buying his Library, which was one of the choicest collection<s> of any private persons whatsoever in England:[4]

---

[1] Held in perpetuity by the owner and his heirs for a fixed annual rent.

[2] Lewisham, near Deptford.

[3] See above, 15 May 1643.

[4] John Cosin, Dean of Peterborough (1594-1672).

I had now also newes that Monsieur the Count de Strade had sent me my Wifes picture from Dynkirk, which he most generously & handsomely did in a large tin case, without any charge: The Picture is of Mr   and is that which has the dog in it; & is to the knees, but has ben something spoild by washing it ignorantly with sope-sudds:

16 I let bloud 9 ounces. 17 Sweate, & bathed, & went to Lond, to take order about my goods ariv'd out of France: I had ben exceedingly troubld with a swelling in my throat & neck, which fore-ran the Piles, & had now for 2 Springs indisposd me, but now prevented, by the Course I tooke & greate evacuations ...

29 Was that celebrated Eclipse of the Sun, so much threatned by the Astrologers, & had so exceedingly alarm'd the whole Nation, so as hardly any would worke, none stir out of their houses; so ridiculously were they abused by knavish and ignorant star-gazers.

30 Came my Bro. Geo: Evelyn & Bro: Rich: with his wife to dine with me, & my little Nephew Geo: Evelyn brought to abide some time with me, if possible to reclaime him of his fondnesse to home, where he miserably lost his time: We went this afternoon to see the Queenes house at Greenewich, now given by the Rebells to Bolstrood Whittlock one of their unhappy Counselors, keeper of pretended Liberties ...

April 9 I went againe to Lond: & next day, passing by Smithfield, there was a miserable Creature burning who had murder'd her husband: I returnd: ...

26: To Lond: to prepare some things against my Wifes coming over, return'd 28. I went next day againe to take order about a Coach, to be made against her Coming, being \<my\> first Coach, the pattern whereof I brought out of Paris ...

May 7 I had Letters from Paris, dated 11th May of my Wifes being with Child of her first ...

June 4 I set out for Rie to meete my Wife, now upon her journey from Paris, after she had obtain'd leave to come out of that Citty, which had now ben besieged some time, by the Pr: of Condys armie, in the Time of the Rebellion: & after she had ben neere 12 Yeares from her owne Country, that is since 5 yeares of age, at which time she went over: ...

11 About 4 in the after-noone, being at bowles on the Greene, we discoverd a Vessel, which proved \<to\> be that in which my Wife was, & got into harbour about 8 a clock that Eveni\<n\>g to my no small joy: They had ben 3 days at Sea, & hardly Escaped the whole Dut\<c\>h Fleete, through which the\<y\> pass'd taken for Fishers; which was a greate good fortune; there being 17 bailes of furniture, & other rich plunder, which I blesse God came all safe to land, together with my Wife, & my Lady Browne her mother, accompanying her Daughter: But my Wife discompos'd with being so long at sea, we set not forth towards home 'til the 14th, when hearing the Smallpox was very rife in and about Lond: and that my Lady had a greate desire to drink Tunbridge Waters; I carried them thither, where I staied in a very sweete place, private & refreshing, and also tooke the Waters my selfe a few daies, 'til the 23d when buisinesse calling me homewards, & to prepare for the reception of my little family (leaving them for the present in their Cottage by the Wells).

The morning growing excessivly hot, I sent my footman some hours before, and so rod negligently, under favour of the shade, 'til being now come to within three miles of Bromely, at a place called the procession Oake, started

out two Cutt-throates, & striking with their long staves at the horse, taking
hold of the reignes, threw me downe, & immediately tooke my sworde, &
haled me into a deep Thickett, some quarter of a mile from the high-way,
where they might securely rob me, as they soone did; what they got of mony
was not considerable, but they tooke two rings, the one an Emrald with
diamonds, an <Onyx>, & a pair of boucles set with rubies & diamonds which
were of value, and after all, barbarously bound my hands behind me, & my
feete, having before pull'd off my bootes: & then set me up against an Oake,
with most bloudy threatnings to cutt my throat, if I offerd to crie out, or make
any noise, for that they should be within hearing, I not being the person they
looked for: I told them, if they had not basely surpriz'd me, they should not
have made so easy a prize, & that it should teach me hereafter not to ride neere
an hedge; since had I ben in the mid way, they durst not have adventur'd on
me, at which they cock'd their pistols, & told me they had long guns too, &
were 14 companions, which were all lies: I begg'd for my Onyx & told them it
being engraven with my armes, would betray them, but nothing prevail'd: My
horses bridle they slipt, & search'd the saddle which they likewise pull'd off,
but let the horse alone to grace, & then turning again bridld him, & tied him to
a Tree, yet so as he might graze, & so left me bound:

The reason they tooke not my horse, was I suppose, because he was mark'd,
and cropt on both Eares, & well known on that roade, & these rogues were
lusty foote padders, as they are cald: Well, being left in this manner,
grievously was I tormented with the flies, the ants, & the sunn, so as I sweate
intollerably, nor little was my anxiety how I should get loose in that solitary
place, where I could neither hear or see any creature but my poore horse & a
few sheepe stragling in the Coppse; til after neere two houres attempting I got
my hands to turn paulme to paulme, whereas before they were tied back to
back, and then I stuck a greate while ere' I could slip the cord over my wrist to
my thumb, which at last I did, & then being quite loose soone unbound my
feete, & so sadling my horse, and roaming a while about, I at last perceiv'd a
dust to rise, & soone after heard the rattling of a Cart, towards which I made,
and by the help of two Country fellows that were driving it, got downe a
steepe bank, into the highway againe; but could hear nothing of the Villains:

So I rod to Colonel Blounts a greate justiciarie of the times, who sent out
hugh & Crie immediately: and 25, The next morning weary & sore as I was at
my wrists & armes, I went from Deptford to Lond, got 500 ticketts printed &
dispers'd, by an officer of Gould Smiths-hall, describing what I had lost, and
within two daies after had tidings of all I lost, except my Sword which was a
silver hilt, & some other trifles: These rogues had paund my Rings &c for a
trifle to a Goldsmiths Servant, before the tickets came to the shop, by which
meanes they scap'd, the other ring was bought by a Victualer, who brought it
to a Goldsmith, that having seene the ticket, seiz'd upon him; but whom I
afterwards discharg'd upon the mediation of friends, & protestation of his
innocency: Thus did God delivr me from these villains, & not onely so, but
restor'd to me what they tooke, as twise before he had graciously don, both at
sea & land, I meane, when I had ben rob'd by Pyrates and was in danger of a
considerable losse at Amsterdam, for which & many, many signal preservations I am eternaly obligd to give thanks to God my Saviour.

There fell this 25t day (after a drowth of neere 4 monethes) so violent a
Tempest of haile, raine, wind, Thunder & lightning, as no man alive had seene
the like in this age: The haile being in some places 4 & 5 Inches about, brake
all the glasse about Lond: especialy at Deptford, & more at Greenewich, where
Sir Tho: Stafford, Vice-Chamberlaine to the Queene, affirm'd some had the

shape of Crownes: others the order of the Gartyr about them; but these were fancies: it was certainely a very prodigious Storme: ...

July 10 I had newes of the taking of one of the knaves who robbd me, & was was summon'd to appeare against him: so as on the 12, I was in Westminster Hall but not being bound over (nor willing to hang the fellow) I did not appeare, comeing onely to save a friends baile who appeard for me; however the man being found <guilty>, was turn'd over to the old bailey:

13 My Wife & her Mother came first to Deptford ...

30 I went to Lond, return'd in the Evening, & the next day againe to take advise about purchasing Sir Richards Interest of those who had bought Sayes Court, returning that night: ...

24 **August**: precisely at one a clock, was my Wife brought to bed of my first Child & son: ...

2d **September** Mr. Owen, sequestred Parson of Eltham christnd my Son, by the Name of Richard (my F. Evelyns & Sir R: Brownes names) Susceptors my Bro: Geo: & sister Evelyn, about 4 in the afternoone, in the little drawing roome, next the Parlor in Says Court, many of my Relations and neighbours present: ...

25 I went to see Dr. Masons house, so famous for the Prospect (for the house is a wretch<e>d one) & description in Barkeleys *Icon Animorum*[1] ...

29 I went to Woodcot intending thence to Wotton & thence into Wiltshire &c with my Wife & Mother in Law, to have visited & rejoiced with my Brothers, & severall of both our Relations, so desirous of our Company; but being gotten to Woodcott it pleased God to visite my Lady with a Scarlet feavar, the Thursday following, of which she died the Wednesday following, which not onely interrupted that designe, but fill'd us with excessive sorrow: so as on the 6: of Octob: we carried her in an hearse to Deptford, & interr'd her in the Church neere Sir Richards Relations, upon the 9th following, accompanied with many Coaches of Friends, & other persons of qualitie; with all decent Ceremonie, & according to the Church Office, which I obtaind might be permitted, after it had not ben usd in that Church of 7 yeares before, to the great satisfaction of that innumerable multitude who were there: Thus ended an excellent and virtuous Lady, from a disconsolate Husband (now besieged & Calamitous in France) & a sad Daughter, but newly return'd into England: Indeede she was universaly lamented, having ben so obliging upon all occasions to those who continualy frequented her house in Paris, which was not onely an Hospital, but the Asylum to all our persecuted & afflicted Countrymen during her 11 yeares residence there, in that honarable Station: ...

December 25 Christmas day [no sermon anywhere, so observd it at home, the next day] we went to Lewsham, where was an honest divine preach'd on 21. Matt: 9. celebrating the Incarnation, for on the day before, no Churches were permitted to meete &c: to that horrid passe were they come: ...

---

[1] Dr, later Sir, Robert Mason (c.1589-1662). The house (66 Croom's Hill, Greenwich), about a mile from Sayes Court, survives; later paintings of the view mentioned by John Barclay (1582-1621) are displayed in the nearby Ranger's House.

1653

January ... 17 I began to set out the Ovall Garden at Says Court, which was before a rude Ortchard, & all the rest one intire fild of 100 Ackers, without any hedge: excepting the hither holly-hedge joyning to the bank of the mount walk: & this was the beginning of all the succeeding Gardens, Walkes, Enclosures & Plantations there:

21 I went to Lond: & seald some of the Writings of my Purchase of Sayes-Court, returnd next day: ...

February 19 I planted the Ortchard at Says-Court, new Moone, wind West.

22 Was perfected the sealing, livery & sesin of my Purchase of Says-Court My Bro: Geo: Glanvill, Mr. Scudamor, Offley, Co: William Glanvill, sonn to Serjeant Glanvil (sometime Speaker of the H: of Commons) Co: Steephens, & severall of my friends dining with me, it being also Shrove Tuesday; I paid for it 3500, my bargaine being 3200 pounds: [cost 3500 pounds 300 pounds more than I bargain'd for:] A bloudy fight now with the Dut<c>h:

24. I was surprized with a severe fit of an Ague which held me neere 12 houres:

3 **March**, my Ague accompanied with a feavor, treated me so rudely, that with much difficulty escaped I with my life, but by the goodnesse of God, & plying with Physick, by advise of Dr. Wilson my Physitian, I began to recover, & was out of danger, after 4 or 5. fitts: but was not cleeare till the 15th: Severall of my Relations & friends coming daily to visite me ...

April 11 I went to take the aire in Hide-Park, where every Coach was made to pay a shill: & horse 6d. by the sordid fellow who had purchas'd it of the State, as they were cald ...

May 12 Came my Bro: Glanvill, brought me his little Sonn, whom I so much longed to see, being the onely child of my deare sister;[1] a very fine, & hopeful boy: ...

18 My Wife perceivd herselfe quick with her 2d Child: ...

July 24 ... Dick had an accesse of an Ague, which greately afflicted us: but it last<ed> not above 3 fits:

August 13 I first began a Course of yearely washing my head with Warme Water, mingld with a decoction of Sweete herbs, & immediately, with cold Spring water, which much refreshd me, & succeeded very well with me divers yeares: ...

September 25 Mr. Owen preached in my Library at Says Court on 18 Luke.7.8. an excellent discourse on the un-just Judge, shewing why Almight<y> God, would sometimes be compared by such similitudes; He administred to us all the Holy Sacrament: ...

---

[1] William Glanville, junior, born January 1650 (d. 1718). His mother, E's sister Jane, had died in a subsequent childbirth, see above, 2 January 1652.

11 of **October** at 10½ houre night, my Sonn John Standsfild was borne, being my second child, & christned on 17th by the name of my Mothers Father, that name now quite extinct, being of Chesshire: Susceptors, my Bro: Glanvill, Wives Unkle Jo: Pretyman, & Aunt Hungerford of Cadenham in Wiltshire: Christned by Mr. Owen in my Library at Says Court: ...

November 7 My Wife was Churched by Mr. Owen, whom I allways made use of on these occasions, because the Parish Minister durst not (or perhaps would not) have officiated according to the form & usage of the Church of England, to which I allwayes adhered: ...

27 My son: J. Standsfild fell into Convulsion fitts, which not long after carried him away: ...

4 **December**: 'Til now I had met with no Phanatical Preachers, but going this day to our Church, I was surprized to see a Tradesman, a Mechanic step up, I was resolv'd yet to stay, & see what he would make of it ... That no danger was to be thought difficult, when God call'd for sheading of blood, inferring that now, the Saints were calld to destroy, temporal Governments, with such truculent, <anabaptisticall> stuff: so dangerous a Crisis were things growne to:

12 I causd an Issue to be made in my little Boy Standfilds neck: which abated his fitts:

14 I kept Court at Warley, lay at Brentwood, return'd next day: ...

25 Christmas-day, no Churches <or> publique Assembly, I was faine to passe the devotions of that blessed day with my family at home:

1654

January 25 Died my Son, J. Standsfield of Convulsion fits, buried at Deptford on the East Corner of the Church, neere his mothers greate Grandfather &c: the Thursday after, being a quarter old, & little more, as Lovely a babe as ever I beheld: ...

February 8 In Contradiction to all Costome & decency, the Usurper Cromwell feasted at the L. Majors on Ash-Wednesday, riding in T<r>iumph through the Citty: ...

13 My Bro: Richard paied me 1000 pounds, which I went to Lond: to receive, return'd next day when I saw a tame Lion play familiarly with a Lamb: The Lion was a huge beast, I thrust my hand into his mouth, & felt his tongue rough like a Catts: A sheepe also that had 6 leggs and made use of 5 of them to walke: A Goose that had 4 leggs, two Cropps, & as many Vents, voyding excrement by both, which was strange: ...

March 11 I went to Lond: to bespeake a new Coach, return'd: ...

13 I had some grudging of an Ague, & thence forwards a Tertian.

18 Came my Bro: and Lady to visite me: next day, being Palme sunday, I op'ne'd a veine, & was in Physick til the 26. when it pleased God to restore me, being even in this short time extreamely weakned, so as I could not go to Church.

May 5 I bound my <Laquay> Tho: Heath Apprentise to a Carpenter, giving with him 5 pounds, and new Cloathing: he thriv'd very well & became rich: I went to Lond, to visite many relations, & return'd not til the 12th, lying at the Temple:

8 I went to Hackny to see my Lady Brooks Gardens, which was one of the neatest, & most celebrated in England: The House also well-furnish'd, but a despicable building: ...

10 My Lady Gerrard treated us at Mulbery-Garden, now the onely place of refreshment about the Towne for persons of the best quality, to be exceedingly cheated at: Cromwell & his partisans having shut up, & seiz'd on Spring Garden, which 'til now had ben the usual rendezvous for the Ladys & Gallants at this season: ...

11 I now observed how the Women began to paint themselves, formerly a most ignominious thing, & used onely by prostitutes: I return'd this evening home: ...

2 **June** I went to [Lond] <to> take leave of severall Relations & friends, resolving to spend some monethes amongst my Wifes friends &c in Wiltshire & other parts, to whom we had ben so uncessantly invited ...

8 My Wife & I set out on our Journey, in Coach & 4 horses &c: din'd at Windsore, and saw the Castle, the Chapell of St. George: where they have laied our blessed Martyr K. Charles in the Vault, just before the Altar ... The Castle it selfe, large in Circumference, but the roomes Melancholy & of antient magnificence: The keepe (or mount) hath besides its incomparable Prospect, a very profound Well, & the Terrace towards Eaton, with the Park, meandring Thames, swete Meadows yeilds one of the most delightfull prospects in the World; So that night we lay at Reading, saw my Lord Cravons House at Causam[1] now in ruines, his goodly Woods felling by the Rebells: ...

27 We all went to see Bathe, where I bathed in the Crosse bathe; amongst the rest of the idle diversions of the Towne, one Musitian was famous for acting a Changling; which indeede he personated strangely: The *Faciate* of this Cathedrall is remarkable for the Historical Carving: The Kings Bath is esteemed the fairest in Europe; The Town is intirely built of stone, but the streetes narrow, uneven & unpleasant: Here we trifled & bath'd, & intervisited with the company who frequent the place, for health &c: till the 30th & then went to Bristoll a Citty emulating London, not for its large extent, but manner of building, shops, bridge: Traffique: Exchange, Market-place &c. The Governor shew'd us the Castle, of no greate concernment: The City wholy Mercantile, as standing neere the famous Severne, commodiously for Ireland and the Western world: Here I first saw the manner of refining Suggar, & casting it into loaves, where we had collation of Eggs fried in the suggar furnace, together with excellent Spanish Wine; but what was most stupendious to me, was the rock of St. Vincent, a little distance from the Towne, the precipice whereoff is equal to any thing of that nature I have seene in the most confragose cataracts of the Alpes: The river gliding betwene them an extraordinary depth: Here we went searching for Diamonds, & to the hot Well of Water at its foote: There is also on the side of this horrid Alp, a very romantic seate: so we returnd that evening to Bathe & on the 1 of July to Cadenam, where on the Sonday, preachd Dr. Hayward Chaplaine to the late A: Bish: Lawde, on 15: Luke 7 describing the Joyes of Heaven at the conversion of a sinner:

---

[1] Caversham, Berkshire..

July 4 Upon a Letter of my Wifes Unkle Mr. Pretyman, I waited back on her to London, passing by Hungerford towne (famous for its Troutes) I ariv'd at Deptford the next day, which was 60 miles, in the extreamity of heate:

6 I saw <my> prety boy, return'd early to Lond, & the next day, met my Wife and company at Oxford, which being on the 7th was the Eve of the Act:[1]

[8] Next day was spent in hearing severall exercises in the Scholes, & after dinner the Procter opened the Act at St. Maries (according to custome) & the Prævaricators their drolery, then the Doctors disputed, & so we supp'd at Waddum Coll:

The 9th Dr. French preechd at St. Maries on 12: Matt: 42, advising the Students the search after true Wisdome, not to be had in the books of Philosophers, but Scriptures: in the afternoone the famous Independent Dr. Owen, perstringing Episcopacy: he was now Cromwells Vice-Chancellor: We din'd with Dr. Ward, Mathematical Professor [since Bish: of Salisbury], & at night Supp'd in Balliol Coll: Hall where I had once ben student & fellow Commoner, where they made me extraordinarily wellcome, but I might have spent the Evening as well.

10 On Monday I went againe to the Scholes to heare the severall faculties, & in the Afternoone tarried out the whole Act in St. Maries. The long speeches of the Proctors: The V: Chancelors, the severall Professars, Creation of Doctors, by the Cap, ring, Kisse, &c: those Ceremonies not as yet wholy abolish'd, but retaining the antient Ceremonies & Institution: Dr. Kendal (now Inceptor amongst others) performing his Act incomparably well, concluded it with an excellent Oration, abating his Presbyterian animositie, which he with-held not even against that Learned & pious divine Dr. Hammond: The Act was closd, with the Spech of the V: Chancellor. There being but 4 In Theologie, 3 in Medicine, which was thought a considerable matter, the times consider'd:

I din'd at on<e> Monsieur Fiats, a student at Excester Coll: & supped at a magnificent Entertainement in Waddum Hall, invited by my excellent & deare Friend Dr. Wilkins, then Warden [now Bishop of Chester]: on the Eleventh was the Latine Sermon which I could not be at, invited, being taken up at All-Soules, where we had Music, voices & Theorbes perform'd by some ingenious Scholars, where after dinner I visited that miracle of a Youth, Mr. Christopher Wren, nephew to the Bishop of Elie: then Mr. Barlow [since Bishop of Lincoln] Bibliothe<c>arius of the Bodlean Library, my most learned friend, who shewd me, together with my Wife, The rarities of that famous place, Manuscrip<t>s, Medails & other Curiosities.

Amongst the MSS an old English Bible wherein the Eunuch mention'd to be baptiz'd by Philip, is cald the Gelding, & Philip & the Gelding went down into the Water &c, also the Original Acta of the Council of Basil, 900 years since, with the Bulla, or leaden Affix, which has a silken Chord, passing thro every parchment: likewise a MS: of Ven: Beades of 800 years antiquity: together with the old *Ritual secundum Usum Sarum*, exceeding voluminous: Then amongst the nicer curiosities: The Proverbs of Solaman written in French, by a Lady every Chapter of a severall Character, or hand, the most exquisitely imaginable: An Hieroglyplical Table, or Carta folded up like a Map, I suppose it painted on Asses hide, extreamely rare: but what is most illustrious, were the no lesse than 1000 MSS: in 19 Languages, espe<c>ialy Oriental, furnishing that new part of the Library, built by A: Bishop Lawd: some of Sir Kenhelme Digby, & the Earle of Pembroch: In the Closset of the Tower, they shew Josephs parti colourd Coat, A Muscovian Ladys Whip, some Indian Weapons,

---

[1] Exercises for the degree of MA and doctorates.

Urnes, Lamps: &c: But the rarest, is the Whole Alcoran written in one large sheet of Calico, which is made up in a Priests Vesture or Cape after the Turkish, & the Arabic Character so exquisitely written, as no printed letter comes neere it: Also a rolle of Magical Charmes or Periapta, divers Talismans, some Medails: Then I led my Wife into the Convocation house finely Wainscoted: The Divinity Schole & gotic Carv'd roofe; The Physick Or Anatomie Schole, adorn'd with some rarities of natural things; but nothing extraordinary, save the Skin of a Jaccal, a rarely Colour'd Jacatroo, or prodigious large Parot, two humming birds, not much bigger than our humble bee: which indeede I had not seene before that I remember. &c.

12 We went to St. Johns, saw the Library, & the 2 Skeletons, which are finely clense'd, & put together: observable are also the store of Mathematical Instruments, all of them chiefly given by the late A: Bishop Lawd, who built here an handsome Quadrangle:

Thence we went to New Coll: where the Chapell was in its antient garb, not withstanding the Scrupulositie of the Times: Thence to Christ-Church, in whose Library was shew'd us an Office of Hen: 8, the writing, Miniature & gilding whereof is equal if not surpassing any curiosity I had ever seene of that kind: It was given, by their founder, the Cardinal Wolsy: The Glasse Windos of the Cathedral (famous in my time) I found much abused: The ample Hall, & Columne that spreads its Capitel to sustaine the roofe as one gos up the Stayres is very remarkable: Next we walked to Magdalen Coll: where we saw the Library & Chapel, which was likewise in pontifical order, the Altar onely I think turn'd Table-wise: & there was still the double Organ, which abominations (as now esteem'd) were almost universaly demolish'd: Mr. Gibbon that famous Musitian, giving us a tast of his skill & Talent on that Instrument: Hence we went to the Physick Garden, where the Sensitive [& humble] plant was shew'd us for a greate wonder. There Grew Canes, Olive Tres, Rhubarb, but no extraordinary curiosities, besides very good fruit, which when the Ladys had tasted, we return'd in Coach to our Lodging.

13 We all din'd, at that most obliging & universaly Curious Dr. Wilkins's, at Waddum, who was the first who shew'd me the Transparant Apiaries, which he had built like Castles & Palaces & so ordered them one upon another, as to take the Hony without destroying the Bees; These were adorn'd with variety of Dials, little Statues, Vanes &c: very ornamental, & he was so aboundantly civill, as finding me pleasd with them, to present me one of these Hives, which he had empty, & which I had afterwards in my Garden at Says-Court,[1] many Yeares after; & which his Majestie came on purpose to see & contemplate with much satisfaction: He had also contrivd an hollow Statue which gave a Voice, & utterd words, by a long & conceald pipe which went to its mouth, whilst one spake thro it, at a good distance, & which at first was very Surprizing: He had above in his Gallery & Lodgings variety of Shadows, Dyals, Perspe<c>tives, places to introduce the Species, & many other artif<i>cial, mathematical, Magical curiosities: A Way-Wiser, a Thermometer; a monstrous Magnes, Conic, & other Sections, a Balance on a demie Circle, most of them of his owne & that prodigious young Scholar, Mr. Chr: Wren, who presented me with a piece of White Marble he had stained with a lively red very deepe, as beautifull as if it had ben naturall.

---

[1] Visiting E's garden Pepys saw 'among other rarities, a hive of bees, so as being hived in glass, you may see the bees making their honey and combs mighty pleasantly' (*Diary*, 5 May 1665).

Thus satisfied with the Civilities of Oxford: Dining at Farington a Towne which had newly ben fir'd, during the Warrs, & passing neere the seate of Sir Walter Pies, we came on the 13th to Cadenam, where on the 16 The Curate preach'd on his former Subject, like a Country parson, that tooke no greate paines:

16 We went to another Uncle & relation of my Wifes, Sir John Glanvill, a famous Lawyer formerly Speaker of the House of Commons; His Seate is at Broad-hinton, Where he now lived but in the Gate-house, his very faire dwelling house, having ben burnt by his owne hands, to prevent the Rebells making a Garison of it: Here my Co: Will: Glanvill (his eldest sonn) shewed me such a lock for a doore, that for its filing, & rare <contrivances>, was a masterpiece, yet made by a Country Black-Smith: But we have seene Watches made by another, with as much curiositie, as the best of that Profession can brag off; & not many yeares after, there was nothing more frequent, than all sorts of Iron-Work, more exquisitely wrought & polish'd, than in any part of Europ; so as a dore lock, of a tollerable price, was esteem'd a Curiositie even among forraine Princes: We went back this evening to Cadenham, & on the 19 to Sir Ed: Bayntons at Spie-Park, a place capable of being made a noble seate; but the humorous old knight, has built a long single house of 2 low stories, upon the precipice of an incomparable prospect, & landing on a bowling-greene in the Park; The house is just like a long barne, & has not a Windo, on the prospect side: After dinner they went to bowles, & in the meane time, our Coachmen made so exceedingly drunk; that returning home, we escaped incredible dangers: Tis it seemes by order of the Knight, that all Gentlemens servants be so treated: but the Custome is barbarous, & much unbecoming a Knight, much lesse a Christian:[1]

On the 20th We proceede to Salisbury; We went to see the Cathedral, which I take to be the compleatest piece of Gotic-Worke in Europe, taken in all its uniformitie; a neate fabric, but the pillars (reputed to be cast) are of stone manifestly cut out of the cuarry: Most observable are those in the Chapter-house: There are some remarkable Monuments, particularly the antient Bishops founders of the church; Knights Templars, the Marques of Hartfords: Also the Cloysters of the Palace & Garden to it, & greate Mural dial.

In the afternoone we went to Wilton, a fine house of the E. of Penbrochs, in which the most observable are the Dining-roome in the modern built part towards the Garden, richly gilded, & painted with story by De Creete, also some other apartments, as that of Hunting Landskips by Pierce: some magnificent chimny-pieces, after the French best manner: Also a pair of arti-ficial winding-stayres of stone, & divers rare Pictures: The Garden (heretofore esteem'd the noblest in all England) is a large handsom plaine, with a Grotto & Waterworks, which might be made much more pleasant were the River that passes through, clens'd & rais'd, for all is effected by a meere force: It has a flower Garden not inelegant: But after all, that which to me renders the Seate delightfull, is its being so neere the downes & noble plaines about the Country & contiguous to it. The stables are well order'd, & yeild a graceful front, by reason of the Walks of limetrees, with the Court & fountaine of the stable adorn'd with the Cæsars heads:

We return'd this evening by the Plaine, & 14 mile-race, where out of my Lords Hare-Waren we were entertain'd with the long course of an hare for neere 2 miles in sight: Neere this a Pergola or stand, built to view the Sports; so we came to Salisbury, and view'd the most considerable parts of that Citty,

---

[1] E suffered this again, see below, 18 March 1669.

the Merket place, which together with most of the streetes are Watred by a quick current & pure streame, running through the middle of them, but are negligently kept, when with small charge they might be purged, & rendred infinitely agreable, & that one of the sweetest Townes in Europe; but as 'tis now, the common buildings are despicable, & the streetes dirty.

22 We departed & dined at a ferme of my U. Hungerfords cald *Darneford magna*,[1] situate<d> in a Vally under the Plaine, most sweetly water'd, abounding in Trowts and all things else requisite, provisions exceeding cheape: They catch the Trouts by Speare in the night, whilst they come wondring at a light set in the sterne: There were Pigeons, Conys, & foule in aboundance, & so we had an excellent dinner at an houres warning: After dinner continuing our returne we passd over that goodly plaine or rather Sea of Carpet, which I think for evennesse, extent, Verdure, innumerable flocks, to be one of the most delightfull prospects in nature and put me in mind of the pleasant lives of the Shepherds we reade of in Romances & truer stories:[2]

Now we were ariv'd at Stone-henge, Indeede a stupendious Monument, how so many, & huge pillars of stone should have ben brought together, erected some, other Transverse on the tops of them, in a Circular arëa as rudly representing a Cloyster, or heathen & more natural Temple: & so exceeding hard, that all with my strength with an hammer, could not breake a fragment: which duritie I impute to their so long exposure: To number them exactly, is very difficult, in such variety of postures they lie & confusion, though they seem'd not to exceede 100, we counted onely 95: As to their bringing thither, there being no navigable river neere, is by some admir'd; but for the stone, there seeme to be of the same kind about 20 miles distant, some of which appeare<s> above ground: About the same hills are divers mounts raisd, conceiv'd to be antient intrenchments, or places of burial after bloudy fights: We now went by the Devizes a reasonable large Towne, so passing over Tan-hill (esteemed one of the highest in England) we came late to Cadenam: We had in this journey some disasters by a stonehorses getting loose: Stonehenge app<e>ares like a Castle at a distance ...

31 Taking leave of Cadenam (where we had ben long & very nobly entertain'd) we went a Compas into Licestershire, where dwelt anoth<er> relation of my Wifes, for I indeede made these excursions to shew her, the most considerable parts of her native Country, who from her childhood had lived altogether in France, as well as for my owne curiosity & information: First we came to Glocester, an handsome Citty, considerable for the Church, monuments, new Librarie, very noble though a private designe; but for nothing so famous as the Whispering place, which is indeede very rare, being thro a passage of 25 yards, in a many angl<e>d Cloister, & was I suppose, either to shew the skill of the Architect, or some invention of a Cunning Priests, who might (standing in a Chapell un-seene in the middle) heare whatever was spoken at either end: This is above the Quire, in which lies buried K. Stephen[3] under a Monument of Irish Oake, not ill carved considering the age: This Minster is a noble fabric: I was also pleasd with the Severne gliding so sweetely by it, The Dukes House, Castle, Workes, now almost quite dismantl'd; nor yet without sad thoughts did I see this Towne, considering how fatal the siege had ben (few yeares before) to our good King: About two

---

[1] Great Durnford, 4 miles north of Salisbury.

[2] This passage recalls Pepys's *Diary* entry for 14 July 1667 on Epsom Downs.

[3] E's error, the tomb is that of Robert, Duke of Normandy, eldest son of William I.

miles e'er we came to Glocester, we have a prospect from woody hills into a most goodly Vale & Country.

August 1 We set out towards Worcester, by the way (thick planted) with Cider-fruit) we deviate to the holy Wells trickling out of a Vally, thro a steepe declivity toward the foote of greate-Maubern hills: They are said to heale many Infirmities, As Kings-evil, Leaprosie &c: sore Eyes: Ascending a greate height above them, to the Trench dividing England from South Wales we had the Prospect of all Hereford shire, Radnor, Brecknock, Monmouth, Worcester, Glocester, Shropshire, Warwick, Derby-shire, & many more: We could discern Tewxbery, Kings-rode towards Bristol &c so as I esteeme it one of the goodliest Vista's in England.

2 This evening we ariv'd at Worcester, The Judges of Assise, & Sherifs just entering as we did: Viewing the Towne the next day, we found the Cathedral extreamely ruin'd by the late Warrs, otherwise a noble structure: The Towne is neatly pav'd and very cleane, The goodly river Severne runing by it: It stands in most fertil Country:

3 We pass'd next thro Warwick, & saw the Castle, which is built on an eminent rock, which gives prospect into a most goodly greene: a Woody & plentifully Watred Country; the river running so delighfully under it, that it may passe for one of the most surprizing seates one should meete with: The Gardens are pretily confus'd, & might be much improv'd; The Castle is the dwelling-house of the Lord Brook, of a Castle-like fabric, the furniture noble: Here they shew us Sir Guys greate two-handed Sword, Staff, horse-armes, Pott, & other reliques of that famous Knight errant. Warwick is a fair old Town, rocky, & hath one Church full of antient Monuments: having view'd these, I went to visite my worth friend Sir H: Puckering at the Abby, & though a melancholy old Seate, yet in a rich soile: Hence to Sir Guys Grott, where they say he did his penances, & dyed, & 'tis certainely a squalid den made in the rock, croun'd yet with venerable Oakes, & respecting a goodly streame, so as were it improv'd as it might <be>, 'twere capable of being render'd one of the most roma<n>tique & pleasant places imaginable: neere this we were shewd his Chapell, and gigantic statue hewn out of the solid rock, out of which there are likewise divers other Caves cut, & some very capacious:

The next place was Coventry, where most remarkeable is the Crosse, for Gotic worke, & rich gilding, comparable to any I had ever seen, excepting that of Cheape side in Lond, now demolish'd: This Citty, has many handsome Churches, a very beautifull Wall, a faire free-Schole & Librarie to it: the streetes full of greate Shops, cleane & well pav'd: At going forth the gate they shew us the bone or rib of a Wild-boare said to have been kild by Sir Guy, but which I take to be the chine of a Whale: [4] Hence riding through a considerable part of Licestershire, an open, rich, <but> unpleasant Country, we came late in the Evening to Horninghold a seate of my Wifes Unkle ...

7 I went to Upingham the Shire-towne of Rutland, pretty & well built of stone, which is a rarity in that part of England, where most of the rural parishes are but of mud, and the people living as wretchedly as in the most impoverish'd parts of France, which the<y> much resemble being idle & <sluttish>: The Country (especialy Licester shire) much in Commune, the Gentry greate drinkers:

9 I went on the ninth, to the old and raged Citty of Licester, large, & pleasantly seated, but despicably built; the Chimnies flues like so many smiths forges: however famous for the Tombs of the Tyrant Rich: the Third, which is now converted to a Cistern at which (I think) catell drink: also here in one of

the Churches lies buried the magnificent Cardinal Wolsey: John of Gaunt has here also built a large, but poore Hospital, neere which a Wretch, has made him an house out of the ruines of a stately Church: We were shew'd also the ruines of an old Roman Temple, thought to be of Janus:[1] Entertain'd at a very fine Collation of Fruite, such as I did not expect to meete with so far north, (especialy very good Melons) we return'd to my Unkles ...

14 I tooke a Journey into the Northern parts: riding thro Ockham, a pretty Towne in Rutlandshire, famous for the Tenure of Barons Harrington, who hold it by taking off a shoe, from every noble-mans horse that passes with his Lord thro the streete: unlesse redeem'd at a certaine piece of mony: a toaken of this, are severall gilded shoes, nailed-up on the Castle Gate: which seemes to have ben large and faire: Hence we went by Brook, a very sweete seate & Parke of the old Lady Camdens: Next Burleigh-house belonging to the Duke of Bouckingham, & worthily reckon'd among the noblest seates in England, situate<d> on the brow of an hill, built *a la modern* neere a Park Waled in, & a fine Wood at the descent. Now we were come to Cottsmore a pretty seate belonging to Mr. Heath, sonn, to the late L. C. Justice of that name; here after dinner parting with the Company that conducted us thus far, I pass'd that Evening by Belvoir Castle built on a round Mount, at the point of a long ridge of hills, which afords a stately Prospect, & is famous for its strenuous resistance in the late Civil Warr; also neere Newark upon Trent, a brave Towne, & Garison; next by Wharton house, belonging to the L: Chaworth, an handsom seate; Then by Home a noble place of the Marq: of Dorchesters, and pass'd the famous River Trent, which divides the South, from the North of England, & so lay that night <at> Notingham.

This whole Towne & County seemes to be but one intire rock as it were, an exceeding pleasant shire, full of Gentry: here I observ'd divers to live in the rocks, & Caves, much after the manner as about Tours in France: The Church is well built on an Eminence: a faire house of the L. Clares, another of Pierepoints, an ample Merkeat place, large streetes full of Crosses: The reliques of an antient Castle, holow'd beneath with many Caverns, especialy that of the Scots-king & his work there; but above all for being the place where his Majestie first erected his standar'd at the beginning of our unhappy differences. The Prospects from this Citty towards the river, & meadows is most delightfull.

[15] We passd next thro Sherewood forest, accounted the most extensive of England: Then Paplewich, a<n> incomparable Vista with the pretty Castle neere it. Thence we saw Newstead Abby belonging to the Lord Biron situated much like *fontaine Beleaw* in France, & capable of being made a noble seate, accommodated as it is with brave Woods, & streames: It has yet remaining the front of a glorious Abby Church: Next by Mansfield Towne, Then Wellbeck the house of the Marquis of New-Castle, seated in a botome in a Park, & invironed with Woods, a noble, yet melancholy seate: The Palace is an handsom & stately building:

Next, Worksop Abby almost demolish'd, The Church has a double flat towre intire, & a pretty Gate. The Mannor belongs to the Earl of Arundel & has to it a faire house at the foote of an hill in a Park that afords a delicate prospect. Blith a Towne: <Tickel> a Towne & Castle and very noble Prospect, all these in Notingham-shire:

[16] so we ariv'd at Doncaster where we lay this night, a large & faire Towne, famous for greate Wax-lights, & good stockings. The next day we

---

[1] Known as the 'Jewry Wall', part of the Roman city baths, still visible.

passe thro Pontfract, as the Castle (famous for many seiges both of late, & antient times, & the death of that unhappy King[1] murder'd in it) was now demolishing by the Rebells: It stands on a Mount, & makes a goodly shew at distance: The Queene has an house here, & many faire seates neere it: Especialy Mr. Pierpoints, built at the foot of an hill out of the Castle ruines: We now all alighted in the high Way, to drink at a Christal Spring, which they call Robinhoods Well, neere it is a Stone Chaire, & an Iron Ladle to drink out of Chain'd to the <Seate>.

Hence we rod to Todcaster at the side of which we have prospect of the Archbishops Palace, which is a noble seate, & in sight of divers other faire Gentlemens houses: This tract is a goodly, fertile, well water'd and Wooded Country, abounding with Pasture & plenty of all Provisions.

17 To YORK the 2d Citty of England, fairely Waled, of a Circular forme, Waterd by the brave river Ouse, bearing Vessels of Considerable burdens, over which a stone bridge, emulating that of London, & built on: The Middle Arch larger than any I have seene in all England, with a rivage or Wharfe all of hewn stone which makes the river appeare very neate: but most remarkeable & worthy seeing, is St. Peters Cathedrall, which alone of all the greate churches in England, had best ben preserv'd from the furie of the sacrilegious, by Composition with the Rebells, when they tooke the Citty, during the many incursions of Scotch & others: It is a most intire, magnificent piece of Gotic Architecture: The Skreene before the Quire is of stone, carv'd with flowers, running work & statues of the old Kings: The Monuments (many of them) very antient: Here as a greate rarity in these dayes, & at this time, they shew'd me a Bible & Common-prayer book cover'd with Crimson Velvet, & richly emboss'd with silver gilt: Also a Service for the Altar of Guilt wrought Plate, flagons, Basin, Eure, Chalices, Patins, &c: with a gorgeous covering for the Altar, Pulpet &c: carefully preserv'd in the Vestrie: in the holow Wall whereof rises a plentifull Spring of excellent Water: I got up to the Toure, where we had Prospect towards Duresme, & could see Rippon, part of Lancashire, & the famous & fatal Marston Moore, the Spaus of Knarsbrough, & all the invirons of that admirable Country.

Sir Ingoldsby has here a large house, Gardens & Tennis-Court; Also the Kings house; & church neere the Castle which was modernly fortified with a Palizad & bastions: The Streetes narrow, ill-pav'd, the shops like London.

[18] We went next day to Beverly, a large Towne, Two stately Churches, St. Johns & St. Maries not much inferior to the best of our Cathedrals. Here a very old Woman shew'd us the Monuments, and being above 100 yeares of age, spake the language of Q: Maries daies in whose time she was born, being the Widdow of a Sexton that had belonged to the Church, an hundred yeares. Hence we passe through a fenny-Country (but rich) to Hull, situate like Calais, modernly & strongly fortified with three Block-houses, of Brick & Earth: It has a good harbour for ships, & Mercat Place: The Water-house is worth seeing: famous also is this Town, (or rather infamous) for Hothams refusing enterance to his Majestie: and here ends the South of Yorkshire, so now we passe the Humber, which is an arme of the Sea, of about 2 leages breadth; [19] the weather was bad, but we cross'd it in a good barque over to Barton the first Towne in that part of Lincoln-shire, all Marsh ground 'til we came to Briggs famous for the plantations of Licoris, & then brave pleasant riding to Lincoln, much resembling Salisbury Plaine.

---

[1] Richard II (1377-99).

LINCOLN an old confusd towne, very long, uneven, & confragose, steepe & raged, but has formerly ben full of good houses, especialy Churches, Abbies, especialy the Minster, comparable to that of Yorke it selfe, abounding with marble pillars, a faire front: Here in was interrd Q. Elianor, loyal & loving Wife to her Husband out of whose wound she succked the poisond arrow: The Abbot founder, with rare carving in the stone: The Greate Bell or Tom as they call it: I went up the steeple to view the Countrie: The Cloyster & Bish: Palace: but the Souldiers had lately knocked off all or most of the Brasses which were on the Gravestones, so as few Inscriptions were left: They told us they went in with axes & hammers, & shut themselves in, till they had rent & torne of some barges full of Mettal; not sparing the monuments of the dead, so helish an avarice possess'd them.

I went to see a Tall woman, that was six foote & 2 Inches high, a comely middle ag'd & well proportiond woman, kept a very neate & cleane Ale house, & got most by peoples coming to see her: The malicious Souldiers had besides the Sacred places and Churches, exceedingly ruined this Citty: from which the Minster yeilds a goodly Prospect all over the Country.

20 From hence we had most pleasant riding over a large heath (like that of Salisbery plaine) to Grantham, a pretty Towne, so well situated on the side of a botome; which is large, & at distance inviron'd with ascending grounds, that for pleasure I think it comparable to most [inland] places of England: famous is the Steeple for the exceeding height of the Shaft, which is of stone: About 18 miles South we passe by a noble seate, & see Boston at distance; here we came to a parish of which the Parson has Tith Ale:

Thence through Rutland we brought night [21] to Horninghold: ...

22 I went a setting, & Hauking, where we had tollerable Sport:

25 I went to see Kirby a very noble house of my Lord Hattons in N.Ha<m>pton -shire; built *a la moderne*: Garden, & stables agreable, but the avenue ungracefull, & the seate naked; return'd that Evening: ...

30 Taking leave of my Friends, who had now feasted me more than a Month, I now with my Wife &c: set our faces towards home, & got this Evening to Peterborow, passing by a stately Palace of <St. Johns> (one deepe in the bloud of our good King) build out of the ruines of the Bishops Palace & Cloyster: The Church of this Citty is exceeding faire, full of monuments of greate antiquity: Here lies Queen Catharine the unhappy Wife of Hen: 8: & the no lesse unfortunate Mary Q: of Scots: On the steeple we viewed the fenns of Lincolnshire, now much inclosed, & drained with infinite expense, and by many sluces, cutts, mounds, & ingenious Mills & like inventions: at which the Citty & Country about it consisting of <a> poore & very lazy sort of people, were much displeas'd: Peterborow is an handsome Towne, & hath another well build church to it:

[31] The next morning through a part of Huntington shire, we passe that Towne, which is a faire antient Towne, a sweete river running by it, and the Country about is so abounding in Wheate, that when any King of England passe thro it, they have a costome to meete his Majestie with an hundred plows: and so this Evening we came early to:

1 **September** Cambridg, & went first to see St. Johns Colledge & Librarie, which I think is the fairest of that Universitie: one Mr. Benlous has given it all the ornaments of *Pietra Commessa*,[1] whereof a Table, and one piece of Perspective is very fine, other trifles there also be of no greate value, besides a

---

[1] Mosaic work.

vast old song book or Service, & some faire Manuscripts: This Coll: is well built of brick: There hangs in the Library the Picture of Williams ABishop of York, & sometime Ld: Keeper, my Kindsman, and their greate benefactor. Next we saw Trinity Coll, esteemed the fairest Quadrangle of any University in Europ, but in truth far inferior to that of Christ-Church Oxford: the Hall is ample, & of stone, the fountaine in the Quadrangle is gracefull, The Chapell and Librarie faire, there they shew'd us the prophetic MS. of the famous Grebner; but the passage & Emblem which they would apply to our late King, is manifestly relating to the Swedish; in truth it seemes to be a meere fantastic rhapsody, however the Title bespeake strange revelations: There is an Office finely miniatur'd MS, with some other antiquities given by the Countesse of Richmond mother of Hen: 7: and the formention<ed> Bishop Williams when Bishop of Lincoln: The Library is pretty well stor'd: Here the Greeke Professor had me into another halfe Quadrangle, cloistred & well built, and gave us an handsome Collation in his owne Chamber:

Then we went to Caius, then to Kings Coll, where I found the Chapel altogether answerable to expectation, especialy the roofe all of stone, which for the flatnesse of its laying & carving may I conceive vie with any in Christendome; The contignation of the roofe (which I went upon), weight, and artificial joyning of the stones is admirable: The lights are also very faire: The library is too narrow: here in one Ile, lies the famous Dr. Collins so celebrated for his fluency in the Latine Tongue: from this roofe we could discry Elie, and the Incampment of Sturbridge faire now beginning to set up their Tents & boothes: also Royston, New-Market &c: houses belonging to the King. Thence we walked to Clare-hall of a new and noble designe, but not finish'd: hence to Peterhouse formerly under the charge & gover<n>ment of my worthy friend Dr. Jo: Cosin; deane of Peterborow, a pretty neate Coll: & delicate Chapell: next to Sidny, a fine College, Kathrine-hall, though meane structure, yet famous for the learned B: Andrews once Master: then to Emanuel Coll: that zealous house, where to the Hall, they have a Parler for the fellows: The Chapell is reform'd *ab origine*, built N. & South, meanely built, as is the Librarie:

Thence to Jesus Coll: one of the best built, but in a Melancholy situation: next to Christ Coll. very <nobly> built, especialy the modern part, built without the Quadrangle towards the Gardens, of exact Architecture: The Schooles are very despicable, & publique Librarie but meane though somewhat improved by the Wainscoting and Books lately added by the Bishop Bancrofts Library & M.SS: They shew'd us little of antiquity: onely K: Jamess Works, being his owne gift, and kept very reverently and was the only rarity shewd us.

The Mercat place of Chambridg is very ample and remarkable for old Hobsons the pleasant Carriers beneficence of a fountaine: But the whole Towne situated in a low dirty unpleasant place, the streetes ill paved, the aire thick, as infested by the fenns; nor are its Churches (of which St. Maries is the best) anything considerable in compare to Oxford which is doubtlesse the noblest Universitie now in the whole World.

From Chambridge we went to Audley End and spent some time in seeing that goodly Palace built by Howard E. of Suffolck, & once Lord Treasurer of England: It is a mixt fabric, 'twixt antique & modern, but observable for its being compleately finish'd, & without comparison one of the statliest Palaces of the Kingdome, consisting of two Courts, the first very large, Wingd with Cloisters: The front hath a double Entrance: The Hall is faire, but somewhat too smale for so august a pile: The Kitchin leaded & Cellars very large &

arched with stone, Celars I never saw any so neate & well dispos'd: These Offices are joynd by a Wing out of the way very handsomely: The Gallery is the most cherefull, & I thinke one of the best in England: a faire dining-roome, & the rest of the Lodgings answerable with a pretty Chapell: The Gardens are not in order, though well inclosed: It has also a Bowling ally, a nobly well walled, wooded & watred Park, full of fine collines and ponds, the river glides before the Palace, to which an avenue of lime-trees; but all this much diminishd by its being placed in an obscure bottome; for the rest a perfectly uniforme structure, & sh<e>wes without like a diademe, by the decorations of the Cupolas & other ornaments on the Pavilions: I observ'd that instead of railes and balusters, there is a bordure of Capital letters, as was lately also on Suffolck house neere Charing Crosse, built by the same L: Tress: This house stands in the Parish of Saffron Walden famous for the aboundance of Saffron there Cultivated and esteem'd the best of any forraine Country.

Having dined here, we passe thro Bishop Stratford a pretty waterd Towne, and so by London late home [3] to Sayes-Court after a parerration of 700 miles, but for the variety an agreable refreshment after my Turmoile & building &c ...

December 25 Christmas-day, were no public offices in Churches, but penalties to the observers: so as I was constrained to celebrate it at home: ...

31 By Gods special Providence we went not to Church, my wife being now so very neere her time: for my little sonne Richard now about 2 yeares old as he was fed with broth in the morning, a square but broad & pointed bone of some part of a ract of Mutton, stuck so fast in the Childs Throate & crosse his Weason, that had certainely choaked him, had not my Wife & I ben at home; for his mayd being alone with him above in the Nurserie, was fallen down in a swone, when we below (going to Prayers) heard an unusual groaning over our head, upon which we went up, & saw them both gasping on the floore, nor had the Wench any power to say what the Child ail'd, or call for any help: At last she sayd, she believed a Crust of bread had choak'd her little master, & so it almost had, for the eyes & face were s<w>ollen, & clos'd, the Mouth full of froath, and gore, the face black — no Chirurgeon neere: what should we doo?, we cald for drink, power it downe, it returnes againe, the poor babe now neere expiring. I hold its head down, incite it to Vomite, it had no strength, In this dispaire, & my Wife almost as dead as the Child, & neere despaire, that so unknown and sad an accident should take from us so pretty a Child: It pleased God that on the suddaine effort & as it were strugling his last for life, he cast forth a bone of this shape & forme:

I gave the child some *Lucotellus Balsome*[1] for his Throat was much excoriated. Ô my Gracious God out of what a tender feare, & sad heart, into what Joy did thy goodnesse now revive us! Blessed be God for this mercy: Wherefore beging pardon for my sinns, & returning Thanks for this grace, I implord his providential care for the following yeare.

---

[1] A medicine, balsam, devised by one Luigi Locatelli (d. 1637).

1655

January 14 About ½ after 10 in the Morning, was my Wife delivered of another Sonn,[1] being my Third, but 2d living: *Benedictus sit deus in donis suis*:[2] 16th I went to Lond: returnd the 18th & the same on foote, returning by Water 20th: I saw a live Camelion ...

26 Was Christned my Sonne John by Sir Jo: Evelyn, Lady Gerrard, & his Unkle Will: Pretyman susceptors, Mr. Owen officiating at Says-Court, according to the rite of the Church of England: ...

February <24> I was shew'd a Table Clock whose balance was onely a Chrystall ball, sliding on paralell Wyers, without being at all fixed, but rolling from stage to stage, till falling on a Spring conceald from sight, it was throwne up to the upmost chanell againe made with an imperceptible declivity, in this continual vicissitude of motion prettily entertaining the eye every halfe minute, and the next halfe minute giving progresse to the hand that shew'd the houre, & giving notice by a small bell; so as in 120 halfe Minuts or periods of the bullets falling on the ejaculatorie Spring the Clock-part struck: This very extraordinary piece (richly adorn'd) had ben presented by some German Prince to our late King, & was now in possession of the Usurper: valued 200 pounds: ...

April 9th ... my Bro: dining with me, we went to see the greate Ship newly built,[3] by the Usurper Oliver, carrying 96 brasse Guns, & of 1000 tunn: In the prow was Oliver on horseback trampling 6 nations under foote, a Scott, Irishman, Dutch, French, Spaniard & English as was easily made out by their several habits: A Fame held a laurell over his insulting head, & the word *God with us*: ...

August <1> I went to Darking to see Mr. Charles Howards Amphitheater Garden, or Solitarie recesse, being 15 Ackers, invirond by an hill: he shew'd us divers rare plants: Caves, an Elaboratory: ...

10 I went to Abburie[4] to visite Mr. Howard, who had begun to build, and alter the Gardens much, he shewed me many rare Pictures, particularly the Moore on horseback; & Erasmus as big as the life of Holbein; also a Madona in miniature by Oliver; but above all the Skull carved out in wood by Albert Durer, he assur'd me his father was offered 100 pounds for it; Also Alberts head by himselfe, with divers rare Achats, Intaglia, & other Curiosities ...

---

[1] John Evelyn (1655-99), E's only son to survive childhood and father of E's heir Sir John Evelyn, baronet, of Wotton (1682-1763).

[2] 'Praised be God in his gifts'.

[3] The *Naseby*, renamed the *Royal Charles* in 1660, E went aboard on 1 July 1665 (see below). It was seized by the Dutch in June 1667 when they sailed up the Medway and attacked the English Fleet, 'I find it is true that the Dutch did heele "The Charles" to get her down, and yet run aground twice or thrice, and yet got her safe away, and have her, with a great many good guns in her ...' (Pepys's *Diary*, 30 June 1667 - Evelyn in his account below on 28 June 1667 does not mention this ship's loss).

[4] Albury Park. This Mr Howard is Henry Howard, later 6th Duke of Norfolk, and elder brother of Charles Howard mentioned under 1 August above.

28 Came that renowned Mathematitian Mr. Oughtred to see me, I sending my Coach to bring him to Wotton, being now very aged: Amongst other discourse, he told me he thought Water to be the Philosophers first matter; & that he was well perswaded of the possibility of their Elixir: He believed the Sunn to be a material fire, the Moone a Continent as appeares by the late Selenographer: He had strong apprehensions of some extraordinary event to happen the following yeare from the Calculation of coincidence with the Diluvian period; & added that it might possible be to convert the Jewes by our Saviours visible appearance or to judge the world, & therefore his word was *parate in occursum:*[1] He said Original Sin was not met with in the Greeke Fathers: yet he believd the thing; this was from some discourse upon Dr. Taylors late booke which I had lent him.

September 17 Received 2600 pounds for the Mannor of Warley Magna in Essex, purchased by me some time since: The Taxes were so intollerable, that they eate up the Rents &c: surcharged as that County had ben above all others during our unnatural War: ...

October ... Sir Nic: Crisp came to Treate with me, about his vast designe of a Mole or Sasse to be made for ships in part of my Grounds &c:[2]

November 27 To Lond about Sir N: Crisps designs: I went to see York-house & Gardens belonging to the former greate Buckingham: But now much ruin'd thro neglect. Thence to visite honest & learned Mr. Hartlib, a Publique Spirited, and ingeni<o>us person, who had propagated many Usefull things & Arts: Told me of the Castles which they set for ornament on their stoves in Germanie (he himselfe being a Lithuanian as I remember) which are furnishd with small ordinance of silver on the battlements, out of which they discharge excellent Perfumes about the roomes, charging them with a little Powder to set them on fire & disperse the smoke: & intruth no more than neede; for their stoves are sufficiently nasty: He told me of an Inke that would give a dozen Copies, moist Sheetes of Paper being pressed on it, & remaine perfect; & a receit how to take off any Print, without injury to the original in the least: This Gent was Master of innumerable Curiosities, & very communicative. I returnd home that evening by water, & was afflicted for it with a Cold, that had almost kil'd me.

This day there also came forth the Protectors Edict or Proclamation, prohibiting all ministers of the Church of England from Preaching, or Teach any Scholes, in which he imitated The Apostate Julian: with the Decimation of all the Royal parties revenues thro-out England ...

1656

February 11 I adventurd to go to White-hall, where of many yeares I had not ben, & found it very glorious & well furnish'd, as far as I could safely go, &

---

[1] Presumably 'Prepare to meet [thy God].' *Amos* IV.12.

[2] See also 16 January 1662. The combination of a mole (artificial breakwater) and sas (lock) seems to imply some sort of drydock or enclosed mooring.

was glad to find, they had not much defac'd that rare piece of Hen 7th & 8th &c. don on the Walles of the Kings Privy Chamber[1] ...

March 4: This night I was invited by Mr. Rog: L'Estrange to heare the incomperable Lubicer on the Violin, his variety upon a few notes [& plaine ground] with that wonderfull dexterity, as was admirable, & though a very young man, yet so perfect & skillfull as there was nothing so crosse & perplext, which being by our Artists, brough<t> to him, which he did not at first sight, with ravishing sweetenesse, & improvements, play off, to the astonishment of our best Masters: In Summ, he plaied on that single Instrument a full Consort, so as the rest, flung-downe their Instruments, as acknowl<e>dging a victory: As to my owne particular, I stand to this houre amaz'd that God should give so greate perfection to so young a person: There were at that time as excellent in that profession as any were thought in Europ: Paule Wheeler, Mr. Mell and others, 'til this prodigie appeared & then they vanish'd, nor can I any longer question, the effects we read of in Davids harp, to charme maligne spirits, & what is said some particular notes produc'd in the Passions of Alexander & that King of Denmark ...

April 6. To Lond: to Celebrate Easter - so greate a snow fell as seldome had I seene a greater, it fell as I was on the way, with two new stone-horses to the Coach, which made them unruly, but we got safe to Lond...

12. Mr Barkley, & Mr. Rob: Boyle that excellent person, & greate Virtuoso, Dr. Taylor & Dr. Wilkins dined with me at Sayes Court, when I presented Dr. Wilkins with my rare Burning-glasse; Afternoone we all went to Coll: Blount to see his new invented Plows: & so went with them to Lond: ...

26 I went to see his Majesties House at Eltham both Palace & Chapell in miserable ruines, the noble woods & Park destroied by Rich the Rebell:[2]

May 12 Was published my *Essay on Lucretius* - with innumerable *Errata* &c; <by> the negligence of Mr. Triplet who undertook the Correction of the Presse in my absence: [little of the Epicurean Philosophy was known then amongst us:][3] ...

28 Againe <to Lond>, to dine with Nieupoort the Holland Ambassador, who received me with extraordinary courtesie: I found him a judicious Crafty & wise man: Gave me excellent cautions as to the danger of the times and Circumstances our Nation was in &c: - remember the Observation he made,

---

[1] Holbein's celebrated painting of Henry VII and Elizabeth of York, Henry VIII and Jane Seymour, destroyed in the Whitehall fire of 1698 (see 2 January 1698). A preparatory drawing for part survives in the National Portrait Gallery.

[2] The Great Hall, now restored, survives.

[3] The publication included E's verse translation of Book I of *De Rerum Natura* and his *Animadversions* on the text. It is evident from the adulatory notices from friends incorporated not only that E had great hopes for the book but also that it had been largely completed by the end of 1653. It was the first published English translation of Lucretius and E had prepared translations of the other books. He was devastated by the typographical errors and his own copy, which survives, is covered in corrections. He was also criticised by some of his clerical friends for taking an interest in pagan expositions of the nature of life and the world. He never issued the rest of the translation.

upon the ill successe of our former Parliaments, by their private animosities, & little care of the publicque: so taking the aire in Hide-parke I went home: ...

July 7 I began my journey to see some parts of the North East of England; but the weather so excessive hot & dusty, I shortned my progresse – I lay this night at Ingulstone,

[8] the next day to Colchester, a faire Towne but now wretchedly demolished by the late Siege; espe<c>ialy the suburbs all burnt & then repairing: The Towne is built on a rising, having faire meadows on one side, & a river, with a strong antient Castle, said to have ben built by K. Coilus father of Helena mother of Constantine the Greate of whom I find no memory, save at the pinacle of one of their Woolstaple houses, where Coilus has a statue of wood wretchedly carvd: The walles are exceeding strong, deeply trenched & fill'd with Earth. It has 6 gates & some Watch toures; & some handsome Churches; but what was shew'd us as a kind of miracle, at the outside of the Castle, the Wall where (Sir Charles Lucas & Sir Geo: Lisle those valiant persons who so bravely behav'd themselves in the late siege, & were barbarously shot to death & murder'd by Ireton in cold blood & after rendission upon articles) the place was bare of grasse for a large space, all the rest of it abounding with herbage: For the rest, this is a raged, factious Towne, & now Swarming in Sectaries. Their trading Cloth with the Dutch, & Baies & saies with Spaine; & is the only place in England where these stuffs are made unsophisticated.

Famous likewise will this Place ever be for the strenuous resistance of those most loyal Gent: &c: against the Rebells, when neere all the strong places & Townes in England had given up to the Conquerors, what time, they expected reliefe from the Scotch Army, defeated with his Majestie at Worcester: It is also famous for Oysters, & Erringo of rootes here about growing & Candied: Henc we went to Dedham a pretty Country Towne, & very faire Church, finely situated, the vally well watred: Here I met with Dr. Stokes a young Gent: but an excellent Mathematician: This is (as most are in Essex) a Clothing Towne, and lies in the unwholsome hundreds.

[9] Hence to Ipswich in Suffolck, which is doubtlesse one of the Sweetest, most pleasant, well built <Towns> in England. It has 12 faire Churches, many noble houses, especialy the Lord D'evorixe's &c – a brave <quay> & commodious harbor, being about 7 miles from the maine: an ample Mercat-place, & here was borne the greate Cardinal Woolsey, who began a palace here, which was not finish'd &c: I returnd to Dedham: At Ipswich I had the curiosity to visite some Quakers there in Prison, a new phanatic sect of dangerous Principles, the<y> shew no respect to any man, magistrate or other & seeme a Melancholy proud sort of people, & exceedingly ignorant: one of these was said to have fasted 20 daies, but another endeavoring to do the like perish'd the 10th, when he would have eaten, but could not:

10: I returnd homeward, passd againe thro Colchester, & by the way saw neere the antient Towne of Chelmsford, saw New-hall built in a parke by Hen: 7th & 8, & given by Q: Eliz: to the Earle of Sussex who sold it to the late greate Duke of <Buckingham> and since seiz'd on by O. Cromwell (pretended Protector) a faire old house, built with brick, low & but of 2 stories, as the manner then was: The Gate-house better: The Court large & pretty: The staire case of extraordinary widenesse, with a piece representing Sir F: Drakes action in 88, an excellent Sea-piece: The galleries are trifling, the hall noble, Garden a faire plot, & the whole seate well accommodated with water; but above all the Sweete & faire avenue planted with stately Lime-trees in 4 rowes for neere a mile in length: It has 3 descents which is the onely fault, & may be reformed: There is another faire walk of the same at the Mall & wildernesse, with a Tenis-Court, & a pleasant Terrace towards the Park, which was well stored with deere, & ponds: From the Towne we saw the antient Maldon (Camelodunum) suppd at Chelmsford, <lay> at Ingolstone & came home by Greenewich ferry, where I saw Sir Jo: Winters new project of Charring Sea-Coale, to burne out the Sulphure & render it Sweete: he did it by burning them in such Earthen-pots, as the glassemen, mealt their Mettal in, so firing the Coales, without Consuming them, using a barr of Yron in each crucible or Pot, which barr has an hooke at one end, that so the Coales being mealted in a furnace, with other crude sea Coales, under them, may be drawn out of the potte, sticking to the Yron, whence they beate them off in greate halfe exhausted Cinders, which rekindling they make a cleare pleasant Chamber fires with, depriv'd of their Sulphury & Arsenic malignity: what successe it may have time will discover: ...

August 3 to Lond, to receive the B: Sacrament, & was the first time that ever the Church of England was reduced to a Chamber & Conventicle, so sharp was the Persecution; The Parish churches filld with sectaries of all sorts, Blasphemous & Ignorant Mechanics usurping the Pulpets every where. In a private house in Fleetestreete Dr. Wild preachd on 14. Luke. 23: The B: Communion succeeded & we had a greate meeting of zealous Christians who were generaly much more devout & religious, than in our greatest propsperity: Afternoone, I went to the French-Church in the Savoy, where I heard Monsieur D'Espagne Catechize: & so returnd to my house: ...

20 Was a confused Election of Parliament cald by the Usurper:

24: ... My son Richard a child of most prodigious hopes was now 4 years old: *Deo gratias.*[1]

September 14 ... Now was old Sir Hen: Vane sent to Carisbrook Castle in Wight for a foolish booke he publish'd:[2] The pretended Protector fortifying himselfe exceedingly, & sending many to Prison: My deare boy, was sick of an Ague: ...

November 23 A very wet day, had the Church office & sermon read to my Family, my Wife not well.

30 An accident keept me at home from Church also: Now indeede that I went at all to Church whilst these usurpers possess'd the Pulpet, was that I might not be suspected for a Papist, & that though the Minister were Presbyterianly affected, he yet was as I understood duly ordaind, & preachd sound doctrine after their way, & besides was an harmelesse & peaceable man.

December 20: The deepe & greate Snow kept us from Church, but not from the publique Office at home.

---

[1] 'Thanks be to God.'

[2] E's error, the book was published by Sir Henry Vane the younger (1613-62). The elder had died in 1655. This kind of error is a consequence of E's writing up the *Diary* from notes many years hence.

1657

January (11) Being not well, could not go to the Parish Church.

18, my Indisposition continued: Dr. Joylife that famous Physitian (& Anatomist, first detector of the lymphatic veins) came to visite me ...

February 5, I din'd at the Holland Ambassadors: he told me that the E. India Comp: of Holland had constantly a stock of 400000 pounds in India, 48 Men of Warr there: of their exact & just keeping their books, Correspondence &c: so as no Adventure<r>s Stock could possibly be lost or defeated: That it was a Vulgar Error of the Hollanders furnishing their Enemies with powder & ammunition for their mony, though ingaged in actual warr; but that they usd to merchandize indifferently, & were permitted to sell to the friends of their Enemies: He laugh'd at our Commitèe of Trade, as compos'd of men wholy ignorant of it, & how they were the ruine of Commerce, by gratifying some for private ends: ...

10 I went to visite the Governor of Havana, a brave sober, valiant Spanish Gent: taken by Capt: Young of Deptford, when after 20 yeares being in the Indias & amassing great Wealth, his lady, & whole family (excepting two <Sonns>) were burnt, destroyed, & taken within sight of Spaine: His Eldest Son, daughter and Wife perishing with immense treasure: One Sonn, with his brother of one yeares old were the onely saved: The young Gent: about 17: was a well complexion'd Youth, not olive colourd: he spake latine handsomly, was extreamely well bred, & borne in the <Charcas> 1000 miles south of the Equinoxial neere the mountaines of Potisi: had never ben in Europe before: The Governor was an antient Gent: of greate Courage, of the order of S: Jago: sore wounded, his arme & rib broken & lost for his owne share 100000 pounds sterling, which he seem'd to beare with exceeding indifference, & nothing dejected; after some discourse I went with them to Arundel house where they dined: They were now going back into Spaine, having obtaind their liberty from Cromewell. An example of human Vicissitude:

March 29 ... The Protector Oliver, now affecting King-ship, is petition'd to take the Title on him, by all his new-made sycophant Lords &c: but dares not for feare of the Phanatics, not thoroughly purged out of his rebell army: ...

April 21 I went to Lond: to consult Dr. Bate about taking preventing Physick: Thence to Visite my Lord Hatton, with whom I dined; at my returne I step'd into Bedlame, where I saw nothing extraordinarie, besides some miserable poore Creatures in chaines, one was mad with making Verses: & also visited the Charter-house, formerly belonging to the Carthusians; now an old neate, fresh solitarie Colledge for decaied Gent: It has a grove, bowling-greene, Garden: Chapell, hall &c where they eate in common: I likewise saw Christ-Church & Hospital, a very goodly building, Gotic: also the Hall, Schoole, Lodgings, in greate order, for the bring<ing> up many hundreds of poore Children of both sexes, & is a<n> exemplary Charity: There is a large picture at one end of the Hall, representing the Governors, founders, & Institution: so on the 23d I returnd home:

25. To Lond ... I had a dangerous fall out of the Coach in Covent Garden, going to my Bro: but without harme, The Lord be praised: ...

May 1 Divers Souldiers quarter'd at my house, but I thank God, went away the next day towards Flanders:

2: I tooke Physick. The next-day (lying at Greenewich on the 4th) I went into Surrey with my Co: G: Tuke, to see Baynards, an house of my Bro: Richards, which he would have hired: We going in a Charriot drawne with unruly young horses, one of which (they said) had already killed two keepers, were often in very greate danger; so as after 20 <miles> riding, we were forced to change our horses. This is a very faire and & noble house of my Bro: built in a park, & having one of the goodliest avenue<s> of Oakes up to it, that ever I saw: There is also a pond of 60 Ackers neere it: The Windos of the chiefe roomes are of very fine painted glasse: but the situation excessively dirty & melancholy: We return'd next day, dining by the way at Wotton: ...

7 **June** My Wife fell in Labour from 2 in the morning till 8½ at night, when my fourth Sonne was borne, it being Sonday: he was Christned on Wednesday on the 10th & named George (after my Grandfathers name) my Bro: Rich: Evelyn: Co: Geo: Tuke & Lady Cotton susceptors &c: Dr. Jer: Taylor officiating in the withdrawing-roome at Says-Court: ...

18 I saw at Greenewich a sort of Catt brought from the East Indies, shaped & snouted much like the Egyptian Ratoone, in the body like a Monkey, & so footed: the eares & taile like a Catt, onely the taile much longer, & the Skin curiously ringed, with black & white: With this taile, it wound up its body like a Serpent, & so got up into trees, & with it, would also wrap its whole body round; It was of a wolly haire as a lamb, exceedingly nimble, & yet gentle, & purr'd as dos the Cat ...

July 3 A ship blown-up at Wapping, shooke my whole house, & the chaire I was sitting & reading in my study[1] ...

September 15 Going to Lond: with some Company, who would needes step in to see a famous Rope-daunser call'd the Turk, I saw even to astonishment the agilities he perform'd, one was his walking bare foote, & taking hold by his toes onely, of a rope almost perpendicular & without so much as touching it with his hands: also dauncing blindfold on the high-roope: & with a boy of 12 yeares old, tyed to one of his feete about 20 foote beneath him dangling as he daunced, & yet moved as nimbly, as it had ben but a feather: Lastly he <stoode> on his head, upon the very top of a very high mast, daunced on a small roope that was very slack, & finaly flew downe the perpendicular, with his head foreward on his breast, his legs & armes extended: with divers other actvities, to the admiration of all the Spectators: I also saw the hairy maid, or Woman wh<om> 20 yeares before I had also seene when a child: her very Eyebrowes were combed upward, & all her forehead as thick & even as growes on any womans head, neatly dress'd: There come also tw<o> lock<s> very long out of Each Eare: she had also a most prolix beard, & mustachios, with long lockes of haire growing on the very middle of her nose, exactly like an Island Dog; the rest of her body not so hairy, yet exceeding long in comparison, armes, neck, breast & back; the <Colour> of a bright browne, & fine as well dressed flax: She was now married, & told me had one Child, that was not hairy, [as] nor were any of her parents or relations: she was borne at

---

[1] De Beer notes that contemporary newspapers reported that it was a barrel of gunpowder, not a ship, that blew up.

Ausburg in Germanie, & for the rest very well shaped, plaied well on the Harpsichord &c: I returnd home:

17 I went to see ... John Tradescants *Musæum*, the chiefest rarities were in my opinion, the antient Roman, Indian, & other Nations Armour, shilds & weapons; Some habits also of curiously colourd & wrought feathers: particula<r>ly that of the Phoenix Wing, as tradition gos: other innumerable things that were too long here to recite, & printed in his Catalogue by Mr. Ashmole, to whom after death of the widdow, they are bequeathe'd: & by him designd a Gift to Oxford: ...

22: To Lond: to visite the Holland Ambassador with whom I had now contracted much friendly corresponden<c>e: usefull to the Intelligence I constantly gave his Majestie abroad: returning, I saw at Dr. Joylifes, two Virginian rattle-snakes alive: they exceeded a yard in length, small heads, & slender tailes but as big as my leg in the middle; when vexed or provoked, swiftly vibrating & shaking theire tailes, they rattled as looud as a childs rattle, or as if on<e> heard a jack going: & this by the collision [or atrition] of certaine grisly Skinns curiously joynted, yet loose, like the Vertebra or back bone; & transparant as parchment; by which they give warning, a providential caution for other creatures to avoid them: They leape cruely: the Doctor tried their biting on ratts & mice which they immediately killed; but their vigour must needes be much exhausted here, where they had nothing to eate, & were in another Climate, kept onely in a barill of bran &c: ...

December 9 I paied in my fi<r>st payment to the E. Ind: stock: There being a Court in Merchant-Taylors hall: ...

25, I went with my Wife &c: to Lond: to celebrate Christmas day. Mr. Gunning preaching in Excester Chapell on 7: Micha 2. Sermon Ended, as he was giving us the holy Sacrament, The Chapell was surrounded with Souldiers: All the Communicants and Assembly surpriz'd & kept Prisoners by them, some in the house, others carried away: It fell to my share to be confined to a roome in the house, where yet were permitted to Dine with the master of it, the Countesse of Dorset, Lady Hatton & some others of quality who invited me: In the afternoone came Collonel Whaly, Goffe & others from Whitehall to examine us one by one, & some they committed to the Martial, some to Prison, some Committed:

When I came before them they tooke my name & aboad, examined me, why contrarie to an Ordinance made that none should any longer observe the superstitious time of the Nativity (so esteem'd by them) I durst offend, & particularly be at Common prayers, which they told was but the Masse in English, & particularly pray for Charles stuard, for which we had no Scripture: I told them we did not pray for Cha: Steward but for all Christian Kings, Princes & Governors: The<y> replied, in so doing we praied for the K. of Spaine too, who was their Enemie, & a Papist, with other frivolous & insnaring questions, with much threatning, & finding no colour to detaine me longer, with much pitty of my Ignorance, they dismiss'd me: These were men of high flight, and above Ordinances: & spake spitefull things of our B: Lords nativity: so I got home late the next day blessed be God: These wretched miscreants, held their muskets against us as we came up to receive the Sacred Elements, as if they would have shot us at the Altar, but yet suffering us to finish the Office of Communion, as perhaps not in their Instructions what they should do in case they found us in that Action: ...

1658

January 27[1] After six fitts of a Quartan Ague it pleased God to visite my deare child Dick with fitts so extreame, especiale one of his sides, that after the rigor was over & he in his hot fitt, he fell into so greate & intollerable a sweate, that being surpriz'd with the aboundance of vapours ascending to his head, he fell into such fatal Symptoms, as all the help at hand was not able to recover his spirits, so as after a long & painefull Conflict, falling to sleep as we thought, & coverd too warme, (though in the midst of a severe frosty season) and by a greate fire in the roome; he plainely expired, to our unexpressable griefe & affliction.

We sent for Physitians to Lond, whilst there was yet life in him; but the river was frozen up, & the Coach brake by the way ere it got a mile from the house; so as all artificial help failing, & his natural strength exhausted, we lost the prettiest, and dearest Child, that ever parents had, being but 5 years <5 months> & 3 days old in years but even at that tender age, a prodigie for Witt, & understanding; for beauty of body a very Angel, & for endowments of mind, of incredible & rare hopes.

To give onely a little tast of some of them, & thereby glory to God, (who out of the mouths of Babes & Infants dos sometimes perfect his praises) At 2 yeare & halfe old he could perfectly reade any of the English, Latine, french, or Gottic letters; pronouncing the three first languages exactly: He had before the 5t yeare or in that yeare not onely skill to reade most written hands, but to decline all the Nounes, Conjugate the verbs, regular, & most of the irregular; learned out *Puerilis*, got by heart almost the intire Vocabularie of Latine & french primitives & words, could make congruous Syntax, turne English into Lat: & vice versa, construe & prove what he read & did, the government & use of Relatives, Verbs Transitive, Substantives &c: Elipses & many figures & tropes, & made a considerable progress in Commenius's *Janua;*[2] began himselfe [to] write legibly, & had a strange passion for Greeke: the number of verses he could recite was prodigious, & what he remembred of the parts of playes, which he would also act: & when seeing a Plautus in ones hand, he asked what booke it was, & being told it was Comedy &c, & too difficult for him, he wept for sorrow: strange was his apt & ingenious application of fables & Morals, for he had read Aesop, & had a wonderfull disposition to Mathematics, having by heart, divers propositions of Euclid that were read to him in play, & he would make lines, & demonstrate them: As to his Piety, astonishing were his applications of Scripture upon occasion, & his sense of God, he had learn'd all his Catechisme early, & understood the historical part of the Bible & N. Test: to a wonder, & how Christ came to redeeme Mankind &c: & how comprehending these necessarys, himselfe, his Godfathers &c were discharged of their promise:

---

[1] This account of the illness and death of E's son Richard is to a large extent derived from the *Epistle Dedicatory* to E's translation of *The Golden Book of St John Chrysostom*, published in 1659 (see *The Writings of John Evelyn*, 1995, p. 39-46). Chrysostom's feast-day is 27 January so it seemes likely that this helped E make his choice of book.

[2] Johan/Jan Amos Komensky. The book is his *Janua linguarum reserata*, published in 1631. This copy survived to the Evelyn Library Sales of 1978, Lot no. 403.

These and the like illuminations, far exceeding his age & experience considering the prettinesse of his addresse & behaviour, cannot but leave impressions in me at the memory of him: When one told him how many dayes a certaine Quaker had fasted in Colchester, he replied, that was no wonder, for Christ had sayd, That Man should not live by bread alone, but by the word of God: He would of himselfe select the most pathetical Psalmes, & Chapters out of Jobe, to reade to his Mayde, during his sicknesse, telling her (when she pittied him) that all Gods Children must suffer affliction: He declaim'd against the Vanities of the World, before he had seene any: often he would desire those who came to see him, to pray by him, & before he fell sick a yeare, to kneele & pray with him alone in some Corner: How thankfully would he receive admonition, how soone be reconciled! how indifferent, continualy cherefull: Grave advise would he be giving his brother John, beare with his impertinences, & say he was but a Child:

If he heard of, or saw any new thing, he was unquiet till he was told how it was made, & brought us all difficulties that he found in booke, to be expounded: He had learn'd by heart divers Sentences in Lat: & Greeke which on occasion he would produce even to wonder: In a word he was all life, all prettinesse, far from morose, sullen, or childish in any thing he said or did: The last time he had ben at Church, (which was at Greenewich) according to costome, I asked him what he remembred of the Sermon: Two good-things Father, replys he: *Bonum Gratiae, & bonum Gloriae* with a just account of what the preacher said:

The day before he died, he cald to me, & in a more serious manner than usualy, Told me, That for all I loved him so dearely, I would give my house, land & all my fine things to his Bro: Jack, he should have none of them, & next morning when first he found himselfe ill, & that I perswaded him to keepe his hands in bed, he demanded, whither he might pray to God with his hands unjoyn'd, & a little after, whilst in greate agonie, whither he should not offend God, by using his holy name so oft, calling for Ease: What shall I say of his frequent pathetical ejaculations utter'd of himselfe, Sweet Jesus save me, deliver me, pardon my sinns, Let thine Angels receive me &c: so early knowledge, so much piety & perfection; but thus God having dressed up a Saint fit for himselfe, would not permit him longer with us, unworthy of the future fruits of this incomparable hopefull blossome: such a Child I never saw; for such a child I blesse God; in whose boosome he is:

May I & mine become as this little child, which now follows the Child Jesus, that Lamb of God, in a white robe whithersoever he goes. Even so Lord Jesus, *fiat Voluntas tua,*[1] Thou gavest him to us, thou hast taken him from us, blessed be the name of the Lord, That I had any thing acceptable to thee, was from thy Grace alone, since from me he had nothing but sinn; But that thou hast pardon'd, blessed be my God for ever Amen:

30 On the Saturday following, I sufferd the Physitians to have him opened: Dr. Needham & Dr. Welles, who were come three days before, & a little time ere he expired, but was past all help, & in my opinion he was suffocated by the woman & maide that tended him, & covered him too hott with blankets as he lay in a Cradle, neere an excessive hot fire in a close roome; for my Wife & I being then below & not long come from him, being come up, & I lifting up the blanket, which had quite cove<re>d the Cradle, taking first notice of his wonderfull fresh colour, & hardly hearing him breath or heave, soone perceived that he was neere overcome with heate & sweate, & so doubtlesse it

---

[1] 'Thy will be done.'

was, & the Child so farr gon, as we could not make him to heare, or once open his eyes, though life was apparently in him: we gave him something to make him neeze but ineffectivly:

Being open'd they they found a membranous substance growing to the cavous part of the liver, somewhat neere the edge of it for the compasse of 3 Inches, which ought not to be; for the Liver is fixed onely by three strong ligaments, all far distant from that part; on which they confidently affirm'd, the Child was (as tis vulgarly cald) liver-growne, & thence that sicknesse & so frequent complaint of his side: & indeede both Liver & Splen were exceedingly large &c: After this I caused the body to be Cofin'd in Lead & reposited him that night, about 8 a clock in the Church of Deptford, accompanied with divers of my relations & neighbours, among whom I distributed rings with this —— *Dominus abstulit:*[1] intending (God willing) to have him transported with my owne body, to be interrd at our Dormitorie in Wotton chur<c>h in my deare native County Surry, & to lay my bones & mingle my dust with my Fathers &c:[2] If God be so gracious to me; & make me as fit for him, as this blessed child was: Here ends the joy of my life, & for which I go even mourning to the grave: The L. Jesus sanctifie this & all others my Afflictions: Amen: ...

February 15 The afflicting hand of God being still upon us, it pleased him also to take away from us this morning my other youngest sonn George now 7 weeks languishing at Nurse, breeding Teeth, & ending in a Dropsie: Gods holy will be don: he was buried in Deptford church the 17th following:——

March ... This had ben the severest Winter, that man alive had knowne in England: The Crowes feet were frozen to their prey: Ilands of Ice inclosed both fish & foule frozen, & some persons in their boates: ...

April 21 Being greately afflicted with the Hemerhoids <bleeding> very much, by reason of the purges which I tooke, stoping this day on a suddain taking cold, I was so ill, that I was not far from death, & so continued to the 23. when being let bloude in the foote, it pleas'd God to restore me after some time ...

May 15 I went to Lond: to divert myselfe from my sadnesse, lay at my Bro: ...

June 2. An extraordinary storme of haile & raine, cold season as winter, wind northerly neere 6 moneths.

3 A large Whale taken, twixt my Land butting on the Thames & Greenewich, which drew an infinite Concourse to see it, by water, horse, coach, on foote from Lond, & all parts: It appeared first below Greenewich at low-water, for at high water, it would have destroyed all the boates: but lying now in shallow water, incompassed with boates, after a long Conflict it was killed with the harping yrons, & struck in the head, out of which spouted blood & water, by two tunnells like Smoake from a chimney: & after an horrid grone it ran quite on shore & died: The length was 58 foote: 16 in height, black-skin'd like Coach-leather, very smalleyes, greate taile, small finns & but 2: a piked snout, & a mouth so wide & divers men might have stood upright in it:

---

[1] 'The Lord has taken away.'

[2] Richard's body was never moved. See below and *The Writings of John Evelyn*, 46, for his epitaph, still at St. Nicholas, Deptford.

No teeth at all, but sucked the slime onely as thro a grate made of that bone which we call Whale bone: The throate <yet> so narrow, as would not have admitted the least of fishes: The extreames of the Cetaceous bones hang downewards, from the Upper <jaw>, & was hairy towards the Ends, & bottom withinside: all of it prodigious, but in nothing more wonderfull then that an Animal of so greate a bulk should be nourished onely by slime, thro' those

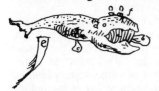

grates: a) The bones making the grate. b) The Tongue, c. the finn: d the Eye: e) one of the bones making the grate (a) f the Tunnells through which, shutting the mouth, the water is forced upward, at least 30 foote, like a black thick mist. &c: ...

August The 10th to Sir Ambros Brown at Betchworth Castle in that tempestious Wind, which threw-downe my greatest trees at Says Court, & did so much mischiefe all England over: It continued all night, till 3 afternoone next day, & was S. West, destroying all our winter fruit ...

September 3 Died that archrebell Oliver Cromwell, cal'd Protector.

5 ... I fell sick of a sore throate & feavor, which made me keepe my bed 4 or 5 dayes: on the 9 let bloud, & my Bro: Richard came to visite me.

16 I tooke a Vomite of <mercury of life>. And this day was published my Translation of *St. Chrysostomes Education of Children*, which I dedicated to both my Brothers, to comfort them upon the losse of their Children:[1]

October 18 I was summoned to Lond. by the Commissioners for new buildings ...

19 To the Commissioners of Sewers, but because there was an Oath to be taken of fidelity to the Government as now constituted without a King: I got to be excus'd & returned home: ...

November 1 I went to dine with the Fefees of the poores stock:[2]

22 To Lond, to visite my Bro: & the next day saw the superb Funerall of the Protectors: [22] He was carried from Somerset-house in a velvet bed of state drawn by six horses houss'd with the same: The Pall held-up by his new Lords: Oliver lying in Effigie in royal robes, & Crown'd with a Crown, scepter, & Mund, like a King: The Pendants, & Guidons were carried by the Officers of the Army, The Imperial banners, Atchivements &c by the Heraulds in their Coates, a rich caparizon'd Horse all embroidred over with gold: a Knight of honour arm'd *Cap a pè* & after all his Guards, Souldiers & innumerable Mourners: In this equipage they proceeded to Westminster μετ <πολλης> φαντασιας[3] &c: but it was the joyfullest funeral that ever I saw, for there was none but Cried, but dogs, which the souldiers hooted away with a barbarous noise; drinking, & taking Tabacco in the streetes as they went: ...

---

[1] All surviving copies of the book (see note above under 27 January 1658) are dated 1659 suggesting that this was in fact the date E submitted the manuscript to the printer.

[2] Foeffees were 'trustees holding land for charitable uses' (de Beer).

[3] 'With great pomp', *Acts* XXV.23.

December 3 I was summoned againe to appeare before the Commissioners about new foundations erected within such a distance of Lond: ...

6 I returnd: Now was publishd my *French Gardiner*[1] the first & best of that kind that introduced the use of the Olitorie Garden to any purpose: ...

23 I went with my Wife to keepe Christmas at my Co: Geo: Tukes at Cressing Temple in Essex, lay that night at Brentwood:

25 Here was no publique Service, but what we privately us'd:

31 I blessed God for his Mercys the yeare past, & 1. **Jan:** beged the Continuance of them: Thus for 3 Sundayes, by reason of the incumbents death, here was neither praying nor preaching: Tho there was a Chapell in the house: where we had good cheere & well come, so as on the 10th I returned home, having ben robbed during my absence of divers things of value, some plate, 20 pounds in mony &c: I also lost a Coach-horse in the journey: lay at Ingulstone & got to Says Court on the 11th: ...

1659

February 21 To Lond, about my erections at Deptford, return'd: ...

April 25 A wonderful & suddaine change in the face of the publique: The new Protector Richard slighted, severall pretenders, & parties strive for the Government, all Anarchy & confusion; Lord have mercy upon us ...

May 5 I went ... to see a new Opera after the Italian way in Recitative Music & Sceanes, much inferior to the Italian composure & magnificence: but what was prodigious, that in a time of such publique Consternation, such a Vanity should be kept up or permitted; I being ingag'd with company, could not decently resist the going to see it, though my heart smote me for it ...

29 Preached Mr. Hienchman on 143 Psal: 10.11. shewing how we should direct our Prayers, submitt our wills &c: & that being in covenant with God, 'twas sufficient argument to move him to heare us: That we should pray the Conduct of the H: Spirit in the Church, raise & quicken our devotion, & thereby engage the heavenly power to deliver us from our Calamities: The Nation was now in extreame Confusion & unsetled, betweene the Armies & the Sectaries: & the poore Church of England breathing as it were her last, so sad a face of things had over-spread us: ...

---

[1] *The French Gardiner: Instructing How to Cultivate all sorts of Fruit-Trees and Herbs for the Garden* ..., E's translation from the French by Nicolas de Bonnefons. This was E's first contribution to the study of horticulture but he named himself as *Philocepos* 'Lover of a garden [or orchard]' on the title page. If this was anonymity for the sake of modesty E made it pointless by signing the *Epistle Dedicatory* with his initials. The second edition of 1669 and those thereafter replaced *Philocepos* with his proper name. E credited his travelling friend Thomas Henshaw (1618-1700; see above, 29 September 1645) with the idea of translating the work.

June 7 To Lond. to take leave of my Bro: & to see the foundations now laying for a long Streete, & buildings in Hatton Garden design'd for a little Towne, lately an ample Garden:[1]

August 14 ... my sonn John was falln very ill of a feavor, & so continued in greate danger, 'til towards the 21: ...

September 1 Came Mr. Rob: Boyle (son to the Earle of Corke) to visite me: I communicated to him my proposal to Errect a [Philosophic] Mathematical College: &c:[2]
26 To Lond: to see Lodgings against winter, my sonn being yet un-recoverd, & now sick of an Ague: return'd the Evening:

October 10 I came with my Wife & family to Lond: tooke Lodgings at the 3 feathers in Russel-streete Covent Garden for all the Winter:
11. Came to Vis<it>e me Mr. William Coventrie, [since Secretary to the Duke <of York>] son to L: Keeper Coventrie: a wise & witty Gent: The Armie now turn'd out the Parliament ...
16 ... We had now no Government in the Nation, all in Confusion; no Magistrate either own'd or pretended, but the souldiers & they not agreed: God Almight<y> have mercy on, & settle us ...
21: Was our private Fast kept by the Church of England Protestants in Towne, to beg of God the removal of his Judgements; with devout Prayers for his mercy to our Calamitous Church ...

November 7 Was publishd my bold *Apologie*[3] for the King, in this time of danger, when it was capital to speake or write in favour of him: It was twice printed, so universaly it tooke:...
12 I went to see the severall Drougs for the confection of Treacle, Diascordium & other Electuaries which an ingenious Apothecarie had not onely prepard, & ranged upon a large & very long table, but coverd every ingredient with a sheete of paper, on which was very lively painted the thing, in miniature very well to the life, were it plant, flower, Animal, or other exotic drough: ...

December 10 I treated privately with Coll: Morley (then Lieutenant of the Tower, & in greate truste & power) concerning delivering it to the King, and the bringing of him in, to the greate hazard of my life; but the Colonel had ben my Schole-fellow & I knew would not betray me: ...

---

[1] The site of Hatton House, built by Sir Christopher Hatton (1540-91), Elizabeth I's Chancellor. It became an élite residential area. E visited it again in 1673, see 23 September 1673.

[2] This is the inception of the Royal Society.

[3] *An Apologie for the Royal Party: Written in a Letter to a Person of the late Councel of State*, By a Lover of Peace and of his Country. E's anonymous attack on parliament was a risky venture but with the tide of change already underway it was perhaps less dangerous than he believed. The text is reproduced in full in my edition of *The Writings of John Evelyn*.

1660

ANNUS MIRABILIS:

January 22 ... I went this afternoone to visite Colonel Morley, then Lieutennant of the Tower: of Lond ... After dinner I discoursd the Colonel, but he was very jealous, & would not believe Monk came in to do the King any service. I told him he might do it without him, & have all the honour: he was still doubtfull, & would resolve on nothing yet: so I tooke leave ...

February 3 ... Generall Monke came now to Lond: out of Scotland, but no man knew what he would do, or declare, yet was he mett on all his way by the Gent: of all the Counties which he pass'd, with petitions that he would recall the old long interrupted Parliament, & settle the Nation in some order, being at this time in a most prodigious Confusion, & under no government, every body expecting what would be next, & what he would do ...

5 ... Now were the Gates of the Citty broken-downe by Gen: Monke, which exceedingly exasperated the Citty; the Souldiers marching up and downe as triumphing over it, and all the old Army of the phanatics put out of their posts, & sent out of Towne.

11 I visited Mr. Boyle, where I met the Earle of Corke. A signal day: Monk perceiving how infamous & wretched a pack of knaves would have still usurped the Supreame power, & having intelligence that they intended to take away his commission, repenting of what he had don to the Citty, & where he & his forces quarterd; Marches to White hall, dissipates that nest of robbers, & convenes the old Parliament, the rump-parliament (so cal'd as retaining some few rotten members of the other) being dissolved; and for joy whereoff, were many thousands of rumps, roasted publiquely in the Streetes at the Bonfires this night, with ringing of bells, & universal jubilee: this was the first good omen.

17: I fell sick, & that very dangerously of a malignant feavor:

From **Feb:** 17th to the 5th of **Aprill** I was detained in Bed, with a kind of double Tertian, the cruell effects of the Spleene & other distempers, in that extremity, that my Physitians Dr. Wetherborn, Needham, Claud, were in greate doubt of my recovery, & in truth I was brought very low; but it pleased God to deliver me also out of this affliction, for which I render him hearty thanks...

During this Sicknesse came innumerable of my Relations & friends to visite me, and it retarded my going into the Country longer than I intended: however I writ, and printed a letter in defence of his Majestie against a wicked forged paper, pretended to be sent from Bruxells,[1] to defame his Majesties person, Virtues, & render him odious, now when every body were in hopes & expectation of the Gen: & Parliaments recalling him, & <e>stablishing the Government on its antient and right basis: In doing which towards the decline

---

[1] *The Late News or Message from Bruxels Unmasked, and His Majesty Vindicated from the Base Calumny and Scandal therein fixed on Him.* E was outraged by a tract called *News from Brussels* which purported to be a letter from a courtier in which the King was described as a cynical political opportunist. The text is reproduced in full along with the *News from Brussels* in my edition of *The Writings of John Evelyn.*

of my sicknesse, & setting-up long in my bed, had caused a small relapse, out of which it pleased God also to free mee, so as by the 14th I was able to go into the Country, which the Physitians advised me to, which I accordingly did to my Sweete & native air at Wotton.

20: I received there the B: Sacrament being good friday, in the house, by reason of my Indisposition, officiating Mr. Higham Minister of the Parish. & 22: preaching on 1. Cor: 10. 16. preparatory to the Sacrament on Easter day &c: also 29: on 18 Jer: 9. 10 concerning Gods Judgements against nations and kingdomes, when not prevented by repentance, applicatory to the time.

30. I was able to ride abroad & went often to take the aire.

May 3 Came the most happy tidings of his Majesties gracious Declaration, & applications to the Parliament, Generall, & People &c and their dutifull acceptance & acknowledgement, after a most bloudy & unreasonable Rebellion of neere 20 yeares. Praised be forever the Lord of heaven, who onely dost wondrous things, because thy mercys indure forever ...

9 I was desired & designed to accompany my Lord Berkeley with the publique Addresse of the Parliament Gen: &c: & invite him to come over, & assume his Kingly government, he being now at Breda; but being yet so weake & convalescent, I could not make that journey by sea, which was not a little to my detriment &c: so I went to Lond to excuse my selfe, returning the 10th, having yet received a gracious message from his Majestie, by Major Scot & Colonel Tuke ...

29 This day came in his Majestie Charles the 2d to London after a sad, & long Exile, and Calamitous Suffering both of the King and Church: being 17 yeares: This was also his Birthday, and with a Triumph of above 20000 horse and foote, brandishing their swords and shouting with unexpressable joy: The wayes straw'd with flowers, the bells ringing, the streetes hung with Tapissry, fountaines running with wine: The Major, Aldermen, all the Companies in their liver<ie>s, Chaines of Gold, banners; Lords & nobles, Cloth of Silver, gold and vellvet every body clad in, the windos and balconies all set with Ladys, Trumpets, Musick, & <myriads> of people flocking the streetes & was as far as Rochester, so as they were 7 houres in passing the Citty, even from 2 in the afternoone 'til nine at night:

I stood in the strand, & beheld it, & blessed God: And all this without one drop of bloud, & by that very army, which rebell'd against him: But it was the Lords doing, *et mirabile in oculis nostris*:[1] for such a Restauration was never seene in the mention of any history, antient or modern, since the returne of the Babylonian Captivity, nor so joyfull a day, & so bright, ever seene in this nation: this hapning when to expect or effect it, was past all humane policy ...

June 4 I received letters of Sir R: Brownes landing at Dov<e>r, & also Letters from the Queene, which I was to deliver at White-hall, not as yet presenting my selfe to his Majestie by reason of the infinite concourse of people: It was indeed intollerable, as well as unexpressable, the greedinesse of all sorts, men, women, & children to see his Majesty & kisse his hands, inso much as he had scarce leasure to Eate for some dayes, coming as they did from all parts of the Nation: And the King on the other side as willing to give them that satisfaction, would have none kept out, but gave free accesse to all sorts of people: Wherefore addressing my selfe to the Duke, I was carried to his Majestie when he was alone, & very few noble-men with him, & kissed his

---

[1] 'And it was wonderful in our eyes.' *Matthew* XXI.42, and *Mark* XII.11.

hands, being very gratiously receivd: which don I returnd home to meet [5] Sir R: Browne, who came not 'til the Eight, after a 19 yeares Exile, during which yet, he kept up in his Chapell, the Liturgie & offices of the Church of England, to his no small honour, & in a time, when it was so low & and as many thought utterly lost, that in many Controversies both with Papists & Sectaries, our divines used to argue for the visibility of the Church from his Chapell & Congregation ...

July 5 I saw his Majestie go with as much pompe & splendor as any Earthly prince could do to the greate Citty feast: (The first they invited him to since his returne) but the exceeding raine which fell all that day, much eclips'd its luster: This was at Guild-hall, and there was also all the Parliament men, both Lords & Comm: the streetes adorn'd with Pageants &c: at immense cost:

6 His Majestie began first to Touch for the Evil according to costome: Thus, his Majestie sitting under his State in the Banqueting house: The Chirurgeons cause the sick to be brought or led up to the throne, who kneeling, the King strokes their faces or cheekes with both his hands at once: at which instant a Chaplaine in his formalities, says, *He put his hands upon them, & he healed them*, this is sayd, to every one in particular: when they have ben all touch'd, they come up againe in the same order, & the other Chaplaine kneeling & having Angel gold, strung on white ribbon on his arme, delivers them one by one to his Majestie: Who puts them about the neck of the Touched as they passe: whilst the first Chaplaine repeates: *That is the true light who came into the World*: Then followes an Epistle (as at first a Gospell) with the Liturgy prayers for the sick with some alteration: Lastly the blessing, And then the Lo: Chamberlaine & Comptroller of the household, bring basin, Ewer & Towell for his Majestie to wash:...

8 Mr. Hinchman on 5: Ephes: 15: From hence forth was the Liturgie publiquely used in our Churches, whence it <had> ben for so many Yea<r>es banish'd: ...

28 I heard his Majesties Speech in the Lords house, passing the bills of Tunnage & poundage, Restauration of my L. Ormond to his estate in Ireland, concerning the Commission of the Sewers, and Continuance of the Excise ...

August 25. Col: Specer, Coll: of a Regiment of horse in our County of Kent, sent to me, & intreated that I would take Commission for a Troope of Horse, & that I would nominate my Lieutennant & Ensigns: but I thanked him for the honour intended me, & would by no meanes embrace the trouble ...

September 13 I saw in Southwark at St. Margarites faire, a monstrous birth of Twinns, both femals & most perfectly shaped, save that they were joyn'd

breast to breast, & incorporated at the navil, having their armes thrown about each other thus: It was reported quick in May last, & produced neere Turne-style Holbourn: well exent<e>rated & preserved till now: We saw also a poore Woman, that had a living Child of one yeare old, who had its head, neck, with part of a Thigh growing out about *Spina dorsi*:[1] The head had the place of Eyes &

---

[1] Backbone.

nose, but none perfected. The head monstrous, rather resembling a greate Wenn;[1] and hanging on the buttocks, at side whereoff, & not in the due place, were (as I remembred) the excrements it avoided, we saw also Monkeys & Apes daunce, & do other feates of activity on the high-rope, to admiration: They were galantly clad *alamode*, went upright, saluted the Company, bowling, & pulling-off their hatts: They saluted one another with as good grace as if instructed by a Dauncing Master. They turned heales over head, with a bucket of Eggs in it, without breaking any: also with Candles (lighted) in their hands, & on their head, without extinguishing them, & with vessells of water, without spilling a drop: I also saw an Italian Wench daunce to admiration, & performe all the Tricks of agility on the high rope, all the Court went to see her: <likewise> here was <her> Father, who tooke up a piece of Yron Canon of above 400 pounds weight, with the haires of his head onely ...

13 In the midst of all the joy & jubilie, dies the Duke of Gloucester of the Small-pox, which put all the Court in Mourning: died the 13th in prime of youthe, a Prince of extraordinary hopes &c: ...

October 6. I paied the greate Tax of Pole-mony, levied for the disbanding of the Army, 'til now kept up; I paid as Esquire 10 pounds & 1s: for every Servant in my house &c: ...

11 I went to Lond: to be sworn a Commissioner of the Sewers; & this day were those barbarous Regicides, who sat on the life of our late King, brought to their Tryal in the old baily, by a Commission of Oyer & terminer: I return'd at night ...

17 This day were executed those murderous Traytors at Charing-Crosse, in sight of the place where they put to death their natural Prince, & in the Presence of the King his sonn, whom they also sought to kill: take<n> in the trap they laied for others: The Traytors executed were Scot, Scroope, Cook, Jones. I saw not their execution, but met their quarters mangld & cutt & reaking as they were brought from the Gallows in baskets on the hurdle: ô miraculous providence of God; Three days before suffered Axtel, Carew, Clements, Hacker, Hewson & Peeters for reward of their Iniquity: I returnd:

18 My Wife receiving a fall from a stoole, miscarried of a fine boy, to our greate trouble ...

29 Going to Lond: about my affaires, My Lord Majors shew stop'd me in cheape-side: one of the Pageants represented a greate Wood, with the royal Oake, & historie of his Majesties miraculous escape at Bosco-bell &c: ...

November I went with some of my Relations to Court, to shew them his Majesties Cabinet and Closset of rarities: The rare miniatures of Peter Oliver after Raphael, Titian & other masters, which I infinitely esteeme: Also that large piece of the Dutchesse of Lennox don in Enamaile by Petito; & a vast number of Achates, Onyxes, & Intaglios, especialy a Medalion of Cæsar, as broad as my hand: likewise rare Cabinetts of Pietra Commessa: A Landskip of Needleworke, formerly presented by the Dutch to K Char: I. Here I saw a vast book of Mapps in a Volume of neere 4 yards large: a curious Ship modell, & amongst the Clocks, one, that shewed the rising & setting of the son in the Zodiaque, the Sunn, represented in a face & raies of Gold, upon an azure skie, observing the diurnal & annual motion, rising & setting behind a landscap of

---

[1] The word can mean a tumour but can also mean an excresence on a tree which is probably what E is comparing the head to.

hills, very divertisant, the Work of our famous Fromantel, & severall other rarities in this royal Cimelium.

3 Arived her Majestie Queene Mother in to England, whence she had ben now banished almost 20 years; together with her illustrious daughter the Princesse Henrietta, divers other Prin<c>es & noble-men accompanying them ...

23 Being this day in the Bed-Chamber of the Princesse Henrietta (where there were many great beauties, & noble-men) I saluted divers of my old friends & acquaintance abroad; his Majestie carying my Wife to salute the Queene & Prin<c>esse, & then led her into his Closet, & with his owne hands shew'd her divers Curiosities ...

27 came down the Cleark Comptroller (by the Lord Stewards appointment) to survey the land at Says-Court, on which I had pretence, & to returne his report:

December 13 I presented my Son John to the Queene Mother: who kissed him, talked with, & made extraordinary much of him ...

21 The Marriage of the Chancellors Daughter being now newly owned, I went to see her: she being Sir R: Browne (my father in laws) intimate acquaintance, when she waited on the Princesse of Orange: She being now at her fathers, at Worcester house in the strand, we all kissed her hand, as did also my Lord Chamberlaine (Manchester), and Countesse of Northumberland: This was a strange change, can it succeed well! I spent the Evening at St. Jamess whither the Princesse Henrietta was retired during the fatal sicknesse of her Sister the Princesse of Orange, now come over to salute the King her brother: The Princesse gave my Wife an extraordinary complement, & gracious acceptance, for the *Character* she had presented her the day before, & which was afterwards printed:[1]

22. I went to Lambeth to visite my kinds-man Sir Rob: Needham: This day died the Princesse of Orange of the Small-pox, which wholy alterd the face & gallantry of the whole Court:

23 ... A robbery attempted at my house, but God deliverd us:

25 Preached at the Abby, Dr. Earles, (clearke of his Majesties Closet, & my deare friend, Deane of Westminster) on 2: luke 13.14. Condoling the breach made in the publique joy, by the lamented death of the Princesse: I receivd the B: Sacrament the Deane officiating: The Service was also in the old Cathedrall Musique: ...

---

[1] This is the marriage, notorious at the time, of Anne Hyde (1637-71), daughter of Edward Hyde, Earl of Clarendon to James, Duke of York. She was already pregnant. The children of this marriage included the Queens Mary II (1662-94) and Anne (1665-1714). It contributed to Clarendon's unpopularity and eventual fall in 1667 (9 December 1667) by allowing his enemies to claim that he had engineered this marriage and that of Charles II to the barren Catherine of Braganza to guarantee that his own descendants would be monarchs, as E observed (see below, 18 September 1683). The Princess of Orange is Mary (1631-60), sister of Charles II and mother of William of Orange, afterwards William III (1650-1702) and husband of Mary II. Her sister the Princess Henrietta (1644-70) is the Duchess of Orleans, otherwise popularly known as 'Madame' (see below 4 November 1670).

Mrs Evelyn's *Character* is not known in published form.

1661

January 6 ... This night was a bloudy Insurrection of some fift-monarchy Enthusiasts, suppressd, & next day examin'd at Council; where the wretchedly abused people could say nothing to extenuate their madnesse, & unwarantable zeale:

I was now chosen (& nominated by his Majestie for one of that Council) by Suffrage of the rest of the Members, a Fellow of the Philosophic Society, now meeting at Gressham Coll: where was an assembly of divers learned Gent: It being the first meeting since the returne of his Majestie in Lond: but begun some years before at Oxford, & interruptedly here in Lond: during the Rebellion: This morning was another rising of the Phanatics in which some were slaine: his Majestie being absent; til the 10th ...

16 I went to the Philosophic Club: where was examin'd the Torricellian experiment: I presented my *Circle of Mechanical Trades*, & had recommended to me the publishing what I had written of *Chalcography*:[1] ...

23. To Lond, at our Society, where was divers Exp: on the Terrella[2] sent us by his Majestie.

25. After divers yeares, that I had <not> seene any Play, I went to see acted the *Scornfull Lady* at a new Theater in Lincolns-in fields ...

30 Was the first Solemn Fast & day of humiliation to deplore the sinns which so long had provoked God against this Afflicted Church & people: orderd by Parliament to be annualy celebrated, to expiate the Gilt of the Execrable Murder of the late King Char: I ... This day (ô the stupendious, & inscrutable Judgements of God) were the Carkasses of that arch-rebell Cromewell, Bradshaw the Judge who condemn'd his Majestie & Ireton, sonn in law to the Usurper, draged out of their superbe Tombs (in Westminster amongst the Kings), to Tyburne, & hanged on the Gallows there from 9 in the morning til 6 at night, & and then buried under that fatal & ignominious Monument, in a deepe pitt: Thousands of people (who had seene them in all their pride & pompous insults) being spectators: looke back at November 22: 1658, & be astonish'd – *And <fear> God, & honor the King, but meddle not with them who are given to change.*[3]

March 11 To our Society: where were experimented divers ways of the rising of water in glasse tubes, above the Super ficies of the stagnant water: either by uniting one part of the water to the other by a kind of natural appetite to joyne its like; or rather by the pressure of the subjacent water by the super stantial ær, to an æquilibrium of Cylinder of the Atmosphere: &c: ...

13 I went to Lambeth with Sir R: Brownes pretence to the Wardenship of Merton Coll: in Oxford, to which (as having about 40 yeares before ben student of that house) he was unanimously elected, one fellow onely excepted: now the statutes of that house being so, that unlesse every fellow agree, the election devolves to the Visitor, who is the A: Bish: of Canterbury, his Grace gave his vote to Sir T. Clayton there, and the Physick Professor; for which I was not at all displeas'd; because though Sir Rich: miss'd it, by much ingratitude and wrong of the Arch-Bishop (Clayton being no fellow) yet it would have hindred Sir Richard from attending at Court, to settle his greater

---

[1] This appeared as *Sculptura*, see below, 10 June 1662.

[2] Magnetic loadstone.

[3] *Proverbs* XXIV.21.

Concernes, and prejudicd me: he being so much inclined to have pass'd his time in a Collegiate life, very unfit for him at that time for many reasons. So I took leave of his Grace, who was Dr. Juxon, formerly L: Treasurer in the reigne of Charles I.

This after noone his hig<h>nesse Prince Rupert shewed me with his owne hands the new way of Graving call'd Mezzo Tinto, which afterwards I by his permission publish'd in my *Historie of Chalcographie*, which set so many artists on Worke, that they soone arived to that perfection it is since come, emulating the tenderest miniature[1] ...

31 This night his Majestie promis'd to make my Wife Lady of the Jewels (a very honorable charge) to the future Queene &c: [but which he never performd, bribd by the Lady Scroope.]

April 19 To Lond: about Says-Court buisinesse: Saw the Bathing & rest of the Ceremonies of the Knights of the Bath preparatory to the Coronation, it was in the Painted Chamber in Westminster: I might have received this honour, but declined it: The rest of the ceremony was in the Chapell at White-hall where their Swords being laid on the Altar, the Bishop deliverd them &c: ...

22 Was the splendid Cavalcade of his Majestie from the Tower of Lond: to White hall: Where I also saw the King in the Banqueting House Create six Earles, & as many Barons viz: Ed: L. Hide L. High Chancellor created Earle of Clarendon, supported by the Earles of Northumberland & Sussex: The Earle of Bedford carried the Cap & Coronet, E: of Warwick the Sword: E: of Newport the Mantle. Next was Capel created Earle of Essex; Brudnell Cardigan: Valencia Angelsea, Greenevill Bath, Howard Caerlisle: The Barons were Denzill Holles, Cornwallis, Booth, Townsend, Cooper, Crew, who were all led-up by severall Peeres, with Garter & Officers of Armes before them, where after Obesience on their severall approches to the Throne, their Patents were presented by Garter K. at Armes, which being received by the L. Chamberlaine & deliver'd his Majestie & by him to the Secretary of State, were read, & then againe delivred to his Majestie & by him to the severall Lords Created, then were they robed, their Coronets & Collers put on by his Majestie, then were they placed in rank on both sides the State & Throne: but the Barons put of their caps & circles and held them in their hands, The Earles keeping on their Coronets as Cousins to the King:

I spent the rest of the Evening in seeing the severall Arch Triumphals built in the streetes at severall Eminent places thro which his Majestie was next day to passe, some of which though tem<p>orarie, & to stand but one Yeare, were of good Invention & architecture, with Inscriptions: ...

23 Was the Coronation of his Majesty Charles the Second in the Abby-Church of Westminster at all which Ceremonie I was present: The King & all his Nobility went to the Tower, I accompanying my L: Vicount Mordaunt part of the Way:

This was on Sunday: 22: but indeede his Majestie went not 'til Early this morning, & proceeded from thence to Westminster in this order: first went the Duke of Yorks Horse guards, Messengers of the Chamber. 136 Esquires to the knights of the Bath, each having two: most richly habited: The knight Harbinger, Searjeant Porter, Sewers of the Chamber, Quarter Waiters, Six-Clearks of Chancery, Cler: of the Signet, Cler: of the Privy-Seale, Clearks of the Council: Cler: of the Parliament, Cler: of the Crowne: Chaplaines in ordinary having dignities 10: Kings Advocats & Remembrancer, Cou<n>cil at

---

[1] *Sculptura*, see below, 10 June 1662.

Law: Master of the C<h>ancery: Puisne Serjeants, Kings Attourney & Solicitor: Kings eldest Serjeant: Secretaries of the French & Latine Tongue: Gent: Ushers daily Waiters: Sewers, Carvers & Cupbearers in Ordinary, Esquires of the body 4. Masters of standing Offices being no Councellers viz. of the Tents, Revells, Ceremonies, Armorie, Wardrob, Ordnance, Masters of Requests, Chamberlaine of the Exchequer, Barons of the Exchequer & Judges: Lord Ch: Baron, L.C. Justice of the Common pleas, Master of the Rolls, L.C. Justice of England: Trumpets, Gent: of the Pr: Chamber, Knights of the Bath 68 in Crimson robes exceeding rich, & the noblest shew of the whole Cavalcade (his Majestie Excepted) Knight Marishall: Treasurer of the Chamber, Master of the Jewells, Lords of the Privy Council: Comptroller of his Majesties Household: Treasurer of the Household: Trumpets, Searjeant Trumpeter: Puirsuivants at Armes 2: Barons: 2: Puirsuivants at Armes: Viscounts, Heraulds 2: Earles. L. Chamb: of the Household. 2 Heraulds: Marqu<i>ses, Dukes: Her: <Clarencieux> and <Norroy>: Lord Chancellor: L.H. Steward of Eng: Two Persons representing the Dukes of Normandy & Aquitain (viz. Sir R: Fanshaw & Sir Herb: Price) in fantastique habits of that time: Gent: Ushers, Garter: Lord Major of Lond: The Duke of York alone: (the rest by twos) L.H. Conestable of Eng: L: Gr: Chamb: of England: The Sword born by the Earle Marishall of Eng: Lastly the KING in royal Robes, & Equipage: Afterwards followd Equerries, Foote-men, Gent: Pensioners, Master of the horse leading an horse richly caparisond: Vice-Chamberlaine: Cap: of the Pensioners: Cap: of the Guard: The Guard, Horse-Gard, The Troope of Voluntieres &c with many other officers, & Gent:

This magnificent Traine on horseback, as rich as Embroidery, velvet, Cloth of Gold & Sil: & Jewells could make them & their pransing horses, proceeded thro the streetes, strew'd with flowers, houses hung with rich Tapissry, Windos & Balconies full of Ladies, The Lond: Militia lining the ways, & the sevrrall Companies with their Banners & Loud musique ranked in their orders: The Fountaines runing wine, bells ringing, with Speeches made at the severall Triumphal Arches: At that of the Temple Barre (neere which I stood) The Lord Major was received by the Baylife of Westminster who in a Scarlet robe made a Speech:

Thence with joyfull Acclamations his Majestie passed to White-hall: [Bonfires at night] & the next day being st. Georges he went by Water to Westminster Abby: when his Majestie was entered, the Deane & Prebends brought all the Regalia, & deliverd them to severall Noble-men, to beare before the King, who met them at the West dore of the church, singing an Antheme, to the Quire: Then came the Peres in their Robes & Coronets &c in their hands, 'til his Majestie was placed in a Throne elevated before the Altar: Then the Bish: of Lond (the A Bishop of Canterbury being sick) went to every side of the Throne to present the King to the People, asking if they would have him for their King, & do him homage, at which they shouted 4 Times *God Save K. Ch: the 2d*: Then an Anthem sung: Then his Majesty attended by 3 Bishops went up to the Altar, & he offerd a pall, & a pound of Gold: Then sate he down in another chaire during the sermon, which was preachd by Dr. Morley then B: of Worcester on   after Sermon the K: tooke his Oath before the Altar, to <mainetaine> the Religion, Mag: Charta & Laws of the Land: Then the Hymn *Veni S. Sp.*, then the Leitany by 2 Bish. Then the L: AB: of Cant (present but <much> indisposd & weake) said, Lift-up your hearts:

Then rose up the King, & put off his robes & upper garments; & was in a Wastcoate so opened in divers places as the A: Bishop might commodiously anoint him, first in the palmes of his hands, then was sung an Antheme &

prayer, Then his breast, & twixt the shoulders, bending of both armes, & lastly on the crowne of the head: with apposite hymns & prayers at each anoynting: Then closed & buttned up the Wastcoate, which was done by the Deane: Then was a Coyfe put on & the Colobium, Syndon or Dalmatic, & over this a Supertunic of Cloth of Gold, with buskins & sandals of the same, Spurrs, The Sword, a prayer being first saied over it by the A.Bish. on the Altar before 'twas girt on: by the L: Chamberlain: Then the Armill, Manteles &c: Then the A: B: placed the Crowne Imperial on the Altar, prayed over it, & set it on his Majesties head, at which all the Peres put on their Coronets &c. Anthems & rare musique playing with Lutes, Viols, Trumpets, Organs, Voices &c. Then the A B: put a ring on his Majesties finger: Then the K. offered his Sword on the Altar: which being redeemed, was drawn & borne before him: Then the AB: deliverd him the Scepters with the Dove in one hand, & the other in the other with the Mond: Then the K. kneeling the A: Bish: pronounc'd the blessing: Then ascending againe his Regal Throne & *Te Deum* singing all the Peeres did their Homage by every one touching his Crowne: The ArchBish & rest of the Bish: first kissing the King: Then he received the H: Sacrament, & so disrobed, yet with the Crowne Imperial on his head, accompanied with all the nobility in the former order, he went on foote on blew cloth, which was spread & reachd from the West dore of the Abby, to Westminster Stayres where he tooke Water in a Triumphall barge to White-hall. where was extraordinary feasting:

24 I presented his Majestie with his Panegyric[1] in the Privy Chamber, which he was pleasd most graciously to accept: &c. also to the L. Chancelor & most of the noble men who came to me for it, & dind at the Marq: of Ormonds now made Duke, where was a magnificent feast, & many greate persons:

25 I went to the Society where were divers Experiments in Mr. Boyls Pneumatique Engine. We put in a Snake but could not kill it, by exhausting the aire, onely made it extreamly sick, but the chick died of Convulsions out right, in a short space: ...

May 1 I went to Hide Park to take the aire, where was his Majestie & an inumerable appearance of Gallantry & rich Coaches &c: it being now a time of universal festivity & joy: &c:

3 I went to see the wonderfull Engine for weaving silk-stockings, said to have ben the Invention of an Oxford Scholler 40 yeares since: return'd by Fromantel the famous Clock maker to see some Pendules: Monsieur Zulichum being with us: This evening I was with my L: Brouncker, Sir Rob: Morray, Sir Pa: Neill, Monsieur de <Zulicum> & Mr. Ball (all of them of our Society, & excellent Mathematicians) to shew his Majestie (who was also present) Saturns Ansatus as some thought, but as Zulicum affirmed with his Balteus (as that learned Gent: had publishd), very neere eclipsed by the Moone, neere the Mons Porphyritis: Also Jupiter & Satelites through the greate Telescope of his Majesties, drawing 35 foote: on which were divers discourses: ...

8 His Majestie rod in state, with his Imperial Crowne on, & all the Peeres in their robes in greate pomp to the Parliament, now newly chosen (the old one disolv'd) & that evening declared in Council his intention to marry the Infanta of Portugal: ...

---

[1] Described by Keynes as an 'eloquent and extravagant prose composition' attributing 'every possible virtue and all known wisdom' to Charles II. Despite being printed it is known from very few copies indeed and was not identified until 1927.

11 My Wife present<e>d his Majestie the Madona she copied in Miniatur after P: Olivers painting after Raphael, which she wrought with extraordinary paines & Judgement. The K. was infinitely pleas'd with it, & caus'd it to be placed in his Cabinet amongst his best Limmings:[1] ...

13 I heard, & saw such Exercises at the Election of Scholars at Westminster Schoole, to be sent to the Universitie, both in Lat: Gr: & Heb: Arabic &c in Theames & extemporary Verses, as wonderfully astonish'd me, in such young striplings, with that readinesse, & witt, some of them not above 12 or 13 yeares of age: & pitty it is, that what they attaine here so ripely, they either not retaine, or improve more considerably, when they come to be men: though many of them do: & no lesse is to be blamed their odd pronouncing of Latine, so that out of England no nation were able to understand or endure it: The Examinants or Posers were Dr. Duport Greek professor at Cambridge: Dr. Fell: Deane of Christchu<rc>h, Oxon: Dr. Pierson, Dr. Alestree, Deane of Westminster & any that would:

14 His Majestie was pleased to discourse with me concerning severall particulars relating to our Society, & the Planet Saturne &c: as he sat at Supper in the withdrawing roome to his Bed-Chamber.

15 We made sevverall experiments on Vipers, & their biting of Dogs & Catts, to make tryall of a stone presented us from the E: Indias a pretended cure:

16. I dined at Mr. Garmus the Resident of Hamburg, who continud his feast neere 9 whole houres, according to the Custome of his Country; though no greate excesse of drinking, no man being obligd: ...

22 Was the Scotch-Covenant burnt by the common hangman in divers places of Lond: ô prodigious change! This after<noone> at our Society were severall discourses concerning poisons. Sir Jo Finch told us of an exquisite poyson of the D: of Florences that kill'd with a drop: That drawing a threit & needle dipt in it thro a hens thigh it perish'd immediatly, but if an hot needle were thrust after it, it cured the wound. This was tried also on a dog, success-fully: That any thing thus killed, the limb affected being suddainly cut off the rest eate most delicately and tender without detriment to the Eater: Hereupon Dr. Charleton affirm'd that having killed a Linnet with *Nux Vomica*[2] suddainly: a Sea-Gull eating that bird died also immediately, & some other animal that prey'd on that Gull the Venume in force after the third Concoction: I return'd home this Evening: ...

29 This was the first Anniversary appointd by Act of Parliament to be observ'd as a day of gen: Thanksgiving for the miraculous Restauration of his Majestie: our Vicar preaching on 118 Psal: ...

June 19 Discourses at our Society about poysons againe. We gave *Nux Vom:* to birds that killed them out-right, afterwa<r>ds, because some writers affirmed Sublimate was its conterpoyson, we tried it on other birds, but it succeded not: ...

July 2 I went to see, the new Spring-Garden at Lambeth a pretty contriv'd plantation: ...

---

[1] Mrs Evelyn certainly had some artistic skill. She designed the frontispiece for E's 1656 edition of Lucretius which was engraved by Hollar.

[2] The seed of the *Strychnos nux-vomica* from which strychnine is derived.

17 I went to Lond. at our Assembly: we put a Viper & slow-worme <or> Aspic to bite a Mouse, but could not irritate them to fasten at all: Mr. Boyle brought 2 polishd Marbles 3 inch diameter: which first well rubb'd, then with a drop of oyle olive, which was afterwards cleane wiped off, the stones claped together stuck close, even so close, that the nether stone having a hook insert<e>d, & the uppe<r> a ring, tooke up 42 pound weight, by the power of contiguity, before they separated: The oyle was added to fill up any possible porositie in the polishd Marbles:

19 We tried our Diving bell, or Engine in the Water Dock at Deptford, in which our Curator contin<ue>d halfe an houre under water: It was made of Cast lead: let downe with a strong Cable: ...

24 ... There was a Camel shewen in our Towne, newly bro<u>ght from the Levant, which I saw, as I had others.

31. To our Society, where a bladder blowne up onely raised a weight of 24 pound; it was at first flaxid & welted on purpose, & the weight hanged at its bottome, then the wind conveyd thro a pipe that had a valve &c:

August 7 Repeating the Experiment of the bladder was raisd 142 pounds & my Laquay, who was an heavy looby of 17 years old &c: A pouder of a plant was brought, which thrown into the fire <flashed> like Gun-powder: ...

9 I tried severall experiments on the Sensitive plant & humilis, which contracted with the least touch of the Sunn, thro a burning Glasse, though it rises & opens onely, when it shines on it: also with *aqua fortis*;[1] but it did not with its fume, nor touch'd with Spirit of Sulphur: I first saw the famous Queen-pine brought from Barbados presented to his Majestie, but the first that were ever seene here in England, were those sent to Cromwell, foure-yeares since: I dined at Mr. Palmers at Grays-Inn, whose curiosity excelled in Clocks & Pendules, especialy one, that had innumerable motions, & plaied 9 or 10 Tunes on the bells very finely; some of them set in parts, which was very harmonious. It was wound up but once in a quarter: he had also good Telescopes, & Mathematical Instruments, choice Pictures & other Curiosities: Thence we went to that famous Montebank, Jo: Punteus ...

14: To Lond: Experiments concerning compression of Water, a letter and a certaine uncombustible Wood was sent the Society from the famous Adeptus Signor Borrhi: This day Sir Kenh<e>lme Digby presented every one of us his discourse of the Vegetation of Plants: And Mr. Henshaw his history of Salt-peter & Gun-powder. I then assisted him to procure his place of French Secretary to the King, which he purchased of Sir Hen: de Vic: I went to that famous Physitian Sir Fr: Prujean who shewed me his Laboratorie, his other workhouse for turning & other Mechanics, also many excellent Pictures, especialy the Magdalen of Carrachio: some incomparable *paisages* don in distemper: He plaied to me likewise on the Polyphone, an Instrument having something of the Harp, Lute, Theorb &c: it was a sweete Instrument, by none known in England, or described by any Author, nor used but by this skillfull & learned Doctor: I returnd home:

15 I went to Tunbridge wells, to visite my Wife, who was there drinking the Waters.

17 Walking about the solitudes <not> far from our Lodging, I greately admired at the extravagant turnings, insinuations, & growthe of sertaine birch trees among the rocks:

---

[1] Nitric acid. The name means literally 'strong water'.

18 ... This afternoone as I was at church and Dr. Burgh going into the Pulpet, I was called out, one of my horses having struck my Coach-man so as he remain'd as dead for a while; I caus'd him to be let bloud, & laying a Cere-cloth to his brest (much brused) & so after a weeke he recovered:

September 14. I presented my *Fumifugium*[1] dedicated to his Majestie who was pleased I should publish it by his special Command; being much pleasd with it: ...

18: To Lond: This day was our Petition to his Majestie for his royal Graunt authorizing our Society to meete as a Corporation &c: with severall privileges, was read: An Experiment of flame in flame was tried: I went home:

October 1 I sailed this morning with his Majestie <on> one of his Yaachts (or Pleasure boates) Vessells newly known amongst us, til the Dut<c>h [E. India Comp.] presented that curious piece to the King, & very excellent sailing Vessels. It was on a Wager betweene his other new Pleasure boate, built fregate-like, & one of the Duke of Yorks, the wager 100 pounds. The race from Greenewich to Gravesend & back: The King lost it going, wind Contrary, but sav'd stakes returning: There were divers noble Person<s> & Lords on board: his Majestie sometimes steering himselfe: There attended his Barge & Kitchin boate: I brake fast this morning with the king, at returne in his smaller Vessell, he being pleasd to take me & onely foure more who were Noble-men with him: but dined in his Yacht, where we all Eate together with his Majestie.

In this passage his Majestie was pleasd to discourse to me about my Book inveing against the nuisance of the Smoke of Lond: & proposing expedients how by removing those particulars I mention'd, it might be reformd; Commanding me to prepare a Bill, against the next session of Parliament; being (as he said) resolved to have something don in it: Then he discoursd to me of the improvement of Gardens & buildings (now very rare in England, comparatively to other Countries) and then commanded to me draw-up the Matter of fact happning at the bloudy Encounter which then had newly happn'd betweene the French & Spanish Ambassador neere the Tower, at the reception of the Sweds Ambassador contending for precedency; giving me order to consult Sir William Compton (Master of the Ordnance) to informe me what he knew of it; & with his favorite Sir Char: Berkeley [after: Earle of Falmoth:] (Cap: of the Dukes life-guard) then present with his Troope, & 3 foote Companies; with some other reflections and Instructions; to be prepard for a Declaration to take off the reports which went about of his Majesties partiality in this affaire, & of his Officers &c: Spectators rudenesse whilst the conflict lasted:

So I came home that night: & went [2] next morning to Lond, where from the Officers of the Towre, Sir William Compton, Sir Ch: Berkeley and others, who were attending at this Meeting of the Ambassadors 3 dayes before, having collected what I could; I drew up a narrative in vindication of his Majestie & carriage of his officers, & standersby &c: on Thursday, his Majestie sent one

---

[1] This is E's invective on atmospheric pollution called, *Fumifugium: or the Inconvenience of the Aer and Smoak of London dissipated.* Probably his most articulate and clearly expressed work it has remained his most durable single piece and is frequently referred to by environmentalists, historians, and journalists alike. The text is reproduced in full in my edition of *The Writings of John Evelyn.*

of the Pages of the Backstayrs for me, to waite on him with my papers, in his Cabinet, where was present onely Sir Henry Bennet (privy purse) [since Secretary of State & E. of Arlington & Lord Chamb:] when I read to his Majestie what I had drawn up: by the time I had read halfe a page, came in Mr. Secretary Morice with a large paper, desiring to speake with his Majestie who told him that he was now very buisy, & therefore order'd him to come againe some other time: The Secretary reply'd, what he had in his hand was of extraordinary importance: So the King rose up, & commanding me to stay, went aside to a Corner of the roome with the Secretary: after a while, the Secretary dispatchd, his Majestie returning to me at the Table, a letter was brought him from Madame out of France, this he read, & bid me proceede where I left off, which I did 'til I had ended all the narrative, to his majesties great satisfaction, and after I had inserted one or 2 more Clauses, in which his Majestie instructed me, commanded that it should that night be sent to the post-house, directed to the Lord Ambassador at Paris, which was the Earle of St. Albans: and then at leasure to prepare him a Copy, which he would publish: This I did, & immediately sent my papers to the Secretary of State; with his Majesties expresse command of dispatching them that night for France: Before I went out of his Majesties Closet, he cal'd me back, to shew me some Ivorie Statues, and other Curiosities that I had not seene before:

3: Next day Evening, being in the withdrawing roome next the Bed-chamber, his Majestie espying me came to me from a greate crowde of noblemen standing neere the fire, & asked me if I had don: told me, he fear'd it might be a little to sharp (on second thoughts) for he had that morning spoken with the French Ambassador who it seemes had palliated the matter, & was very tame; & therefore directed me where I should soften a period or two, before it were publish'd &c [(as afterward it was)]. This night also spake to me to give him a sight of what was sent, and to bring it to him in his Bed Chamber, which I did, & received it againe from him at dinner next day: By Saturday having finish'd it with all his Majesties notes, the King being gon abroad, I sent the papers to Sir Hen: Bennet (privy-Purse, & a greate favorite) and slip'd home, being my selfe much indisposs'd & harrass'd, with going about, & sitting up to write, &c: ...

29 I saw the Lord Major passe in his Water Triumph to Westminster being the first solemnity of this nature after 20 yeares: ...

31 I was this day <41> yeares of age: for which I render thanks to Almighty God, & implore his favour for the yeare to come ...

November 15 I dind with the Duke of Ormond: his Grace told me there were no Moules in Ireland, nor any Ratts 'till of late, & that but in one County; but a mistake that Spiders would not live there; onely not poyson<ous>: Also that they frequently took Salmon with dogs:

16 I presented *Naudaus* concerning *Liberaries* to my Lord Chancelor; but it was miserably false printed:[1] ...

---

[1] This is E's translation of *Instructions Concerning Erecting of a Library: Presented to my Lord the President De Mesme*, from the French by Gabriel Naudé [Naudeus]. E spent a lifetime trying to organise his own rambling and enormous library made up from his own collection and that of his father-in-law, Sir Richard Browne. He never succeeded and I have been able to show from the press-marks in his surviving books that he had at least three attempts at emulating Naudé's schemes, none of which was ever instigated in a comprehensive and catalogued way. See *The Book Collector*,

20 To Lond: the discourse was about a Vernish that should resist all Weathers, & preserve yron from rust; but fire would not dry it, nor boyling water fetch it off:

24 ... This night his Majestie fell into discourse with me Concerning Bees &c:[1]

26: I saw Hamlet Pr: of Denmark played: but now the old playe began to disgust this refined age; since his Majestie being so long abroad: ...

December 3 By universal suffrage of our Philosophic Assembly, an order was made, & registred, that I should receive their Publique Thanks for the honorable mention I made of them by the name of *Royal Society*, in my Epistle Dedicatory to the Lord Chancellor, before my Traduction of *Naudeus*: Too greate an honour for a trifle:

4 I had much discourse with his highnesse the Duke of York concerning strang Cures. He affirmed that a Woman who swallow'd a whole Eare of Barly, had it worke out at her side. I told him of the knife swallow'd, & the pinns: &c: I tooke leave of the Bish: of Cap-Verde now going in the fleete to bring over our new Queene:

7: I din'd at Arundell house, the day when the greate contest in Parliament was concerning the restoring of the Duke of Norfolck; however 'twas carried for him. I also now presented my little trifle of Sumptuary Laws intitled *Tyrannus*:[2] ...

16 Saw a French Comedy acted at White-hall:[3] ...

Volume 43, no, 4, Winter 1994. Library organisation was an esoteric skill and way beyond Pepys who tried to follow the book, 'I abroad to the office and thence to the Duke of Albemarle, all my way reading a book of Mr. Evelyn's translating and sending me as a present, about directions for gathering a Library; but the book is above my reach, but his epistle to my Lord Chancellor [Clarendon] is a very fine piece' (Pepys's *Diary*, 5 October 1665).

[1] E had a special beehive in his garden. Pepys was intrigued because 'being hived in glass, you may see the bees making their honey and combs mighty pleasantly (*Diary*, 5 May 1665). E had seen these at Oxford, see 13 July 1654.

[2] One of E's more curious pieces *Tyrannus, Or the Mode: In a Discourse of Sumptuary Lawes* is a would-be humorously xenophobic invective against the slavish pursuit of French fashions in Restoration England. In this respect it contrasts with his celebration of the superiority of French customs in his 1659 *A Character of England* (published anonymously and not mentioned in the *Diary*) and thus illustrates the schizophrenic approach towards France exhibited by many of his contemporaries. Even more ironically in my annotated edition of the text in *The Writings of John Evelyn* I have been able to show that the tract was heavily derived from at least three *Essaies* by the French essayist Michel de Montaigne. E's own, annotated, copy survives at the Bodleian Library in Oxford, and has been issued in facsimile form, edited by J.L. Nevinson in 1951.

[3] This is probably a farce presented by a French company which Pepys saw in the summer of 1661 (Pepys's *Diary*, 30 August 1661: the post-Restoration notice of a foreign company playing in London).

1662

January 6 ... This evening (according to costome) his Majestie opned the Revells of that night, by throwing the Dice himselfe, in the Privy Chamber, where was a table set on purpose, & lost his 100 pounds: the yeare before he won 150 pounds: The Ladys also plaied very deepe: I came away when the Duke of Ormond had won about 1000 pounds & left them still at passage, Cards &c: at other Tables, both there and at the Groome-porters, observing the wiccked folly vanity & monstrous excesse of Passion amongst some loosers, & sorry I am that such a wretched Custome as play to that excesse should be countenanc'd in a Court, which ought to be an example of Virtue to the rest of the kingdome.

9 I saw acted the <2>d part of the *Seige of Rhodes*: In this acted the faire & famous Comœdian call'd Roxalana for that part she acted, & I think it was the last; then taken to be the E. of Oxfords Misse (as at this time they began to call lew'd women) it was in Recitativa Musique.

10 Being called into his Majesties Closet, when Mr. Cooper (the rare limmer) was crayoning of his face & head, to make the stamps by, for the new mill'd money, now contriving, I had the honour to hold the Candle whilst it was doing; choosing to do this at night & by candle light, for the better finding out the shadows; during which his Majestie was pleasd to discourse with me about severall things relating to Painting & Graving &c:[1]

11 I dined this day at Arundell-house, where I heard excellent Musique, perform'd by the ablest Masters both French & Eng, on Theorba, Viols, Organs & Voices as an Exercise against the comming of the Queene, as purposly composd for her chapell &c: After which my Lord Aubignie (her Majesties Almoner to be) shewed us his elegant Lodging; & his wheele-chaire for Ease & motion, with divers other Curiosities, especialy a kind of artificial Glasse or Porcelan adorn'd with relievo's of Past, hard & beautifull: My L: Aubigny, bro: to the Duke of Lenox, was a person of good sence, but wholy abandon'd to Ease & effeminancy &c. I received of Sir Peter Ball (the Queenes Attourney) a draught of an Act, against the nuisance of the Smoke of Lond, to be reformed by removing severall Trades, which are the cause of it, & indanger the heal<t>h of the K: & his people &c: which was to have ben offered to the Parliament, as his Majestie commanded:

15 Was Indicted a generall Fast through the whole Nation, & now celebrated at Lond: to avert Gods heavy judgement on this Land, there having falln so greate raine without any frost or seasonable cold: & not onely in England, but in Sweden & the most northern parts; it being here neere as warme as at Midsomer some yeares: The wind also against our Fleete which lay at greate expenses, for a gale to to carry it to Portugal for the new Queene; and also to Land the Guarnison we were sending with the Earle of Peterborow at Tangier, now to be put into our hands, as part of the Q: portion: This solemn Fast was held for the House of Commons, at St. Margarites: ... The effect of this fast appeard, in an immediate change of wind, & season: so as our Fleete set-saile this very afternoone, having laine wind-bound a moneth:

---

[1] E offered the inscription, now on modern £1 coins, ' I suggested the *Decus & Tutamen* [an ornament and protection] out of a Viniet in Cardinal de Richlieu's Greek testament' to discourage 'this injurious Practice of Clippers' (*Numismata*, 1697, 225).

16 Having notice of his R: Highnesse the Duke of Yorks intention to visite my poor habitation and Garden this day, I returned; where he was pleasd to do me that honour of his owne accord: and to stay some time viewing such things as I had to entertaine his curiosity; after which he caused me to dine with him at the Treasurer of the Navys house, & to sit with him coverd at the same table: There were with his Highnesse The Duke of Ormond & severall Lords: Then they viewed some of my Ground, about a project of a Sasse or receptacle for ships to be moored in; which was laied aside, as a fancy of Sir Nic: Crisp &c: After this I accompanied the Duke to an East India vessel that lay at Black-Wall, where we had Entertain<me>nt of several curiosities: among other spiritous drinks, as Punch &c, they gave us Canarie that had ben carried to, & brought back from the Indies, which was indeede incomparably good: So I returnd to Lond, with his highnesse. This night was acted before his Majestie the *Widow*, a lewd play:

18 I came home to be private a little, not at all affecting the life & hurry of Court.

22: To Lond: at our Society divers tryals about the declination of the Needle; & discourses concerning the reduction of time and Measures to a certaine standard, as by Vibration of Pendules & other proportions.

24 His Majestie entertaind me with his intentions of building his Palace of Greenewich & quite demolishing the old; on which occasion I declard him my thoughts ...

February 17 I went with my Lord of Bristol to see his house at Wimbledon (newly bought of Queene Mother) to help contrive the Garden after the moderne. It is a delicious place for Prospect, & the thicketts, but the soile cold & weeping clay: returned that evening with Sir Hen: Bennet.

17 This night was buried in Westminster the Queene of Bohemia (after all her sorrows & afflictions being come to die in her Nephews armes the King) & this night, & the next day fell such a storme of Haile, Thunder & lightning, as never was seene the like in any mans memorie; especialy the tempest of Wind, being South-West, which subverted besids huge trees, many houses, innumerable Chimnies, among other that of my parlor at Says Court, & made such havoc at land & sea, as severall perish'd on both: Divers lamentable fires were also kindled at this time: so exceedingly was Gods hand against this ungratefull, vicious Nation, & Court.

19. at our Assembly, discourses of Vegetation without Earth, for which I was ordered to prepare some experiments: It was therefore affirmed of an English Lady, who sweate so excessively, that a quart of water, might at any time be taken out of the Palmes of her hands, not smelling ill, & proportionably from the rest of her body: Also of a little Woman at Rome who pissed about 200 weight of Water every 24. hours and dranke nothing, upon which were divers discourses & conjectures of the resolution of aire.

20 I returned home to repaire my miserably shatt<er>ed house by the late Tempest:[1] ...

March 22. I made an accord with Mr. Scott for 150 pounds for the rectifying my son Johns crooked leg, & knee-pan: ...

---

[1] E refers to the damage caused to his garden in *Sylva*, 1664. See my edition of *The Writings of John Evelyn*, 263.

24. I returned home, with my whole family, which had ben most part of the Winter since october at London in Lodgings neere the Abby of Westminster.

May 7 I waited on Prince Rupert to our Assembly, where we tried severall experiments in Mr. Boyles Vaccuum: a man thrusting in his arme, upon exhaustion of the ayre had his flesh immediatly swelled, so as the bloud was neere breaking the vaines, & unsufferable: he drawing it out, we found it all speckled: ...

14 To Lond, being chosen one of the Commissioners about reforming the buildings, wayes, streetes, & incumbrances, & regulating the Hackny-Coaches in the City of Lond: taking my Oath before my Lord Chancelor, & then went to his Majesties Surveyors Office in Scotland Yard, about naming & establishing officers, adjourning til: 16: when I went to view, how St. Martines Lane might be made more passable into the strand. There were divers Gent: of quality in this Commission: ...

30 The Queene[1] arivd, with a traine of Portugueze Ladys in their mo<n>strous fardingals or Guard-Infantas: Their complexions olivaster, & sufficiently unagreable: Her majestie in the same habit, her foretop long & turned aside very strangely: She was yet of the handsomest Countenance of all the rest, & tho low of stature pretily shaped, languishing & excellent Eyes, her teeth wronging her mouth by stiking a little too far out: for the rest sweete & lovely enough: This day was solemnly kept the Anniversary of his Majesties Birth, & restauration: Dr. Alestree preaching in the Chapell: ...

June 2: The L: Mayor & Aldermen made their Addresses, presenting her 1000 pounds in Gold: Now saw I her Portuguesse Ladys, & the *Guarda Damas* or mother of her maides; & the old knight, a lock of whose haire quite covered the rest of his bald-pate, bound on by a threit, very oddly:

I had newes sent me from home, that a Swarme of my Bees tooke flight, & hived them selves betweene a Cabine in his Majesties ship, the Oxford fregat; which telling the King of he tooke for a good omen; desiring me that none should disturb them.

I saw the rich Gudola sent his Majestie from the state of Venice, but it was not comparable for swiftnesse to our common wherries, though managed by Venetians: &c: ...

9 I heard the Q: Portugals Musique, consisting of Pipes, harps, & very ill voices.

Hampton Court is as noble & uniforme a Pile & as Capacious as any Gotique Architecture can have made it: There is incomparable furniture in it, espe<c>ialy hangings design'd by Raphael & very richly with gold: also many rare Pictures, especialy the Cæsarian Triumphs of Andr: Mantegna: formerly the Duke of Mantuas; & of the Tapissrys the story of Abraham, & Tobit: than which I believe the whole world shews nothing nobler of that kind: The Gallery of Hornes is very particular for the vast beames of staggs &c: Elkes, Antelops &c: The Queenes bed was an Embrodery of silver on Crimson Velvet, & cost 8000 pounds, being a present made by the states of Holland, when his Majestie returned, & had ben formerly given by them to our Kings sister, the Princesse of Orange, & being bought of here againe, now presented to the King: The greate looking-Glasse & Toilet of beaten & massive Gold

---

[1] Catherine of Braganza (1638-1705). She had no children by Charles II and thus the crown passed to his brother James on Charles's death in 1685.

was given by the Q: Mother &c: The Queene brought over with her from Portugal, such Indian Cabinets and large trunks of Laccar, as had never before ben seene here: The Greate hall is a most magnificent roome: The Chapell roofe incomparably fretted & gilt: I was also curious to visite the Wardrobe, & Tents, & other furniture of State: The Park formerly a flat, naked piece of Ground, now planted with sweete rows of lime-trees, and the Canale for water now neere perfected: also the hare park: In the Garden is a rich & noble fountaine, of Syrens & statues &c: cast in Copper by Fanelli, but no plenty of water: The Cradle Walk of horne-beame in the Garden, is for the perplexed twining of the Trees, very observable &c: Another Parterr there is which they call Paradise in which a pretty banqueting house, set over a Cave or Cellar; all these Gardens might be exceedingly improved, as being too narrow for such a Palace:

10: I returned to Lond: &c: presented my *Historie of Chalcographie*[1] (dedicated to Mr. Boyle) to our Society: ...

19 I went to Albury in Surrey, to visite Mr. Henry Howard [since Duke of Norfolk], soone after he had procured the Dukedome to be restored &c: This Gent: had now compounded a debt of neere 200000 pounds, contracted by his Grandfath<e>r: I was much obliged to that greate virtuoso and to this young Gent: so as I staied a fortnight with him ...

July 2: We hunted and killed a Buck in the Park, Mr. Howard inviting most of the Gent: of the Country neere him.

3. The 3d my Wife meeting me at Woodcot, whither Mr. Howard accompanied me, to see my sonn John, who had ben much brought up amongst Mr. Howards Children at Arundel house, 'til for feare of their perverting him, in the popish religion, I was forc'd to take him home; where I came late at night:

28: His Majestie going to sea to meete Queene-mother (now coming againe for England), met with such ill-weather, as greately indangerd him. I went to Greenewich to waite on the Queene now landed.

30: To Lond: at our Society, where was a meting about Charitable Uses, & particular to enquire how the Citty had dispos'd of the revenues of Gressham Colledge; & why the Salaries of the Professors there was no better improv'd: I was of this Commission, & so were divers Bishops & Lords of the Council, but little was the progresse we could make.

31. I sate with the Commissioners about reforming the buildings & streetes of London, & we ordered the Paving of the Way from st. James's north, which was a quagmire, & also of the Hay-market about Piqudillo,[2] and agreed upon Instructions to be printed & published for the better-keeping the Streetes cleane: so returnd home: ...

August 13 To Lond. Our Charter being now passed under the Broad-Seale, constituting us a Corporation under the Name of the Royal-Society, for the improvement of naturall knowledge by Experiment: to Consist of a President, Council, Fellows, Secretaries, Curators, Operators, Printer, Graver & other

---

[1] *Sculptura: or the History and Art of Chalcography and Engraving in Copper* issued on the strength of a paper presented earlier to the Royal Society on the 16 January 1661 (see above). Pepys admired it as 'a very pretty book' (Pepys's *Diary*, 3 November 1665).

[2] Piccadilly.

officers, with power to make laws, purchasse land, have a peculiar Seale & other immunities & privileges &c: as at large appears in our Graunt, was this day read, & was all that was don this afternoone, it being very large:

14 ... This After-noone her Majestie Queene-Mother (with the Earle of St. Albans, & many greate Ladys & persons) was pleased to honour my poor Villa with her presence, & to accept of a Collation, being exceedingly pleased, & staying 'till very late in the Evening:

[15] The day following Came also my Lord Chancellor Earle of Clarendon (& Lady) his purse, & Mace borne before him, to Visite me, who likewise Collation'd with us, & was very merry: They had all been our old acquaintans in Exile, during the Rebellion; & indeede this greate person was ever my friend &c: his sonn, my L: Corneberry was here too:

17 Being the Sonday when the Common-prayer-booke reformed, was ordered to be used for the future, was appointed to be read: & the Solemn League & Covenant to be abjured by all the Incumbents of England, under penalties of loosing their Livings &c: our Viccar, accordingly read it this morning, and then preached an excellent Sermon on 1. Pet: 2. 13. pressing the necessity of obedience to Christian Magistrates, & especialy Kings: There were strong Guards in the Citty this day, apprehending some Tumult, many of the Presbyterian Ministers, not conforming:

I din'd at Mr. V. Chamberlaines, & then went to see the Q: Mother, who was pleased to give me many thanks for the Entertainement she receiv'd at my house, after which she recounted to me many observable stories of the Sagacity of Dogs that she had formerly had.

20: To Lond: I was this day admitted, & then Sworne one of the present Council of the Royal Society, being nominated in his Majesties Original Graunt, to be of this first Council, for the regulation of <the> Society, & making of such Laws & statutes as were conducible to its establishment & progresse: for which we now set a part every Wednesday morning, 'till they were all finished: My Lord Vicount Brounchar (that excellent Mathematitian &c) being also, by his Majestie, our Founders, nomination, our first <President>: The King being likewise pleas'd to give us the armes of England, to beare in a Canton, in our Armes, & send us a Mace of Silver guilt of the same fashion & bignesse with those carried before his Majestie to be borne before our President on Meeting-daies &c: which was brought us by Sir Gilbert Talbot, Master of his Majesties Jewelhouse ...

23 I this day was spectator of the most magnificent Triumph that certainly ever floted on the Thames, considering the innumerable number of boates & Vessels, dressd and adornd with all imaginab<l>e Pomp: but, above all, the Thrones, Arches, Pageants & other representations, stately barges of the Lord Major, & Companies, with vari<o>us Inventions, musique, & Peales of Ordnance from both the vessels & shore, going to meet & Conduct the new Queene from Hampton Court to White-hall, at the first time of her Coming to Towne, <far> exceeding in my opinion, all the Venetian Bucentoro's &c on the Ascention, when they go to Espouse the Adriatic: his Majestie & the Queene, came in an antique-shaped open Vessell, covered with a State or Canopy of Cloth of Gold, made in forme of a Cupola, supported with high Corinthian Pillars, wreathed with flowers, festoones & Gyrlands: I was in our new-built Vessell, sailing amongst them ...

29 The Council & Fellows of the R: Society, went in Body to White hall, to accknowledge his Majesties royal grace, in granting our Charter, & vouchsafing to be himselfe our Founder: when our President, my L: Brounchar

made an eloquent Speech, to which his Majestie gave a gracious reply, & then we all kissed his hand:

[30] Next day, we went in like manner with our addresse to my Lord High-Chancelor, who had much promoted our Patent &c: who received us with extraordinary favour: In the Evening I went to Queene-Mothers Court & had much discourse with her Majestie & so returnd home late ...

September 17 I went to our Councel to passe severall other statutes: We had now resolved upon the Armes of the Society: that it should be a field Argent, with a Canton of the armes imperial of England: the Supporters two Talbots, argent: The Crest an Eagle or, holding a Shield with the like armes of England, viz: 3. Lions: The Word, *Nullius in Verba*, which was presented to his Majestie for approbation, & orders Given to Garter K. at Armes to passe the Diploma of their office for it. I returnd home:

October 1 To Lond: There were Vipers brought to the Society, Mr. Boyle produced 2 cleare liquors, which being mingled became a clear hard stone: There was also brought the Hippomanes or Mare-poyson: I returned home:

3. To Lond. invited to the Colledge of Physitians, where Dr. Meret a learned man, and Library-keeper shewed me the Library, Theater for Anatomies, & divers natural Curiosities, especialy the Devil Fish (as he call'd it) which being very strong, had when taken nothing in its head save sheere water, & no other braine: There were also divers skelletons: I much admired the thigh bone of an Ostridge: The Statue & epigraph under it of that renouned Physitian Dr. Harvey, inventor of the Circulation of blood: ...

15 I this day delivered my Discourse concerning Forest-trees to our Society upon occasion of certain Queries sent us by the Commissioners of his Majesties Navy: being the first Booke that was Printed by Order of the Society, & their Printer, since it was a Corporation:[1] ...

21. To Q: Mothers Court: where her Majestie related to us divers Passages of her Escapes during the Rebellion & Warre in England: I dined at Court:

22d I went to my L. Tressurers, & then to our Society, where Dr. Charleton brought in his discourse of Birds, relating to the names of such, as being mention'd in divers Authors, were reduced to known birds, for rectifying the defects in most Dictionaries: Also the jaw of a Pike, wherein 'twas observed that every-other tooth was moveable upon a Muscle, the rest fix't: Dr. Whistler shewed, that the wormes breeding in Timber, were the very same with mites in cheese, onely much leaner; which produced a discourse concerning æquivocal generations, and some experiments ordered to be made about it. Next day I went home ...

29 Was my L. Majors shew with a number of sumptuous pageantry, speeches & Verses: I was standing in an house in Cheape side, against the place prepared for their Majesties. The Prince & heire of Denmark [after: King of Denmark] was there, but not our King: There were also the Maids of honor: I went to Court this Evening and had much discourse with Dr. Basiers one of his Majesties Chaplains the greate Travellor, who shewed me the Syngraphs & original subscriptions of divers Eastern Patriarchs & Asian Churches to our Confession &<c>: ...

November 4 I was invited to the Wedding of Sir Geo: Carteret the Tressurer of the Navy, & Kings Vice-Chamberlains Daughter married to Sir Nich:

---

[1] Published as *Sylva*, see 16 February 1664 below.

Slaning knight of the Bath, married by the Bish. of London in the Savoy chapell, after which was an extraordinary feast &c:

5. The Council for the R: So: met to make an end of the statute, & dined together: afterward meeting at Gressham Coll: there was discourse suggested by me, about planting his Majesties Forest of Deane with Oake now so much exhausted of the choicest ship-timber in the world: ...

21. Spent the Evening at Court, Sir Kenhelme Digby giving me greate thanks for my *Sylva*: & then returned home the next morning ...

27 I went to Lond: to see the Enterance of the Russian Ambassador, whom his Majestie ordered should be received with much state, the Emperor his Master having not onely ben kind to his Majestie in his distresse, but banishing all Commerce with our Nation during the Rebellion: & first then the Citty Companies & Traind bands were all in their stations, his Majesties Army & Guards in greate order: his Excellency came in a very rich Coach, with some of his chiefe attendants; many of the rest on horse back, which being clad in their Vests, after the Eastern manner, rich furrs, Caps, & carrying the present, rendred a very exotic and magnificent shew: Some carrying Haukes, furrs, Teeth, Bows, &c: ...

December 1. Having seene the strange, and wonderfull dexterity of the sliders on the new Canall in St. James's park, perform'd by divers Gent: & others with Scheets, after the manner of the Hollanders, with what pernicitie & swiftnesse they passe, how sudainly the<y> stop in full carriere upon the Ice, before their Majesties: I went home by Water but not without exceeding difficultie, the Thames being frozen, greate flakes of yce incompassing our boate: ...

21: <one> of his Majesties Chaplains preachd: after which, instead of the antient grave and solemn wind musique accompanying the Organ was introduced a Consort of 24 Violins betweene every pause, after the French fantastical light way, better suiting a Tavern or Play-house than a Church: This was the first time of change, & now we no more heard the Cornet, which gave life to the organ, that instrument quite left off in which the English were so skilfull: ...

29 To Lond: Saw the Audience of the Moscovy Ambassador, which was with extraordinary state: for his retinue being numerous, all clad in vests of several Colours, & with buskins after the Eastern manner: Their Caps of furr, & Tunicks richly embrodr<e>d with gold & pearle, made a glorious shew: The King being sate under the Canopie in the banqueting house, before the Ambassador went in a grave march the Secretary of the Embassy, holding up his Masters letter of Credence in a crimson-taffaty scarfe before his forehead: The Ambassador then deliverd it, with a profound reverence to the King, the King to our Secretary of State; it was written in a long & lofty style: Then came in the present borne by 165 of his retinue, consisting <of> Mantles & other large pieces lined with Sable, Black fox, Ermine, Persian Carpets, the ground cloth of Gold and Velvet, Sea-morce teeth aboundance, Haukes, such as they sayd never came the like: Horses, said to be Persian, Bowes & Arrows &c: which borne by so long a traine rendred it very extraordinary: Wind musick playing all the while in the Galleries above: This finish'd & the Ambassador conveyed by the Master of Ceremonies to York house, he was treated with a banquet, that cost 200 pounds, as I was assured, &c: ...

1663

January 7 I went to Council at the R: Society: dind with our Councel: &c: at night saw the Ball, in which his Majestie daunced with severall greate Ladys:

8: I went to see Sir S: Tuke (my kindsmans) Comedy acted at the Dukes Theater, which so universaly tooke as it was acted for some weekes every day, & twas believed would be worth the Comedians 4 or 5000 pounds: Indeede the plot was incomparable but the language stiffe & formall ...

February 15 ... This night some villans brake into my house & study below & robb'd me to the Value of 60 pounds in plate, mony & goods.

18 To Lond: when I brought his Majestie a Copy of what pass'd at Tower-hill at the reception of the Sweeds Ambassador, to assert the reasons why for the future his Majestie would have that Ceremonie of the Coaches of foraine Ministers to be of the Introducers: ...

March 18. To Lond: our Council of R: So: ordered their Printer to print my *Sylva*, & was the first printed by their order: I returnd: ...

April 30 Came his Majestie to honor my poore Villa with his presence, viewing the Gardens & even every roome of the house: & was then pleased to take a small refreshment: There was with him the Duke of Richmont, E: of St. Albans, L: Lauderdail & severall Persons of quality: ...

May 4: To Lond: & to take leave of Mr Howards & bring home my sonn John, who had ben the whole winter with the Gent: his sonns at Arundel house, & for feare he might be perverted with their religion: returned the 7th: ...

17: ... I saluted the old Bishop of Durham, Dr. Cosin, to whom I had ben kind & assistant in his exile, but which he little remembred in his greatenesse: I din'd with the Secretary Bennet: ...

30 This morning was pass'd My Lease from the Crowne of Says-Court, for the finishing whereof I had ben obligd to such frequent journeys to Lond: I returned this Evening, having seene the Russ: Ambassador take leave of their Majesties with greate solemnity: ...

July 1 To Lond: To our Society were brought severall Insects described by Mr. Hooke with the Microscop and reduced to a scale, which we ordered should be cut in Brasse in order to his printing his industrious description of them: ...

4: I saw his Majesties Guards being of horse & foote 4000 led by the Generall, The Duke of Albemarle, in extrordinary Equipage & gallantrie, consisting of Gent: of quality, & Veterane Souldiers, excellently clad, mounted & ordered, drawn up in batallia before their Majesties in Hide-parke, where the old Earle of Cleavela<n>d trailed a Pike, & led the right-hand file in a foote Company commanded by the Lord Wentworth his sonn, a worthy spactacle & example, being both of them old & valiant Souldiers: This was to shew the French Ambassador Monsieur Cominges: There being a greate Assembly of Coaches &c in the Park: In the Evening I went home: ...

7: Din'd at the Comptrollers, after dinner we met at the Commission about the streetes, & to regulate Hackny Coaches, also to make up our Accompts to passe the Exchequer: I return'd: ...

19 ... This evening came Mrs. Bennet (sister to Mr. Secretary) to visite us: we all sup'd at Sir Geo: Carterets Tressurer of the navy, who had now maried his daughter Caroline to Sir Tho: Scot of Scots hall: This Gent: thought to be begotten by Prince Rupert ...

August 2 ... This Evening I accompanied Mr. Tressurer & Vice Chamberlaine Carteret to his lately married Son in Laws Sir Tho: Scot to Scots hall in Kent; wee took barge as far as Grays-in,[1] thence by Post to Rochester, whence in Coach & six horses to Scots hall, a right noble seate, uniformely built, handsome Gallery, it stands in a Park well stored, fat & good land: we were exceedingly feasted by the young knight & in his pretty Chapell heard an excellent sermon by his Chaplaine ... In the Churchyard of the Parish-Church I measurd an over-grown Yew-tree that was 18 of my paces in compasse out of some branches of which, torne off by the Winds, were divers goodly planks sawed:

10: We returned by Sir Nortons, whose house is likewise in a park: This gent: is a worthy person and learned Critic espe<c>ialy in the Gr: & Heb: Passing by Chattam we saw his Majesties Royal Navy, dined at Commissioner Pets Master builder there, who shewed me his study & Models, with other curiosities belonging to his art, esteemed for the most skillfull *Naupœgus*[2] in the World: he has a prety Garden & banqueting house, potts, status, Cypr<e>sses, resembling some villa about Rome; after a greate feast we rod post to Graves-End, & sending the Coach to Lond, came by barge home that night: ...

20 I din'd at the Comptrollers, with the Earle of Oxford & Mr. Ashburnham: It was saied it should be the last of the publique Diets or Tables at Court, now determining to put down the old hospitality, at which was greate murmuring, considering his Majesties vast revenue, and plenty of the Nation: hence I went to sit in a Committè of which I was one, to consider about the regulation of the Mint at the Tower, in which some small progresse was made ...

25 To Lond: having severall affaires at Court; where I saw her Majestie take leave of the greate-men & Ladys in the Circle, being the next morning to set out towards the Bath: ...

27: din'd at Sir Ph: Warwicks Secretary to my L: Tressurer, who shewed me the Accompts & other private matters, relating to the Revenue: Thence to the Commissioners of the Mint, particularly about Coynage, & bringing his Majesties rate from 15 to 10 shill: for every pound weight of Gold: &c: & went home next day: ...

31 I was invited to the Translation of Dr. Sheldon Bish: of London from that see to Canterbury; the Ceremonie perform'd at Lambeth: First went his Graces Mace-bearer, Steward, Tressurer, Comptroller all in their Gownes & with white-staves; next the Bishops in their habites, eight in number: next Dr. Sweat Deane of the Arches, Dr. Exton Judge of the Admiralty, next Sir William Merick, Judge of the Prerogative Court, with divers Advocates in Scarlet: After divine service in the Chapell perform'd with Musique extraordinary: Dr. Franck & D. Stradling (his Graces Chaplaines) said prayers: The A Bish: in a private roome looking into the Chapel, the Bishops who were

---

[1] Gravesend, Kent.
[2] Ship-builder.

Commissioners went up to a Table plac'd before the Altar & sat about it in chaires:

Then Dr. Chawworth presented the Commission under the broad-seale to the Bish: of Winchester, which was read by Dr. Sweat; Then the Vicar-Generall went to the Vestery, & brought his Grace into the Chapell, his other officers marching before, he, being presented to the Commissioners, was seated in a greate arm'd Chaire at one end of the Table: Then was the Definitive Sentence read by the Bishop of Winchester, & subscribed by all the Bishops & Proclamation three-times made at the Chapell dores, which were then set-open for any to enter, & give their exceptions, if any they had: This don, we all went to dinner in the Greate hall to a mighty feast of 500 pounds expense. There were present all the Nobility in Towne, the Lord Maior of Lond: Sheriffs, Duke of Albemarle &c: My Lord A Bishop did in particular most civily welcome me &c. So going to visite my Lady Needham who lived at Lambeth I went over to Lond: ...

September 10. I dind with Mr. Tressurer of the Navy, where sitting by Mr. Secretary Moris we had much discourse about Bookes & Authors, he being a learned man, & had a good collection: ...

October 24 Mr. Edw: Philips, came to be my sonns præceptor:[1] This Gent: was Nephew to Milton who writ against Salmasius's Defensio, but not at all infected with his principles, & though brought up by him, yet no way taint<e>d:

November 2 To Lond: to receive a dividend from the East India Stock: ...

30 Was the first Anniversary our Society for the Choice of new Officers, according to the Tenor of our Patent, & Institution; it being St. Andrews day, who was our Patron, each fellow wearing a St. Andrews Crosse of ribbon on the crowne of his hatt, after the Election was over, we all dined together, his Majestie sending us Venison: ...

December 16 To Lond: To our Society, where Mr. P. Balle our Treasurer on this Election, presented the Society with an Iron Chest with 3 Locks, & in it an hundred pounds as a Gift & benefactor: ...

29: my sonn John was let bloud 3 ounces, for his feavour: ...

---

[1] Edward Phillips (1630- c. 1696), John Milton's nephew. The relationship was of no value to E who disapproved of Milton's association with those who defended the execution of Charles I. Phillips left E's service on 27 February 1665. On 4 April 1665 E wrote to Christopher Wren seeking his recommendation for a new tutor for his son, expressing his desire that a candidate be a 'perfect Grecian and ... more than vulgarly mathematical ... the boy is capable beyond his years.' John Evelyn junior became an accomplished linguist producing, amongst other works, a translation from the Greek of the *Life of Alexander* to a translation of Plutarch's *Parallel Lives* published in 1685 by Jacob Tonson.

1664

January <17>: ... And this day was my Wife brought to bed of a sonn borne exactly at 2 in the afternoone: blessed be God for this mercy to her, who had ceased from bearing some yeares: ...

27 Was Christned my sonn Richard [2d. of that name] by his Grandfather Sir Rich: Browne, my Lord Vicount Mordaunt & my Lady Warwick being Sponsors &c: Dr. Breton officiating in the greate Chamber at Says Court.

February 10 To Lond: my *Sylva*[1] being now in the presse: ...

16. I went to Lond: presented my *Sylva* to the Society. & 17: To his Majestie to whom it was dedicated, to my Lord Treasurer, & Lord Chancellor: ...

26: Din'd at my Lord Chancellors who invited me. Thence to Court, where I had greate thanks for my *Sylva* & long discourse with him of divers particulars.

March 2 I went to Lond, to distribute some of my Books amongst friends, return'd: ...

6 ... This Spring I planted the home field & West field about Says-Court, with Elmes; being the same Yeare that the Elmes were also planted by his Majestie in Greenewich park.

9 I went to the Tower of Lond, to sit in Commission about regulating the Mint, & now it was the fine new Milled Coyne both of White-mony & Ginnies was established: returnd: ...

26: It pleased God to take-away my sonn Richard, being now a moneth old, yet without any sicknesse of danger perceivable, being to all appearance a most likely child; so as we suspected the Nurse had over-layne him to our extreame sorrow, being now againe reduc'd to one: Gods will be don:

---

[1] *Sylva, or a Discourse of Forest Trees, and the Propagation of Timber in His Majesties Dominions*, published following a paper presented to the Royal Society on 15 October 1662. E had been charged by the Royal Society, along with Dr Jonathan Goddard, John Winthrop, and Christopher Merret, to deal with inquiries by the Royal Navy about the management of woodland following the depradations of the Interregnum. E's role was to synthesize all the findings. The resulting book, the first published by the Society, was the basis of E's contemporary and subsequent reputation. The text, derived from anecdotal evidence gathered from Pliny the Elder, Cato, Varro, and various medieval authorities as well as from E's correspondents and his own experience, forms one of the first serious attempts at a practical handbook. E prepared three further editions (1667, 1679, and 1706) in his own lifetime and the book was re-issued in various amended forms throughout the eighteenth and early nineteenth centuries. All the original editions were accompanied by E's short work *Pomona* on fruit-trees and a gardening calendar called *Kalendarium Hortense*. It has been claimed that the information in *Sylva* was partly responsible for creating the resources essential to the building of Nelson's navy. The complete text of the 1664 edition is included in my edition of *The Writings of John Evelyn* and is the only comprehensively annotated version of any of the texts of *Sylva* to have appeared since 1664.

27: our Curate on: 11: Matt: 28: After evening prayer was my child buried neere the rest of his brothers, my deare children: ...

April 17: ... In the afternoone I went with Sir Sam. Tuke to Epsam, & staied with my Bro: at Woodcot 'til tuesday, when Sir R: Browne & my Wife fetched me home in the Coach:

27: To Lond about buisinesse: supp'd at Mr. Secretary Bennets; saw a facecious Comedy Cald *Love in a Tub* ...

May 5 I went with some company a journey of Pleasur on the Water, in barge, with Musick & at Mortlack had a greate banquet, returning late: The occasion was Sir Robert Carr now Courting Mrs. Bennet, sister to the secretary of state &c:

June 8 I went to our Society, to which his Majestie had sent that wonderfull horne of the fish, which struck a dangerous hole in the keele of a ship, in the India Sea, which being broake off with the violence of the fish, & left in the timber, preserv'd it from foundring: ...

22 One Tomson a Jesuite shewed me such a <Collection> of rarities, sent from the Jesuites of Japan & China to their order at Paris (as a present to be reserved in their *Chimelium*, but brought to Lond; with the East India ships for them) as in my life I had not seene: The chiefe things were very large Rhinoceros's hornes, Glorious Vests, wrought & embrodered on cloth of Gold, but with such lively colours, as for splendor & vividnesse we have nothing in Europe approches: A Girdill studdied with achats, & balast rubies of greate value & size, also knives of so keene edge as one could not touch them, nor was the mettal of our Couler but more pale & livid: Fanns like those our Ladys use, but much larger, & with long handles curiously carved, & filled with Chineze Characters: A sort of paper very broad thin, & fine like abortive parchment, & exquisitely polished, of an amber yellow, exceeding glorious & pretty to looke on, & seeming to be like that which my L: Verulame describes in his *Nova Atlantis*; with severall other sorts of papers some written, others Printed: Also prints of Landskips, of their Idols, Saints, Pagoods, of most ougly Serpentine, monstrous & hideous shapes to which they paie devotion: Pictures of Men, & Countries, rarely painted on a sort of gumm'd Calico transparant as glasse: also Flowers, Trees, Beasts, birds &c: excellently wrought in a kind of sleve-silk very naturall. Divers Drougs that our Drougists & physitians could make nothing of: Especialy, one which the Jesuite called *Lac Tygridis*, it look'd like a fungus, but was weighty like metall: yet was a Concretion or coagulation of some other matter: ...

July 7: To Court, where I subscribed to Sir Arthyr Slingsbys loterey, a desperate debt owing me long since in Paris: ...

14: I went to take leave of the two Mr. Howards now going to Paris & brought them as far as Bromely, thence to Eltham to see Sir John Shaws new house now building, the place is pleasant, if not too wett, but the house not well contrived, especialy the roofe, & roomes too low pitch'd, & Kitchins where the Cellars should be: The Orangerie & Aviarie handsome, & a very large plantation about it.[1]

---

[1] The house survives almost unaltered from the outside in Eltham as the headquarters of the Royal Blackheath Golf Club.

19. To Lond. to see the event of the Lottery, which his Majestie had permitted Sir Arth: Slingsby to set up for one day in the Banqueting house at whitehall: I gaining onely a trifle, as well as did the King, Queene Consort, & Q: Mother for neere 30 lotts: which was thought to be contriv'd very un-handsomely by the master of it, who was in truth a meer shark: ...

August 3: To Lond: This day was a Consort of Excellent Musitians espe<c>ialy one Mr. Berkenshaw that rare artist, who invented a mathematical way of composure very extraordinary: True as to the exact rules of art, but without much harmonie ...

8. came the sad and unexpected newes of my Lady Cotton, Wife to my Bro: Geo: a most excellent Lady: ...

22. I went back to Wotton to assist at the Funerall of my sister-in Law, the Lady Cotton buried in our Dormitorie there, she being put up in Lead: Dr. Owen preaching ... a profitable & pathetic discourse, concluding with an Elogie of that virtuous, pious, & deserving Lady &c: it was a very solemn funerall of about 50 mourners: I came back next day: with my Wife to Lond:

25. To Deptford: my foote-man lingering at some distance behind the Coach, was robb'd, & bound <it> being night: ...

October 5. To Lond: at our Society Experiments on severall bodys descent in Water, by vibrations of a pendule, also was brought a new invented Instrument of Musique, being an harpsichord with gut-Strings, sounding like a Consort of Viols with an Organ, made vocal by a Wheele, & a Zone of parchment that rubb'd horizontaly against the Strings: ...

15 Dined, at L: Chancelors, where was also the Duke of Ormond, Earle of Cork, and Bishop of Winchester: After dinner my Lord Chancellor & Lady carried me in their Coach to see their Palace (for now he lived at Worcester-house in the Strand) building at the upper end of St. James's Streete; & to project the Garden: Then went with my Lady to St. James's house to see her Grand-Children, the Lady Mary & a sonn, &c, children of the Dutchesse of Yorke; & this Evening presented his Lordship with my booke of *Architecture*,[1] as before I had don to his Majestie & Queene Mother, both of whom were pleasd to say it was the usefullest booke on that subject of any extant: My L: Chamberlaine caused me to stay with him in his bed chamber,

---

[1] *A Parallel of the Antient Architecture with the Modern, In a Collection of Ten Principal Authors who have written upon the Five Orders* ... E's translation from the French by Roland Fréart, Sieur de Chambray. E brought a copy back from France in 1651 but waited for the opportunity to have suitable plates made up from the original to reproduce the engravings which are essential. He appended his own *Account of Architects and Architecture*. E's interest in the revival of classical architecture dated back to the 1650s following his travels in the 1640s. He published comments on London's architecture in *A Character of England*, praising Inigo Jones's Banqueting House and facade for the old St Paul's, and discarding the rest as gothic (see *The Writings of John Evelyn*, 79).

The book did not attract immediate widespread attention and enough sheets were left over for a re-issue in 1680. Nevertheless E prepared a second edition which was published posthumously in 1707, with further editions appearing in 1723 and 1733, reflecting the book's value once Palladianism began to come to the fore in the eighteenth century. The book is easily the most attractive of all E's publications.

discoursing of severall matters, very late, even 'til he was going into his bed: ...

17. I went with my L: V. Count Cornbury to Cornebury in Oxfordshire, to assist the Planting of the Park & beare him company, with Mr. Belin, both virtuous & friendly Gent: also with Mr. May, in Coach & six horses, din'd at Uxbridge, lay at Wicckam:

18 at Oxford, went through Woodstock where we beheld the destruction of that Royal Seate & Park by the late Rebels;[1] & ariv'd that Evening at Cornbury, an house built by the Earle of Denby, in the middle of a Sweete dry Park walled with a Dry-wall: The house of excellent free stone, abounding in that park, a stone that is fine, but never swets or casts any damp: tis of ample receite, has goodly Cellars, the paving of the hall admirable, for the close laying of the Pavement: We design'd an handsome Chapell that was yet wanting, as Mr. May had the stables which indeede are very faire, having set out the Walkes in the Park, & Gardens: The Lodge is a prety solitude, and the Ponds very convenient; The Park well stored.

Hence on the 20: we went to see the famous Wells natural, & artificial Grotts & fountains calld Bushells Wells at Ensham: this Bushell had ben Secretary to my L: Verulam: It is an extraordinary solitude: There he had two Mummies, a Grott where he lay in an hamac like an Indian: Hence we went to Dichley an antient seate of the Lees, now Sir Hen: Lees, a low antient timber house, with a pretty bowling greene: My Lady gave us an extraordinary dinner: This Gent: Mother was Countesse of Rochester, who was also there, & Sir Walt: Saint Johns: There were some pictures of their ancestors not ill Painted; the Gr: Grandfather had ben Knight of the Gartyr, also the Picture of a Pope & our Saviours head: so we returned to Cornbury: ...

24: We dined at Sir Tim: Tyrills at Shotover: this Gent married the daughter & heyre of Bishop Usher A:B: of Armagh that learned Prælate: th<e>y made a greate entertainement: There is here in the Grove, a fountain of the coldest water I ever felt: 'tis very cleere, his plantations of Oakes &c is commendable: so we went this Evening to Oxford, lay at Dr. Hides Principal of Magdalen Hall (related to my L:) bro: to the L: Ch: Justice, and that Sir Henry Hide that lost his head for his Loyalty: we were handsomly entertained two dayes.

25 ... I went to visit Mr. Boyle now here, whom I found with Dr. Wallis & Dr. Chr: Wren in the Tower at the Scholes, with an inverted Tube or Telescope observing the Discus of the Sunn for the passing of Mercury that day before the Sunn; but the Latitude was so greate, that nothing appeared: So we went to see the rarities in the Library, where the Library keepers, shewed me my name, among the Benefactors: They have a Cabinet of some Medails, & Pictures of the Muscular parts of Mans body: Thence to the new Theater, building now at an exceedingly & royal Expense by the L:A:B: of Canterbury, to keepe the Acts in for the future, 'til now being in St. Maries church: The foundation being but newly laied & the whole, Design'd, by that incomparable genius, & my worthy friend Dr. Chr: Wren, who shewed me the Model, not disdaining my advise in some particulars: Thence to see the Picture on the Wall over the Altar at All-Soules, being the largest piece of Fresco painting (or rather in Imitation of it, for tis in oyle [of Terpentine] in England, & not ill design'd, by the hand of one Fuller: yet I feare it will not hold long, & seemes too full ๐๋

---

[1] The site was handed over by Anne to the Duke of Marlborough, w๋
February 1705 shortly after the Battle of Blenheim, for the bu๋
Palace.

nakeds for a Chapell: Thence to New-Coll: & the Painting of Magdalens Chapell, which is on blue cloth in *Chiaro Oscuro* by one Greeneborow, being a *Cœna Domini* & Judgement <on> the Wall by Fuller, as is the other, somewhat varied: Next to Waddam, & the Physik Garden where were two large Locust Trees, & as many Platana, & some rare Plants under the Culture of old Bobart.

26: We came back to Beaconsfield, next day to Lond. where we dined at my L: Chancelors with my L: Belasis & divers greate persons:

<28> Being casualy in the Privy Gallery at White-hall, his Majestie gave me thanks (before divers Lords & noble men) for my Book of *Architecture* & *Sylva* againe: That they were the best designd & usefull for the matter & subject, the best printed & designd (meaning the *Tallè doucès* of the *Paralleles*) that he had seene: then caused me to follow him alone to one of the Windows, he asked me if I had any paper about me un-written, & a Crayon; I presented him with both, & then laying it on the Window stoole, he with his owne hands, designed to me the plot for the future building of White-hall, together with Roomes of State, & other particulars, which royal draft, though not so accurately don, I reserve as a rarity by me: After this he talked to me of severall matters, & asking my advice, of many particulars, in which I find his Majestie had an extraordin<ar>y talent, becoming a magnificent Prince:

The same day, at Council (there being Commissioners to be made, to take care of such sick & Wounded, & Prisoners of War, as might be expected upon occasion of a succeeding Warr, and Action at sea; a War being already declared against the Hollanders) his Majestie was pleasd to nominate me to be one; amongst three other Gent: of quality, Parliament men: Viz: Sir William D'oily knight & Baronet, Sir Tho: Clifford [since L: Tressurer of England], & Bullein Rhemys Esquire, with a Sallary of 1200 pounds amongst us, besides extraordinares &c: for our care & attendance in time of action, each of us appointed his particular District, & mine falling out to be Kent, [&] Sussex: with power to constitu<t>e Officers, Physitians, Chirurgeons, Provost Martials &c: dispose of halfe of the Hospitals thro England: after which I kissed his Majesties hand, as did the rest of my Collegues when the Council was up: At this Council, I heard Mr. Solicitor Finch [since L: Chan] plead most elegantly the Merchants Cause, trading to the Canaries, that his Majestie would grant them a new Charter.

29 Was the most magnificent triumph by Water & Land of the Ld: Major, I dined at Guild-hall: the feast said to cost 1000 pounds: at the upper Table, placed next to Sir H: Bennet Secretary of State, just opposite to my L: Chancelor & the Duke of Buckingham, who sate between Mr. Comminges the Fr: Ambassador, Lord Tressurer, Dukes of Ormond, of Albemarle, E: of Manchester Lord Chamberlaine & the rest of the great officers of State: My Lord Major came twice up to us, first drinking in a Golden Goblett his Majesties health, then the French Kings (as a Complement to his Ambassador). Then we return'd my L: Majors health, the Trumpets, Drumms sounding: for the rest, the Cheere was not to be imagind for the Plenty & raritie, an infinitie of Persons at the rest of the Tables in that ample hall, so I slip'd away in the crowd & came home late: ...

November 2: To Lond: Her Majestie Queene-mother came crosse the Gallerie in White-hall to give me thanks for my Book of *Architecture*, which I had presented to her, with a complement that I did by no means deserve: returnd that evening: ...

7: To Lond: about our Commission, took leave of his R: Highnesse the Duke now going to sea, Generall of the fleete against the Dut<c>h: [&] I kissd his hand in his bed-chamber & returnd home: ...

15: To Lond. We chose our Treasurer, Clearks, Messengers, appointed our seale, which I ordered should be the good Samaritan, with this motto, *fac similiter*:

24: His Majestie was pleasd to tell me what the conference was with the Holland Ambassador which (as after I found) <was part of> the heads of the Speech he made at the reconvention of the Parliament, which now began: 24: I dined with the Commissioners for Sick & Wounded, & sate at Painters hall: ...

December 2. Sir William D'Oylie & myselfe deliverd the Pr: Councils letters to the Governors of St. Thomas Hospital in Southwark, that a mo<ie>tie of the house should be reserved for such sick & wounded as should from time to time be sent from the Fleete, during the War: This being dellivr<e>d at their Court, the President & severall Aldermen Governors of that Hospital invited us to a greate feast in Fishmong<e>rs hall: ...

13 To Lond: Sate at Painters hall, where we perfected the Method for disposing of the sick.

14: met at the R: Society, where we had severall letters read, from correspondents beyond sea, about the Comet which now appeared: orders were given for accurate observations to our Curator &c: ...

22: I went to the Launching of a new ship of two bottomes, invented by Sir William Petty by a Modell of Sir William Petty on which were various opinions: his Majestie present, gave her the name of the Experiment: so I came home, where I found Sir Humphrie Winch, & Mr. Phil. Packer who dined with me: This yeare I planted the Lower grove next the Pond: ...

1665

January 2 [To Lond] This day was publishd by me that part of the *Mysterie of Jesuitisme* translat<e>d & collected by me, though without name, containing the Imaginarie Heresy with 4 letters & other Pieces.[1] I dind at my L: Chancelors, to whom I recomended Sir Roger Langlys my kindsmans contest with Sir Tho: Osborne [since L. Tress of England] about being a knight for Yorkshire: Then, my Lord Chiefe Justice recommended a relation of his to be one of my officers, so I returnd ...

4 I went in Coach (it being excessive sharp frost & snow) towards Dover, & other parts of Kent, to settle Physitians, Chirurgeons, Agents, Martials & other

---

[1] Μυστήριον τῆς 'Ανομίας, *That is, Another Part of the Mystery of Jesuitism, Publickly maintained At Paris, in the College of Clermont, the XII of December MDCLXI. Declar'd to all the Bishops of France. According to the Copy printed at Paris. Together with The Imaginary Heresie in three Letters, With divers other Particulars relating to this Abominable Mysterie. Never before published in English*, translated from the French of A. Arnauld and P. Nicole. The work castigated the Catholic church for its hypocritical claims of purity and for equating the powers of the Pope with those of God. Despite this E was nowhere nearly as anti-Catholic as many of his contemporaries.

offices in all the Sea-Ports, to take care of such as should be set on shore, Wounded, sick or Prisoner &c in pursuance of our Commission, reaching from the North foreland in Kent, to Portsmouth in hampshir: the rest of the Ports in England, from thence, to Sir Will: D'oily, to Sir Tho Clifford [afterwards L: Tressurer of England], Bulleyn Rhemes: so that evening I came to Rochester, where I delivered the Privy Councils letter to the Major to receive orders from me:

5. I arived at Canterbury, [6] being Epiphanie, when I went to the Cathedrall, exceedingly well repaired since his Majesties returne:

<7>: To Dover, where Col: Stroode Lieutennant of the Castle, (having receiv'd the Letter I brought him from the Duke of Albemarle) invited me, and made me lodge in the Castle, & was splendidly treated, assisting me from place to place: here I settled my first Deputy:

8: I heard an excellent sermon in the chiefe Church on<e> Dr. Hynd, on 12: Rom: 6. The Major, & Officers of the Costomes were very civel to me:

9 To Deale, settled Agent, & matters there:

10: To Sandwich, a pretty towne about 2 miles from the sea, a river: The country sandy: here the Major also very dilligent to serve me: I visited the forts in the way: Thence that night back to Canterbury,

11 To Rochester, where I tooke orders to settle Officers at Chatham.

12. To graves end, where having dispatch'd with the Governor of the Block-house, & Major, relating to my Instructions, I returned home, a Cold, buisy, but not unpleasant Journey:

15 ... To Lond: to meete my Bro: Commissioners & give accompts what we had don in our severall districts:

18: At the R: Society came in severall schemes & observations about the Comet: Mr. Hooke produc'd an Experiment of fire, shewing that the aire was but a certainly disolving menstrue:

<19> I din'd at the L: Majors, a prodigious feast, it being a day when the Companies were received &c: I waited on Q: Mother: ...

26: Met at Commission for Sick & Wounded: This night being at White hall, his Majestie came to me standing in the Withdrawing roome, & gave me thanks for publishing the *Mysterie of Jesuitisme*, which he said he had carried 2 days in his pocket, read it, & encouragd me, at which I did not a little wonder; I suppose Sir Robert Morray had given it him ...

February 2 I had a kind audience of my L: Chancellor about a buisinesse: Saw a fine Mask at Court perform'd by 6 Gents: & 6 Ladys surprizing his Majestie, it being Candlemas day: ...

8 Ashwednesday I visited our Prisoners at Chelsey Colledge, & to examine how the Martial & Suttlers behaved themselves: These were Prisoners taken in the Warr; They onely complain'd that their bread was too fine: I din'd at Sir Hen: Herberts Master of the Revells:

9 Dined at my L: Treasure<r>s the Earle of Southampton in Blomesbury, where he was building a noble Square or Piazza & a little Towne: his owne house stands too low, some noble rooms, a pretty Cedar Chapell, a naked Garden to the north, but good aire: I had much discourse with his Lordship whom I found to be a person of extraordinary parts, but Valetudinarie:

I went to St. Ja: Parke, where I examin'd the Throate of the *Onocratylus* or Pelecan, the tongue scarce appearing, the Peake above 2 foote long, crooked at the very point & a little red at the tip: the neck rough, a fowle betweene a Storke & Swan & neere as big as a Swan; a Melancholy water foule: brought from Astracan by the Russian Ambassador: it was diverting to see how he would tosse up & turne a flat-fish, plaice or flounder to get it right into its gullet, for it has one at the lower beake which being filmy stretches to a prodigious widenesse when it devours a greate fish &c: Here was also a small Water-fowle that went almost quite erect, like the Penguin of America: It would eat as much fish as its whole body weighed, I never saw so unsatiable a devourer, I admir'd how it could swallo<w> so much & swell no bigger: I believe it to be the most voracious creature in nature, it was not biger than a More hen: The Solan-Geece here also are greate devourers, & are said soone to exhaust all the fish of a pond: Here were a curious sort of Poultry, not much exceeding a tame pidgeon, with legs so short, as their crops seem'd to touch the Earth: also a milk-white Raven, a good<l>y bird: here was also a Stork, which was a raritie at this season, seing he was loose, & could flie loftily: Also 2 Balearian Cranes, one of which having had one of his leggs broken and cut off above the knee, had a wodden or boxen leg & thigh with a joynt for the <knee> so accurately made, that the poore creature could walk with it, & use it as well as if it had ben natural: It was made by a souldier: The Parke was at this time stored with infinite flocks of severall sorts of ordinary, & extraordinary Wild foule, breeding about the Decoy, which for being neere so greate a Citty, & among such a concourse of Souldier<s>, Guards & people, is very diverting: There were also Deere of severall countries, W<h>ite, spotted like Leopards, Antelope: An Elke, Red deeres, Robucks, Staggs, Guinny Goates; Arabian sheepe &c: The supporting the Withy potts or nests for the Wild foule to lay in, a little above the surface of the water was very pretty.

27: Mr. Phillips præceptor to my sonn, went to be with the E: of Penbroch sonn my L. Herbert:[1] ...

March 2. I went with his Majestie into the Lobbie behind the house of Lords, where I saw the King & the rest of the Lords robe themselves, & getting into the Lords house in a corner neere the Woolsackes, that on which the L: Chancellor sate next below the Throne, The King sate in all the <Regalia>, the Crown Imperial on his head, Scepter & Mond &c: The D: of Albemarle bare the sword, the D: of Ormond the Cap: of dignity: The rest of the Lords rob'd & in their places, the Lords spiritual &c. A most splendid & august convention: Then came in the Speaker & H: of Comm: & at the barr made a speech, after which he presented divers bills, read by the Cleark, the King by a nod onely passing them, the Cleark saying *le Roy le veult*, this to the Publique bills, the Private bills, *Soit fait comme il est desirè*, being in all 26 bills, Then his Majestie made a very handsome, but short speech, commanding my Lo: Privy-Seale to prorogue the Parliament, which he did, my L: Chancelor being absent & ill: so all rise: I had not before seene the manner of passing Laws ...

9 Went to receive the poore burnt Creatures that were saved out of the London fregat in which were blowne up above 200 men by an axident and so perish'd on<e> of the bravest ships in Europe: returning this evening I saw a pillar of Light, of a very strange Colour, & position, being to appearance upright from the body of the setting sunn 7 or 8 yards long & 2 foote broade ...

15 ... Afternoone at our Society, where was tried some of the Poysons sent from the King of Macassar out of E. India, so famous for its suddaine operation: we gave it a wounded dog, but it did not succeede ...

---

[1] See note above for 24 October 1663.

April 4: Lond: Commiss: to take order about some Prisoners sent from Cap: Allens ship, taken in the Solomon, viz. the brave Man who defended her so gallantly.

5. return'd, which was a day of humiliation pub: & for successe of this tirrible Warr, begun doubtlesse at seacret instigation of the French &c to weaken the States, & Protestant Interest &c: prodigious preparations on both sides: our Doctor preached on 4. James 10. concerning the effect of true humiliation &c: ...

19 Invited to a greate dinner at Trinity house in Lond: where I had buisinesse with the Commissioners of the Navy, & to receive the second 5000 pounds imprest for his Majesties Service of the Sick & Wounded & Prisoners: &c: Thence to our Society where were divers poisons experimented on Animals:

20: To White-hall, to the King, who call'd me into his Bed-Chamber as he was dressing, to whom I shew'd the Letter written to me from his R: Highness the Duke of York from the Fleete, giving me notice of Young Evertse, & some other considerable Commanders (newly taken in fight with the Dartmouth & Diamond fregats) whom he had sent me as Prisoners at Warr: I went to know of his Majestie how he would have me treate them: who commanded me to bring the Young Cap: to him, &, to take the Dutch Ambassadors Word (who yet remained here) for the other, that he should render himselfe to me when ever I cald, & not stir without leave: Upon which I desired more Guards, the Prison being Chelsey house: I went also to my L: Arlington (viz. Mr. Secretary Bennet, lately made a Lord) about another buisinesse; dined at my L: Chancelors, none with him but Sir Sackvill Crow (formerly Ambassador at <Constantinople>) where we were very cherefull, & merry:

21 Went home, having taken order with my Martial about my Prisoners; & with the Doctor & Chirurgeon to attend the Wounded, both Enemies, & others of our owne: Next day to Lond: againe I visited my Charge, severall their legges & armes off, miserable objects God knows: ...

24 I presented Young Cap: Everse, eldest sonn of Cornelius, Vice-Admirall of Zealand, & Nephew of John now Admiral, a most valiant person, to his Majestie, being in his bed-chamber: the K. gave his hand to kisse, gave him his liberty, asked many quest: concerning the fight (it being the first bloud drawne) his Majestie remembring the many civilities he had formerly received from his relations abroad, and had now so much Interest in that Considerable Province: Then I was commanded to go with him to the Holl: Ambassador, where he was to stay for his pass-port, & ordered me to give him 50 pieces in broad gold: Next day I had the Ambassadors Parole for the other Cap: taken in Cap: Allens fight <before> Cales &c:

26: I gave his Majestie Accompt of what I had don, & desired the same favour for another Cap: which his Majestie gave me: ...

May 16: To Lond to consider of the poore Orphans & Widdows made by this bloudy beginning, & whose Husbands & Relations perished in the London fregat: whereof 50 Widdows, & of them 45 with child: ...

26: To treat with the Holl: Ambassador at Chelsey, for the release of divers Prisoners of Warr, in Holland, upon Exchange here. After dinner, being calld into the Council Chamber at White hall, I gave his Majestie an accompt what I had don, informing him of the vast charge upon us, being now amounted to no lesse than 1000 pounds weekely; desiring our Treasurer might have another Privy-Seale for 500 pounds speedily, then went home: ...

29 I went (with my little boy) to visite my District over Kent, & to make up Accompts with my Officers; & so by Coach to Rochester, lay at Sitingburne,

[30] din'd at Canterbury, next to Dover, visited the Governor at the Castle where I had some Prisoners: My son went to sea but was not sick.

31 To Deale: ...

June 1 finished my Accompts at Deale: visited the small forts:

2. returnd to Canterbury.

3. Through Roch: Sittingb: Grave<s>end, & the Fleete being just now Engaged gave special orders for my Officers to be ready to receive the Wounded & Prisoners: returned late home by boate: ...

5 To Lond: to speake with his Majestie & D: of Albemarle for Horse & foote Guards for the Prisoners of War committed more particularly to my Charge, by a Commission a part, under his Majesties hand & seale:

<7?> I went againe to his Grace, thence to the Council, and moved for another Privy-seale for 20000 pounds: That I might have the disposal of the Savoy Hospital for the sick & Wounded: all of which was granted: hence to our R: Society to refresh among the Philosophers:

8 Came newes of his Highnesse Victory over the Enemie, & indeede it might have ben a compleate one, & at once ended the Warr, had it ben pursued: but the Cowardize of some, Tretchery, or both frustrated that: we had however bonfires, bells, & rejoicing in the Citty &c.

9: Next day I had instant orders to repaire to the Downes; so as I got to Rochester this evening, dined next day at Canterbury,

[10] lay at Deale where I found all in readinesse: but the fleete hindred by Contrary winds, I came away: having staied there the 11: ...

12: I went back to Dover, din'd with the Governor at the Castle, returnd to Deale: next day, hearing the Fleete was at Sold-bay, I went homeward, lay at Chattham, in which journey, my Coach, by a rude justle against a Cart, was dangerously brused: ...

15: Came Monsieur Brizasiere eldest sonn to the Pr: Sec: of State to the French King, with much other companie to dine with me: After dinner I went with him to Lond to speake to my Lord Gen: for more Guards, [16] & gave his Majestie an account of my journey to the Coasts, under my inspection: I also waited on his R: Highness now come triumphant from the fleete; goten in to repaire: See the whole history of this Conflict in my Hist: of the Dutch Warr:[1] so on Saturday got home being 17: June.

20: To Lond: represented the state of the S<ick> & Wo<unded>: to his Majestie being in Council; for want of mony, who orderd I should apply to my L: Tressurer & Chan: of Exchequer upon what fonds to raise the mony promised: at which time we also presented to his Majestie divers expedients for retrenchment of the charge: This Evening making my Court to the Duke, I spake with Monsieur Cominges the French Ambassador & his highnesse granted me six Prisoners Embdeners, who were desirous to go to the Barbados with a Merchant:

22: We waited on the Chancellor of the Exchequer; & got an order of the Council for our mony, to be paied to the Tressurer of the navy to our Receiver: ...

23 The Duke of Yorke told us, that his dog sought out absolutely the very securest place of all the vessel, when they were in fight:...

---

[1] *Navigation and Commerce* (1674), see 18 June 1670 and 18 August 1674.

28: To Lond: to R: Society, the Assembly now prorogued to Michaelmas, according to costome; & the sooner, because the Plague in Lond much increased:

29 went home, &c:

30 I went to Chattam:

1 **July** downe to the fleete, with my Lord San<d>wich now Admiral, with whom I went in a Pinnace to the Buy of the Noore[1] where the whole fleete rod at anker: went on board the Prince a vessel of 90 brasse ordnance, (most whole canon) & happly the best ship in the world both for building & sailing: she had 700 men: They made a great huzza or shout at our approch 3 times: here we dined with many noble men, Gent: and Volunteeres; served in Plate, and excellent meate of all sorts: after dinner came his Majestie & the Duke & Prince Rupert: & here I saw him knight Cap: Cuttance, for behaving himselfe so bravely in the late fight: & was amaz'd to <behold> the good order, decency, & plenty of all things, in a vessell so full of men: The ship received an hundred Canon shot in her body:

Then I went on board the Charles, to which after a Gun was shot off, came all the flag-officers to his Majestie, who there held a generall Council, determining his R: Highness should adventure himselfe no more this summer: I spake with Sir Geo: Ayscogh, Sir William Pen &c: Sir William Coventry (secretary to the Duke) about buisinesse, and so came away late, having seene the most glorious fleete, that ever spread saile: here was also among the rest the Royal Sovraigne: we returned in his Majesties Yacht with my L: Sandwich & Mr. V: Chamberlaine landing at Chattam on Sunday morning: ...

3. I tooke order for 150 men to be carried on board, (who had ben recovered of their wounds & sicknesse) the *Clove-tree, Carolus quintus & Zeland*, ships that had ben taken by us in the fight: & so returnd home ...

7: To Lond: to Sir William Coventrie & so to Sion, where his Majestie sat at Council (during the Contagion): when my buisines was over I viewed that seate, belonging to the E: of Northumberland built out of an old Nunnerie, of stone, & fair enough, but more celebrated for the Garden than it deserves; yet there is excellent Walle fruit, & a pretty fountaine, nothing else extraordinarie: returnd that day:

9: I went to Hampton Court where now the whole Court was: my buisinesse was to solicite for mony, to carry letters intercepted, to conferr againe with Sir W: Coventrie, the Dukes Secretary, & so home, having dined at Mr. Sec: Morice.

16. To Hampton-Court againe, hearing a fragment of a sermon there by Dr. Turner: There died of the Plague in Lond: this Weeke 1100:

23. There perished this weeke above 2000, & now there were two houses shut up in our parish: ...

August 2. Was the Solemn Fast through England to deprecate Gods displeasure against the Land by Pestilence & War: ...

4: ... I went to Wotton to carry my sonn & his Tutor Mr. Bohune, a fellow of New Coll: (& recommended to me by Dr. Wilkins & the President of Trinity Coll: in Oxford) for feare of the Pestilence still increasing both in Lond: & invirons: ...

7. I returned home, calling at Woo<d>cot, & Durdens by the way: where I <found> Dr. Wilkins, Sir William Pettit, & Mr. Hooke contriving Charriots,

[1] The Buoy of the Nore, in the Thames Estuary.

new rigges for ships, a Wheele for one to run races in, & other mechanical inventions, & perhaps three such persons together were not to be found else where in Europ, for parts & ingenuity:

8: To Lond: where I waited on the D: of Albemarle, who was resolv'd to stay at the Cock-pit in St. James Parke: who had sent me a Letter about buisinesse for his Majesties service: There dying this Week in Lond: 4000:

13 was so tempesteous that we could not go to church:

13. There perished this Weeke 5000: ...

28 The Contagion growing now all about us, I went my Wife & whole family (two or three of my necessary Servants excepted) to Wotton to my Brothers, being resolved to stay at my house my selfe, & to looke after my Charge, trusting in the providence & goodnesse of God ...

September 7 Came home, there perishing now neere ten-thousand poore Creatures weekely: however I went all along the Citty & suburbs from Kent streete to St. James's, a dismal passage & dangerous, to see so many Cofines exposed in the streetes & the streete thin of people, the shops shut up, & all in mournefull silence, as not knowing whose turn might be next: I went to the D: of Albemarle for a Pest-ship, to waite on our infected men, who were not a few: ...

10: ... I dined with the Commissioners of the Navy, retreated hither, & with whom I had buisinesse:[1] ...

17: Receiving a Letter from his Excellency my L: Sandwich of a defeate given to the Dut<c>h, I was forc'd to travell all Sonday, when by the way calling in to see my other Bro: at Woodcot, as I was at dinner, I was surpriz'd by a fainting fit: which much a'larm'd the family, as well it might, I coming so lately from infected places; but I blesse God it went off, so as I got home that night; but was exceedingly <perplex'd>, to find that there were sent me to dispose of neere 3000 Prisoners at Warr; so as on the 18 I was forc't to go to Lond: & take orders from my Lord Gen: what I should do with them, they being more than I had places fit to receive & guard, he made me dine with them, & then we consulted about it: ...

23. My L: Admirall being come from the Fleete to Greenewich, I went thence with him to the Cock-pit to consult with the Duke of Albemarle: I was peremptory, that unlesse we had 10000 pounds immediately, the Prisone<r>s would sterve, & 'twas propos'd it should be raised out of the East India Prises, now taken by my L: Sandwich: They being but two of the Commissioners & so not impower'd to determine, sent an expresse to his Majestie & Council to know what they should do: In the meane time I had 5 Vessels with Competent Guards to keepe the Prisoners in for the present, & to be placed as I should think best: ...

28 To the L: Generall to acquaint him againe of the deplorable state of our men, for want of provisions, return'd with orders:

29. To Erith to quicken the Sale of the Prizes lying there, by orders, to the Commissioners who lay on board, til they should be disposed of, 5000 pounds being proportiond for my quarters: Then I also deliverd the Dut<c>h Vice Admirall, who was my Prisoner, to Mr. Lo, of the Marshallsea he giving me bond of 500 pounds to produce him at my call: I exceedingly pittied this brave, unhappy person, who had lost with these Prizes 40000 pounds, after 20 yeares negotiation in the East Indies: I dined in one of these Vessels of 1200 tunn, full of riches, and return'd home:

---

[1] This bald account contrasts with Pepys' entry for the same day, see p. 6.

October 1 ... This afternoone as I was at Evening prayer, tidings were brought to me, of my Wifes being brought to bed at Wotton of a Daughter (after 6 sonns) borne this morning 1. Octob: in the same Chamber, I had first tooke breath in, and at the first day of that moneth, in the morning, as I was on the last: 45 yeares before: & about the very same houre, being 1/3 aft<e>r 4: Sonday:[1]

4 Was the monethly fast, Mr. Plume on: 16: Numb: 46, of the sinn of rebellion against Magistrates & Ministers:

7: I went to see my Wife.

8: ... before Dinner, was my Daughter Christnd Mary in the Chamber cald the red chamb<e>r, where borne, Her Grandfath<e>r Sir R: Bro: my Aunt Hunger-ford of Cadenam (by proxy) & my Neepce Mary (& God-daught<e>r) being Gossips:[2]

10 I returned to Lond: I went thro the whole Citty, having occasion to alight out of the Coach in severall places about buisinesse of mony, when I was invironed with multitudes of poore pestiferous creatures, begging almes; the shops universaly shut up, a dreadfull prospect: I dined with my L: Gen: was to receive 10000 pounds & had Guards to convey both my selfe & it, & so returned <home>, through Gods infinite mercy: ...

17 I went to Gravesend, next day to Chattam, thence to Maidstone, in order to the march of 500 Prisoners to Leeds-Castle which I had hired of my Lord Culpeper, and [19] dined with Mr. Harlakingdon, a worthy Gent: of Maidstone, being earnestly desired by the Learned Sir Roger Twisden & Deputy Lieutenants, to spare that town from quartering any of my sick flock: Here Sir Ed: Brett sent me some horses to bring up the rere, which returned that night to Rochester:

20: This County from Rochester to Maidstone by the Medway river, is very agreable, the downes & prospect:

21 I came from Gravesend where Sir Jo: Griffith the Governor of the fort, entertaind me very handsomly: ...

November 27: I went to the D: of Albemarle having buisinesse to recommend to his grace, going now to Oxford, where both Court, K & Parliament had ben most part of the summer: There was no small suspicion of my Lord Sandwiches permitting divers Commanders that were in the fight & action, at the taking of the E. India prizes, to break bulk, and take to their owne selves many rich things, Jewels, Silkes &c: though I believe some I could name, fill'd their pockets, my L: Sandwich himselfe had the least share: however he underwent the blame of it, & it created him Enemies, & prepossessed the L: Generall, for he spake to me of it with much zeale & concerne, & I believe laied load enough on Sandwich at Oxford ...

December 8 To my L: of Albemarles (now return'd from Oxon) who was also now declared Generall at Sea, to the no small mortification, of that Excellent Person, the Earle of Sandwich: Whom the Duke of Albemarle, not onely suspected faulty about the prizes, but lesse Valiant: himself imagining how easie a thing it were to confound the Hollander, as well now, as when heretofore he fought against them, upon a more disloyal Interest:

---

[1] Mary Evelyn (1665-85). She died of smallpox on 14 March 1685. Her epitaph is on the same stone as E's son Richard's, still at St Nicholas, Deptford.

[2] A sponsor at a baptism establishing a spiritual relationship with the child.

10 A stranger preached at Greenewich on 13 Luke. 1. 2. and 5. not to judge uncharitably of others, for our owne Escape: applied to those who survived the Contagion &c: a seasonable discourse: ...

23. To Wotton to see my Wife, & kept Christmas with my hospitable Brother:

25 ... Now blessed be God, for his extraordinary mercies & preservations of me this Yeare when thousands & ten thousands perish'd & were swept away on each side of me: There dying in our Parish this yeare 406 of the Pestilence:

1666

January 2 I supped in None-such house (whither the Office of the Exchequer was transferrd, during the Plague) at my good friends Mr. Packer: & tooke an exact view of the Plaster Statues & *Bass-relievos* inserted twixt the timbers & poincons of the outside walles of the Court, which must needes have ben the work of some excellent Italian: admire I did how much it had lasted so well & intire as since the time of Hen: 8, exposd, as they are to the aire, & pitty it is they are not taken out, & <preserved> in some dry place, a gallerie would become them: there are some *Mezzo relievi*[1] as big as the life, & the story is of the heathen Gods, Emblems, Compartiments, &c:

The Palace consists of two Courts, of which the first is of stone Castle like, by the Lord Lumlies (of whom 'twas purchas'd) the other of Timber a Gotique fabric, but these walls incomparably beautified: I also observed that the appearing timber punchions, *entretices* &c were all so covered with Scales of Slate, that it seemed carved in the Wood, & painted, the Slat fastned on the timber in pretty figures, that has preserved it from rotting like a coate of armour: There stand in the Garden two handsome stone Pyramids, & the avenue planted with rows of faire Elmes, but the rest of those goodly Trees both of this & of Worcester-Park adjoyning were fell'd by those destructive & avaritious Rebells in the late Warr, which defac'd one of the stateliest seates his Majestie had.[2]

After much, & indeede extraordinary mirth & cheere, all my Brothers, our Wives & Children being together, & after much sorrow & trouble during this Contagion, which separated our families, as well as others, I returned to my house, but [12] my Wife went back to Wotton, I not as yet willing to adventure her, the Contagion, though exceedingly abated, not as yet wholy extinguish'd amongst us:

29 I went to waite on his Majestie (now return'd from Oxford to Hampton Court) where the Duke of Albemarle presenting me to him, he ran towards me, & in most gracious manner gave me his hand to kisse, with many thanks for my Care, & faithfullnesse in his service, in a time of that greate danger, when every body fled their Employments; he told me he was much oblig'd to me, &

---

[1] Carvings in half-relief.

[2] In 1670 Charles II gave Nonsuch to the Duchess of Cleveland who sold it for demolition in 1682 to George, Lord Berkeley, for £1,800 when 'several large Squares of Historical Relieve ... upon the Demolition of that Royal Fabrick, I hear, have been translated, and ornamently plac'd ... at his delicious Villa Durden's in Surry, not far from Nonsuch' (E's *An Account of Architects and Architecture*, 1697, 54.)

said he was severall times concern'd for me, & the peril I under-went, & did receive my service most acceptably: Though in truth I did but what was my duty, & ô that I had perform'd it as I ought: After this his Majestie was pleas'd to talke with me alone neere an houre, of severall particulars of my Employment, & ordred me to attend him againe the thursday at White-hall: Then the Duke came towards me & embrac'd me with much kindnesse, & told me, if he had but thought my danger would have ben so greate, he would not have sufferd his Majestie to employ me in that Station: then came to salute me, my L. of St. Albans, L. Arlington, Sir William Coventrie & severall greate persons, after which I got home, not being very well in health ...

February 6 My Wife & family return'd to me now out of the Country, where they had ben since August by reason of the Contagion, now almost universaly ceasing: Blessed be God for his infinite mercy in preserving us; I having gon through so much danger, & lost so many of my poore officers, escaping still my selfe, that I might live to recount & magnifie his goodnesse to me: ...

8 To Lond. had another gracious reception of his Majestie who call'd me into his bed-chamber, to lay-before, & describe to him my project of an Infirmarie, which I read to him, with greate approbation, recommending it to his R: Highnesse, & so I returned home ...

20: To the Commissioners of the Navy, who having seene the project of the Infirmary, encouragd the worke, & were very earnest it should be set about speedily: but I saw no mony, though a very moderate expense, would have saved thousands to his Majestie and ben much more commodious for the cure & quartering our sick & wounded, than the dispersing of them into private houses, where many more Chir<ur>giones, & tenders were necessary, & the people tempted to debaucherie &c: ...

March 1 To Lond: presented his Majestie with my booke, intituled, *The Pernicious Consequences of the new Heresy of the Jesuites, against King & States:*[1]

April 10. To Lond: to visite Sir W: D'Oylie, surpriz'd with a fit of Apoplexie & in extreame danger:

11: ... As his Majestie came from Chapell, he call'd me in the lobby, & told Me he must now have me Sworn for Justice of Peace (having long since made me of the Commission) for preventing some dissorder in our parish at this time; I replied, that it was altogether inconsistent with the other service I was ingag'd in, during this hostility with Dutch & French and humbly desir'd to be excus'd, notwithstanding he persisted: After dinner waiting on him I gave him the first notice of the Spaniards referring the umpirage of the Peace 'twixt them, & the Portugal to the French King, which came to me in a letter from France before the Secretaries of State had any newes of it: After this againe his Majestie asked me, if I had found out any able person about our Parts, that might supplie my place of Justice of Peace (the thing in the world, I had most industriou<s>ly avoided to act in hitherto, in reguard of the perpetual trouble thereoff in this numerous Parish &c) on which I nominated one, whom his Majestie commanded me to give immediate notice of to my L: Chancellor, & I

---

[1] Like his earlier translation of an anti-Catholic work by Pierre Nicole this was also issued by E anonymously. In his *Dedicatory Preface* and correspondence E makes it clear that his patron was Edward Hyde, Earl of Clarendon and Lord Chancellor.

should be excus'd: for which I rendred his Majestie many thankes: After dinner, I went to the D: of Albemarle about some complaints I had against the Cleark of the Passage at Dover: Thence to my L: Chancelors to do his Majesties Command: Thence to the R: Society where I was chosen by 27 Voices to be one of their Council for the ensuing yeare, but upon my earnest suite, in respect of my other affairs, I got to be excused, & so got home: ...

15 ... Our Parish now was more infected with the Plague, than ever, & so was all the Countrie about, though almost quite ceased at London:

18 ... that night my poore Wife Miscarried of a Sonn, being but young with Child: ...

May 7 I went to Rochester:

8 To Queenborow where finding the Richmond fregate I sailed to the Buy of the Noore to my L: Gen: & Prince Rupert where was the Rendezvous of the most glorious Fleete in the World, now preparing to meete the Hollander: having received orders & settled my buisinesse there, I return'd on the 9th to Chattham at night: next day I went to visit my Co: Hales at a sweetely watred place near Bochton at Chilston: The next morning to Leeds-Castle, once a famous hold &c. now hired by me of my Lord Culpeper for a Prison: here I flowed the drie moate and made a new draw bridge, brought also Spring Water into the Court of the Castle to an old fountaine, & tooke order for the repaires: ...

June 1. Being in my Garden & hearing the Greate gunns go thick off: I immediately tooke horse, & rod that night to Rochester it being 6 at Evening when I set out:

[2] Thence next day towards the Downes & Sea-Coast: but meeting with the Lieutennant of the Hantshire fregat, who told me what pass'd, or rather not pass'd, I returned to Lond: (there being no noise, nor appearance at Deale or the Coast of any engagement) this recounting to his Majestie whom I found at St. James's [Park] impatiently expecting) & [I] knowing that Prince Rupert was loose, about 3 at St. Hellens point at N. of Wight, it greately rejoic'd him: but was astonish'd when I assur'd him they heard nothing of the Gunns in the Downes, nor the Lieutennant who landed there by five that morning.

3: Whitsonday: ... after sermon came newes, that the Duke of Albemarle was still in fight & all Saturday; & cap: Harmans ship (the Henrie) like to be burnt: Then a letter from Mr. Bertie that Pr: Rupert was come up with his Squadron (according to my former advice of his being loose & in the way) & put new courage into our fleete now in a manner yeilding ground; so as now we were chasing the chacers: That the D: of Alb: was slightly wounded, & the rest in greate danger 'til now; so having ben much wearied with my journey, I slip'd home, the Gunns still roaring very fiercely:

5 I went this morning to Lond: where came severall particulars of the fight:

6: came Sir Dan: Harvey from the Generall & related the dreadfull encounter, upon which his Majestie commanded me to dispatch away an extraordinary Physitian, & more Chirurgions: 'Twas on the solemn fast day, when the newes came, his Majestie being in the Chapell made a suddaine Stop, to heare the relation, which being with much advantage on our side, his Majestie commanded that Publique Thanks should immediately be given as for a Victory; The Deane of the Chapell going down to give notice of it to the other Deane officiating; & so notice was likewise sent to St. Paules and Westminster abbey: But this was no sooner over, but newes came that our losse was very great both in ships & men: That the Prince fregat was burnt &

so a noble vessel of 90 brasse Guns lost: together with the taking of Sir Geo: Ayscue & exceeding shattring of both fleetes, so as both being obstinate, both parted rather for want of ammunition & tackle than Courage, our Generall retreating like a Lyon, which exceedingly abated of our former jolitie: There was however order given for bone-fires & bells, but God knows, it was rather a deliverance than a Triumph: so much it pleased God to humble our late over Confidence, that nothing could withstand the Duke of Albemarle: who in good truth made too forward a reckoning of his successe, now, because he had once beaten the Dutch in another quarrell: & being ambitious to out-do the Earle of Sandwich, whom he had prejudice <to> as defective of Courage: ...

7 I sent more Chirurgions, linnen, medicaments &c: to the severall ports in my District: din'd at my Lord Cornburies, returned home with my Wife:

8. Dined with me Sir Alex: Frasier (prime Physitian to his Majestie) after dinner went on board his Majesties pleasure-boat where I saw the London fregate launched (a most statly ship built by the Cittie, to supply that which was burnt by accident some time since) The King: L. Major & Sherifes being there, with a greate Banquet: I presented my Sonn to his Majestie: ...

15 I went to Chattham:

16 in the Jemmy Yach't (an incomparable sailer) to sea, arived by noone at the Fleete in the B of Nore, dined with Pr: Rupert & Generall:

17: Came his Majestie, Duke, & many Noblemen; after Council, we went to Prayers: having dispatch'd my buisinesse, I return'd to Chattham having layne but one night at sea, in the Royal Charles, we had a tempestuous sea; I went on shore at Sheere-Nesse, where they were building an Arsenal for the Fleete, & designing a royal Fort, with a receptacle for greate ships to ride at Anker; but here I beheld that sad spectacle, namely more than halfe of that gallant bulwark of the Kingdome miserably shatterd, hardly a Vessell intire, but appearing rather so many wracks & hulls, so cruely had the Dutch mangled us: when the losse of the Prince (that gallant Vessell) had ben a losse to be universaly deplor'd, none knowing for what reason we first ingagd in this ungratefull warr: we lost besids 9 or 10 more, & neere 600 men slaine, & 1100 wounded 2000 Prisoners, to balance which perhaps we might destroy 18 or 20 of the Enemies ships & 7 or 800 poore men:

18 weary of this sad sight I came home: ...

July 2. Came Sir Jo: Duncomb & Mr. Tho: Chichley both Privy Councellors & Commissioners of his Majesties Ordinance to give me a visite, & to let me know his Majestie had in Council nominated me to be one of the Commissioners for regulating the farming & making of Salt-peter through the whole Kingdome, & that we were to sit in the Tower the next day &c: When they were gon, came to see me Sir Jo: Cotton (heire to the famous Antiquarie Sir Robert) a pretended greate Gretian, but had by no meanes the parts or genius of his Grandfather: with him were severall other knights & Gent:

3 I went to sit with the Commissioners at the Tower of Lond, where our Commiss: being read, we made some progresse in buisinesse: Sir G: Wharton being our Secretary, that famous Mathematitian, & who writ the yearely Almanac, during his Majesties troubles:

Thence to Painter hall to our other Commiss: & dined at my L: Majors:

4: ... After Sermon I waited on my L: A: Bish: of Cant and B: of Winchester; where the Deane of Westminster spake to me about putting into my hands the disposal of 50 pounds which the Charitable people at Oxford had sent to be distributed among the sick & wounded seamen &c: since the battaile: Thence I went to my L: Chancellor to joy him of the Royal Highnesse second sonne now born at St. James's, and to desire the use of the Star-chamber for our Commissioners to meete in, painters hall not being so convenient ...

11 ... to the R: Society, where was an experiment of vibrating two [concave] Globes fill'd with sand, of severall dimensions, to represent the motion of the Earth & Moone about it, which the sand issuing out of the bottome described on the floore: Triall againe of the saddle Charriot, & fountaine to water Gardens & tops of tallest trees: &c: ...

22 I went to Greenewich to Prayers: our Parish still exceedingly infected with the Contagion:

29 The Pestilence now a fresh increasing in our Parish, I forbore going to Church: In the <Afternoon> came tidings of our Victorie over the Hollanders, sinking some, and driving others on ground, & into their ports:

August 6 To Lond:, din'd with Mr. Povy, & then went with him, to see a Country house he had bought neere Brainford, returning by Kensington, which house I saw standing to a very gracefull avenue of trees; but tis an ordinary building, especialy one part. I returnd to Lond: ...

12 The pestilence still raging in our Parish, I durst not go to Church ...

17: Din'd with L: Chancellor whom I intreated to visite the Hospital of the Savoy, & reduce it (after the greate abuse had ben continued) to its original institution, for the benefit of the poore, which he promised to do ...

23. Sat at Star-Chamber, Din'd at Sir William D'Oylies now recovered as it were miraculously: In the afternoone Visited the Savoy Hospital, where I staied to see the miserably dismembred & wounded men dressed & gave some necessary orders: Then to my L: Chancelor, who had (with the Bish: of Lond & others in Commission) chosen me one of the three Surveyors of the repaires of Paules, & to consider a model for the new building, or (if it might be) repairing of the Steeple, which was most decayd: & so I returned home.

26 Contagion still continuing, we had the Church Office at home &c:

27 I went to St. Paules Church in Lond: where with Dr. Wren, Mr. Prat, Mr. May, Mr. Tho. Chichley, Mr. Slingsby, the Bish: of Lond., the Deane of S. Paule, & severall expert Workmen, we went about to survey the generall decays of that antient & venerable Church, & to set downe the particulars in writing, what was fit to be don, with the charge thereof: giving our opinion from article to article: We found the maine building to receede outward: It was Mr. Chichleys & Prats opinion that it had ben so built *ab origine* for an effect in Perspective, in reguard of the height; but I was with Dr. Wren quite of another judgement, as indeede ridiculous, & so we entered it: We plumbed the Uprights in severall places: When we came to the Steeple, it was deliberated whither it were not well enought to repaire it onely upon its old foundation, with reservation to the 4 Pillars: This Mr. Chichley & Prat were also for; but we totaly rejected it & persisted that it requird a new foundation, not onely in reguard of the necessitie, but for that the shape of what stood was very meane, & we had a mind to build it with a noble Cupola, a forme of church building, not as yet knowne in England, but of wonderfull grace: for this purpose we offerd to bring in a draught & estimate, which (after much contest) was at last assented to, & that we should nominate a Committè of able Workemen to examine the present foundation: This concluded we drew all up in Writing, and so going with with my L: Bishop to the Deanes, after a little refreshment, went home ...

September 2: This fatal night about ten, began that deplorable fire, neere Fish-streete in Lond:

2: I had pub: prayers at home: after dinner the fire continuing, with my Wife & Sonn took Coach & went to the bank side in Southwark, where we beheld that dismal speectaccle, the whole Citty in dreadfull flames neere the Water side, & had now consumed all the houses from the bridge all Thames Streete & up-wards towards Cheape side, downe to the three Cranes, & so returned exceedingly astonishd, what would become of the rest:

3 The Fire having continud all this night (if I may call that night, which was as light as day for 10 miles round about after a dreadfull manner) when consp<ir>ing with a fierce Eastern Wind, in a very drie season, I went on foote to the same place, when I saw the whole South part of the Citty burning from Cheape side to the Thames, & all along Cornehill (for it likewise kindled back against the Wind, as well <as> forward) Tower-Streete, Fen-church-streete, Gracious Streete, & so along to Bainard Castle, and was now taking hold of St. Paules-Church, to which the Scaffalds contributed exceedingly:

The Conflagration was so universal, & the people so astonish'd, that from the beginning (I know not by what desponding or fate), they hardly stirr'd to quench it, so as there was nothing heard or seene but crying out & lamentation, & running about like distracted creatures, without at all attempting to save even their goods; such a strange consternation there was upon them, so as it burned both in breadth & length, The Churches, Publique Halls, Exchange, Hospitals, Monuments, & ornaments, leaping after a prodigious manner from house to house & streete to streete, at greate distance one from the other, for the heate (with a long set of faire & warme weather) had even ignited the aire, & prepared the materials to conceive the fire, which devoured after a<n> incredible manner, houses, furniture, & everything: Here we saw the Thames coverd with goods floating, all the barges & boates laden with what some had time & courage to save, as on the other, the Carts &c carrying out to the fields, which for many miles were strewed with moveables of all sorts, & Tents erecting to shelter both people & what goods they could get away: ô the miserable & calamitous speectacle, such as happly the whole world had not seene the like since the foundation of it, nor to be out don, 'til the universal Conflagration of it, all the skie were of a fiery aspect, like the top of a burning Oven, & the light seene above 40 miles round about for many nights: God grant mine eyes may never behold the like, who now saw above ten thousand houses all in one flame, the noise & crakling & thunder of the impetuous flames, the shreeking of Women & children, the hurry of people, the fall of towers, houses & churches was like an hideous storme, & the aire all about so hot & inflam'd that at the last one was not able to approch it, so as they were force'd <to> stand still, and let the flames consume on which they did for neere two whole mile<s> in length and one in bredth: The Clowds also of Smoke were dismall, & reached upon computation neere 50 miles in length:

Thus I left it this afternoone burning, a resemblance of Sodome, or the last day: It call'd to mind that of 4 Heb: *non enim hic habemus stabilem Civitatem:*[1] the ruines resembling the picture of Troy: London was, but is no more: Thus I return'd:

4. The burning still rages; I went now on horse back, & it was now gotten as far as the Inner Temple, all Fleetestreete, old baily, Ludgate Hill, Warwick Lane, Newgate, Paules Chaine, Wattling-streete now flaming & most of it reduc'd to ashes, the stones of Paules flew like granados, the Lead mealting

---

[1] 'For here have we no continuing city.' *Hebrews*, correctly, XIII.14.

down the streetes in a streame, & the very pavements of them glowing with a
fiery rednesse, so as nor horse nor man was able to tread on them, & the
demolitions had stopped all the passages, so as no help could be applied; the
Easter<n> Wind still more impetuously driving the flames forewards: Nothing
but the almighty power of God was able to stop them, for vaine was the help of
man: on the fift it crossed towards White-hall, but ô the Confusion was then at
that Court:

It pleased his Majestie to command me among the rest to looke after the
quenching of fetter-lane end, to preserve (if possible) that part of Holborn,
whilst the rest of the Gent: tooke their several posts, some at one part, some at
another, for now they began to bestirr themselves, & not 'til now, who 'til now
had stood as men interdict, with their hands a crosse, & began to consider that
nothing was like to put a stop, but the blowing up of so many houses, as might
make a <wider> gap, than any had yet ben made by the ordinary method of
pulling them downe with Engines: This some stout Seamen proposd early
enought to have saved the whole Citty: but some tenacious & avaritious Men,
Aldermen &c. would not permitt, because their houses must have ben <of> the
first: It was therefore now commanded to be practised, & my conerne being
particularly for the Hospital of st. Bartholomeus neere Smithfield, where I had
many wounded & sick men, made me the more diligent to promote it; nor was
my care for the Savoy lesse: So as it pleased Almighty God by abating of the
Wind, & the industrie of people, now when all was lost, infusing a new Spirit
into them (& such as had if exerted in time undoubtedly preserved the whole)
that the furie of it began sensibly to abate, about noone, so as it came no
farther than the Temple West-ward, nor than the enterance of Smithfield
North; but continued all this day & night so impetuous toward Cripple-Gate,
& The Tower, as made us even all despaire; It also brake out againe in the
Temple: but the courage of the multitude persisting, & innumerable houses
blown up with Gunpowder, such gaps & desolations were soone made, as also
by the former three days consumption, as the back fire did not so vehemently
urge upon the rest, as formerly:

There was yet no standing neere the burning & glowing ruines neere a
furlongs Space; The Coale & Wood wharfes & magazines of Oyle, rozine,
[chandler] &c: did infinite mischiefe; so as the invective I but a little before
dedicated to his Majestie & publish'd,[1] giving warning what might probably
be the issue of suffering those shops to be in the Citty, was lookd on as
prophetic: but there I left this smoking & sultry heape, which mounted up in
dismall clowds night & day, the poore Inhabitans dispersd all about St.
Georges, Moore filds, as far as higate, & severall miles in Circle, Some under
tents, others under miserab<l>e Hutts and Hovells, without a rag, or any
necessary utinsils, bed or board, who from delicatnesse, riches & easy
accommodations in stately & well furnishd houses, were now reduc'd to
extreamest misery & poverty: In this Calamitous Condition I returnd with a
sad heart to my house, blessing & adoring the distinguishing mercy of God, to
me & mine, who in the midst of all this ruine, was like Lot, in my little Zoar,
safe and sound:

6 Thursday, I represented to his Majestie the Case, of the French Prisoners
at War in my Custodie, & besought him, there might be still the same care of
Watching at all places contiguous to unseized houses: It is not indeede
imaginable how extraordinary the vigilanc<e> & activity of the King & Duke
was, even labouring in person, & being present, to command, order, reward,

---

[1] *Fumifugium*, see above 14 September 1661.

and enourage Workemen; by which he shewed his affection to his people, & gained theirs: Having then disposed of some under Cure, at the Savoy, I return'd to white hall, where I dined at Mr. Offleys, Groome-porter, who was my relation, together with the Knight Martial, where I also lay that night.

7 I went this morning on foote from White hall as far as London bridge, thro the Late fleete streete, Ludgate hill, by St. Paules, Cheape side, Exchange, Bishopsgate, Aldersgate, & out to Morefields, thence thro Cornehill, &c: with extraordinary difficulty, clambring over mountaines of yet smoking rubbish, & frequently mistaking where I was, the ground under my feete so hott, as made me not onely Sweate, but even burnt the soles of my shoes, & put me all over in Sweate: In the meane time his Majestie got to the Tower by Water, to demolish the houses about the Graft,[1] which being built intirely about it, had they taken fire, & attaq'd the white Towre, where the Magazines of Powder lay, would undo<u>btedly have not onely beaten downe & destroyed all the bridge, but sunke & torne all the vessells in the river, & rendred the demolition beyond all expression for severall miles even about the Country at many miles distance: At my returne I was infinitly concern'd to find that goodly Chur<c>h St. Paules now a sad ruine, & that beautifull Portico (for structure comparable to any in Europ, as not long before repaird by the late King) now rent in pieces, flakes of vast Stone Split in sunder, & nothing remaining intire but the Inscription in the Architrave which shewing by whom it was built, had not one letter of it defac'd: which I could not but take notice of: It was astonishing to see what imense stones the heate had in a manner Calcin'd, so as all the ornaments, Columns, freezes, Capitels & proje<c>tures of massie Portland stone flew off, even to the very roofe, where a Sheete of Leade covering no lesse than 6 akers by measure, being totaly mealted, the ruines of the Vaulted roofe, falling brake into St. Faithes, which being filled with the magazines of bookes, belonging to the Stationer<s>, & carried thither for safty, they were all consumed burning for a weeke following: It is also observable, that the lead over the Altar at the East end was untouch'd; and among the divers monuments, the body of one Bishop, remained intire.

Thus lay in ashes that most venerab<l>e Church, one of the <antientest> Pieces of early Piety in the Christian world, beside neere 100 more; The lead, yronworke, bells, plate &c mealted; the exquisitely wrought Mercers Chapell, the Sumptuous Exchange, the august fabricque of Christ church, all the rest of the Companies Halls, sumptuous buildings, Arches, Enteries, all in dust. The fountaines dried up & ruind, whilst the very waters remained boiling; the Voragos of subterranean Cellars Wells & Dungeons, formerly Warehouses, still burning in stench & dark clowds of smoke like hell, so as in five or six miles traversing about, I did not see one load of timber unconsum'd, nor many stones but what were calcind white as snow, so as the people who now walked about the ruines, appeard like men in some dismal desart, or rather in some greate Citty, lay'd wast by an impetuous & cruel Enemy, to which was added the stench that came from some poore Creaturs bodys, beds & other combustible goods:

Sir Tho: Gresshams Statue, though falln to the ground from its nich in the R: Exchange remain'd intire, when all those of the Kings since the Conquest were broken to pieces: also the Standard in Cornehill, & Q: Elizabeths Effigies, with some armes on Ludgate continud with but little detriment, whilst the vast yron Chaines of the Cittie streetes, vast hinges, barrs & gates of Prisons were many of them mealted, & reduc'd to cinders by the vehement

---

[1] The Tower Moat.

heats: nor was I yet able to pass through any of the narrower streetes, but kept <to> the widest, the ground & aire, smoake & fiery vapour, continud so intense, my hair being almost seinged, & my feete unsufferably surbated: The bielanes & narrower streetes were quite fill'd up with rubbish, nor could one have possibly knowne where he was, but by the ruines of some church, or hall, that had some remarkable towre or pinacle remaining:

I then went towards Islington, & high-gate, where one might have seene two hundred thousand people of all ranks & degrees, dispersed, & laying along by their heapes of what they could save from the *Incendium*, deploring their losse, & though ready to perish for hunger & destitution, yet not asking one penny for reliefe, which to me appeard a stranger sight, than any I had yet beheld: His Majestie & Council indeeade tooke all imaginable care for their reliefe, by Proclamation, for the Country to come in & refresh them with provisions: when in the middst of all this Calamity & confusion, there was (I know not how) an Alarme begun, that the French & Dutch (with whom we were now in hostility) were not onely landed, but even entring the Citty; there being in truth, greate suspicion some days before, of those two nations joyning, & even now, that they had ben the occasion of firing the Towne:

This report did so terrifie, that on a suddaine there was such an uprore & tumult, that they ran from their goods, & taking what weapons they could come at, they could not be stop'd from falling on some of those nations whom they casualy met, without sense or reason, the clamor & perill growing so excessive, as made the whole Court amaz'd at it, & they did with infinite paines, & greate difficulty reduce & apease the people, sending Guards & troopes of souldiers, to cause them to retire into the fields againe, where they were watched all this night when I left them pretty quiet, & came home to my house, sufficiently weary & broken: Their spirits thus a little sedated, & the affright abated, they now began to repaire into the suburbs about the Citty, where such as had friends or opportunit<i>e got shelter & harbour for the Present; to which his Majesties Proclamation also invited them. Still the Plage, continuing in our parish, I could not without danger adventure to our Church.

10: I went againe to the ruines, for it was now no longer a Citty:

11 Sat at Star Chamber, on the 13, I presented his Majestie with a Survey of the ruines, and a Plot for a new Citty, with a discourse on it,[1] whereupon, after dinner, his Majestie sent for me into the Queenes Bed-chamber, her Majestie & the Duke onely present, where they examind each particular, & discoursed upon them for neere a full houre, seeming to be extreamly pleasd with what I had so early thought on: The Queene was now in her Cavaliers riding habite, hat & feather & horsemans Coate, going to take the aire; so I took leave of his Majestie & visiting the Duke of Albemarle, now newly return'd from Sea, I went home ...

29 Michaelmas-day, I went to visite my Bro: Richard, who was now indisposd in his health:

---

[1] *London Redivivum or London Restored.* The composition remained unpublished in E's lifetime but E submitted a further draft to the Royal Society. This was probably the version used by William Maitland in his 1756 *History of London from its Foundation to the Present Time.* An annotated version of this text was published by E.S. de Beer in 1938 and the full text with added notes is included in my *Writings of John Evelyn.* A copy of E's map can be found in Barker, F., and Jackson, P., 1990, *The History of London in Maps*, 36.

October 2: I gave my Bro: of Wotton a Visite, being myself also not well, & returnd the 4th, so as I entred into a Course of Steele, against the Scorbut:

10 This day was indicted a Generall fast through the nation, to humble us, upon the late dreadfull Conflagration, added to the Plage & Warr, the most dismall judgements could be inflicted, & indeede but what we highly deserved for our prodigious ingratitude, burning Lusts, profane & abominable lives, under such dispensations of Gods continued favour, in restoring Church, Prince, & people from our late intestine calamities, of which we were altogether unmindfull even to astonishment: This made me resolve to go to our Parish Assemblie, where our Doctor preached on 19 Luke: 41 &c: piously applying it to the occasion, after which followd a Collection for the poore distressed loose<r>s in the late fire, & their present reliefe ...

18 To Lond: Star-Chamber: thence to Court, it being the first time of his Majesties putting himselfe solemnly into the Eastern fashion of Vest, changing doublet, stiff Collar, [bands] & Cloake &c: into a comely Vest, after the Persian mode with girdle or shash, & Shoe strings & Garters, into bouckles, of which some were set with precious stones, resolving never to alter it, & to leave the French mode, which had hitherto obtained to our greate expense & reproch: upon which divers Courtiers & Gent: gave his Ma<jesty> gold, by way of Wager, that he would not persist in this resolution: I had some time before indeede presented an Invectique against that unconstancy, & our so much affecting the french fashion, to his Majestie in which <I> tooke occasion to describe the Comelinesse & usefullnesse of the Persian clothing in the very same manner, his Majestie clad himselfe; This Pamphlet I intituled *Tyrannus* or the mode, & gave it his Majestie to reade; I do not impute the change which soon happn'd to this discourse, but it was an identitie, that I could not but take notice of:[1]

This night was acted my Lord Brahals Tragedy cal'd Mustapha before their Majesties &c: at Court: at which I was present, very seldom at any time, going to the publique Theaters, for many reasons, now as they were abused, to an atheisticall liberty, fowle & undecent; Women now (& never 'til now) permitted to appeare & act, which inflaming severall young noble-men & gallants, became their whores, & to some their Wives, witnesse the Earle of Oxford, Sir R: Howard, Pr: Rupert, the E: of Dorset, & another greater person than any of these, who fell into their snares, to the reproch of their noble families, & ruine both of body & Soule: I was invited to see this Tragedie, exceedingly well writ, by my Lord Chamberlain, though in my mind, I did not approve of any such passe time, in a season of such Judgements & Calamitie: ...

21 Our Viccar on his former subject: This season (after so long & extraordinary a drowth in September, & Aug: as if preparatory for the dreadfull fire) was so very wett & rainy, as many feared an ensuing famine: ...

28 ... The Pestilence now through Gods mercy, began now to abate in our Towne considerably.

30 To Lond. to our Office, & now had I on the Vest, & Surcoate, or Tunic as 'twas cald, after his Majestie had brought the whole Court to it; It being a comely, & manly habite: to<o> good to hold, it being impossible for us to leave the Monsieurs Vanitys in good earnest long:

November 14 I went my Winter Circle through my district, Rochester & other places wher I had men quartered & in Custody:

---

[1] See note above for the 7 December 1661.

15. To Leedes Castle.

16 I musterd them being about 600 Dutch & French, ordred their proportion of Bread to be augmented, & provided cloths & fuell: Monsieur Colbert Ambassador at the Court of England, having also this day sent mony from his Master the French King to every Prisoner of that nation under my Guards: I lay at Chilston at my Co: Hales's.

17: I return'd to Chattham, my Charriot overturning on the steepe of Boxley-Hill, wounded me in two places in the head, but slightly, my sonn Jack being with me, & then but newly out of long Coates, was like to have ben Worse cutt, by the Glasse, of the Charriot dores, but I thank God, we both escaped without much hurt, though not without exceeding danger ...

23. I heard an extraordinary Case before a Committeè of the whole house of Commons, in the Commons house of Parliament, betweene one Cap: Taylor, & my Lord Vicount Mordaunt; where after the Lawyers had pleaded, & the Witnesses examin'd, such foule & dishonorable things were produced against his Lordship of Tyrannie during his goverment of Windsore Castle, of which he was Constable, Incontinence & suborning, of which last one Sir Rich: Breames was most concerned, that I was exceedingly concernd for his Lordship, who was my special friend, and husband of the most virtuous Lady in the world: We sate 'till neere ten at night, & yet but halfe the Council had don, on behalfe of the plaintife: The question then was put, for the bringing in of lights to sit longer, which lasted so long a time before it was determind, & raisd such a confused noise among the Members, that a stranger would have ben astonished at it: & I admire, that there is not a Rationale to regulate such trifling accidents, which yet I find consume a world of time, & is a reproch to the gravity of so greate an Assembly of sober men: ...

27: Sir Hugh Pollard, Comptroller of the household died at W: Hall, & his Majestie Conferred the White-Staffe on my bro: Commissioner for Sick & Wounded, on Sir Tho: Clifford, [since Lord high Tressurer of England] a bold young Gent: of a meane fortune in Devon: but advanc'd by my L: Arli<n>gton Sec: of State: to the greate astonishment of all the Court: This gent: was some what related to me, by the marriage of his mother, to my neerest Kindsman Greg: Coale, & was ever my noble friend; a valiant & daring person, but by no meanes fit for a soupple & flattering Courtier: ...

December 2 dind with me Monsieur Kiviet, a Dut<c>h Gent: Pensioner of Roterdam, who came over hither for protection, being of the Prince of Oranges party, now not well-come in Holland: The King knighted him for some merit in the princes behalfe: he should (if caught) have ben beheaded with Monsieur Buat, & was brother in Law to Van Tromp, the Sea Generall &c: with him came downe Mr. Gab: Sylvius, & Mr. Williamson, Secretarie to my L: Arlington: Sir Kiviet came downe to examine, whither the soile about the river of Thames would be proper to make Clinkar brick with & to treate with me about some accommodations in order to it:

9: To Lond: & returned the 14:[1]

30: Dr. Dolben deane of Westminster, & now made Bishop of Rochester our

---

[1] E's entry should be compared with Pepys for the same day (the 14th). Pepys evidently thought more of their meeting that day than E did, and recorded, '... So I to Westminster Hall, and there met my good friend Mr. Evelyn, and walked with him a good while, lamenting our condition for want of good council, and the King's minding of his business and servants ... staied in Westminster Hall till the rising of the

Diocese, preached at our Parish-Church his first sermon on 1. Tim: 3.16, of the wonder of our B:S: Incarnation &c: after sermon Confirmed many young children, solemnly prepar'd the weeke before, among whom my sonn John was bro<u>ght, and then his Lordship dined at my house.

1667

January 9 To the R: Soc:, which since the sad Conflagration, were now invited to sit at Arundel house in the strand, by Mr. Howard; who upon my instigation likewise bestowed on the Society that noble Library, which his Grandfath<er> especialy, & all his Ancesters had collected: this Gent: having so little inclination to bookes, that 'twas the preserving them from imbezilment: We had divers Experiments for improving Pendule Watches: & for winding up huge Springs by the force of powder; with an invention for the letting down, & taking up any Earth, Corall, or what ever it met with at the bottome of the sea &c: ...

24 Din'd at Sir Ph: Warwicks, visited my L: Chancelor, & presented my son John to him, now preparing to Go to Oxford, of which his Lordship was Chancelor: This Evening I heard rare Italian voices, 2 Eunuchs & one Woman, in his Majesties greene Chamber next his Cabinet: ...

29 To Lond: in order to my sonns Oxford Journey, who being very early entered both in the Lat: & Greeke, & prompt to learne beyond most of his age, I was perswaded to trust him under the tutorage of Mr. Bohune fellow of New Coll: who had ben his Præceptor in my house some years before; but at Oxford, under the inspection of Dr. Batthurst President of Trinity where I placed him: My son not as yet 13 yeares old:

30: ... Jack set out this day to Oxford with his Tutor:

February 7: My L: of Carlisle treated with me for the proposal of a marriage betweene his Eldest sonn, & my Nieece Ann Evelyn ...

13: Arundel house where Dr. Croone produced his Calesh or new invented Charriot, the Carriage a single deale board onely instead of the Pearch: his Majestie was well pleas'd with it as he told me this Evening: As to the Lamp: it was a Globe so order'd as just to counterpoise the oyle in it, so as it never sunk: The Globe shewing also by its revolution (as the oyle Wasted) the houre of the night &c ...

15 My little booke in answer to Sir Geo: Makenzys *Solitude*,[1] was now published: ...

19 Lond: star: cha: in the afternoone I saw a Wrestling-match for 1000 pounds in St. James's Parke before his Majestie &c: twixt the Western & Northern men: Mr. Secr: Morice & Lo: Gerard being the Judges; befor a world

---

house, having told Mr. Evelyn, and he several others, of my Gazette which I had about me that mentioned in April last a plot for which several were condemned of treason at the Old Bayly ...' Pepys does not appear in E's *Diary* until 10 June 1669, a few days after Pepys had ended his.

[1] *Publick Employment and an Active Life preferr'd to Solitude.* Pepys was unimpressed, 'I do not find much of good matter, though it be pretty for a bye discourse.' (*Diary*, 26 May 1667).

of Lords, & other Spectators. The Western-men won: <many> greate summs were abetted:

18 I saw a magnificent Ball or Masque in the Theater at Court, where their Majesties & all the greate Lords & Ladies daunced infinitely gallant: the Men in their richly imbrodred, most becoming Vests:

22 I began to be very feavorish, & so continued til the 24th, when letting blood, I grew better ...

March 10: ... Greate frosts, snow & winds, prodigious at the vernal aequinox; indeede it had hitherto ben a yeare of nothing but prodigies in this Nation: Plage, Ware, fire, raines, Tempest: Comets: ...

22 Dined at Mr. Secretarie Morices, who shewed me his Librarie, which was a well chosen Collection: I had this afternoone audience of his Majestie concerning the proposal I made of building the Key: & so return'd: ...

26 Sir John Kiviet dined with me, we went to search for brick-Earth, in order to a greate undertaking.

28: To Lond. at Ar<undel>: house the Society experimented the transfusion of bloud, out of one animal into another; it was successfully don out of a sheepe into a dog, 'til the sheepe died, the dog well, & was ordered to be carefully looked to ...

April 4 The cold so intense, as hardly a leafe on a tree ...

[23] In the morning his Majestie went to Chapell, with the Knights all in their habits, & robes, ushered by the Heraulds: After the first service they went in Procession, the youngest first, the Sovraigne last, with the Prelate of the Order, & Deane, who had about his neck the book of the Statutes of the Order, & then the Chancelor of the Order, (old Sir H: De Vic.) who wore the Purse about his: then Heraulds & Gartyr King at Armes, <Clarenceux>, Black-rod: but before the Praelate & Deane of Winsor, went the Gent: of Chapell, Choristers &c. singing as they marched, behind them two Doctors of Musick in damask robes: This proceeding was about the Courts of White-hall, then returning to their Stalles & Seates in the Chapell, placed under each knights coate armour, & Titles: Then began Second Service, then the King Offered at the Altar, an Anthem sung, then the rest of the knights offerd, & lastly proceeded to the Banqueting house to a greate feast: The King sate on an elevated Throne at the uper end, at a Table alone: The Knights at a Tab: on the right-hand reaching all the length of the roome; over against them a cuppord of rich gilded Plate &c: at lowere end the Musick; on the balusters above Wind musique, Trumpets & kettle drumms: The King was se<r>ved by the Lords, & pensioners, who brought up the dishes: about the middle of dinner, the Knights drank the Kings health, then the King theirs: Then the trumpets, musique &c: plaied & sounded, the Gunns going off at the Tower: At the banquet came in the Queene & stood by the Kings left hand, but did not sit: Then was the banqueting Stuff flung about the roome profusely: In truth the crow'd was so greate, that though I staied all the supper the day before, I now staied no longer than this sport began for feare of disorder: The Cheere was extraordinary, each knight having 40 dishes to his messe: piled up 5 or 6 high: The roome hung with the richest Tapissry in the World &c: ...

25. Visited againe the Duke of New-Castle, whom I had ben acquainted with long before in France, & had obligation to my Wives mother, for his marriage, there, That is his Dutchesse had, who was Sister to my L: Lucas, & maide of honor then to Q: Mother; married in our Chapel in Paris, & in gratitude had often & solemnly promis'd to give my wife 1000 pounds: but

now all was forgotten of that nature: My Wife being with me, the Duke & Dutchesse both would needes bring her to the very Court.

26. My Lord Chancellor shewed me all his newly finished & furnished Palace, & Librarie;[1] Then we went to take the aire in Hide-park:

27 I had a greate deale of discourse with his Majestie at dinner. Afternoone I went againe with my Wife to the Dutchesse of N. Castle, who received her in a kind of Transport: suitable to her extravagant humor & dresse, which was very singular; Then came in the Bish: of Winchester, my Lo: Percy, & so we came away, & returned home: ...

May 18 dined there, had buisinesse with L: Chancellor for Sir Ri: Browne now sick of the Gowt, returned home: My Son: John came with his Tutor to see me from Oxford: ...

June I went to Greenewich where his Majestie was trying divers Granados shot out of Cannon at the Castle hill, from the house in the Park: which broke not till they hit the mark; the forged ones brake not at all, but the Cast ones very well: The inventor was a Germane there present: At the same time was a ring shewed her Majestie pretended to be a projection of mercury & maleable, & said by the gent: to be fixed with the Juice of a Plant: ...

11: To Lond: alarm'd by the Dutch, who were falln on our Fleete, at Chattam by a most audacious enterprise entering the very river with part of their fleete, doing us not onely disgrace, but incredible mischiefe in burning severall of our best Men of Warr, lying at Anker & Moored there, & all this thro the unaccountable negligence of our negligence in setting out our fleete in due time: This alarme caused me (fearing the Enemie might adventure up the Thames even to Lond, which with ease they might have don, & fired all the Vessells in the river too) to send away my best goods, plate &c: from my house to another place; for this alarme was so greate, as put both my County and Citty in to a pan<i>que feare & consternation, such as I hope I shall never see more: for every body were flying, none <knew> why or whither: Now then were Land forces dispatched with Lord Duke of Albemarle, L: Midleton, Pr: Rupert & the Duke to hinder the Dut<c>h comming to Chattham, fortifying Upnore Castle, & Laying chaines & bombs, but the resolute Enemy brake through all, & set fire on our ships, & retreated in spight, stopping up the Thames, the rest of their Fleete lying before the mouth of it:

14: I went to see the Work at Woolwich, a batterie for to defend them from coming up to Lond: which Pr: Rupert commanded, & sunk some ships in the river ...

17 This night about 2 a clock, some chipps & combustible matter prepared for some fireships, taking flame, in Deptford yard, made such a blace, and caused such an uprore in the Towne, it being given out that the Dutch fleet were come up, & had landed their me<n>, & fired the Towne, as had like to have don much mischiefe before people would be perswaded to the Contrary, & believe the accident: every body went to their armes, & all my family alarm'd with the extraordinarie light, & confusion &c: These were sad, & troublesome times ...

24 I was before the Council (the Dutch fleete still continuing to stop up the river of Thames, so as nothing could stirr out, or come in) and commanded by his Majestie that I with some others, should search about the invirons of the Citty, now exceedingly distressed for want of fuell, whither there could be any

---

[1] See above 16 October 1664, and below 19 June 1683.

Peate or turfe, fit for use, could be found: & the next day I went, & found enough, & made my report, that there might be found a greate deale, &c: but nothing was now farther don in it:

So on the 28 I went to Chattham, and thence to view not onely what Mischiefe the Dutch had don, but how triumphantly their whole Fleete, lay within the very mouth of the Thames, all from North-foreland, Mergate, even to the Buoy of the Noore, a Dreadfull Spectacle as ever any English men saw, & a dishonour never to be wiped off: Those who advised his Majestie to prepare no fleete this Spring, deserv'd I know what! but -

Here in the river of Chattam, just before the Towne lay the Carkasse of the Lond: (now the 3d time burnt) the Royal Oake, the James &c yet Smoking, & now when the mischiefe was don, we were making trifling forts on the brink of the river: Here were yet forces both of horse & foote with Gen: Midleton, continualy expecting the motions of the Enemys fleete: I had much discourse with him, an experien<c>'d Commander: I told him I wondered the King did not fortifie Sheerenesse, [since don:] & the Ferry, both abandon'd: and so returned home: ...

July 2: Cald upon by my L: Arlington, as from his Majestie, about the new fuell; the occasion why I was mention'd, was from something I had said about a sort of fuell, for a neede, printed in my *Sylva* 3 yeares before, which obstructing a pattent my Lord Carlingford had ben seeking for himselfe; he was seeking to bring me into the project, & proffered me a share: I met my Lord, & on the 4th by an order of Council, went to my Lord Major, to be assisting: In the meane time, they had made an experiment of my receite of Houllies which I mention in my booke, to be made at Maastricht, with a mixture of charcoale dust & loame, which was tried with Successe at Gressham Colledge (which then was the Exchange, for meeting of the Merchants, since the fire of London) for every body to see: This don, I went to the Lords Commissioners of the Tressury about a supply of 12000 pounds for the Sick & Wounded yet on my hands: next day we met againe about the Fuell, at Sir Ja Armorers in the Mewes, & thence home ...

8 My Lord Brereton & severall gentlemen dined at my house, where I shewed them profe of my new fuell; which was very glowing, & without Smoke or ill Smell: ...

10: I went to se<e> Sir Samuel Morelands inventions & Machines, Arithmetical Wheele: Quench-fires, new harp: &c: returnd home ...

24 I went to Gravesend, (The Dutch fleete at anker still before the River) where I saw 5 ships of his Majesties men of Warr, encounter above 20 of the Dutch, in the bottome of the Hope, chacing them with many broad sides given & retur<n>ed, towa<r>ds the buoy of the Noore, where the body of the Fleete lay, which lasted til about midnight: There was one of their ships fired, suspected as don by the Enemie, she being run on high ground: having seene this bold action, & their braving us so far up the river, I went home the next day, not without indignation at our negligence & nations reproch: 'Tis well knowne who of the Commissioners of the Treasury gave advice that the charge of setting forth a Fleete this yeare, might be spared: Sir W<illiam>: C<oventry>: by name: ...

August 1 To Arundell house, thence home: where I received the sad newes of Abraham Cowlys death, that incomparable Poet, & Virtuous Man, my very deare friend and greately deplored &c: ...

3. Went to Mr. Cowleys funerall, whose Corps Lay at Wallingford house, & was thence conducted to Westminster Abby in an Hearse with 6 horses, & all funebral decency, neere an hundred Coaches of noble men & persons of qualitie following, among these all the Witts of the Towne, Divers Bishops & Cleargy men: &c. He was interred next Jeofry Chaucer & neere Spencer &c: [a goodly Monument since erected.] I returned home: ...

6 ... to the Lords Commissioners of the Tressury: gave accompt of the Souldiers under my care: The King discoursed with me much about swimming &c:

7: proceeded on my Accompt in Star-chamber: Dined at the middle Temple invited by my old friend Serjeant Barton, now Reader: Now did his Majestie againe dine in the Presence, in antient State, with Musique & all the Court ceremonies, which had ben interrupted since the late warr:

8: Home, by the way visiting Mr. Oldenburg now close Prisoner in the Tower, for having ben suspected to write Intelligence &c: I had an order from my L: Arlington secr: of state, which made me be admitted: this Gent: was Secretary to our Society, & will prove an innocent person I am confident: [Soon after released.] ...

20: To Lond: about the Executor ship of my Co:Tuke: There was now a very gallant horse to be baited to death with doggs, but he fought them all, so as the fiercest of them, could not fasten on him, till they run him thro with swords; This wiccked and barbarous sport, deserv'd to have ben published in the cruel Contrivers, to get mony, under pretence the horse had killed a man, which was false: I would not be perswaded to be a Spectator:

21 I dined at the V: Chancellor & afterwards attended the Lords Commissioners for mony: saw the famous Italian puppet play, for 'twas no other.

22 at Star Chamber: thence home: There was also now an Hermaphrodite shew'd both Sexes very perfectly, the Penis onely not perforated, went for a woman, but was more man, of about 21 yeares of Age: divers curious persons went to see her, but I would not:

24. I was appointed with the rest of my brother Commissioners to put in Execution an order of Council, for the freeing of the Prisoners of war at Leedes Castle, & taking off his Majesties extraordinary charge, having called before us the French & Dutch Agents: I returned, the Peace being now proclaimed according to usual forme by the Heraulds at Armes: Sir Sam: Moreland, Sir Jo: Kiviet & some others dining with me this joyfull day: ...

27: Visited L: Chancellor to whom his Majestie had sent for the Seales a few daies before: I found him in his bed Chamber very Sad: The Parliament had accused him, & he had enemies at Court, especialy the boufoones & Ladys of Pl<e>asure, because he thwarted some of them & stood in their way, I could name some of the chiefe, The truth is he made few friends during his grandure among the royal Sufferers, but advanced the old rebells, that had mony enough to buy places: he was however (though no considerable Lawyer,) one who kept up the forme & substance of things in the nation with more solemnity than some would have, & was my particular kind friend on all occasions: but the Cabal prevailed, & that ingredient in Parliament: Greate division in Court concerning him, & divers greate persons interceeding for him:

28 I dined with my Late L: Chancellor where dined also Mr. As<h>burnham, Mr W: Leg of the Bed Chamber, & his Lordship pretty well in heart, though now many of his friends & Sycophants abandon'd him: Afternoone I went againe to the Lords: Comm for mony; & thence to the Audience of a Russian Envoyè in the Queens Presence chamber: introduced with much State, the Souldiers, Pensionars, Guards in their order; his letter of

Credence brought by his Secretary in a Scarfe of Sarsenett; their vests Sumptuous much embroid<er>ed with pearle. He delivered his Speech in the Russe language alowd, but without the least action or motion of his body (besides his tongue) which was immediately interpreted alowd also by a German that Spake good English; halfe of it consisted in repetition of the Zarrs titles which were very haughty & oriental; & the substance of the rest, that he onely sent to see the King & Queene & know how they did &c: with much compliment & froth of Language, then they kissed their Majesties hands, & went as they came: but their real errand was to get mony:

29 We now met at Star: Cham: about exchange & release of Prisoners, I dined with the Maides of honour, & so late home: ...

September 13 'Twixt the houres of 12 and one at night, was borne my second daughter[1] ...

17: My Daught<e>r was Christned Elizabeth by my Sister Evelyn, A: Pretyman, & Sir R: Bro: her Grandfather by Dr. Breton our Viccar, in my house at Says Court: ...

19 To Lond: & with Mr. Hen: Howard of Norfolck: of whom I obtained the gift of his Arundelian Marbles, Those celebrated & famous Inscriptions Greeke and Latine, with so much cost & Industrie gathered from Greece, by his Illustrious Grandfather the magnificent Earle of Arundel, Thomas E. Marishall of England, my noble friend whilst he lived: These precious Monuments, when I saw miserably neglected, & scattred up & downe about the Gardens & other places of Arundell-house, & how exceedingly the corrosive aire of London impaired them, I procured him to bestow on the Universite of Oxford; This he was pleasd to grant me, & now gave me the Key of the Gallery, with leave to marke all those stones, Urnes, Altars &c: & whatever I found had Inscriptions on them that were not Statu<e>s: This I did, & getting them removed & piled together, with those which were incrusted in the Garden walles, I sent immediately letters to the Vice-Chancelor what I had procured, & that if they esteemed it a service to the University (of which I had ben a Member) they should take order for their transportation: ...

21. I accompanied Mr. Howard to his Villa at Alburie, where I designed for him the plat[2] for his Canale & Garden, with a Crypta thro the hill &c:

October 8 Came to dine with me Dr. Bathurst Deane of Wells, Pres: of Trinity Coll, & sent by the Vice Chancelor of Oxon: in the name of both him, & the whole University, to thanke me for procuring the Inscriptions, & to receive my directions what was to be don, to shew their gratitude to Mr. Howard &c.

10: To Lond: dined with the Swedish Resident: where was a disection of a dog, the poore curr, kept long alive after the Thorax was open, by blowing with bellows into his lungs, & that long after his heart was out, & the lungs both gashed & pierced, his eyes quick all the while: This was an experiment of more cruelty than pleased me:

11 I visited Lo: Arlington, ill of a fall: Afternoone I went to see my Lord Clarendon (late L: Chancelor, & great<e>st Officer in England) in continual apprehension what the Parliament would determine concerning him, upon divers Articles exhibited of his mal-Administration: returned home: ...

---

[1] Elizabeth Evelyn (1667-85). She eloped in 1685 but died soon afterwards from smallpox, see 27 July 1685, and entries for August 1685.

[2] Plot.

25 Were delivered to me two Letters, from the Vice-Chancelor of Oxford with the Decree of the Convocation, attested by the Publique Notarie, ordering <four> Doctors of Divini<t>y & Law to accknowledge the obligation the Universite had to me (the originals whereoff I keepe) for procuring the *Marmora Arundeliana*, which was solemnly don, by Dr. Barlow Provost of Queens: [since B: of Lincoln] Dr. Jenkins Judge of the Admiralty, [since Secretary of State] Dr. Lloyd, Obadia Walker of University Coll: [since head of that Coll:] who having made me a large Compliment from the University, delivered me the Decree ...

31. I was this day 47 yeares of age: Blessed <be> God for his mercys: I went to Lond: dined with my Bro: made the Royal Society a present of the Table of Veines, Arteries & Nerves which with greate Curiositie I had caused to be made in Italy, out of the natural humane bodies, by a learned Physit: & the help of Vestlingius professor at Padoa, from where I brought them 1646,[1] for which I received the publique thanks of the Society, & are hanging up in their Repositary; with an Inscription; I lay this night at Arundell house: ...

December 9: To Lond: to visite my late Lord Chancelor, I found him in his Garden at his new built Palace sitting in his Gowt wheel chayre, & seeing the Gates towards the North & fields setting up: he looked & spake very disconsolately, after some while deploring his condition to me, I tooke my leave, & the next morning heard he was gon: though I am perswaded had he gon sooner, though but to Cornbery & there lay quiet, it would have satisfied the Parliament: That which exasperated them was his presuming to stay, & contest the Accusation as long as twas possible, & that they were upon the point of sending him to the Tower &c: ...

21 I saw one Carr Piloried at Charing-Crosse for libelling, which was burnt before him by the Hangman, dined in the Citty, returned home:

1668

January 8: Wednesday I saw deepe & prodigious gaming at the Groome-porters, vast heapes of Gold squandered away in a vaine & profuse manner: This I looked on as an horrid vice, & unsuitable to a Christian Court: ...

15 Petition'd the Lords Commissioners of the Treasury, about the Enlargement of my Back-yard at Sayes Court ...

24: We went to stake out ground for the building a Colledge for the R: Society at Arundel house, but did not finish it, which we shall repent of: ...

February 4: To Lond: This Evening I saw the Trajedie of Horace (written by the virtuous Mrs. Philips) acted before their Majesties: 'twixt each act a Masque & Antique: daunced: The excessive galantry of the Ladies was infinite, Those especialy on that ...[2] Castlemaine esteemed at 40000 pounds & more: & far out shining the Queene &c:[3] ...

---

[1] See above, January 1646.

[2] This is E's gap, presumably to denote some derogatory term such as 'strumpet', or 'whore', which he could not bring himself to write down. But see 2 April 1668 below.

[3] Despite the note above E appears to be indicating that he thought the Countess

March 3. Was launched at Deptford that goodly Vessel the Charles: I was now neere his Majestie, she is longer than the Sovraine, & carries 110 brasse Canon: built by old Shish, a plained honest Carpenter (Master builder of this Dock) yet one that can give very little account of his art by discourse, as hardly capable to reade, yet of greate abilitie in his calling: They <have> ben Ship-Carpenters in this Yard above 100 yeares: ...

April 2 To the R: Society where I subscribed 50000 bricks, towards the building of a Coll: Amongst other Libertine Libells, there was now printed & thrown about a bold Petition of the poore Whores, to the Lady Castlemaine &c: I came home ...

9: Lond: about buisinesse, namely the finishing my grand Accompt of the Sick & Wounded & Prisoners at War, amounting to above 34000 pounds: ...

24 I transferred 500 pounds to Signor Palavicini in the East India Comp: as part of his Wifes Portion, in which I was a Trusteè: for her Mother I heard Sir R: Howard impeach Sir William Pen in the H. of Lords, for breaking bulk, & taking a way rich goods out of the E. India Prizes formerly taken by my L: Sanwich: ...

28 Lond: being now about the Purchase of Ravensbourn Mills & Land, about it in upper Deptford, of one Mr. Beecher &c.

May 6. To Lond: to transfer a Mortgage to my Bro: Geo: Evelyn, returned next day: ...

13 Invited by that expert Commander Cap: Cox (Master of the lately built *Charles the 2d*, & now best vessell of the fleet) design'd for the Duke of York; I went to Erith, where we had a greate dinner: I return'd in the Evening: ...

June 19. To a new play, with severall of my Relations, the *Evening Lover*, a foolish plot, & very prophane, so as it afflicted me to see how the stage was degenerated & poluted by the licentious times: ...

July <5> ... Sir Sam: Tuke Baronet & the Lady he had married but this day came & beded her at night at my house, many friends accompanying the Bride:

10: I went to Lond: 11 about petitioning his Majestie to enlarge my Court with a small slip of Land out of the brick-Close: returnd: ...

23. Went to R: Society, where were presented divers *Glossa Petra's*,[1] & other natural Curiosities, found in digging to build the fort at Sheere-Nesse, they were just the same, <as> what the<y> bring from Malta, pretending them to have ben Vipers teeth, whereas they are in truth of a Shark: as we found by comparing them to one in our Repository: home this Evening: ...

August 14 His Majestie was pleased to grant me a lease of a slip of ground out of Brick-Close, to enlarge my fore Court; for which I now gave him thanks; & then entering into other discourse, he talked to me of a new Invention of a

---

attractive. Pepys was certainly impressed and dreamed about her 'the best that ever was dreamed - which was, that I had my Lady Castlemayne in my armes and was admitted to use all the dalliance I desired with her ...' (Pepys's *Diary*, 15 August 1665).

[1] 'Shiny stones', in this context fossil teeth.

Vernish for ships, instead of Pitch, and of the Guilding with which his new
Yacht was beautified with all: I also shewed his Majestie the Perpetual motion
sent me by Dr. Stokes from Collen, and then came in Monsieur Colbert the
French Ambass: &c:

19 I saw the magnificent Entrie of the Fr: Ambassador Colbert received in
the Banqueting house: I had never seene a richer coach than what he came in
to Whitehall. Standing by his Majestie at dinner in the Presence, There was of
that rare fruite called the King-Pine, (growing in Barbados & W. Indies), the
first of them I had ever seen; His Majestie having cut it up, was pleasd to give
me a piece off his owne plate to tast of, but in my opinion it falls short of those
ravishing varieties of deliciousnesse, describ'd in Cap: Liggons history &
others; but possibly it might be, (& certainely was) much impaired in coming
so farr: It has yet a gracefull accidity, but tasts more of the Quince and Melon,
than of any other fruite he mentions: ...

28 To Lond: Publishd my booke of the Perfection of *Painting*,[1] dedicated to
Mr. Howard: after other buisinesse, return'd the 29: ...

September 17: I entertained Signor Muccinigo The Venetian Ambassador &
one of the noblest families of that State, this being the day of making his
Publique Enterie, setting forth from my house, with severall Gent: of Venice
& others in a very glorious traine: With me he staied til the Earle of Anglesea,
Sir Cha: Cotterell (Master of the Ceremonies) &c came with the Kings Barges
to carry him to the Tower, where the Gunns went off at his Landing, & then
entered his Majesties Coach, follow'd by many others of the nobility: I
accompanied him to his house, where there was a most noble Supper to all the
Companie of six Courses: After the extraordinarie Compliment to me & my
Wife for the civilities he receiv'd at my house, I tooke leave of his Excellency
& return'd: he is a very much accomplish'd person: [since Ambassador at
Rome.] ...

November 14 To Lond ... went to a most sumptuous dinner in the hall, where
was the Duke of Buckingham, Judges, Secretaries of State, Lord Keeper,
Counsell, Noblemen, & such an infinity of other Companie, as were honourers
of this incomparable man, the most universaly beloved of all that knew him:
This being her Majesties Birthday, greate was the galantrie at White-hall, and
the night celebrated with very fine fireworks &c:

My poore Bro: continuing ill, I went not from him til the 17th: when dining
at the Groome Porters, I heard Sir Edw: Sutton play excellently on the Irish-
harp: & indeede plaies gently, but not approaching my worthy friend Mr.
Cleark a Gent of Northumberland, who makes it exceeding Lute, Viol, & all
the harmonie an Instrument is capable of, pitty 'tis that is not more in use: but
indeede to play well, it takes up the whole man, as Mr. Clark assur'd me, who
tho a Gent: of Quality & parts, was yet brought up to that Instrument from 5
Yeares old, as I remember he told me: ...

---

[1] *An Idea of the Perfection of Painting: Demonstrated From the Principles of Art, and
by Examples conformable to the Observations, which Pliny and Quintilian have made
upon the most celebrated Pieces of the Ancient Painters, Parallel'd with some Works
of the most famous Modern Painters* ... Written in French By Roland Fréart, Sieur de
Chambray, And rendred English By J.E. Esquire, Fellow of the Royal Society.

27. I dined at my Lord Ashleys [since Earle of Shaftsbury & L. Chan:] where the Match of my Niepce was proposed, for his onely sonn, in which my assistance was desired for my Lord: ...

30: St. Andrews Day we chose Officers at the R: Society, & I of the Council for this yeare; We dined together, the King sending us Venison: ...

December 17 At the Ro: Society, some experiments about the Principle of Motion, viz. Elastic, & that where was not spring, there could be no motion; tried by a pendule ball of solid Glasse, vibrating against wyre strings & catts-gutts; it making a much greater & quicker rebound from the Wyre, than from the fiddle strings, t<h>o equaly stretched: & died suddanly against wood, or Yron, where there was no Spring:

19. I went to see the old play Cataline acted, having ben now forgotten 40 yeares almost:[1] ...

20: ... I dined with my Lord Cornbury at Clarendon house, now bravely furnish'd; especialy with Pictures of most of our Antient & Modern Witts, Poets, Philosophers famous & learned English-men, which Collection of my L: Chancelors, I much commended, and gave his Lordship a Cataloge of more to be added: ...

1669

January 29 I went to see a tall gigantic Woman, that measured 6 foote 10 Inches hight, at 21 years old, the rest proportionable, borne at the Busse in the Low Countries:

February 5 home by Water, & our Whirrie running <thwart> an hauser,[2] I was like to be drawne over board: but blessed by God, I <e>scaped: ...

13 I presented his Majestie with my *Historie of the foure Imposters*,[3] he told me of other like cheates: gave my booke to L: Arlington to whome I dedicated it &c: It was now he began to tempt me about writing the Dutch-Warr &c: ...

March 18, I went with my L: Howard of Norfolk to visite Sir William Ducy at Charleton,[4] where we dined: The servants made our Coach-men so drunk, that they both fell-off their boxes upon the heath, where we were faine to leave them, & were droven to Lond: by two Gent: of my Lords: This barbarous Costome of making their Masters Wellcome, by intoxicating the Servants had now the second time happn'd to my Coachman: My sonn came from Oxon: for altogether: ...

---

[1] *Catiline his Conspiracy*, by Ben Johnson, first performed in 1611.

[2] E's boat became entangled with a mooring rope.

[3] 'Foure' is E's error - the full title is *The History of the Three late famous Imposters, viz. Padre Ottomano, Mahomed Bei, and Sabati Sevi ... together with the Cause of the Final Extirpation, Destruction and Exile of the Jews out of the Empire of Persia.*

[4] At Charlton House (built 1607). It survives intact and is now a community centre owned by the London Borough of Greenwich.

April 1 At R: Soc: an handsome discourse touching the pulse of the bloud &c: There was a Lobster discected:

2 Din'd at Mr. Tressurer where was my L: Newport Comptroller, L. Asshley, Lauderdaill, Bishop of Chester, Coll: Titus of the bedchamber (author of that famous piece against Crom-well, *Killing no Murder*) & other greate persons: I now placed Mr. Wase,[1] with Mr. Williamson Secretary to the secretary of state, & Cleark of the Papers:

May 19 To Lond: next day at a Council of the R: Society our Graunt was finished in which his Majestie gives us Chelsey Colledge & some Land about it: & it was ordered that five should be a quorum for a Council: There were then also Sworne the Vice-President the first time: & It was also then proposed how we should receive the Prince of Tuscanie, who desired to visite the Society.

20 This Evening returning, I found my Wife in Labour, but was delivered within an houre at 10 a clock at night, being Ascention day, when was borne my third Daughter[2] ...

25 Was baptisd my Daughter Susanna (by the name of her Godmother her Aunt Hungerford of Cadenam): Godfather her Grandfather Sir R: Browne ...

June 10: Came my Lord Cornbery, Sir William Poultny & others to visite me; I went that evening to Lond: to carry Mr. Pepys to my Bro: (now exceedingly afflicted with the Stone in the bladder) who himselfe had ben successfully cut; & carried the Stone (which was as big as a tenis-ball) to shew him, and encourage his resolution to go thro the operation[3] ...

30 ... My Wife being gon on a journey of Pleasure downe the River as far as the Sea, with Mrs. Howard, & her daughters the Maids of Honor, amongst whom, that excellent creature Mrs. Blagge: I now built the long wall which separates my Court from the brick-close, newly granted me of the King: ...

July 7 I went towards Oxford, lay at little Wicckam ...

9 In the morning was celebrated the *Encenia*[4] of the New Theater so magnificently built by the munificence of Dr. Gilbert Sheldon Arch-Bishop of Canterbery, in which was spent 25000 pounds, (as Sir Chr: Wren the Architect as I remember told me) & yet was never seene by the Benefactor, my L: A

---

[1] Christopher Wase (c.1625-90), related to Lady Browne. He is said to have composed E's son Richard's epitaph (see above 27 January 1658). E thought him an 'incomparable Interpreter' (*Sylva*, 1664, 73, or my edition of *The Writings of John Evelyn*, 279).

[2] Susanna Evelyn, afterwards Draper (1669-1754). Unlike her sisters she survived smallpox and was the only one of E's eight children born alive to outlive him. She married William Draper of Addiscombe, see below, 27 April 1693. There are a number of living descendants of this marriage.

[3] This is E's first reference to Samuel Pepys. The men were already well-known to one another through E's association with naval affairs and Pepys's job as Clerk of the Acts at the Navy Office. Pepys's *Diary* makes this clear with several references to social and business occasions when they met. Pepys, ironically, had closed his *Diary* ten days before on 31 May and thus we are deprived of separate descriptions by the two greatest diarists of the age of each other on the same occasion.

[4] A dedicatory festival of inauguration.

Bish: having upon occasion told me, that he never did, nor never would see it. It is in truth a fabrique comparable to any of this kind of former ages, and doubtlesse exceeding any of the present, as this Universitie dos, for Colledges, Libraries, Scholes, students & Order all the Universities in the World:

To the Theater is <joined> the famous [Sheldonian] Printing-house: This being at the Act, and the first time of opening the Theater (Acts being formerly kept in St. Maries-Church, which might be thought undecent, as being soly set a part for the immediate worship of God, & was the inducement of building this noble Pile) it was now resolv'd, to celebrate its dedication with the greatest splendor & formalitie that might be, & therefore drew a world of strangers & other Companie to the University from all parts of the Nation: The Vice-Chancelor then, Heads of Houses, & Doctors being seated in magisterial seates, the Vice-Chancellors Chaire & Deske, Proctors &c: covered with Brocatell & Cloth of Gold: the Universitie Register read the Founders Grant & gift of it to the Universitie, for their Scholastic Exercises upon these solemn occasions: Then follow'd Dr. South the Universities Orators Eloquent Speech upon it; it was very long, & not without some malicious & undecent reflections on the Royal Society as underminers of the University, which was very foolish and untrue, as well as unseasonable, (but to let that passe, from an ill natured man) the rest was in praise of the Arch Bish: and the ingenious Architect: This ended, after loud Musique, from the Corridor above, (where was placd an Organ) there follow'd divers Panegyric Speeches both in Prose & Verse interchangeably pronounc'd by the young students, plac'd in the *Rostrum, Suggestum, Plutea's* &c Some in *Pindarics, Ecclogas, Heroics* &c: mingled with excellent Musique both vocal, & Instrumental to entertaine the Ladys &c: then was a spech made in praise of Academical Learning; all of which lasted from 11 in the morning till 7 at night, which was likewise concluded with Bells ringing, & universal joy & feasting.

10 The next day began the more solemn Lectures in all the Faculties which were perform'd in their several Scholes, where all the Inceptor Doctors did their Exercises, the Professors having first ended their reading: The Assembly now return'd to the Theater, the *Terræ filius*[1] or Universitie bouffoone, entertaind the Auditorie with a tedious, abusive, sarcastical rhapsodie, much unbecoming the gravity of the Universitie, & that so grossly, as that unlesse it be suppress'd, will be of ill consequence, as I plainly expressed my sense, both to the Vice Chancelor and severall heads of houses afterwards, who were perfectly ashamed of it, and resolv'd to take care of it for the future, for they had left the facetious old way of raillying upon the Questions: &c & fell wholy upon persons; so as in good earnest 'twas rather licentious lying, & railing than genuine & noble witt: In my life I was never witnesse of so shamefull entertainement. After this ribauldry, The Proctors made their Speeches:

Then began the Musick Act, Vocal, & Instrumental, above in the Balustred Corridore, opposite to the Vice-Chancelors seate: Then Dr. Wallis the Mathematical Professor made his Oration, and created one Doctor of Musique, according to the usual Ceremonies, of Gowne (which was white Damask) Cap: Ring, kisse &c: Next follow'd the Disputation of the Inceptor Doctors in Medicine, the Speech of their Professor Dr. Hyde, & so in Course their respective Creations: Then Disputed the Inceptors of Law, the Speech of their Professor & Creation: Lastly, Inceptors in Theologie, Dr.Compton (bro: to the Earle of Northampton) being Junior began, with greate modesty, & applause: & so the rest: After which Dr. Tillotson, Dr. Sprat &c: & then Dr. Alestreès

---

[1] 'Son of the Earth.'

(the Kings Professors) Speech, & their respective Creations: Last of all the Vice-Chancelors shuting up all in a Panegyrical Oration celebrating their Benefactor, & the rest apposite to the occasion: Thus was the Theater Dedicated by the Scholastic Exercises in all the faculties with infinite solemnity, & the night (as the former) entertaining the new Doctors friends, in feasting & Musique: I being invited by Dr. Barlow, the worthy & learned Provost of Queenes Coll: ...

11 The Act Sermon was this forenoone preach'd by Dr. Hall in St. Marie's in an honest practical discourse against Atheisme on Rom. In the afternoone, the Church was so crowded, that coming not so early, I could not approch to heare: ...

13 I dined on Tuesday at the V. Chancelors, & spent the afternoone in seeing the rarities of the Pub: Librarie, & visiting the noble Marbles & Inscriptions now inserted in the Walles that compasse the Area of the Theater, which were 150 the most antient, and worthy treasure in the Learned World of that kind, procur'd by me for them some time before: now observing that people, approaching them too neere, some Idle people began to Scratch and injure some of them, I advis'd that an hedge of holly, should be planted at the foote of the wall, to be kept breast-high onely, to protect them, which the V: Chancelor promisd to see don the next season:

14 Came Dr. Fell (Deane of Christchurch) Vice-Chancellor, [now Bish: of Oxon] with Dr. Alestree, K<ing>s Professors; Beadles & Maces before them, to Visite me at my Lodging: Then I went to Visite My L: Howards sonns at Magdalen Coll: who also repaied me theirs:

[15] Having two daies before notice that the Universitie intended me the honor of Doctor-ship, I was this morning attended by the Beadles belonging to the Law, who carried me to the Theater, where I found the Duke of Ormond (now Chancelor of the Universitie,) with the Earle of Chesterfild, & Mr.Spencer brother to the late Earle of Sunderland: Thence we marched to the Convocation house, a Convocation having ben cald on Purpose: Here being all of us rob'd in Scarlet, with Caps & hoods &c: in the Porch, we were led in by the Professor of Laws, & presented respectively by name & a short elogie &c: to the Vice-Chancelor who sate in the Chaire, with all the Doctors & heads of houses & Masters about the roome, which was exceeding full: Then began the Publique Orator, his speech, directed chiefly to the Chancelore, the Duke of Ormond, in which I had also my Compliment in Course: This ended, we were called up, and Created Doctors according to the forme, and seated by the Vice-Chancelor amongst the Doctors, on his right hand: Then made the Vice-Chancelor a short spech, & so saluting our Bro: Doctors the Pageantry concluded, & the Convocation desolved: So formal a Creation of Honorarie Doctors, had seldome ben seene, that a Convocation should be cald on purpose, & Speeches made by the Orator &c: But they could do no lesse, their Chancelor being to receive, or rather do them this honour: I had ben made Doctor with the rest at the Publique Act; but their expectation of the Duke their Chancelor made them deferr it; so I was led with my Bro: Doctors, to an extraordinary Entertainement at Dr. Mewes, head of St. Johns Coll: & after aboundance of feasting & complements, having visited the V: Chancelor & other Doctors & given them thanks for the honours don me, [16] I went towards home the next day, & got as far as Windsor, & to my house [17] the next ...

27 I went to see my poor afflicted Bro: at Woodcot, returnd that evening: ...

August 4. I was invited by Sir Hen. Peckham to his Reading feast Mid: Temp: a pompous Entertainement: where was the A Bish: of Cant: all the greate Earles & Lords &c: I had much discourse with my Lo: Winchelsea, a prodigious talker; and the Venetian Ambassador Signor Moccinigo, whom I was acquainted with, a very fine Gent: at night I went home: ...

17: To Lond: spending almost the intire day in surveying what progresse was made in rebuilding the ruinous Citty, which now began a little to revive, after its sad calamitie:

23 I went to visite my most excellent & worthy neighbour, the L. Bish: of Rochester at Bromely, which he was now repairing, after the dilapidations of the late rebellion, returned after dinner:

29 ... I was this day very ill, of a paine in my limbs: which continued most of this weeke, & was increased, by a visite I made [September] to my old acquaintance the Earle of Norwich, at his house in Epping forest: There are many very good pictures, put into the Wainscot of the roomes, which Mr.Baker his Lordships predecessor there, brought out of Spaine: especialy the Historie of Joseph: The Gardens were well understood, I meane the Pottagere: here is also an excellent picture of the pious & learned Picus Mirandula &c & one of old Breugle incomparable: I return'd late [in] the Evening, ferrying over at Grenewich:

September <5> My Indisposition hindred me from Church, & B: Sacrament to my greate sorrow.

7 I let bloud, purged, drew blisters, but Leaches did me most good exceedingly pa<i>ned with my Teeth: ...

26 To Church to give God thanks for my recovery: ...

October 21. To the Ro: Society meting now the first time after a long recesse during Vaccation, according to costome: where were red many letters from our Philosophical Correspondents; also a Map, and description of the prodigious irruption & Incendium of Ætna, together with a large box of the severall materials, mettals, cinders, salts, &c: throwne out of that mountain which burnt in a flowing river of Sulphur 30 miles in Length & 12 in bredth, as far as Catanea & even into the sea it selfe, a greater eruption never was recorded in any historie: Sir <Robert> Southwell likewise presented Balsomes & other Curiosities out of Portugal: & our English Itinerant an account of his Autumnal peregrination about England (for which we hired him) of dried foules, Fish, Plants, Animals &c: ...

29: Afternoone at the R: Society, where was produc'd Mr. Hooks pendule Clock going 12 moneths to a second as affirm'd: proposals were now made, for the more accurate measuring a Degree in the Earth, from that in the heavens: There was shew'd also a stain'd Wollan Cloth in imitation of Tapissry, as also a relation of the Salt-pits at Namptwich: My deare Brother continued extreamely full of paine: the Lord be gracious to him: ...

November 14: went home (having ben the night before at the funeral of Mrs Pepys:[1] &c:)

---

[1] Elizabeth Pepys (1640-69), wife of the diarist, at St. Olave's, Hart Street. She had been taken ill in Flanders while travelling with her husband in autumn 1669, and died on 10 November shortly after their return.

December 8: To Lond: upon the second Edition of my *Sylva*, which I presented to the R: Society[1] ...

1670

January 7: so extraordinary a storme of wind, as had seldome ben known, that did much harme: all over the nation almost: ...

26 I had much discourse with the Venetian Ambassador concerning the excessive Cold weather they often had in Italy, & especialy this Winter &c: ...

March 3 Finding my brother in such exceeding torture, & that he now began to fall into Convulsion fits, [4] I solemnly set the next-day a part, to beg of God to mitigate his sufferings, & prosper the onely meanes which yet remained for his recovery; or if otherwise; that it would please Almighty God to prepare him for himselfe, he not onely being very much wasted, but exceedingly, & all along averse from being cut, which he was advised to undergo from time to time, with extraordinary probability of successe: but when it came to the operation, & all things prepared, his spirit & resolution failed, & there was now lesse hopes than ever.

5. I went to visite my poore afflicted brother, whom I found almost in the last agonies:

6 Dr. Patric in Covent Garden Church, on his former Text. I participated of the blessed Sacrament, recommending the deplorable condition of my bro: his agonies still increasing: In the Afternoone, a stranger made an excellent sermon against Atheists: &c. I watched late with my Bro: this night, yet not imagining his end to be so neere; but so it pleased God, to deliver him out of this miserable life, towards five this moneday morning, to my unspeakeable griefe & sorrow, being a Bro: whom I most dearely loved for many Virtues; & that was but two yeares Younger than my-selfe, a sober, prudent, & worthy Gent: he had married a great fortune, and left one onely daughter, & a most noble seate, at Woodcot neere, Epsom in Surrey &c:

7: I staied all the next day to comfort my sister in Law, his Wife:

8 On Tuesday he was ordred to be opened; but it was not a specctacle I desir'd to be present at; & therefore returned home this evening full of sadnesse, & to bemoane my losse:

10: To Lond: My Bro: being opened, a stone was taken out of his bladder, not much bigger than a nutmeg, somewhat flatt, & oval, not sharp, one part excepted, which was a little rugged: but his Livar so faulty, that in likelyhood <it could not> have lasted much longer, and his kidnis almost quite consum'd: all of this doubtlesse the effects of his intollerable paine proceeding from the stone: & that perhaps by his drinking too excessively of Epsom Waters, when in full health, & that he had no neede of them, being all his lifetime of a sound & healthy constitution, &c: I returnd, & came up againe to visite my sister, & being one of the Overseeres of the Will, to order about the funeral, which kept me in towne 'til the 12th ...

18 To Lond: In order to my deare Bro: funeral ...

21. We all accompanied the Corps of my deare Bro: to Epsome Church, where he was decently interred in the Chapell belonging to Woodcot his

---

[1] The actual books bear the date 1670.

house: There were a greate number of Friends & gent: of the Country & innumerable people, about 20 Coaches of six-horses; so as yet we return'd to Lond: that night, somewhat late.

22: I went to Westminster where in the house of Lords, I saw his Majestie on his Throne, but without robes; all the Peeres sitting also with their hatts on: The buisinesse of the day being about the Divorce of my Lord Rosse: such an occasion & sight had not ben seene in England since Hen: 8th ...

May 26: Came my Bro: Geo: Evelyn & Niepce Marie my God-daughter to dine with me. This afternoone receiving a letter from Phil: Howard [since Cardinal of Norfolk] Lord Almoner to the Queene that Monsieur Evelin (first Physitian to Madame, who was now come to Dover to visite the King her brother) was come to Lond: greately desirous to see me, & his stay so short, that he could not come to me; I went with my Bro: to meete him at the Toure of Lond: where he was seeing the Magazine and other Curiosities, having never ben before in England: There was with him the Marishal de Plessis Prasline, & the Bishop of Tournon his Bro: where we re-newed our aliance & friendship, with much regret on both sides that being that Evening to returne towards Dover, we could enjoy one another no longer: How this French Familie Ivelin of Eveliniere, their familie in Normandie, & of a very antient & noble house is grafted into our Pedegree; see in your Collection, brought from Paris 1650.[1] &c: ...

June 5 ... My son John, having ben at Dover to see the intervieu of Madame & his Majestie & accompanied that Court at her returne into France, as far as Calais, was now come home:

9 To Lond: return'd: There was this day produced in the R: Society, an invention by intromitting the Species into a dark large box, to take the profile of ones face as big as the life; which it did performe very accurately: ...

16 I was forc'd to accompanie some friends to the Beare-garden &c: Where was Cock fighting, Beare, Dog-fighting, Beare & Bull baiting, it being a famous day for all these butcherly Sports, or rather barbarous cruelties: The Bulls did exceedingly well but the Irish Wolfe dog exceeded, which was a tall Gray-hound, a stately creature in deede, who beat a cruell Mastife: One of the Bulls tossd a dog full into a Ladys lap, as she sate in one of the boxes at a Considerable height from the Arena: There were two poore dogs killed; & so all ended with the Ape on horse-back, & I most heartily weary, of the rude & dirty passetime, which I had not seene I think in twenty years before: ...

18 at Goring-house whither my L: Arlington carried me from W: hall, with the Marquis of Worcester; there we found my L. Sandwich, Vicount Stafford [since beheaded], The Lieutennant of the Tower & others:

After dinner, my Lord, communicated to me his Majesties desire, that I would undertake to write the Histories of our Late War with the Hollander, which I had hitherto declin'd; This I found was ill taken, & that I should disoblige his Majestie who had made choice of me to do him that service, & that if I would undertake it, I should have all the Assistance the Secretarie Office & others could give me, with other encouragements, which I could not decently refuse: Note, that at Dinner, my Lord Vicount Stafford rose from Table in some Disorder, because there were roses stuck about the fruite, when the Discert came in & was set on the table: such an Antipathie it seemes he had to Roses, as once my Lady Selenger also had, & to that degree, that, as Sir

---

[1] With this note E makes clear his *Diary* was written for his descendants.

Kenhelme Digby tells us, laying but a rose upon her Cheeke, when she was a sleepe it raisd a blister: but Sir Kenhelme was a teller of strange things: I went home this evening ...

29 To Lond: in order to my Niepce Evelyns Marriage, daughter to my Late Brother of Woodcot, with the Eldest Son of Mr. Attourney Montague, which was celebrated at Southampton house Chapell, after whch a magnificent Entertainement, Feast & dauncing, diner & supper in the greate roome there; but the bride &c was bedded at my Sisters Lodging in Drurie-Lane &c: ...

July 18 I went to Lond, to accompany my worthy friend, that excellent man (Sir Rob. Morray) with Mr. Slingsby Master of the Mint, to see his Seate & Estate at Burrow Greene in Cambridge-shire: desiring our advice for the placing of a new house Mr. Slingsby was resolv'd to build:

19 We set out in a Coach & six horses, with him & his Lady: dined about midway at one Mr. Turners where we found a very noble dinner, Venison, Musique, and a circle of Country Ladys & their Gallants: so after dinner we proceeded, and came to Borrow Greene that night: This had ben the antient seate of the Cheekes (whose daughter Mr. Slingsby married) formerly Tutor to K: Edw: the Sixt: The old house large & ample & built for antient hospitalitie, ready to fall down with age; plac'd in a dirty hole, a stiffe Clay, no Water &c: & next a Church-Yard adjoyning, & other inconveniences: so we pitch'd upon a spot, on a rising ground, & adorn'd with venerable woods, a dry & sweete prospect E: & West, & fit for a Parke, at some mile distant, but no running water to be found:

<21> We went to dine at my Lord A<r>lingtons, who had newly built a house of greate cost, (his Architect Mr. Pratt) I believe little lesse than 20000 pounds, seated in a Parke, with a Sweete Prospect & stately avenue, water still defective: The house has also its infirmities; thence we went back to Mr. Slingsbies: my Lord A<r>lington [since Conestable of the Tower] having very nobly entertaind us.

22 We rod out to see the greate Meere or Levell of recovered fenland not far off: In the way we met my Lord Arlington going to his house in Suffolck accompanied with Count Ogniati (the Spanish Minister) & Sir Bernard Gascoigne: My Lord was exceedingly importunate with me to go with him to Euston, being but 15 miles distant: but in reguard of my Companie I could not: so passing through New-Market, we alighted, to see his Majesties house there now new building, the arches of the Cellers beneath, are exceedingly well turned, by the Architect Mr. Samuel, the rest meane enough, & hardly capable for a hunting house: Many of the roomes above had the Chimnies plac'd in the angles & Corners, a Mode now introduc'd by his Majestie which I do at no hand approve of, & predict it will Spoile many noble houses & roomes if followed; it dos onely well in very Small & trifling roomes, but takes from the state of greater: besids this house is plac'd in a dirty Streete; without any Court or avenue, like a common Burgers: whereas it might & ought to have ben built at either end of the Towne, upon the very Carpet, where the Sports are Celebrated; but it being the purchase of an old wretched house of my Lord Tumonds, his Majestie was perswaded to set it on that foundation, the most improper imaginable for an house of Sport & pleasure:

We went to see the Stables and fine horses, of which many were here kept, at vast expense, with all the art & tendernesse Imaginable: Being ariv'd at Some meeres, we found my Lord Wotton & Sir Jo: Kiviet about their draining Engines, having it seemes undertaken to do wonders, on a vast piece of March-ground, they had hired of Sir Tho: Chichley, Master of the Ordinance: They much pleasd themselves with the hopes of a rich harvest of Hempe & Cole-seede, which was the crop expected: Here we visited Engines & Mills, both for Wind & Water, draining it thro two rivers or grafts cut by hand, & capable of considerable barges, which went thwart one the other, discharging the water into the Sea, such as this Spot had ben the former winter, which was now drie, & so exuberant & rich as even astonish'd me to see what increase there was; Weedes grew as high as horse & man almost upon the bankes:

Here my Lord & his Partner had built two or 3 roomes with flanders white brick, very hard; one of the greate Engines was in the Kitchin, where I saw the fish swimm up even to the very Chimny hearth, by a small cut derived thro the roome, & running within a foote of the very fire: having after dinner rid about that vast levall, pesterd with heate & swarmes of Gnatts, we returnd over New-market-heath, the way being most of it a sweete Turfe, & down, like Salisbery plaine, the Jockies breathing their fine barbs & racers, & giving them their heates.

Having ben very much made <of> at Borrow-Greene on 23 we return'd to Lond: staying some time at Audlie End to see that fine Palace: It is indeede a cherefull piece of Gotic-building, or rather antico-moderno, but placed in an obscure bottome: The Cellars, & Gallerie are very stately; It has a river by it, a pretty avenue of Limes, & in a parke: This is in Saffron Walden Parish famous for that usefull plant, with which all the Countrie is covered: so dining at Bishops Stratford we came late to London: ...

August 5 There was sent me by a Neighbour, the Servant-maid of a friend of hers, who the last moneth as she was sitting before her mistris at work (I think 'twas sewing) felt a seacret stroke upon her arme a little above her wrist, the upper part for a pretty height, the smart of which as if she had ben strock with another hand, caus'd her to hold her arme a while, 'til it was somewhat mittigated; but so it put her into a kind of convulsion fit, or rather Hysteric: A gentleman coming casualy in, looking on her arme, found that part poudred with red Crosses, set in most exact & wonderful order

```
            x
        x       x
    x       x       x
        x       x
            x
```

neither swelled up, nor depressed, about this shape and bignesse

neither seeming to be any ways made by artifice; of a redish colour, not so red as bloud, the skin over them smooth, but the rest of the arme livid & of a mortified hue with certaine prints as it were of the stroke as of fingers: This had hapned three severall times in July at about 10 days intervall, the Crosses beginning to ware out, but the successive ones set in other different (yet uniforme) order: The Maid seem'd very modest, no Phanatic, but well disposd to the Church established: she was borne northward and came from Lond: to Deptford with her Mistris to avoid the discourses & importunity of curious people; made no gaine by it, pretended no religious fancies, had never any commerce with the Popish Priests &c but seemed to be a plaine, ordinary, silent working wench, somewhat fat, short, & high colourd: she told me divers

Divines & Physitians had seene her, but were unsatisfied; That she had taken some remedies against her fits, but did her no good, that she never had any fits 'til this happn'd; but that she once since seemed in her sleepe, to heare one say to her, that she should tamper no more with them, nor trouble herself with any thing that happn'd; but put her trust in the Merits of Christ onely: This being the substance of what she told me, & of what I saw, & curiously examin'd (being formerly acquainted with the impostorious Nunns of Loudune in France, which made such noise in the World amongst Papists,) I thought worth the notice: I remember Monsieur Monconis, (that curious Travellor & a Roman Catholick) was by no meanes satisfied with the stigmata of those Nunns, because they were so shie of letting him scrape the Letters, which were Jesus, Maria, Joseph, (as I think) observing they began to scale off with it: whereas this poore Wench was willing to submit to any trial; so as I professe, I knew not what to think of it; nor dare I pronounce it any thing supernaturall; though (as I told her) I did by no meanes conceive it have ben sent, as any mark to encourage her to change her Religion; which I told her might probably be the temptation of subtile priests; but rather to engage her to a constancy in the Christian Profession, & particularly of the Church of England who have respect to the Crosse, & beare it on their foreheads as soone as made Christians, & that this might be a seasonable admonition, now in a time of so many Heresies, Sects, & Atheistical men: &c: ...

24. To Lond: Thence to Windsore:

26, I supped with Duke of Monmoth; & the next day, invited by my Ld: Arlington dined with the same Duke & divers Lords: After dinner my Lord & I had conference of more than an houre alone in his Bed-chamber, to engage me in the Historie, I shew'd him some thing that I had drawn up, to his greate satisfaction, & then he desired me to shew it to the Tresurer also &c:

28 ... I din'd with the Tressurer, consulted with him, what pieces I was to add &c. & in the afternoone his Majestie tooke me aside into the Balconie over the Tarice, extreamely pleased with what had ben told him I had begun in order to his commands, & enjoyning me to proceede vigorously in it; & told me he had ordered the Secretaries of state to give me all necessary assistance of papers & particulars relating to it, & enjoyning me to make it a little keene, for that the Hollanders had very unhandsomely abused him, in their pictures, books & libells. &c: I went in the Evening to Eaton to visite the Provost Dr. Alestrie Professor Regius Oxon:

29 returned home. Note, that Windsor was now going to be repaired, being exceedingly ragged and ruinous: Prince Rupert Constable had begun to trim up the Keepe or high round Tower, & handsomly adorn'd his hall, with a furniture of Armes, which was very singular; by so disposing the Pikes, Muskets, Pistols, Bandilers, [holster<s>], Drumms, Back, brest & head pi<e>ces as was very extraordinary: & thus those huge steepe stayres ascending to it, had the Walls invested with this martial furniture, all new & bright, & set with such study, as to represent, Pillasters, Cornishes, Archi-traves, Freezes, by so disposing the bandalliers, holsters, & Drums, so as to represent festoones, & that with out any Confusion, Trophy like: from the Hall, we went into his Bedchamber & ample roomes which were hung with tapissrie, curious & effeminate Pictures, so extreamely different from the other, which presented nothing but Warr & horror, as was very Surprizing & Divertissant. The King passed most of his time in hunting the Stag, & walking in the Parke which he was now also planting with walks of Trees, &c: ...

September 6 I went to the Wedding of my neighbour Mrs. Jeakel married to Colonel Midleton, one of the Commissioners of the Navy; at Grays-Inn Chapell, & dined in Suffolck-streete, returned.

8 I went with my Wife & Children to visite my Bro: at Wotton in Surrey: ...

23 To Alburie to see how that Garden proceeded, which I found exactly don according to the Designe & plot I had made, with the Crypta through the mountaine in the parke, which is 30 pearches in length, such a *Pausilippe*[1] is no where in England besides: The Canals were now digging, & Vineyards planted ...

October 15. I spent the whole afternoone in private with the Treasurer, who put into my hands those seacret pieces and Transactions concerning the Dutch war, & particularly the Expedition of Bergen in which he had himselfe the chiefe part; & gave me instructions &c, 'til the King arriving from New market, we both went up into his Majesties Bed-Chamber, it being now almost night, after which I went home, the weather uncomfortable: ...

21. Din'd at the Tressurers & after dinner were shut-up together, I received other advises, & ten paper-bookes of Dispatches & Treaties, to returne which againe, I gave a note under my hand to the Master of the Paper Office Mr. Jos: Wiliamson & so return'd home ...

26: To Lond: din'd with Mr. Vice-Chamberlaine, return'd next day, having caled at the Ro: Society, it being the first time of meeting since their recesse; where were several Curiosities of nature sent us from New England, & a learned discourse from Bolognia of some starrs disappearing in the Constellation of the Ship, starrs of the 2d Magnitude, which were wont to be conspicuous with the bare Eye; Also was presented with a noble Piece of Chrystal from Iseland sent from Copenhagen with a book: ...

November 1 ... We met this day as Foefeès for the poore, according to Costome:

3: Lond: at our Society where there was an Experiment about cracking a thin & ordinary bell glasse with the shrillnesse of the voice onely.

4. Dined at the Groome-porters, return'd that Evening, having seene the Prince of Orange, newly come to see his Unkle the King: he has a manly couragious wise Countenance, resembling both his Mother, & Duke of Glocester both deceased: I now also saw that famed beauty (but in my opinion of a childish simple & baby face) Madamoiselle Quirreval,[2] lately maide of honour to Madame,[3] & now to be so to the Queene: ...

26 I had a Tryall in Guild-Hall againest on<e> Cock who had exceedingly wronged me in an Accompt of monies going through his hands: but there being many Causes, 'twas respited til Wednesday following: ...

29, To Lond: in order to our Tryal; but by perswasion of Judge Hales (that excellent good Man) I was willing to put it to arbitration &c:

30: St. Andrews day we proceeded to Elections in the Society, where I was chosen of the Council for the following yeare, then dined all together according to costome, his Majestie & Lord Howard sending the Venison: ...

---

[1] De Beer notes that the word relates to tunnel of the Grotta di Posilippo in Italy (II, 338).

[2] Louise de Kéroualle (1649-1734), created the Duchess of Portsmouth in 1673.

[3] Henrietta Anne (1644-70), Duchess of Orléans, Charles II's sister. She died in June 1670.

December 15 To Lond: It was the thickest, & darkest fogg on the Thames, that was ever know<n> in the memory of man, & I happned to be in the midst of it: I supped with Monsieur Zulestein late Governor to the Young Pr: of Orange, with severall other greate persons, & had a greate entertainement: next day, at the Ro: Society, where was present<ed> an Inscription in a stone found on the Keepe at Winsore, which covered the Skelleton of a child; with an Urne full of old Coynes &c:[1] ...

1671

January 5 My long Consumptive Servant J: Smith died, a faithfull honest servant:

10 Mr. Bohune my sonns Tutor, having now ben 5 yeares in my house, & now Batchelor of Laws & Fellow of New Coll: went from me to Oxford to reside there, having well & faithfully perform'd his Charge &c: ...

16 To Lond: about buisinesse, dined in Hatton Garden at the first-fruits Office:

18 I this day first acquainted his Majestie with that incomparable young man, Gibson,[2] whom I had lately found in obscure place, & that by meere accident, as I was walking neere a poor solitary thatched house in a field in our Parish neere Says-Court: I found him shut in, but looking into the Window, I perceiv'd him carving that large Cartoone, or Crucifix of Tintorets, a Copy of which I had also my selfe brought from Venice, where the original Painting remaines: I asked if I might come in, he opned the doore civily to me, & I saw him about such a work, as for the curiosity of handling, drawing, & studious exactnesse, I never in my life had seene before in all my travells: I asked why he worked in such an obscure & lonesome place; he told me, it was that he might apply himselfe to his profession without interruption; & wondred not a little how I came to find him out: I asked if he were unwilling to be made knowne to some Greate men; for that I believed it might turne to his profit; he answerd, he was yet but a beginner; but yet would not be sorry to sell off that piece; I asked him the price, he told me 100 pounds. In good earnest the very frame was worth the mony, there being nothing even in nature so tender, & delicate as the flowers & festoones about it, & yet the worke was very strong; but in the Piece above 100 figures of men &c: I found he was likewise Musical, a very Civil, sober & discreete in his discourse: There was onely an old Woman in the house; so desiring leave to visite him sometimes, I took my leave: Of this Young Artist, together with my manner of finding him out, I acquainted the King, and beged of his Majestie that he would give me leave to bring him & his Worke to White-hall, for that I would adventure my reputation with his Majestie that he had never seene any thing approch it, & that he would be exceedingly pleased, & employ him: The King sayd, he would himselfe go see him: This was the first notice his Majestie ever had of Mr. Gibbons.

20: His Majestie <came> to me the Queenes Withdrawing roome, from the Circle of Ladies, to talke with me what advance I had made in the Dutch

---

[1] The burial was probably Roman in date.

[2] Grinling Gibbons (1648-1720), the celebrated wood-carver and sculptor.

Historie: I dined with the Tressurer & after we went to the Secretaries Office, where we conferred about divers particulars:

21. I was directed to go to Sir Geo: Downing who (being a pub: Minister in Holland, at the beginning of the War) was to give me light in some material passages: so returned home with my Lady Tuke who gave my Wife a Visite for some daies:...

30 Was our late good Kings Anniversary & Martyrdome, our Doctor preached on 7: Act: ultimo: He shew'd the antiquity & duty of kneeling at Prayers, reprehending the late irreverenc: The Examples of praying for, & forgiving Enemies: The sinn of Cursing them, clearing those Texts in some of the Prophetical Psalmes, as against the Children mocking Elias, Judas, Simon Magus & others; as being predictions rather then maledictions: Then exaggerated the monstrousnesse of the Crime of Murdering the King, so good a king, & how it became the sinn of the whole nation, which was yet to expiate it by serious Repentance, to prevent the ruine threatned &c and in truth the leudnesse of our greatest ones, & universal luxurie, seemed to menace some yet more dreadfull vengeance: we have had a plague, a Warr, & such fire, as never was the like in any nation since the overthrow of Sodome, and this very yeare so Wett, Stormy & unseasonable, as had not ben knowne in many yeares: The Lord be gracious to us, we that are yet the most happy, are withall the most unthankfull & undeserving people of the Universe: ...

February 9: I saw the greate Ball danced by the Queene & greate Ladies at White hall Theater: & next day was acted there the famous Play, cald the Siege of Granada two days acted successively: there were indeede very glorious scenes & perspectives, the work of Mr. Streeter, who well understands it: ...

19 ... This day dined with me Mr. Surveyor Dr. Chr: Wren, Mr. Pepys Clerk of the Acts, two extraordinary ingenious, and knowing persons, and other friends; I carried them to see the piece of Carving which I had recomended to the King ...

27 To Lond: to the funerall of Sir Jo: Minnes Comptroller of the Navy, a pleasant man:

28: The Treasurer acquainted me his Majestie was graciously pleased to nominate me one of his Council of forraine Plantations, & <had> given me a salarie of 500 pounds per Annum to encourage me.

29: I went to thanke the Tressurer who was my greate friend, and loved me; I dined with him, & much company there: Thence to my Lord Arlington Secretary of state, in whose favour I likewise was: upon many occasions, though I cultivated neither of their friendships with any meane submissions: I kissed his Majesties hand, upon his making me one of that new Establish'd Council: ...

March 1. I caused Mr. Gibbon to bring to Whitehall his excellent piece of Carving where being come, I advertised his Majestie who asked me where it was, I told him, in Sir R: Brownes (my F. in Laws) Chamber, & that if it pleased his Majestie to appoint whither it should be brought (for 'twas large, and though of Wood, yet heavy) I would take care for it: No says the King; shew me the Way, Ile go to Sir Richards Chamber: which his Majestie immediately did, walking all along the Enteries after me as far as the Ewrie til he came up into the roome where I also lay: & no sooner was he entred, & cast his eye on the Worke but he was astonish'd at the curiositie of it, & having considred it a long time, & discours'd with Mr. Gibbon, whom I brought to kisse his hand; he commanded it should be immediately carried to the Queenes side to shew her Majestie, so it was carried up into her bed-chamber, where she and the King looked on & admired it againe, the King thus leaving us with the Queene being now caled away, I think to Council, believing that she would have bought it, it being a Crucifix; but when his Majestie was gon, a French pedling woman, one Madame de boord, that used to bring peticoates & fanns & baubles out of France to the Ladys, began to find faults with severall things in the worke, which she understood no more than an Asse or Monky; so as in a kind of Indignation, I caused the porters who brought it, to carry it to the Chamber againe, finding the Queene so much govern'd by an ignorant french woman: and this incomparable Artist <had> the labour onely for his paines, which not a little displeased me; so he was faine to send it downe to his cottage againe, though he not long after sold it for 80 pounds, which was realy, (even without the frame) worth an hundred: Sir Geo: Viner buying it of him, as his first Essay, and his Majesties Surveyor Mr. Wren faithfully promising me to employ him for the future; I having bespoke his Majestie also for his Worke at Windsore which my friend Mr. May (the Architect there) was going to alter and repaire universaly: for on the next day, I had a faire opportunity of talking to his Majestie about it, in the Lobby next the Queenes side, where I presented him with some Sheetes of my historie, & thence walked with him thro St. James's Parke to the Garden, where I both saw and heard a very familiar discourse betweene <the King> & Mrs. Nellie as they cal'd an impudent Comedian, she looking out of her Garden on a Tarrace at the top of the Wall, & <the King> standing on the greene Walk under it: I was heartily sorry at this scene: Thence the King walked to the Dutches of Cleavelands, another Lady of Pleasure & curse of our nation: It was on a Council day, & so I went back & on the 4th to my house ...

May 2. To Lond: The French King being now with a greate Army of 28000 about Dynkirk divers of the grandees of that Court, & a vast number of Gentlemen & Cadets in fantastical habites, came flocking over to see our Court, & complement his Majestie. I was present when they were first conducted into the Queenes withdrawing roome where saluted their Majesties The Duke of Guise, The D: of Longuville, of Ballion, Marq: Arignie, Monsieur Le Grand, Monsieur Le Premiere & innumerable more of the first sort: so I went home: ...

10 To Lond: din'd at Mr. Treasurers where dined Monsieur de Gramont & severall French noblemen: & one Bloud that impudent bold fellow, who had not long before attempted to steale the Imperial Crowne it selfe out of the Tower, pretending onely curiositie of seeing the Regalia there, when stabbing (though not mortaly) the keeper of them, he boldly went away with it, thro all the guards, taken onely by the accident of his horses falling. How he came to be pardoned, & even received to favour, not onely after this, but severall other exploits almost as daring, both in Ireland and here, I could never come to understand: some believed he became a spie of severall Parties, being well with the Sectaries & Enthusiasts, & did his Majestie services that way, which none alive could so well as he: But it was certainely as the boldest attempt, so the onely Treason of this nature that was ever pardon'd: The Man had not onely a daring but a vilanous un-mercifull looke, a false Countenance, but very well spoken, & dangerously insinuating:

11 I went to Eltham to sit as one of the Commission about the subsidie given his Majestie by Parliament: returnd: ...

18 dined at Mr. Tressurers with the E: of Arlington, Ca<r>lingford, Lord Arundel of Wardoer, Lo: Almoner to the Queene; a French Count, and two

Abbots with severall more of French nobility: And now by something I had lately observed of Mr. Treasurers conversation & discourse on occasion I suspected him a little warping to Rome: ...

25. I dined at a feast made for me & my Wife by the Trinity Company, for our Passing a fine about the Land, Sir R: Bro: my Wifes Father, freely gave to found & build their Colledge or Almes houses on, at Deptford; it being my Wifes after her Father: It was a good & a Charitable Worke & gift, but much better bestowed on the poore of that Parish, than on the seamens Widdows, the Trinity Company being very rich, & the rest of the poore of the Parish exceedingly Indigent:

26: Meeting all at Queenes streete at the Earle of Bristols house (which we had lately taken, & furnish'd with rich hangings of the Kings, 7 roomes on a floore with a long Gallery, Gardens, &c:) The Duke of Buckingham, E: of Lauderdail, L: Culpeper, Sir Geo: Carteret Vice-Chamberlaine & my selfe, had our Oathes given us by the Earle of Sandwich our President: To Advise & Counsel his Majestie to the best of our abilities &c: for the well Governing of his Majesties forraine Plantations &c. The forme very little differing from what is given the Privy Council: Then we tooke all our Places in the Council Chamber at the board: The roome very large, & furnished with Atlases, Mapps, Charts, Globes &c: Then came the Lord Keeper Sir Orlando Bridgeman, E: of Arlington Pr: Secretary of State: Lord Ashley, Mr. Treasurer, Sir Jo: Trevor the other Pr: Secretary, Sir Jo: Duncomb, Lord Allington, Mr. Grey, sonn to the Lord Grey, Mr. Hen: Broncher, Sir Humfry Winch; Sir John Finch, Mr. Waller, Coll: Titus of the Bed chamber, Mr. Slingsby the Secretary to the Council, & two Clearks of the Council, who were all Sworne some dayes before: being all set, our Patent was read, & then the additional Patent, in which was recited this new establishment: Then was delivered to every one of us a Copy of the Patent, & of our Instructions: after which we fell to debate matters; & first agreed on a forme for Circulating Letters to be immediately despatched to all his Majesties Plantations & Territories in the West Indies & Ilands thereof; to give them notice to whom they should apply themselves on all occasions, & to render us an account of their present state, & Government, & therefore the Letters were directed to the respective Governors: but most we insisted on, was to know in what condition New-England was; which appearing to be very independent as to their reguard to old England, or his Majestie, rich & strong as now they were, greate were the debates, in what style to write to them: for the Condition of that Colonie was such, as they were able to contest with all our Plantations about them, & feare there was, of their altogether breaking from all dependance on this nation: His Majestie therefore recommended this afaire more expressly: We therefore thought fit, in the first place, to acquaint our selves as well as we could of the state of that place, by some who we heard of, that were newly come from thence, & to be informed of their present posture & Condition; because some of our Council were for sending them a menacing Letter which those who better understood the touchy & peevish humor of that Colonie, were utterly against. Then a letter was red which came from Sir Tho: Modiford Governor of Jamaica, & then the Council brake up: My agreement with Cock not succeeding, I went to take advise of that famous Lawyer Mr. Jones of Grays Inn: & 27: had a Trial before the L: C. Justice Hales for a summ on mony owing me; so after the Lawyers had wrangled sufficiently, It was againe referred to a new Arbitration: This being the very first Suite at Law, that ever I had with any Creature before and ô that it might be the Last: from hence I returned to my house:

June 6: I went to Council, where was produc'd a most exact and ample Information of the state of Jamaica, and of the best expedients to reduce New-England, on which there was a long debate, & whether it were fit <to> send a Letter & certaine curious Queries relating to the seacrets of the Government: but 'twas concluded in the negative, & that if any, it should be onely a conciliating paper at first, or civil letter 'til we had better information of the present face of things; since we understood they were a people al most upon the very brink of renouncing any dependance on the Crowne: - I din'd at my Brothers, & went home ...

20: To carry Coll: Midleton to White hall to my L: Sandwich our President, for some information he was able to give the Council of the state of the Colonie in N. England, & return'd: Next day to Council againe, where one Coll: Cartrite a Notinghamshere man, (formerly in Commission with Coll: Nichols) gave us a considerable relation of that Country. Upon which the Council concluded, that if policy would not reduce the disaffected there, force should: that yet in the first place, a letter of amnestie should be dispatch'd, with an intention to fortifie a certaine Iland in the mouth of the chiefe river; & to purchase the maine of that part of the Plantation belonging to Ferdinando Gorges, which would inable the King to curb Boston: I went home:

24 Came Constantine Hugens S<e>igneur of Zulechom, that excellent learned man, Poet & Musitian, & now neere 80 yeares of age a vigorous brisk-man, to take leave of me before his returne into Holland, with the Prince, whose Secretary he was: ...

26 To Lond: to Council, where my Lo: Arlington being present, acquainted us that it was his Majesties Proposal, we should every one of us contribute 20 pounds a piece, towards the building of a Council-chamber and conveniences some where in White-hall, to the end, that his Majestie himselfe might come and sit amongst us & heare our debates; The mony we laied out to be reimbours'd us out of the contingent monies already set apart for us, viz: 1000 pounds yearley: To which we unanimously consented. There came also an uncertaine brute from Barbados, of some disorder there: so I went home, steping in at the Theater, to see the new Machines for the intended scenes, which were indeede very costly & magnificent:

July 4: To Lon: to Council: where we drew up & agreed to a letter to be sent to N: England & made some proposals to Mr. Gorges for his Interest &c: ...

24: To Lon: Council: Mr. Surveyor brought us a plot for the building of our Council-Chamber to be erected at the end of the Privy-Garden in White-hall which was all was don: I returned ...

August 19 To Lond: & Council: The letters of Sir T: Mudiford were read, giving relation of the Exploit at Panamà, which was very brave: They tooke & burnt, and pilag'd the Towne of vast Treasures, but the best of the booty had been ship'd off, & lay at anker in the South Sea, so as after our Men had ranged the Countriy 60 miles about, they went back to Nombre de Dios, & embarq'd to Jamaica; Such an action had not ben don since the famous Drake: I dined at the Resident of Hambroghs, & after dinner at the Christning of Sir Sam: Tukes Son Charles which was don at Somerset house by a Popish Priest with many odd Ceremonies, Spittle & anointings: Godfathers the King: L: Arundell of Wardoer, &c Countesse of Huntington: after which I went home ...

29 <Aug> To Lond: with some more papers of my progresse in the Dutch Warr, delivered to the Treasurer: on 1. **September** when I dined with him, my

L: Arlington, Halifax, Sir Th: Strickland: & next day went home, [2] being the Anniversarie of the late dreadfull fire of London ...

13. This night fell a dreadfull tempest.

14. I spent this morning privately with Mr. Tres: and 15 Afternoone at Council, where leters were read from Sir Ch: Wheeler concerning the resigning his Government of St. Christophers: There was a very warme contest betweene my L: Sandwich our President, & Mr. Slingsby our Secretary, about some unkind expressions, wherein I think the Latter was to blame: I returned home: ...

21. I dined in the Citty, at the fraternity feast in yron-mongers hall, where the 4 stewards chose their successors of the next yeare with a solemn procession, garlands about their heads & musique playing before them, so coming up to the uper Tables where the gentlemen sate, they drank to the new <stewards> &c: and so we parted.

22. I dind at the Tressurers where I had discourse with Sir Hen: Jones (now come over to raise a regiment of horse) concerning the French Conquests in Lorraine: He told me the King sold all things to the Souldiers, even to an handfull of hay: My L: Sunderland was now nominated Ambassador for Spaine. After dinner the Tressurer carried me to Lincolns Inn to one of the Parliament Clearks, to obtaine of him that I might carry-home, with me and peruse some of the Journals, which I had delivered to me to examine about the late Dutch war &c: Returning home I went on shore to see the Costome-howse now newly rebuilt since the dreadfull Conflagration ...

October 8 ... I went after Evening Service to Lond: in order to a journey of refreshment with Mr. Treasurer to Newmarket &c where his Majestie was &c:

9 We set out on the 9th in his Coach of 6 brave horses, which we changed thrice: & first at Bishop Stratford, & last at Chesterford so as by night we got to N.Market, where Mr Henry Jermin (Nephew to the Earle of St. Albans) lodged me very Civily: We went immediately to Court (the King & all the English Gallantes being here at their autumnal sports) supped at my L: Chamberlaines, & next day after dinner went on the heath, where I saw the greate match run betweene Wood-cock & Flat-foot the Kings, & Mr. Eliots of the Bedchamber, many thousands being spectators, a more signal race had not ben run of many yeares:

This over, I went that night with Mr. Tressurer to Euston, a palace of my Lo: <Arlingtons> [10] where we found Monsieur Colbert (the French Ambassador) & the famous new french maid of honor, Mademoisell Quierovil now comeing to be in greate favour with the K-: here was also the Countesse of Sunderland, & severall Lords & Ladies more who lodged in the house: during my stay here with my Lord Arlington neere a fortnight; Came his Majestie almost every second day with the Duke, who commonly returnd againe to New-market; but the King lay often here, during which time I had twice the honor to sit at Dinner with him, with all freedome: It was universaly reported that the faire Lady - was bedded one of these nights, and the stocking flung, after the manner of a married Bride: I acknowledge she was for the most part in her undresse all day, and that there was fondnesse, & toying, with that young wanton; nay 'twas said, I was at the former ceremonie, but tis utterly false, I neither saw, nor heard of any such thing whilst I was there, though I had ben in her Chamber & all over that appartment late enough; & was my selfe observing all passages with curiosity enough: however twas with confidence believed that she was first made a Misse as they cald these unhappy creatures, with solemnity, at this time &c: ...

16 Came all the greate Men from N:Market & other parts both of Suffolck, & Norfolck to make their Court; the whole house fill'd from one end to the other, with Lords, Ladys, & Gallants, and such a furnished Table had I seldome seene, nor any thing more splendid & free: so as for 15 dayes there were entertain'd at the Least 200 people, & halfe as many horses, besids Servants, Guards, at Infinite expense: In the mornings we went a hunting & hauking; In the afternoone 'til almost morning to Cards & dice &c yet I must say without noise, swearing, quarell or Confusion of any sort: I who was no Gamster, had often discourse with the French Ambassador Colbert, & went sometimes abroad on horse back with the Ladys to take the aire, & now & then to hunting; thus idly passing the time, but not without more often recesse to my prety apartment, where I was quite out of all this hurry, & had <leasure>, when I would to converse with bookes; for there is no man more hospitably easy to be withall than my L: Arlington, of whose particular friendship & kindnesse I had ever a more than ordinary share:

My Lord Chamberlaines house is a very noble pile consisting of 4 greate pavilions after the french, beside a body of a large house, & though not built altogether, but form'd of additions to an old house (purchasd by his Lordship from of one Sir T Rookwoods) yet with a vast expence, made not onely capable & roomesome, but very magnificent & commodious, as well within as without, nor lesse splendidly furnish'd: The Stayre case is very elegant, the Garden handsome, the Canale beautifull, but the soile drie, barren, & miserably sandy, which flies in drifts as the wind sets: Here my Lord was pleasd to advise with me about the ordering his Plantations of firs, Elmes, limes &c up his parke, & in all other places & Avenues; I perswaded him to bring his Parke so neere, as to comprehend his house with in it, which now he resolved upon; it being now neere a mile to it: The Water furnishing the fountaines is raised by a pretty Engine or very slight plaine Wheele, which likewise serves to grind his Corne, from a small cascade of the Canale, the invention of Sir Sam: Moreland: In my Lords house, & especialy above the Stayre Case, the greate hall & some of the Chambers & roomes of State, is painted in fresca, by the hand of Signor Virrio [the same who has painted all Winsor] being the first worke which he did in England.

17 My Lord Hen: Howard coming this night to visite my Lord Chamberlain, & staying a day, would needes have me go along with him to Norwich; promising to convey me back againe after a day or two; This as I could not refuse, so I was not hardly perswaded to, having a desire to see that famous Scholar & Physition Dr. T. Browne author of *Religio Medici* & *Vulgar Errors* &c: now lately knighted: Thither then went my Lord & I in his flying Charriat with 6 horses; & by the way discoursing to me of severall of his Concernes, he acquainted me of his going to marry his Eldest sonn to one of the Kings natural daughters, by the Dutchess of Cleaveland; by which he reckon'd he shall come into might<y> favour: he also told me that though he kept that idle Creature & common - Mrs. B[1] - & would leave 200 pounds a yeare to the sonne he had by her; he would never marry her, & that the King himselfe had caution'd him, against it: All the world knowes, how he kept this promise; & I was sorry at heart to hear what now in confidence he confessed to me; & that a person & a family (which I so much honou<re>d, for [the sake of] that noble & illustrious friend of mine, his Grandfathers) should dishonour and polute them both, with those base, & vicious Courses he of late had taken, & was falln into, since the death of Sir Sam: Tuke, & that of his own virtuous Lady

---

[1] Jane Bickerton (c. 1644-93).

my L: Ann Somerset (sister to the Marquesse) who whilst they lived, preserv'd this Gentleman by their example & advice, from those many extravagances that impaird both his fortune & reputation:

Being come to the Ducal Palace, my Lord made very much of me, but I had little rest, so exceedingly desirous he was to shew me the contrivances he had made, for the entertainement of their Majesties & whole Court not long before, & which, though much of it, but temporary appartments fram'd of boards &c onely, were yet standing: As to the Palace, tis an old wretched building, & that part of it, newly built of brick, is very ill understood; so as I was of opinion, it had ben much better to have demolish'd all, & set it in a better place than to proceede any farther; for it stands in the very Market place, & though neere a river, yet a very narrow muddy one & without any extent: here before we went to bed, my Lord fell-out with his Carpenter, about measuring of a roome, & grew into such a passion, as in my life, I had never seene any mortal man; so much beneath his dignitie, & for so wretched a trifle; my Lord saying the dimension was so many foote, the Workman so many: This conflict lasting from 8 till 1 at night, was grievous to me:

Next morning I went to see Sir Tho: Browne (with whom I had sometime corresponded by Letters tho never saw before) whose whole house & Garden being a Paradise & Cabinet of rarities, & that of the best collection, especialy Medails, books, Plants, natural things, did exceedingly refresh me after last nights confusion: Sir Thomas had amongst other curiosities, a collection of the Eggs of all the foule & birds he could procure, that Country (especialy the promontorys of Norfolck) being (as he said) frequented with severall kinds, which seldome or never, go farther into the Land, as Cranes, Storkes, Eagles &c: & variety of Water-foule: He likewise led me to see all the remarkeable places of this antient Citty, being one of largest, & certainely (after London) one of the noblest of England, for its venerable Cathedrall, number of stately Churches, Cleanesse of the streetes; & buildings of flint, so exquisitely headed & Squared, as I was much astonish'd at; Sir Tho: told me they had lost the art, of squaring the flint, which once they <were> so excellent in: & of which the Churches, best houses, & Walls are built: The Castle is an antique extent of ground, which they now call marsfield, & had ben a fitting area to have placed the Ducal Palace in: The suburbs are large, the prospect sweete, & other amoenities, not omiting the flower-gardens, which all the Inhabitans excell in of this Citty, the fabric of stuffs, which it affords the Merchants, & brings a vast trade to this populous Towne:

Being return'd to my Lords, who had ben with me all this morning, he advis'd with me concerning a plot to rebuild his house, having already (as I said) erected a front next the streete, & a left wing, and now resolving to set up another wing, & pavilion next the Garden, & to convert the bowling greene into Stables: In summ, my advise was to desist from all, & to meditate wholy on the rebuilding an handsome Palace at Arundell house in the Strand, before he proceeded farther here; & then to place this in the Castle, that ground belonging to his Lordship: One thing I observ'd of remarkable in this Citty, that most of the Church-yards (though some of them large enough) were filled up with earth, or rather the congestion of dead bodys on<e> upon another, for want of Earth &c to the very top of the Walls, & many above the wales, so as the Churches seem'd to be built in pitts:

18 I return'd to Euston next day (leaving my Lord Howard at Norwich) in my Lords Coach, & in company with a very ingenious Gent: one Mr. White, whose Father & Mother (daughter to the late Lord Treasurer Weston [Portland]) I knew at Rome, where this gent: was borne, & where his Parents

lived & died with much reputation, During their banishment in our Civil broiles:

In this journey my L: Howard told me he would go to Church & become Protestant & recover his title of Earle Martial of England; & at another time, that he would have his sonn Harry go to Church &c: (for he thought most Religions alike) but that being the head of his family, it would not so well become himselfe to change: 'Tis great pitty, that a person, not onely of so eminent birth, but of such excellent natural parts, & smo<o>th a tongue; should have so little Judgement, & be so very inconstant, for he has fits of good resolution, greate generositie, &c, & then of things of quite contrary &c: my time now being short

<19> Leaving Euston, I lodged this night at Newmarket, where I found the jolly blades, Racing, Dauncing, feasting & revelling, more resembling a luxurious & abandon'd rout, than a Christian Court: The Duke of Buckingham was now in mighty favour, & had with him here that impudent woman, the Countesse of Shrewsbery, with his band of fidlars &c.

Next morning (in Company with Sir Bernard Gascoyne & my L: Hawly) I came in the Tressurers Coach, to Bish: Stratford, where the Tressurer gave us a noble supper, and next day to London & so home:

November <20> ... to Council, where Sir Cha: Wheeler (late Governor of the Lee-ward Ilands in America) having ben complaind of, for many indiscreete managements; it was resolv'd (upon the Scanning many of the particulars &c), to advise his Majestie to remove him; & consult what was to be don to prevent those inconveniencys he had brought things to: This buisinesse staied me in Lond, almost a weeke, being either in Councill, or Committee every Morning till the 25

December 6 Came Sir William Haywood to visite me, a greate pretender to English antiquities &c: ...

<5> ... In the afternoone at the R: Society were examind some draughts of arches to sustaine a Cupola:[1] ...

14 At the R: Society, whence to see the Duke of Buckingams ridiculous farce & <Rhapsody> called the *Recital*, bouffoning all Plays yet prophane enough[2] ...

21: I din'd with the Gent: of the Kings Bed-chamber, thence to the R: Society, where Mr. Hooke read his new method of the Art of Musique, and part of Malphigiu's *Anatomie of Vegetables*, sent us in MS; from Bolognia, which we intended to have published: next day home: ...

---

[1] Almost certainly connected with the debate over the new St Paul's. Wren presented his 'Great Model' design which included this feature in 1673, derived ultimately from St Peter's in Rome.

[2] Actually called *The Rehearsal*. De Beer points out that E uses the word 'Rhapsody' in a now-obsolete form to indicate a 'confused ramble'.

1672

January 12 His Majestie renewed us our Lease of Says-Court Pastures for 99 yeares &c: but ought according to his solemn promise (as I hope he will still performe) have passed them to us in Fee-farme[1] ...

23 To Lond: in order to Sir R:Bro: my F. in Laws resigning his Clerke of the Councils Place to Sir Joseph Williamson, which he did in the Council Chamber in his Majesties Presence, according to the usual forme of taking the Oathes of Supr: & Alegiance & then that of the Cl: of the Council, after which his Majestie knighted him: This Place his Majestie had promised me many yeares before, but upon consideration of 1000 pounds; and our lease of 500 pounds per ann: at fourty shill<ings> rent, without fine for 99 yeares, I chose to part with it to Sir Joseph who gave us, & the rest of his bro: Clearkes an handsome supper at his house, & after supper, a Consort of Musique:

25 To the R: Society; where were produc'd new invented Perspectives, a letter from Grene-Land, of recovering men that had ben drown'd, we had also presented us from Iseland some of the *Lapis Obsidialis*:[2]

February 3: I went to Lond: an extraordinary Snow ... The rest of the Weeke was taken up in consulting about the Commission, & Instruction to our Officers, in order to a second War with the Hollanders, his Majestie having made choice of [some of] the former Commissioners & amongst them my selfe againe ...

12. At the Council of Plant: we entred upon enquiries about improving his Majesties American Dominions by Silk, Galls, Flax, Senna &c & considered how Nutmegs & Cinamon might be obtaind, & brought to Jamaica, that Soile & Climat promising successe; upon this Dr. Worsley being called in spake many considerable things to encourage it: We also tooke order to send to the Plantations, that none of their ships should adventure homeward single, but stay for company & Convoyes, in reguard of the late indicted War &c: we also deliberated of sending some fit Person to goe as Commissioner to Inspect their actions at New-England, & from time to time to make report by Letters, & to give us information how that Nation stood affected: This we had formerly in deliberation: Then adjourn'd for the future to meete at White-hall, & 13 I returned home ...

March 1 To Lond: at our Council of Plant: where was present his Royal Highnesse the Duke: Pr: Rupert, D: of Buckingham, both the Secretaries of state &c: & divers Lords of the Privy Council: Debating of our saving the Lee-ward Ilands, now in danger of the French, who had taken some of our Ships, & began to interrupt our trade; as also about the power of the new Governor of st. Christophers, whither he should be Subordinate to the Governor of Barbados &c: The Debates were serious & long: ...

12 To Lond: Now was the first blow given by us against the Dutch Convoy of the Smyrna fleete, by Sir Robert Holmes & my Lord Ossorie, in which we received little save blows, & a worthy reproch, for atacquing our neighbours ere any war was proclaim'd & then pretending the occasion to be, that some time before, the Merline Yacht chancing to saile thro the whole Dutch fleete,

---

[1] Held in perpetuity by the owner and his heirs for a fixed annual rent.
[2] Volcanic rock.

their Admiral did not Strike to that trifling vessel: Surely this was a quarel
slenderly grounded, & not becoming Christian neighbours, & of a Religion:
and we are like to thrive accordingly: My Lord Ossory several times deploring
his being ingaged in it to me, & he had more justice & honour than in the least
to approve of it, though he had ben over perswaded to the expedition, & there
is no doubt, but we had surpriz'd this exceeding rich fleete, had not the avarice
and ambition of Holmes & Sprag, separated themselv<e>s & willfully divided
our fleete, on presumption that either of them were strong enough to deale
with the Dutch Convoy, without joyning & mutual help; whilst the Dutch
Convoy so warmly plied our divided fleete, that whilst they were in Conflict,
the Merchants saild away & got safe into Holland:

It was a few daies before this that the Treasurer of Majesties Howshold
(Sir Tho: Clifford) hinted to me (as a Confident) that his Majestie would shut
up the Chequer, & accordingly his Majestie made use of infinite Treasure
there to prepare for an intended rupture; but says he, it will soon be open
againe, & every body satisfied: for this bold man (who had ben the sole
adviser to the King, to invade that sacred stock, though some pretend it was
my Lord Ashleys counsel (Chancelor then of the chequer) was so over
confident of the successe of this unworthy designe against the Smyrna
Merchants; as to put his Majestie on an action which not onely lost the hearts
of his subjects, & ruined many Widdows & Orphans whose stocks were lent
him, but the reputation of his Exchequer for ever, it being before in such
Credit, that his Majestie before this seizure, might have commanded halfe the
wealth of the nation:

The Credit of this bank being thus broken, did exceedingly discontent the
people, & never did his Majesties afaires prosper to any purpose after it, for as
it did not supply the expense of the meditated war, so it mealted away I know
not how. And to this succeded his Majesties declaration for an universal
Tolleration; Papists & Swarmes of sectaries now boldly shewing themselves in
their publique meetings; & this was imputed to the same Council, Clifford
warping to Rome, as was believe'd, nor was my Lord Arlington cleare of
suspicion, to gratifie that partie, but, as since it has prov'd & was then
evidently fore-seene, to the extreame weakning the Church of England & its
Episcopal Government; as 'twas projected:

I speake not this as my owne sense, but what was the discourse & thoughts
of others, who were lookers on: for I think, there might be some relaxations
without the least prejudice to the present Establishment, discreetely limited,
but to let go the reines in this manner, & then to imagine they could take them
up againe as easily, was a false politique, & greately destructive; The truth is
our Bishops slipt the occasion; since had they held a steady hand on his
Majesties restauration, as easily they might have don, The Church of England
had emerg'd & flourish'd without interruption; but they were then remisse, &
covetous after advantages of another kind, whilst his Majestie suffer'd them to
come into an harvest, which without any injustice he might have remunerated
innumerable gallant Gentleman with for their services, who had ruin'd
themselves for him in the late rebellion: ...

21. I went to the Co<a>sts in my District of Kent, lay this night at
Gravesend, where I visited divers wounded & langwishing poore men that had
ben in the Smyrna conflict: I went over to see the new begun Fort of Tilbery, a
Royal work indeede, & such as will one day bridle a greate Citty to the
purpose, before they are aware: ...

22, To Rochester. <23>: Cap: Cox one of the Commissioners of the Navy,
furnishing me with a Yacht, on the 23, I sailed to Sheere Nesse to see that fort

also, now newly finished; severall places on both sides the Swale & Medway to Gillingham & Upnore being also provided with redouts & batteries, to secure the station of our Men of War at Chatham, & shut the doore when the steedes were stollen, & so returned to Rochester.

24: I din'd with Mr. Commissioner Cox having seene that morning my Chirurgeon cut off a poore creaturs Leg, a little under the knee, first cutting the living & untainted flesh above the Gangreene with a sharp knife, and then sawing off the bone in an instant; then with searing & stoopes stanching the blood, which issued aboundantly; the stout & gallant man, enduring it with incredible patience, & that without being bound to his chaire, as is usual in such painefull operations, or hardly making a face [or crying oh]: I had hardly such courage enough to be present, nor could I endure to se<e> any more such cruel operations.

The leg was so rotten & gangreen'd, that one might have run a straw through it; but neither did this the cure, for it not being amputated high-enough, the gangreene prevaild upon the knee, & so a second amputation of the Thigh, cost the poore Creature his life, to my very greate sorrow: I do not remember that ever in my life I smelt so intollerable a stink as what issu'd from the part <that> was cut off, & which I ordered should immediately be buried in the Garden: Lord, what miseries are mortal men obnoxious to, & what confusion & mischiefe dos the avarice, anger, and ambition of Princes cause in the world, who might be happier with halfe they possesse: This stoute man, was but a common sailer.

25 I proceeded to Canterbery, said my Prayers at the Cathedral, & next morning to Dover, saluted the Governor of the Castle,

27 To Deale: next to the Isle of Thannet by Sandwich & so to Margate where I was handsomely entertain'd & Lay at my Deputies Cap: Glovers: here we had aboundance of miserably wounded men, his Majestie sending to meete me, Serjeant Knight, his Majesties chiefe Chirurgeon, & Dr. Waldrond who attended me all this journey, so having taken such order for the accommodation of the Wounded as was requisite, I came back through a Country the best cultivated of any that in my life I had any where seene, every field lying as even as a bowling greene, & the fences, plantations, & husbandrie in such admirable order, as infinitely delighted me, after the sad & afflicting specctacles & objects I was come from: observing almost every tall tree, to have a Weather-cock on the top bough, & some trees halfe a dozen, I learned, that on a certain holy-day, the Farmers feast their Servants, at which solemnity they set up these Cocks in a kind of Triumph &c:

Being come back towards Rochester, I went to take order about building a strong & high Wall about an house I had hired of a Gent: at a place called Hartlip, for a Prison, paying 50 pounds yearely rent: here I settled a Provost Martial, & other officers, returning by Feversham ... & so got to Says-Court by the first of **Aprill**.

April 2: To Lond: to give his Majestie an account of my Progresse.

4: I went to see the fopperies of the Papists at Somerset house, & York-house, where now the French Ambassador had caused to be represented our B: Saviour, at the Pascal Supper, with his Disciples, in figures & puppets made as big as the life, of wax work, curiously clad, & sitting round a large table, the roome nobly hung, & shining with innumerable Lamps & Candles, this exposed, to the whole world, all the Citty came to see; such liberty had the Roman Catholicks at this time obtained ...

May 2: My sonne John was specialy admitted of the Middle Temple by Sir Fra: North, his Majesties Solicitor general [Since Lord Chancelor]: I pray God blesse this begining, my intention being he should seriously apply himselfe to the study of the Law: ...

10: To Lond: din'd with Sir W: D'Oylie when came a Letter from the Council, that I was forthwith to repaire to his Majestie whom I found in the Pal-Mal in St. Ja: Park, where his Majestie coming to me from the companie, he commanded me to go immediately to the Sea-Coast, & to observe the motion of the Dutch Fleete & ours, the Duke, & so many of the flower of our Nation being now under saile coming from Portsmouth thro the Downes, where 'twas believed there might be an encounter; so as I went on the next day (11) to Chatham:

12 heard a sermon at the Cathedrall of Rochester, din'd at Coll: Midletons:

13 To Canterbury, Visited Dr. Bargrave my old fellow Travelor in Italy & greate Virtuoso.

14: To Dover where I staied in attendance of the Fleete from Portsmouth, but which appear'd not til the 16: Ascension Day, when the Duke of York with his, & the French Squadron, in all 170 ships, of which above 100 Men of War, sailed by after the Dutch, who were newly withdrawn: Such a gallant & formidable Navy never I think spread saile upon the seas, it was <a> goodly, yet tirrible sight, to behold them as I did passing by the straits, twixt Dover & Calis eastward, in a glorious day: The wind was yet so high, that I could not well go on board, & they were soone gotten out of sight:

So the next day having visited our Prisoners at the Castle & saluted the Governor, I tooke horse [17] for Margate, where from North-foreland lighthouse top (which is a pharos built of Bricque, having on top a Cradle of yron, in which one attends a greate Sea-Coale fire, all the yeare long when the nights are darke, for the safe-guard of Sailers) we could see our fleete as it lay at Anker; & the morning weighing, sailed out of sight to the N: East: ...

20 I was carried to see a gallant Widow a Farmoresse, & I think of Gygantic race, rich, comely, & exceedingly Industrious: She put me in mind of Debora, and Abigal; her house was so plentifully stored with all manner of Countrie provisions, all of her own groth, & all her conveniences so substantiall, neate & well understood; She herselfe so jolly & hospitable, & her land, so trim, & rarely husbanded, that it struck me with a kind of admiration at her Oeconomie:

21 This towne much consists of Brewers of a certaine heady Ale; & deale much in mault &c: for the rest tis raggedly built, & an ill haven, with a small fort of little concernement, nor is the Iland well disciplin'd, but as to the husbandry & rural part, far exceeding any part of England, & I think of the whole world for the accurate culture of their ground, in which in truth they exceede even to Curiosity & emulation: We passed by Richborow, & in sight of Reculvers, & so came thro a sweete garden as it were to Canterbery, hearing no noise from the sea:

[22] at Canterbery after Prayers and Sermon I came on to Rochester, & [23] next day to my house:

24 I went to Lond, gave his Majestie an account of my Journey, and that I had put all things in a readinesse, upon all events, & so returned home sufficiently wearied: ...

31. I received another Command to repaire to the seaside againe, so I went to Rochester, where I found many both Wounded, sick, and Prisoners newly put on shore, after the Engagement of the 28, in which the Earle of Sandwich, that incomparable person, & my particular friend & divers more whom I

loved, were lost: My Lord (who was Admiral of the <Blew>) in the *Prince* which was burnt, being one of the best Men of War, that ever spread canvas on the sea: Lost likewise with this brave man, was Sir Charles Coterell<'s> Sonn, whose Father was Master of the Ceremonies, & Sir Ch: Harbord sonn of his Majesties Surveyor generall, two valiant, & most accomplish<ed> youths, full of virtue & Courage, & that might have saved themselves, but would perish with my Lord, whom they honor'd & loved above their owne lives:

And here I cannot but make some reflection upon things past: Since it was not above a day or two, that going at White-hall to take my leave of his Lordship (who had his Lodgings in the Privy Gardens) shaking me by the hand bid me *god buy*, he should he thought see me no more, & I saw to my thinking something boading in his Countenance; no says he, they will not have me live: Had I lost a Fleete (meaning on his return from Bergen, when he tooke the E. India prise) I should have fared better; but be it as please God; I must do I know not what, to save my reputation; something to this effect, he had hinted to me; but thus I took my leave: and well I remember, that the Duke of Albemarle, & now my Lord Clifford, had I know not why, no greate opinion of his Courage, becaue in former Conflicts, being an able & experienc'd sea-man (which neither of them were) he allwayes brought of his Majesties ships, without losse, though not without as many markes of true Courage as the stoutest of them; & I am witnesse, that in the late War, his owne ship was pierced like a Culender: But the buisinesse was, he was utterly against the War from the beginning, & abhor'd the attacquing of the Smyrna fleete; He did not favour the brutish & heady expedition of Clifford at Bergin; nor was he so stupidly furious, & confident as was the D: of Albemarle, who believed he could vanquish the Hollander with one Squadron:

My L: Sandwich was prudent as well as Valiant, & allways govern'd his afairs with successe, and little losse, he was for deliberation, & reason, they for action & slaughter without either; & for this, whisperd it, as if my L: of Sandwich were not so Gallant, because he was not rash & knew how fatal it were to loose a Fleete, such as was that under his Conduct, & for which these very persons would have censurd him on the other side: This it was which I am confident griev'd him, & made him enter like a Lion, & fight like one too, in the middst of the hottest service, where the stoutest of the rest, seing him ingagd, & so many ships upon him, durst not, or would not, come into his succour, as some of them, whom I know, might have don:

Thus this gallant Person perish'd to gratifie the pride & envy, of some I named: & deplorable was the losse, of one of the best accomplish<ed> persons, not onely of this Nation but of any other: He was learned in the Mathematics, in Musique, in Sea affaires, in Political: Had ben divers Embassies, was of a sweete obliging temper; Sober, Chast, infinitly ingenious, & a true noble man, an ornament to the Court, & his Prince, nor has he left any that approch his many Virtues behind him: He had I confesse serv'd the Tyrant Cromwell, when a young man, but 'twas without malice, & as a souldier of a fortune, & readily submitted & that with joy, bringing an intire fleet with him from the Sound, at the very first tidings of his Majesties restauration: nor praise I him for what he did then amisse, but for the signal services he since had don, & verily believe him as faithfull a Subject as any that were his not his Friends: I am yet heartily griev'd at this mighty losse, nor do I call it to my thoughts without emotion.

June 2 Trinity Sonday I passd at Rochester, & on the 5, was buried in the Cathedral Monsieur Rabiniere *tres le bois*,[1] Reare Admiral of the French Squadron (a very gallant person) of his Wounds received in the fight: I went to visite him languishing some time before, & now this Ceremonie lay on me, which I perform'd with all the decency I could; inviting the Mayor & Aldermen to come in their formalities: Sir Jonas Atkins there with his Guards, the Deane & Prebends; one of his Countriemen, pronouncing a funeral Oration, at the brink of his Grave, which I caused to be in the Quire, with all decent solemnity, as it was more at large describd in the Gazzet of that day, Colonel Reymes, (my Collegue in Commission) assisting, who was so kind as to accompany me from Lond: though it was not his district: for indeede, the stresse of both these Warrs, lay more on me, by far, than on any of my breatheren, who had little to do in theirs:

7 I went to see Upnore Castle, which I found pretty well defended, but of no greate moment: Nex<t> day I sailed to the Fleete now riding at the buoy of the Noore, where I met his Majestie, the Duke, L. Arlington & all the greate men in the Charles, lying miserably shatterd; but the misse of my Lord Sandwich redoubled the losse to me, as well as the folly of hazarding so brave a fleete, & loosing so many good men, for no provocation in the World but because the Hollander exceeded us in Industrie, & all things else but envy: Here at Sheere-Nesse, I gave his Majestie [& R: Hig<hn>esse] an account of the Charge under my inspection, & so returned that night to Quinborow, & the next day (being Sonday) din'd at Major Dorels Governor of Shere Nesse, at his Country house, who treated me with greate Civility, thence to Rochester ...

July 3: To Lond: din'd at my Sister Evelyns, & then to my L: Sandwiches funerall, which was by Water in solemn pomp to Westminster: ...

31 I entertaind the Maids of honour (among whom there was one[2] whom for her many & extraordinary virtues, I did infinitely esteeme) at a Comedy, this afternoone, & so went home:

August 1. I was at the Marriage of my L: Arlingtons onely Daughter (a Sweete Child, if ever there was any) to the Duke of Grafton, natural sonn, of the King, by the Dutchesse of Cleaveland, The Archbishop of Cant: officiating, the King & all the grandees present: I had a favour given me by my Lady, but tooke no greate joy for many reasons: ...

11: Came to see my Wife, the Queenes Maides of honour, and amongst them my particular Devota, Mrs. Blagge, they returned late in the Evening ...

September 1 ... I spent this weeke in soliciting for monies, & in reading my papers of the first Holland War to my Lord Clifford &c: And now our Council of Plantations met at my Lord Shaftsberys (chancelor of the Exchequer) to reade, and reforme the draght of our new Patent, joyning the Council of Trade to our political capacities: after which I returned home, in order to another Excursion to the sea side, to get what recovered men on board the fleete was

---

[1] Des Rabesnières-Treillebois.

[2] One of E's first references to a meeting with Margaret Blagge, later Mrs Godolphin (1652-78), and now about twenty years old. He had already been aware of her for some time as his wording makes obvious. Apart from dining with her on 22 July 1672, his only prior notice is that she went on a journey with his wife (30 June 1669).

possible; so as 8: I lay at Gravesend, thence to Rochester, returning on the 11th ...

[26] I carried with me to dinner my Lord: H: Howard, now to be made Earle of Norwich, and L: Marishal of England, to Sir Rob: Claytons now Sherif of Lond: where we had a greate feast: in his new House, built indeed for a greate Magistrate at excessive cost: The Cedar Dining roome is painted with the Historie of the Gyants War, incomparably by Mr. Streeter; but the figures are too neere the Eye:

October 4: Supped with my deare friend Mrs. Blagge and the Countesse of Sunderland: ...

8 My Lord Sunderland now Ambassador at Paris, I went to take my Leave of my Lady, who was now going over to him: she made me stay dinner at Lycester house, & after dinner sent for Richardson the famous Fire-Eater, who before us devourd Brimston on glowing coales, chewing and swallowing them downe: he also mealted a beere glasse & eate it quite up: then taking a live Coale on his tongue, put on it a raw oyster, which coale was blown on with billows till it flam'd & sparkled in his mouth, & so remain'd til the Oyster gaped & was quite boiled: Then he mealted pitch & Wax with Sulphure, which he drank downe as it flamed; I saw it flaming in his Mouth a good while: he also tooke up a thick piece of Yron, such as Laundresses use to put in their Smoothing boxes, & when 'twas fiery hot, he held it betweene his teeth, <then> in his hand, & threw it about like a stone: but this I observ'd he car'd not to hold very long: Then he stood on a small pot, & bending his body, tooke a glowing Yron with his mouth from between his feete, without <touching> either pot or ground with his hands; with divers other prodigious feates: ...

16 My Devout, & deare Friend declaring her condition to me for want of one she could trust, to govern & manage her competent stock; and earnestly desiring my poore assistance; I promised to do my best to serve her, & from that time forwards, I reckond her as my Child; for none did ever shew greater esteeme for a Father, than did this incomparable Creature to me, worthy of all the returnes I could ever make, for the many lasting obligations I received from her; a rare example of so much piety, & Virtue in so greate a Witt, beauty & perfection; This Miracle of a Young Lady in a licentious Court & so deprav'd an age: She now delivered me the★under her owne hand,[1] & it shall be Inviolable ...

30 My Lord of Ossory, having newly received the Order of the Garter carried me in his Coach with him to Clarenden house where I dined with my Lord Duke his father. &c: In the afternoone we met at the R: Society, where were made divers Microscopic observations on Plants &c: ...

---

[1] Inserted in the *Diary* manuscript at this point is an ink sketch of an altar surmounted by an inverted heart with a halo of six-pointed stars. On the altar is the inscription in Margaret Blagge's hand: 'XVI.OCTOB.M.D.C.LXXII. Marg^t: Blagge. be this the symbol of our friendshipe in I.+H.S.... for my Brouther Evelyn'. On the left side in E's hand is '*Mediocria firmæ*' and on the right '*Meliora retinete*', a variation on his motto (see p.15-16). At the bottom is the five-pointed star, the pentangle: ★ . This drawing, presumably the original made on the occasion recorded in the *Diary* and *The Life of Mrs Godolphin* (see, for example, 1847, 36-7), is reproduced by de Beer (III, 628).

November 15 Was a Council, many Merchants being summond about the Consulage of Venice, which caused great dispute; the most considerable thought it Uselesse; but it was dismiss'd to another hearing on friday when they were to produce their proposals: This being the Queen Consorts birth day, There was an extraordinary appearance of Gallantrie & a Ball danced at Court: ...

December 29 ... My poore <Laquey> Adames died of a Pleurisie: ...

1673

January 1. After pub: Prayers in the Chapell at W:hall, & my humble supplication to God for his blissing the Yeare now entering, I went to see + not well, & so returned home, having my lately deceased Servant to bury, & some neighbours to entertaine:

   <5> ... My Sonn now publish'd his version of *Rapinus Hortorum* &c dedicated to the Ear: of Arlington:[1]

February 6 To Council about reforming an abuse of the diers with Saunders & other false drogues, exam<in>ing divers of that trade &c: ...

March 26 I was sworn a Younger-brother of the Trinity Company with my most worthy & long acquainted noble friend My Lord Ossorie Eldest sonn to the Duke of Ormond: Sir Richard Browne my F. in Law, being now Master of that Society; after which there was a greate Collation &c: ...

   29 I carried my Sonn to the Bishop of Chichester that learned & pious man, Dr. Peter Gunning, to be instructed by him before he received the holy Sacrament, when he gave him most excellent advise, which I pray to God may influence, and remaine with him as long as he lives; and ô that I had been so blessed, and instructed when first I was admitted to that Sacred Ordinance!

   30: Easter-day preached in the morning one Mr. Field ... a Resurrection sermon with much eloquence: The Blessed Communion followd, at which both my selfe, & my Sonne received, it being his first time, & with that whole weekes more extraordinary preparation, I besech God make him a sincere good Christian, whilst I endeavor to instill into him the feare & love of God, & discharge the Duty of a Father: The Sermon *Coram Rege* this day, was by Dr. Sparrow Bishop of Excester; but he spake so very low, & the crowde so greate, that I could not heare him: however I staied to see whither (according to costome) the Duke of York did Receive the Communion, with the King, but he did not, to the amazement of every body; This being the second yeare he had forborn & put it off, & this being within a day of the Parliaments sitting, who had Lately made so severe an Act against the increase of Poperie, gave exceeding griefe & scandal to the whole Nation; That the heyre of it, & the

---

[1] *Of Gardens. Four Books. First written in Latine Verse by Renatus Rapinus, And now made English by J.E.* E included part of the text in the third and subsequent editions of *Sylva*. The boy was not quite eighteen when this, his first published work (apart from a Greek poem appended to the second edition of *Sylva* in 1670), appeared.

sonn of a Martyr for the Protestant Religion, should apostasize: What the Consequence of this will be God onely knows, & Wise men dread: ...

April 20 ... This Evening Mrs. Thornhill, sister to the Earle of Bath, & a relation of ours, shewed my Wife and me her Majesties rich Toylet in her Dressing roome, which being all of Massie Gold,[1] & presented her by the King, was valued at 4000 pounds ...

24 I was sent by his Majestie into the Citty to borrow ten-thousand Pounds, upon the third quarter Tax, per advance for the Sick & Wounded & Prisoners at War: &c ...

<27> ... at St. Martines the Minister on 1. Cor: 11. 29 the holy Sacrament following: which I partooke of upon Obligation of the Late Act of Parliament, injoyning every body in Office Civil or Militarie, under penalty of 500 pounds, to receive the holy Sacrament within one moneth, before two authentique Wittnesses: so as I had besides Dr. Lamplughs the Viccars hand, the two Church-Wardens also ingrossed in parchment to be afterwards producd in the Court of Chancery or some other Court of Record: which I did at the Chancery barr, as being one of the Council of Plantations & Trade, [**May** 3] taking then also the Oath of Allegiance & Supremacy, signing the clause in the said Act against Transubstantiation. Dined at Mr. Herveys the Queens Tressurer with Mr. Sid: Godolphin ...

21: Came to see us & Dine with me, my Lord Jo: Berkeley and his Lady, my deare Friends Mrs. Blagg, Mr. Sidny Godolphin (a grome of the Bedchamber) Sir Robert Morray, Mr. Lucie Gore, & Sir Elis Leighton &c: ...

28 I carried one Withers an ingenious Shipwright, to the King, to shew his Majestie some new method of building &c: ...

June 12 Came to Visite and dine with me, my Lord V: Count Cornbery & his Lady, My Lady Francis Hyde Sister to the Duchesse of York, Mrs. Dorothy Howard Mayd of Honour: We all went after dinner to see the formal, & formidable Camp, on Black-heath, raised to invade Holland, or as others suspected for another designe &c-: Thence to the Italian Glasse-house at Greenewich, where was Glasse blowne of finer mettal, than that of Muran ...

17 Din'd with Mrs. Blagg, at B: house, thence to Mr. Dicksons the Painters, to whom she sate the first time for her picture, which I desired her to give to me:[2]

19 ... Congratulated the new Lord Tressurer Sir Tho: Osborn, a Gent: whom I had ben intimately acquainted with at Paris, & who was every day at my F in Laws house & Table there; on which account I was too Confident of succeeding in his favour, as I had don in his Predecessors; but such a friend never shall I find, & I neglected my time, far from believing that my Lord Clifford would have so rashly laied down his staffe as he did, to the amazement of all the World; when it came to the test of his receiving the Communion; which I am confident he forbore, more for some promise he had entered into, to gratifie the Duke, than for any prejudice to the Protestant Religion, though I found him wavering of a prety while: ...

---

[1] Solid gold.

[2] Reproduced in W.G. Hiscock, 1951, *John Evelyn and Mrs Godolphin*, opposite p. 64, and T. Lever, 1952, *Godolphin, his Life and Times*, opposite p. 8.

26: Came my Bro: Evelyn, my Sister of Woodcott, my Niepce Montague & severall persons of quality from Court, to dine with me, and see the army, still remaining Encamp'd on Black-heath: ...

July 25 I went to Tunbridge Wells, to visite my Lord Clifford, Late L: Tressurer, who was ther to divert his mind, more than body, that he had so engag'd himselfe to the Duke (as was believed) that rather than take the Test, without which he could be capable of no office, he would resigne that greate & honorable station; This, I am confident grieved him to the heart, & at last broke it; for though he carried with him musique & people to divert him, & when I came to see him, Lodged <me> in his owne appartmen<t>, & would not let me go from him, I found he was struggling in his mind, & being of a rough & ambitios nature, could not long brooke the necessitie he had brought on himselfe of submission to this conjuncture; besides that he saw the Dutch-Warr, which was made much by his advise, as well as the shutting up of the Exchequer, very unprosperous: These things his high spirit could not support.

26. I went to the Wells with my Lord, & visited my Lady Henrietta Hyde:

27: Sonday, was no [pub:] prayers in the morning: but in the afternoone I heard Prayers at my Lady Henriettas: so having staied here two or 3 daies I obtain'd leave of my Lord, that I might returne, by the way I saw my Lord of Dorsets house at Knowle neere Sevenock a greate old fashiond house &c ...

31 ... I went through Cheape side to see the Pictures of all the Judges & Eminent men of the Long robe newly painted by Mr. Write, & set up in Guild-hall costing the Citty 1000 pounds: most of them are very like the Persons they are made to represent, though I never tooke Write to be any considerable artist ...

August 18 To Lond: to speak with his Majestie: My Lord Clifford being about this time returned from Tunbridge where I left him, & now preparing for Devonshire, I went to take my leave of him at Wallingford house, where he was packing up of Pictures, most of which were of hunting wild beasts, & vast pieces of bull-baiting, beare baiting &c: with other furniture: I found him in his study, & restored to him several papers of state, & other importances, which he had furnished me with, upon ingaging me to write the historie of the Holland War; with other private letters of his acknowledgements to my L: Arlington, who of a private Gent: of a very noble family, but inconsiderable fortune, had advanc'd him from almost nothing:

The first thing was his being a Parliament man, then knighted, then made one of the Commissioners of the Sick & Wounded, upon which occasion we sate long together: then on the death of Hugh Pollard, he was made Comptroller of the Household & Privy Counselor, yet still my bro: Commissioner: after the death of my L: Fitzharding Treasurer of the Houshold, which (by letters of his my L: Arlington has shew'd me) he beging of his Lordship to obtaine for him as the very height of his ambition, with such submissions, & professions of his patronage, & being totaly his creature, as I had never seene more accknowledging: The Earle of Southampton then dying, & he with others made one of the Commissioners of the Treasury, his Majestie inclining to put it into one hand, my L: Clifford under pretence of making all his Interest for his Patron my L: Arlington, cutt the Grasse under his feet & procur'd it for himselfe, assuring the King, that my L: A: did not desire it, & indeed my Lord A: has himselfe protested to me, that his Confidence in my L: Clifford, made him so remisse, & his affection to him so particular that was absolutely minded to devolve it on my L: Clifford, that was his Creature, all the world knowing how himselfe affected Ease & quiet, now growing into Yeares, but yet little thinking of go-by: This was the onely great ingratitude which my L: Clifford shew'd, keeping my L: Ar: in ignorance, whom he <continualy> assurd, he was pursuing his Interest, which was the Duke, into whose greate favour Clifford was now gotten, but which did certainely cost him the losse of all; namely his going so irrevocably far in his Interest: &c:

For the rest my Lord Clifford was a valiant, uncorrupt gent: ambitious, not Covetous, generous, Passionate, and a most constant sincere friend to me in particular; so as when he lay'd down his office, I was at the end of all my hopes, and endeavors; which were not for high matters, but to obtaine what his Majestie was realy indebted to my F. in law, which was the uttmost of my ambition, and which I had undoubtedly don, if this friend had stood; he who succeeded him, Sir Thomas Osborn, though much more obliged to my F in Law & his family, & my long & old acquaintance; being of a more haughty & far less obliging nature, & from which I could hope for little; a man of excellent natural parts, but nothing generous or grateful:

Well, thus taking Leave of my L: Clifford, wringing me by the hand, & earnestly looking on me, he bid me *god buy*, adding, Mr. E: I shall never see thee more; no <said> I my L: whats the meaning of this? I hope I shall see you often, and as greate a person againe; No Mr. E: do not expect it, I will never see this Place, this Citty or Court againe, or words of this sound: In this manner, not without mutual tears almost I parted from him: nor long was it after, but the newes was, that he was dead; and as I have heard from some that I believe knew, made himselfe a way, after an extraordinary Melancholy: This is not confidently affirm'd; but a servant who lived in the house, & afterward with Sir Ro: Clayton L: Mayor, did report it, as well as others; & when I hinted some such thing to Mr. Prideaux one of his Trustees, he was not willing to enter into that discourse: but tis reported with these particulars, That causing his Servant to leave him one morning unusualy, locking himselfe in, he strangled himselfe with his Cravett, upon the bed Tester: His Servant not liking his manner of dissmissing, & looking through the key hole (as I remember) & seeing his Master hanging, brake in before he was quite dead, & taking him downe, vomiting out a greate deal of bloud, was heard to utter these words; Well, let men say what they will, there is a God, a just God above, after which he spake no more &c: This if true, is dismal, and realy, he was the chiefe occasion of the Dutch Warr, & of all that bloud which was lost at Bergen, in attaquing the Smyrna fleete, & that whole quarrell &c: ...

September 23 To Lond: dining with Mrs. Bl: we went to see Paradise, a roome in Hatton Garden furnished with the representations of all sorts of animals, handsomely painted on boards or cloth, & so cut out & made to stand & move, fly, crawll, roare & make their severall cries, as was not unpretty: though in it selfe a mere bauble, whilst the man who shew'd, made us Laugh heartily at his formal poetrie ...

October 30 I sat with the Commissioners of Sewers in Southwark, & returned home:

November 5 ... This night the youths of the Citty burnt the Pope in Effigie after they had made procession with it in greate triumph; displeased at the D: for altering his Religion, & now marrying an Italian Lady &c: ...

December 1 In the morning to the Council of Plant: & thence to Gressham Coll: whither the Citty had invited to the Royal Society, by severall of their chiefe Aldermen & Magistrates and gave us a Collation, to wellcome us to our first place of Assembly, from whence we had ben driven to give place to the Citty to make it their Exchange upon the dreadfull Conflagration, 'til their new exchange was now finished: the Society having til now ben entertaind & met at Arundel house: This day we also Chose Officers, St. Andrews day being on the Sonday & day before:

2 I dined with ★ & visited the sick, thence to an Almeshouse, where was prayers, & reliefe, some very sick & miserable: returning prayers, and it was one of the best daies I ever spent in my life: There was this day at Dinner my Lo: Lockart design'd Ambassador for France, a gallant & a sober person ...

20 I had some discourse with certaine strangers, not unlearned, who had ben born not far from the old Niniveh: They assur'd me the ruines being still extant, & vast, wonderfull was the buildings, Vaults, Pillars, & magnificent fragments now buried, & remaining: but little could they say of the Toure of Babel that satisfied me: but the description of the amœnitie & fragrancy of the Country for health & cherefullnesse, did almost ravish me; so sensibly the<y> spake of the excellent aire & climat, in respect of our cloudy & splenetic Country: ...

1674

January 5, I saw an Italian Opera in musique, the first that had ben in England of this kind: ...

9 Sent for next morning to Lond: by his Majestie to write some thing against the Hollanders, about the Duty of the flag & fisherie; so returned with some papers.

May 4 Came the Queenes Maids of honour & my friend to dine with us at Says-Court: ...

6 Carried my La: Berkely & Mrs. Blagg to see the Repositary of the Royal Society.

7: I visited my L: Mordaunt at Parsons Greene it being his Wedding-day & a greate feast with much Companie &c: ...

June 27: Mr. Dryden the famous Poët, & now Laureat came to give me a Visite: It was the Anniversarie of my Marriage, & the first day I went into my new little Cell, & Cabinet which I built below the South Court, at East end of the Parlor: ...

July 9: To Lond: to pay Dr. Jacomb 360 pounds for his sonn now of age: for his part of the purchase of the Mills & Land, I bought of the Beechers in Deptford: returnd the 10: ...

22 I went to Winsore with my Wife & sonn, to see my Daughter Mary who was there with my Lady Tuke; & to do my Duty to his Majestie: next day to a greate entertainement at Sir Robert Holmes's at Cranburne Lodge in the forest: There were his Majestie, Queene, Duke, Dutchesse & all the Court: I returned the Evening with Sir Jos: Williamson now declared Secretary of state: Sir Jos:

was sonn of a meane Clergyman some where in Cumberlandshire, brought up at Queenes Coll: [Oxon:] of which he came to be a fellow; ...

August 6 I went to Groomebridge to see my old friend Mr. Packer, the house built within a Moate & in a woody Valy: The old house had ben the place of Confinement of that duke of Orleance taken by one Waller (whose house this then was) at the Bataile of Agencourt; but now demolish'd, a new <w>as built in its place; though a far better had ben on the south of the wood on a graceful ascent: At some small distance is a large Chapell not long-since built by Mr. Packers father, upon a Vowe he made to do it, upon the Returne of Charles the first, out of Spaine 1625. & dedicated it to St. Charles: but what saint there was then of that name, I am to seeke; for being a Protestant, I conceive it was not Borrhimeo ...

9 ... I went to the Wells at Southborrow to visite my deare friend Mrs. Blagg, then drinking the Waters with my Lady Berkeley: ...

18 To Lond, and next day to Winsore about buisinesse with my Lord Tressurer: next day his Majestie told me how exceedingly the Dutch were displeased, at my Treatise of historie of *Commerce*; that the Holland Ambassador had complained to him of what I had touch'd of the flag, & fishery &c: & disired the booke might be caled in: whilst on the other side, he assur'd me he was exceedingly pleased with what I had don & gave me many thanks: However it being just upon conclusion of the Treaty of Breda, (for indeed it was designed to be published some moneths before, & when we were at defyance) his Majestie told me, he must recall it formaly, but gave order that Copies should be publiquely seiz'd to pacifie the Ambassador should immediatly be restord to the Printer, & that neither he nor the Vendor should be molested:[1]

The truth is, that which touch'd the Hollander, was much lesse, than what the King himselfe furnish'd me with, & oblig'd me to publish, having caus'd it to be read to him 'ere it went to the presse: but the error was, it should have ben publish'd before the peace was proclaim'd: The noise of this books suppression, made it be presently bought up, & turn'd much to the Stationer<'s> advantage: Nor was it other, than the meere preface, prepard'd to be præfix'd to my Historie of the whole Warr; which I now pursu'd no farther.

21 There was approches, & a formal seige, against a Work with Bastions, Bullwarks, Ramparts, Palizads, <Graft>, hornworks, Conter-scarps &c: in imitation of the Citty of Maestrict, newly taken by the French: & this being artificialy design'd & cast up in one of the Meadows at the foote of the long Terrace below the Castle, was defended against the Duke of Monmouth (newly come from that real seige) who [with the Duke of York] attaqu'd it with a little army, to shew their skill in Tactics: so on Saturday night, They made their approches, opened trenches, raised batteries, [took] the Conter-scarp, Ravelin, after a stout Defence. Greate Gunns fir'd on both sides, Granados shot, mines Sprung, parties sent out, attempts of raising the seige, prisoners taken, Parlies, & in short all the Circumstances of a formal seige to appearance, & what is most strange, all without disorder, or ill accident, but to

---

[1] *Navigation and Commerce, Their Original and Progress, Containing A Succinct Account of Traffick in General* ... Even if the book was withdrawn enough copies remained in circulation, as E goes on to point out, for it to be not unobtainable even today.

the greate satisfaction of a thousand spectators, when being night it made a formidable shew, & was realy very divertisant:

This mock seige being over, I went with Mr. Pepys back to Lond: where we arived about 3 in the morning: & at St. Martines heard a sermon [<23>] on 26: Matt: 74: The very same sermon, by the same preacher, I happn'd to heare againe at St. Jamess this Afternoone: ...

September 3. I went to Lond: about sealing writings in Trust for Mrs. Blagge, & then home ...

15 To Council, about the fetching off the English left at Syrenam &c since our reconciliation with Holland: I visited ★, gave her the deedes about the 500 pounds I had disposed of for her &c ...

23. I went to <see> the greate losse that my Lord Arlington had received by fire, at Goring-house, now this night consum'd to the ground, with exceeding losse of hangings, plate, rare pictures and Cabinets, in a word, nothing almost was saved, of the best & most princely furniture that any subject had in England: My Lord & Lady being both absent at the Bathe; so returned home full of astonishment at the uncertaintie of worldly enjoyments: ...

October 20: Lond: Council, dind with ★ at my L: Berkeleys where I had discourse with Sir Tho: Modiford, Late Governor of Jamaica, & with Coll: Morgan who undertooke that gallant exploit from Nombre de Dios to Panamà on the Continent of America: he told me 10000 men would easily conquer all the Spanish Indies, the<y> were so secure: greate was the booty they tooke, & much, nay infinitly greater had it been, had they not ben betraied & so discovered before their approch, as they had time to carry on board the vast Treasure, which they put off to sea, in sight of our Men, that had no boates to follow &c: They set fire of Panamà, and ravag'd the Country 60 miles about. The<y> were so supine, & unexercis'd, that they were afraid to give fire to a greate gun &c: ...

November 15 The Anniversary of my Baptisme I first heard that famous & Excellent Preacher Dr. Burnet (Author of the *Historie of the Reformation*) on 3: Coloss: 10: with such a floud of Eloquence, & fullnesse of matters as shew'd him to be a person of extraordinary parts: The B: Comm: followed: & din'd with my friend Dr. Needham: This night being her Majesties Birth-day: the Court was exceeding splendid, in Clothes & Jewells to the height of excesse:

17 A Council in the morning, din'd with ★, & Council also in the afternoone still about the buisinesse of Surenam, where the Dutch had detained some English in prison, ever since the first War 1665.

19 I heard that stupendious Violin Signor Nicholao (with other rare Musitians) whom certainly never mortal man Exceeded on that Instrument: he had a stroak so sweete, & made it speake like the Voice of a man; & when he pleased, like a Consort of severall Instruments: he did wonders upon a note: was an excellent Composer also: here was also that rare Lutinist Dr. Wallgrave: but nothing approch'd the Violin in Nicholas hand: he seem'd to be *spiritato'd* & plaied such ravishing things on a ground as astonish'd us all:

December 2: heard Signor Francisco on the Harpsichord, esteem'd on<e> of the most excellent masters in Europe on that Instrument: then came Nicholao with his Violin & struck all mute, but Mrs. Knight, who sung incomparably, & doubtlesse has the greatest reach of any English Woman: she had lately ben roming in Italy: & was much improv'd in that quality: There was other Musique, & this Consort was at Mr. Slingsbys Master of the Mint, my worthy friend, & greate lover of Musique: ...

15 To Lond: to Council: Saw a Comedie at night, at Court, acted by the Ladys onely, viz: The Lady Mary & Ann his R: hig<h>nesses two Daughters, & my deare friend Mrs. Blagg, who having the principal part, perform'd it to admiration: They were all covered with Jewels:[1]

17 Mrs. Blagg, with the two Maids of honor, Mrs. Howarde, & my Wife, came to house warming to my new Lodging: ...

22 Lond: to Council, & for the poores mony: was at the repetition of the Pastoral, on which [occasion] my friend Mrs. Blagg, had about her neere 20000 pounds worth of Jewells, of which one she lost, borrowed of the Countesse of Suffolck, worth about 80 pounds, which the Duke made good; & indeede the presse of people was so greate, that it was a wonder she lost no more: ...

1675

January 20 Visited ★ - pr: & to see Mr. Streeter that excellent Painter of Perspective &c: & Landscip, to comfort, & encourage him to be cut of the stone, with which that honest man was exceedingly afflicted: ...

29 All the Queenes Mayds of honor came to dine with mee: ...

March 4 ... I supped at Mr. Secretarie Williamsons with severall of our Society: among whom Mr. Sheeres Sonn of Cap: Sheres of our Parish, who undertooke and best succeeded in the Mole of Tanger, affirmed, that if a Scorpion were placed within a Circle of fire, or so invirond with danger as no way to escape, he would sting himselfe to death: he spake of the prodigious bignesse of Locusts in Africa: That all the Teeth of Elephants grew downewards, & not as commonly painted: That the Camelion preied chiefly on flys by a violent Suction first so exhausting its own body of breath & aire as to reduce itselfe to as thin as the edge of a knife in appearance, & then sudainly relaxing and violent suction of the aire, filling himselfe againe drew in with it, the flies that were within it<s> Spheare & opposite to him: ...

24: ... I supped at Sir William Pettys, with The Bish: of Salisbury, & divers honorable persons: we had a noble entertainement, in a house gloriously furnished; The Master & Mistris of it extraordinary Persons: Sir Will: being the sonn of a meane man some where in Sussex, was sent from Schole to Oxon: where he studied Philos: but was most eminent in Mathematics & Mechanics, proceeded Doctor of Physick, & was growne famous as for his Learning, so for his recovering a poore wench that had ben hanged for felonie, the body being beged (as costome is) for the Anatomie lecture, he let bloud, put to bed to a warme woman, & with spirits & other meanes recovered her to life; The Young Scholars joyn'd & made her a little portion, married her to a Man who had severall children by her, living 15 yeares after, as I have ben assured: He came from Oxon: to be <pedagogue> to a neighbour of mine;

---

[1] The daughters of James II, when Duke of York, by Anne, née Hyde: subsequently the Queens Mary II (1688-94) and Anne (1702-14).

Thence when the Rebells were dividing their Conquests in Ireland, he was employed by them to measure & set out the Land, which he did upon an easy contract so much per Acker: which he effected so exactly, & so expeditiously, as not onely furnish'd him with a greate summ of money, but enabled him to purchas an Estate worth 4000 pounds a yeare; he afterwards married the Daughter of Sir Hardresse Waller, she an extraordinary witt, as well as beauty, & a prudent Woman: Sir William amongst other inventions author of the Double-bottom'd ship; which though it perishd, & he censur'd for rashnesse; yet it was lost in the bay of Biscay in a storme when, I think 15 more Vessels misscarried: The Vessell was flat-bottom'd, of exceeding use to put into shallow Ports, & ride over small depths of water; It consisted of two distinct Keeles crampt together with huge timbers &c: so as a violent streame ran between: It bare a monstrous broad saile; & he still persists it practicable & of exceeding use, & has often told me he would adventure himselfe in such another, could he procure sailors, and his Majesties Permission to make a second Experiment, which name the King gave it at the Launching:

The Map of Ireland made by Sir William is bilieved to be the most exact that ever was yet made of any Country: he did promise to publish it: & I am told it has cost him neere 1000 pounds to have it ingrav'd at Amsterdam. There is not a better Latine poet living, when he gives himselfe that Diversion; nor is his Excellency less in Counsil, & prudent matters of state: &c: but is so extraordinary nice in scifting, & examining all possible contingences, that he adventures at nothing, which is not Demonstration: There were not in the whole world his equal for a superintendent of Manufacturs, & improvement of Trade; or for to govern a Plantation: If I were a Prince, I should make him my second Counselor at least: There is nothing difficult to him; besides he is Coragious, on which account I cannot but note a true storie of him: That when Sir Aleyn Brodrick sent him a Challenge, upon a difference twixt them in Ireland: Sir Will: though, exceedingly purblind, accepted the challenge, & it being his part to propound the Weapon, defied his Antagonist, to meete him with an hatchet or Axe in a darke Cellar; which he refusing, was laught at, for challinging one whom every body knew was so short sighted:

Sir William was with all this facetious, & of Easy Conversation, friendly, & Courteous & had such a faculty to imitate others, that he would take a Text, and preach now like a grave orthodox Divine, then fall-into the Presbyterian way, thence to the Phanatical, the Quaker, the Moonk, & frier, the Popish Priest, with such admirable action, & alteration of voice & tone, as it was not possible to abstaine from wonder, & one would sweare, to heare severall persons, or think he were not in good earnest an Enthusiast & almost beside himselfe, when he would fall out of it in to a serious discourse &c which was very divertisant: but it was very rarely he would be courted to oblige the company with this faculty, unlesse among most intimate friends: My Lord Duke of Ormond once obtain'd it of him, & was almost ravished with admiration of it; but by & by he fell upon a serious reprimand of the faults & miscarriages of some Princes & Governors, which though he named none, did so sensibly touch my L: Duke, who was then Lieutenant of Ireland; that my Lord began to be very uneasy, & wish'd the spirit alayed; for he was neither able to indure such truths, nor could he for his heart but be delighted; so at lasted he mealted his discourse to another more ridiculous subject & came do<w>ne from the joyne stoole; but my Lord, would heare him preach no more. He could never get to be favoured at Court; because he outwitted all the projecturs that came neere him: In my life having never know<n> such a Genius, I cannot but mention these particulers, among multitude of others, which I could produce: When I have ben in his splendid Palace, who knew him in meaner Circumstances, he would be in admiration himselfe how he ariv'd to it; nor was it his value <or> inclination to splendid furnitur & the curiositie of the age: but his Elegant Lady, who could indure nothing meane, & that was not magnificent; whilst he was very negligent himselfe & of a Philosophic temper: Lord, would he say, what a deale of do is here; I can lie in straw with as much satisfaction: & was indeede rather negligent of his person &c: Sir William is the Author of the ingenious deductions from the bills of Mortality who go under the name of Mr. Graunt: also of that usefull discourse of the manufactur of Wooll, & severall other, in our Register of the R: Society: The Author of that Paraphrase on 104 Psal: in Latin Verse, which gos about in MSS: & is inimitable: In a word, there is nothing impenetrable to him ...

April 29 I read my first discourse of *Earth & Vegetation* before the Royal Society, as a lecture in Course after Sir Rob: Southwell had reade his the weeke before on Water: I was commanded to print it by our President & the Suffrage of the Society:[1] returned home that evening: ...

May 16 ... This day was my deare friend Mrs. Blagg married to Mr. Sidny Godolphin Groome of the Bed-Chamber to his Majestie at the Temple Church by Mr. Leake Chap: to the Duke:[2] ...

31 I went with my L. Ossorie to Deptford where we chose him Master of the Trinity Companie ... Thence by barge, to Lond: where at the Trinity house we had a magnificent feast, & divers greate persons: I thence went with his Lordship to his Lodging in White-hall: ...

June 2 At a Conference of the Lords & Comm: in the painted Chamber upon a difference about imprisoning some of their Members I was present: Din'd at the Duke of Ormonds, with the Duke of Munmoth & severall greate men.

3: I was at another Conference, where the Lords accused the Commons for their transcended misbehaviour, breach of Privelege, Magna Charta, Subversion of Government, & other high & provoking & diminishing Expressions; shewing what duties & subjections they owed to the Lords in Parliament by record Hen: 4th &c. which was like to create a notable disturbance: I din'd at the Master of the Mints, went to R: Society: The discourse being of Fountaines &c & so to my owne house: ...

20: ... This afternoone came Monsieur Quierwill[3] & his Lady Parents to the famous beauty & <the King's> favorite at Court, to see Sir Rich: Bro: my F. in Law, with whom they were intimately acquainted in Bretagne, what time Sir Richard was sent to Brest, to supervise his Majesties sea affaires during the later part of his Majesties banishment abroad: This Gent: house being not a mile from Brest; Sir Richard made an acquaintance there, & being used very Civily, was oblig'd to returne it here, which we did in a Collation: after which

---

[1] *A Philosophical Discourse of Earth, Relating to the Culture and Improvement of it for Vegetation, and the Propagation of Plants, &c. as it was presented to the Royal Society, April 29. 1675,* published in 1676. Later editions prefixed *Terra*.

[2] She did not reveal her marriage to E until 3 May 1676. But note that E subsequently refers to her as Mrs Godolphin, for example 6 July below, indicating that the *Diary* had been written up retrospectively.

[3] Comte de Kéroualle, Guillame de Penancoët, father of Louise, Duchess of Portsmouth.

they returned to Lond: He seem'd a souldierly person, & a good fellow, as the Bretons generaly are, his Lady had ben very handsom, & seem'd a shrew'd understanding woman: Conversing with him in our Garden, I found severall words of the Breton language the same with our Welch: His daughter was now made Dutchesse of Portsmouth and in the height of favour; but we never made any use of it: &c: ...

28 My F in Law had a Tryal before the L: Chancelor, to advantage; but the Register prevaricated in the minutes, which is a shamefull abuse: & ought to be reform'd, by causing them to be read in Court: I visited Mrs. G - pr:

29 I went with Mrs. Godolphin to my house at Says-Court, where she staied a weeke with us: pr: ...

July 5 Came to dine with us Mr. Sidny Godolphin to see his Lady, with the two Howards Ma: of honour, & returned that Evening:

6: I carried Mrs. Godolphin to Lond: & set her downe at my Lord Sunderlands.

8 I went with Mrs. Howard & her two daughters towards Northampton Assises about a Tryal at Law, in which I was Concerned for them as a Trusteè. We lay this night at Henly on the Thames at our Attourney Mr. <Stephens's> who entertain'd us very handsomely: Thenc next day dining at Shotover at Sir Tim: Tyrills a sweete place, we lay at Oxford it being the Act: when Mr. Rob: Spencer Unkle to the Earle of Sunderland and my old acquaintance in France, entertain'd us at his appartment in Christ-Church (where he had hired one of the Canons Lodgings,) entertain'd us all the while, with exceeding generosity:

10: The Vice-Chancelor Dr. Bathurst, (who had formerly taken particular care of my Sonn) President of Trinity, invited me to Dinner, & did me greate honour all the time of my stay: The next day he also invited me & all my Company, though strangers to him, to a very noble Dinner: I was at all the Academique Exercises: <Sunday>, at St. Maries preached a fellow of Brasen nose on 2: Tit: 15., not a little magnifying the dignity of Church-man: In the afternoone one of New Coll: but the heat and presse was so greate I could not hear &c: & was faine to go out:

We heard the Speeches & saw the Ceremonie of Creating Doctors in Divinity, Law, Physique &c: I had in the morning early heard Dr. Morison Botanic Professor, reade on divers Plants in the Physic Garden; & saw that rare Collection of natural Curiosities, of Dr. Plots of Magdalen hall: Author of the Natural hist: of Oxford-shire; all of them collected in that shire, & indeede extraordinary, that in one County, there should be found such varietie of Plants, Shells, Stones, Minerals, Marcasites, foule, Insects, Models of works &c: Chrystals, Achates, Marbles: he was now intending to Visite Staffordshire & as he had of Oxfordshire to give us the Natural, Topical, Political, Mechani<c>al history: & pitty it is, more of this industrious mans genius were not employed so to describe every County of England, since it would be one of the most usefull & illustrious Workes that was ever produc'd in any age or nation: I visited also the Bodlean library & my old friend the Learned Obadia Walker head of Universitie Coll: which he had now almost quite rebuilt or repair'd: So taking leave of the V: Chancelor, Dr. Alestree the Kings Professor in Divinity, Deane of Christ Church Dr. Fell, we proceeded to Northampton where we arived next day:

In this journey went part of the way Mr. Ja: Grahame [Since privy purse to the Duke], a Young Gent: exceedingly in love with Mrs. Dorothy Howard one of the Mayds of honor in our Company: I could not but pitty them both: The Mother not much favouring it: This Lady was not onely a greate beauty, but a most virtuous & excellent Creature, & worthy to have ben Wife to the best of men: My advice was required, & I spake to the advantage of the young gent: more out of pitty, than that I thought she deserv'd no better; for though he was a gent: of a good family, yet there was greate inequalitys &c:

14 I went to see my Lord Sunderlands seat at Althorp, 4 miles from the ragged Towne of Northampton [Since burned & well rebuilt]: tis placed in a pretty open bottome, very finely watred & flanqued with stately woods & groves in a Park with a Canale, yet the water is not running, which is a defect: The house a kind of modern building with Free stone: within most nobly furnish'd: The Apartments very commodious, & Gallerie & noble hall: but the Kitching for being in the body of the house, & Chapell too small were defects: There is an old, yet honorable Gate house standing a wry, & outstanding meane, but design'd to be taken away: It was Moated round after the old manner, but is now dry & turf'd with a sweete Carpet: above all are admirable & magnificent the severall ample Gardens furnish'd with the Choicest fruite in England, & exquisitely kept: Great plenty of Oranges, and other Curiosities: The Parke full of Fowle & especialy Her<o>nes, & from it a prospect to Holmby house, which being demolished in the late Civil Warre, shews like a Roman ruine shaded by the trees about it, one of the most pleasing sights that ever I saw, of state & solemne:

15 Our Cause was pleaded in behalfe of the Mother Mrs. Howard & Daughters before baron Thurland, who had formerly been Steward of Courte for me: We carried our Cause, as there was reason; for here was an imprudent as well as disobedient sonn, against his Mother by instigation doubtlesse of his Wife, one Mrs. Ogle (an antient Maid) whom he had clandestinly married, & who brought him no fortune, he heire aparent of the Earle of Berkshire. After dinner we went towards Lond: Lay at Brickhill in Bedfordshire & came late next day to our journeys end.

This was a journey of Adventure & knight errantry, one of the Ladys servants being as desperatly in love with Mrs. Howards Woman, who riding on horsback behind his Rival, the amorous & jealous Youth, having a little drink in his pate, had certainly here killed himselfe, had he not ben prevented; for alighting from his horse & drawing his sword, he endeavored to fall upon it twise or thrice, but was interrupted; <by> our Coach-man & stranger that passed by, after which running to his rival, & snatching another sword from his side (for we had beaten his owne out of his hand) & on the suddaine pulling down his Mistriss, would have run both of them through; but we parted them, though not without some blood: This miserable Creature Poyson'd himselfe for her not many daies after they came to Lond: ...

20 ... I had the un-wellcome newes of my sonns being falln ill of the Small-pox: but God was mercifull to him in all his sicknesse.[1]

25 ...My Sonn recovers blessed be God ...

August 9 My Coach-house was broken open this night, & the Glasses & Damaske Cushions, Curtaines &c: taken away: Went to Wimbledon to see my Lord of Bristoll & return'd in the Evening: ...

29 our Viccar on his old beaten Text: Afternoone the Curate on 9: Pro: 8:

30: To Lond: return'd next day; found Mrs. Blagge there, she gave me a

---

[1] Smallpox killed two of E's daughters in 1685, see 7 March and 16 August for that year.

letter of Attourney about her Concernes & return'd to Twicknam that evening, my Wife bringing her a good part of the way:

September 2 I went to see Dullwidge Colledge, being the pious foundation of one Allen a famous Comœdian in K. James's time: The Chapell is pretty; The rest of the Hospital very ill contriv'd; it yet maintaines divers poore of both sexes, 'tis in a melancholy part of Camerwell Parish; I came back by certaine Medicinal Spa Waters at a place called Sydname Wells in Lewisham Parish; much frequented in Summer time: ...

9 I went to Lond: to see a sick [poore] person taken suddenly ill of a dumb Palsy.

10 I was Casualy shewed the Dutchesse of Portsmouths splendid Appartment at Whitehall, luxuriously furnished, & with ten times the richnesse & glory beyond the Queenes, such massy pieces of Plate, whole Tables, Stands &c: of incredible value &c: ...

29: I went to Parsons Greene to visite my Lord Mordaunt with my Wife & Mrs. Godolphin: Saw the Italian *Scaramucchio* act before the King at Whitehall; People giving monye to come in, which was very Scandalous, & never so before at Court Diversions: having seene him act before in Italy many yeares past, I was not averse from seeing the most excellent kind of that folly: ...

October 15 I got an extreame cold, such as was afterwards so epidemical, as not onely afflicted us in this Iland, but was rife all over Europe, & raged like a Plague; note that it was after an exceeding dry Summer & Autumn.

16: Anniver.★ pr: when I settled affaires my sonn being to go into france with my Lord Berkeley, designed Ambassador Extraordinary for France, & Plenipotentiary for the gen: Treaty of Peace at Nimegen: ...

27 My Lord Berkeley now in precinct for his departure into France, coming to the Council fell downe in the Gallery at White-hall of a fit of Apoplexie, & being carried into my L: Chamberlaines Lodgings employed all that night severall famous Doctors & with much adò was at last recovered to some sense by applying hot fire-pans & Spirit of Amber to his head, but nothing was found so effectual as cupping on the shoulders: an almost miraculous restauration: The next day he was carried to B: house. This stopped for the present his journey, & caused my stay in Towne, into whose hands he had put all his Affaires & whole estate in England during his absence, which though I was very unfit to undertake, in reguard of <many> buisinesses then which tooke me up; yet upon the greate importunity of my Lady, & Mrs. Godolphin (to whom I could refuse nothing) I did; It seemes when he was Deputy (not long before in Ireland) he had ben much wronged by one he left in trust with his affaires, & therefore wished for some unmercenary friend, who would take that trouble on him; which was to receive his Rents, looke after his Houses & Tennants, solicite for Supplies from the L: Tressurer &c: Correspond weekely with him, more than enough to employ any drudge in England: but what will not friendship & love make on<e> do! ...

November 9 I din'd at B: house, & went home: the next day being the time appointed for my L: Ambassador to set forth, [10] I met them with my Coach at New-Crosse: There was with him my Lady his Wife, & my deare friend Mrs. Godolphin who, out of an extraordinary friendship, would needes accompany my Lady to Paris & stay with her some time, which was the chiefe induce-ment of my permitting my Sonn to Travell; but I knew him safe under her inspection, & in reguard my Lord himselfe had so promis'd me to take him into his special care, who had intrusted all he had to mine: Thus we set out 3 Coaches, 3 Wagons, and about 40 horse besides my Coach: It being late and my Lord but valetudinarie yet, we got but to Dartford the first day, & [11] the next to Citinburne; by the Way the Major of Rochester Mr. Cony, who was then an Officer of mine for the Sick & Wounded of that place &c, entertain'd the Ladys with an handsome present of refreshments, as we came by his house:

12 We came to Canterbery, where next morning Mrs. Godolphin & I went to the Cathedrall to prayers, and thence to Dover: There was in my Lady Ambassadors Company also my Lady Hammilton, a Spritefull young Lady, who was much in the good-graces of that family, & wife of that valiant & worthy Gent: Geo: Hammilton not long after slaine in the Warrs; she had ben a Maid of Honor to the Dutchesse, & now turn'd Papist:

13 At Dover Mrs. Godolphin delivered me her Will, which her Husband had given her leave to make, & absolutely to dispose of all her fortune, which was in value better than 4000 pounds: then after prayers,

[14] the next morning my Lord having delivered me before his Letters of Attourney, Keyes, Seale, & his Will, (it being Sonday-morning and a glorious day) We tooke solemn leave of one another upon the Beach, the Coaches carrying them into the sea to the Boatts, which delivered them to Cap: Gunmans Yacht the Mary: & so I parted with my Lord, my sonn, & the person whom I esteemed as my owne life Mrs. Godolphin; being under saile, the Castle gave them 17 Gunns, & Cap: Gunman answered with 11: Hence I went to Church to beg a blessing on their Voyage: The Ministers text was 1. Joh:5.4: I dined at the Majors, who was also an officer of mine in this port: & lay that night at his house: ...

December 2 I visited my La: Mordaunt at P: Greene, my Lord her sonn being sick: After dinner this pious woman delivered me 100 pounds to bestow as I thought fit for the release of poore Prisoners, & other Charitable uses: I returned home: ...

23 To Lond: return'd: My Lady Sunderland gave me ten Ginnies, to bestow in Charities:

1676

February 19 At the R: Society Experiments to prove that the force of gunpowder was from the compression of aire in the Cornes.

20. Dr. Gunning Bish: of Elie (Coram Rege) 20 Joh:21.22.23. Chiefly against an anonymous Booke called *Naked Truth*, a famous & popular Treatise against the Corruption in the Cleargie, but not sound as to its quotations; supposed to have ben the Bish: Herefords; & was answered by Dr. Turner: it endeavoring to prove an Equality of Order of Bish: & Presbyter: Dr. Gunning asserted the difference of their functions, as divine & absolutely necessarie; implying that their antagonists were Sismatics: I received the B: Com: at St. Jamess in the morning ...

27: ... I tooke leave of my young Lo: Mordaunt going into France, & sent a recommendatory letter to Mrs. Godolphin, to have some eye over him: ...

March <20?> Dining at my La: Sunderlands, I saw a fellow swallow a knife, & divers greate pibble stones, which shaking his stomach, would make a plaine rattling one against another: The Knife was in a sheath of horne to bend in: ...

24 Goodfriday St. Martines Dr. Doughty (the Dukes Chap:) 1. Pet.2.21 incomparably describing the incomparable sorrows of our Saviours ...

Note, that this was the first time Duke appeared no more in the Chappell, to the infinite griefe and threatnd ruine of this poore Nation: I went to Says-Court ...

April 4 I went to Lond: Visited my L: Marshall, Lord Shaftsbery where I found the Earle of Burlington: I had now notice that Mrs. Godolphin was returning from Paris & landing the 3d at Dover; so I din'd with my L: Sunderland expecting her:

6 Came my dearest Friend to my greate joy; whom after I had welcom'd, I gave accompt to of her buisinesse, & return'd home ...

26 Din'd with★, discovered her Marriage by her sister:

27 My Wife entertaind her Majestie at Deptford, for which the Queene gave <me> thanks in the Withdrawing roome at White-hall.

28 The University of Oxford presented me with the *Marmora Oxon: Arundell:* the Bish: of Oxford writing to me, that I would introduce Mr. Prideaux the Editor (a most learned young man in Antiquities) to the Duke of Norfolck, to present another, dedicated to his Grace, which I did, & we both din'd with the Duke at Arundel house: & supped at the Bish: of Rochesters with Isa: Vossius ...

May 1 The meeting for the Trustees of the poore, we din'd together ...

3 Visited Mrs. Godolphin expostulated with her about the concealement, & was satisfied, it was not her intention: ...

11. I din'd with Mr. Charleton; went to see Mr. Montagues new Palace neere Bloomesbery, built by Mr. Hooke of our Society, after the French manner: Spake with my Lord Treasurer about Mony &c ...

13 returned home, & found my sonn returned out of France, praised be God; for my deare friend Mrs. Godolphin coming thence I had no desire he should stay there any longer for many reason<s>: ...

22 Trinity Monday preached a Chaplaine of my L: Ossories, after which we tooke barge to Trinity house in Lond, where was a greate feast, Mr. Pepys (Secretary of the Admiralty) chosen Master, & succeeding my Lord ...

June 2 I went with my L: Chamberlaine to see a Garden at Enfield towne; Thence to Mr. Secretary Coventries Lodge in the Chace, which is a very pretty place, the house commodious, the Gardens handsome, & our entertainment very free; there being none but my Lord & my selfe: That which I most admir'd at, was, that in the compasse of 25 Miles (yet within 14 of Lond) there is never an house, barne, Church, or building, besides three Lodges: To this Lodge there are 3 greate ponds, & some few inclosures, the rest a solitarie desert, yet stored with no lesse than 3000 deare &c: These are pretty retreates for Gent: especialy that were studious & a lover of privacy: We return'd in the Evening by Hamsted, where we diverted to see my Lord Wottons house & Garden; built with vast expense by Mr. Oneale an Irish Gent: who married his Mother, the Lady Stanhop: The furniture is very particular for Indian Cabinets, Porcelane, & other solid & noble moveables, The Gallery very fine: The Gardens very large, but ill kept; yet Woody & chargeable; the mould a cold weeping clay, not answering the expense: ...

12 I went to Sir Tho: Bonds new & fine house by Pecham, the place is on a flat, yet has a fine Garden, & prospect thro the meadows towards Lond:

13 To Lond: about Mrs. Godolphins Lease at Queenes Council: ...

27 My Marriage Anniversarie, I din'd with Mrs. Godolphin at Berkeley-house, being the first day of her house-keeping since her Marriage & returne into England ...

July 3 din'd with my Lo: Chamberlaine, & sealed the Deedes of Mortgage for security of 1000 pounds lent by my friend Mrs. Godolphin to my Lord Sunderland ...

19 dind at L: Chamb: Went to Sir William Sandersons funerall (husband to the Mother of the Maides, & author of two large, but meane Histories of KK. James & Charles the first): he was buried at Westminster: ...

August 25 Din'd with Sir Jo: Banks's at his house in Lincolns Inn fields: upon recommending Mr. Upman to be Tutor to his sonn going into France: This Sir Jo: Bankes was a Merchant, of small beginnings, but by usurie &c: amass'd an Estate of 100000 pounds &c.

26 I din'd at the Admiralty, with Sec: Pepys: Supp'd at L: Chamberlaines, here was Cap: Baker, who had ben lately on the attempt of the Nor-west passage: he reported prodigious depth of yce, blew as a Saphire & as transparant: That the thick mists was their chiefe impediment, & cause of returne: [I went home.] ...

September 2 I paied 1700 pounds, to the Marquis de Sissac, which he had lent to my L: Berkeley &c: which I heard the Marqu<i>s lost at play <within> a night or two: ...

6 Supp'd at L: Chamberlains, where also supped the famous beauty & errant Lady, the Dutchesse of Mazarine (all the world knows her storie)[1] the Duke of Monmouth, Countesse of Sussex, both natural Children of the Kings, by that infamous Adulteresse the Dut: of Cleaveland: & the Countesse of Derby a vertuous Lady, daughter to my best friend, the Earle of Ossorie; ...

12 To Lond: to take order about the building of an house, or rather an appartment, which had all the conveniences of an house; for my deare friend Mr. Godolphin & Lady: which I undertooke to Contrive, & Survey, & employ workmen in, til it shold be quite finished: It being just over against his Majesties Wood-yard, by the Thames side, leading to Scotland yard: I din'd with★pr: [returned.]

17: ... There dined with me Mr. Flamested the learned Astrologer & Mathematitian, whom now his Majestie had established in the new Observatorie in Greenewich Park, and furnish'd with the choicest Instruments: an honest, sincere man &c: ...

18 To Lond, to survey my Workemen, dined with★- pr: and [19] then with Mrs. Godolphin to Lambeth, to that rare magazine of Marble, to take order for chimny-pieces &c: The Owner of the workes, had built him a pretty dwelling: This Dutchman, had contracted with the Genoezes for all their Marble &c: We

---

[1] Cardinal Mazarin's niece, Hortense Mancini (1646-99). Until 1660 she had hoped to marry Charles II. In 1661 she married the future Duc de Mazarin. She published an autobiographical account of her unhappy marriage and came to England in 1675, becoming one of the King's mistresses. She had no children by Charles and was temporarily expelled in 1677 for a liaison with the Prince de Monaco.

also saw the Duke of Bouckingams Glasse worke, where they made huge Vasas of mettal as cleare & pondrous & thick as Chrystal, also Looking-glasses far larger & better than any that come from Venice: I din'd with Mr. Godolphin & his Wife: ...

October 9 I went with Mrs. Godolphin & my Wife to Black-wall to see some Indian Curiosities, & as I was walking thro a streete, the way, being s<l>ipperie & misty, I fell against a piece of Timber, with such violence, as quite beate the breath out of my body, so as being taken up, I could not speake, nor fetch any breath, for some space, & then with greate difficulty, coming to my sense, after some applications, being carried into an house, & let bloud: I was carried to the water side, & so home, where after a daies rest, I recovered, though my bruse was not quite healed: This being one of the greatest deliverances that ever I had, The Lord Jesus make me ever mindfull, & thankfull: ...

30 To Lond: about the building; Mrs. Ann Howard Mayd of honor to the Queene, whom I went to Visite, related to me the strang<e> Vision she saw: which was thus: One of her maides being lately dead & one whom I well knew, had in her life time told her Mistris, that when she died she would certainly appeare to her: This Wench, being deepely in love with a young man, dying, a little while after appeared to her Mistris, as she lay in <bed>, drawing the Curtaine, siting downe by her, & beckning to her; her Mistris being broad awake, & sitting up at the affright, called alow'd for her maid to come to her, but no body came; The Vision, now going from her, she still continued to call her Maid, who lying in another chamber next to her, rose & came at last to her Mistris: begging her pardon that she did not come at her first call; for said shee, I have ben in a most deadly fright, & durst not stirr for Mistress Maundy (for so was her name) who has appear'd to me, and looked so wistly on me, at the foote of my bed, that I had not the power to rise or answer: These two, Mistris Howard & her Woman Davis, affirming it so positively, & happning to see it, neere the same time, & in severall chambers, is a most remarkable thing: & I know not well how to discredit it, Mrs. Howard being so extraordinary a virtuous & religious Lady.

31 Being my Birth-day, & 56 yeare, I spent the morning in Devotion, surveying my accompts & imploring Gods protection, with solemn thanksgiving for all his signal mercys to me, especialy for that escape which concern'd me this Moneth at Blackwall: I din'd with Mrs. Godolphin & return'd home this Evening, thro a prodigious & dangerous Mist &c: ...

November 16 My sonn & I dining at my Lo: Chamberlaines, he shewed us, amongst others, that incomparable piece of Raphaels, being a Minister of state dictating to Guicciardine, the earnestness of the Secretary looking up in expectation of what he was next to write, is so to the life, & so naturall, as I esteeme it for one of the choices<t> pieces of that admirable Artist: There was an other womans head of Leonardo da Vinci; a Madona of old Palma, & two of Van-Dykes, of which one was his owne picture at length when young, in a leaning posture, the other an Eunuch singing; but rare pieces indeede: ...

30: Was our Anniversarie Elections at the R: Society, where I was againe chosen of the Council: having in the morning before ben to visite & Com: with a poore sick person: ...

December 10 Fell so deepe a Snow, as hindred us from Church &c:

12: To Lond: in so greate a snow, as I remember not to have ever seene the like: supped with Mrs. Godolphin: ...

16 ... dind with Lo: Clarendon, Lady Henrietta Hyde, Mr. Andr: Newport, & with much a doe got home through the snow:

17 More Snow falling, I was not able to get to church &c:

19: To Lond: about buisinesse: dind at Mrs. Godolphins; fell ill of a feavorish distemper &c: which confin'd me to bed two daies: ...

1677[1]

February 8 Went to Rohampton with my Lady Dutchesse of Ormond: The Garden & perspective is pretty, the Prospect most agreable, I went home that Evening: ...

March 31 Mrs. Godolphin remov'd to the Buildings I had finished in W: hall from Berkeley house:

June 12 I went to Lond: to give the L: Ambassador Berkeley (now return'd from the Treaty at Nimegen) an accompt of the greate Trust repos'd in me during his absence, I having received & transmitted to him no lesse than 20000 pounds: to my no small trouble, & losse of time, that during his absence, & when the Lord Tressurer was no greate friend, I yet procurd him greate Summs, very often soliciting his Majestie in his behalfe, looking after the rest of the Estate & concernes intirely; without so much as accepting any kind of acknowledgement, purely upon the request of my deare friend Mrs. Godolphin.

13 I din'd with Mrs. Godolphin & return'd, with aboundance of thanks & professions [16] from my Lord Berkeley & Lady &c: ...

24 My Lord Berkeleys troublesome buisinesses being now at an end & I delivered from that intollerable servitude & Correspondence; I had leasure to be somewhat more at home, & to myselfe: ...

July 16 I went to Wotton to see my deare Brother.

22: Mr. Evans Curate at Abinger, preach'd an excellent sermon on 5.Matt:12. In the Afternoone Mr. Higham at Wotton Cathechiz'd:

23. I went to see Albury, a sweete Villa of the Duke of Norfolcks, the plot of which Garden & Crypta through the mountaine, I had first design'd &c:

26 I din'd at Dr. Duncombs at Sheere whose house stands inviron'd with very sweete & quick streames: ...

August 21. To Lond, to meete with one about a proposal of a Match for my Sonn:

---

[1] The full *Diary* for the first part of this year is notable for its mostly very brief entries concerned either with sermons or dining with Mrs Godolphin. The contrast is very marked with the rest of the manuscript and indicates either that he had effectively given up most of his other activities or had no time to make notes of them.

27 To Lon: designing to Visite my Lord Chamberlaine in Suffolck:

28 whither I came on Tuesday, his Lordship sending his Coach & 6 horses, to meete me at, & bringing me from St. Edmondsbury[1] to Euston:

29, We went a hunting in the Park, & killed a very fat Buck:

31 I went a Hauking:

September 2: ... There din'd this day at my Lords, one Sir Jo: Gaudy a very handsome person, but quite dumb: yet very intelligent by signes, & a very fine Painter: so civil, & well bred he was, as it was not possible to discerne any imperfection by him; his Lady & children were also there, & he was at church in the morning with us:

4: I went to visite my Lord Crofts, now dying at St. Edmonsbery, and tooke this opportunity to see this antient Towne, & the remaines of that famous Monasterie & Abby; There is little standing intire save the Gate-house, which shews it to have ben a vast & magnificent Gotique structure, & of greate extent: The Gates are Wood, but quite plated over with jron: There are also two stately Churches, one especialy.

5. I went to Thetford the Borrogh Towne, where stands likewise the ruines of another religious house; & there is a round mountaine artificialy raised, either for some Castle or Monument, which makes a pretty Landscape: As we went & return'd a Tumbler shew'd his extraordinary addresse in the Warren: I also saw the Decoy, much pleased with the stratagem &c:

9: A stranger preached at Euston Church on 1. Thess: 5. 21. Prove all things, that is examine your faith, your life, your actions, & that of others, to imitate the best;[2] & then fell into an handsome Panegyric on my Lords new building the Church, which indeede for its Elegance and cherefullnesse is absolutely the prettiest Country Church in England: My Lord told me that his heart smote him, after he had bestow'd so much on his magnificent Palace there he should see Gods-house in the ruine it lay; he has also rebuilt the Parsonage house all of stone, very neately & ample:

10 My Lord: to divert me, would needes carry me to see Ipswich, where we dined at one Mr. Manns by the way, Recorder of the Towne: There was in our Company my Lord Huntingtore, sonn to the Dutchesse of Lauderdail, Sir Ed: Bacon, a learned Gent, of the family of the greate Chancellor Verulame, & Sir Jo: Felton with some other knights & Gent: After dinner came the Baylifs, & Magistrates in their formalitie<s> & Maces, to Complement my Lord, & invite him to the Towne-house, where they presented us a noble Collation of dried Sweetemeates & Wine, Bells ringing &c:

Then we went to see the Towne, & first the L: Vicount Herefords house which stands in a Parke neere the Towne, like that at Bruxelles in Flanders: The house not greate, yet pretty, especialy the Hall: & the stewes of fish succeeding one anoth<e>r & feeding one the other, all paved at bottome: There is a good picture of the B: Virgin in one of the parlours, seeming to be of Holbein, or some good Masters.

Then we saw the Haven, 7 miles from Harwich: There is no River, but it dies at the Towne running out every day with the tide; but the bedding being soft mudd, it is safe for ships, & a station: The Trade of Ipswich is for most part, New-Castle Coales which they supply London with; but was formerly Cloathing: There is not any beggar dos aske any Almes in the whole Towne; a

---

[1] Bury St Edmunds, Suffolk.

[2] This passage is the source of E's motto *Omnia explorate, meliora retinete.*

thing very extraordinary; so ordered by the prudence of the Magistrates: It has in it 14 or 15 very beautifull Churches, in a word 'tis for building, cleanesse & good order, one of the sweetest Townes in England: Cardinal Wolsey was a butchers sonne of this Towne, but there is little of that magnificent Prælates foundation here besides a Schole, &, I think a Library: which I did not see; but his intentions were to build some greate thing &c: Thus we return'd late to Euston, having travelled above 50 miles this day:

Since first I was at this place,[1] seated in a bottome betweene two gracefull swellings, I found things exceedingly improved: The maine building being now made in the figure of a Greeke Π with 4 pavilions two at each corner & a breake in the front, rail'd & balustred at the top, where I caused huge jarrs of Earth to be plac'd full of Earth to keep them steady <on> their <Piedestalls>, betweene the statues, which make as good a shew, as if they were of stone; and though the buildng be of brick & but two stories, besides Cellars & Garrets, covered with blew Slate, yet there is roome enough for a full Court, the Offices & out-houses being so ample & well disposed: The Kings appartment is both painted *a fresca*, & magnificently furnish'd: There are many excellent Pictures in the roomes of the greate Masters: The Gallery is a pleasant noble roome, & in the breake or middle, a Billiard Table; but the Wainscot being of firr, & painted dos not please me so well as Spanish Oake without painting: The Chapell is pretty, & Porch descending to the Gardens:

The Orange-Garden is very fine, & leads into the Green-house, at the end whereoff is a sall to eate in, & the Conservatory very long (some hundred feete) adorn'd with Mapps, as the other side is with the heads of Cæsars ill cut in alabaster: over head are severall appartments for my Lord, Lady, & Dutchesse, with Kitchins & other offices below in a lesser volume, with lodgings for servants, all distinct, for them to retire to when they please, & that he would be in private & have no communication with the Palace, which he tells me he will wholly resigne to his Sonn in Law, & Daughter, that Wise, & charming young Creature:[2]

The Canale running under my Ladys dressing chamber window, is full of Carps, & fowle, which come & are fed there with greate diversion: The Cascade at end of the Canale turnes a Corne-mill which finds the family, & raises with water for the fountaines & offices: To passe this Chanal into the opposite Meadows, Sir Sam: Moreland has invented a Skrew Bridge, which being turned with a Key land<s> you 50 foote distant, at entrance of an ascending Walke of trees for a mile in length: as tis also on the front into the Park, of 4 rows of Ashes & reaches to the Parke Pale which is 9 miles in Compas, & the best for riding & meeting the game that ever I saw, There were now of red & fallow deere almost a thousand, with good Covert, but the soile barren & flying sand in which nothing will grow kindly: The Tufts of Firr & much of the other wood were planted by my direction some yeares before:

In a word, this seate is admirably placed for field sports, hauking, hunting, racing: The mutton small, but sweete: The stables are capable of 30 horses & 4 Coaches: The out offices make two large quadrangles, so as never servants liv'd with more ease & convenience, never Master more Civil; strangers are attended & accomodated as at their home in pretty apartments furnish'd with

---

[1] 10 October 1671.

[2] Henry Fitzroy (1663-90), 1st Duke of Grafton, Charles II's son by the Duchess of Cleveland and Isabella Bennet (c. 1667-1723). E attended their marriage on 1 August 1672, and their remarriage on 6 November 1679, when the bride was 12 years old.

all manner of Conveniences & privacy: There are bathing roomes, Elaboratorie, Dispensatorie, what not: Decoy & places to keepe & fat foule &c: He had now in his new Church (neere the Garden) built a Dormitory or Vault with severall repositories to burie in his family: In the expense of this pious structure, I meane the church, exceedingly laudable, most of the houses of God in this Country resembling rather stables & thatched Cottages than Temples to serve God in: He has also built a Lodge in the Park to house for the Keeper, which is a neate & sweete dwelling, & might become any gentleman of quality, the same he has don for the Parson, little deserving it, for his murmuring that my Lord put him for some time out of his wretched hovell, whilst it was building: he has also built a faire Inn at some distance from his Palace, a bridge of stone over a River neere it, and repaired all the Tennants houses, so as there is nothing but neatenesse, and accomodations about his estate, which yet I think is not above 1500 pounds a yeare: I believe he had now in his family 100 domestic servants.

His Lady (being one of the Bredrodes daughters; grandchild to a natural sonn of Henry Fred: Prince of Orange) is a good natured, & obliging woman. They love fine things, & to live easily, pompously, but very hospitable; but with so vast expense plunges my Lord into debt exceedingly; My Lord himselfe is given to no expensive vise but building & to have all things rich, polite, & Princely: he never plays, but reades much, having both the Latine, French & Spanish tongues in perfection: has traveled much, & is absolutely the best bred & Courtly person his Majestie has about him; so as the publique Ministers more frequent him than any of the rest of the nobility:

Whilst he was secretary of state & prime Minister he had gotten vastly, but spent it as hastily, even before he had established a funds to maintaine his greatenesse, & now beginning to decline in favour (the Duke being no greate friend of his) he knows not how to retrench: He was the sonn of a Doctor of Laws whom I have seene, & being sent from Westminster Schole to Oxon: with intention to be a divine, and parson of Arlington a Village neere Brainford, when Master of Arts, the Rebellion falling out, he followd the Kings Army, & receiving an honorable wound in the face, grew into favour & was advanc'd from a meane fortune at his Majesties restauration, to an Earle, & knight of the Garter: L: Chamb: of the Household, first favorite for a long time, during which the King married his Natural Sonn the Duke of Grafton, to his onely Daughter & heiresse: worthy for her beauty & vertue of the greatest Prince in Christendom: My Lord is besids all this a prudent & understanding person, in buisinesse, speakes very well: Unfortunate yet in those he has advanc'd, proving ungratefull most of them: The many obligations & civilities I have to this noble gent: exacts from me this Character, and I am sorry he is in no better Circumstances.

Having now pass'd neere three weekes at Euston, to my greate Satisfaction, with much difficulty he sufferd me to looke homewards; being very earnest with me to stay longer, & to engage me, would himselfe have carried & accompanied me to Lynn regis,[1] a Towne of important Trafique about 20 miles beyond, which I had never seene, as also the *Travelling Sands*, about 10 miles wide of Euston, that have so damaged the Country, rouling from place to place, like the Sands in the desarts of Lybia, quite overwhelmed some gentlemens whole Estates, as the relation extant in print, and brought to our Society describes at large:

---

[1] King's Lynn, Norfolk.

The 13 of September my Lords-Coach conveyed me to Berry: & thence baiting at New Market, stepping in at Audly end, to see that house againe, I lay at Bishops Stratford, & the next day home, accompanied in my Jo<u>rney with one Major Fairfax of a Younger house of the Lord Fairfax, a Souldier, a Traveller, an excellent Musitian, good natured, well bred gent: ...

October 12 With Sir Robert Clayton to Marden, an estate he had lately bought of my kindsman Sir John Evelyn of Godstone in Surry: which from a despicable farme house Sir Robert had erected into a Seate with extraordinary expense: Tis seated in such a solitude among hills, as being not above 16 miles from Lond, seemes almost incredible, the ways also to it so winding & intricate: The Gardens are large & walled nobly, & the husbandry part made so convenient, & perfectly understood, as the like I had not seene: The barnes, the stacks of Corne, the Stalls for Cattell, Pidgeon house, &c of most laudable example: Innumerable are his plantations of Trees, espe<c>ialy Wallnuts, the Orangerie & Gardens very curious; large & noble roomes in the house. He & his Lady (very curious in Distilling &c) entertain'd me 3 or 4 dayes very freely: I earnestly suggested to him, the repairing of an old desolate delapidated Church, standing on the hill above the house, which I left him in good disposition to do, & endow it better, there not being above 4 or 5 inhabitants in the Parish besids this prodigious rich Scrivenor: This place is exceeding sharp in Winter, by reason of the serpenting of hills, & wants running water, but the solitude exceedingly pleased me: all the ground is so full of wild Time, Majoram & other sweete plants, as is not to be overStock'd with Bees, so as I think he had neere 40 hives of that industrious Insect:
14. I went to Church at Godstone, where on 30 Psal.4 the Minister made a good sermon: After sermon I went to see old Sir Jo: Evelyns Dormitory, joyning to the Church, pav'd with Marble, where he & his Lady lie on a very stately Monument at length, in Armor &c: white Marble: The Inscription (being onely an account of his particular branch of our family) is on black Marble[1] ...
23 To Lond: dind with ★. I saw againe the Prince of Orange: his Marriage with the Lady Mary (eldest Daughter to the Duke by Mrs. Hyde the late Dutchesse) was now declared[2] ...

November 11 ... I was all this Weeke in composing matters betweene old Mrs. Howard, and Sir Gabriel Sylvius, upon his long & earnest addresse to Mrs. Ann, her second daughter Mayd of Honor: my friend Mrs. Godolphin (who exceedingly loved the young Lady) was most industrious in it, out of pitty to the languishing Knight; so as (though there were greate differences in Yeares) it was at last effected, & they married on the 13. in Hen: 7th Chapell, by the Bish: of Rochester, there being besides my wife & Mrs. Graham her sister by Mrs. Godolphin very few more: We din'd at the old Ladys, & supp'd at Mr. Grahame's at St. James's: I likewise dined there the next day, & supp'd at Sir Jos: Williamsons among severall of our Society.
15 The Queenes birth-day, & of my Baptisme; a greate Ball at Court, where the Prince of Orange & his new Princes daunc'd: I dind with ★.
17 I din'd with Mr. Godolphin & his Wife, at which time he sealed the Deedes of settlement on his Lady, in which I was a Trustee: &c: ...

---

[1] Sir John Evelyn (1591-1644), E's cousin by his grandfather's first marriage.
[2] Subsequently William III (1688-1702) and Mary II (1688-94) of England.

19 The Prince & Princesse of Orange went away, and I saw embarqued my Lady Sylvius who now went also into Holland with her Husband, made Hoffmaester to the Prince a considerable Charge: We parted with greate sorrow, for the greate respect and honour I bore to the Lady, a most pious and virtuous creature &c: I dind with my Lord Berkely at his house.

20 At Mrs. Godolphins, then visited Mr. Rob: Boyle, where I met Dr. Burnet & severall Scots Gent: Mr. Boyle now shewing us his new Laboratorie: ...

30: To the R: Society, it being our Anniversary Election day, where we chose Sir Joseph Williamson (now prin: Secretary of state) President for the next yeare, after my Lord Vicount Brounchar had possessed the Chaire now 16 yeares successively: & therefore now thought fit to change &c: that prescription might not prejudice &c: we had a greate Entertainment this night ...

December 20 To Lond: din'd at Lo: Chamb: Carried my Lord Treasurer an account of the Earle of Bristols Librarie at Wimbleton, which my Lord thought of purchasing, til I acquainted him, it was a very broken Collection, consisting much in books of Judicial Astrologie, Romances & trifles &c: Thence to our Society, where were experiments of the incumbency & gravitation of the Aire on Mercury for the Barometer. Peper wormes were first shewed us in the Microscope &c:

23 ... I gave my Sonn an Office,[1] with Instructions how to govern his Youth, I pray God give him the Grace to make a right use of it &c: ...

1678

January 4 My Lord Ossory going now Into Holland, sent his Barge to bring me to his Yacht, now under saile; I went with him a good part of the way towards Gravesend, & after dinner returned with my Lord, it beginning to be stormie &c: ...

Din'd 22 with Mrs. Godolphin, and next day with the Duke of Norfolck; being the first time I had seene him since the Death of his elder Bro: who died at Padoa in Italy where as being lunatic, he had ben kept above 30 yeares: The Duke had now newly declard his Marriage to that infamous Woman his Concubine, whom he promised me he would never marry: I went with him to see the Duke of Buckingam, thence to my Lord Sunderlands now Secretary of State, to shew him that rare piece of Vostermans (sonn of old Vostermans) which was a View or Landscip of my Lords Palace &c: at Althorp in Northamptonshire ...

February 18 My Lord Treasurer sent to me that I would accompanie him to Wimbledon which he had lately purchased of the Earle of Bristoll, so breaking fast with him privately in his Chamber (at what time he was very like to be choaked in drinking too hastily) I accompanied him, with two of his daughters,

---

[1] A devotionary book. Another devotionary book by E, not this one, was published in a limited edition from the original manuscript in 1936 by Walter Frere.

my L: Conway, & Sir Bernard Gas<c>ogne & having surveied his Gardens & alterations, returned late at night: ...

March 22 I went to Graves-end about a Pay & Accompt, for the quarte<r>s of men, during the late Warr, where to my extraordinary affliction, I found my Agent there had missbehaved himselfe: I returned home next day: ...

April 18 I went to see New Bedlam Hospital, magnificently built, & most sweetely placed in Morefields, since the dreadfull fire of Lond: dined with★: ...

May 16 Being the Wedding Anniversarie of my excellent friend Mrs. Godolphin, she, with my Lady Sylvius & her sister Grahame came to visite, & dine with me; returning in the Evening, & was the last time, that blessed Creature ever came to my house, now being also greate with Child, & seldome stirring abroad: ...

June 28 I went to Windsor with my Lord Chamberlain (the Castle now new repairing with exceeding Cost &c) to see the rare Worke of Virrio, & incomparable Carving of Gibbons:
   29 returned with my Lord &c: by Hownslow heath where we saw the new raised Army encamp'd, designed against France, in pretence at least, but gave umbrage to the Parliament: his Majestie & a world of Company in the field, & the whole Army in Batallia, a very glorious sight: now were brought into service a new sort of souldier called Granadiers, who were dextrous to fling hand granados, every one having a pouch full, & had furr'd Capps with coped crownes like Janizaries,[1] which made them looke very fierce, & some had long hoods hanging down behind as we picture fooles: their clothing being likewise py bald yellow & red: so we returned to Lond: ...

July 20 I went to the Tower to try a Mettal at the Say-Masters, which onely proved Sulphur: then saw Monsieur Rotiere that incomparable Graver belonging to the Mint, who emulates even the Antients in both mettal & stone; he was now moulding of an Horse for the Kings statue to be cast in silver of a Yard high: I dined with Mr. Slingsby Master of the Mint. Visite<d> L: Brouncker: ...
   23 Return'd, having ben to see Mr. Elias Ashmoles Library & Curiosities at Lambeth, he has divers MSS, but most of them Astrological, to which study he is addicted, though I believe not learned; but very Industrious, as his History of the Gartir shews, he shewed me a Toade included in Amber: The prospect from a Turret is very fine, it being so neere Lond: & yet not discovering any house about the Country. The famous John Tradescant, bequeath'd his Repositary to this Gent: who has given them to the University of Oxford, & erected a Lecture on them &c: over the Laboratorie, in imitation of the R: Society: My deare friend Mrs. Godolphin & my Wife were with us: I think it was the last of her going abroad:
   25 I went to Lond: to the wedding of my Bro: in Law Glandvills Niepce, married to Cap: Fowler &c: Thence to R: Society: supp'd with Mrs. Godolphin whose husband was now made Master of the Robes to the King.
   There was now sent me 70 pounds from some <one> whom I knew not to be by me distributed among poore people at my discretion; I came afterwards

---

[1] Turkish soldiers.

to find it was from that heavenly creature my deare friend: who had frequently given me large Summs to bestow on Charities &c: ...

August 23 Upon Sir Rob: Readings importunity, I went to Visite the Duke of Norfolck at his new Palace by Way bridge; where he laied out in building neere 10000 pounds, on a Copyhold, & in a miserable barren sandy place by the streete side, never in my daies had I seene such expense to so small purpose: The roomes are Wainscoted, & some of them richly parquetted with Cedar, Yew, Cypresse &c. There are some good Pictures, especialy, that <incomparable> painting of Holbens where The Duke of Norfolck, Charles Brandon, & Hen: the 8: are dauncing with the three Ladys, such amorous countenances, & spritefull motion did I never see expressed: 'Tis a thousand pitties (as I told my Lord of Arundel his sonn) that jewell should be given away to the present broode, & not to be fixed to the incontaminate issue:

24 I went to see my L: <St. Albans's> house at Byfleete, an old large building; and thence to the Paper-mills, where I found them making a Course white paper: First they cull the raggs (which are linnen for White paper, Wollen for browne) then they stampe them in troughs to a papp, with pestles or hammers like the powder mills: Then put it in a Vessel of Water, in which they dip a frame closely wyred, with wyer as small as an haire, & as cloose as a Weavers reede: upon this take up the papp, the superfluous water draining from it thro the wyres: This they dextrously turning shake out like a thin pan-cake on a smoth board, betweene two pieces of flannell; Then presse it, betweene a greate presse, the <flannel> sucking out the moisture, then taking it out ply & dry it on strings, as they dry linnen in the Laundry, then dip it in allume water, lastly polish, & make it up in quires: &c: note that the<y> put some gumm in the water, in which they macerate the raggs into a pap: note that the marks we find in the sheetes is formed in the wyres.

25 ... After Evening prayer Visited Mr. Sheldon (Nephew to the late Archbish: of Cant: where I found the Bish: of Rochester) and his pretty melancholy Garden, I tooke notice of the largest *Arbor Thuyæ*[1] I had ever seene: The place is finely water'd, & there are many curiosities of India which we were shew'd in the house: There was at Way-bridge the Dutchesse of Norfolck, My Lord Thomas Howard (a worthy & virtuous gent, with whom my sonn, was sometime bred up in Arundel house) who was newly come from Rome where he had ben some time; also one of the Dukes Daughters by his first Lady: My Lord leading me about the house, made no scrupule of shewing me all the *Latebræ*[2] & hiding places for the popish Priests, & where they said Masse, for he was no bigoted Papist: He told me he never trusted them with any seacret; & used Protestants onely in all buisinesses of importance: I went with my L. Duke this evening to Windsore, where was a magnificent Court, it being the first time of his Majesties removing thither, since it was repaired:

27: ... dined at Mr. Hen: Brounchers at the Abby of Sheene formerly a Monastery of Carthusians, there yet remaining one of their solitary Cells with a Crosse: within this ample inclosure are severall pretty Villas, and fine Gardens of the most excellent fruites, Especialy Sir William Temples, lately Ambassador into Holland, & the Lord Liles sonn to the Earle of Licester, who has divers rare Pictures, above <all> that of Sir Brian Tukes of Holbein:

---

[1] Citrus tree, from the Greek θυια.

[2] Priest-holes in this context.

After dinner I walked to Ham, to see the House & Garden of the Duke of Laderdaile, which is indeede inferiour to few of the best Villas in Italy itselfe, The House furnishd like a great Princes; The Parterrs, flo: Gardens, Orangeries, Groves, Avenues, Courts, Statues, Perspectives, fountaines, Aviaries, and all this at the banks of the sweetest river in the World, must needes be surprizing &c: Thence I went <to> my worthy friends Sir Hen: Capels (bro: to the Earle of Essex) it is an old timber house, but his Garden has certainely the Choicest fruite of any plantation in England, as he is the most industrious, & understanding in it: from hence To Lond: & [28] next day to Says-Court; after a most pleasant & divertisant Excursion, the weather bright & temperate:

29 I was cald againe to London to waite againe on the Duke of Norfolck who having at my request onely, bestow'd the Aru<n>delian Library on the Royal Society, sent me to take charge of the Bookes & remove them; onely that I would suffer the Heraulds Chiefe Officer Sir W: Dugdale to have such of them as concernd Herauldry & Martials Office As bokes of Armorie & Geneologies; the Duke being Earle Marishal of England: I procured for our Society besides Printed bookes, neere 700 MSS: some in Greeke of greate concernement; The Printed books being of the oldest Impressions, are not the lesse valuable; I esteeme them almost equal with MSS: Most of the Fathers printed at Basil &c: before the Jesuites, abused them with their Expurgatorie Indexes: There is a noble MSS: of Vitruvius: Many of these Bookes had ben presented by Popes, Cardinals & greate Persons to the Earles of Arundell & Dukes of Norfolck; & the late magnificent Tho: E: of Arundel bought a noble Library in Germanie, which is in this Collection; nor should I for the honour I beare the family, have perswaded the Duke to part with these, had I not seene how negligent he was of them, in suffering the Priests, & every body to carry away & dispose of what they pleased: so as aboundance of rare things are gon, & irrecoverable:

Having taken Order here, I went to the R: Society, to give them an account of what I had procured, that they might call a Council, & appoint a day to waite on the Duke to thank him for this munificent gift:

There were this afternoone also severall Experiments shewn, and divers learned & curious discourses: as first, Concerning a Woman that in Lions had ben 24 yeares with Child, which had ben dead 7 yeares before the Mother, who lived to 60: Also that this Child was found out of the Womb: Also of another Conceiv'd out of the Womb, lying in the hollow of the body, during which the Mother conceiv'd & brought forth another Child: the first coming forth by piecemeale, bones, & putrid flesh, through severall ulcers in severall parts below: This was in England: An other (abroad) who went divers yeares with an Embrio in her body, at last brought forth, a Child whose head and limbs were halfe petrified: Divers learned Physitians now present held, that these extra-Utrine Conceptions happn'd through the Eggs passing out of the *Ovarium* or Fallopian Tubes, by some occult *meatus*,[1] besides that into the womb:

There being a discourse of Iseland; It was affirm'd, that the bodys of men when dead, are piled up for severall moneths without corruption, frozen as hard as marble; till the Thaws come, & then buried: the ground being 'til then too hard to dig: The same is sayd of Muscovy, & that they commonly remaine so expos'd til about mid-May: Dr. Croone affirmed that Freezing is not by any <gradual> conjelation of the Water, but an instantaneous action or operation,

---

[1] Course or motion.

so as listning attentively, one may heare a kind of obscure sharp frizling noise when it shoots the Icy skin or first Epidermis which is swift as thought: This he tried by a glasse of Water. Also <that> all water shoots into the shape of branches infinitely multiplied at right angles, & resembling the veines in the Leafe of a Vegetable: That Snow by accression did grow by falling, & shot like a tree, at right angles also, besides the Stellifying of every individual atome of it *. It was by some there also assured us, that the Greeneland Whale when struck hastens to the shore, a Vast fish in Thicknesse with a huge head & jawes: That the Bermudas is longer & more slender, with a sharp snout, & he being smitten contrarie to the other, hastens out to sea, for they find them at a certaine season, among the rocks neerer the Iland; & being gotten out no rope is long enough to fasten to their harping Irons; so as it was so difficult to kill them, that the trade (which is very Considerable) had certainly failed there, had not an halfe drunken fellow, after he had flung his speare & wounded a Whale, desperately ho<p>ped out of his boate upon the fishes back, where he so hacked him, as killed him before he could get to sea; & this is now familiarly practised by those of the Bermudas ever since. This story was affirmed me for a certaine truth by Sir Rob: Clayton who has one of the most considerable Plantations in that fertil Iland: I returned home this evening: ...

September 3 I went to Lond: to dine at Mrs. Godolphins according to my custome every Tuesday, and found her in Labour; & staye'd 'til they brought me word the infant was borne, a lovely boy, the Mother exceedingly well laied to all appearance, Mr. G: (the Father) being at Windsore with the Court:

5 It was christned, The Susceptors being Sir Will: Godolphin (head of the family) Mr. Jo: Hervey Tresurer to the Queene, & Mrs. Boscawen (sister to Sir William & the Father); and named after the Gra<n>dfathers name Francis:[1] It was baptiz'd in the Chamber where it was borne, in the mothers presence, at White-hall, by the Chaplaine who used to officiate in her pretty family; so I returned this evening home with my Wife, who was also come up to see her & congratulate.

8: our Curate (in absence of the Viccar) preaching on his former Text, whilst I was at Church this morning came a Letter from Mr. Godolphin (who had ben sent for from Winsore the night before) to give me notice that my deare friend, his Lady, was exceedingly ill, & desiring my Prayers & assistance, his affliction being so extreme: so my Wife and I tooke boate immediately, & went to White-hall, where to mine unexpressable sorrow I found she had ben atacqu'd with the new feavor then reigning, this excessive hot Autumne, which being of a most malignant nature, & prevailing on her now weakned & tender body, eluded all the skill & help of the most eminent Physitians; and <surprizing> her head, so as she fell into deliriums, & that so vilontly & frequent, that unlesse some (almost mira<c>ulous) remedy were applied, it was impossible she should hold out; nor did Doctors dare prescribe such remedies as might have ben proper in other cases, by reason of her condition, then so lately brought to bed; so as the paroxysmes increasing to

---

[1] The boy survived to succeed his father in 1712 as 2nd Earl of Godolphin, dying in 1766. He married on 23 April 1698 Henrietta Churchill (1681-1733), daughter and heir of John Churchill, Duke of Marlborough, and Duchess of Marlborough in her own right in 1722 by Act of Parliament. Their daughter Mary married Thomas Osborne, 4th Duke of Leeds and through this line there are a number of living descendants of Margaret Godolphin.

greater height, it was now despair'd that she should last many houres, nor did she continue many minutes, without repeated fitts, with much paine & agonie, which carried her off [9] the next day, being moneday, betweene the houres of one & two in the afternoone, in the 26t yeare of her Age: to the unexpressable affliction of her deare Husband, & all her Relations; but of none in this world, more than my selfe, who lost the most excellent, & most estimable Friend, that ever liv'd:

I cannot but say, my very Soule was united to hers, & that this stroake did pierce me to the utmost depth: for never was there a more virtuous, & inviolable friendship, never a more religious, discreete, & admirable creature; beloved of all, admir'd of all, for all the possible perfections of her sex: But she is gon, to receave the reward of her signal Charity, & all other her Christian graces, too blessed a Creature to converse with mortals, fitted (as she was) by a most holy Life, to be receiv'd into the mansions above:

But it is not here, that I pretend to give her Character, who have design'd, to consecrate her worthy life to posterity: I must yet say, she was for witt, beauty, good-nature, fidelitie, discretion and all accomplishments, the most choice & agreable person, that ever I was acquainted with: & a losse to be more sensibly deplored by me, as she had more particularly honord me with a friendship of the most religious bands, & such, as she has often protested she would even die for with cherefullnesse:

The small services I was able to do her in some of her secular concernes, was immensly recompenc'd with her acceptance onely; but how! ah how! shall I ever repay my obligations to her for the infinite good offices she did my soule, by so o'ft ingaging me to make religion the termes & tie of the friendship which was betweene us: She was certainely the best Wife, the best Mother, the best Mistris, the best friend that ever Husband, Child, Servant, friend [or] that ever any creature had, nor am I able to enumerate her vertues: Her husband fell downe flat like a dead man, struck with unspeakeable affliction, all her Relations partooke of the losse; The King himselfe & all the Court express'd their sorrow, & to the poore and most miserable it was irreparable; for there was no degree, but had some obligation to her memorie:

So virtuous & sweete a life she lead, that in all her fitts, (even those which tooke away her discernement); she never was heard to utter any syllable unbecoming a Christian, or uninnocent, which is extraordinary in delirious persons: So carefull, & provident she was to prepare for all possible accidents, that (as if she fore-saw her end), she received the heavenly *Viaticum*[1] but the Sunday before, after a most solemn recollection; & putting all her domestic Concerns in the exactest order, left a Letter directed to her Husband (to be opened in case she died in Child-bed) in which, with the most pathetic and indearing expressions of a most loyal & virtuous wife, she begs his kindness to her Memorie, might be continu'd; by his care and esteeme of those she left behind, even to her very domestic servants, to the meanest of which she left considerable Legac<i>es, desiring she might be buried in the Dormitorie of his family neere 300 miles from all her other friends; And as she made use of me to convey innumerable & greate Charities all her lifetime, so I paied 100 pounds to her chiefe woman, 100 to a kindswoman in declining circumstances: To her sister<?s> the value of 1000 pounds: In diamond rings to other of her friends, 500 pounds: & to severall poore people, widows, fatherlesse, Prisoners & indigents, pensions to continue: ô the passionate, humble,

---

[1] Journey.

mealting disposition of this blessed Friend; how am I afflicted for thee! my heavenly friend:

It was now seaven yeares since she was maid of Honor to the Queene that she reguarded me as a Father, a Brother, & (what is more) a Friend: we often prayed, visited the sick & miserable, received, read, discoursed & communicated together in all holy Offices together without reproch: She was most deare to my Wife, affectionate to my Children, intrested in my Concernes, in a word, we were but one Soule, as aboundance of her professions & letters in my hands testifie: But she is gon, & the absence so afflicting to me, as I shall carry the sense of it to the last: This onely is my Comfort, that she is happy, & I hope in Christ, I shall shortly behold her againe in the boosome of our deare Saviour, where she is in blisse, & whence we shall never part:

The excessive affliction of this losse did so exceedingly afflict her husband, and other neere Relations, that knowing in what profession of a most signal Friendship, she ever own'd me; The Fees to the Physitians, The intire Care of her funeral, was wholy comitted to me; so as having closed the Eyes, & drop'd a teare upon the Cheeke of my blessed Saint, Lovely in death, & like an Angel; I caused the Corps to be embaulmed, & wrap'd in Lead, with a plate of Brasse sothered on it, with an Inscription & other Circumstanc<e>s due to her worth, with as much dilligence & care as my grieved heart would permitt me; being so full of sorrow, & tir'd with it, that retiring home for two daies, I spent it in solitude, & sad reflections: ...

16 I went to Lond: in order to the funeral of my deare Friend: so as on the 17th in an herse with 6 horses, & two other Coaches of as many, & with about 30 people of her relations & servants, we as privately, & without the least pomp (as expressly required by her) proceeded towards the place, where she would be buried: There accompanied her hearse her husbands Bro: Sir Will. & two more of his Bro: & 3 Sisters: Mr. G: her husband, so surcharg'd with griefe, that he was wholy unfitt to Travell so long a journey 'til he should be more composed, & for this reason, after I had waited on the companie as far as Hounslow heath, with a sad heart, I was oblig'd to returne, upon some indispensable affaires: The Corps was ordred to be taken out of the hearse & decently placed in the house, with tapers about it, & her servants attending, every night during all the way to the foote of Cornewell, neere 300 miles, & then as honorably interred in the Parish Church of Godolphin.[1] This funerall, private as it was, costing her deare husband not much lesse than 1000 pounds; and ô that ten thousand more might have redeemed her life! Returning back, I caled in to visite & Condole with my Lady Berkeley, my Lord, being also newly dead, which repeated sorrowes:

18 I spent most of the afternoone with disconsolate Mr. Godolphin, in looking over & sorting his Ladys Papers, most of which consisted of Prayers, meditations, Sermon-notes, Discourses & Collections on severall religious subjects, & many of her owne happy Composing, & so pertinently digested, as if she had ben all her life a student in Divinity: There we found a Diarie of her solemn resolutions, all of them tending to Institution of life, & practical virtue; with some letters from select friends &c all of them put into exact method; so

---

[1] The grave is marked in the floor of Breage church near Godolphin House with a brass plate installed by her descendant George Osborne (1862-1927), 10th Duke of Leeds, including the note 'the friend of John Evelyn who has told the story of her noble life' and the pentangle (see note above for 16 October 1672).

as it even astonish<ed> us to consider what she had read, & written, her youth considered, few Divines having taken halfe that paines, or to better purpose; for what she read, or writt, she liv'd, full of Charity, and Good works which she did. 19 I return'd home to my house:

22: Our Viccar & Curate, on their former Texts: My Family being also this crazy season, much discomposed with sicknesse ...

October 1 I went with my Wife to Lond: The Parliament being now alarm'd with the whole Nation, about a conspiracy of some Eminent Papists, for the destruction of the King, & introducing Popery; discovered by one Oates and Dr. Tongue, which last, I knew, being the Translator of the Jesuites Morals: I went to see & converse with him, now being at White-hall, with Mr. Oates, one that was lately an Apostate to the Church of Rome, & now return'd againe with this discovery: he seem'd to be a bold man, & in my thoughts furiously indis-creete; but everybody believed what he said: & it quite chang'd the genius & motions of the Parliament, growing now corrupt & intrested with long sitting, & Court practises; but with all this Poperie would not go downe: This discovery turn'd them all as one man against it, & nothing was don but in order to finding out the depth of this &c: Oates was encourag'd, & every thing he affirm'd <taken> for Gospel: The truth is, The Roman Chath: were Exceeding bold, & busy every where, since the D<uke of York>: forbore to go any longer to the Chapell &c:

2: I went to Parsons Greene to visite my Lady Mordaunt, & condole with her for my Deare Mrs.G: ...

17: I went to Lond: to make up Accompts with Mr. Godolphin, as on the 16, I was constantly wont to do with his Lady, when she lived: He then requested me to continue the trust she reposed in me, in behalfe of his little sonne, & would by no meanes alter anything; conjuring me to transferr the kindnesse & friendship I had for his deare wife, on him & his: ...

21 The barbarous murder of Sir Edmund Bery-Godfry, found strangled about this time, as was manifest by the Papists, (he being a Justice of the Peace, and one who knew much of their practises, as conversant with Coleman, a Servant of the ... now accus'd) put the whole nation in a new fermentation against them:- I din'd with my Lady Tuke ...

31. Being the 58th of my age, requir'd my humble addresses to Almighty God, & that he would take off his heavy hand still on my family, and restore comforts to us, after the losse of my Excellent friend: I also now review'd & new made my Will: ...

November 5. Dr. Tillotson before the house of Commons at St. Margarits: 'Tis since Printed: 'Twas now he sayed, the Papists were ariv'd to that impudence, so as to deny there was ever any such thing as the Gun-powder Conspiresy: To this he affirm'd, he had himselfe severall letters written by Sir Everard Digby (one of the Traytors) in which he glories that he was to suffer for it; & that it was so contriv'd, that of the Papists, not above 2 or 3 should have ben blown up, & they such, as were not worth the saving:

10 I went to St. James's in the morning Synax: Cor: Rege at W:hall Dr. Butler on 5. Gal:1, shewing by way of Paralell, the Case of the Protestants, wavering betweene us & the Papists: he spake very home to his Majestie, exhorting to stedfastnesse in the Faith, & Liberty, in which Christ had made us free in this Land especialy, reckning up the heavy Yoake of Popish bondage &c.

13 Was an Universal Fast; That God would avert his Judgements, & bring to naught the Conspirators against the K: & Government: In the morning preach'd to The Lords, the A:Bishop of Cant: in the Abby on 57:Psal:1. shewing how safe the Church & People of God were in the midst of the most iminent dangers, under the wings of the Almighty: This was also Printed.

15 The Queenes birthday &c: I never saw the Court more brave, nor the nation in more apprehension, & Consternation &c: It was also my Baptismal Anniversary: ...

24: ... Now had Coleman ben try'd, & one Staly, both Condemn'd & Executed: Oates on this grew so presumptuous as to accuse the Queene for intending to Poyson the King; which certainly that pious & vertuous Lady abhorred the thought off, & Oates his Circumstances, made it utterly unlikely in my opinion: 'Tis likely he thought to gratifie some, who would have ben glad his Majestie should have married a more fruitfull Lady: but the King was too kind an husband to let any of these make impression on him. However, Divers of the Popish Peres sent to the Toure, as accused by Oates, all the Ro: Cath: Lords were by a new Act, for ever Excluded the Parliament: which was a mighty blow: The Kings, Queenes & Dukes servants banished, & a Test to be taken by every body, who pretended to enjoy any Office of publique Trust, or not be suspected of Popery: This was so Worded That severall good Protestants scrupled; & I went with Sir W: Godolphin (a Member of the Commons house) to Bish: of Ely (Dr. Pet: Gunning) to be resolved, whether Masse were Idolatry, as the Test expressed it: for Sir William (though a most learned Gent: & excellent Divine himselfe) made some doubt of it: but the Bishops opinion was he might take it, & that the Papists could not excuse themselves from Idolatry; though he wished it had ben otherwise worded in the Test: ...

December 8 I tooke Physick being indisposed, & stirr'd not out all this weeke:

15 Preach'd Mr. Saunders on 5. Eccles: Shewing the reverence due to the house of God: a seasonable discourse there being some in our Congregation not so reverent at prayers, as they should be.

16 To Lond: the nation exceedingly disturb'd at the publique commotions: for now was also the Lo: Treasurer Danby impeach'd &c: ...

29 Being very ill of Gripings I was faine to keepe my bed: Divers of my Neighbours invited &c: according to Costome:

31 I gave God thanks for his goodnesse to me the yeare past, & begg'd that I might make a sanctified use of those Afflictions I had pass'd thro for the losse of a deare friend.

1679

January 12: ...When so strange a Clowd of darknesse came over, & especialy, the Citty of London, that they were faine to give-over the publique service for some time, being about 11 in the forenoone, which affrited many, who consider'd not the cause, (it being a greate Snow, & very sharp weather,) which was an huge cloud of Snow, supposed to be frozen together, & descending lower than ordinary, the Eastern wind, driving it forwards: ...

14 Din'd with Mr. Godolphin now newly return'd from the funeral of his deare Wife, which he follow'd after some daies of its setting forth from

London, he being then not able to <have> accompanied <it> on the way, for very griefe: ...

25 Was the Long Parliament (which now had sate ever-since his Majesties restauration) disolv'd by perswasion of the L: Tressurer: though divers of them were believed to be his Pensioners; at which all the polititians were at a stand: they being very eager in pursuite of the late plot of the Papists: ...

February <25?> ... My Bro: Evelyn of Wotton was now chosen knight for the County of Surrey, carying it against my Lord Longford and Sir Adam Browne of Bechworth Castle; The Country coming-in to give their suffrages for my bro: were so many, that I believe they eate & dranke him out neere 2000 pounds by a most abominable costome: ...

April 16 ... the Bish: of Lond: Confirm'd many Children & others, & amongst them my Daughter Mary, now about 14 yeares old: ...

27 ... His Royal highnesse the Duke, Voted against by the Commons for his Recusancy, went over into Flanders, which made much discourse among the Politicians: &c: ...

June 4. To Lond: Din'd with Mr. Pepys at the Tower, whither he was committed by the house of Commons, for misdemeanors in the Admiralty, where he was Secretary; but I believe unjustly: Here I saluted my Lord Stafford & Peters who were also committed for the Popish Plot: ...

7: I saw the magnificent Cavalcade and Entery of the Portugal Ambassador: din'd at L: Chamberlaines: ...

17 I was Godfather to a Sonn of Sir Chr: Wren Surveyor of his Majesties building<s>, that most learned & excellent person; with Sir William Fermor & my Lady Vicountesse Newport wife of the Treasurer of the household: Thence to Chelsey with Sir Steph: Fox and my Lady, in order to his purchas of the Co: of Bristols house ther, which she desired me to procure a Chapman for: ...

22: ... There were now divers Jesuites executed about the Plot; & a Rebellion in Scotland of the Phanatics there; so as there was a sad prospect of publique affaires: ...

July 3. Sending a piece of Venison to Mr. Pepys Sec: of the Admiralty, still a Prisoner, I went & dined with him; Thence to the R: Society, where was both a discourse, & experiment of innumerable wormes or Insects in the Sperme of an horse by the Microscope: And also of a Liquor, in which flesh, or fish being boiled, the bones were rendred as soft as marrow, yet neither over boiled, or ill relished, all by the Contrivance of a Digestorie, with very inconsiderable expense as to fire: This by Dr.Papin of our Society: I went home in the Evening: ...

6: ... Now were there Papers, Speeches, Libels, publiquely cried in the streetes against the Duke of York, & Lauderdail &c obnoxious to the Parliament, with too much, & indeede too shamefull a liberty; but the People & Parliament had gotten head, by reason of the vices of the greate ones:

There was now brought up to Lond. a Child (sonn of one Mr. Wotton formerly *Amanuensis* to Dr. Andrews Bish: of Winton) who both read & pefectly understood Heb: Gr: Latine, Arab: Syriac, & most of the Modern Languages; disputed in Divinity, Law, all the Sciences, was skillfull in Historie both Ecclesiastical & Prophane, in Politic &c, in a word so universaly & solidly learned at 11 yeares of age, as he was looked on as a Miracle: Dr. Lloyd (one of the most deepe learned Divines of the nation, in all sorts of literature) with Dr. Burnet who had severely Examin'd him, came away astonish'd and told me, they did not believe there had the like appeared in the world since Adame to this time: He had onely ben instructed by his Father, who being himselfe a learned person, confessed that he knew all he knew to a tittle: but what was more admirable was not so much his vast memorie, but his judgement & invention, he being tried with divers hard questions which required maturity of thought & experience: he was also dextrous in Chronologie, Antiquities, in the Mathematics &c: in summ a<n> *Intellectus Universalis* beyond all that we reade of Picus Mirandula & other precoce witts: &c: with all this a very humble Child:[1] ...

18 I went early to the old-Baily Sessions-house to the famous Trial of Sir Geo: Wakeman (one of the Queenes Physitians) & 3 Benedictine Monkes; The first (whom I was well acquainted with, & take to be a worthy gent: abhorring such a fact) for intending to poyson the King: The other as complices to carry on the Plott, to subvert the Government, & introduce Poperie: The Bench was crowded with Judges, Lo: Major, Justices, & innumerable spectators: The chiefe Accusers Dr. Oates (as he called himselfe) <and> one Bedlow, a man of inferior note; but their testimony were not so pregnant, & I feare much of it from heare-say, but sworne positively to some particulars, which drew suspicion upon their truth; nor did Circumstances so agree, as to give either the bench or Jurie so intire satisfaction as was expected:

After therefore a long & tedious tryal of 9 houres, the Jury brought them in not guilty to the extraordinary triumph of the Papists, & not without sufficient disadvantage & reflections on the Witnesses, especialy Oates & Bedlow: And this was an happy day for the Lords in the Tower, who expecting their Triall (had this gon against the Prisoners at the barr) would all of them <have> ben in uttmost hazard: For my part, I do looke on Oates as a vaine, insolent man, puff'd up, with the favour of the Commons, for having discovered something realy true; as more especialy detecting the dangerous intrigue of Coleman, proved out of his owne letters: & of a generall designe, which the Jesuited party of the Papists, ever had, & still have to ruine the Church of England; but that he was trusted with those great seacrets he pretended, or had any solid ground for what he accused divers noble men of, I have many reasons to induce my contrary beliefe; That amongst so many Commissions as he affirm'd he delivered to them from P: Oliva & the Pope, he who made no scruple of opening all other Paper, letters & seacrets, should not onely, not open any of those pretended Commissions, but not so much as take any Copy, or Witnesse, of any one of them, is <almost> miraculous: But the Commons (some leading persons I meane of them) had so exalted him, that they tooke for Gospell all he said, & without more ado, ruin'd all whom he nam'd to be Conspirators, nor did he spare whomsoever came in his way;

But indeed the Murder of Sir Ed: Godferie (suspected to have ben compassed by the Jesuite party, for his intimacy with Coleman (a buisy person whom I also knew) & the feare they had he was able to have discovered some thing to their prejudice) did so exasperate, not onely the Commons, but all the nation; That much of these sharpnesses against even the more honest Ro: Catholicks who lived peaceably, is to be imputed to that horrid fact: The Sessions ended I dined, or rather indeede supped, (so late it was) with the Judges, in the large <roome> annexed to the Place, & so returned to my house: And tho it was not my <Custome> or delight, to be often present at any Capital Trials, we having them commonly, so exactly published, by those who take

---

[1] He grew up to be William Wotton, the scholar (1666-1727).

them in short hand; Yet I was inclined to be at this signal one, that by the occular view of the carriages, & other Circumstances of the Manegers & parties concerned I might informe my selfe, and regulate my opinion of a Cause that had so alarm'd the whole Nation, & filled it with such expectations: ...

23. To Court, after dinner I visited that excellent Painter Verrio whose work in Fresca, the Kings Palace at Winsor, will celebrate as long as those walls last: Signor Verrio shewed us his pretty Garden, choice flowers & curiosities, he himselfe being a skillfull Gardner; after an herty Collation with him, I went to Clifden that stupendious natural Rock, Wood, & Prospect of the Duke of Buckinghams, & building of extraordinary Expense: The Grotts in the Chalky rock are pretty, 'tis a romantic object, & the place alltogether answers the most poetical description that can be made of a solitude, precipice, prospects & whatever can contribute to a thing so very like their imaginations: The <house> stands somewhat like Frascati as to its front, & on the platforme is a circular View to the uttmost verge of the Horison, which with the serpenting of the Thames is admirably surprising: The Staire Case, is for its materials, singular: The Cloisters, Descents, Gardens, & avenue through the wood august & stately: but the land all about wretchedly barren, producing nothing but ferne: & indeede, as I told his Majestie that evening, (asking me how I liked Clifden?) without flattery: that it did not please yet me so well as Windsore, for the Prospect & the Park, which is without compare; There being but one onely opening, & that but narrow, which let one to any Variety, where as That of Winsore is every where greate & unconfin'd:

Returning I called in at my Co: Evelyns, who has a very pretty seate in the Forest, 2 miles behether Cliffden, on a flat, with sweete Gardens, exquisitly kept though large, the house a stanch good olde building; & what was singular some of the roomes floor'd Dovetailed wise without a naile; so exactly cloose, as I was exceedingly pleas'd with the manner of it, one of the Closets being

parquetted with plaine deale set in Diamond thus exceeding

stanch & pretty: but my Kindsman & Lady being from home, I went back to Winsor, & next morning followed the King to Hampton Court, where was a Council, at which I had affaires: thence dining at Kingstone I returned that night to Says-Court: not at all displeased at the journey:

August 1. I went on board his Majesties Yach't, his Majestie saling towards Portsmouth, Mr. Henry Thynn & Mr. Brisbane, the one Secretary to Mr. Coventry Sec: of state, & the other, to the Admiralty, dining with me: afterward to Lond: to see my deare friend, Mr. Godolphins little sonn, who was sick, & with my Wife came back at night ...

8 I went this morning to see my L: Chamberlaine, his Lady, & the Dutchesse of Grafton, the incomparable work of Mr. Gibbons the Carver whom I first recommended to his Majestie, his house being furnish'd like a Cabinet, not onely with his owne work, but divers excellent Paintings of the best hands: Thence to Sir St: Foxes where I dined with my Lord, & all our Company, & so home: ...

24 ... Dr. Needham came to see my Sonn, now indispos'd, & next day was sent for to Windsore the King being sick, & he one of his Physitians in Ordinarie: ...

September 25 Came to visite & dine with me Mr. Slingsby Master of the Mint & Signor Verrio the famous Painter, to whom I gave China oranges of my owne trees, as good as were ever eaten I think, to Signor Verrios no small admiration: ...

November 4 ... in the Evening went to the funerall of my pious, deare & antient learned friend Dr. Jasper Needham; he was buried at St. Brides Church; he was a true & holy Christian, & one who loved me with greate affection: ... I lost in this person one of my dearest remaining sincere friends.[1]

5 I was invited to dine at my Lord Tividales (a Scotch Earle of my acquaintance, a learned & knowing noble man) we afterwards went to see Mr. Montagues new Palace neere Blomesbery, built by our Curator Mr. Hook, somewhat after the French; it was most nobly furnished, & a fine, but too much exposed Garden:

6 Dind at the Co: of Sunderlands, & was this evening at the remarriage of the Dutchesse of Grafton to the Duke (his Majesties natural son) she being now 12 yeares old: The Ceremonie was perform'd in my Lord Chamberlaines (her fathers Lodgings) at Whitehall below, by the Bish: of Rochester, his Majestie Present: a suddaine, & unexpected thing (when every body believed the first marriage, would have come to nothing:) But the thing being Determined, I was privately invited by my Lady her mother, to be present: but I confesse I could give her little joy, & so I plainely told her; but she told me, the King would have it so, & there was no going back: & this sweetest, hopfullest, most beautifull child, & most vertuous too, was Sacrific'd to a boy, that had ben rudely bred, without any thing to encourage them, but his Majesties pleasure: I pray God the sweete Child find it to her advantage; who if my augurie deceave me not, will in few yeares be such a paragon, as were fit to make the Wife of the greatest Prince in Europe: I staied Supper, where his Majestie sate betweene the Dutchesse of Cleaveland (the incontinent mother of the Duke of Grafton) & the sweete Dutchesse the Bride, with severall greate Persons & Ladies, without Pomp; my Love to my Lord Arlingtons family, & the sweete Child made me behold all this with regret: Though as the Duke of Grafton affects the Sea, to which I find his father intends to use him; he may emerge a plaine, usefull, robust officer; & were he polish'd, a tollerable person, for he is exceedingly handsome, by far surpassing any of the Kings other naturall Issue: ...

18 I dined at my Lo: Majors, being desired by the Countesse of Sunderland to carry her thither on a Solemn Day, that she might see the Pomp & Ceremonie of this Prince of Citizens, there never having ben any, who for the statlinesse of his Palace, prodigious feasting & magnificence exceeded him: This Lord Majors acquaintance had ben from the time of his being Apprentice to Mr. Abbot (his Unkle) who being a Scrivenor, & an honnest worthy man, (one who was condemn'd to die [(but escaped)] at the beginning of the Troubles 40 yeares past, as concerned in the Commission of Aray, for K. Char: 1:) I often used his assistance in mony matters: Rob: Clayton (now Major) his Nephew, then a boy, became after his Unkle Abbotts death, so prodigiously

---

[1] Needham was E's family doctor and had hurried through the snow in 1658 to treat E's son Richard (see 27 January 1658). His presentation copy of *Sylva* (1664) eventually entered the Evelyn Library and was sold in 1978 (Lot 1708), bearing the inscription 'For my honor'd Friend Dr. Needham from his most humble servant IEvelyn.'

rich & opulent, that he was reckoned on<e> of the welthiest Citizens: he married a freehearted Woman, who also became his hospitable disposition, & having no Children, with the accession of his Partner & fellow Apprentice, who also left him his Estate; he grew Excessively rich, was a discreete Magistrate, & though, envied, I thinke without much cause: some believ'd him gilty of hard-dealing, especialy with the Duke of Buckingham, much of whose estate he had swallow'd: but I never saw any ill by him, considering the trade he was off: The reputation, & known integrity of his Unkle Abbot, brought all the Royal party to him, by which he got not onely greate credite, but vast riches; so as he passed this Office with infinite magnificence & honor:

20 I dined at the Master of the Mints with my Wife, invited to heare Musique which was most exquisitely performed by 4 <of> the most renouned Masters, Du Prue a French-man on the Lute: Signor Batholomeo Ital: on the Harpsichord: & Nicolao on the Violin; but above all for its swetenesse & novelty the Viol d'Amore of 5 wyre-strings, plaied on with a bow, being but an ordinary Violin, playd on Lyra way by a German, than which I never heard a sweeter Instrument or more surprizing: There was also a Flute douce now in much request for accompanying the Voice: Mr. Slingsby Master of the house (whose Sonn & Daughter played skillfully) being exceedingly delighted with this diversion, had these meetings frequently in his house: ...

28: Came over the Duke of Munmoth from Holland unexpectedly to his Majestie whilst the D: of Yorke was on his Journey to Scotland, whither the King sent him to preside, & governe &c: The Bells & Bone-fires of the Citty at this arival of D: M: publishing their joy to the no small regret of some at Court; This Duke (whom for distinction they cal'd the Protestant Duke, though the sonn of an abandoned woman) the people made their Idol of: ...

December 4 I dined (together with my L: Ossorie & E: of Chesterfild) at the Portugal Ambassadors now newly come, at Cleaveland house: a noble Palace, too good for that infamous ———: The Staire Case is sumptuous & Gallerie: with the Garden: but above all the costly furniture belonging to the Ambassador, especialy the rich <Japan> Cabinets of which I think there were a dosen; & a Billiard table with as many more hazards as ours commonly have: the game being onely to prosecute the ball til hazarded, without passing the port or touching the pin: If one misse hitting the balle every time, the game is lost, or if hazarded: & 'tis more difficult to hazard a ball though so many, than in our Tables, by reason the board is made so exactly Even, & the Edges not stuff'd: The balls also bigger, & they for the most part use the sharp & small end of the billiard-stick, which is shod with brasse or silver: The Entertainement was exceeding Civile, but besids a good olio, the dishes were trifling, hash'd & Condited after their way, not at all fit for an English stomac, which is for solid meate: There was yet good fowle, but roasted to Coale; nor were the sweetemeates good: I had much discourse with the Secretary, who seem'd an understanding person ...

30 I went to Lond, to meete Sir John Stonehouse, and give him a particular of the settlement on my Sonn, who now made his addresses to the Young Lady his Daughter in Law; & so returned home: ...

1680

January 11 I tooke Physick my face & eye swelled by a Cold:

25 ... Coram Rege Dr. Pellin, 49 Isa:23. a Prerogative discourse, but very honestly shewing what obedience is due from Subjects to their Princes; it being in a Conjuncture when there was a very ill understanding 'twixt the Court & Countrie upon his Majesties unwillingnesse to let the Parliament sit.

26 I went to Counsel for the settling my Estate on my Sonn, now in treaty about a marriage, with my Lady Stonehouse's Daughter: ...

February 19 Were the Writings for the Settling Joynture, & other Contracts of Marriage of my Sonn finish'd and sealed &c: at White-hall Mr. Thursby & Melldecot being our Counsel, Sir John Stonehouse & Nephew Glanvill being Trustees: The Lady was to bring 5000 pounds in consideration of a settlement of 500 pounds a yeare present maintenance, - Which was likewise to be her joynture, & 500 pounds, after myne & my Wifes decease: though with Gods blessing it will be at least 1000 pounds a yeare more in few yeares; I pray God make him worthy of it, and a Comfort to his excellent Mother, who deserves much from him: ...

24 It being Shrove tuesday was my Sonne married to Mrs. Martha Spencer Daughter to my Lady Stonehouse by a former Gent: at St. Andrews in Holborn by our Viccar, (borrowing the Church of Dr. Stillingfleete Deane of St. Paules who was the present incumbent) & afterward dined <at> an House in Holborn; & after the solemnity & Dauncing was don, They were beded at Sir Jo: Stonehouses Lodging in Bow streete Covent Garden: I would very faine have had the marriage deferr'd til after the Lent; but severall accidents requiring it now, it was left to the disposall of her friends, & their convenience: ...

March 4 I went home, to receive my new Daughter in Law & her husband my sonn, with his Wifes Relations, who all dined with us, & returning to Lond: in the Evening, left my Daughter in Law with us for altogether ...

16 To Lond: to receive 3000 pounds of my Daughter in Laws Portion, which was paied in Gold: ...

18 At the Ro: Society was a letter from Surenam of a certaine small Eele that being taken with hooke & line at 100 foote length, did so benumb, & stupifie the limbs of the Fisher, that had not the line suddainly beene cutt, by one of the Iland (who was acquainted with its effects) the poore man had immediately died: There is a certaine wood growing in the Country, which put into a Waire or Eele-pot, dos as much intoxicate the fish as *Nux Vomica*[1] dos other fish, by which this mortiferous Torpedo is not onely caught, but becomes both harmelesse, & excellent meate: I this day introduc'd Mr. Bridgeman (Secretary to the E: of Sunderland now Pr: Sec: of state) to be a member of the R: Society, he being a very ingenious Person: ...

26 ... the D: of Sarum on a Text he entred on 5. Feb: viz: 45 Jer: 5. Not to seeke greate things to our selves, Gods counsel to Baruc, in time of distresse: In which he assembled so many Instances out of heathen histories, and greate persons, who had quitted the Splendor and opulence of their births, fortunes, and grandures, that he seemed for an houre and halfe to do nothing else but reade Common-places, without any thing of Scripture almost in his whole sermon, which was not well: ...

---

[1] See note above for 19 June 1661.

April 17 I went to Lond. and the next day, upon the earnest invitation of the Earle of Essex went with him to his house of Cassioberie in Hartford-shire: It was on Sunday, but going early from his Lordships house in the Square of St. Jamess we ariv'd by ten a clock; but my Lord, thinking it too late to go to Church, we had prayers in his Chapell: The House is new, a plaine fabric, built by my friend Mr. Hugh-May; there are in it divers faire & good roomes, excellent Carving of Gibbonss, especialy the chimny <piece> of his Library: There is likewise a painting in the porch or Enterance of Signor Virrios, Apollo & the Illiberal Arts: One roome parquetted with yew which I liked well: The Chimny mantles are some of them of a certaine Irish Marble (which his Lordship brought with him when he was Lieutennant of Ireland not long before) not much inferior to Italian: The Tympanum or Gabel at the front is a *Bass-relievo* of Diana hunting cut in Portland stone handsomely enough: The middle Dores being round I did not approve of: but when the Hall is finishd as his Lordship designs it, being an Oval Cupol'd, together with the other wing, it will be a very noble Palace: The Library is large, & very nobly furnish'd, & all the books richly bound & gilded: No Manuscripts, except of the Parliament Rolls, and Journals, which his Lordship assured me cost him 500 pounds transcribing & binding:

No man has ben more industrious than this noble Lord in Planting about his seate, adorn'd with Walkes, Ponds, & other rural Elegancies; but the soile is stonie, churlish & uneven, nor is the Water neere enough to the house, though a very swift & cleare streame run within a flight-shot from it in the vally, which may fitly be cald cold-brook, it being indeede excessive Cold, yet producing faire Troutes: In a word, 'tis pitty the house was not situated to more advantage; but it seemes it was built just where the old one was, & which I believe he onely meant to repaire at first, which leads men into irremediable errors, & saves but little:[1]

The Land about it is exceedingly addicted to Wood, but the coldnesse of the place hinder<s> their growth: onely Black-Cherry trees prosper even to Considerable Timber, some being 80 foote long: The<y> make also very handsome avenues: There is a pretty Oval at the end of a faire Walke, set about with treble rows of Spanish firr-trees: The Gardens are likewise very rare, & cannot be otherwise, having so skillfull an Artist to governe them as Mr. Cooke, who is as to the Mechanic part not ignorant in Mathematics, & pretends to Astrologie: Here is an incomparable Collection of the choicest fruits:

As for my Lord, he is a sober, wise, judicious & pondering person, not illiterate beyong the rate of most noble-men in this age, very well Versed in our English Histories & Affaires, Industrious, frugal, Methodical, & every way accomplished: His Lady (being sister to the late Earle of Northumberland) is a wise [yet somewhat] melancholy woman, setting her heart too much upon the little Lady her daughter, of whom she is over fond: They have a hopefull sonn, at the Academie: My Lord was now not long since come over from his Lieutenancy of Ireland, where he shew'd his abillities in Administration & government there; as well as prudence in considerably augmenting his Estate, without reproch: He had also ben Ambassador Extraord: in Denmark; & in a

---

[1] E here indirectly refers to problems he had had at Sayes Court which he subsequently recorded in an MS now at Christ Church: 'I repaired the ruined house ... to my great cost, and better had I done to have pulled all down at first ... (quoted in some Bray editions of the Diary, e.g. John Forster's for Routledge, 1906, 711).

word, such a person as becomes the sonn of that worthy Hero his Father, the late Lord Capel, who lost his life for K: Charles the first: We spent our time in the mornings in Walking or riding about the Grounds & Contriving; The Afternoones in the Library among the Books; so as I passed my time for 3 or 4 daies with much satisfaction: He was pleased also during this Conversation, to impart to me divers particulars of state relating to the present times; but being no friend to the D - was now laied aside; his integritie & abillities being not so sutable in this Conjuncture: ...

22 I din'd at my L: Arlingtons, & thence to the R: Society, where was read a letter out of Germanie, with some haire inclos'd, that had ben taken from a Corps long buried, that was totaly covered with it, of an Inch in length, exceeding thick, and somewhat harsh & reddish: It seem'd to grow on the skinn like Mosse upon a Tree, the rest of the Cadaver being totaly consum'd. Then a Physitian present, shew'd us a Tooth, or rather a trebble Grinder, with its roote, which he affirmed to have ben found in the Testicle of a Woman whom he Discected: ...

May 13: I was at the funerall of old Mr. Shish Master Shipwrite of the Kings Yard here in this Parish,[1] an honest and remarkable man, & his death a publique losse, for his excellent successe in building Ships, (though illiterate altogether) & for the breeding up so many of his Children to be able Artists: I held up the Pall, with three knights who did him that honour, & he was worthy of it: ... It was the Costome of this good man, to rise in the night, and to pray kneeling in his owne Cofin; which many yeares he had lying by him: he was borne that famous yeare of the Gunpowder Plot 1605: ...

29 His Majesties Birth & returne; but there was so thin a Congregation, that our Viccar who came prepar'd to Preach, omitted it: so soone do we slight & forget Gods benefits: ...

June 14 Came to Dine with us the Countesse of Clarendon, Dr. Lloyd Deane of Bangor [since Bish: of St. Asaph.] and Dr. Burnet author of the *Hist: of Reformation*, & my old friend Mr. Henshaw. After dinner we all went to see the Observatory & Mr. Flamsted; where he shewed us divers rare Instruments, especialy, the greate Quadrant: ...

July 11 A stranger on 9: Mar: 43. 44. The advantage of parting with the greatest pleasure to secure Eternal life: He spake of the Death they put Malefactors to in Egypt, the cutting them asunder, and <setting> the upper halfe of the body on a hot plate: the suffering mans paine expressed in weeping teares, and gnashing of teeth, which he applied to the paine of Hell-fire ... The excessive heate made me extreame sleepy: ...

24 Sir Will: Godolphin lending me his six-horses, I went with my Wife & Daughter to Winsore, to see that stately Court, now neere finished: there was now erected in the Court, the King on Horse-back lately cast in Coper, & set upon a rich Piedestal, of white Marble, the worke of Mr. Gibbons &c: at the expense of Toby Rustat, a Page of the Back stayres, who by his wonderfull frugality had arived to a greate Estate in Mony, & did many works of Charity; as well as this of gratitude to his Master; which cost him 1000 pounds; he is a very simple, ignorant, but honest & loyal creature: We all dined at the Countesse of Sutherlands, afterwards to see Signor Virios garden; thence to Eaton Coll to salute the Provost, & heard a Latine Speech of one of the

---

[1] Jonas Shish (1605-80). His monument is still in the nave at St Nicholas, Deptford.

Alumni (it being at the Election) were invited to supper, but tooke our leaves, and got to Lond: that night in good time: ...

26 my most noble & illustrious friend, the Earle of Ossorie espying me this morning after sermon, in the Privy Gallerie, calling to me, told me he was now going his journey; (meaning to Tangier, whither he was designed Governor, & Generall of the Forces, to regaine the losses we had lately suffer'd from the Moores, when Inchequeene was Governor): I asked his Lordship if he would not call at my house (as he allways did when ever he went out of England on any exploit) I feare I shall not said his Lordship, for I foresee I must embarque at Portsmouth; wherefore I pray, I let you & I dine together to day, I am quite alone, and have something to impart to you: I am not well, & have taken a little Physick this morning; & so shall be private, & I desire your Company: Being retird to his Lodgings & sat down on the Couch, he sent to his secretary for a Copy of a Letter, which he had written to my Lo: Sunderland (secretary of state) wishing me to reade it; and it was to take notice, how ill he resented it, That he should tell the King before my L: Ossories face, That Tangier was not to be kept, but would certainly be lost; & yet added, that twas fit, my L: Ossorie should be sent, that they might give some account of it to the world, meaning (as supposed,) the next Parliament, when all such miscarriages would probably be examin'd, This my L: O: tooke very ill of my L: S. & not kindly of his Majestie, who resolving to send him with an incompetent force, seem'd (as his Lordship tooke it) to be willing to cast him away upon not onely an hazardous Adventure, but, in most mens opinions Impossible; seing there was not to be above 3 or 400 horse & 4000 foote, for the Garison & all, both to defend the Towne, forme a Campe, repulse the Enemie, & fortifie what ground they should get in: This touch'd my Lord deeply, that he should be so little consider'd, as to put him on a buisinesse, in which he should probably, not onely loose his reputation, but be charg'd with all the miscarriages & ill successe; where as at the first they promis'd him 6000 foote & 600 horse effective:

My Lord, being an exceeding brave & valiant person, & that had so approv'd himselfe in divers signal batailes, both at Sea, & Land; so beloved, so esteem'd by the people, as one they depended on upon all occasions worthy such a Captaine; looked on this as too greate an indifference in his Majestie after all his services (& the merits of his father the Duke of Ormond) & a designe of some who envied his Virtue; And it certainly, tooke so deepe roote in his mind, that he who was the most void of feare in the world (and assur'd me he would go to Tangier with ten men, if his Majestie Commanded him) could not beare up against this unkindnesse: Having disburdned himselfe of this to me after dinner, he went with his Majestie to The Sherifs, at a greate supper in Fishmongres Hall; but my Lord, finding himselfe ill, tooke his leave immediately of his Majestie & came back to his Lodging, without staying at all at the Sherifs:

Not resting well this night, he was perswaded to remove to Arlington house for better accommodation where being no longer able to sustaine his indisposition, it manifestly turn'd to a Malignant feavor; which increasing to violence, after all that six of the most able Physitians could do to save him, beginning now and then to be somewhat delirious, at other times with intervalls of better sense: Dr. Lloyd (now Bish: of St. Asaph) administring then to him the holy Sacrament, (of which I also participated) he died the friday after, about 7 in the Evening, being the 30th of July, to the universal griefe of all that either knew, or ever heard of his greate worth: nor had any greater losse than my selfe, he being so much my friend; Oft would he say I was the oldest acquaintance he had in England (when, his Father was in Ireland) it being now of 30 yeares, contracted abroad, when he rid at the Academie in Paris, & that we were seldom asunder: Surely his Majestie never lost a worthier Subject; nor Father, a better, & more dutifull sonn, a loving, goodnatured, generous and perfectly obliging friend, & one who had don innumerable kindnesses to severall persons, before they so much as kn<e>w it: nor advanc'd he any but such as were worthy; None more brave, more modest, none more humble, sober, & every way virtuous: Ô unhapy England! in this illustrious persons losse: Universal was the Mourning for him, the Elogies on him, nor can I sufficiently deplore him: I staied night & day by his bedside to his last gasp to close his deare Eyes: ô sad Father, Mother, Wife & Children!

What shall I add? he deserved all that a sincere friend, a brave Souldier, a Virtuous Courtier, a Loyal Subject, an honest man, a bountifull Master, a good Christian could merit of his Prince & Country: One thing more let me note, That he often expressed to me, the abhorrance he had, of that base & unworthy action, which he was put upon, of Engaging the Smyrna fleete in time of Peace, which, though he behaved himselfe like a greate Captaine; yet he told me was the onely blot of his life, & troubled him Exceedingly: for though he was commanded, & niver examin'd it farther, when he was so: yet allways spake of it with regret, & detestation:

30 I went home very sad: & then write his Countesse a letter giving her an Account of what pass'd in his sicknesse, she being then at her Daughters the Countesse of Derby, at his seate almost 200 miles off: ...

August 30: Lond: I went to visite a French Stranger, one Monsieur Jardine[1] [since Knighted by his Majestie & made Denison of England] who having ben thrice at the East Indias, Persia & other remote Countries, came hither in our returne ships from those parts; and it being reported he was a very curious man, & knowing, I was desir'd by the Ro: Society in their name, to salute him, & to let him know how glad they should be to receive him, if he pleased to do them that honour: &c: There were appointed to accompanie me Sir Jo: Hoskins & Sir Chr: Wren &c.

We found him at his lodging, in his Eastern habite, a very handsom person, extreamely affable, not inclin'd to talke Wonders, but exceedingly modest, & a well bred man: It seemes he traveld in search of Jewels, & was become extreamely rich: He spake Latine, understood the Greeke, Arabic & Persian by 11 yeares Conversation in those Parts, yet seem'd he not to be above 36 yeares of age: After the usual Civilities, we told him, we much desired an account of the extraordinary things he must have seene; having (as we understood) trav<e>ld over land, those places, where few, if any northern Europeans used to go, as about the Black & Caspian Sea, Mingrelia, Bagdat, Ninive, <Persepolis> &c: He told us the things most worthy of our sight, would be, the draughts he had caused to be made of some noble ruines &c: for that (besides his little talent that way) he had carried two very good Painters along with him, to draw Landskips, Measure, and designe the remainders of the Palace which Alexander burnt in his frolique at Persepolis, with divers Temples, Columns, Relievos, & statues, yet extant, which he affirm'd were Sculptures far exceeding, any thing he had observ'd either at Rome, [Greece] or any other part of the World, where Magnificence was in estimation: That there was there an Inscription, of Letters not intelligible, though exceedingly intire; but was extreamely sorry he could not gratifie the Curiosity of the Society, at present,

---

[1] Sir John Chardin (1643-1712).

his things, not being yet out of the ship; but would take the first opportunity to waite on us with them, at his returne from Paris, whither he was hastning the very next morning, but with intention, to be suddenly back againe, & stay longer in our Country, the persecution in France not suffering Protestants, & such he was, to be quiet: so we failed of seeing his Papers; but it was told us by others, that he durst indeede not open or shew them, 'til he had first shew'd them to the French King; though of this he himselfe said notthing:

On farther discourse, he told us that Nineveh was a vast Citty, all now buried in her ruines, and the Inhabitants building on the subterranean Vaults, which were (as appeared) the first stories of the old Cittie; That were frequently <found>, huge Vasas of fine Earth, Columns, & other Antiquities &c: That the straw which the Egyptian Pharoah so tyrannicaly requir'd of the Israelites, was not to burne, or Cover their rowes of brick, as we use; but being chopp'd small, to mingle with the Clay, which drying in the Sunn (for they bake not in the furnaces) would else cleave asunder: That in Persia are yet a race of Igniculi, that still Worship the Sunn, & the fire as Gods: That the Women of Georgia & Mingrelia were Universaly, & without any compare, the most beautifull Creatures for shape, features, & figure in the whole world, & that therefore The Grand Signor, & Bashaws &c had thence most of their Wives & Concubines: That there had within these 100 yeares ben Amazons amongst them (that is) a sort or race of Valiant Women, given to Warr: That Persia was infinitely fertile. He spake also of Japon, & China, & of the many greate errours of our late Geographers &c: as we suggested occasion to discourse; & so we tooke our leaves, & made report to our Society: & I returned home: ...

September 2: I went to Lond: because of an Opportunity I had of his Majesties being yet at Winsor, to see his private Library at Whitehall, which I now did at my full Ease; and went with expectation of finding some Curiosities: But tho there were about a thousand Volumes, there were few of any greate importance, or which I had not perused before; they consisting chiefely of such bookes as had from time to time ben dedicated, or presented him: Few Histories, some Traveles, & french bookes, Aboundance of Mapps & Sea <Charts>: Entertainements, & Pomps; buildings, & Pieces relating to the Navy: some Mathematical Instruments &c: But what was most rare were 3 or 4 Romish Breviaries with a greate deale of Miniature & Monkish Painting & Gilding: one of which is most exquisitely don, both as to the figures, Grotescs & Compartiments, to the uttmost of that curious art: There's another in which I find written by the hand of Henry the 7th, his giving it to his deare Daughter Margarite, afterwards Queene of Scots ([Greate] mother of our K. James, & greate greate Grandmother to the successive Kings, uniting the two Kingdomes) in which he desires her to pray for his soule, subscribing his Name at length:

There is also the Process of the Philosophe<r>s greate Elixir, represented in divers pieces of incomparable miniature; but the Discourse is in high-Dut<c>h & a MSS: Also another MS. in quarto of above 300 yeares old in French, being an Institution of Physic, & in the Botanical part, the Plants are curiously painted in Miniature: There is likewise a Folio Manuscript of a good thicknesse, being the severall exercises, as Theames, Orationes, Translations &c: of K. Edward the sixt, all written & subscrib'd by his owne hand, & with his name very legibly, & divers of the Greeke, interlin'd, & corrected, after the manner of Schole-boys exercises, & that exceedingly well & proper, with some Epistles to his Præceptor &c, which shews that Young Prince to have ben extraordinarily advanc'd in learning, & as Cardan that greate Wit &c (who had ben in Englan'd) affirmed, stupendiously knowing for his age: There is likewise his Journal, no lesse testif<y>ing his early ripenesse & care about the affaires of state: [Dr. Burnet has transcribed many remarks out of this in his *Hist of the Reformation.*]

There are besides many other pompous Volumes, some emboss'd with Gold, & Intaglios on Achats, Medailes &c: I spent 3 or 4 intire daies locked up, & alone among these bookes &c: There is in the rest of the Private Lodgings contiguous to this, divers of the best pictures of the greate Masters, Raphael, Titian &c (& in my esteeme) above all the *Noli me tangere*[1] of our B: Saviour to M: Magdalen, after his Resurrection, of Hans Holbeins, than which, in my life, I never saw so much reverence & kind of Heavenly astonishment, expressed in Picture: There are also divers curious Clocks, Watches & Penduls of exquisite work, and other Curiosities: An antient Woman, who made these lodgings Cleane, & had all the Keyes, let me in at pleasure, for a small reward, by the meanes of a friend:

5 I found our late affected fantastical Curate Mr. Al<derson> preaching in the Chapel at W:hall on 119 Psal: 175 ver: that mens soules were certainely immortal, distinct from the animal life &c: It was not <possible> to heare him without astonishment at his Confidence & formalitie: He was a boy of our Parish, that from a poore grammar schole, turn'd Preacher; & at last got the degree of Batchelor of Art, by a Mandamus, at Cambridge, where he had ben 2 or 3 daies, in his whole life: when he came back, that people might take notice of his degree, he ware his lambskin not onely 2 whole Sundays in the Church, but going all over the Towne, and Every streete, with a wonderfull traine of boys & girls running after him, (as they do when the Beares are led about) came to give me a visite in his formalities, at which I could not <possibly> contain my Countenance: This yet I must say of Mr. A<lderson> that he has together with a vast stack of Confidence, a prodigious Memorie, & strong lungs, & some are taken with his Preachment, that know not the man out of the Pulpet: In a word he is a most singular person, & exceedingly conceited of his abilities: ...

6 I din'd with Sir St: Fox, now one of the Lords Commissioners of the Treasury: This Gent: came first a poore boy from the Quire of Salisbury, then was taken notice of by Bish: Duppa, & afterwards waited on my Lord Percy (bro: to Algernon E: of Northumberland) who procured for him an inferior place amongst the Clearks of the Kitchin & Greene-Cloth side: Where he was found so humble, diligent, industrious, & prudently to behave himselfe, that his Majestie in Exile, & Mr. Fox waiting, both the King & Lords about him, frequently Employed him about their affaires, trusted him both with receiving and paying the little mony, they had: Returning with his Majestie into England after greate Wants, & greate sufferings: his Majestie ...

The Diary *text is broken here*

... so honest & industrious, & withall so capable & ready; that being advanced, from Cl: of the Kitchin to that of the Greene-Cloth &c: he procured to be pay-Master to the whole Army, & by his dexterity, & punctual dealing <obtained> such credit amongst the Banquers, that he was in short time, able to borrow vast summs of them, upon any exigence; The continud Turning thus of mony, & the souldiers moderate allowance to him, for his keeping touch

---

[1] '[Jesus saith unto her] Touch me not.' *John* XX.17.

with them, did so inrich him; that he is believed to be worth at the least 200000 pounds honestly <gotten>, & unenvied, which is next to Miracle, & that with all this he still continues as humble, & ready to do a Courtesie, as ever he was; nay he is generous, & lives very honorably, of a sweete nature, well spoken, & well bred, & so very highly in his Majesties Esteeme, & usefull, that being long-since made a Knight, he is also advanc'd to to be one of the Lords Commissioners of the Treasury: & has the reversion of the Coferers place after Harry Brounckar: He has married his Eldest Daughter to my Lord Cornwallis, & gave her 12000 pounds & restored that intangled family besides; Match'd his Eldest Sonn to Mrs. Trallop who brings with her (besides a greate summ) neere, if not altogether 2000 pounds per annum: Sir Stephens Lady (an excellent Woman) is sister to Mr. Whittle one of the Kings Chirurgions: In a word, never was man more fortunate than Sir Stephen; & with all this he is an handsom person, Vertuous & very religious, & for whom I have an extraordinary esteeme: ...

13 My Lord the Earle of Chesterfield now Justice in Iyre;[1] sent me a fat Buck out of New-Park, which I presented to my Bro: & we eate among severall good friends & gent: of the neighbourhood: ...

23 Came to my house some German strangers, & Signor Pietro a famous Musitian, who had ben long in Sweden in Queene Christinas Court: he sung admirably to a Guitarr & has a perfect good tenor & base &c: & had set to Italian composure, many of Abraham Cowleys Pieces which shew'd extreamely well: He told me the heate [some part] in summer was as excessive as the Cold in in winter in Sweden; so cold he affirm'd, that the streetes of all the townes are desolate, no creature stirring in them for many moneths, all the inhabitans retiring to their stoves: He spake high things of that romantic Queene, her Learning, skill in Languages, the Majestie of her behaviour, her Exceeding Wit, & that the Histories she had read of other Counteries, especialy of Italy & Rome made her despize her owne: That the real occasion of her resignation of the Crowne to her Cousin, was the Noblemens importuning her to Marie, and the Promise which the Pope had made her of procuring her to be Queene of Naples, which also caused her to change her Religion, but she was cheated by his crafty holinesse, working on her ambition: That the reason of her Killing her secretarie at Fontain Beleaw, was his revealing that Intrigue with the Pope: But after all this, I rather believe it was her mad prodigality & extreame Vanity, which had Consum'd all those vast treasures, the greate Adolphus (her father) had brought out of Germany, during his enterance there, & wonderfull successes: & that if she had not voluntarily resign'd (as for-seeing the Event) the States of her Kingdome would have compell'd her.

October <30> I went to Lond: [to be private:] My Birth-day being the next; & I now arived to the sixtieth yeare of Age; [31] upon which, I began a more solemn survey of my whole Life, in order to the making, and confirming my peace with God, by an accurate Scrutinie of all my actions past, as far as I was

---

[1] 'Iyre' = eyre: the court circuit; Chesterfield, one of E's oldest friends (see above, 7 May 1650) held this office in royal forests south of the Trent from 1679-85. E now gave him a copy of the 1679 edition of *Sylva*. It survives (sold through Maggs Brothers Ltd in 1993), bearing the inscription 'For the Rig^t: Honble The Earle of Chesterfield Lord Justice of Eire & of all his Maties Woods & Forests in ye Kingdome of England: from his most humble Servant JEvelyn.'

able to call them to min'd: And oh, how difficult, & uncertaine, yet most necessarie worke; The Lord be mercifull to me & accept me. Who can tell how oft he offendeth? Teach me therefore so to Number my daies, that I may apply my heart to wisdome, making my calling & election secure: Amen Lord Jesus: I spent this whole day in Exercise &c: ...

November 1. I began, and spent this whole Weeke in examining my life, beging pardon for my faults, Assistance & blessing for the future, that I might in some sort be prepared for the time that now drew neere, & not have the greate worke to begin, when one can worke no longer: The Lord Jesus help & assist me: I therefore stirred little abroad til the 5t ...

30 The Anniversary Elections at the R: Society brought me to Lond: where was chosen Præsident, that excellent person, & greate Philosopher Mr. Robert Boyle who indeed, ought to have ben the very first; but neither his infirmitie, nor modestie could now any longer excuse him: I desir'd I might for this yeare be left out of the Council, by reason my dwelling was in the Country; The Society, according to Costome, din'd together: This signal day, began the Trial of my Lord Vicount Stafford for conspiring the Death of the King, and was likewise his Birth-day.

December 2. I was curious to see & heare the famous Triale of my L: Stafford [second] sonn to my Lord Thomas Howard, Earle of Arundel & Surry, Earle Marishall of England, & Grandfather to the present Duke of Norfolck, whom I so well knew, & from which excellent person, I received so many favours:

The Trial was in Westminster Hall, before the King, Lords & Commons, just in the same manner as just 40 yeares past, the greate & wise Earle of Strafford (there being but one letter differing their names) received his Tryal (for pretended ill government in Ireland) in that famous Parliament [and same place]: This Lord Staffords Father being High-Steward &c: Onely the Place of sitting was now exhalted some considerable height from the Paved flore of the Hall, with a stage of boards, His Majesties Throne or state, the Woolsacks for the Judges, long formes for the Peeres, Chaire of the Lord Steward *pro tempore*, exactly ranged as in the House of Lords: All the sides on both hands Scaffolded to the very roofe, for the Members of the H: of Commons: At the upper end, & right side of the Kings state, was a box for his Majestie, others for the Greate Ladys on the left hand; and over head a gallerie for Ambassadors & Pub: Ministers: At the lower-end or Enterance was a Barr, & place for the Prisoner, The Lieutennant of the Toure of London, the Axe-bearer & Guards, My Lord Staffords two Daughters, the Marchionesse of Winchester being one. There was likewise a Box for my Lord to retire into: At the right hand in another box some what higher, stood the Witnesses, at the left, the Manegers, who were to produce & manege the Evidence & whole processe in the name of the Commons of England: viz: Serjeant Maynard, (the greate lawyer, the same who prosecuted the Cause against the Earle of Strafford 40 years before in the same place, being now neere 80 yeares of age) Sir William Jones, (late Attourney Gen:) Sir Fran: Winnington (a famous Pleader) & Mr. Treby (now Recorder of Lond:) not appearing in their gownes as Lawyers, but in their cloakes & swords, as representing the Commons of England. To these were joyn'd Mr. Hamden, Mr. Sechevarell, Mr. Poule, Coll: Titus, Sir Tho: Lee all Gentlemen of Qualitie & noted Parliament men:

The first two dayes (in which was read, the Commission, & Impeacchment) was but a very tedious enterance into Matter of fact, the Charge, at which I was little present: But on Thursday being commodiously seated amongst the

Commons, when the wittnesses were sworn, & deposed, of which the principle were Mr. Oates (who cal'd himselfe Doctor) Mr. Dugdale & Turberville: Oates tooke his Oath, that he delivered a Commission to V. Count Stafford from the Pope, to be Pay-Master Generall, to an Army intended to be raised &c: Dugdale, that being at my Lord Astons, the <Prisoner> dealt with him plainely to Murder his Majestie, & Turbervile, that at Paris also he proposed the same to him &c.

3 Friday was spent in Depositions of my Lords Wittnesses, to invalidate the Testimonie of the Kings Witnesses, which being very slight persons, though many, viz, 15 or 16: tooke up all that day: and in truth they rather did my Lord injurie than service, & made but little for him.

4: Saturday came other Witnesses of the Commons, to corroborate the Kings, of which some were Peeres, & some Commons, with other of good qualitie, who tooke off all the former days objections, & set the Kings Witnesses *recti in Curia*, & then adjourn'd 'til moneday:

6 Moneday, being the 6 of December I went againe to the Trial, where I heard the Evidences summ'd up by Sir William Jones, which was very large; and when he had don, & said all he could to exaggerate the charge succeeded all the rest of the Lawyers Manegers; Then began Mr Hen: Poule in a vehement Oration, as to the profes of the Jesuitical doctrine, of holding it not onely lawfull, but meritorious to Murder an Heretic King; which my Lord, had in his plea denyed:

After this my Lord (as upon all occasions, & very often he did during the whole Trial) spake in his owne defence, denying the Charge altogether; that he never in his life saw either Turbervile or Oates at the time, and manner affirmed; & in truth their Testimonie did little weigh with me; Dugdales onely seemed to presse hardest; To which my Lord spake a greate while, but without any method, & confus'dly:

One thing my Lord said, which I confesse did exceedingly affect me, as to Titus Oates, That a Person, who, during his depositions, should so vauntingly as he did, brag that though he went over to the Church of Rome, yet he was never a Papist, nor of their Religion, all the time that he seem'd to Apostasize from the Protestant; but onely as a spie; Though he confess'd he tooke their Sacraments, Worship'd Images, went through all the Oathes & discipline of their Proselytes, swearing seacrecy, & to be faithfull, but with intention to come over againe & betray them:

That such an Hypocrite, that had so deeply prevaricated, as to turne even Idolater, (for so we of the Church of England esteem'd it) attesting God so solemnly, that he was intirely theirs, & devoted to their interests, & consequently (as he pretended) trusted; I say that the Witnesse of such a proflygate wretch should be admitted, against the life of a Pere; This my Lord, looked upon as a monstrous thing, & such as must needes redown'd to the dishonor both of our Religion & Nation: And verily, I am of his Lordships opinion; Such a mans Testimonie should not be taken against the life of a Dog: 'Tis true, many Protestants had defected, & return'd againe; but we know of none, (nor if any, can approve them) who when they turned Papists, did not heartily believe they were in the right, 'til they were convinc'd to the Contrary: But this is not Oates his case, he went thro all the mysteries of their Religion, thro all their Oat<h>es, Execrations on himselfe, Sacraments &c, whilst by his owne Confession, he disembl'd all; This he affirmed & I know not on what occasion it escaped from him, no lesse impiously: than foolishly:

From this moment foreward, I had quite lost my opinion of Mr. Oates. But the merite & service of something material which he discovered against

Coleman at first, put him in such esteeme with the Parliament &c: that now I fancy, he stooke at nothing, & thought that every body was to take what he said for Gospel afterwards: The Consideration of this, and some other Circumstances began to stagger me; particularly how 'twas possible, that one who went among the Papists with such a designe, & pretended to be intrusted with so many letters, & Commissions from the Pope & party, nay & delivered them to so many greate Persons, should not reserve one of them to shew, or produce, nor so much as one Copie of any Commission; which he who had such dexterity in opening letters &c, might certainely have don, to the undenyable Conviction of those whom he accus'd: But, as I said, he gained Credit upon Coleman, but as to others whom he so madly flew upon, I am little inclined to believe his testimonie; he being so slight a person, so passionate, ill-bred, & [of] impudent behaviour: nor is it at all likely, such piercing politicians as the Jesuites should trust him with so high, & so dangerous seacrets.

[7] On Tuesday I was againe at the Trial, when Judgement was demanded, and after my Lord had spoken what he could in denying of the fact &c: The Manegers answering the objections &c: The Peeres adjourned to their House, & within two houres, return'd againe: There was in the meane time this farther question put, whither there being but one witnesse to any single Crime or act, it could amount to convict a man; upon this, the Judges being cald on to give their opinion, unanimously declar'd, that in case of Treason, they all were overt acts; for though no man should be condemn'd by one witnesse for any one act, yet for severall acts to the same intent, it was valid, which was my Lord Staffords Case, for one sware he practised him to Kill his Majestie at Paris, another at my L: Astons, a Third that he delivered him a Commission from Rome, but to neither of there were <there> above one Witnesse, so it was overruled:

This being past, and The Peres in their seats againe, my Lord [Chancelor] Finch (who was this day High Steward) removing to the Wool-sack next his Majesties state, after summoning the Lieutennant of the Tower to bring forth his Prisoner, and Proclamation made for silence; demanded of every Peere (who were in all 86) whither William Lord Vicount Stafford were Guilty of the Treason Laied to his Charge, or not Guilty: Then the Peere (spoken to) standing up, & laying his right hand upon his breast, sayed Guilty, or Not Guilty Upon his honour; & then sat downe: & so another 'til all were asked: the L: Steward noting their severall Suffrages as they answered upon a paper:

When all had don, the number of not Guilties being but 31, the Guiltys 55, after Proclamation for silence againe; The Steward directing his speech to the Prisoner (against whom the Axe was turn'd edge ways towards him, & not before) in aggravation of his Crime, he being enobled by his Majesties Father, & since received many favours & graces from his present Majestie: That came of such a stock, & noble family, had appeared in his defence in time of the late rebellion &c: & all that could signifie to the charge of his ingratitude & disloyalty: Then inlarged on the honor & justice of their Proceedings against him with a Christian exhortation to Repentance, & Confession, deploring first his owne unhapinisse, that he who never Condemned any man before, should now be necessitated to begin with him, &c: & then Pronounced Sentence of Death, by Hanging, Drawing & Quartering (according to forme) with greate solemnity, and dreadfull gravity; last of all, after a short pause; Told the Prisoner, That he believed the Lords would interceede with his Majestie that some Circumstances of his sentence, might be omitted, beheading onely excepted & then breaking his White-staff, the Court disolved.

My Lord Stafford during all this later part spake very little, & onely Gave their Lordships thanks, after the sentence was pronounc'd; & indeede behav'd himselfe modestly, and as became him: 'Twas observ'd, that all his owne Relations, & of his Name & family Condemn'd him, excepting onely his Nephew the Earle of Arundel; sonn to the D: of Norfolck: and it must be acknowledg'd that the whole Trial was carried on from first to last, with exceeding gravity, & so stately and august appearance I had never seene; for besides innumerable spectators of Gent: & forraine Ministers &c: who saw & heard all the proceedings, the Prisoner had the Consciences of all the Commons of England for his Accusers, and all the Peeres to be his Judges & Jury: He had likewise the assistance of what Counsel he would to direct him in his plea, that stood by him: And yet I can hardly think, a person of his age & experience, should engage men, whom he never saw before, (& one of them that came to visite him as a stranger, at Paris), *point blanque* to Murder the King: God onely, who searches hearts, can discover the Truth, & to him it must be left: My Lord Stafford, was not a man belov'd, Especialy of his owne family, & had ben suspected, & in danger to by it, of a Vice in Germanie, which neede not be nam'd, and I doubt not but he had seriously repented ...

12 Our Viccar & Curate proceeded on their former Texts: This Evening looking out of my Chamber Window towards the West, I first saw a Meteor, (or what ever Phænomenon it was) of an obscure bright Colour (if so I may call it without a solecisme) resembling the brightnesse of the Moone when under a thin Clow'd, very much in shape like the blade of a sword, whose point to the starre in appearance, bending Northwards towards London, not seeming at the Horizon to be above a yard in bredth, & so pyramidal, the rest of the skie, very serene & cleere; The Moone new, but not appearing, the Weather exceeding sharp, hard frost with some snow falling 2 daies before: What this may Portend (for it was very extraordinarie) God onely knows; but another such Phænomen<on> I remember I saw, which went from North to South, & was much brighter, & larger, but not so Ensiforme in the yeare 1640, about the Triall of the greate Earle of Strafford, præceeding our bloudy Rebellion: I pray God avert his Judgements; we have had of late severall Comets, which though I believe appeare from natural Causes, & of themselves operate not, yet I cannot despise them; They may be warnings from God, as they commonly are for-runners of his Annimadversions: After some daies this plainly appeared to be headed with a small hazy-starr distant from Venus 23°-'58 & the bright st: of Aquila 28-15-½-5°-90 Latitude - 9°-44 South, the taile or point extending to the middle of Sagitta above a degree broad, & was 35 deg: long.

17 This day being friday, at exactly halfe an <houre> after one at noone, was my Daughter in Law brought to bed of a Sonn, a very fine babe; for which I gave God Thanks: ...

[19] being the last Sonday of Advent; was Christned my little Grandsonn, by the name of Richard: his <great> Grandfather Sir Rich: Browne & my Bro: Geo: Evelyn being Susceptors with my Lady Stonehouse mother of my Daughter in Law:

22 Was the solemn Publique Fast thro out England, that God would prevent all popish plotts, avert his Judgements, & give a blessing to the proceedings of the Parliament now assembled, & which struck at the Succession of the Duke of York &c: ...

29, was the unhappy ViCount Stafford beheaded on Tower Hill ...

1681

January 2 ... After many daies & nights of Snow, Clowdy & dark weather, the Comet was gotten as far as the head of Andromeda & not above 23 deg: long, much wasted: ...

February 10 I was at the Wedding & Marriage of my Nephew Jo: Evelyn of Wotton, married by my L: Bish: of Rochester at Westminster (in Hen: 7th Chapell) to the daughter & heyre of Mr. Erskin of Sussex, her portion 8000 pounds: I wish it may <prove> happy to him,[1] & the familie, having first proposed it to my Bro: & that she is like to be a proper beautifull young Lady, & of an honourable familie: The solemnity was kept with a few select friends only, at my Lady Beckfords mother of the Lady: ...

March 27 ... The Parliament now conven'd at Oxford: Greate expectation of his Royal Highnesses Case, as to Succession, against which the house was set:
An extraordinary sharp, cold Spring, not yet a leafe on the trees, frost & snow lying: whilst the whole nation was in a greate ferment ...

April 12 I din'd at Mr. Brisbans Secretary to the Admiralty, a learned & industrious person: whither came Dr. Burnet to thank me for some Papers I had contributed towards his excellent *Historie of the Reformation*: Thence to the R: Society, next day home: ...
26 I dined at Dom Piedro Ronquillos the Spanish Ambassador at Wild house, used me with extraordinarie Civility: After dinner (which was plentifull, halfe after the Spanish, & halfe after the English way) he led me into his Bed-chamber, where we both fell into a long discourse about Religion; in which, though he was a learned man in Politiques, & an Advocate; I found him very ignorant, & unable to defend any point of Controversy, blindly recurring at every foote, to the Churches Infallibility, & Tradition - he was however far from being fierce; onely at parting earnestly wishing that I would humbly apply my selfe to the Blessed Virgin to direct me, & that he had know<n> divers that had ben averse from the Roman Catholique religion, be wonderfully inlightned & convinced by her Intercession. This was a pretty Postulatum; he would have one be a papist, that he might be a Papist: They have not a weaker tenet in all their Religion, than this error of Invocation of Saints & Adoration: so I tooke leave of the Ambassador, who importun'd me to come & visite him often: ...
29 I gave in my grand Accompt to the Lords Commissioners of the Treasury, & so home, but one showre of raine all this Moneth, the whole yeare dry &c: ...

May 5 Came to visite & dine with me Sir William Fermor, of N:hamptonshire, & Sir Chr: Wren, his Majesties Architect & Surveyor, now building the Cathedrall of St. Paules, & the Columne in memorie of the Citties Conflagration, & was in hand with the building of 50 Parish Churches: a <wonderfull> genius had this incomparable Person: ...

---

[1] It did not. The young man died in 1691 of the effects of over-indulgence (see 21 May 1691). By the time his father died in 1699 there were no living male descendants and the estate passed to his uncle, the diarist, and his heirs (see 4 October 1699).

16 Came my Lady the Countesse of Sunderland, to desire me, that I would propose a Match to Sir Stephen Fox, for her sonn, my Lord Spencer, to Marry Mrs. Jane Sir Stephens daughter: I excused it all I was able; for the truth is, I was afraid he would prove an extravagant man; for though a youth of extraordinary parts, & that had all the Education imaginable to render him a worthy man; yet his early inclinations to vice made me apprehensive I should not serve Sir St: Fox in it, like a friend: This being now his onely Daughter, so well bred, & who was like to receive a large share of her fathers kindnesse, as far as opulence & mony could expresse it: For Sir Stephen is my Friend, & for whom I have much esteeme; & I consider'd that My Lord Sunderland, being much sunke in his Estate, by Gaming & other prodigalities, it could not at this time answer Sir Stephens expectations; for my Lord, was now no longer secretary of state, but was falln in displeasure with the King, for his siding with the Commons &c: about the Succession; but which, I am very well assured he did not do, out of his owne inclination, or for the preservation of the Protestant religion; but by mistaking a party, which he believed would have carried it, & perhaps had good reason to think so: For otherwise Sir Stephen did not stand so much upon a rich fortune for his Favorite daughter, but was willing to marry her to a noble familie, both to fortifie his interests, & better his allyance:

However so earnest & importunate was the Countesse that I would use my interest, & breake it to him; that I was over come, and did accordingly promise it: so next day, I tooke an opportunitie to introduce the proposal: Sir Stephen (who knew nothing of the young gallants inclinations, but that he was as to appearance, one of the loveliest & spiritous Youths in England) professed to me, that no man in England's recomendations should be sooner receiv'd than mine; but told me That it was too greate an honour to him, that his Daughter was very Young, as well as my Lord, & he was fully resolv'd never to marry her, without the parties mutual liking, which she could not judge of 'til more advanc'd in age, with other difficulties and objections that I neither could, nor would contradict:

I told him how I was ingag'd, & that I would serve them both, if he thought good to proceede, and take what measures he should give me in this matter; I onely told him that I was my Lady Sunderlands friend, one that she trusted with many <of> her concernes, & did Confesse their condition as to Estate was impair'd; but that I verily believ'd, that if it were set-free, they would husband things better for the future, & that he would do an act of greate Generositie, & as already he had, (by marrying his Eldest Daughter with a vast Portion,) redeem'd my Lord Cornwallis's intangled estate, (& who proved a very worthy gent:) so it would be his glory to set up the Earle of Sunderlands family againe; with how greate an obligation it would be to those who sought his Alyance:

This did a little worke upon Sir Stephens good nature, who I am sure might have had his choice in any of the best families in England: However he desired me to write to the Countesse, & to expresse the greate sence he had of the honour don him; that his Daughter & her sonn were too Young, that he would do nothing without her liking, which he did not think her capable of expressing judiciously, 'til she should arive to the age of 16 or 17: of which she now wanted 4 yeares; & in short, that I would put it off as civily as I could for the present; which indeede I did: But my Lady, (now that I had broken the ice,) continues to conjure my assistance, & that I would not leave it in this posture: ...

20 ... There had scarce fallen yet any raine since Christmas: ...

June 12 ... My exceeding drowsinesse hindred my attention, which I feare proceeded from Eating too much, or the drinesse of the season & heate, it still continuing so greate a drowth, as was never knowne in Eng: & was said to be universal: ...

19 ... The dry weather had now withered every thing, & threatned some universal dirth &c: ...

July 21 My Wife & Daughter Mary &c: went to Tunbridge to drinke the Waters: &c: ...

August 4. To Lond: about severall affaires: Went to R: Society where was produced by Dr. Slaer (one of the Members) an extraordinary Experiment: He prepared a matter, which without exposure to the Sunn, or light, (as other Phosphorus's were) shoone as bright as the flame of a Candle: It was a substance of the Colour of mouth glew; had an urinous smell; with this he wrote on a sheete of paper, <nothing> in the least appearing, but being put into a dark place, shoone forth in a bright & delicate stroke these two words *Vivat Rex Carolus*, which remain'd above halfe an hour, & longer than we were willing to stay: A beame of the Sunn was not more perspicuous, it did not flame up, but remained close to the paper, in a neate stroake about the bignesse <of> Text letters, so as to give a pretty light about it; The very motion of drawing it on a paper, (as one would write with a black-lead pen) seting it on this lambent fire: & when it was almost quite spent, rubbing it a little with ones hand or finger, it would rekindle, yet without taking holding of, or leaving any track on the paper, when exposed to the day againe: Many Phosphorus had I seene, as that famous *Lapis illuminabilis*[1] of Bologna, which I went there to see being in Italy many yeares since; but never did I see any comparable to this: Washing my hands & face with it, I appeared in the darke like the face of the moone, or rather like some spirit, or strange apparition; so as I cannot but attribute it to the greate providence of God, that it was not first found out by the Papists; for had they the seacret onely, what a miracle might they make it, supposing them either to rub the Consecrated Wafer with it, or washing the Priests face & hands with it, & doing the feate in some darke Church or Cloyster, proclaime it to the Neighbour hood; I am confident the Imposture would bring thousands to them, & do an infinity of mischiefe, to the establishing of the common error of Transubstantiation; all the world would ring at the miracle &c:

This matter being rubbed very hard on paper or board, set it in a devowring flame, which I never saw any Phosphorus do but this, & it being of a nature to spend it selfe, or if a little warmed either by the fire or the Sunn, would flame out right, & burne most fiercely, but being kept continualy in a glasse of water, lasted without impaire: He affirm'd it to be chymicaly & with extraordinary preparation, composed of Urine & humane bloud: which gives greate light to Dr. Willis &c notions of the *flamula Vitalis*[2] which animates the bloud, & is, for ought we know, the animal life it selfe of all things living:

It is certainely a most noble Experiment; first excogitated & hinted (as this Doctor Confessed) by Mr. Boyle, with whom this industrious young Physitian, some time wrought in his Laboratory: He tooke a small portion, not bigger than a small peper Corne, layed it on a dry piece of fir board, & with the flatt

---

[1] 'Stone with light.'
[2] 'Spark of life.'

of a knife bruised it, as one would spread a Plaister, & immediately rose up in a fierce flame, & consum'd the board: Then he had a Phiol of Liquor, which he said was made of a disolution of this, which dropping into a beere glasse of Ale, conceived a flame, so soone as it touched & mingled with the Ale: of this I drank, & seem'd to me to be of an agreable amber scent, with very little altering the tast of the Ale: The Doctor pretends to bring it into a usefull & precious Medicine or Panaceam: This liquor was red:

This noble Experiment, exceeded all that ever I had seene of this nature, unlesse that which my learned Friend, & fellow Traveler Mr. Hensheaw & I accidentaly beheld a certaine Mountebank at Rome in the *Piazza Navona* (formerly Circus Maximus)[1] now the Market place; here, whilst the other Charlatans, invited people to their stages, by Monkies, Jack-puddings & Pantomimes; This Fellow onely tooke from his finger a Ring (w<h>ither gold, brasse or silver, I could not examine, nor did I mind) which seem'd to have a lump of blackish wax upon it, about the bignesse & of the shape, of those we call Toade stones, (which are indeede, but the grinders of the shark-fish). This he no sooner touched with the tip of his finger, which he seemed to wet with spittle at his mouth onely (though perhaps dip'd in some oyle or other menstrue before) but it immediately rose into a flame, as big & bright as any Wax light; This we saw him two or three times blow out, & accend againe, with the least touch of his finger, & then put the ring on his finger, & having by this surprizing trick, gotten Company about him, he fell to prating for the vending of his pretended Remedies &c:

But a thousand times have we deplored, that whatever it Cost, we had not purchased this rare receit; Tis mentioned how to make the like both in Wecker & Jo: Bap: Porta &c: but on many tryals, it did not succeede: & what stupidity should seaze & possesse us, that all the time we were in Rome, we should never think of this, 'til some yeares after we were nearer home, We have both admir'd: The matter of fact is true, & I wish I knew how to make the like for a greate summ of mony; since, <if> it could be made without exceeding Cost, it would be an expeditious way to kindle any fire, light a Candle, & use upon a thousand occasions, abroad or at home: ...

14: Our Viccar still indisposed, the Curate preached on 3: Apocalyps. 19. No Sermon this afternoone, which I think did not happen twice in this parish these 30 yeares; so gracious had God ben to it, & indeede to the whole Nation: God Grant, we abuse not this greate privelegdge: either by our wantonesse, schismes, or Unfruitfullnesse under such meanes, as he has not favoured any nation under heaven besides: ...

23 I went to visite my deare Bro: at Wotton, the place of my birth: & Country:

24 I was invited to Mr. Denzil Onslows at his seate at Purford, where was much company, & such an extraordinary feast, as I had hardly ever seene at any Country Gent: table in my whole life; but what made it more remarkeable was, that there was not any thing, save what his Estate about it did not afford; as Venison, Rabb<i>ts, hairs, Pheasants, Partridge, [pigeons,] Quaile, Poultrie, all sorts of fowle in season (from his owne Decoy neere his house) all sorts of fresh fish: so Industrious is this worthy Gent: After dinner we went to see sport at the decoy, I never saw so many herons &c. The seate stands on a flat, the ground pastures, rarely watred, & exceedingly improved; since Mr. Onslow

---

[1] E is wrong. The *Piazza* was once the Circus of Domitian and follows exactly the former plan of the track. The Circus Maximus is elsewhere in Rome.

bought it of Sir Rob: Parkhurst, who spent a faire Estate &c: The house is Timber, but commodious, & with one ample dining roome, & the hal<l> adorned with paintings of fowle, & huntings &c: the work of Mr.Barlow, who is excellent in this kind from the life: It stands neere part of Guildford river, within 12 or 14 miles of Lond: we returned to Wotton in the Evening: ...

30 I went to visite Mr. Hussey a neere neighbour of my Bro: who has a very prety seate, delicately watred, & he certainely the neatest husband for curious ordering his Domestic & field Accommodations, & what pertaines to husbandry, that in my life I have ever seene, as to his severall Graneries, Tackling, Tooles & Utensils, Ploughs, Carts, Stables, Woodpiles, Woork house, even to the hen rosts & hog troughs: so as I mithought I saw old Cato or Varro in him:[1] all substantial, all in exact order, which exceedingly delighted me: The sole inconvenience he lies under, is the greate quantities of sand, which his streames bring along with them, which fills his chanales & receptacles of fish too soone: The rest of my time of stay at Wotton was spent in walking about the grounds & goodly Woods, where I have in my Youth entertained my solitude &c: & so on the 2d of September I returned to my home, being two daies after my Wife &c was returned from Tunbridge, where they had ben, I blesse God, with good successe, now neere five weekes: ...

September 6. Died my pretty Grand-child at Nurse of the gripes.

8. My good neighbour Mr. Turner was buried, our Viccar preached on 126. Psal.7: when <likewise> was interred our little Child:

9: I sadly remembred the losse of another deare friend: This afternoone came the Bish: of Rochester & his Lady to visite us: ...

14. Din'd with Sir Steph: Fox: Who proposed to me the purchasing of Chelsey Coll; which his Majestie had some time since given to our Society, & would now purchase it of us againe, to build an Hospital [Infirmary] for Souldiers there; in which he desired my assistance as one of the Council of the R: Society: ...

October 11 I went to Fulham to visite the Bish: of Lond: in whose Garden I first saw the *Sedum arborescens*[2] in flowre, which was exceeding beautifull: I called in at Parsons Greene to see our Charge, my L: Vic: Mordaunts Children: ...

18 My Coach-house was robbed, they ript off the Velvet &c: There was this day a meeting with the rest of the Trustees, upon my Young Lord Vicount Mordaunts offer to procure 20000 pounds for the payment of his Bro: & sisters portions, in consideration that we would possesse him of Parsons Greene, & the Coale-farme, which were worth 3000 per Annum: This tooke up long debates with our Council, who were for us Sir William Jones late Attourney Gen: and Mr. Keck: There were with me the Earle of Clarendon, Mr. Newport, & Mr. Herbert: but nothing concluded ...

November 15 I went to Visite, & dined with the Earle of Essex, who after dinner in his study sitting alone with him by the fire, related to me how much he had ben scandaliz'd & injur'd in the report of his being privy to the Marriage of his Ladys Niepce, the rich young Widdow of my late Lord Oagle,

---

[1] Cato and Varro's respective works on agriculture and cultivation were amongst E's favourite sources for his *Sylva* and *Kalendarium Hortense*.

[2] The tree houseleek.

sole daughter of the Earle of Northumberland; shewing me a letter of Mr. Thinns excusing himselfe for his not communicating his Marriage to his Lordship; acquainting me also with the whole storie of that unfortunate Ladys being betraied by her Grandmother the Countesse of N-humb: & Coll: Bret for mony; and that though upon the importunitie of the Duke of Monmoth, he had delivered [to the Grandmother] a particular of the Joynture, which Mr. Thynn pretended he would settle on the Lady; yet he totaly discourag'd the proceeding, as by no means a competent Match, for one that both by her birth, & fortune might have pretended to the greatest Prince in Christendome: That he also proposed the Earle of Kingston (a kinds man of mine) or the Lord Cranborn; but was by no meanes for Mr. Thynn:

24. I was at the Audience of the Russia Ambassador which was befor both their Majesties in the Banqueting-house: The presents were carried before them, held up by his followers standing in two rankes towards the Kings state, & consisted of Tapissry (one suit of which was doubtlesse brought from France as being of that fabric, this Ambassador having passed through that Kingdom as he came out of Spaine) a large Persian Carpet, Furrs of Sable & Ermine &c: but nothing was so splendid & exotick, as the Ambassador Who came soone after his Majesties restauration:[1] This present Ambassador was exceedingly offended that his Coach was not permited to come into the Court; til being told that no Kings Ambassadors did, he was pacified, yet requiring an attestation of it under Sir Ch: Cotterells the Master of the Ceremonies hand; being it seemes afraid he should offend his Master if he omitted the least puntillo: 'Twas reported he condemn'd his sonn to loose his head, for shaving off his beard, & putting himselfe in the French mode at Paris, & that he had executed it, had not the french King interceeded: of this quære: ...

28 Several Fellows of our Society met at diner in the Citty, to consult about Electing a fit Secretarie, & to regulate some other defects: This Evening I got Dr. Slaer to shew my Lord Chamberlaine, the Duke & Dutchesse of Grafton, the Earle of Chesterfild, Conde de Castel Melior & severall others, that admirable and stupendious experiment of both the liquid & drie Phosphorus, at which they were all astonish'd:

30 Being St. Andrews day, we continued Sir Chr: Wrenn our President, elected a new Council according to the Statute, of which I was one; & chose Mr. Austine secretary with Dr. Plott, the ingenious Author of the Natural Hist. of Oxfordshire: There was a most illustrious appearance:

December 1 I went home to my house, after neere a Moneths absence upon buisinesse with Sir Denis Gauden, & Commissioners of the Navy: ...

15 The Duke of Grafton invited me to a magnificent Feast at the Trinity house:

1682

January 11 To Lond: Saw the Audience of the Morroco Ambassador: his retinue not numerous, was receivd in the Banqueting-house both their Majesties present: he came up to the Throne without making any sort of Reverence, bowing so much as his head or body: he spake by a Renegado

---

[1] On 29 December 1662.

English man, for whose safe returne there was a promise: They were all Clad in the Moorish habite Cassocks of Coloured Cloth or silk with buttons & loopes, over this an Alhaga or white wollan mantle, so large as to wrap both head & body, a shash or small Turban, naked leg'd & arm'd, but with lether socks like the Turks, rich Symeters, large Calico sleev'd shirts &c: The Ambassador had a string of Pearls odly woven into his Turbant; I fancy the old Roman habite was little different as to the Mantle & naked limbs: The Ambassador was an handsom person, well featur'd, & of a wise looke, subtile, and extreamely Civile: Their Presents were Lions & Estridges &c: Their Errant, about a Peace at Tangire &c: But the Concourse & Tumult of the People was intollerable, so as the Officers could keepe no order; which they were astonish'd at at first; There being nothing so regular exact & perform'd with such silence &c, as [in] all these publique occasions of their Country, & indeede over all the Turkish dominions: ...

24 To Lond: where at the Council of the R: Soc: we passed a new Law, for the more accurate consideration of Candidates before admission, as whither they would realy be Usefull: & also concerning Honorarie Members, that none should be admitted but *per diploma*:[1] An exper: for the describing any Parabola line whatsoever.

This Evening I was at the Entertainement of the Morroco <Ambassador> at the Dut: of Portsmouths glorious Appartment at W.hall, where was a greate banquet of Sweetemeates, & Musique &c but at which both the Ambassador & Retinue behaved themselves with extraordinary Moderation & modestie, though placed about a long Table a Lady betweene two Moores: viz: a Moore, then a Woman, then a Moore &c: and most of these were the Kings natural Children, viz: the Lady Lichfield, Sussex, DD of Portsmouth, Nelly &c: Concubines, & catell of that sort, as splendid as Jewells, and Excesse of bravery could make them: The Moores neither admiring or seeming to reguard any thing, furniture or the like with any earnestnesse; and but decently tasting of the banquet: They dranke a little Milk & Water, but not a drop of Wine, also they drank of a sorbett & Jacolatte: did not looke about nor stare on the Ladys, or expresse the least of surprize, but with a Courtly negligence in pace, Countenance, & whole behaviour, answering onely to such questions as were asked, with a greate deale of Wit & Gallantrie, & so gravely tooke leave, with this Compliment That God would blesse the D: of P: and the Prince her sonn, meaning the little Duke of Richmon'd: The King came in at the latter end, just as the Ambassador was going away: In this manner was this Slave (for he was no more at home) entertained by most of the Nobility in Towne; & went often to Hide-Park on horse back, where he and his retinue shewed their extraordinary activity in Horsmanship, and the flinging & Catching their launces at full speede; They rid very short, & could stand up right in full speede, managing their speares with incredible agility. He also went sometimes to our Theaters, where when upon any foolish or fantastical action he could not forbeare laughing, he endeavored to hide it with extraordinary modesty & gravity: In a word, the Russian Ambassador, still at Court behaved himselfe like a Clowne, compar'd to this Civil Heathen:

27 This Evening Sir St. Fox acquainted me againe with his Majesties resolutions of proceeding in his Erection of a Royal Hospital for Emerited Souldiers on that spot of ground The Ro: Society had sold his Majestie for 1300 pounds & that he would settle 5000 pounds per Annum on it, & build to the value of 20000 pounds for the reliefe & reception of 4 Companies, viz. 400

---

[1] 'Through a letter of recommendation.'

men, to be as in a Coledge or Monastrie: I was therefore desired by Sir Stephen (who had not onely the whole menaging of this, but was (as I perceiv'd) himselfe to be a grand benefactor, as well it became him, who had gotten so vast an Estate by the Souldiers &c) to assist him & Consult what Method to Cast it in, as to the Government: So in his Study, we set downe the Governor, Chaplaine, Steward, Housekeeper, Chirurgion, Cooke, Butler, Gardner, Porter & other Officers, with their severall salaries & entertainements: I would needes have a Librarie, & mentioned severall books &c. since some souldiers might possibly be studious, when they were at this leasure to recolect: Thus we made the first Calculations, & set downe our thoughts to be considered & digested better to shew his Majestie & the Archbishop: He also engaged me to consider of what Laws & Orders were fit for the Government, which was to be in every respect as strickt as in any religious Convent &c: After supper, came in the famous Trebble Mr. Abel newly return'd from Italy, & indeede I have never heard a more excellent voice, one would have sworne it was a Womans it was so high, & so well & skillfully manag'd: being accompanied with Signor Francesco on the Harpsichord:

28 Mr. Pepys (late Sec: to the Admiralty) <shewed me> a large folio containing the whole Mechanic part, & art of Building royal ships & Men of Warr; made by Sir Anth: Deane, being so accurate a Piece, from the very keele to the lead block, rigging, Gunns, Victualing, Manning, even to every individual Pin & naile, in a Method so astonishing & curious; with the draughts both Geometrical, & in Perspective, & severall sections; That I do not think the Whole World can shew the like; I esteeme this one booke above any of the Sybillas, & it is an extraordinary Jewel: hence I returned home ...

31 To Lond: but tooke such a cold that the next day returning from our Society (where we had the Phosphorus experimented in *Vaccuo Boyliano*[1] which greately surprized me) to my Lodging at White-hall, I was attaq'd with a fit of an *Ague Tertian* for 3 fitts, which so exceedingly weaken'd me, that I was not able to stirr out til Sunday when:

February 5 I went to Chapell ... My fitts continuing with much violence I sent my Wife to fetch me home in the Coach: There came & sent to Visite me my L: Chamberlaine, Dutchesse of Grafton, Countesse of Bristol & Sunderland, Sir William Godolphin, & severall of my friends almost daily:

7. I went home: My Daughter Mary now first began to learne Musick of Signor Bartholomeo, & Dauncing of Monsieur Isaac, both reputed the best Masters &c: I continu'd ill for 2 fitts after, and then bathing my leggs to the knees in Milk made as hott as I could endure it, & sitting so in it, in a deepe Churn or Vessell, Covered with blanquets & drinking Carduus posset, then going to bed & sweating, I not onely missed that expected fit, but had no more; onely continued so weake that I could not go to church 'til Ash-wednesday, which I had not missed I think so long in twenty yeares, so long had God ben gracious to me:

After this warning & admonition, I now began to looke-over & methodize all my Writings, Accompts, Letters, Papers, &c: Inventoried the goods &c of the house, & to put things into the best order I could; & also new made my Will: That growing now in yeares, I might have none of these secular things & Concernes, to distract me, whensoever it should please Almighty God to call me from this transitorie life: And with this prepared me some special

---

[1] Boyle's vacuum chamber, see above, 7 May 1662.

Meditations & devotions for the time of sicknesse: The Lord Jesus grant them Salutary for my poore Soule at that day, that I may obtaine Mercy & acceptance ...

March 1 Was my second Grand-child borne, exactly at Sunn-rising; & Christned the next day by our Viccar at Sayes-Court, his Susceptors being My Selfe with my Nephew Jo: Evelyn of Wotton, by the Name of John: his God-mother was Mrs. Anderson, sister to his Mother: I beseech God to blesse him.[1]

10: ... There was this day Executed Coll: Vrats & some of his Complices, for their Execrable Murder of Mr. Thynn, set on by the principal Konings-marke <who> went to Execution like an undaunted Hero, as one that had don a friendly office for that base Coward C. Coningsmark, who had hopes to marry his Widdow the rich Lady Ogle; & was acquitted by a Corrupt Jury, & so got away: Vrats told a friend of mine, who accompan<y>ing him to the Gallows & gave him some advice; That dying he did not value a rush, & hoped & believed God would deale with him like a Gentleman; never man went so gallant, & so unconcern'd to his sad fate: ...

19 ... I was this day exceedingly paind in both my kidnies, which gave me apprehension of some farther evil, which God in mercy avert: ...

22: I dined with severall of the R: Society ... I went hence to see the Corps of that obstinate Creature, Coll. Vratz the German murderer of Mr. Thynn (set on by the Principal Count Koningsmark) the King permitting his body should be transported to his owne Country, (being it seemes a person of a good family) it being one of the first, which was embaulmed by a particular art invented by one Will: Russell a Coffin Maker; which preser<v>ed the body without disboweling or using to any appearance any bituminous matter; The flesh florid, soft and full, as if the person were onely sleeping: The Cap: having now ben dead neere 15 daies: He lay exposed in a very rich Coffin, lined with lead: &c to<o> magnificently for so daring, & horrid a Murderer: ...

April 5: To Lond: our Society, where at a Council, was regulated what Collections should be monethly published, as formerly the Transactions, which had of late ben discontinued; but were now much desired & called for by the Curious both from abroad, & home: ...

12 ... I went this Afternoone to a Supper, with severall of the R: Society, which was all dressed (both fish & flesh) in Monsieur Papins Digestorie; by which the hardest bones of Biefe itselfe, & Mutton, were without water, or other liquor, & with lesse than 8 ounces of Coales made as soft as Cheeze, produc'd an incredible quantity of Gravie, & for close, a Gellie, made of the bones of biefe, the best for clearnesse & good relish, the most delicious that I had ever seene or tasted; so as I sent my Wife a glasse of it, to the reproch of all that the ladys ever made of the best Harts-horne &c: We Eate Pick & other fish with bones & all without any impediment: but nothing exceeded the Pigeons, which tasted just as if baked in a pie, all these being stewed in their owne juice, without any add<i>tion of water, save what swam about the <digester> as in balneo: The natural juice of all these provisions, acting on the grosser substances, reduct the harder bones to this tendernesse: but it is best described (with infinite more particulars for extracting tinctures, preserving & stewing fruite &c, & saving fuel) by Dr. Papins booke, published, & dedicated to our Society, of which he is a member, though since gon to Venice with Signor   late Resident for that State here, & a member also of our Society, who

---

[1] John, later Sir John, Evelyn of Wotton (1682-1763), cr. baronet in 1713, E's heir.

carried this excellent Mechanique Philos: & Physitian, to set up a Philos: meeting in that Citty: By this Experiment it is plaine, that the most obdurate bones are but the more compacted & closer parts of the same matter (by juxtaposition) which composes the tenderest flesh & Muscular parts; & reduces them to a friable, rather than glutinous substance, which disolves into gravy, or composes the Gelly: These bones then, breaking as it were into crumbs, one may strew on bread & eate without harme: This Philosophical Supper, raised much mirth amongst us, & exceedingly pleased all the Companie: ...

16 ... As now I grew in yeares, I becam much subject to sleepe in the Afternoones, which I formerly censured in some others, and believed impossible; I beseech God to pardon & help me: Seldome & rarely did I sleepe in the morning Exercises &c:

23 ... I stirr'd not forth this Weeke, but tooke Physick, the season unusualy wet, with such stormes of Raine & Thunder, as did greate damage: ...

May 25 *Dies Ascentionis*:[1] I was desired by Sir St: Fox, & Sir Chr: Wren, his Majesties Surveior, and Architect, to accompanie them to Lambeth, with the plot, & designe of the College to be built at Chelsey for emerited Souldiers, to have the Archbishops approbation: It was a quadrangle of 200 foote square, after the dimensions of the larger quadrangle of Christ Church in Oxon for the accommodation of 440 Persons with Governor & Officers: This being fix'd, & agreed upon, we went to dinner, & then returned: ...

June 20 To our Society, where Mr. Hook read to us his ingenious Hypothesis of Memorie, which he made to be an Organ of sense, distinct from any of the five; placed somewhere in the braine, which tooke notice of all Ideas & reposited them; as the rest of the senses do of their peculiar objects:

The Bantame or East India Ambassadors (for we had at this time in Lond together The Russian, Morrocan, & Indian Ambassador) being invited to dine at my Lord Geo: Berekeleys (now created Earle) I went to the entertainement, to Consider the exotic guests: They were both very hard favour'd, & much resembling in Countenance to some sort of Munkeys: We eate at two Tables, The Ambassador & Interpreter by themselves: Their Garments were rich Indian silks flowred with gold, viz, a Close Wast-Coate to their knees, Drawers, Naked leggs; and on their heads Capps made just in fashion like fruit baskets; They Ware poison'd Daggers at their boosome, the haft carved with some ougly serpents or devils head, exceeding keene, & of damasco mettal: they wore no sword: The second Ambassador (sent it seemes to succeede, in case the first should die by the Way in so tedious a journey) having ben at Méca (for they were Mahumetans) ware a Turkish or rather Arab Shash, a little part of the linnen hanging downe behind his neck, With some other diference of habite; & was halfe a negro; bare legg'd & naked feete; esteem'd a very holy man: They sate Crosse-legd like Turks, & some-times in the posture of Apes & Munkys; Their nailes & <Teeth> black as any jeat & shining, which being the effect of perpetual chewing betell, to preserve them from the Toothatch more raging in their Country, is esteem'd beautifull: The first Ambassador was of an Olive hue, had a flatter face & narrow eyes, squat nose & morish lips, haire none appeared: Wore severall rings of silver, gold, coper on their finger, which was a toaken of Knighthood or nobility: They were of *Java major*, whose Princes have ben turn'd Mahumetans not above 50

---

[1] Ascension Day.

yeares since, The Inhabitans stil Pagans & Idolaters: They seem'd of a dul & heavy Constitution, not wondering at any thing they saw; but exceedingly astonish<ed> to understand, how our Law's gave us propriety in our Estates, & so thinking we were all Kings; for they could not be made to Comprehend, how subjects could possess any thing but at the pleasure of their Prince, they being all slaves but infinitly surprized at it, & pleased with the notion, & admiring our happinesse; They were very sober, & I believe subtile in their way: Their meate was cook'd, carried up, & they attended on, by severall fat slaves, who had no Covering save drawes, their whole body from the girdle upward stark naked, as well as their leggs, which appeared very uncouth, & lothsom; They eate their pilaw & other spoone-meate without spoones, taking up their pottage in the hollow of <their> fingers, & very dextrously flung it into their mouthes, without spilling a drop: ...

July 30 ... We went ... to visite our good neighbour Mr. Bohune, whose whole house is a Cabinet of all elegancies, especialy Indian, and the Contrivement of the <Japan> Skreenes instead of Wainscot in the Hall, where an excellent Pendule-Clock inclosed in the curious flower-work of Mr. Gibbons in the middst of the Vestibule, is very remarkable; and so are the Landskips of the Skreenes, representing the manner of the living, & Country of the Chinezes &c: but above all his Ladys Cabinet, adorn'd on the fret, Ceiling & chimny-piece with Mr. Gib: best Carving; there is also some of Streeters best painting, & many rich Curiosities of Gold & sil: growing in the Mine: &c: Besides the Gardens are exactly kept, & the whole place very agreable & well watred: The Owners good and worthy neighbours, & he has also builded, & endowed an Hospital for Eight poore people, with a pretty Chapell, & all accommodations:

August 9 To Lond: R: Society, where Dr. Tyson produced a *Lumbricus Latus*,[1] which a Patient of his voided, of 24 foote in length, it had severall joynts, at lesse than one inch asunder, which on examination prov'd so many mouthes & stomachs in number 400 by which it adhered to & sucked the nutrition & juice of the Gutts, & by impairing health, fills it selfe with a white Chyle, which it spewed-out, upon diping the worme in spirit of Wine; nor was it otherwise possible a Creature of that prodigious length should be nourish'd, & so turgid, with but one mouth at that distance: The part or joynt towards the head was exceeding small: We ordered the Doctor to print the discourse made upon it: The Person who voided it, indured such torment in his bowels, that he thought of killing himselfe: There were likewise the Anatomies of other Wormes bred in humane bodys, which though strangly small, were discovered apparently to be male & female, had their Penis, Uterus, Ovaries and seminal Vessels &c: so as no likely hood of æquivocal generations: There was also produced Millipedes newly voided by Urine, *per penem*,[2] it having it seemes stuck in the neck of the blader & yard, giving a most intollerable itching to the patient; but the difficulty was, how it could possibly passe-through the bloud and the Heart, & other minute ductus's & strainers through the kidnies to the blader; which being looked on as impossible, was believed to be produced by an Egg in the bladder; The person who voided it, having ben prescribed Millipedes against suppression of Urine: &c: The Dr. King presented a sharp pointed stone that a day or two before had ben taken out of the Ureters of a

---

[1] 'Broad', or 'extended', worm, i.e. a tapeworm.
[2] Through the penis.

Gent, who <had> no kidney at all: The Council this day had recomended to them the being Trusteès & Visitors or Supervisers of the Academie which Monsieur Faubert did hope to procure to be builded by the subscription of worthy Gent: & noblemen, for the Education of Youth, & to lessen the vast expense the nation is yearely at, by sending their Children into France, to be taught these militarie Exercises: We thought therefore good, to give him all the Encouragement our recommendation could procure: After this we Adjourned our meetings 'til Michaelmas according to Costome at this season: so I went home, where I found my Aunt Hungerford come to Visite us: ...

October 25 To Lond, din'd with the R: Society (now againe <meeting> after recesse). After dinner a French-man produced some experiments for the raising of Water: Also we found, that Water put in *Vaccuo Boyliano*[1] & the glasse hermeticaly sealed, if jogged & shaken, made the same noise as if so many pibble stones had ben in the glasse, or some solid body beaten against the bottom & sides of it: The reason; because the aire being exhausted both out of the water & the Vessel, the Contact of the water, was more immediate, & the body more solid; for it had ben easie to have broken the bottle with the water onely.

27 I suppd at the Earle of Clarendons, with my L: Hide his bro, now the greate favorite, who now invited himselfe to dine at my house the tuesday following: ...

<31> Being my Birth-day, and I now entering my greate Climacterical of 63, after serious Recollection of the yeares past, giving Almighty God thankes for all his mercifull preservations & forbearance; beging pardon for my sinns & unworthinesse, & his blessing & mercy on me the Yeare entering: I went with my Lady Fox, to survey her Bu<i>lding, and give some direction for the Garden at Chiswick: The Architect is Mr. May, somewhat heavy & thick; & not so well understood: The Garden much too narrow, the place without water, neere an high way, & another greate house of my Lord Burlingtons; little Land about it; so as wonder at the expence; but Women will have their Will ...

November 5 The Anniversarie of the Powder-plot Mr. Bohun preaching on 1. Cor: 10. 7. Comparing Popish Idolatrie, to that of the Heathen: The peril of their doctrine; Their wicked & pernicious Conspiracys, The danger of their late Dissenters least they bring us againe into that corrupt religion, by provoking God to take away the light we have so long abused: ...

25 I was invited by Monsieur Lionberg The Swedish Resident, who made a magnificent Entertainement it being the Birth-day of his King: There dined the Duke of Albemarle, D:Hamilton, Earle of Bathe, E: of Alesbery, Lord Arran, Lord Castlehaven, the sonn of him who was executed 50 yeares before for Enormous Lusts &c: & sevveral greate persons: I was exceedingly afraide of Drinking, (it being a Dutch feast) but the Duke of Albemarle being that night to waite on his Majestie Excesse was prohibited; & to prevent all, I stole away & left the Company as soone as we rose from Table: ...

28: I went to Council of R: Society, for the Auditing the last yeares Accompts, where I was surpriz'd with a fainting fit, that for the present tooke away my sight; but God being mercifull to me, I recovered it after a short repose:

30: St. Andrews day, being our Anniversar<i>e for the Choice of new President; I was exceedingly indangr'd & importuned, to stand this Election,

---

[1] Boyle's vacuum chamber. See 7 May 1662, and 31 January 1682.

having so many Voices &c: But, by favour of my friends & reguard of my remote dwelling, & now frequent Infirmities, I desired their Suffrages for me, might be transferr'd on Sir John Hoskins, one of the Masters of the Chancery, a most learned virtuoso, as well as Lawyer, who accordingly was elected; & then we all dined together according to Costome: ...

December 10: ... I was this whole Weeke transacting buisinesse with Mr. Brent, about my Arrere due from his Majestie & made severall Visites:

17: ... I went to Visite, & Congratulate my Lord Hyde (the greate favorite) newly made Earle of Rochester, & lately marrying his Eld: Daughter to the Earle of Ossorie:

18 I sold my East India Adventure of 250 pounds, Principal for 750 pounds after it had ben in that Companie 25 yeares, to my extraordinary Advantage: & by the blessing of God:

20: To our Society, where was an Experiment of the puritie of the Æther and a learn'd Discourse of Dr. Tysons red: proving that according to the newest & most accurate Anatomists, The Embrio was Nourish'd onely by the Mouth, of the liquor in the Amnion (not by the navil onely as the vulgar error) for that there was onely that liquor found in its Stomack & Intestines: & that the Umbilical Vessells carried blood onely, impregnated with nitrous aire for the supplie of life, but not at all for nourishment &c: ...

1683

January <1> ... on the first, besought the continuance of <Gods> mercy & protection for the yeare now entering & which was my grand Climacterical.

3. I went to Lond: about my E: India stock, which I had sold to the Royal Society for 750 pounds: it being not to be paied 'til the 25 of Mar: returned that evening: & Entertained severall of my Neighbours, according to costome: ...

February 1 Returning with Sir William Godolphin from Visiting Dr. Barnet & P: Church-Yard among the Bookes, being stop'd in Fleetestreete; a Paver, or inferior Labourer, working in a deepe Channell, by St. Dunstans in Fleete-streete flung in a greate stone to the coach, and brake a greate glasse in pieces, which was drawn up, without doing either of us other harme, we being on the brink of the pit:

2 I made my Court at St. Jamess where I saw the Sea Charts of Cap: Collins, which that industrious man now brought to shew the Duke, having taken all the Coastings from the mouth of the Thames as far as Wales, & exactly measuring every Creeke, Iland, Rock, Soundings, harbors, Sands, Tides & intending this next Spring, to proceede til he had finish<ed> the <whole> Iland: & that measured by Chaine, & other Instruments: a most exact & usefull undertaking: He affirmed, that of all the Mapps, put out since, there are none extant, so true as those of Jo: Norden, who gave us the first in Q: Eliz: time &c: all since him erroneous: hence I returned home: ...

12 This morning being at Mr. Packers, I received the newes of the death of my Father in Law, Sir Rich: Browne knight & Baronet, who dyed at my house at Says-Court this 12th of Feb: at 10 in the morning, after he had labour'd under the Gowt, and Dropsie for neere 6 monethes, in the 78th yeare of his

Age, upon which I returned home to comfort my disconsolate Wife; & take order about his Funerall.

18 I went not to Church, obeying the Custome of keeping at home 'til the Ceremonies of the Funerall were over: which were solemniz'd, on the 19th at Deptford with as much Decency, as the Dignity of the Person, & our Relation, required: There being invited the Bishop of Rochester, severall Noble Men, knights, & all the fraternity of the Trinity Companie (of which he had ben Master) & others of the Country &c: The Viccar preaching on 39: Psal: 10, a short, but Proper discourse upon the frailty of our mortal Condition, Concluding with an ample, & well deserving Elogie upon the Defunct, relating to his honorable Birth, & Ancestors, Education, Learning in Gre: & Latin, Modern Languages, Travells, Publique Employments, Signal Loyaltie, Character abroad, & particularly the honour of supporting the Church of England in its publique Worship, during its pers<e>cution by the late Rebells Usurpation, & Regicide, by the Suffrages of divers Bishops, Doctors of the church & others, who with it, found such an Asylum in his house & family at Paris, that in their disputes with the Papists &c (now triumphing over it, as utterly lost) they us'd to argue for its Visibility & Existence from Sir R: Brownes Chapell & Assembly there: Then he spake of his greate & loyal sufferings during 19 yeares Exile with his present Majestie, his Returne with him, the signal yeare 1660; his honourable employment at home, his timely Recesse, to recollect, his greate Age, Infirmity, Death; He gave that land, to the Trinity Corporation in Deptford, to build upon it, those Almes houses, now standing for 24 Widdows of Emerited Sea-men &c: He was borne the famous yeare of the Gun-powder Treason 1605; & being the last of his Family, left my Wife his onely Daughter heire:

His Grandfather Sir Rich: Browne was the greate Instrument under the greate Earle of Licester (favorit to Quene Eliz,) in his government of the Nether-Lands: He was Master of the household to King James; & Coferer; (I think) was the first who regulated the Compositions through all England, for the Kings houshold provisions, Progresse &c, which was so high a service & gratefull to the whole Nation, as he had accknowledgements & publique thanks sent him from all the Counties; finaly he died by the rupture of a Veine in a vehement speech he made about the Compositions, in a Parliament of K. James's. By his Mothers side he was a Gunson, Treasurer of the Navy in Hen: 8th: Q:Marys, Q:Eliz: reigne; & as by his large & noble Pedegree appears, related to divers of the English peeres & nobility: too tedious here to reherse: &c: Thus ended this honorable Person after infinite Changes & tossing too & froo, in the same house and place where he was borne: Lord teach us so to number our daies, that we may apply our hearts to Wisdome, & sit so loose to the things & employments of this world, as to be ready & prepared for a better: Amen: By an especial Clause in his last Will, he ordered to be buried in the Church-Yard under the South-East Window of the Chancel, joyning to the burying places of his Ancestors, since they came out of Essex to Says-Court: being much offended at the novel Costome of burying every body within the body of the Church & chancel, as a favour heretofore onely granted to Martyrs, & greate Princes, this excesse of making Churches Charnel-houses being of ill & irreverent example, & prejudicial to the health of the living: besides the continual disturbance of the Pavement, & seates, the ground sinking as the Carcases consume, & severall other undecencies: Dr. Hall, the pious Bish: of Norwich would also so be interr'd, as may be read in his Testament: ...

March 16 I went to see Sir Josiah Childs prodigious Cost in planting of Walnut trees, about his seate, & making fish-ponds, for many miles in Circuite, in Eping-forest, in a Cursed & barren spot; as commonly these over growne & suddainly monied men for the most part seate themselves: He from an ordinary Merchants Apprentice, & managements of the E.India Comp:Stock, being arived to an Estate of (tis said) 200000 pounds: & lately married his daughter to the Eldest sonn of the Duke of Beaufort, late Marques of Worcester, with 30000 pounds portion at present, & various expectations: This Merchant most sordidly avaricious &c:

I dined at one Mr. Houblons a rich & gentile french Merchant, who was building an house in the Forest neere Childs, in the place where the Late Earle of Norwich dwelt some time, & which came from his Lady, the Widow of Mr. Baker: & where I had formerly ben with his Lordship: It will be a pretty Villa, about five miles from White-Chapell: ...

[20] ... Din'd at Dr. Whistlers at the Physitians Coll: with Sir Tho: Mellington, both most learned men, Dr. Wistler the most facetious man in nature; & now Censor of the Colledge. I was here consulted, where they should erect their Librarie: 'Tis pitty this Colledge is bu<i>lt so neere new-gate Prison, & in so obscure an hole, a fault in placing most of our Publique buildings & Churches in the Citty, through the avarice of some few men, & his Majestie not over-ruling it, when it was in his powre after the dreadfull Co<n>flagration &c: ...

April 17 I was at the Launching of the last ship of the 30, ordred to be new built, by Act of Parliament, & named the *Neptune*, a 2d rate, one of the goodliest vessels of the whole Navy, & of the world, & built by my kind neighbour [young] Mr. Shish, his Majesties Master Ship-Wright of this Dock:

May 1 ... went to Black-heath, to see the new faire, being the first, procured by the L:Dartmoth, this being the first day, pretended for the sale of Cattell; but, I think in truth to inrich the new Tavern at the bowling-greene, erected by Snape his Majesties farrier, a man full of projects: There appeared nothing but an innumerable assemblie of drinking people from Lond, Pedlers &c: & I suppose it too neere Lond; to be of any greate use for the Country: March was unaccostomably hott & drie this spring and all April hitherto, excessively Wet; I planted all the out limites of the Garden, & long Walks, with Holly: ...

9: Din'd at Sir Gab: Sylvius, & thence went to visite the Duke of Norfolck, & to know whither he would part with any of his Cartoones & other Drawings of Raphael & the greate masters: He answered me, he would part with & sell any thing for mony, but his Wife (the Dutchesse &c) who stood neere him; & I thought with my selfe, That if I were in his condition, it should be the first thing I would be glad to part with: In conclusion he told me, if he might sell them altogether, he would; but that the late Sir Peter Lely (our famous painter) had gotten some of his best: The person who desir'd me to treate with the Duke for them was Van der Douse, (Grand-son to that greate Scholar, Contemporarie, & friend of Jos:Scaliger,) a very ingenious Virtuoso: &c: ...

<13> Our Viccar on 1.Peter:2.11.12. Curate on his former Text: I was so exceedingly drowsy (as usualy I now am in the decline of my age) that I could hardly hold mine Eyes open: The Lord be gracious to me ...

23 To Lon: R:Society when Mr. Baker[1] (a most ingenious young man) that had ben at St. Helenas, shewed us some Experiments of the Variation of the

---

[1] E's error for Edmund Halley, the astronomer (1656-1742).

Needles plac'd betweene t<w>o equal Magnets, and Dr. Tyson brought in the Anatomie of a greene Lizard: I return'd that Evening ...

June 6 To Lond: our Society: an Experiment on the Magnes, which immersed in filings, they so sated it, that it would take up nothing more, 'til it was perfectly clensed from them: Mr. Hake brought a small Magnes, that being formerly of great activity, being laied a side for severall yeares, lost all its Virtue, as if sterv'd for want of foode; which being by little & little applied to steele, from 2 ounces weight that it would hardly take up, now suspended an yron of six pound, still augmenting in power, as it recovered strength, he applying weight after weight, & by degrees, not at once, as they treat famished people, to whom if at first, they give their fill of Victuals, it indangers their lives: ...

18 I was present, & saw & heard the humble Submission & Petition of the Lord-Major Sherifs & Aldermen in behalfe of the Citty of London, upon the *Quo Warranto*[1] against their Charter, which they delivered to his Majestie in the presence Chamber: It was delivered kneeling; & then the King & Counsel, went into the Council-Chamber, the Major & his Brethren attending still in the Presence: After a short space, they were called in, & my Lord Keeper made a speech, to them, exaggerating the dissorderly & royotous behaviour in the late Election & polling for Papillon & du Bois, after the Common hall had been formaly disolv'd, with other misdemeanors, Libells on the Government, &c for which they had incurr'd upon themselves his Majesties high displeasure; and that but for this submission, and under such Articles which the King should require their obedience to: he would certainely, Enter Judgement against them; which hitherto he had suspended: which were as follows: That they should neither Elect Major, Sheriff, Alderman, Recorder, Common Serjeant, Towne-Cleark, Coroner or Steward of Southwark, without his Majesties approbation; and that if they presented any, his Majestie did not like, they should proceede in wonted manner to a second choice, if that were disapprov'd, his Majestie to nominate them; & if within five daies they thought good to assent to this, all former miscarriages should be forgotten &c: & so they tamely parted, with their so antient privileges, after they had dined & ben treated by the King &c: This was a signal & most remarkable period; what the Consequence will prove time will shew, whilst there were divers of the old & most learned Lawyers & Judges, were of opinion that they could not forfaite their Charter, but might be personaly punish'd for their misdemeanors; but the pluralitie of the younger Judges, & rising Men, judg'd it otherwise:

The Popish Plot also (which had hitherto made such a noise) began now sensibly to dwindle, through the folly, knavery, impudence & giddynesse of Oates; so as the Papists began now to hold up their heads higher than ever, & those who were fled flock'd to Lond: from abroad: Such suddaine Changes & eager doings there had ben, without any thing of steady, or prudent for these last seaven yeares:

19: I returned in Coach with the Earle of Clarendon, when passing by the glorious Palace his father built, but few years before, which they were now demolishing, being sold to certaine undertakers &c: I turn'd my head the Contrary way til the Coach was gon past it, least I might minister occasion of

---

[1] 'By what warrant?' - a writ served on someone or a body requiring them to explain by what warrant they held a charter or franchise.

speaking of it, which must needs have grieved his Lordship that in so short a time, their pomp was fallen &c:[1] ...

28 After the Popish-plot &c there was now a new (& as they call'd it,) Protestant-Plot discover'd, that certaine Lords, & others should design the Assacination of his Majestie & the Duke, as they were to come from New-Market, with a general rising of several of the nation, and especialy the Citty of Lond: disafected to the present Government &c: Upon which were committed to the Tower the Lord Russel, Eldest sonn of the Earle of Bedford: Earle of Essex, Mr. Algernon Sydnie, sonn to the old Earle of Licester; Mr. Trenchard, Hambden: Lord Howard of Eskrick & others; with Proclamation out against my Lord Grey, the Duke of Munmouth, Sir Tho: Arme-Strong, and one Ferguson who had escaped beyond sea &c: of which some were said to be for the Killing of his Majestie, others for only seasing on him, & perswading him to new Counsils, on pretence of the danger of Poperie, should the Duke live to succeede &c: who was now admitted to the Councils, & Cabinet seacrets againe &c: Much deplor'd were my Lords Essex & Russell, few believing they had any evil Intention against his Majestie or the Church, & some that they were cunningly drawn in by their Enemies, for not approving some late Councils, & management of affaire<s>, in relation to France, to Popery, to the prosecution of the Dissenters &c. They were discovered by the Lord Howard, & some false breathren of the Clubb, & the designe happily broken; since had all taken effect; it would in all appearance have indangered the Government to unknowne & dangerous Events: which God avert:

28 Was borne about 3 in the Afternoone, my Grand-Daughter at Says Court, & Christned by the name of Martha Maria, by her two Grand-mothers, the Lady Stonehouse & my Wife &c: our Viccar Officiating: ...

July 13 <Friday>, as I was visiting Sir Tho: Yarbrow & Lady in Covent Garden, that astonishing newes of the Earle of Essex having Cut his owne Throat was brought to us, having now ben but three dayes prisoner in the Tower, & this happning on the very day & instant that the Lord Russel was on his Trial, & had sentence of death: This accident exceedingly amaz'd me, my Lord of Essex being so well know<n> by me to be a person of so sober & religious a deportment, so well at his ease, so much obliged to the King.

It is certaine the King & Duke were at the Tower & pass'd by his Window about the same time this morning, when My Lord asking for a rasor, he shut himselfe into a closet, & perpetrated the horrid fact: It was wondred yet by some how it was possible he should do it, in the manner he was found; for the wound was so deepe & wide, as being cut through the Gullet, Wind-pipe, & both the jugulars, it reached to the very Vertebræ of the neck, so as the head held to it by a very little skin as it were, which tack'd it from being quite <off>; The gapping too of the rasor, & cutting his owne fingers, was a little strange, but more, that having passed the Jugulars he should have strength to proceede so farr, as an Executioner could hardly have don more with an axe, and there were odd reflections upon it:

This fatal newes coming to Hicks-hall upon the article of my L: Russels Trial, was said to have no little influenc'd the Jury, & all the bench, to his prejudice: Others said, he had himselfe upon some occasions hinted, that in case he should <be> in danger of having his life taken from him, by any publique misfortune, those who thirsted for his Estate, should misse of their aime, & that he should long since speake favourably of that D: of

---

[1] Clarendon House, Piccadilly, see 15 October 1664, and 18 September 1683.

Northumberland & some others who made away themselves: But these are discourses so very unlike his sober & prudent Conversation, that I have no inclination to credit them: what might instigate him to this develish fact I am not able to conjecture; since (as my Lord Clarendon his bro: in Law, who was with but the day before assur'd me) he was then so very cherefull, & declared it to be the Effect of his innocence & loyalty: & most believe his Majestie had no severe intentions against him; however he was altogether inexorable as to my Lord Russell & some of the rest:

For my owne part I believe the crafty & ambitious Earle of Shaftsbery had brought them into some dislike of the present carriage of matters at Court, not with any designe of destroying the Monarchy (which Shaftsbery has in Confidence & for unanswerable reasons, told me, he would support, to his last breath, as having seene & felt the miserie of being under [a] Mechanic Tyrannie &c) but perhaps of setting up some other, whom he might govern, & frame to his owne Platonic fancie, without much reguard to the Religion establish'd under the Hierarchie, for which he had no esteeme: But when he perceiv'd those whom he had engag'd to rise, faile of his expectations, & the day past, reproching his Complices, that a second day for an Exploit of this nature, was never successfull, he gave them the slip, & got into Holland, where the fox died, three moneths before these unhappy Lords & others were discovered or suspected: Every creature deplored Essex, & Russell, especialy the last, as being thought to be drawn in on pretence onely of endeavoring to rescue the King from his present Counselors, & secure Religion, from Popery, & the Nation from Arbitrary government, now so much apprended; whilst the rest of those who were fled, especialy Ferguson & his gang, had doubtless some bloudy designe, set up a Commonwealth, & turne all things topsie turvy; of the same tragical principles is Sidney &c: ...

The whole Nation was now in greate Consternation, upon the late Plot & Conspiracy; his Majestie very Melancholic, & not stirring without redoubled Guards, all the Avenues & private dores about White-hall & the Park shut up; few admitted to walke in it: The Papists in the meane while very jocond, & indeede they had reason, seeing their owne plot brought to nothing, & turn'd to ridicule & now a Conspiracy of Protestants, as they cald them: The Turk likewise in hostility against the German Emperor, almost Master of the upper Hungarie & drawing towards Vienna; on the other side the French (who tis believed brought in the Infidel) disturbing their Spanish, & Dutch Neighbours, & almost swallowed, all Flanders, pursuing his ambition of a fift [& Universal] Monarchy; & all this blood, & dissorder in Christendome had evidently its rise from our defections at home, in a Wanton peace, minding nothing but Luxurie, Ambition, & to procure Mony for our Vices: To this add our irreligion & Atheisme, greate ingratitude & selfe Interest: the Apostacie of some, & the Suffering the French to grow so Greate, and the Hollanders so Weake. In a word we were Wanton, madd, and surfeiting with prosperity, every moment unsettling the old foundations, & never constant to any thing. The Lord in mercy avert the sad Omen; & that we do not provoke him farther, 'til he beare it no longer:

This summer did we suffer 20 French-men of Warr to passe our Chanell towards the Sound, to help the Dane against the Swede, who had <abandoned> the <French> Interest; we having not ready sufficient to guard our Coasts, or take Cognizance of what they did; so as though the Nation never had more, or better Navy, the Sea never had so slender a Fleete: ...

19 George Prince of Denmark, who landed this day, came to Mar<r>y the Lady Anne daughter to the Duke: so I return'd home; having seen the young Gallant at dinner at Whitehall.

20 Severall of the Conspirators, of the lower forme, were Executed at Tyburn-

21 And the next day was the Lord Russell decapitated in Lincolns in fields, the Executioner giving him 3 butcherly strokes: The Speech he made & Paper he gave the Sherif, declaring his Innocence, the noblenesse of the family, the piety & worthynesse of the unhappy Gent: wrought effects of much pitty, & various discourses on the plot &c: ...

25 I went to Lond: saw againe Prince George, he had the Danish Countenance, blound; a young gent of few words, spake French but ill, seemed somewhat heavy; but reported Valiant, & indeede had bravely rescued & brought off his brother the K. of Denmarke in a battaile against the Swede, when both those Kings, were engaged very smartly:...

28 Prince Geo: was married to the Lady Ann at White-hall: Her Court & household to be moduled just as the Dukes her fathers &c: & to continue in England:[1] ...

August 1 Came to see me Mr. Flamested the famous Astrologer from his Observatorie at Greenewich, to draw the Meridian for my Pendules &c: ...

8 A Woman, who came from Lond: to speake with my Wife, was Arested for debt in my Hall, by one who pretended to be a Porter, & to deliver her a letter; but I rescued her from the Insolence &c: ...

28 Died my sweete little Grand-child Martha Maria of Convulsion fitts, an extraordinary pretty & foreward child: Gods will be don:

Came also this morning to take his leave of us his Grace the Archbishop of Yorke now preparing for his Journey: & reside in his Province.

29 Was buried our Grand-child, amongst the rest of our sweete Infants in the Parish-Church: ...

September 3 I went (together with my Wife &c) to Chelsey, to see my Charge, the Daughters, and Children of my deare friends, the late V.Countesse Mordaunt: After dinner I walked to survey what had ben don as to repaires &c, by the Duke of Beaufort upon his late purchased house at <Chelsey>, of which I had once the selling for the Countesse of Bristol: I found he had made greate alterations, but might have built a better house with the Materials & that cost: at my returne to our Company, I found the Countess of Monte Feltre, whose husband I had formerly known, & was a subject of the Popes, but Changing from his Religion, & become Protestant, resided here in England, & married into the familie of the Savells of York-shire: The Count (her late husband) was a very learned Gent: a greate Polititian; a goodly man: she was accompanied with her Sister, exceedingly skild in painting; nor indeede did they seeme to spare for Colour on their owne faces: They had a greate deale of Wit, one of them especialy, who talked of a sparrow she had at home not inferior to Lesbias.

9 ... My little Grand-Child was very ill all yesterday, so as we feared his life, 'til this day, that God was pleas'd to give us hopes:

---

[1] Anne became Queen in 1702 but the death of her son William, Duke of Gloucester (see 7 July 1700) occasioned the Hanoverian Succession.

15 Came to visite & dine'd with us Sir W:Godolphin and my sweete charge, little Francis: also his Unkle Henry & Aunt Boscawen: came also <to> visite me the learned Anatomist Dr. Tyson with some other fellows of our Society: ...

18 I went to Lond: to visite & waite on the Dutchesse of Grafton now greate with Child, a most vertuous & beautifull Lady, & dining with her at my Lord Chamberlains met my Lo: of St. Albans, now growne so blind, that he could not see to the taking his meate: It is incredible how how easy a life this Gent: has lived, & in what plenty even abroad, whilst his Majestie was a sufferer; nor lesse, the immense summs he has lost at play, which yet at about 80 yeares old he continues, having one that sets by him to name the spot in the Chards: He eate & dranke with extraordinary appetite. He is with all this a prudent old Courtier, & much inrich'd since his Majesties returne.

After dinner I walked to survey the sad demolitions of Clarendon house that costly & onely sumptuous Palace of the late L.Chancelor Hydes, where I have often ben so cherefull with him, & so sad; hapning to make him a visite but the day before he fled from the angry Parliament, accusing him of mal-administration, & envious at his grandure, who from a private lawyer, came to be fatherinlaw to the Duke of York; &, as some would suggest, designing his Majesties marriage with the Infanta of Portugal, not apt to breede: To this they imputed much of our unhapinesse, & that being sole Minister & favorite at his Majesties Restauration he neglected to gratifie his Majesties suffering party, for the rewards he received of his richer, & disloyal subjects, who were the cause of our troubles: But perhapps as many of these were injuriously laied to his charge; so he kept the Government far steadier than since it has proved: I could name some others who I thinke contributed greately to his ruine, The bouffones, and the Misses to whom he was an Eye sore: 'Tis true he was of a jolly temper, after the old English fashion; but France had now the ascendant, & we become quite another nation. The C<h>ancellor gon, & dying in Exile, the Earle his successor sold that which cost 50000 pounds building to the Young Duke of Albemarle for 25000, to pay his debts, which how contracted remaines yet a Mysterie, his sonn being no way a prodigal; some imagine the Dutchesse his daughter had ben chargeable to him; however it were, this stately Palace is decreede to ruine, to support the prodigious Wast the D: of Albemarle had made of his Estate, since the old man died; so as selling it to the highest bidders, it fell to certaine inferior people, rich bankers & Mechanics, who gave for it & the ground about it 35000 pounds; who designing a new Towne as it were, & the most magnificent Piazza in Europ, 'tis said have already materials toward it, with what they sould of the house alone, more worth than what they paied for it: See the Vicissitude of earthly things: I was plainely astonish'd as at this demolition, so noe lesse, at the little armie of Labourers, & Artificers in levelling ground, laying foundations, & contriving greate buildings at an expense of 200000 pounds, if they perfect their designe:

20 did some buisinesse among the Lawyers, having a troublesome suite of an Accompt, with Mr. Pretiman my Wifes Unkle, pretending bills of Exchange not paied, during her Fathers Residence in France:[1] This Controversie having

---

[1] E's father-in-law, Sir Richard Browne, was owed money by the King for expenses in France prior to 1660. Browne's brother-in-law, William Prettyman, was suing the Evelyns for cash he had sent to France to help them. Prettyman was himself in debt to the King. Evelyn's idea was to accept a reduction of Prettyman's debt in lieu of money owed to Browne. A part settlement came on 2 June 1687 (see below).

now lasted for many Yeares, coming now to be defended by me, upon My Fa: in Laws decease, as executor in right of my Wife (whose land was engag'd, & Writings <kept> from us, on an imaginary debt) to put it to a final Issue, I was now to commence all a new; & for that end, did this day (among other Council) retaine Mr. North, brother to my L: Keeper, & so referr the issue to the good providence of God, & return'd home to my house: Note, that by the way, I stepped in to a Gold-beaters work-house, who shewed me the wonderfull ductilitie of that spreading & oylie Metall: he said it must be finer than the standard; such as was old Angel gold: & that of such he had once to the value of 100 pounds, stamp'd with the Agnus Dei, & coyn'd at the time of the holy-War, which had ben found in a ruin'd Wall some where in the north, neere to Scotland: some of which he beate into leaves, & the rest sold to the Curiosi of Antiquities & Medails.

23 ... We had now the wellcome tidings of the K: of Polands &c raising the siege before Vienna, which gave terror to all Europe, & uttmost reproch to the French, who 'tis believed brought him in, for diversion, that he might the more easilie swallow Flanders, & pursue his unjust conquests on the Empire &c, whilst we sate unconcerned, & under a deadly charme from somebody: There was this day a Collection for the rebuilding of New-Market Consum'd by an accidental fire, which removing his Majestie thence sooner than was intended, put by the Assassinates, who were dissapointed of their Rendezvous & expectation, by a wonderfull providence: This made the King more earnest to render Wi<n>chester the seate of his Autum<n>al field diversions of the future, designing a Palace there, where the antient Castle stood, infinitely indeede preferrable to New-Market, for Prospect, aire, pleasure, & provisions; The Surveior having already begun the foundations for a palace of 35000 pounds & his Majestie purchasing ground about it, to make a Parke &c:

My right arme of late yeares becoming very cold & weakened, it passed now into my left, with paine, & such weakenesse, that I had little force left in it, yet without the least appearance of any thing outwardly: ...

October 4: ... Following his Majestie this morning through the Gallerie, <I> went (with the few who attended him) into the Dutchesse of Portsmouths dressing roome, within her bed-chamber, where she was in her morning loose garment, her maides Combing her, newly out of her bed: his Majestie & the Gallants standing about her: but that which ingag'd my curiositie, was the rich & splendid furniture of this woman's Appartment, now twice or thrice, puld downe, & rebuilt, to satisfie her prodigal & expensive pleasures, while her Majestie dos not exceede, some gentlemens Ladies furniture & accommodation:[1] Here I saw the new fabrique of French Tapissry, for designe, tendernesse of worke, & incomparable imitation of the best paintings; beyond any thing, I had ever beheld: some pieces had Versailles, St. Germans & other Palaces of the French King with Huntings, figures, & Landscips, Exotique fowle & all to the life rarely don: Then for Japon Cabinets, Skreenes, Pendule Clocks, huge Vasas of wrought plate, Tables, Stands, Chimny furniture, Sconces, branches, Braseras &c, they were all of massive silver, & without number, besides of his Majesties best paintings: Surfeiting of this, I din'd yet at Sir Steph: Foxes, & [5] went contentedly home to my poore, but

---

[1] It is typical of E that though he makes it clear he was very aware the Duchess was half-dressed he goes out of his way to stress how much more interested, he would like the reader to believe, he was in the furniture.

quiet Villa. Lord what contentment can there be in the riches & splendor of this world, purchas'd with vice & dishonor: ...

31 Being determin'd to passe this winter in London with my family, by reason of many important affaires; I invited divers of my Neighbours to dinner: <it> was likewise my Birth-day & the 63d or greate Climacterical, to w<h>ich through Gods infinite goodnesse I was now arived, & for which his holy name be praised ...

November 11 ... I visited Sir William Hooker: whose Lady related to us of a Child laied to sleepe, & [that] whilst the Nurse was a little absent, a Monkey had bitten out its Eyes, torne the face, & eaten the head into the braine: Those mischievous animals should not be kept by Ladies that have young children, this being the second accident of that nature I have ben told of, one of which happned in this Parish, a vile Monkey had killd a Nurse child in the cradle almost after the same manner, whilst the nurse went but out to draw a bucket of water: & what was most deplorable, it was the onely child remaining of one who had lost severall.

17 I came with my whole Family (except my little Grandson, & his Nurse & some servants to looke after the house) to be in London the rest of this Winter, having many important concernes to dispatch which I could not so well attend at home [& for the education of my daughters]: I tooke therefore the house of one of Mr. Dive's, in Villars streete in Yorke-buildings in the Strand ...

23 I went home to Says Court to see my little family, and return'd next day: The Duke of Monmoth 'til now proclaim'd Traytor upon the pretended plot, for which my L:Russell lately was be headed: Came this evening to white-hall & rendered himselfe, [24] upon which were various discourses: ...

26 I went to complement the Dutchesse of Grafton now laying of her first child, which was a sonn, which she cald for me to see with greate satisfaction: She was become more beautifull (if it were possible) than before, & full of vertue & sweetnesse, discoursed with me of many particulars with greate prudence, & gravity beyond her yeares: ...

December 5 I was this day invited to a Wedding of one Mrs. Castle, to whom I had some obligation, & it was to her fift Husband, a Lieutennant Coll: of the Citty: The woman was the daughter of one Burton a Broome-man & of a Mother who sold Kitchin stuff in Kent Streete, Whom God so blessed, that the Father became a very rich & an honest man, was Sherif of Surrey, where I have sat on the bench with him: Another of his daughters was Married to one Sir Jo: Bowles; & this Daughter a jolly friendly woman: There was at the Wedding the Lord Major, the Sherif, severall Aldermen and persons of quality, & above all Sir Geo: Jeoffries newly made Lord Chiefe Justice of England, with Mr. Justice Withings, daunced with the Bride, and were exceeding Merrie: These greate men spent the rest of the afternoone til 11 at night in drinking healths, taking Tobacco, and talking much beneath the gravity of Judges, that had but a day or two before Condemn'd Mr. Algernoon Sidny, who was executed on the 7th on Tower hill upon the single Wittnesse of that monster of a man the L: Howard of Eskrick, and some sheetes of paper taken in Mr. Sidnys study, pretended to be writen by him, but not fully proov'd, nor the time when, but appearing to have ben written before his Majesties restauration, & then pardon'd by the Act of Oblivion: So as though Mr. Sidny was known to be a person obstinately averse to government by a Monarch (the subject of the paper, in answer to one of Sir E: Filmer) yet it was thought he had very hard measure: There is this yet observable, that he had ben an inveterate enemy to the last King, & in actual rebellion against him: a man of greate Courage, greate sense, greate parts, which he shew'd both at his trial & death; for when he came to the scaffold, in stead of a speech, he told them onely, that he had made his peace with God; that he came not hither to talk but to die, put a paper into the Sherifs hand, & another into a friends, sayed one prayer as short as a grace, laied downe his neck, & bid the Executioner do his office: The Duke of Monmouth now having his pardon, refuses to accknowledge there was any Treasonable plot, for which he is banish'd to White-hall: This was a greate dissappointment to some, who had prosecuted the rest, namely Trenchard, Hampden &c: that for want of a second wittnesse were come out of the Tower upon their *Habeas Corpus*. The King had now augmented his guards with a new sort of dragoons, who also carried granados & were habited after the polish manner with long picked Caps very fierce & fantastical; & was very exotic: ...

20 I went to Deptford, return'd the 22d in very cold & severe weather: My poore Servant Humphry Prideaux being falln sick of the small-pox some days before:

23 ... This night died my poore excellent servant of the small pox, that by no remedies could be brought out, to the wonder of the Physitians: It was exceedingly mortal at this time; & the season was unsufferably cold. The Thames frozen, &c:

26 I dined at my Lord Clarendons where I was to meete that most ingenious and learned Gent: Sir Geo: Wheeler, who has publish'd that excellent description of Attica & Greece, and who being a knight of a very faire estate & young had now newly entred into holy Orders: I also now kissed the Princesse of Denmarks hand, who was now with Child.

27 I went to visite Sir J. Chardin that French gent,[1] who had 3 times travelled into Persia by Land, and had made many curious researches in his Travells, of which he was now setting forth a relation. It being in England this yeare one of the most severe frosts that had happn'd of many yeares, he told me, the Cold in Persia was much greater, the yce of an incredible thicknesse: That they had little use of Iron in all that Country, it being so moist (though the aire admirably cleare & healthy) that oyle would not preserve it from rusting immediately, so as they had neither clocks nor Watches, some padlocks they had for doors & boxes &c:

1684

January 1 ... My Daughter Susan had some few small pox come forth on her, so as I sent her out of the Family;[2] The Weather continuing intollerably severe, so as streets of Boothes were set up upon the Thames &c: and the aire so very cold & thick, as of many yeares there had not ben the like: The small pox being very mortal, many feared a worse Contagion to come &c:

2 I dined at Sir St: Foxes, after dinner came a fellow that eate live charcoale glowingly ignited, quenching them in his mouth, & then champing &

---

[1] E had already met him, see above, 30 August 1680.

[2] She survived but her elder sisters died the following year from smallpox.

swallowing them downe: There was a dog also that seemed to do many rational actions ...

6 I went home to Says-Court to see my Grandson, it being extreame hard weather, and return'd the next day by Coach the river being quite frozen up: ...

9 I went crosse the Thames upon the Ice (which was now become so incredibly thick, as to beare not onely whole streetes of boothes in which the<y> roasted meate, & had divers shops of wares, quite crosse as in a Towne, but Coaches & carts & horses passed over): So I went from Westminster stayers to Lambeth and dined with my L. Archbishop, where I met my Lord Bruce, Sir Geo: Wheeler, Coll: Coock, and severall Divines; after dinner, and discourse with his Grace 'til Evening prayer, Sir Geo: and I returnd, walking over the Ice from Lambeth stayres to the Horse Ferry, and thence walked on foote to our Lodgings:

10: I visited Sir Rob: Reading, where after supper we had musique, but none comparable to that which Mrs. Bridgeman made us upon the Gittar, which she master'd with such extraordinary skill, and dexterity, as I hardly ever heard any lute exceede for sweetenesse ...

16 Was my first tryal befor my L: Keeper at the Chancery for a rehearing of my Cause: I went thence to the Bishops of Lond, with whom I dined: endeavouring to procure some of his Majesties Charity for the poore of our Parish, the severe weather still continuing, & now the Thames was filled with people & Tents selling all sorts of Wares as in the Citty it selfe: ...

24 The frost still continuing more & more severe, the Thames before London was planted with bothes in formal streetes, as in a Citty, or Continual faire, all sorts of Trades & shops furnished, & full of Commodities, even to a Printing presse, where the People & Ladys tooke a fansy to have their names Printed & the day & yeare set downe, when printed on the Thames: This humour tooke so universaly, that 'twas estimated the Printer gained five pound a day, for printing a line onely, at six-pence a Name, besides what he gott by Ballads &c: Coaches now plied from Westminster to the Temple, & from severall other staires too & froo, as in the streetes; also on sleds, sliding with skeetes; There was likewise Bull-baiting, Horse & Coach races, Pupet-plays & interludes, Cookes & Tipling, & lewder places; so as it seem'd to be a bacchanalia, Triumph or Carnoval on Water, whilst it was a severe Judgement upon the Land: the Trees not onely splitting as if lightning-strock, but Men & Catell perishing in divers places, and the very seas so locked up with yce, that no vessells could stirr out, or come in: The fowle [Fish] & birds, & all our exotique Plants & Greens universaly perishing; many Parks of deere des-troied, & all sorts of fuell so deare that there were greate Contributions to preserve the poore alive; nor was this severe weather much lesse intense in most parts of Europe even as far as Spaine, & the most southern tracts: London, by reason of the excessive coldnesse of the aire, hindring the ascent of the smoke, was so filled with the fuliginous steame of the Sea-Coale, that hardly could one see crosse the streete, & this filling the lungs with its grosse particles exceedingly obstructed the breast, so as one could scarce breath: There was no water to be had from the Pipes & Engines, nor could the Brewers, and divers other Tradesmen work, & every moment was full of disastrous accidents &c: ...

30...The frost still raging as fircely as ever, the River of Thames was become a Camp, ten thousands of people, Coaches, Carts, & all manner of sports continuing & increasing: miserable were the wants of poore people, Deare universaly perished in most of the parks thro-out England, & very much Cattell: ...

February 4 I went to Says-Court to see how the frost & rigorous weather had dealt with my Garden, where I found many of the Greenes & rare plants utterly destroied; The Oranges & Myrtils very sick, the Rosemary & Lawrell dead to all appearance, but the Cypresse like to indure it out: I came to Lond: the next day when it fir<s>t of all began to Thaw, and pass'd over without alighting in my Coach from Lambeth to the Horse-ferry at Mill-bank at Westminster; the Weather growing less severe, it yet began to freeze againe; but the boothes were allmost-all taken downe; but there was first a Map or Landskip cut in copper representing all manner of the Camp, & the several actions, sports and passe-times thereon in memory of this signal Frost: ...

8...I went this Evening to visite that greate & knowing Virtuoso Monsieur Justell: The weather now was set to an absolute Thaw & raine, but the Thames still hard: ...

12 The E: of Danby late L:Tressurer together with the Rom:Cath: Lords impeach'd of high Treason in the popish-plot, had now their *Habeas Corpus*, and came out upon Baile, after 5 yeares Imprisonment in the Toure: Then were also Tried and deeply fin'd Mr. Hambden & others, for being supposed of the late Plot, for which my L:<Russell> and Coll:<Sidney> suffered: As also the person, who went about to prove that the E: of <Essex> had his Throat Cut in the Tower by others: likewise Mr. Johnson, the Author of that famous piece cald Julian.[1]

13 Newes of the P: of Oranges having accus'd the Deputies of Amsterdam of *Crimen Læsæ Majestatis*,[2] & being Pensioner to France.

Dr. Tenison communicating to me his intention of Erecting a Library in St. Martines parish, for the publique use, desird my assistance with Sir Chr: Wren about the placing & structure thereof: a worthy & laudable designe: He told me there were 30 or 40 Young Men in Orders in his Parish, either, Governors to young Gent: or Chaplains to Noble-men, who being reprov'd by him upon occasion, for frequenting Taverns or Coffè-houses, told him, they would study & employ their time better, if they had books: This put the pious Doctor upon this designe, which I could not but approve of, & indeede a greate reproch it is, that so great a Citty as Lond: should have never a publique Library becoming it: There ought to be one at S. Paules, the West end of that Church, (if ever finish'd), would be a convenient place: ...

23 I went to Sir John Chardins, who desired my Assistance for the ingraving of the plates, the translation & Printing of his historie of that wonderfull Persian monument neere Persepolis, & other rare Antiquities, which he had Caus'd to be drawne from the originals, at his 2d journey into Persia: which we now concluded upon:[3] And afterwards I went to Dr. Tenison (with Sir Chr: Wren) where we made both the draught & estimate of the Library to be begun this spring,[4] neere the Mewes: ...

---

[1] Samuel Johnson (1649-1702), divine and author of various pro-Protestant works. This piece on the Emperor Julian the Apostate (360-63) was an attack on the Duke of York. He had also been Russell's chaplain.

[2] The crime of offending against the sovereignty.

[3] E had listened keenly to Chardin's tales on 30 August 1680.

[4] De Beer notes (1955, I, 73) that this is one of the earliest entries in the *Diary* which indicates that it was now being written up on a more or less daily basis, E having now completed writing up the earlier sections.

March 28 Good friday ... There was so greate & eager a concourse of people with their children, to be touch'd of the Evil, that 6 or 7: were crush'd to death by pressing at the Chirurgions doore for Tickets &c. The weather began now onely to be more mild & tollerable, but there was not the least appearance of any Spring.

30 Easter-day, I received the B:Sacrament at white-hall early, with the Lords & household: the B: of Lond: officiating: Then went to St. Martines wher Dr. Tenison (now first coming abroad after his recovery of the small-pox) preached on 16:Psal:11:- Hence I went againe to White Hall, where *coram Rege*, preach'd the B: of Rochester on a Text out of Hosea 6.2. touching the subject of the day: After which his Majestie, accompanied with 3 of his natural Sonns, (viz. the Dukes of Northumb: Richmond & St. Albans, base sonns of Portsmouth, Cleaveland, Nelly, prostitute Creatures) went up to the Altar; The three Boyes entering before the King within the railes, at the right hand, & 3 Bishops on the left: viz: Lond: (who officiated) Durham, Rochester, with the sub-Deane Dr. Holder: The King kneeling before the Altar, making his offering, the Bishops first received, & then his Majestie, after which, he retir'd to a Canopied seate on the right hand &c: note, there was perfume[1] burnt before the office began: ...

April 4 After 5 monethes being in Lond: this severe winter, I return'd home with my family this day: My sonn with his wife &c: continuing behind, upon pretence of his applying himselfe more seriously to his studying the Law, but wholy without my approbation: - hardly the least appearance of any Spring ...

12 Being much indispos'd this weeke, I tooke Physick, & a Vomite, which did greately restore me, blessed be God: ...

May 10th. I went to visite my Brother in Surrey ...

11 One Mr. Crawly preached in the morning at Abinger on 13 Heb:18: In the Afternoone I went to visite Mr. Higham now sick in his Climacterical, whereof he died [about] 3 days after: his Grandfather & Father (who Christn'd me) with himselfe had now ben 3 generations Parsons of the Parish an hundred and foure yeares this May: viz: from 1584.

12 I returned to Lond: where I found the Commissioners of the Admiralty abolished, & the Office of Admiral restord to the Duke,[2] as to the disposal & ordering all sea buisinesse: But his Majestie signing all the Petitions, Papers, Warrants & Commissions, that the Duke not acting as Admiral by Commission, or Office, might not incurr the penalty of the late Act against Papists & Dissenters holding Office or refusing the Oath & Test: &c: every body was glad of this Change: Those in the late Commission being utterly ignorant of their duty, to the greate damage of the Navy royal:

July 2 I went to the Observatorie at Greenewich, where Mr. Flamstead tooke his observations of the Ecclipse of the sunn, now hapning to be almost 3 parts obscur'd: So greate a drowth still continu'd, as never was since in my memorie: ...

---

[1] i.e. Incense, normally a Roman Catholic custom.

[2] The Duke of York resigned his offices in 1673 due to the Test Act of that year. See above 30 March 1673 when to E's horror James refused to participate in Protestant communion.

August 24 St. Bartholomews day our Viccar & Curate preached on their former Text, much of it repetition onely: I was exceedingly drowsy this afternoone it being most excessively hot: we having not had above one or two considerable showres (& they stormes) these eight or nine moneths so as the trees lost their leafe like Winter, & many of them quite died for want of refreshment ...

September 26 I went to Lond, to Congratulate my deare friend Mr. Sidny Godolphins being created a Baron of England, the King being now returned from Winchester, there was a numerous Court at White-hall where I saluted divers of my acquaintance: There was at this time a remove of the Earle of Rochester from the Treasury to the presidentship of the Council, & my L: Godolphin made first Commissioner of the Treasury in his place, my Lord Midleton a Scot, made Secretary of state. These Alterations (being very unexpected & mysterious) gave greate occasion of discourse among the Politicians: I supped this night at my La: Sylvius, with Dr. Tenison, & the afternoone taking the aire in Hide Parke, saw two bucks encounter each other very fiercely for a long willes 'til one was quite vanquished: ...

29 I was let bloud about 8 ounces for the dizzinesse of my head ...

October 22 Sir William Godolphin and I went to see the Rhinocerous (or Unicorne) being the first that I suppose was ever brought into England: It more ressembled a huge enormous Swine, than any other Beast amongst us; That which was most particular & extraordinary, was the placing of her small Eyes in the very center of her cheekes & head, her Eares in her neck, and very much pointed: her Leggs neere as big about as an ordinarie mans wast, the feete divided into claws, not cloven, but somewhat resembling the Elephants, & very round & flatt, her taile slender and hanging downe over her Sex, which had some long haires at the End of it like a Cowes, & was all the haire about the whole Creature, but what was the most wonderfull, was the extraordinary bulk and Circumference of her body, which though very Young, (they told us as I remember not above 4 yeares old) could not be lesse than 20 foote in compasse: she had a set of most dreadfull teeth, which were extraordinarily broad, & deepe in her Throate, she was led by a ring in her nose like a Buffalo, but the horne upon it was but newly Sprowting, & hardly shaped to any considerable point, but in my opinion nothing was so extravagant as the Skin of the beast, which hung downe on her hanches, both behind and before to her knees, loose like so much Coach leather, & not adhering at all to the body, which had another skin, so as one might take up this, as one would do a Cloake or horse-Cloth to a greate depth, it adhering onely at the upper parts; & these lappets of stiff skin, began to be studdied with impenetrable Scales, like a Target of coate of maile, loricated like Armor, much after the manner this Animal is usually depicted: she was of a mousse Colour, the skin Elephantine; Tame enough, & suffering her mouth to be open'd by her keeper, who caus'd her to lie downe, when she appeared like a [greate] Coach overthrowne, for she was much of that bulke, yet would rise as nimbly as ever I saw an horse: T'was certainly a very wonderfull creature, of immense strength in the neck, & nose especialy, the snout resembling a boares but much longer; to what stature she may arive if she live long, I cannot tell; but if she grow proportionable to her present age, she will be a Mountaine: They fed her with Hay, & Oates, & gave her bread. She belonged to Certaine E. Indian Merchants, & was sold (as I remember) above two-thousand pounds:

At the same time I went to see a living Crocodile, brought from some of the W: Indian Ilands, in every respect resembling the Egyptian Crocodile, it was not yet fully 2 yards from head to taile, very curiously scaled & beset with impenetrable studds of a hard horny substance, & most beautifully ranged in works especialy on the ridge of the back & sides, of a dusky greene Colour, save the belly, which being tender, & onely vulnerable, was of a lively & lovely greene, as lizards are, whose shape it exactly kept: The Eyes were sharp & piercing, over which it could at pleasure draw up a thin cobweb skinn: The rictus was exceeding deepe set with a tirrible rank of sharp & long teeth: We could not discerne any tongue, but a small lump of flesh at the very bottome of its throate, which I suppose helped his swallowing: the feete were divided into long fingers as the Lizards, & he went forward wadling, having a chaine about the neck: seemed to be very tame; I made its keeper take up his upper jaw which he affirmed did onely move, & so Pliny & others confidently report; but it did not appeare so plaine to me, whither his keeper did not use some dexterity in opening his mouth & placing his head so as to make it seeme that the upper chap, was loose; since in that most ample & perfect sceleton in our Repositarie at the R: Society, it is manifestly fixed to the neck & Vertebræ: the nether jaw onely loose: They kept the beast or Serpent in a longish Tub of warme Water, & fed him with flesh &c: If he grow, it will be a dangerous Creature.

23 I dined at Sir Stephen Foxes with the Duke of Nor<t>humberland another of his Majesties natural sonns, by that strumpet Cleaveland: He seemed to be a Young gent, of good capacity, well bred, civile, & modest, had ben newly come from Travell, & had made his Campagne at the siege of Luxemburg, Of all his Majesties Children, (of which he had now 6 Dukes) this seemed the most accomplished, and worth the owning; he is likewise extraordinary handsome & perfectly shaped: what the Dukes of Richmond, & St. Albans, base sonns of the Dutchesse of Portsmouth a French Lasse, and of Nelly, the Comedian & Apple-woma<n>s daughter, will prove their youth dos not yet discover, farther than that they are both very pretty boys, & seeme to have more Witt than [most of] the rest:

26 ... I dined at my sonns, now newly being come to his new house & house-keeping: My Daughter in Law ready to lie-in of her 4th Child: ...

26 I attended the Chancery in Westminster Hall, where I had a Cause pleaded, giving reasons for the changing of the Master who had made an injurious Accompt, in the difference betwixt me & Mr. Pretyman: my L: Chan: was pleas'd to grant our plea:

27 I din'd & went to Visite my Lord Chamberlaine now returnd from the Countrie, where dined the black Baron, & Monsieur Flamerin, who had so long ben banish'd France for a duel:

28 Being S.Sim: & Judes, I carried my Lord Clarendon through the Citty amidst all the Squibbs & barbarous bacchanalia of the Lord-Majors shew, to the R:Society, where he was proposed a Member, and then Treated him at dinner: ...

November 2 Our Viccar proceeded on his former Text: the holy Comm: followed at which I was participant: So suddaine an alteration from temperate warm weather to an excessive cold, raine, frost, snow & storme, as had seldome ben knowne, this Winter weather beginning as early & fi<e>rce, as the past did late, & neere christmas, till which there had hardly ben any winter at all: Buda in Hungary yet besieg'd by the DD: of Lorrain & Bavaria, to the losse of many brave commande<r>s & men: ...

15 Being the Queenes Birth-day, there was such fire works upon the Thames before White-hall, with pageants of Castles, Forts, & other devices of Gyrandolas, Serpents, The King & Queenes Armes & mottos, all represented in fire, as had not ben seene in any age remembred here: but that which was most remarkable was the several fires & skirmishes in the very water, which actualy moved a long way, burning under the water, & now and then appearing above it, giving reports like Muskets & Cannon, with Granados, & innumerable other devices: It is said this sole Triumph cost 1500 pounds: which was concluded with a Ball, where all the young Ladys & Gallants daunced in the greate Hall: The Court had not ben so brave & rich in apparell since his Majesties restauration: ...

26 Was my Sons Wife brought to bed of a Daughter[1] at h<e>r house in Arundel streete neere Norfolck house, & Christned by the Curate of St. Clements in the Chamber, the Godfather my Nephew Glanvil, Godmother the Lady Anderson, & my Niepce Mary Evelyn, who named it Elizabeth, the name of my Lady Anderson: ...

December St. Andrews day being on the Sonday, our Election & meeting of the R: Society was on [1] Moneday, when I brought the Duke of Norfolck & Earle of Clarendon to the Society, who being first ballotted & chosen, tooke their places, & were after chosen also of the Council for this yeare, as was also myselfe: Mr. Pepys, Secretary of the Admiralty elected President ...

7 ... I went to see the new church St. James', elegantly indeede built, especialy adorn'd was the Altar, the white Marble Enclosure curiously richly carved, & the flowres & Garlands about the Walls by Mr. Gibbons in Wood, a Pelican with her young at her breast just over the Altar in the Carved Compartment and bordure, invironing in the purple-velvet, richly frenged, with IHS richly embrodred, & most noble Plate were given by Sir R:Geere - to the value (as was said) of 200 pounds: such an Altar was no w<h>ere in any Church in England, nor have I seene any abroad more handsomly adorn'd:

17 Early in the morning I went into St. James's Park to see three Turkish or Asian Horses, brought newly over, and now first shewed his Majestie: There were 4 of them it seemes in all, but one of them died at sea, being 9 weekes coming from Hamborow: They were taken from a Bashaw at the seige of Vienna in Austria, the late famous raising that Leaguer: & with mine Eyes never did I behold so delicate a Creature as was one of them, of somwhat a bright bay, two white feete, a blaze; such an head, [Eye,] eares, neck, breast, belly, buttock, Gaskins, leggs, pasterns, & feete in all reguards beautifull & proportion'd to admiration, spiritous & prowd, nimble, making halt, turning with that sweiftnesse & in so small a compasse as was incomparable, with all this so gentle & tractable, as called to mind what I remember Busbequius speakes of them; to the reproch of our Groomes in Europ who bring them up so churlishly, as makes our horse most of them to retaine so many ill habits &c: They trotted like Does, as if they did not feele the Ground; for this first Creature was demanded 500 Ginnies, for the 2d 300, which was of a brighter bay, for the 3d 200 pound, which was browne, all of them choicely shaped, but not altogether so perfect as the first.

In a word, it was judg'd by the Spectators, (among whom was the King, Prince of Denmark, the Duke of Yorke, and severall of the Court noble persons skilled in Horses, especialy Monsieur Faubert & his sonn & Prevost, Masters of the Accademie and esteemed of the best in Europ), that there were

---

[1] Elizabeth Evelyn (1684-1760), afterwards wife of Simon Harcourt.

never seene any horses in these parts, to be compared with them: Add to all this, the Furniture which consisting of Embrodrie on the Saddle, Housse, Quiver, bow, Arrows, Symeter, Sword, Mace or Battel ax *a la Tur<c>isque*: the Bashaws Velvet Mantle furr'd with the most perfect Ermine I ever beheld, all the Yron worke in other furnitur being here of silver curiously wrought & double gilt, to an incredible value: Such, and so extraordinary was the Embrodery, as I never before saw any thing approching it, the reines & headstall crimson silk, covered with Chaines of silver gilt: There was also a Turkish royal standard of an horses taile, together with all sorts of other Caparison belonging to a Generals horse: by which one may estimate how gallantly & <magnificently> those Infidels appeare in the fild, for nothing could certainely be seene more glorious, The Gent: (a German) who rid the horse, being in all this garb: They were shood with yron made round & closed at the heele, with an hole in the middle about as wide as a shilling; the hoofes most intire: ...

18 Mr. Faubert having newly railed in a Manage & fitted it for the Academy, I went with my Lord Cornwallis to see the Young Gallants do their Exercise: There were the Dukes of Norfolck & Northumberland, Lord Newburge, and a Nephew of the Earle of Feversham: The exercises were first running at the ring, next flinging a Javlin at a Mores head, 3d discharging a Pistol at a Mark, lastly, the taking up a <Gauntlet> with the point of the Sword, all these <Exercises> performed in full speede: The D: of Northumberland, hardly miss'd succeeding in every one a douzen times as I think: Next the D: of Norfolck did exceeding bravely: Newburge & Duras seemed to be nothing so dextrous: here I saw the difference of what the French call *bell-homme a Chevall*, & *bonn homme a Chevall*, the D: of Norfolck being the first, that is rather a fine person on an horse; the D: of Northumberland being both, in perfection, namely a most gracefull person, & excellent rider: But the Duke of Norfolck told he had not ben at this exercise this twelve yeare before: There were in the fi<e>ld the Prince of Denmark & the L:Lansdown, sonn of the Earle of Bath, who had ben made a Count of the Empire last summer for his service before Vienna.

20 I returned home to my house to keepe Christmas now approching:

A villanous Murder perpetrated by Mr. St.Johns, (eldest sonn to Sir Walter, a worthy Gent:) on a knight of quality in a Tavern: The Offended being Sentenced, & Repriv'd, so many horrid murders & Duels about this time being committed (as was never heard of in England) gave much cause of complaint & murmure universaly.

21 St. Thomas's day & Sonday, my Rheume & cold was so greate, that it kept me from Church: ...

1685

January 1 ... It proved so sharp weather and so long & cruel frost that the Thames was frozen crosse, but the frost often dissolved, & froze againe: ...

25. ... [I saw this evening such a sceane of profuse gaming, and luxurious dallying & prophanesse, the King in the middst of his 3 concubines, as I had never before:][1] ...

---

[1] This unusually (even for E) critical comment is entirely a marginal afterthought.

February 4 I went to Lond, hearing his Majestie had ben the moneday before surpriz'd in his bed chamber with an Apoplectical fit, & so, as if by Gods providence, Dr. King (that excellent chirurgeon as well as Physitian) had not ben accidentaly present [to let him bloud] (with his lancet in his pocket) his Majestie had certainely died that moment, which might have ben of direfull consequence, there being no body else with the King save this doctor & one more, as I am assured: It was a mark of the extraordinary dexterity, resolution, & presentnesse of Judgment in the Doctor to let him bloud in the very paroxysme, without staying the coming of other physitians, which regularly should have ben don, & the not doing so, must have a formal pardon as they tell me: This rescued his Majestie for that instant, but it prov'd onely a reprieve for a little time; he still complain'd & was relapsing & often fainting & sometimes in Epileptical symptoms 'til Wednesday, for which he was cupp'd, let bloud againe in both jugularies, had both vomit & purges &c: which so relieved him, that on the Thursday hops of recovery were signified in the publique Gazett; but that day about noone the Physitians conjectur'd him somewhat feavorish; This they seem'd glad of, as being more easily alaied, & methodicaly to be dealt with, than his former fits, so as they prescrib'd the famous Jesuits powder; but it made his Majestie worse; and some very able Doctors present, did not think it a feavor, but the effect of his frequent bleeding, & other sharp operations used by them about his head: so as probably the Powder might stop the Circulation, & renew his former fitts, which now made him very weake: Thus he pass'd Thursday night with greate difficulty, when complaining of a paine in his side, the<y> drew 12 ounces more of blood from him, this was by 6 in the morning on friday, & it gave him reliefe, but it did not continue; for being now in much paine & strugling for breath, he lay doz'd, & after some conflicts, the Physitians desparing of him, he gave up the Ghost at halfe an houre-after Eleaven in the morning, being the 6 of Feb: in the 36t yeare of his reigne, & 54 of his age:

[Feb:6] 'Tis not to be express'd the teares & sorrows of Court, Citty & Country: Prayers were solemnly made in all the Churches, especialy in both the Court Chapells, where the Chaplaines relieved one another every halfe quarter of an houre, from the time he began to be in danger, til he expir'd: according to the forme prescribed in the Church office: Those who assisted his Majesties devotion were the A:Bish: of Cant: of London, Durrham & Ely; but more especialy the B: of Bath & Wells. It is sayd they exceedingly urged the receiving the H:Sacrament but that his Majestie told them he would Consider of it, which he did so long, 'til it was too late: others whispered, that the Bishops being bid withdraw some time the night before, (except the Earls of Bath, & Feversham), Hurlston the Priest, had presum'd to administer the popish Offices; I hope it is not true; but these buisie emissaries are very forewarde upon such occasions:[1] [see September 16:] He gave his breeches & Keys to the Duke, who was almost continualy kneeling by his bed side, & in teares; he also recommended to him the care of his natural Children, all except the D: of Monmoth, now in Holland, & in his displeasure; he intreated the Queene to pardon him, [(Nor without cause)] who a little before had sent a Bishop to excuse her not more frequently visiting him, in reguard of her excessive griefe, & with all, that his Majestie would forgive it, if at any time

---

[1] John Huddlestone, priest (1608-98). He had aided the King's flight from Worcester in September 1651. See also 2 October 1685 when Pepys reveals to E his evidence for Charles's Catholicism.

she had offended him: He spake to the Duke to be kind to his Concubines the DD: of Cleveland, & especialy Portsmouth, & that Nelly might not sterve; I do not heare he said any thing of the Church or his people, now falling under the government of a Prince suspected for his Religion, after above 100 yeares the Church & Nation had ben departed from Rome:

Thus died K.Charles the 2d, of a Vigorous & robust constitution, & in all appearance capable of a longer life. A prince of many Virtues, & many greate Imperfections, Debonaire, Easy of accesse, not bloudy or Cruel: his Countenance fierce, his voice greate, proper of person, every motion became him, a lover of the sea, & skillfull in shipping, not affecting other studys, yet he had a laboratory and knew of many Empyrical Medicines, & the easier Mechanical Mathematics: Loved Planting, building, & brought in a politer way of living, which passed to Luxurie & intollerable expense: He had a particular Talent in telling stories & facetious passages of which he had innumerable, which made some bouffoones and vitious wretches too presumptuous, & familiar, not worthy the favors they abused: He tooke delight to have a number of little spaniels follow him, & lie in his bed-Chamber, where often times he suffered the bitches to puppy & give suck, which rendred it very offensive, & indeede made the whole Court nasty & stinking: An excellent prince doubtlesse had he ben lesse addicted to Women, which made him uneasy & allways in Want to supply their unmeasurable profusion, & to the detriment of many indigent persons who had signaly serv'd both him & his father: Easily, & frequently he changed favorites to his greate prejudice &c: As to other publique transactions and unhappy miscarriages, 'tis not here I intend to number them; but certainely never had <a> King more glorious opportunities to have made himselfe, his people & all Europ happy, & prevented innumerable mischiefs, had not his too Easy nature resign'd him to be menag'd by crafty men, & some abandoned & prophane wretches, who corrupted his otherwise sufficient parts, disciplin'd as he had ben by many afflictions, during his banishment: which gave him much experience, & knowledge of men & things; but those wiccked creatures tooke him [off] from all application becoming so greate a King: the History of his Reigne will certainely be the most wonderfull for the variety of matter & accidents above any extant of many former ages: The [sad tragical] death of his father, his banishment, & hardships, his miraculous restauration, conjurations against him; Parliaments, Warrs, Plagues, Fires, Comets; revolutions abroad happning in his time with a thousand other particulars: He was ever kind to me & very gracious upon all occasions, & therefore I cannot without ingratitude [but] deplore his losse, which for many respects (as well as duty) I do with all my soule: [See 2.Octob:1685:]

His Majestie dead, The Duke (now K.James the 2d) went immediately to Council, before entering into any buisinesse, passionately declaring his sorrow, Told their Lordships, That since the succession had falln to him, he would endeavor to follow the example of his predecessor in his Clemency & tendernesse to his people: That however he had ben misrepresented as affecting arbitrary power, they should find the contrary, for that the Laws of England had made the King as greate a Monarch as he could desire; That he would endeavour to maintaine the Government both in Church & state as by Law establish'd, its Principles being so firme for Monarchy, & the members of it shewing themselves so good & Loyal subjects; & that as he would never depart from the just rights & prerogative of the Crown, so would he never Invade any mans propriety: but as he had often adventured his life in defence of the Nation, so he would still proceede, & preserve it in all its lawfull rites & libertyes:

This being the substance of what he said, the Lords desired it might be published as containing matter of greate satisfaction to a jealous people, upon this change: which his Majestie consented to: Then were the Counsel sworn, & proclamation ordered to be publish'd, that all officers should continue in their station; that there might be no failure of publique Justice, 'til his farther pleasure should be known:

Then the King rose, the Lords accompanying him to his bed Chamber, where, whilst he reposed himselfe (tired indeede as he was with griefe & watching) They immediately returned againe into the Council-Chamber to take order for the Proclayming of his Majestie which (after some debate) they consented should be in the very forme, his Grandfather K.James the first was, after the death of Q:Elizabeth, as likewise that the Lords &c: should proceede in their Coaches through the Citty for the more solemnity of it; upon this was I and severall other Gent: (waiting in the privy Gallerie), admitted into the Council Chamb: to be wittnesse of what was resolv'd on: & Thence with the Lords (the Lord Martial & the Herraulds & other Crowne Officers being ready) we first went to Whitehall gate, where the Lords stood on foote beareheaded, whilst the Herauld proclaimed His Majesties Titles to the Imperial Crowne, & succession according to the forme: The Trumpets & Kettle drumms having first sounded 3 times, which after also ended with the peoples acclamations:

Then an Herauld called the Lords Coaches according to ranke, my selfe accompanying the solemnity in my Lord Cornwallis Coach, first to Temple barr, where the Lord Major & his breathren &c met us on horseback in all their formalities, & proclaymed the King; Thence to the Exchange in Cornhill, & so we returned in the order we set forth: being come to White-hall, we all went and kissed the King & Queenes hands, he had ben on the bed, but was now risen, & in his Undresse. The Queene was in bed in her appartment, but put forth her hand; seeming to be much afflicted, as I believe she was, having deported herselfe so decently upon all occasions since she came first into England, which made her universally beloved: Thus concluded this sad, & yet Joyfull day:

[I am never to forget the unexpressable luxury, & prophanesse, gaming, & all dissolution, and as it were total forgetfullnesse of God (it being Sunday Evening) which this day sennight, I was witnesse of; the King, sitting & toying with his Concubines Portsmouth, Cleaveland, & Mazarine: &c: A french boy singing love songs, in that glorious Gallery, whilst about 20 of the greate Courtiers & other dissolute persons were at Basset round a large table, a bank of at least 2000 in Gold before them, upon which two Gent: that were with me made reflexions with astonishment, it being a sceane of uttmost vanity; and surely as they thought would never have an End: six days after was all in the dust.] ...

10 Being sent to by the Sherif of the County, to appeare, & assist the Proclayming the King; [11] I went the next day to Bromely, where I met the Sherif, and the Commander of the Kentish Troope, with an appearance of (I suppose) above 500 horse, & innumerable people: Two of his Majesties Trumpets, & a serjeant, with other officers, who having drawn up the horse in a large field neere to towne, march'd thence [with swords drawne] to the Market place, where making a ring, after sound of Trumpets, & silence made, the high Sherif read the Proclaming Titles, to his Bailife, who repeated it alow'd, & then after many shouts of the people &c: his Majesties health being

drunk in a flint glasse of a yard-long, of the Sherif, Commanders, Officers & chiefe Gent: they all disperc'd and I returned: ...

14 The King was [this night] very obscurely buried in a Vault under Hen: 7th Chapell in Westminster, without any manner of pomp,[1] and soone forgotten after all this vainity, & the face of the whole Court exceedingly changed into a more solemne and moral behaviour: The new King affecting neither Prophanesse, nor bouffonry: All the Greate Officers broke their white-Staves on the Grave &c: according to forme: ...

The 2d sermon (which should have ben before the King, who to the great griefe of his subjects, did now the first time go to Masse publicly in the little Oratorie at the Dukes lodgings, the doores set wide open) was by Mr. Fox, a young quaint Preacher, who made a very profitable sermon on Pro: Fooles make a mock at sin, against prophanes & Atheisme; now reigning more than ever through the late dissolutenesse of the Court: ...

18 I was carried by my Lord Privy-Seale to congratulate my Lord Tressurer who [19] the next day, together with the other new Officers, were all sworne at the Chancery barr, & at the Chequer: I return'd home in the Evening.

The late King having the revenue of Excise, Costomes, & other late duties granted for his life onely; were now farmed & let to severall persons upon an opinion that the late K: might let them for 3 yeares after his decease (some of the old Commissioners refusing to act) The major part of Judges, (but as think, not the best lawyers) pronounced it legal; but 4 dissenting: The lease was made but the day before his Majesties death; which seemes by the words of the statute to be invalid:

Note that the Clearke of the Closset, had shut-up the late Kings private Oratory next the Privy-Chamb: above; but the King caus'd it to be open'd againe, & the Prayers should be said as formerly: The Papists now swarmed at Court. &c:

22 Severall most usefull tractates against Dissenters, Papists & Fanatics, & resolution of Cases, were now publish'd by the London divines: ...

March 5 To my griefe I saw the new pulpet set up in the popish oratory at W-hall, for the Lent preaching, Masse being publiqly saied, & the Romanists swarming at Court with greater confidence than had ever ben seene in England since the Reformation, so as every body grew Jealous to what this would trend; A Parliament was now also summond, and greate industry used to obtaine Elections which might promote the Court Interest: Most of the Corporations being now by their new Charters in power to make what returnes of members they pleased: Most of the Judges likewise having given their opinions that his Majestie might still take the Costomes, which to foure Judges (<esteem'd> the best Lawyers) seemed against the Act of Parliament which determines it with the Kings life:

Now came over divers Envoyès & greate Persons to condole the Death of the late King: The Q: Dowager received them on a bed of mourning, the whole Chamber seiling & floore hung with black, tapers lighted; so as nothing could be more Lugubrous & solemn: The Q:Consort sat out under a state on a black foot-cloth, to entertaine the Circle as the Q: used to do, & that very decently: ...

---

[1] The grave to this day is marked by no more than a small inscribed stone in the floor with similar monuments for William III, Mary II, and Anne.

7 Newes coming to me that my Daughter Mary was falln ill of the Small Pox, I hastned home full of apprehensions, & indeede found her very ill, still coming-forth in aboundance, a wonderfull affliction to me, not only for her beauty, which was very lovely, but for the danger of loosing one of extraordinary parts & virtue. &c: Gods holy will be don.

8 ... My Deare Child continuing ill, by reason of the Disseases fixing in the Lungs, it was not in the power of physick without more plentiful expectoration to recover her, insomuch as [9] Dr. Short (the most famous approved & famous Physition of all his Majesties Doctors) gave us his opinion, that she could not escape, upon the Tuesday; so as on Wednesday she desired to have the B: Sacrament given her (of which she had yet participated the Weeke before) after which disposing her selfe to suffer what God should determine to inflict, she bore the remainder of her sicknesse with extraordinary patience, and piety & with more than ordinary resignation, and marks of a sanctified & blessed frame of mind, rendred [up] her soule to the Lord Jesus on Saturday the 14 of March, exactly at halfe-an houre after Eleaven in the fore noone, to our unspeakable sorrow & Affliction, and this not to ours (her parents) onely, but all who knew her, who were many of the best quality, greatest and most vertuous persons:

How unexpressable losse I and my Wife sustain'd, the Virtues & perfections she was endow'd with best would shew; of which the justness of her stature, person, comelinesse of her Countenance and gracefullnesse of motion, naturall, & unaffected (though more than ordinaryly beautifull), was one of the least, compar'd with the Ornaments of her mind, which was truely extraordinary, especialy the better part: Of early piety, & singularly Religious, so as spending a considerable part of every day in private devotion, Reading and other vertuous exercises, she had collected, & written out aboundance of the most usefull and judicious periods of the Books she read, in a kind of Common place; as out of Dr. Hammonds N. Test: and most of the best practical Treatises extant in our tonge:

She had read & digested a considerable deale of History, & of Places, the french Tongue being as familiar to her as English, she understood Italian, and was able to render a laudable Account of what she read & observed, to which assisted a most faithfull memory, & discernement, & she did make very prudent & discreete reflections upon what she had observe'd of the Conversations among which she had at any time ben (which being continualy of persons of the best quality), she improved: She had to all this an incomparable sweete Voice, to which she play'd a through-base on the Harpsichord, in both which she ariv'd to that perfection, that of all the Schollars of those Two famous Masters, Signor Pietro and Bartolomeo: she was esteem'd the best; [for] the sweetenesse of her voice, manegement of it, adding such an agreeablenesse to her Countenance, without any constraint and concerne, that when she sung, it was as charming to the Eye, as to the Eare; this I rather note, because it was a universal remarke, & for which so many noble & judicious persons in Musique, desir'd to hear her; the last, being at my Lord Arundels of Wardours, where was a solemn Meeting of about twenty persons of quality, some of them greate judges & Masters of Musique; where she sung with the famous Mr. Pordage, Signor Joh: Battist touching the Harpsichord &c: with exceeding applause: What shall I say, or rather not say, of the cherefullnesse & agreeablenesse of her humor, that she condescending to the meanest servant in the family, or others, she kept still her respect without the least pride: These she would reade to, examine, instruct and often pray with, if they were sick; so as she was extreamely beloved of every body: Piety was so prevalent an ingredient in her constitution (as I may say) that even amongst superiors, as equals, she no sooner became intimately acquainted; but she would endeavour to improve them by insinuating something of Religious, & that tended to bring them to a love of Devotion; and she had one or two Confidents, with whom she used to passe whole dayes, in fasting, reading and prayers, especialy before the monethly communions, & other solemn occasions:

She could not indure that which they call courtship, among the Gallants, abhorred flattery, & tho she had aboundance of witt, the raillery was so innocent and ingenuous, as was most agreable; She sometimes would see a play, but since the stage grew licentious, tooke greate scandal at them, & express'd her being weary of them, & that the time spent at the Theater was an unaccountable vanity, nor did she at any time play at Cards, without extreame importunity & for Company; but this was so very seldome, that I cannot number it among any thing she could name a fault:

No body living read prose, or Verse better & with more judgement, & as she read, so she writ not onely most correct orthography, but with that maturitie of judgement, and exactnesse of the periods, choice expressions, & familiarity of style, as that some letters of hers have astonish'd me, and others to whom she has occasionaly written: Among other agreablenesses she had a talent of rehersing any Comical part or poeme, as was to them she might decently be free with, more pleasing than the Theater; She daunc'd with the most grace that in my whole life I had ever seene, & so would her Master say, who was Monsieur Isaac; but she very seldome shew'd that perfection, save in the gracefullnesse of her Carriage, which was with an aire of spritefull modestie, not easily to be described; Nothing of haughty, nothing affected, but natural and easy, as well in her deportment, as her discourse, which was allways material, not trifling, and to which the extraordinary sweetenesse of her tone, even in familiar speaking, was very charming: Nothing was so pretty, as her descending to play with little Children, whom she would caresse, & humor with greate delight:

But she most of all affected to be [with] grave, and sober men, of whom she might learne something and improve herselfe: I have my selfe ben assisted by her, both reading & praying by me; and was comprehensive of uncommon notions, curious of knowing every thing to some excesse, had I not indeavor'd to represse it sometimes; Nothing was therefore so delightfull to her, as the permission I ever gave her to go into my Study, where she would have willingly spent whole days; for as I sayd, she had read aboundance of History, & all the best poets, even to Terence, Plautus, Homer, Vergil, Horace, Ovide, all the best Romances, & modern Poemes, and could compose very happily, & put in her pretty Symbol, as in that of the *Mundus Muliebris*,[1] wherein is an enumeration of the immense variety of the Modes and ornaments belonging to the Sex:

But all these are vaine trifles to those interior vertues which adorn'd her Soule, For she was sincerely Religious, most dutifull to her parents, whom she lov'd with an affection temper'd with greate esteeme, so as we were easy & free, & never were so well pleased, as when she was with us, nor needed we other Conversation: She was kind to her Sisters, and was still improving them, by her constant Course of Piety:

---

[1] A poem by Mary which made fun of contemporary manners called '*Mundus Muliebris: or the Ladies Dressing-Room unlock'd*'. E published it in 1690.

Ô deare, sweete and desireable Child, how shall I part with all this goodnesse, all this Vertue, without the bitternesse of sorrow, and reluctancy of a tender Parent! Thy affection, duty & love to me was that of a friend, as well as of a Child: passing even the love of Women, the Affection of a Child: nor lesse dearer to thy Mother, whose example & tender care of Thee was unparalleled; nor was Thy returnes to her lesse conspicuous: Ô how she mourns thy losse! ô how desolate has Thou left us, Sweete, obliging, happy Creature! To the grave shall we both carry thy memory — God alone (in whose boosome thou art at rest & happy) give us to resigne Thee, & all our Contentments (for thou indeede wert all in this world) to his blessed pleasure: ô let him be glorified by our submission, & give us Grace to blesse him for the Graces he implanted in thee, thy vertuous life, pious & holy death, which is indeede the onely remaining Comfort of our soules, hastning through the infinite love and mercy of the Lord Jesus, to be shortly with Thee deare Child, & with Thee (and those blessed Saints like thee,) glorifie the Redemer of the World to all Eternity. Amen:

It was in the nineteenth yeare of her Age, that this sicknesse happn'd to her, at which period Dr. Harvy somewhere writes, all young people should be let blood; and to this we advised her; whilst to all who beheld her she looked so well, as her extraordinary beauty was taken notice of, the last time she appeared at Church: but she had so greate an aversion to breathing a veine, as we did not so much insist upon it as we should: being in this exceeding height of health, she was the more propence to change, & had ever ben subject to feavors; but there was yet another accident that contributed to the fixing it in this dissease; The apprehension she had of it in particular, & which struck her but two days before she came home, by an imprudent Gentlewomans telling my Lady Faulkland (with whom my daughter went to give a Visite) after she had entertained them a good while in the house, that she had a servant sick of the small pox above, who died the next day; This my poore Child accknowledged made an impression on her spirits, it being with all [of] a mortal & spreading kind at this time about the towne:

There were now no lesse than foure Gent: of Quality offering to treate with me about Marriage; & I freely gave her her owne Choice, knowing she was discreete: One (against which I had no exceptions) and who most passionately lov'd her, but was for a certaine natural blemish that rendered him very disagreable, she would in complyance to me have married, if I did injoyne her; but telling me she should never be happy with him (observing it seemes a neerenesse in his nature, and a little under-breeding) I would not impose it; for which she often expressed her satisfaction, & thanks to me in the most obliging & respectfull manner: The other was one Weston a Stafford shire Gent: of the same family, & I thinke heire (within one) to the Earles of Portland: This was but now just beginning:

But the person who first made love to her, was Mr. Wilbraham a Chesshire Gent: of a noble Family, whose extreamely rich & sordid Fathers demands of a Portion, I could by no meanes reach, without injury to the rest of my daughters, which this pious, & good natured Creature, would never have suffered, and so that match stood in suspense; I say in suspense, for the young Gent: still pursu'd, & would have married her in private, if either my Daughter, or We had don so disingenuously: She & we had principles that would by no meanes suffer us to harken it: At last he's sent for home, continues his Affection, hop<e>s to bring his father to reasonable termes: My Child is taken with his Constancy, his Virtuous breeding, and good nature, & discretion, having beene a fortnight together in my house: This, made us not forward to embrace any other offers, together with the extraordinary indifferency she ever shewed of Marrying at all; for truely says shee to her Mother, (the other day), were I assur'd of your lives & my deare Fathers, never would I part from you, I love you, & this home, where we serve God, above all things in the world, nor ever shall I be so happy: I know, & consider the vicissitudes and changes of the world, I have some experience of its vanities, & but for decency, more than inclination, & that You judge it expedient for me, I would not change my Condition, but rather add the fortune you designe me to my Sisters, & keepe up the reputation of our family: This was so discreetely & sincerely utter'd as, could not proceede but from an extraordinary Child, & one who loved her parents without example: ...

... there was a designe of my Lady Rochester & Clarendon to make her Mayd of <honour> to the Queene, so soone as there was a place empty: but this she did not in the least set her heart upon, nor indeede upon any thing so much as the service of God, <as> a quiet regular life, & how she might improve herselfe in the most necessary accomplishments, & to which she was arived in so greate a measure, as I acknowledge (all partiality of relation layed aside) I never saw, or knew her equal, considering how universal they were; save in one onely Creature of her Sex, Mrs. Godolphin, (late the wife of my Lord Godolphin, whose life for the singular piety, Vertue & discretion, (& that she was to me a Friend, in all the peculiar transcendencys of that relation) I have written at large,[1] and consign'd to my Lady Sylvius (whom she loved above all her Sex) & who requested it of me: And this I mention here, because the Example of that most religious Lady: made I am assured deepe impressions in my deare Child; and that I was told, she caused it to be read to her, at the very beginning of her sicknesse, when She had taken that bed, out of which she never risse, to my insupportable griefe & sorrow; though never two made more blessed ends: But all this sorrow is selfe-love, whilst to wish them here againe, were to render them miserable who are now in happinesse, and above:

This is the little History, & Imperfect Character of my deare Child, whose Piety, Virtue, & incomparable Endowments, deserve a Monument more durable than brasse & Marble: Precious is the Memorial of the Just - Much I could enlarge on every period of this hasty Account, but thus I ease & discharge my overcoming passion for the present, so many things worthy an excellent Christian & dutifull Child, crowding upon me: Never can I say enough, ô deare, my deare Child whose memory is so precious to me.

This deare child was born at Wotton in Surry, in the same house and roome where I likewise first drew breath, (my wife being retir'd to my bro: there, the greate sicknesse yeare) upon the first of that moneth, & neere the very houre, that I was borne, upon the last: viz: October:

16 Was my deare Daughter interr'd in the south east end of the church at Deptford neere her Grand mother & severall of my Younger Children and Relations: my desires were she should have ben carried & layed among my owne Parents & Relations at Wotton, where our Family have a Vault, where she was born, & where I have desire to be interred my selfe, when God shall call me out of this uncertaine transitory life; but some Circumstances did not permit it; & so she was buried here.[2] Our Viccar Dr. Holden preaching her Funerall Sermon on: 1. Phil: 21. *For to me to live is Christ, & to die is gaine,*

---

[1] *The Life of Mrs Godolphin*, first published in 1847.

[2] Her epitaph is still at St Nicholas, Deptford.

upon which he made an apposit discourse (as those who heard it assure me, for griefe suffer'd me not to be present) concluding with a modest recital of her many vertues, and especialy her signal piety, so as drew both teares, & admiration from the hearers, so universaly was she beloved, & known to deserve all the good that could be sayd of her: & I was not altogether unwilling something of this should be spoken of her, for the edification & encouragement of other young people: There were divers noble persons who honor'd her Obsequies, & funerall, some in person, others in sending their Coaches, of which there were 6 or 7. of six horses viz. Countesse of Sunderland, Earle of Clarendon, Lord Godolphin, Sir St. Fox; Sir William Godolphin, Vis<c>ount Falkland &c [following the hearse of 6 horses &c] there were (besides other decenc<i>es distributed among her friends about 60 rings: Thus lived, died, & was buried the joy of my life & ornament both of her sex & my poore family: God Almighty of his infin<i>te mercy grant me the grace thankfully to resigne my selfe & all I have, or had, to his divine pleasure, & in his good time, restoring health & Comfort to my Family, teach me so to number my days, as I may apply my heart to Wisdome, & be prepared for my dissolution, & that into the hands of my blessed Saviour I may recommend my Spirit. Amen:

Having some days after opened her Trunks, & looked into her Closset, amazed & even astonished we were to find that incredible number of papers and Collections she had made of severall material Authors, both Historians, Poets, Travells &c: but above all the Devotions, Contemplations, & resolutions upon those Contemplations, which we found under her hand in a booke most methodicaly disposed, & much exceeding the talent & usage of [so] young & beautifull women, who consume so much of their time in vaine things: with severall prayers, Meditations, & devotions on divers occasions; with a world of pretty letters to her confidents & others savoring of a greate witt, & breathing of piety & honor: There is one letter to some divine (who is not named) to whom she writes that he would be her Ghostly Father & guide, & that he would not despise her for the many errors & imperfections of her Youth, but beg of God, to give her courage, to acquaint him with all her faults, imploring his assistance, & spiritual direction: & well I remember, that she often desired me to recommend her to such a person, but (though I intended it) I did not think fit to do as it yet, seeing her apt to be scrupulous, & knowing the great innocency & integrity of her life; but this (it seemes) she did of her selfe: ... But as she was a little miracle whilst she lived, so she died with out Example:

26 I was invited to Cap: Gunmans Funerall, that excellent Pilot, & sea-man, who had behav'd himselfe so valiantly in the Dut<c>h-Warr: taken away by the gangreene which happn'd in his cure, upon his unhappy fall from the peere of Calais: This was the Cap: of the yacht, whom they accused for not giving timely warning, on the Dukes (now the King) going into Scotland, when his ship split upon the Sands, when so many perished: But of which I am most confident, the Cap: was no ways guilty, either through negligence, or designe; as he made appeare not onely at the Examination of the matter of fact; but in the Vindication he shewed me some time since, which must needes give any-man of reason satisfaction: ... He was a sober, frugal, cherefull & temperat man; we have few such sea-men left:

There <came> to Condole the death of my deare Daughter this Weeke moneday, & friday: The Countesse of Bristoll, Sunderland, La: Sylvius, Mrs. Penelope Godolphin: Sir Stephen Fox & his Lady &c:

29 ... A servant mayd of my Wifes fell sick of the very same disease, of the same sort of S:pox, & in all appearance in as greate danger, though she never came neere my daughter: we removed her into the Towne with care:

April 5 ... Drowsinesse much surpriz'd me: The Lord be gratious to me:

The mayd, by Gods greate mercy, but with extraordinary difficulty, recovered: Blessed be God:

7 Being now somewhat compos'd after my greate affliction, I went to Lond: to heare Dr. Tenison (it being [8] a Wednesday in Lent) at Whitehall: who preached on 3. Gen: 3: I returned in the Evening: I observ'd that though the King was not in his seate above in the Chapell, the Doctor made notwithstanding his three congèes, which they were not us'd to do, when the [late] King was absent, making then one bowing onely: I asked the reason; it was sayd, he had special order so to do: The Princesse of Denmarke yet was in the Kings Closset, but sat on the left hand of the Chaire, the clearke of the Closset standing by his Majesties Chaire as if he had ben present: [I met Q:Dowager going now first from W.hall to dwell at Somerset house.] ...

23 Was the day of his Majesties Coronation, the Queene was also crown'd, the solemnity very magnificent, as the particulars are set forth in print: The Bish: of Ely preached, but (to the greate sorrow of the people) no Sacrament, as ought to have ben: However the King beginns his reigne with greate expectations and hopes of much reformation as to the former vices, & prophanesse both of Court & Country:

Having ben present at our late Kings Coronation, I was not ambitious of seing this Ceremonie; nor did I think it fit to leave my poore Wife alone, who was yet in greate sorrow: ...

May 7th: I was in Westminster Hall when Oates (who had made such a stirr in the whole Kingdome, (upon his revealing a plot of the Papists) as alarm'd several Parliaments, & had occasion'd the execution of divers persons, priests, noble men &c:) was tried for Perjurie at the Kings-bench; but it being exceedingly tedious, I did not much endeavor to see the issue of it, considering that it would certainely be publish'd: Aboundance of R:Cath: were now in the Hall, in expectation of the most gratefull conviction & ruine of a person who had ben so obnoxious to them; & as I verily believe had don much mischiefe & greate injurie to several by his violent & ill grounded proceedings, whilst he was at first so unreasonably blowne-up, & encourag'd, that his insolence was no longer sufferable: ...

16 Was sentenc'd Oates to be whip'd & pilloried with uttmost severity: ...

21. Din'd at my Lord Privy-Seales, with Sir Will: Dugdale the <Garter> K: at Armes, Author of the *Monasticon*,[1] & greate Antiquarie; with whom I had much discourse: he told me he was 82 yeares of age, had his sight & memory &c: There was shew'd a dra<u>ght of the exact shape & dimensions of the Crowne the Queene had ben crown'd withall, together with Jewells & Pearles, their weight & value, which amounted to 100650 pounds sterling, an immense summ: attested at the foot of the paper by the Jeweller and Gooldsmith who set the Jewells &c:

22 In the morning, I went (together with a French gent, a person of quality) with my Lord Pr: Seale to the house of Lords, where we were both plac'd by

---

[1] *Monasticon Anglicanum*, also author of the *Baronage of England* a fundamental resource for genealogists.

his Lordship next the barr just below the Bishops very commodiously both for hearing and seeing: After a short space came in the Queene & Princesse of Denmark, & stood next above the Arch-Bishops, at the side of the house on the right hand of his Majesties Throne: In the interim divers of the Lords (who had not finish'd before) tooke the Test, & usual Oathes, so as her Majestie (Spanish Ambassador & other forraine Ministers who stood behind the state) heard the Pope, & worship of the Virg: Mary &c: renounc'd very decently, as likewise the following Prayers, standing all the while:

Then came in the King, the Crowne on his head &c and being sate, The Commons were let in, so the house being fill'd, he drew forth a Paper, containing his speech, which he <read> distinctly enough to this effect: That he resolved to call a Parliament from the moment of his brothers decease, as the best meanes to settle all the concernes of the Nation so as might be most easy & happy to himselfe & his subjects: That he would confirme what ever he had said in his declaration at the first Council, concerning his opinion of the principles of the Church of England, for their Loyaltie, & would defend & support it, and preserve its government, as by Law now establish'd: That as he would Invade no mans property, so he would never depart from his owne prerogative: & as he had <ventur'd> his life in defence of the nation so he would proceede to do still: That having given this assurance of his Care of our Religion (his word was your Religion) & propertie, (which he had not said by chance, but solemnly) so he doubted not of suitable returnes of his subjects duty & kindnesse, especialy as to the settling his Revenue for life for the many weighty necessities of the government which he would not suffer to be precarious: That some might possibly suggest that it were better to feede & supply him from time to time onely, out of their inclination to frequent Parliaments; but that that, would be but a very improper Method to take with him; since the best way to engage him to meete oftener, would be allways to use him well; & therefore expected their compliance speedily, that this session being but short, they might meete againe to satisfaction:

At every period of this, the house gave loud shouts &c: Then he acquainted them with that mornings news of Argiles being landed in the West-highlands of Scotland from Holland, and the Treasonous declaration he had published, which he would communicate to them, & that he should take the best care he could it should meete with the reward it deserv'd, not questioning of the parliaments Zeale & readinesse to assist him, as he desired: At which There followed another *Vive le roy*, & so his Majestie retired: &c: & I went into the Court of Requests &c:

So soone as the Commons were return'd, & put themselves, into a grand Committè they immediately put the Question, & unanimously voted the Revenue to his Majestie during life: Mr. Seamour made a bold speech against many Elections, and would have had those Members who (he pretended) were obnoxious, to withdraw, 'til they had cleared their being legaly return'd, but no body seconded him: The truth is there were very many of the new Members, whose Elections & returnes were universaly censur'd; being divers of them persons of no manner of condition or Interest in the nation, and places for which they served, especialy in the Counties of Devon, Cornwell, Norfolck, &c, said to have ben recommended from the Court, and effect of the new charters, changing the Electors:

It was reported my L: of Bath, carried-down with him no fewer than 15 Charters, so as some cald him the Prince Elector: whence Seaymor told the house in his speech, that if this were digested, they might introduce what Religion & Lawes they pleased, & that though he never gave heede to the feares & jealosies of the people before, he now was realy apprehensive of Popery &c: The truth is, by printed List of Members of 505, there did not appear to be above 135 who had ben in former Parliaments, especialy that lately held at Oxon:

In the Lords house, my Lord Newport made but an impertinent exception against two or three [young] Peeres, who wanted some moneths, & some onely 4 or 5 daies being of age:

The Popish Lords (who had some time before ben released from their Confinement about the Plot) were now discharg'd of their Impeachment: of which I gave my L. Arundel of Wardoer joy:

Oates, who had but two days before ben pilloried at severall places, & whip't at the Carts taile from New-gate to Algate; was this day placed in a sledge (being not able to go by reason of his so late scourging) & dragd from prison to Tyburn, & whip'd againe all the way, which some thought to be very severe & extraordinary; but in case he were gilty of the perjuries, & so of the death of many innocents, as I feare he was; his punishment was but what he well deserv'd: I chanc'd to passe in my Coach, just as Execution was doing on him: *A strange revolution.*

Note, that there was no speech made by my Lord Keeper, after his Majesties as usualy: It was whispered, he would not long be in that station; & many believing the bold Chiefe Justice Jeofries (now made Baron of Wen in Yorkshire, & went through-stitch in that Tribunal) stood faire for that Office: I gave him joy the morning before of his new honor, he having always ben very civil to me &c:

24 ... We had hitherto [not] any raine for many monethes, insomuch as the Caterpillar had already devoured all the Winter fruite through the whole land, & even killed severall greate & old trees; such two Winters, & Summers I had never known:

June 4. Came to visite, and take leave of me Sir Gab: Sylvius now going Envoyè Extraordinary into Denmark: with his secretary, & chaplaine, a french-man who related the miserable persecution of the Protestants in Fr: not above ten Churches left them, and they threatned to be also demolish'd: That they were commanded to christen their children within 24 houres after birth, or else a Popish-priest was to be call'd, & then the Infant brought-up in popery: and that in some places they were 30 leagues from any Minister or opportunity: That this persecution had dispeopled the most industrious part of the nation and dispers'd them into Swisse, Burgundy, Hollond, Ger: Denmark, England, Plantations & where not. There were with Sir Gab: his Lady, Sir William Godolphin, and sisters, & my Lord Godolphins little son, (my Charge): I brought them to the water side, where Sir Gab: embarked for his Voyage, & the rest return'd to Lond: ...

14 There was now certaine Intelligence of the Duke of Monmoths landing at Lyn[1] in Dorset shire, & of his having set up his standart as K. of England: I pray God deliver us from the confusions which these beginnings threaten:

Such a drowth for want of raine, was never in my memory:

17 To Lond: at which time the D: of Monmoth invaded this nation landing with but 150 men at Lyme in Dorsetshire, which wonderfully alarm'd the whole Kingdome, fearing the joyning of dissafected people; many of the train'd bands flocking to him: he had at his landing published a Declaration, charging his Majestie with Usurpation, & severall horrid crimes, upon

---

[1] Lyme Regis.

pretence of his owne title, and the calling of a free-Parliament: This Decl: was condemn'd to be burnt by the hang-man, the Duke proclaim'd Traytor, a reward of 5000 pounds to him that should kill him &c: Now were also those words in the Inscription about the Pillar (intimating the Papists firing the Citty) erased and cut out &c:

The exceeding Drouth still continued: God grant a successfull conclusion to these ill-boded beginnings: I tooke the Chaire as Vice-President at the R: Society.

July 8 To Lond: Came now the newes of Monmouths Utter defeate, and the next day of his being taken by Sir William Portman & Lord Lumley, with the Militia of their Counties. It seemes the horse commanded by my Lord Grey, being newly raised, & undisciplin'd, were not to be brought in so short a time to indure the Fire, which exposed the foote to the Kings: so as when Monmoth had led the foote in greate silence and order thinking to surprise my Lord Feversham Lieutenant General newly incamped, and given him a smart charge, interchanging both greate & small shot; The horse breaking [their owne] ranks; monmoth gave it over, and fled with Grey, leaving their party to be cut into pieces: to the number of 2000: the whole number reported to be about 8000: The Kings but 2700: The slaine were most of the Mendip-miners, who did greate Execution with their tooles, and sold their lives very dearely: whilst their leaders flying were pursu'd and taken the next morning, not far from one another: Mon: had walked 16 miles on foote changing his habite with a poore coate, & was found by L. Lumley in <a> dry-ditch cover'd with fern-braken, but neither with sword, pistol, or so much as any Weapon, and so might happly have passed for some country man, his beard being grown so long, & so gray, as hardly to be known, had not his George discovered him, which was found in his Pocket: Tis said he trembled exceedingly all over not able to speake: Grey was taken not far from him: Most of his party were Anabaptists, & poore Cloth-workers of the Country, no Gent: of account being come into him: The Arch-bouttefew Ferguson, Matthews &c: were not yet found: The 5000 pounds to be given to whomsoever should bring Monmouth in by Proclamation, was to be distributed among the Militia by agreement twixt Sir William Portman & Lumley: The battail ended, some words first in jeast then in heate [passing] twixt Sherrington Talbot a worthy Gent, (son to Sir Jo. Talbot, & who had behav'd himselfe very handsomly) and one Capt: Love, both commanders of the Militia forces of the Country, whose souldiers fought best: both drawing their Swords, & passing at one another Sherrington was wounded to death upon the spot; to the greate regret of those who knew him, being also his fathers onely son:

9 Just as I was coming into the Lodgings at Whitehall a little before dinner my Lord of Devonshire standing very neere his Majesties bed-Chamber-doore in the lobby: came Coll: Culpeper & in a rude manner looking my Lord in the face, Asked whether this were a time and place for Excluders to appeare, my Lord tooke little notice of what he said at first, knowing him to be a hot-headed fellow; but reiterating it againe, Asked Culpeper whether he meant him? he said, yes, he meant his Lordship: My Lord told him he was no Excluder (as indeede he was not) the other affirms it againe: My Lord told him he Lied; on which Culpeper struck him a box o'th'Eare, my Lord him another and fell'd him downe; upon which being soone parted: Culpeper was seiz'd and commanded by his Majestie (who was all the while in the B: chamber) to be carried downe to the Greenecloth Officer, who sent him to the Martialsea, as he deserv'd: My L: Devon had said nothing to him ...

15 ... This day was Monmoth brought to Lond: examin'd before the King to whom he made greate submission, accknowledg'd his seduction by Fergusson the Scot, whom he named the bloudy Villain: thence sent to the Tower, had an enterview with his late Dutchesse, whom he received coldly, having lived dishonestly with the Lady Hen: Wentworth for two years; from obstinatly asserting his conversation with that debauched woman to be no sin, seing he could not be perswaded to his last breath, the Divines, who were sent to assist him, thought not fit to administer the holy Communion to him: for the rest of his faults he professed greate sorrow, and so died without any apparent feare, would make use of no cap, or other circumstance, but lying downe bid the fellow do his office better than to my late Lord Russell, & gave him gold: but the wretch made five Chopps before he had his head off, which so incens'd the people, that had he not ben guarded & got away they would have torne him in pieces: He made no Speech on the Scaffold (which was on Tower-hill) but gave a paper (containing not above 5 or 6 lines) for the King, in which he disclaimes all Title to the Crowne, accknowledges that the late King (his Father) had indeede told him, he was but his base sonn, & so desire'd his Majestie to be kind to his Wife & Children: This relation I had from the Mouth of Dr. Tenison Rector of St. Martines, who with the Bishops of Ely & Bath & Wells, was one of the divines his Majestie sent to him, & were at the execution: Thus ended this quondam Duke, darling of his Father, and the Ladys, being extraordi<na>rily handsome, and adroit: an excellent souldier, & dauncer, a favorite of the people, of an Easy nature, debauched by lust, seduc'd by crafty knaves who would have set him up onely to make a property; tooke this opportunity of his Majestie being of another Religion, to gather a party of discontented; failed of it, and perished:

He was a lovely person, had a vertuous & excellent Lady that brought him greate riches & a second Dukedome in Scotland; Was Master of the Horse, Gen. of the K. his fathers Army, Gent: of the Bed chamber: Knight of the Garter, Chancellor of Camb: in a Word had accumulations without end: Se<e> what Ambition and want of principles brought him to. He was beheaded on Tuesday the 14th July: His mother (whose name was Barlow, daughter of some very meane Creatures) was a beautifull strumpet, whom I had often seene at Paris, & died miserably, without anything to bury her: Yet had this Perkin ben made believe, the King had married her: which was a monstrous forgerie, & ridiculous: & to satisfie the world the iniquitie of the report, the King his father (if his Father he realy were, for he most resembled one Sidny familiar with his mother) publiquely & most solemnly renounced it, and caused it to be so entred in the Council booke some yeares since, with all the Privy Counsel<o>rs attestation ...

27 This night when we were all asleepe went my Daughter Eliz: away, to meete a young fellow, nephew to Sir Jo: Tippet (Surveyor of the Navy: & one of the Commissioners) whom she married the next day being Tuesday;[1] without in the least acquainting either her parents, or any soule in the house: I was the more afflicted & <astonish'd> at it, in reguard, we had never given this Child the least cause to be thus dissobedient, and being now my Eldest, might reasonably have expected a double Blessing: But it afterward appeared, that this Intrigue had ben transacted by letters long before, & <when> she was with my Lady Burton in Licester shire, and by private meetings neere my

---

[1] Apart from this description the young man is otherwise unknown, including his name.

house: She of all our Children had hitherto given us least cause of suspicion; not onely for that she was yet young, but seemed the most flattering, souple, and observant; of a silent & particular humor; in no sort <betraying> the levity & Inclination which is commonly apparent in Children who fall into these snares; having ben bred-up with the uttmost Circumspection, as to principles of severest honour & Piety: But so far it seemes, had her passion for this Young fellow made her forget her duty, and all that most Indulgent Parents expected from her, as not to consider the Consequence of her folly & dissobedience, 'til it was too late: This Affliction went very neere me & my Wife, neither of us yet well compos'd for the untimely losse of that incomparable & excellent Child, which it pleased God to take from us by the small pox a few monethes before: But this farther Chastizement was to be humbly submitted to, as part of the burden God was pleased to lay farther upon us; in this yet the lesse afflictive, That we had not ben wanting in giving her an Education every way becoming us: We were most of all astonish'd at the suddainesse of this action, & the privatenesse of its manegement; the Circumstances also Consider'd & quality, how it was possible she should be flattered so to her dissadvantage: He being in no condition sortable to hers, & the Blessing we intended her: The thing has given us much disquiet, I pray God direct us, how to govern our Resentments of her dissobedience; and if it be his will, bring good out of all this Ill:

August 2 So had this Affliction descompos'd us, that I could not be well at Church next Lords day; though I had prepared for the B:Sacrament: I hope God will be more gracious to my onely remaining Child, whom I take to be of a more discreete, sober and religious temper: that we may have that comfort from her, which is deny'd us in the other:
   This Accident caus'd me to alter my Will; as was reasonable; for though there may be a reconciliation upon her repentance, and that she has suffer'd for her folly; yet I must let her see what her undutifullnesse in this action, deprives her of; as to the provision she else might have expected; solicitous as she knew I now was of bestowing her very worthily: ...
   16 Came newes to us that my undutifull daughter was visited with the small-pox, now universaly very contagious: I was yet willing my Wife should go visite & take care of her: ...
   22 I went to Lond, to see my unhappy Child, now in greate danger, and carried our Viccar with me, that according to her earnest desire, (being very sensible & penitent for her fault) he might administer to her the H: Sacrament, which he did; & after some time, and her greate submissions & agonies, leaving her to the mercys of God, & her mother with her I returned in the Evening: We had now the newes of the Newhausels being taken by the Christians: There was also this day an universall appearance of the Kings forces at Brainford:[1] ...

---

[1] Between this day and the next entry E wrote to his wife saying that he had refrained from seeing his daughter because he did not want to see 'the injurious Man, who has (in great part ben the occasion of this redoubt'd Affliction, whether the poore Creature live or die; and truely that has ben the only cause of hindering me from being so often with her ... I have most earnestly besought Almighty God to me Mercifull to, & spare her life, if he think fit; and in all Events to accept of this severe Chastisement for all her errors, that she may be happy in another, and better World ...' (*Evelyn Papers*, uncatalogued and unpublished). The letter can be interpreted as either

28 My poore unhappy Daughters sickness increasing, a violent feavor succeeding when her other distemper appeared to be past danger; I went up againe to see, & comfort her, together with our Minister: My disconsolate Wife I left with her, who had ben almost all her sicknesse with her; so I return'd home in greate doubt how God would deale with her, whom the next morning he was pleased to take out of this vale of misery, I humbly trust, to his infinite mercy, though to our unspeakeable affliction, loosing another Child in the flower of her age, who had never 'til now given us cause of any displeasure, but many hopes of Comfort: & thus in lesse than 6 moneths were we depriv'd of two Children for our unworthinesse, & causes best known to God, whom I beseech from the bottome of my heart that he will give us grace to make that right use of all these chastisements that we may become better, and intirely submitt [in] all things to his infinite wise disposal.

She departed this life on <Saturday> 29: Aug: at 8 in the Morning: fell sick [& died] on the same day of the weeke, that my other most deare & dutifull daughter did, and as also one of my servants (a very pious youth) had don the yeare before: I beseech God of his mercy Sanctifie this and all my other Afflictions & dispensations to me. His holy will be don Amen.

30 This sad accident kept me from the publique service this day being Sonday.

September My Child was buried by her sister on 2d September in the Church of Deptford:[1]

The 3 of Sep: I went to Lond, being sent to by a Letter from my Lord Clarendon (Lord privy-seale) to let me know that his majestie being pleased to send him Lord Lieutennant into Ireland, was also pleased to Nominate me one of the Commissioners to execute the office of Privy-Seale during his Lieutenancy there: It behoving me [4] to waite upon his Majestie & give him thanks for his greate honor (returning home that Evening) I accompanied his Lordship [5] the next morning to Windsore (dining by the Way at Sir Hen: Capels at Cue) where his Majestie receiving me with extraordinary kindnesse, I kissed his hands: I told him how sensible I was of his Majesties gracious favour to me: that I would endeavour to serve him with all sincerity, dilligence & loyalty, not more out of my duty, than Inclinations: He said, he doubted not of it, & was glad he had this opportunity to shew the kindnesse he had for me: After this came aboundance of the greate Men to give me Joy, particularly L: Tressurer, L: Sunderland, L. Peterborrow, L: Godolphin, L: Falkland & every body at Court who knew me: ...

15 I went to Lond: accomp<a>nied Mr. Pepys (Secretary of the Admiralty) to Portsmouth, Whither his Majestie was going the first time since his coming to the Crowne, to see in what state the Fortifications were. Wee tooke Coach & 6 horses, late after din<n>er, yet got to Bagshot that night: whilst supper was making ready I went & made a Visite to Mrs. Grahames, some time Maide of honor to the queen Dowager, now wife to Ja: Gr: Esquire of the Privie-purse to the King: her house being a Walke in the Forest, within a little quarter of a mile from Bagshot Towne: very importunate she was that I would sup, &

---

extraordinarly stoic or a damning comment on E's capacity to be repressively judgemental. He appears to regard her impending death as a logical punishment for her actions.

[1] This implies that E did not attend the funeral. Elizabeth was not awarded the honour of an epitaph in the church as Richard and Mary had been.

abide there that night: but being oblig'd by my companion, I return'd to our Inn, after she had shew'd me her house which was very commodious, & well furnish'd, as she was an excellent housewife, a prudent & vertuous Lady: There is a parke full of red deare about it: Her eldest sonn, was now sick there of the small pox, but in a likely way of recovery; & other of her Children ran about, & among the infected, which she said let them do on purpose that they might whilst young, passe that fatal dissease, which she fancied they were to undergo one time or other, & that this would be the best: The severity of this cruel dissease so lately in my poore family confirming much of what she affirm'd:

16 The next morning early seting out, we ariv'd early enough at Winchester to waite on the King, who was lodged at the Deanes, (Dr. Megot) I found very few with him besides my Lord Feversham, Arran, Newport, & the Bishop of Bath & Wells to whom his Majestie was discoursing Miracles, & what strange things the Saludadors would do in Spaine, as by creeping into [heated] ovens with[out] hurt &c: & that they had a black Crosse in the roofe of their mouthes: but yet were commonly, notorious & prophane wretches: upon which his Majestie farther said, that he was so extreamely difficult of Miracles, for feare of being impos'd on, that if he should chance to see one himselfe, without some other wittnesse, he should apprehend it some delusion of his senses:

Then they spake of the boy who was pretended to have had a wanting leg restor'd him, so confidently asserted by Fr: de Santa Clara, & others: To all which the Bishop added a greate Miracle happning in that Citty of Winchester to his certaine knowledge, of a poore miserably sick & decrepit Child, (as I remember long kept un-baptized) who immediately on his Baptisme, recover'd; as also of the sanatory effect of K. Charles his Majesties fathers blood, in healing one that was blind: As to that of the Saludador (of which likewise I remember Sir Arthir Hopton, formerly Ambassador at Madrid had told me many like wonders) Mr. Pepys passing through Spaine, & being extreamely Inquisitive of the truth of these pretended miracles of the Saludadors; found a very famous one of them at last, whom he offered a considerable reward to, if he would make a trial of the Oven, or any other thing of that kind, before him: The fellow ingenuously told him, that, finding he was a more than ordinary curious person, he would not deceive him, & so accknowledg'd that he could do none of those feates, realy; but that what they pretended, was all a cheate, which he would easily discover, though the poore superstitious people were imposed upon: yet have these Imposters, an allowance of the Bishops, to practise th<e>ir Juggleings:

This Mr. Pepys affirm'd to me; but said he, I did not conceive it fit, to interrupt his Majestie, who told me what they pretended to do, so solemnly: Then there was something said of the second-sight, happning to some persons, especialy Scotch: Upon which both his Majestie & (I think) my Ld: Arran, told us, that Monsieur a French Nobleman lately here in England, seeing the late Duke of Monmoth, come into the Play-house at Lond: suddainly cryed out to some sitting in the same box: *Voila Messieurs comme il entre sans tete*:

After this his Majestie speaking of some Reliques, that had effected strange cures, particularly a Thorne of our B: S: Crosse; that healed a Gentlewomans rotten nose by onely touching; & speaking of the Golden Crosse & Chaine taken out of the Coffin of St. Edward the Confessor at Westminster, by one of the singing-men, who as the scaffolds were taking-down, after his Majesties Coronation, espying an hole in the Tomb, & something glisten; put his hand in, & brought it to the Deane, & he to the King: his Majestie began to put the

Bishop in mind, how earnestly the [late] King (his brother) call'd upon him, during his Agonie, to take out what he had in his pockett: [See Feb: 6:] I had thought (says the King) it had ben for some keys, which might lead to some Cabinets, which his Majestie would have me secure; but (says he) you well remember that I found nothing in any of his pockets but onely a Crosse of Gold, & a few insignificant papers; & thereupon shewed us the Crosse, & was pleased to put it into my hand; it was of Gold about 3 Inches long, having on one side a Crucifix enameled & embossed, the rest was graved & garnished with gold-smith worke & two pretty broad table Amethists (as I conceived) & at the bottome a pendant pearle; within was inchas'd a little fragment (as was thought) of the true Crosse: & a latine Inscription, in Gotic & roman letters:

How his Majestie came by it I do not remember; for more company coming in this discourse ended: Onely I may not forget, a Resolution which his Majestie there made, & had a little before entered upon it, at the Counsels board at Windsor or White-hal: That the Negros in all the Plantations should be Baptized, exceedingly declaiming against that impiety, of their Masters prohibiting it, out of a mistake opinion, that they were then *ipso facto* free: But his Majestie persists in his resolution to have them Christn'd, which piety the Bishop, deservedly blessed him for; and so I went out, to see the New Palace his late Majestie had began, and brought almost to the Covering: It was placed on the side of the Hill, where formerly stood the old Castle: a stately fabrique of 3 sides, & a Corridor, all built of brique, & Cornished, windoes, Columns at the break & Entrance, of freestone: intended for a Hunting House, when his Majestie came to those parts, & having an incomparable prospect: I believe there had already ben 20000 pounds and more expended; but now his Majestie did not seem to encourage the finishing of it; at least for a while; & it is like to stand:

Hence I went to see the Cathedrall, a reverend pile, & in good repaire: There is still the Coffines of the 6 Saxon kings, whose bones had ben scattered by the sacrilegious Rebells of 1641, in expectation (I suppose) of finding some valuable Reliques; & afterward gather'd-up againe & put into new chests, which stand above the stalls of the Quire: Here lies the body of their Founder, of Card: & severall other Bishops &c: & so I went to my Lodging, very wett, it having rained the whole day:

17 Early next morning we went to Portsmouth, some thing before his Majestie arived: we found all the way full of people, the Women in their best dresse, multitudes of all sorts, in expectance of seeing his Majestie passe by, which he did, riding on horse-back, a good part of the way: We found the Major, his Aldermen with their Mace, & in their formalities standing at the Entrance of the Fort, a Mile on this side of the Towne, where he made a speech to the King, & then went off the Guns of the fort, as did all those of the Garison, so soone as he was come into Portsmouth, all the souldiers (which were neere 3000) drawn up, and lining the streetes, & platforme to Gods-house (which is the name of the Governors house) where (after his Majestie had viewed the new Fortifications, & Ship-yard) he was Entertained at a Magnificent dinner, by Sir <Henry> Singsby, the Lieutenant Governor; all the Gent: of any quality, in his traine setting downe at Table with him, & which I had also don, had I not ben before engag'd to Sir Robert Holmes (Governor of the Isle of Wight) to dine with him at a private house, where likewise we had a very sumptuous & plentifull repast of excellent Venison, Fowle, Fish, fruit, & what not: After dinner I went to waite on his Majestie againe, who was pulling on his boots in the Town hall joyning to the house where he dined, & then having saluted some Ladys &c: that came to kisse his hand; he tooke horse for

Winchester, whither he returned that night: This hall is artificialy hung round, with Armes of all sorts, like the Hall & keepe of Windsor, which looks very finely:

I went hence to see the Ship-yard, & Dock, the Fortifications, and other things: What I learned was, the facility of an armies taking the Ile of Wight, should an attempt be made by any Enemy, for want of due care in fortifying some places of it, & the plenty of the Iland, able to nourish 20000 men, besides its inhabitants: Portsmouth when finished will be very strong, & a Noble Key: There were now 32 Men of war in the Harbour: I was invited by Sir R: Beach, the <Commissioner> where after a greate supper, Mr. Secretary and my selfe lay-all that night: & the next morning set out for Gildford [18] where we arived in good houre, & so the day after to Lond: whence [19] taking leave of Mr. Pepys, I came home to my house, after a journey of 140 miles:

I had twice before ben at Portsmouth, Ile of Wight &c: many yeares since: I found this part of Hampshire bravely wooded; especialy about the house and estate of Coll: Norton, who (though now in being, having formerly made his peace by meanes of Coll Legg) was formerly a very fierce Commander in the first Rebellion: His house is large, & standing low, as one goes from Winchester to <Portsmouth>:

By what I observed in this Journey; I find that infinite industry, sedulity, gravity, and greate understanding & experience of affaires in his Majestie, that I cannot but predict much happinesse to the Nation, as to its political Government, & if he so persist (as I am confident he will) there could be nothing be more desired, to accomplish our prosperity, but that he were of the national Religion: for certainly such a Prince never had this Nation since it was one:

20: ... My Wifes & Daughter Susans pictures were drawn: This Weeke: ...

October 2 I spent this morning in Devotion, preparing for the Communion, when having a letter sent me by Mr. P<epys>, with this expression at the foote of it: *I have something to shew you, that I may not have againe another time*: &c & that I would not fail to dine with him: I went accordingly:

After dinner he had me, and one Mr. Houblon (a very rich & considerable Merchant, whose Fathers had fled out of Flanders upon the persecution of the Duke of Alva) into a private roome: & being sate downe, told us that being lately alone with his Majestie and upon some occasion of speaking concerning my late Lord Arlingtons dying a R: Cath, who had all along seemed to professe himselfe a Protestant, taken all the Tests &c: 'til the day (I think) of his death: His Majestie say'd, that as to his inclinations he had known him long wavering, but <for> feare of loosing his places [he] did not think convenient to declare himselfe: There are (says the King) who believe the Ch: of R: gives Dispensations, for going to church, & many like things; but that it was not so; for if that might have ben had, he himselfe had most reason to make use of it: Indeede he said, As to some Matrimonial Cases, there are now & then Dispensations, but hardly in any Cases else:

This familiar discourse encourag'd Mr. P: to beg of his Majestie (if he might aske it, without offence, and for that his Majestie could not but observe how it was whispered among many), [whither] his Late Majestie had ben reconcil'd to the C. of Rome: He againe humbly besought his Majestie to pardon his presumption, if he had touch'd upon a thing, did not befit him to looke into &c: The King ingenuously told him, That he both was, & died a R: Cath: & that he had not long since declared it was upon some politic & state reasons, best known to himself [(meaning the King his Brother)] but that he was of that persuasion, he bid him follow him into his Closett, where opening a Cabinet, he shew'd him two papers, containing about a quarter of a sheete on both sides, written in the late Kings owne hand, severall Arguments opposite to the Doctrine of the Church of Eng: Charging her with heresy, novelty, & [the] phan<tas>ticisme of other Protestants: The chiefe whereoff (as I remember) were, our refusing to accknowledge the Primacy & Infallibility &c of the Church of Rome, how impossible it was so many Ages should never dispute it, til of late; how unlikely our B: Saviour would leave his Church without a Visible Head & guide to resort to during his absence, with the like usual Topics; so well penn'd as to the discourse, as did by no means seeme to me, to have ben put together by the Late King: Yet written all with his owne hand, blotted, & interlin'd, so as if indeede, it were not given him by some Priest; they happly might be such Arguments and reasons as had ben inculcated from time to time, & here recollected, & in the conclusion shewing his looking on the Protestant Religion, (& by name the Church of Eng:) to be without foundation, & consequently false & unsafe:

When his Majestie had shew'd him these Originals, he was pleas'd to lend him the Copies of those two Papers, attested at the bottome in 4 or 5 lines, under his owne hand: These were the papers I saw & read: This nice & curious passage I thought fit to set downe; Though all the Arguments, and objections were altogether weake, & have a thousand times ben Answerd irreplicably by our Divines; though such as their Priests insinuate among their Proselytes, as if nothing were Catholique but the C. of Rome, no salvation out of that, no Reformation sufferable &c: botoming all their Errors on St. Peters Successors unerrable dictatorship; but proving nothing with any sort of Reason, or the taking notice of any Objection which could be made against it: Here was all taken for granted, & upon it a Resolution & preference it implied:

I was heartily sorry to see all this; though it were no other, than what was long suspected, by his late Majesties too greate indifference, neglect & course of Life, that he had ben perverted, & for secular respects onely, profess'd to be of another beliefe; [See 6: Feb 1684/5] & thereby giving infinite advantage to our Adversaries, both the Court, & generaly the Youth, & greate persons of the nation becoming dissolute & highly prophane; God was incensed to make his Reigne very troublesome & improsperous, by Warrs, plagues, fires, losse of reputation by a universal neglect of the publique, for the love of a voluptuous & sensual life, which a vitious Court had brought into credit. I think of it with sorrow & pitty, when I consider of how good & debonaire a nature that unhappy prince was, what opportunities he had to have made himselfe the most renouned King, that ever sway'd the British Scepter; had he ben firme to that Church, for which his Martyred & Bl: Father suffer'd; & gratefull to Almighty God, who so miraculously Restor'd him, with so excellent a Religion had he endeavored to owne & propagate it, as he should, not onely for the good of his Kingdomes, but all the Reformed Churches in Christendome, now weaken'd, & neere utterly ruind, through our remissnesse, & suffering them to be supplanted, persecuted & destroyed; as in France, which we tooke no notice of: The Consequence of this time will shew, & I wish it may proceede no farther: The Emissaries & Instruments of the C. of R: will never rest, 'til they have crush'd the Church of Eng: as knowing that alone able to cope with them: and that they can never answer her fairely, but lie aboundantly open to <irresistible> force of her Arguments, Antiquity, & purity of her doctrine: so that albeit it may move God (for the punishment of a Nation so unworthy) to eclipse againe the profession of her here; & darknesse & superstition prevaile; I am most confident the Doctrine of the Church of

Eng: will never be extinguish'd, but to remaine Visible, though not Eminent, to the consummation of the World: I have innumerable reasons that confirme me in this opinion, which I forbeare to mention here:

In the meane time, as to This discourse of his Majestie with Mr. Pepys, & those Papers; as I do exceedingly preferr his Majesties free & ingenuous profession, of what his owne Religion is, beyond all Concealements upon any politique accounts what so ever; so I think him of [a] most sincere, and honest nature, upon whose word, one may relie, & that he makes a Conscience of what he promises, to performe it: In this Confidence I hope, the Church of England may yet subsist; & when it shall please God, to open his Eyes, & turne his heart (for that is peculiarly in the Lords hands) to flourish also: In all events, whatever do become of the C. of Eng: It is certainely of all the Christian professions on the Earth, the most Primitive, Apostolical, & Excellent: ...

8 To Lond: return'd that Evening: I had my picture drawn this Week: [by the famous Kneller:][1] ...

14 I went to Lond: about my Suite, & finishing my Lodgings at White-hall.

15 Being the Kings birth-day, was a solemn Ball at Court; And Musique of Instruments & Voices before the Ball: At the Musique I happen<ed> (by accident) to stand the very next to the Queene, & the King, who ta<l>ked with me about Musick: ...

The King was now building all that range from East to west by the Court & Garden to the streete, & making a new Chapel for the Queene, whose Lodgings this new building was: as also a new Council Chamber & offices next the South end of the Banqueting-house: ...

22 I accompanied my Lady Clarendon to her house at Swallowfield in Berkeshire, dining by the way at Mr. Grahams's Lodge at Bagshot: Where his Lady (my excellent & long acquaintance when maide of honour) entertain'd us at a plentifull dinner: The house, new repaired, and capacious of a good family, stands in a Park: Hence we went to Swallow-fild the house is after the antient building of honourable gent: houses where they kept up the antient hospitality: But the Gardens & Waters as elegant as 'tis possible to make a flat, with art & Industrie and no meane Expenses, my Lady being so extraordinarily skilld in the flowry part: & the dilligence of my Lord in the planting: so that I have hardly seene a seate which shews more toakens of it, then what is here to be found, not onely in the delicious & rarest fruits of a Garden, but in those innumerable & plentifull furniture of the grounds about the seate of timber trees to the incredible ornament & benefit of the place:

There is one Ortchard of a 1000 Golden & other cider Pepins: Walks & groves of Elms, Limes, Oake: & other trees: & the Garden so beset with all manner of sweete shrubs, as perfumes the aire marvelously: The distribution also of the Quarters, Walks, Parterre &c is excellent: The Nurseries, Kitchin-garden, full of the most desireable plants; two very noble Orangeries well furnish'd; but above all, The Canale, & fishponds, the one fed with a white, the other with a black-running water, fed by swift & quick river: so well & plentifully stor'd with fish, that for Pike, Carp, Breame, & Tench; I had never seene any thing approching it: we had Carps & Pikes &c of size fit for

---

[1] Kneller painted E four years later (see 9 July 1689) for Pepys, a painting which survives. The whereabouts of this painting is unknown but as the artist's name is a marginal addition here E may have made a mistake, and the artist may have been a different one.

the table of a Prince, every meale, & what added to the delight, the seeing hundreds taken in the drag, out of which the Cooke standing by, we pointed what we had most mind to, & had Carps every meale, that had ben worth at London twenty shill a piece: The Waters are all flag'd about with *Calamus arromaticus*;[1] of which my Lady has hung a Closset, that retaines the smell very perfectly: Also a certaine sweete willow & other exotics: There is to this a very fine bowling-greene; Meadow, pasture, Wood, in a word all that can render a Country seate delightfull: ...

28 I went to the R: Society, being the first meeting after our Summer recesse, & was very full: An Urn full of bones, was presented, for the repository, dug up in an high way, by the repairers of it: in a field in Camberwell in Surry: This Urn & cover was found intire among many others; believed to be truely Roman & antient: Sir Ri: Bulkeley, described to us a model of a Charriot he had invented, which it was not possible to overthrow, in whatsoever uneven way it was drawn: giving us a stupendious relation, of what it had perform'd in that kind; for Ease, expedition, & Safty: There was onely these inconveniences yet to be remedied; that it would not containe above one person; That it was ready to fire every 10 miles, & being plac'd & playing on no fewer than 10 rollers, made so prodigious noise, as was almost intollerable: These particulars the Virtuosi were desir'd to excogitate the remedies, to render the Engine of extraordinary Use: &c:

31 I dined at our greate Lord Chancellors, who us'd me with greate respect: This was the late L: C. Justice Jeofries, who had ben newly the Western Circuite, to trie the Monmoth Conspirators; & had formerly don such severe Justice among the obnoxious in Westminster Hall &c for which his Majestie dignified him with creating him first a Baron, & now L. Chancellor: He had some yeares past, ben conversant at Deptford: is of an assur'd & undaunted spirit, & has serv'd the Court Interest upon all the hardiest occasions: [of nature cruell & a slave of this Court.]

I had now accomplish'd the 65t yeare of my Age: Lord teach me to Number my daies, so as to employ their remainder to thy glory onely. Amen: ...

November 3 I returned home: The French persecution of the Protestants, raging with uttmost barbarity, exceeding what the very heathens used: Innumerable persons of the greatest birth, & riches, leaving all their earthly substance & hardly escaping with their lives, dispers'd thro' all the Countries of Europe: The Fr: Tyrant, abrogating the Edicts of Nants &c in favour of them, & without any Cause on the suddaine, demolishing all their Churches, banishing, Imprisoning, sending to the Gallies all the Ministers: plundring the common people, & exposing them all sorts of barbarous usage, by souldiers sent to ruine & prey upon them; taking away their children; forcing people to the Masse, & then executing them as Relapsers: They burnt the libraries, pillag'd their goods, eate up their filds & sustenance, banish'd or sent to the Gallies the people, & seiz'd on their Estates:

There had now ben numbred to passe through Geneva onely, from time to time by stealth onely (for all the usual passages were strictly guarded by sea & land) fourty thousand, towards Swisserland: In Holland, Denmark, & all about Germany, were dispersed some hundred thousands besids here in England, where though multitude of all degrees sought for shelter, & wellcome, as distressed Christians & Confessors, they found least encouragement; by a fatality of the times we were fall'n into, & the incharity & indifference of

---

[1] Sweet calamus, a type of reed.

such, as should have embrac'd them: and I pray, it be not laied to our Charge: The famous Claude fled to Holland: Alex & severall more came to Lond: & persons of mighty estates came over who had forsaken all: But France was almost dispeopled, the bankers so broaken that the Tyrants revenue exceedingly diminished: Manufacture ceased, & every body there save the Jesuites &c. abhorring what was don: nor the Papists themselves approving it; what the intention farther is time will shew, but doubtlesse portending some extraordinary revolution:

I was now shew'd the Harangue that the Bishop of Valentia on Rhone, made in the name of the Cleargie, celebrating the Fr: King (as if he were a God) for his persecuting the poore protestants; with this Expression in it: That as his Victories over Heresy was greater than all the Conquests of Alexander & Caesars &c: it was but what was wished in England: & that God seem'd to raise the French King to this power & magnanimous action, that he might be in capacity to assist the doing of the same here: This paragraph is very bold & remarkable; severall reflecting on AB: Ushers Prophecy as now begun in France, & approching the orthodox in all other reformed Churches: &c: One thing was much taken notice of, That the Gazetts which were still constantly printed twice a weeke, & informing us what was don all Europ over &c: never all this time, spake one syllable of this wonderfull proceeding in France, nor was any Relation of it published by any, save what private letters & the persecuted fugitives brought: Whence this silence, I list not to conjecture, but it appeared very extraordinary in a Protestant Countrie, that we should know nothing of what Protestants suffered &c: whilst greate Collections were made for them in forraine places more hospitable & Christian to appearance.

5 It being an extraordinary wett morning, & I indisposed by a very greate rheume, I could not go to Church this day, to my greate sorrow, it being the first Gunpouder conspiracy Anniversary, that had ben kept now this 80 yeares, under a Prince of the Roman Religion: Bonfires forbidden &c: What dos this portend? ...

9 Began the Parliament; The King in his Speech requiring continuance of a standing force in stead of a Militia, & indemnity & dispensation to Popish Officers from the Test; Demands very unexpected & unpleasing to the Commons; He also requird a Supply of Revenue, which they granted; but returned no thanks to the King for his Speech 'til farther consideration: ...

20 Was the Parliament adjourn'd to ffeb: Severall both of Lords & Commons, excepting against some passage of his Majesties Speech, relating to the Test, & continuance of Popish Officers in Command: This was a greate surprize to a Parliament, which people believed would have complied in all things:

Popish pamphlets & Pictures sold publiqly: no books or answers against them appearing &c: [till long after:] ...

December 15 Dining at Mr. Pepyss Secretary of the Admiral<ty>, & still president of our Society: Dr. Slayer shew'd us an Experiment of a wonderfull nature; pouring first a very cold liquor into a Matras, & superfusing on it another (to appearance) cold & cleare liquor also, it first produced a white clowd, then boiling, divers Corruscations & actual flames of fire mingled with the liquor, which being a little shaken together fixed divers sunns and starrs of real fire perfectly globular upon the walls of the Glasse to our greate astonishment, & which there stuck like so many Constellations burning most vehemently, & exceedingly resembling starrs & heavenly bodyes, & that for a long space: It seem'd to exhibite a Theorie of the eduction of light out of the

Chäos, & the fixing or gathering of the universal light, into luminous bodys: This matter of Phosphorus, was made out of human blood & Urine, elucidating the Vital flame or heate in Animal bodys: a very noble Experiment: ...

18 I dind at the greate entertainement his Majestie gave the Venetian Ambassadors Signors Zenno & Justiniani, accompanied with 10 more Noble Venetians of their most illustrious families Cornaro, Maccenigo &c, who came to Congratulate their Majesties coming to the Crowne &c: The dinner was one of the most magnificent & plentifull that I have ever seene, at 4 severall Tables with Music, Trumpets, Ketle-drums which sounded upon a whistle at every health: The banquet was 12 vast Chargers pild up so high, as those who sat one against another could hardly see one another, of these Sweetemeates which doub<t>lesse were some dayes piling up in that exquisite manner, the Ambassadors touched not, but leaving them to the Spectators who came in Curiosity to see the dinner, &c were exceedingly pleas'd to see in what a moment of time, all that curious work was demolish'd, & the Comfitures &c voided & table clear'd: Thus his Majestie entertain'd them 3 dayes, which (for the table onely) cost him 600 pounds as the Cleark of the Greene-Cloth Sir W: Boreman assur'd me: Dinner ended, I saw their procession or Cavalcade to W:hall, innumerable Coaches attending: The 2 Ambassadors had 4. Coaches of their owne & 50 footemen, as I remember, besides other Equipage as splended as the occasion would permitt, the Court being still in mourning, Thence I went to the Audience which they had in the Queenes presence Chamber: The banqueting-house being full of goods & furniture til the Galleries on the Garden side, Council Chamber & new Chapell, were finish'd, now in building: They went to their Audience in those plaine black Gownes, [& Caps] which they constantly weare in the Citty of Venice: I was invited to have accompanied the two Ambassadors in their Coach to supper that night, returning now to their owne Lodgings, as no longer at the Kings expense, but being weary, I excus'd my selfe: ...

22 Our pattent for executing the Office of the Lord Privy-Seale, during the absence of the L: Lieutennant of Ireland, being this day sealed by the L: Chancellor: We went afterwards to St. James's, where the Court then was, upon occasion of the building at White-hall, where his Majestie deliverd The Seale to My L: Tiveat & my-selfe (the other Commissioner being not come) and then, gave us his hande to kisse: There was the 2 Venetian Ambassadors & a world of Company, amongst the rest, The first Popes Nuntio Signor <Ferdinando conte D'Adda> that had ever ben in England since the Reformation; so wonderfully were things chang'd, to the universal jealosie &c:

24 We were all three Commissioners sworn on our knees by the Cleark of the Crowne before my Lord Chancellor, 3, severall Oathes, Allegeance, Supremacy, & the oath belonging to the L: Privy-Seale, which we onely tooke standing: After which the L. Chancellor invited us all to dinner; but it being Christmas Eve, we desir'd to be excus'd; at 3 in the afternoone intending to Seale divers things which lay ready at the Office: So attended by three of the Clearks of the Signet, we met, & sealed; amongst other things, one was a Pardon to West, who being privy to the late Conspiricy, had reveald the Complices, to save his owne neck: There was also another pardon, & two Indenizations: & so agreeing to a fortnights vaccation, I return'd home to my house: ...

31 Recollecting the passages of the yeare past [I] made up Accompts, humbly besought Almighty God, to pardon those my sinns, which had

provok'd him to discomposse my sorrowfull family, that he would accept of our humiliation, & in his good time restore comforte to it: I also blesse God for all his undeserved mercys & preservations, beging the continuance of his grace & preservation: The winter had hitherto ben extraordinarily wett, & mild:

1686

January 6 I went to Lond: to our Office, din'd with the L. Arch-Bish: of Yorke, where was Peter-Walsh that Romish Priest, who was so well known for his moderation; professing the Ch: of England to be a true member of the Chatholique Church; he is used to go to our publique prayers without scrupule, did not acknowledge the Popes Infallibility, & onely primacy of Order &c. I returned this Evening: ...

19 I went to Lond: pass'd the Privie Seale amongst others, the Creation of Mrs. Sidly (concubine to ...)[1] Countesse of Dorchester, which 'tis certaine the Queene tooke very grievously: so as for two dinners, standing neere her, she hardly eate one morsel, nor spake one word to the King, or to any about her, who at all other times us'd to be extreamely pleasant, full of discourse & good humor: The Roman Cath: were also very angrie, because the<y> had so long valu'd the Sanctite of their Religion & Prosleytes &c:

Dryden the famous play-poet & his two sonns, & Mrs. Nelle (Misse to the late <King>) were said to go to Masse; & such purchases were no greate losse to the Church. This night was burnt to the Ground my Lord Montagues Palace in Bloom<s>bery; than which for Painting & furniture, there was nothing more glorious in England: This happen'd by the negligence of a servant, airing (as they call it) some of the goods by the fire, in a moist season; for indeede so wett & mild a Winter had scarce ben ever seene in mans memory:

At this Seale there also passed, the creation of Sir H: Walgrave to be a Lord: He had married one of the Kings natural Daughters, begotten on Mrs. Churchil: These two Seales, my Bro: Commissioners pass'd in the morning before I came to Towne, at which I was not at all displeas'd; We likewise pass'd privy seales for 276000 pounds upon severall accounts, Pensions, Guards, Wardrobes, Privie purse &c, besids divers Pardons: & one more which I must not forget (& which by providence, I was not present at) one Mr. Lytcott, to be Secretarie to the Ambassador to Rome: we being three Commissioners [any] two were a Quorum ...

February 6: Being his Majesties day, on which he began his Reigne; By Order of Council, it was to be solemniz'd with a particular Office, & sermon, which the Bis: of Ely preached at W:hall: on 11: Numbers: 12: a Court-Oration, upon the Regal Office &c: It was much wonder'd at; that this day which was that of his late Majesties death, should be kept as festival, & not the day of the present Kings Coronation: It is said, that it had formerly ben the costome, though not 'til now, since the Reigne of K. James. 1 ...

March 1 Came Sir Gilb: Gerrard to treate with me about his sons marying my Daughter Susanna; The father being obnoxious, & in some suspicion &

---

[1] E politely leaves the King's name out of any association with Catherine Sedley.

displeasure of the King, I would receive no proposal, 'til his Majestie had given me leave, which he was pleas'd to do: but after severall meetings, we brake off, upon his not being willing to secure any thing competant for my daughter<s> Children: besides that I found his estate to be most of it in the Coale-pits as far as N.Castle, & leases from the Bishop of Durrham, who had power to make concurrent Leases with other difficulties, so as we did not proceede to any conclusion: ...

12 There was a doquett to be sealed importing a Lease of 21 yeares to one Hall, who styled himselfe his Majesties Printer (& lately turn'd Papist) for the printing Missals, Offices, Lives of Saints, Portals, Primers &c: books expressly forbidden to be printed or sold, &c by divers Acts of Parliament: which I refused to put the seale to, & made my exceptions against, so it was laied by: ...

16 I was at the [review of the] Army about Lond: which was in Hide-parke, the whole consisting of about 6000: horse & foote in excellent order &c: his Majestie & an infinity of people present:

17 I went to my house in the Country, refusing to be present at what was to passe the next day at the Privy-Seale: ...

28 ... I supped this night at my L: Tressurers: discoursed with my Lady Tennet, who pretended to some more than ordinary talent of knowledge &c: ...

A Briefe was read in all the Churches for Relieving the French Protestants who came here for protection, from the unheard-off, cruelties of their King: ...

April 15 ... Little Fr:Godolphin was now sick of the small pox, I pray God be gracious to that precious Chld:

The Arch-Bish: of Yorke now died of the small-pox, aged 62 yeares, a Corpulent man; My special loving Friend, & whilst our Bish: of Rochester (from whence he was translated) my excellent Neighbour, an unexpressible losse to the whole Church, & that Province especialy, he being a learned, Wise, stoute, and most worthy prelate; so as I looke on this as a greate stroke to the poore Church of England now in this defecting period:

18 ... Afternoone I went to Camberwell to visite Dr. Par: but sate so inconveniently at Church, that I could very hardly heare his Text, which was 5.Heb:9: After sermon I went to the Doctors house, where he shew'd me The life and Letters of the late learned Primate of Armagh, Usher, and among them that letter of Bish: Bramhals to the Primate, giving notice of the popish practices to pervert this nation, by sending an hundred priests &c into England, who were to conforme themselves to all Sectaries, and Conditions for the more easily dispersing their doctrine amongst us: This Letter was the cause of the whole Impressions being seiz'd on, upon pretence, that it was a political or historical account, of things, not relating to Theologie, though it had ben licenc'd by the Bish: &c: which plainely shewe'd what an Interest the Popish now had, that a Protestant Booke, containing the life, & letters of so eminent a man was not to be publish'd. There were also many letters to & from most of the learned persons his correspondents in Europ: but The Booke will, (I doubt not) struggle through this unjust impediment.

20 To Lond: a seale – & to see little Godolphin now, I blesse God, in an hope full way of Escape: Severall Judges put out, & new complying ones put in.

24 I returned home, found my Coach-man dangerously ill of vomiting greate quantities of blood: ...

May 5 To Lond: There being a Seale, it was feared we should be required to passe a Doquett, Dispensing with Dr. Obadia Walker & 4 more, wheroff one an Apostate Curate at Putney, the other Master of University Coll: Ox: to hold their Masterships, fellowships & Cures, & keepe pub: schooles & enjoy all former emoluments &c. notwithstanding they no more frequented, or used the pub: formes of Prayers, or Communion with the Church of England, or tooke the Test, & oathes of Allegeance & Supremacy, contrary to 20 Acts of Parliaments &c: which Dispensation being likewise repugnant to his Majesties owne gracious declaration at the begining of his Reigne, gave umbrage (as well it might) to every good Protestant: nor could we safely have passed it under the Privy-Seale: wherefore it was don by Immediate warrant, sign'd by Mr. Solicitor &c at which I was not a little glad: This Walker was a learned person, of a munkish life, to whose Tuition I had more than 30 yeares since, recommended the sonns of my worthy friend Mr. Hyldiard of Horsley in Surry: believing him to be far from what he proved, an hypocritical concealed papist, by which he perverted the Eldest son of Mr. Hyldyard, Sir Ed. Hales's eld: son & severall more [&] to the greate disturbance of the whole nation, as well as the University, as by his now publique defection appeared: All engines being now at worke to bring in popery amaine, which God in mercy prevent:

This day was burnt, in the old Exchange, by the publique Hang-man, a booke (supposed to be written by the famous Monsieur Claude) relating the horrid massacres & barbarous proceedings of the Fr:King against his Protestant subjects, without any refutation, that might convince it of any thing false: so mighty a power & ascendant here, had the French Ambassador: doubtlesse in greate Indignation at the pious & truly generous Charity of all the Nation, for the reliefe of those miserable sufferers, who came over for shelter: ...

I procur'd of my L.president of the Council, the nomination of a son of Mrs. Cock, a Widdow (formerly living plentifully, now falln to want) to be chosen into the Charter-house Schoole, which would be a competent subsistence for him: ...

8 Died my sick Coachman of his feavor, to my greate griefe, being a very honest, faithfull servant: I beseech the Lord, to take-off his afflicting hand, in his good time ...

12 To Lond: Memorand, I refus'd to put the P: Seale to Dr. Walker<s> licence for the printing & publishing divers Popish Books &c: of which I complain'd both to my L: of Canterbury (whom I went to advise with, which was in the Council-chamber) and to my Lord Treasurer that evening at his lodging: My Lord of Cantorburies advise was that I should follow my owne Conscience therein; my Tressurer, that if in Conscience I could dispence with it; for any hazard, he believed there was none: Notwithstanding which I persisted not to do it: ...

16 A stranger on: 2: Zeph: 1.2.3. Afternoone, on: 2.Tit:11.12 &c: both practical sermons exhorting to Repentance upon prospect of the ruines threatning the Church, & drawing on for our prodigious Ingratitude, & doubtlesse Never was England so perverted, through an almost universal face of prophanesse, perjury, luxurie, unjustice, violence, hypocrisie, Atheisme, & dissolution: A kingdome & a people so obliged to God, for its long prosperity, both in Church & state: so signaly delivered, and preserved: & now threatn'd to be destroyed, by our owne folly & wickednesse: How strangely is this nation fallen from its antient zeale & Integritie! ô unhappy, unthankfull people! ...

June 2 To Lond: passing divers Pardons & other doquetts:

Such stormes, <raine> & foule weather hardly ever know<n> at this season: The Camp now on Hounslo-Heath forc'd for sicknesse and other Inconveniences of Weather to retire to quarters: ...

9 To Lond: a Seale, most pardons, & discharges, of Knight Baronets fees; which having ben pass'd over for so many yeares, did greately dissoblige several families who had serv'd his Majestie. – The Camp now at Brainford [Hounslow] after exceeding <wet> & stormy weather, now as excessively hott; many grew sick: greate feasting there, especialy in my L:Dunbarton<s> quarters: many jealosies & discourse what the meaning of this incampment of an army should be: – L:Terconell gon to Ireland with greate powers & commissions – giving as much cause of talke as the other: especialy 19 new Pr:Councelors being now made & Judges, among which but three protestants: & Terconell made [L.] Generall: New-Judges also here, among which Milton a papist, & bro: to the Milton who wrot for the Regicides, who presum'd to take his place, without passing the Test: – Scotland, refuse to grant Liberty of Masse to the Papists in Scotland: – The French persecution more inhumane than ever &c: The Protestants in Savoy, successfully resist the French Dragoons, perfidiously murdering them. – The booke written by Monsieur Claude to informe the world of the cruel persecution by France: Translated here burnt by the hangman, so greate was the Interest of the Fr: Ambassador, as was said: It seem'd to relate onely matter of fact, very modestly: & was thought a severe treatement; his Majestie having both given protection, & reliefe to the Refugies: It was thought hard, that the people should not know for what & to whom they gave so bountifully. – The Kings chiefe physitian in Scotland, Apostasizing from the protestant Religion, dos of his owne accord publique Recantation at Edenbrugh. -

11 I went to see Midletons – receptacle of Waters at the New River:[1] & the new Spa wells neere it ...

July 12 I went to visite Dr. Godolphin vice-Provost of Eton, & dined with him in the Colledge: among the Fellows: It is an admirable foundation:

13 I return'd to Lond: Note, that standing by the Queene at Basset (Cards) I observ'd that she was exceedingly concern'd for the losse of 80 pounds: her outward affability much changed to statelinesse & since she has ben exalted: ...

14 Was sealed at our Office the Constitution of certaine Commissioners to take upon them the full power of all Ecclesiastical Affaires, in as unlimited a manner, or rather greater, than the late High-Commission Court, abbrogated by Parliament: for it had not onely faculty to Inspect & Visite all Bishops diocesses, but to change what lawes & statutes they shold think fit to alter, among the Colledges, though founded by private men; to punish [suspend] fine &c give Oathes, call witnesses, but the maine drift was to <suppresse> zealous Preachers &c – In summ, it was the whole power of Viccar General, note the Consequence – The Commissioners were of the Cleargy, the A Bish of Cant: Bishops of Duresme, Rochester:- of the Temporal: L:Tressurer, Chancellor (who alone was ever to be of the quorum) Chiefe Justice, L:President: ...

---

[1] A 38 mile long channel begun in 1609 and completed in 1613 by Sir Hugh Myddleton (c. 1560-1631) to bring Hertfordshire water to London with a reservoir ('receptacle') at New River Head, Clerkenwell.

21 ... Evening, having ben at the R:Society, where was a Wind Gun brought & tried, which first shot a bullet with a powder Charge, & then discharged 4 severall times with bullets, by the wind onely, every shoote at competent distance piercing a thick board: The Wind-Chamber was fastned to the barrill through the stock, with Valves to every <charge> so as they went off 4 successive times: I<t> was a very curious piece, made at Amsterdam, not bigger than a pretty Birding piece: Note, that the drawing up of the Cock alone <admitted> so much aire into a small receptacle at the britch of the piece out of the Chamber or magazine of aire underneath as suffic'd for a charge, which was exploded by pulling downe the Cock by the Triccker: (a) the wind Chamber [of brasse], to scrue into the barrell thro the stock, at (b): note, that it was fill'd with an [aire] pumpe:

27 This day was bound Apprentice to me, & serve as a Gardner, Jonathan Mosse, to serve from 24 June 1686: to 24 June –92, being six yeares: ...

August 8 ... I went to visite the Marquis de Ruvignie now my Neighbour at Greenewich, he had <been> 'til this cruel persecution in France (whence he was now retir'd) the Deputy of all the Protestants of that Kingdome in the Parliament of Paris, & severall times Ambassador in this & other Courts; a Person of greate Learning & experience: ...

September 8 ... The Bish: of Lond was on Monday suspended on pretence of not silencing Dr. Sharp of St. Giles's, for something of a sermon, in which he zealously reproov'd the Doctrine of the R.C. The Bish: having consulted the Civilians, who told him, he could not by any Law proceede against Dr. Sharp, without producing wittnesses, & impleading according to forme &c: But it was over-ruled by my L:Chancelor & the Bishop sentenc'd, without so much as being heard to any purpose: which was thought a very extraordinary way of proceeding, & universaly resented; & so much the rather, for that 2 Bish: Durham, & Rochester, sitting in the Commission, & giving their suffrages: The AB: of Cant: refusing to sit amongst them: What the issue of this will be, Time will shew: ...

October 14: His Majesties Birth day, I was at his Majesties rising in his Bed-Chamber: Afterwards in the [Hide] Parke where his Majesties 4: Comp: of Guards were drawn up: Such horse & men as could not be braver: The Officers &c: wonderfully rich & gallant: They did not head their troops, but their next officers; the Colonels &c: being on Horse <back> by the King, whilst they marched: The Ladys not lesse splendid at Court, where was a Ball that night; but small appearance of qualitie: This day all the shops both in Citty & suburbs shut up, and kept as solemnly as any holy-day: Bone-fires at night in Westminster &c: but forbidden in the Citty: ...

22 To Lond: the next day with my Lady the Countesse of Sunderland, I went [23] to Cranburne, a Lodge & walke of my Lord Godolphins, in Windsor parke: there was one roome in the house, spared in the pulling-downe the old one, because the late Dutchesse of Yorke, was borne in it, the rest was build & added to it by Sir Geo: Carteret, Tressurer of the Navy: & since the whole

purchased by my Lord Godolphin, who spake to me to go see it, and advise what trees were fit to be cut downe, to improve the dwelling, it being invironed with old rotten pollards, which corrupt the aire: It stands on a knowle, which though insensibly rising, gives it a prospect over the keepe of Windsore, which is about three miles north-east of it: The ground is clayy & moist, the water stark nought: The Park is pretty; The house tollerable & gardens convenient: after dinner we came back to Lond, having 2 Coaches both going and coming, of 6 horses a-piece, which we changed at Hounslow: ...

November 16 I went with part of my family to passe the melancholy winter in Lond: at my sonns house in Arundel Buildings: ...

26 I din'ed at my L.Chancelors, where being 3 other Serjants at Law, after dinner being cherefull & free, they told their severall stories, how long they had detained their clients in tedious processes, by their tricks, as [if] so many highway thieves should have met & discovered the severall purses they had taken: This they made but a jeast of: but God is not mocked: ...

December 16 I carried the Countesse of Sunderland to see the rarities of one Mr. Charleton at the Middle Temple, who shewed us such a Collection of Miniatures, Drawings, Shells, Insects, Medailes, & natural things, Animals whereoff divers were kept in glasses of Sp: of wine, I think an hundred, besids, Minerals, precious stones, vessels & curiosities in Amber, Achat, chrystal &c: as I had never in all my Travells abroad seene any either of private Gent: or Princes exceede it; all being very perfect & rare in their kind, espec<i>aly his booke of Birds, Fish: flowers, shells &c drawn & miniatured to the life, he told us that one book stood him in 300 pounds: it was painted by that excellent workeman whom the late Gastion duke of Orleans emploied: This Gent:'s whole Collection (gathered by himselfe travelling most parte of Europe) is estimated at 8000 pounds: He seem'd a Modest and obliging person:

1687

January 5 The French K. now sayd to be healed or rather patch'd up of the *fistula in Ano*,[1] for which he had ben severall times cut: &c: The persecution still raging:

I was to heare the Musique of the Italians in the new Chapel, now first of all opned at White-hall publiquely for the Popish Service: Nothing can be finer than the magnificent Marble work & Architecture at the End, where are 4 statues representing st. Joh: st. Petre, st. Paule, & the Church, statues in white marble, the worke of Mr. Gibbons, with all the carving & Pillars of exquisite art & greate cost: The history or altar piece is the Salutation, The Volto, in fresca, the Asumption of the blessed Virgin according to their Traditions with our B:Saviour, & a world of figures, painted by Verio. The thrones where the K. & Q: sits is very glorious in a Closset above just opposite to the Altar: Here we saw the Bishop in his Miter, & rich Copes, with 6 or 7: Jesuits & others in Rich Copes richly habited, often taking off, & putting on the Bishops Miter, who sate in a Chaire with Armes pontificaly, was adored, & censed by 3

---

[1] Rectal ulcer.

Jesuits in their Copes, then he went to the Altar & made divers Cringes there, censing the Images, & glorious Tabernacle placed upon the Altar, & now & then changing place; The Crosier (which was of silver) put into his hand, with a world of mysterious Ceremony the Musique pla<y>ing & singing: & so I came away: not believing I should ever have lived to see such things in the K. of Englands palace, after it had pleas'd God to inlighten this nation; but our greate sinn, has (for the present) Eclips'd the Blessing, which I hope he will in mercy & his good time restore to its purity. This was on the 29 of December: ...

17 ... Greate expectations of severall greate-mens declaring themselves Papists: and L:Tyrconell gon to succeede my Lord Lieutennant in Ireland, to the astonishment of all sober men, & to the evident ruine of the Protestants in that Kingdome, as well as of its greate Improvement: Much discourse that all the White-staff-Officers and others should be dismissed for adhering to their Religion: Popish Justices of Peace established in all Counties of the meanest of the people: Judges ignorant of the Law, and perverting it: so furiously does the Jesuite drive, & even compell Princes to violent courses, & distruction of an excellent Government both in Church & State: God of his infinite mercy open our Eyes, & turne our hearts, Establish his Truth, with peace: the L: Jesus Defend his little flock, & preserve this threatned church & Nation ...

30 ... I heard the famous Cifeccio (Eunuch) sing, in the new popish chapell this afternoone, which was indeede very rare, & with greate skill: He came over from Rome, esteemed one of the best voices in Italy, much crowding, little devotion: ...

March 2 ... Came out now a Proclamation for Universall liberty of Conscience in Scotland and dispensation from all Tests & Lawes to the Contrary; as also capacitating Papists to be chosen into all Offices of Trust: &c. *The Mysterie operats* ...

10 His Majestie sent to the Commissioners of the Privy-Seale this morning into his bed-chamber, & told us that [tho] he had thought fit to dispose of the Seale, into a single hand, yet he would [so] provide for us, as it should appeare how well he accepted of our faithfull & loyal service, with many gracious expressions to this effect: upon which we delivered the Seales into his Majesties hands – It was by all the world both hoped & expected his Majestie would have restor'd it to my Lord Clarendon againe; but they were astonish'd to see it given to my L. Arundel of Wardour, a zealous Rom: Catholique: & indeede it was very hard, and looked very unkindly, his Majestie (as my L:Clarendon protested to me, going to visite him & long discoursing with him about the affaires of Ireland) finding not the least failor of duty in him during all his government of that Kingdome: so as his recalling, plainely appeared to be from the stronger Influence of the Papists, who now got all the preferments:

Most of the greate officers both in Court, [& Country] Lords & others, dismissed, who would not promise his Majestie their consent to repealing the Test, & penal statutes against the Romish recusants: There was to this end most of the Parliament men, spoken to in his Majesties Closset, & such as refused, if in any place, or office of Trust, Civil, or military, put out of their Employments: This was a time of greate trial: Hardly one of them assenting, which put the Popish Interest much backward: The English Cleargy, every where very boldly preaching against their Superstition & errors, and wonderfully follow'd by the people, not one considerable proselyte being made in all this time. The party so exceedingly put to the worst by the preaching & writing of the Protestants, in many excellent Treatises, evincing the doctrine & discipline of the Reformed Religion, to the manifest disadvantage of their Adversarys: & to which did not a little contribute [13] the Sermon preached now at W-hall before the Princesse of Denmark, & an innumerable crowde of people, & at least 30 of the greatest nobility, by Dr. Ken:Bish: of Bath & Wells, upon 8:John:46 (the Gospel of the day) all along that whole discourse describing the blasphemies, perfidie, wresting of Scriptures, preference of Traditions before it, spirit of persecution, superstition, Legends & fables, of the Scribes & pharisees; so as all the Auditory understood his meaning of paralleling them with the Romish Priests, & their new Trent Religion: Exhorting the people to adhere to the Written-Word, & to persevere in the Faith tought in the Church of England, whose doctrine for Catholique & soundnesse, he preferr'd to all the Communit<i>es & Churches of Christians in the whole-world; & concluding with a kind of prophesy, that whatsoever it suffer'd, it should after a short trial Emerge to the confusion of her Adversaries, & the glory of God:

I went this Evening to see the order of the Boys & children at Christs hospital, there was neere 800 of them, Boys & Girles: so decently clad, cleanely lodged, so wholesomly fed, so admirably taught, some the Mathematics, Especialy the 40 of the late Kings foundation; that I was plainly astonished to see the progresse some little youths of 13 & 14 yeares of age, had made: I saw them at supper, visited their dormitories, admired the order, Oeconomie, & excellent government of this most charitable seminary: The rest, some are tought for the Universitie, others designed for seamen, all for Trades & Callings: The Girles instructed in all such worke as became their Sex, as might fit them to make good Wives, Mistresses, & a blessing to their generation: They sung a Psalme before they sat downe to supper in the greate hall, to an Organ which played all the time, & sung with that cherefull harmony, as seem'd to me a vision of heavenly Angels: & I came from the place with infinite Satisfaction, having never in my life seene a more noble, pious, & admirable Charity: All these consisting of Orphans onely: The foundation (which has also had & still has many Benefactors) was of that pious Prince, K. Edward the 6: whose picture, (held to be an original of Holbeins) is in the Court, where the Governors meete to consult of the affairs of the Hospital, & his stat<u>e in White-marble stands in a Nich of the Wall below, as you go to the Church which is a modern noble & ample fabric ...

10th Saw the trial of those devlish murdering mischiefe-doing engines Bombs, shot out of the Morter piece on black-heath: The distance that they are cast, the destruction they make where ever they fall is most prodigious: ...

25 ... There came in a man (whilst we were at divine service) with his sword drawn to neere the middle of the Church, with severall others in that posture; which in this jealous time, put the Congregation into a wonderfull Confusion; but it appear'd to be one who fled into it, for Sanctuary, being pursued by Baylifs &c:

April 10 ... There having the last weeke ben issu'd forth a dispensation from all Obligations & Tests, by which dissenters & Papists especialy, had publique liberty of exercising their severall ways of Worship, without incurring the penalty of the many Laws, & Acts of Parliament to the Contrary ever since the Reformation; & this purely obtained by the Papists, thinking thereby to ruine the C. of England, which now was the onely Church, which so admirably & strenuously oppos'd their Superstition; There was a wonderfull concourse at the Dissenters meeting house in this parish, and the Parish-Church left exceeding thinn: What this will end in, God Almighty onely knows, but <it> lookes like confusion, which I pray God avert: ...

19 I heard the famous Singer the Eunuch Cifacca, esteemed the best in Europe & indeede his holding out & delicatenesse in extending & loosing a note with that incomparable softnesse, & sweetenesse was admirable: For the rest, I found him a meere wanton, effeminate child; very Coy, & prowdly conceited to my apprehension: He touch'd the Harpsichord to his Voice rarely well, & this was before a select number of some particular persons whom Mr. Pepys (Secretary of the Admiralty & a greate lover of Musick) invited to his house, where the meeting was, & this obtained by peculiar favour & much difficulty of the Singer, who much disdained to shew his talent to any but Princes: ...

May 12 I came downe with the Countesses of Bristol & Sunderland, whose husband being Lord President [& Secretary of state] was made knight of the Gartir, & prime favorite: The two Countesses &c: dined at my house: Memorandum: this day was such a storme of wind as had seldome happened in an age for the extreame violence of it, being as was judg'd a kind of Hurocan: It also kept the floud out of the Thames that people went on foote over several places above bridge, the tide was so low. I return'd this evening with the Ladys: ...

17: Lond: about my P: Seale &c: stayed all this weeke: An Earthquake in severall places of England about the time of the great storme 11th past: ...

June 2: I went to Lond: it having pleas'd his Majestie to grant me a Privy-Seale for 6000 pounds, for the discharging the Debt, I had ben so many years persecuted for. It being indeede for Mony drawne over by my F. in Law Sir R: Browne during his Residence in the Court of France, & so (with a much greater summ, due to Sir Richard from his Majestie & now this part of the Arrere payed) there remaining yet due to me (as Executor to Sir Richard) about 6500 more: But this determining a tedious & expensive Chancery suite, has ben so greate a mercy & providence to me (through the kindnesse & friendship of my L. Godolphin one of the Lords Commissioners of the Treasury), that I do accknowledge it, with all imaginable thanks to my gracious God: ...

12 ... There was about this time brought into the Downes, a Vast treasure which after 45 yeares being sunk in a Spanish Galioon, which perish'd somewhere neere Hispaniola [or B<a>hama Ilands] coming home; was now weighed up, by certaine Gentlemen & others, who were [at] the Charge of Divers &c: to the suddaine enriching of them, beyond all expectation: The Duke of Albemarles share came (tis believed) to 50000, & some private Gent: who adventured but 100 pounds & little more, to ten, 18000 pounds, & proportionably; [his Majesties tenth to 10000 pounds:] ...

16 I went to Lond: thence to Hampton-Court to give his Majestie thanks for his late gracious favour, though it was the granting but what was a due debt to me, [18] & so return'd home: Whilst I was in the Council-chamber came in a formal person, with a large roll of Parchment in his hand, being an Addresse (as he said, for he introduc'd it with a Speech) of the people of Coventry, giving his Majestie their greate Acknowledgements for his granting a liberty of Conscience: He added, that this was not onely the Application of one party, but the unanimous Addresse of C. of England men, Presbyterians, Independents, & Anabaptists, to shew how extensive his Majesties Grace was, as taking all parties to his Indulgence & protection, had also taken a way all

dissentions & animosit<i>es, which would not onely unite them in bonds of Christian Charity, but exceedingly incourage their future Industry to the Improvement of Trade in his Majesties dominions, & spreading of his glory through out the world, & that now he had given God his Empire, God would establish his, with Expressions of greate loyaltie & submission: & so gave the King the roll: which being return'd him againe, his Majestie caused him to reade: The Addresse was short, but much to the substance of the speech of their foreman: To whom the K. (pulling off his hatt,) sayed; That what he had don in giving liberty of Conscience, was, what ever his judgement ought to be don, & that as he would preserve them in their injoyment of it during his reigne; so he would indeavor so to settle it by Law, that it should never be alter'd by his successors: After this he gave them his hand to kisse: It was reported the subscribers were above 1000: But this is not so remarkeable as an Addresse of the Weeke before (as I was assured by one present) of some of the Family of Love; His Majestie asked what their Worship consisted in, & how-many their party might consist of: They told him, their costome was to reade the Scriptures, and then to preach, but did not give any farther account, onely sayed, that for the rest, they were a sort of refined Quakers, but their number very small, not consisting (as they sayed) of above threescore in all, and those chiefly belonging to the Ile of Ely: ...

August 27 I went to Lond, to resigne a Mortgage of 1000 pounds to my Lord Sunderland, being mony lent him in my name, but belonging to my Lord Godolphin, as part of his late Wifes (my ever dearest friend) portion: & now by his Lordships desire lent to the <Exchequer>, in my name againe, the product both of this and 2000 pounds more, for the maintenance of his sonn & heire Francis Godolphin &c: I returned this Evening: ...

October 6 I was Godfather to sir Jo: Chartins sonn (the greate French Traveller), with the Earle of Bath, and the Countess of Carlile: The Child was Christn'd in Greenewich Church with much solemnitie, and it was named John, which was also my L: of Bathes name &c: we all dined at sir Johns in the Queenes house, where was the Marquisse of Ruvignie, Young Lord Carteret, Sir Jo: Fenwick, & other persons of qualitie: ...

29 Was an Anabaptist very odd ignorant Mechanic, I thin<k> a made Lord Mayor; The K: Q: Invited to feast at Guild-hall, together with Dadi, the Popes Nuncio – ô strange turne of affaires, That these who scandaliz'd the Church of England, as favourers of Popery (the Dissenters) should publiqly invite an Emissary from Rome, one who represented the very person of their Antichrist! ...

December 1 I went to severall of my friends, & returned home [2] The next day, leaving both my poore Wife & daughter very much Indisposed: ...

10 I went to Lond to see my Wife who was Indisposed with a rhume, & staying some while to take the physitians Advice: My Son was now returned out of Devon Shire, where he had ben upon a Commission, from the Lords of the Tressury, about a Concealement of Land: I dined with the Secretary of the Admiralty [upon a petition for Mr. Fowler:] & returned home late: ...

20 I went with my Lord Chiefe-Justice Herbert, to see his house at Walton on the Thames: It is a barren place, he had built, to a very ordinary house a very handsome Library, designing more building to it, than the place deserves in my opinion: He desired my advice about the laying out of his Gardens &c: next day, we went to Waybridge, to see som pictures of the Dutchesse of

Norfolcks, especialy the statue, or Christo in Gremio, said to be of M:Angelos; but, there are reasons to think it rather a copy, from some proportion in both the figures ill taken: I<t> was now exposed to sale: I came to Lond: the thursday after, having be<en> exceedingly well treated by my L.C.Justice: and so ...

1688

January 15 Was a solemn & particular office used at our, & all the Churche<s> of London, & 10 miles about it, for thanksgiving to God for her Majesties being with child: ...

February 12 ... Wednesday before My Daughter Evelyn, going in the Coach to visite in the Citty, a Jolt (the doore being not fast-shut) flung her quite out of the Coach upon her back, in such manner, as the hind-wheles passed over both her Thighes a little above the knees: Yet it pleased God, besides the bruse of the Wheele upon her flesh, she had no other harme: We let her blood, anointed, & made her keepe bed 2 dayes, after which <s>he was able to walke & soone after perfectly well: Through God Almightys greate mercy to an Excellent Wife & a most dutifull & discreete daughter in Law:

17 ... I now receiv'd the sad tidings of my Niepce Montagues death, who died at Woodcot the 15th: There had ben unkindnesses & Injuries don our family by my Sister-in-Law, her mother, which we did not deserve; & it did not thrive to the purposes of those who instigated her, to cause her da<u>ghter to cut-off an Intaile clandestinely: But Gods will be don, she has seene the ill effect of it, & so let it passe:[1] ...

March 23 ... The Bish: of Oxford, Parker who so lately published, his extravagant Treatise about Transubstantiation & for abbrogating the Test & penal Laws, died: esteem'd a Violent, passionate haughty man, but being [yet] pressed to declare for the C. of Rome; he utterly refus'd it: A remarkable end:

The Fr: Tyrant, now finding he could make no proselytes amongst those Protestants of quality & others whom he had caused to be shut up in Dungeo<n>s & confin'd to Nunneries & Monastries; gave them after so long Tryal a general releasement, & leave to go out of the Kingdom, but Utterly taking away their Estates, & their Children; so as greate numbers came daily into England & other places, where they were received & relieved with very Considerable Christian Charity: This providence and goodnesse of God to those who thus constantly held out; did so work upon those miserable poore soules, who to avoy'd the persecution, sign'd their renuntiation, & to save their Estates, went to Masse; That reflecting on what they had don, grew so afflicted in their Consciences, as not being longer able to support it; They Unanimously in infinite number thro all the french provinces; Acquaint the Magistrates & Lieutenants that being sorry for their Apostacy; They were resolved to returne to their old Religion, that they would go no more to Masse, but peaceably assemble where they could, to beg pardon & worship God, but so without weapons, as not to give the least umbrage of Rebellion or sedition, imploring their pitty & commisseration: And accordingly meeting so from

---

[1] See below, 17 May 1688.

time to time, The Dragoon Missioners, popish Officers & Priests, fall upon them, murder & put to death who ever they could lay hold on, who without the least resistance embrace death, torture & hanging, with singing <psalmes> & praying for their persecutors to the last breath; yet still continuing the former Assembly of themselves in desert places, suffering with incredible Constancy, that through Gods mercy they might obtaine pardon for this Lapse: Such Examples of Christian behaviour has not been seene, since the primitive Persecution, by the Heathen: & doub<t>lesse God will do some signall worke in the end, if we can with patience & christian resolution hold out, & depend on his Providence: ...

28 I went to Lond: in the Evening, the next morning with Sir Charles Littleton to Sheene an house & estate given him by my Lord Brounchar, one who was ever noted for an hard, vicious man, had severall Bastards; but for his worldly Craft, & skill in gaming &c: few exceeding him: Coming to die, he bequeathed all his Land, House, furnitur &c intirely to Sir Charles, to whom he had no manner of Relation, but an antient friendship, contracted at the famous siege of Colchester 40 yeares before: It is a pretty place, fine gardens and well planted, & given to one worthy of them, Sir Charles being an honest Gent, & souldier; & brother to Sir Hen: Littleton of Worster shire, whose greate Estate he is to Inhe<r>ite, his Bro: being without Children: They are <descendants> of the greate Lawyer of that name & give same Armes & motto: He is married to one <Mrs.> Temple (formerly maide of Honor to the late Queene,) a beautifull Lady, & has many fine Children; so as none envy his good fortune.

After dinner (at his house) we went to see Sir William Temples, neere to it: The most remarkeable thing, is his Orangerie & Gardens; where the wall Fruite-trees are most exquisitely nailed & applied, far better than in my life I had ever noted:

There are many good Pictures, especialy of V. dykes, in both these houses, & some few statues & small busts in the later:

From hence we went to Kew, to Visite Sir Hen: Capels, whose Orangerie & Myrtetum, are most beautifull, & perfectly well kept: He was contriving very high palisados of reedes, to shade his Oranges in during the Summer, & painting those reedes in oyle: ...

May 13 ... The Hollanders did now al'arme his Majestie with their fleete, so well prepar'd & out before we were in any readinesse, or had any considerable number to have encounter'd them had there ben occasion, to the greate reproch of the nation, whilst being in profound peace, there was a mighty Land Army, which there was no neede of, & no force by Sea, where onely was the apprehension; [at present, but was doub<t>lesse kept & increased in order to bring in & Countenance Popery, the K beginning to discover his intention by many Instances, perverted by the Jesuites against his first seeming resolution to alter nothing in the Church Established, so as it appeared that there can be no relyance <o>n Popish promises.]

17 I went to Lond, to meete my Bro: G. Evelyn about our mutual concerne in the will of my Bro: Richard, by which, my Niepce Montague, dying without issue, a considerable Estate ought to have returned to our Family, after the decease of her husband: but thro the fraude & unworthy dealing of her mother, (my sister-in-Law), the intaile had ben cut off, & a recovery pass'd & consequently the Estate given to her husband Montag<u>e, through the perswasion of my sister, contrary to the intent of her husband my brother, & that to a son-in law who had lived dissolutly & Scandalously with another

woman, & his dishonesty made publiquely notorious: What should move my sister in Law, professing so greate love to the memory of her husband, to [cause my Niepce to] give away not onely this, but considerably more, to a son in law, who had no Issue, from all her husbands relations, was strangely spoken off, especialy to one who had so scandalously & so basely abused her da<u>ghter:

18 The King injoyning [the ministers] the Reading his declaration for giving liberty of Conscience (as it was styled) in all the Churches of England: This Evening six Bishops, Bath & Wells, Peterborow, Ely, Chichester, St. Asaph, & Bristol, (in the name of all the rest) came to his Majestie to petition him that he would not impose the reading of it to the severall Congregations under their diocesse: not that they were averse to the publishing of it, for want of due tendernesse towards dissenters, in relation to whom they should be willing to come to such a temper, as should be thought fit, when that matter might come to be consider'd & settled in parliament & Convocation: But the declaration being founded upon such a dispencing power, as might at pleasure set aside all Lawes Ecclesiastical & Civil, it appeared to them Illegal, as doing so to the parliaments in -61 & 72; & that it was a point of such Consequence, as they could not so far make themselves parties to it, as the Reading of it in the Church in the time of divine service amounted to.

The King was so far incensed at this Addresse, that he with threatning expressions commanded them to obey him in reading of it at their perils, & so dismis'd them: ...

25 I visited Dr. Tenison, Secretary Pepys, of the Admiralty, Mr. Boile, Coll: Philips and severall of my Friends, all the discourse now being about the Bishops refusing to reade [the injunction for the abbrogation of] the Test &c: It seemes the Injunction came so crudely from the Secretarys office, that it was neither sealed nor sign'd in forme, nor had any Lawyer ben consulted; so as the Bishops who tooke all imaginable advice, put the Court to greate difficulties how to proceede against them: Greate were the Consults, and a Proclamation expected all this day; but no thing don: The action of the Bishop<s> universaly applauded, & reconciling many adverse parties, Papists onely excepted, who were now exceedingly perplex'd, & violent courses every moment expected: Report was the Protestant Secular Lords & nobility would abett the Cleargy: God knows onely the event.

The Queene Dowager obstinately bent hitherto on her returne into Portugal, now on the suddaine, upon pretence of a greate debt owing her by his majesties, declares her resolution to stay:

June 8 This day were the Arch-Bishop of Canterbery together with the Bishops of Ely, Chichester, St. Asaph, Bristol, Peterborow & Bath & Wells, sent from the Privy Council, Prisoners to the Tower, for refusing to give baile for their appearance (upon their not reading the Declaration for Liberty of Conscience) because in giving baile, they had prejudiced their Peerage: Wonderfull was the concerne of the people for them, infinite crowds of people on their knees, beging their blessing & praying for them as they passed out of the Barge; along the Tower wharfe &c:

10 A young prince borne &c. [which will cost dispute.] ...

About two a clock, we heard the Toure Ordnance discharge, & the Bells ringing; for the Birth of a Prince of Wales; This was very surprizing, it being universaly given-out, that her Majestie did not looke til the next moneth: ...

13 I went to the Tower to see the Bishops now there in Prison, for not complying with his Majesties commands to Cause his declaration to be read in

their Diocesse; where I visited the A:Bish: B: of Ely, Asaph, & Bath & Wells: ...

15 The Bish: came from the Tower to Westminster upon their *Habeas Corpus* & after divers houres dispute before the Judges, by their Counsel, upon security to appeare friday fortnight, were dismiss'd: Their Counsel alledged false Imprisonment & abatement of their Committment for want of some words: Denyed the paper given privately to the K. to be a seditious libel or that it was ever published: but all was over-ruled: W<r>ight, Alibon, Hollowell & Powell were the Judges: Finch, Sawyer, Pollixfen & Pemberton, their Counsel, who pleaded incomparably, [so as the Jury quitted them.] There was a lane of people from the Kings Bench to the water-side, upon their knees as the Bishops passed & repassed to beg their blessing: Bon fires made that night, & bells ringing, which was taken very ill at Court and an appearance of neere 60 Earles & Lords &c upon the bench in honor of the Bishops, & which did not a little comfort them; but indeede they were all along full of Courage & cherefull:

Note that they denyed to pay the Lieutennant of the Tower: (Hales who us'd them very surlily) any Fees, denying any to be due: ...

July 8 ... In the meane time more viru<le>ntly did the popish priests, in their sermons against the C. of England, raging at the successe of the Bishops, as being otherwise no ways able to carry their Cause against their learned Adversaries confounding them by both disputes & writings: ...

12 The 2 Judges, who favour'd the Cause of the Bish: had their writ of Ease: greate wroth meditating against the Bish: Cleargy & Church:

Coll: Titus, Sir H. Vane (son of him who was executed for his Treason) & some others of the Presbyt: & Indep: party, Sworn of the Privy Council, hoping thereby to divert that party, from going-over to the Bishops & C: of England, which now they began to do: as forseeing the designes of the papists to descend & take in their most hatefull of heretiques (as they at other time believed them) to effect their owne ends, which was now evidently, the utter extirpation of the C. of Eng: first, & then the rest would inevitably follow: ...

17 I went to Lond: with my Wife &c: & This night were the fire-works plaied, which were prepar'd for the Queenes up-sitting: We stood at Mr. Pepys's Secretary of the Admiralty to greate advantage for the sight, & indeede they were very fine, & had cost some thousands of pounds about the pyramids & statues &c: but were spent too soone, for so long a preparation: ...

29 ... My Wife was ataqu'd with a suddaine fit of fainting, at dinner, but without any sensible convulsion; which yet to prevent, she was immediately let blood, & I blesse God soone restored: ...

August 10 To Lond. Din'd with Sir William Godolphin, return'd: [Dr. Tenison now told me there would suddainly be some greate thing discovered, which happened to be the P: of O: intended coming:] ...

[15] ... to Althorp in Northamptonshire, it being 70 miles, which in 2 Coaches one [of 4 horses] that <tooke> me & my son up at white-hall & carried us to Dunstaple, where we arived & dined at noone, & another there of 6 horses, which carried us to Althorp 4 miles beyond N-hampton, by 7 a clocke that evening; both these Coaches laied for me alone, by that noble Countesse of Sutherland, who Invited me to her house at Althorp, where she entertaind me & my son with very extraordinary kindnesse, and convey'd us back againe to London in the very same noble manner, both going & coming, appointing a Dinner for us, at Dunstaple, as soone as we came to the Inn: ...

18 Dr. Jessup the Minister of Althorp, who was my Lords Chaplaine, when Ambassador in France, preached on the shortest discourse I ever heard: but what was defective in the amplitude of his sermon, we found supplied in the largenesse, & convenience of the Parsonage house, which the Doctor (who had in spiritual advancements, at least 600 pounds per Annum) had new-built, fit for any person of quality to live in, with Gardens & all accommodations) according.

20 My Lady carried us to <Castle Ashby> my Lord of Northamptons Seate, a very strong large house built of stone, not altogether modern: they were now inlarging the Gardens, in which was nothing extraordinary but the Yron gate, opening into the Parke, which is indeede very good worke, wrought in flowers, painted with blew & gilded; & there is a very noble Walke of Elmes towards the front of the house by the Bowling Greene: I was not in any roomes of the house besides a lobby looking into the Garden, where my Lord, and his new Countesse (Sir St: Foxes daughter, whom I had known from a very Child) entertained the Countesse of Sunderland & her daughter the Countesse of Arran, (newly married to the son of the Duke of Hamilton) with so little good grace, & so dully, that our Visite was very short, & so we return'd to Althorp: which is 12 miles distant:

The Earle of Sunderlands House, or rather palace at Althorp, is a noble uniforme pile, in forme of an 𝍖 built of brick & freestone, balustred, & a la moderne; The Hale is well, the Staircase incomparable, the roomes of State, Gallerys, Offices, & Furniture such as [may] become a greate Prince: It is situated in the midst of Gardens, exquisitely planted & kept, & all this in a parke wall'd with hewn stone; planted with rowes & walkes of Trees; Canales & fish ponds, stored with Game: & what is above all this, Govern'd by a Lady, that without any shew of solicitude; keepes every thing in such admirable order both within & without, from the Garret, to the Cellar; That I do not believe there is any in all this nation or any other, exceeds her: all is in such exact order, without ostentation, but substantialy greate & noble; The meanest servant lodged so neate & cleanely, The Services at several Tables, the good order & decenccy, in a word the intire Oeconomie perfectly becoming, a wise & noble person, & one whom for her distinguishing esteeme of me from a long & worthy friendship; I must ever honour & Celebrate: & wish, I do from my Soule; The Lord her Husband (whose parts & abilit<i>es are otherwise conspicuous) were as worthy of her, as by a fatal Apostacy, & Court ambition, as he has made himselfe unworthy: This is what she deplores, & renders her as much affliction, as a Lady of a greate Soule & much prudence is capable of: The Countesse of Bristol her mother, a grave & honorable Lady has the comfort of seing her daughter & Grand-children under the same Oeconomie, especialy, Mr. Charles Spencer, a Youth of extraordinary hopes, very learned for his age & ingenious, & under a Governor of Extraordinary worth: Happy were it, could as much be said, <of> the Elder Bro: the Lord Spencer, who rambling about the world, dishonors both his name & family, adding sorrow to sorrow, to a Mother, who has taken all imaginable care of his Education: but vice more & more predominating, gives slender hopes of his reformation: He has another sister very Young, married to the Earle of Clancartie to a greate & faire Estate in Ireland, which [yet] gives no greate presage of worth; so universaly contaminated is the youth of this corrupt & abandoned age: But this is againe recompens'd by my Lord Arran, a sober & worthy Gent: & who has Espoused the Lady Ann Spencer, a young lady of admirable accomplishments & vertue:

23d I left this noble place, & Conversation on the 23d, passing through Northampton, which having lately ben burnt & reedified, is now become a Towne, that for the beauty of the buildings especialy the Church, & Townehouse, may compare with the neatest in Italy itselfe:

24 Hearing my poore wife, had ben ataqu'd with her late Indisposition I hasted home this morning, & God be pra<i>sed found her much amended.

Dr. Sprat: Bish of Rochester, writing a very honest & handsome letter to the Commissioners Ecclesiastical; excuses himselfe from sitting no longer amongst them, as by no meanes approving of their prosecution of the Cleargy who refus'd to reade his Majesties declaration for liberty of Conscience, in prejudice of the Church of England &c: ...

The Dutch make extraordinary preparations both at sea & land which (with the very small progresse popery makes amongst us) puts us to many difficulties: ...

After long trials of the Doctors, to bring up the little P: of Wales by hand (so-many of her Majesties Children having died Infants) not succeeding: A country Nurse (the wife of a Tile-maker) is taken to give it suck: ...

September 18 I went to Lond: where I found the Court in the uttmost consternation upon report of the Pr: of Oranges landing, which put White-hall into so panic a feare, that I could hardly believe it possible to find such a change:

Writs issued now in order to the Parliament, & a declaration to back the good order of Elections, with greate professions of maintaining the Ch: of England: but without giving any sort of satisfaction to people, who now began to shew their high discontent at several things in the Government: how this will end, God onely can tell: ...

30 ... The Court &c in [so] extraordinary consternation upon assurance of the Pr: of Oranges intention of Landing, as the Writs which were sent forth to choose Parliament men, were recalled &c: ...

October 6: I went to Lond: [7] The next day being Sonday Dr. Tenison viccar of St. Martins, preached on 2: Tim: 3.16. shewing the Scripture to be our undoubted & onely Rule of Faith, & its perfection above all other Traditions & Writings, most excellently proved; after which the Communion was celebrated to neere 1000 devout people. This sermon chiefly occasioned by an impertinent Jesuite who in their Masse-house the Sunday before had disparaged the Scripture & railed at our Translation with extraordinary. ignorance & impudence; which some present contradicting, they pulled him out of the Pulpit, & treated him very coursely, insomuch as it was like to create a very greate disturbance in the Citty:

Hourely dreate on expectation of the Pr: of Oranges Invasion still heightned to that degree, as his Majestie thought fit to recall the Writes of Summons of Parliament; to abbrogate the Commission for the dispencing power, [but retaining his owne right still to dispense with all Laws &] restore the ejected Fellows of Magdalen College Oxon: But in the meane time called over 5000 Irish, 4000 Scots; continue<s> to remove protestants & put papists into Portsmouth & other places of Trust: & retaines the Jesuites about him, which gave no satisfaction to the nation, but increasing the universal discontent, brought people to so desperate a passe as with the uttmost expressions even passionately seeme to long for & desire the landing of that Prince, whom they looked on as their deliverer from popish Tyrannie, praying uncessantly for an Easterly Wind, which was said to be the onely remora of his expedition, with a numerous Army ready to make a descent; To such a strange temper & unheard of in any former age, was this poore nation reduc'd, & of which I was an Eye witnesse: The apprehension was (& with reason) that his Majesties Forces, would neither at land or sea oppose them with that viggour requisite to repell Invaders:

The late Imprisoned Bishops, were now called to reconcile matters, & the Jesuites hard at worke to foment confusions amongst the Protestants, by their usual tricks &c: [Leter sent the AB. of Cant informing from a good hand what was contriving by the Jesuits: &c:]

9 I return'd the 9th – A paper of what the Bishops advised his Majestie [was publish'd]

A [forme of] prayer, the Bishops were injoy<n>'d to prepare [an office] against the feared Invasion.

A pardon published: Souldiers & Mariners daily pressed &c.

14 The Kings Birth-day, no Gunns from the Tower, as usualy: The sunn Eclips'd at its rising: This day signal for the Victory of William the Conqueror against Herold neere Battel in Sussex: The wind (which had hitherto ben West) all this day East, wonderfull expectation of the Dutch fleete ...

<28> I din'd with Sir W: Godolphin: [A Tumult in Lond on the rabble demolishing a popish Chapell set up in the Citty.]

29 My Lady Sunderland acquainted me at large his Majesties taking away the Seales from her husband, & of her being with the Queene to interceede for them: It is conceiv'd he grew remisse of late in pursuing the Interest of the Jesuitical Counsels, some reported one thing, some another; but there was doubtlesse some seacret betraied, which time may discover:

There was a Council now cald, to which were summon'd the A:Bish of Cant. &<c>: Judges, Lord Major &c: Q:Dowager, all the Ladies & Lords, who were present at the Q:Consorts labour, upon oath to give testimonie of the Pr: of Wales's birth, which was recorded, both at the Council board, & at the Chancery a day or two after: This procedure was censur'd by some, as below his Majestie to condescend to, upon the talke of Idle people: Remarkable on this occasion, was the refusal of the A: Bish: Marq: Halifax, Earles of Clarendon & Notinghams refusing to sit at the Council Table in their places, amongst Papists, & their bold telling his Majestie that what ever was don whilst such sate amongst them was unlawfull, & incurr'd præmunire: if at least, it be true, what I heard: ...

Visited Mr. Boile, where came in Duke Hamilton & E. of Burlington: The Duke told us many particulars of Mary Q: of Scots, and her amours with the Italian favorite &c: ...

November 1 ... Continual al'armes of the Pr: of Oranges landing, but no certainty; reports of his greate losses of horse in the storme; but without any assurance. A Man was taken with divers papers & printed Manifests, & carried to Newgate after examination at the Cabinet-Council: There was likewise a declaration of the States, for satisfaction of all publique Ministers in their Dominions, the reason of their furnishing the Prince with their Vessels & Militia on this Expedition, which was delivered to all the Ambassadors & publique Ministers at the Hague except to the English & French:

There was in that of the Princes, an expression as if the Lords both Spiritual & Temporal &c had invited him over, with a deduction of the Causes of his enterprise: This made his Majestie Convene my L: of Cant: & the other Bishops now in Towne, to [give] them an account of what was in the

Manifesto: & to enjoyne them to cleare themselves by <some> publique writing of this disloyal charge.

2 It was now certainly reported by some who saw the Pr: imbarke, and the fleete, That they sailed from Brill on Wednesday Morning, & that the Princesse of Orange was there, to take leave of her Husband, [3] & so I returned home.

4 ... Fresh reports of the Pr: being landed somewher about Portsmouth or Ile of Wight: whereas it was thought, it would have ben north ward: The Court in greate hurry – ...

8 I went to Lond: heard the newes of the Princes of Oranges being landed at Tor-bay, with a fleete of neere 700 saile, so dreadfull a sight passing through the Channell with so favorable a Wind, as our Navy could by no meanes intercept or molest them: This put the King & Court into greate Consternation, now employed in forming an Army to incounter their farther progresse: for they were gotten already into Excester, & the season, & wayes very improper for his Majesties forces to march so greate a distance:

The A Bish of Cant, & some few of the other Bishops, & Lords in Lond. were sent for to White-hall, & required to set forth their abhorrency of this Invasion, They assured his Majestie they had never invited any of the Princes party or were in the least privy to this Invasion, & would be ready to shew all testimonies of their Loyalty &c: but as to a publique declaration, they being so few, desired that his majestie would call the rest of their brethren & peeres, that they might consult what was fit to do on this occasion, not thinking it convenient to publish any thing without them, & untill they had themselves seene the Princes Manifest, in which it was pretended he was invited in by the Lords Sp: & temporal: This did not please his Majestie: So they departed: There came now out a Declaration, prohibiting all people to see or reade the Princes Manifest; in which was at large set-forth the cause of his Expedition, as there had ben on<c>e before one from the States: These are the beginnings of Sorrows, unlesse God in his Mercy prevent it, by some happy reconciliation of all dissentions amongst us, which nothing in likelihood can Effect but a free Parliament, but which we cannot hope to see, whilst there are any forces on either side: I pray God protect, & direct the King for the best, & truest Interest of his People: [I saw his Majestie touch for the Evil, Piters the Jesuit & F. Warner officiating in the Banqueting house] ...

11 ... My deare Wife fell very ill of the gravell &c in her kidnies this afternoone. God in mercy give her ease & comfort:

The Pr. of Orange increases every day in forces, several Lords go in to him; The King gos towards Salisbery with his Army; doubtfull of their standing by him, Lord Cornbery carrys some Regiments from him, marches to Honiton, the Princes head quarters; The Citty of Lond: in dissorder by the rabble &c who pull-downe the Nunery at St. Johns, newly bought of the Papists of my Lord Berkeley: The Queene [prepare<s> to] <go> to Portsmouth for safty: to attend the issue of this commotion, which has a dreadfull aspect:

18 ... The King gos to Salisbery to rendevouze the Army, and returning back to Lond: Lord De la Mare appears for the Pr: in Cheshire: The nobility meete in Yorkshire: The ABish & some Bishops, & such peeres as were in Lond: addresse to his Majestie to call a Parliament: The King invites all forraine nations to come over: The French take all the Palatinat, & alarme the Germans more than ever: ...

29 I went to the R: Society, we adjourn'd Election of Præsident til. 23. Aprill by reason of the publique commotions, yet dined together as of custome on this day:

December 2 ... Visited my L. Godolphin, then going with the Marquis of Halifax, & E: of Notingham as Commissioner to the Prince of Orange: He told me, they had little power: Plymoth declared for the Prince & L: Bath: Yorke, Hull, Bristoll, all the eminent nobility & persons of quality throout England declare for the Protestant Rel<i>gion & Laws, & go to meete the Prince; who every day sets forth new declarations &c: against the Papists: The Greate favorits at Court, priest<s> & Jesuites, flie or abscond: Every thing (til now conceiled) flies abroad in publique print, & is Cryed about the streetes: Expectations of the Pr: coming to Oxon: Pr: of Wales & greate Treasure sent daily to Portsmouth, Earle of Dover Governor: Addresse from the Fleete not gratefull to his Majestie: The Popists in offices lay down their Commissions & flie: Universal consternation amongst them: it lookes like a Revolution: Herbert, beates a french fleete: ...

13 I went to Lond: [The rabble people demolish all Papists Chapells & severall popish Lords & Gent: house<s>, especialy that of the Spanish Ambassador, which they pillaged & burnt his Library, &c:]

16 ... I din'd at my L. Clarendons: The King flies to sea, [putts in at Feversham for ballast is rudely detained by the people: comes back to W<hite>hall.]

The Pr: of Orange now advanc'd to Windsor, is invited by the King to St. James, the messenger sent was the E. of Feversham the general of the forces: who going without Trumpet or passeport is detained prisoner by the Prince: The Prince accepts the Invitation, but requires his Majestie to retire to some distant place, that his owne Guards may be quartered about the palace & Citty: This is taken heinously, so the King gos away privately to Rochester: Is perswaded to come back: comes on the Sunday; Goes to masse & dines in publique, a Jesuite says grace: [I was present] That night a Council, [17] his Majestie refuses to assent to all proposals; gos away againe to Rochester:

18 The Pr: comes to St. James, fills W-hall (the King taking barge to Gravesend at 12 a Clock) with Dut<c>h Guard: A Council of Peres meete about an expedient to call a parliament: Adjourne to the House of Lords: The Chancelor, E. of Peterbor, & divers Priests & other taken: E: of Sunderlands flies & divers others, Sir E: Hales, Walker & other taken & secured: All the world go to see the Prince at St. James where is a greate Court, there I saw him & severall of my Acquaintance that come over with him: He is very stately, serious & reserved: The Eng: souldiers &c. sent out of Towne to distant quarters: not well pleased: Divers reports & opinions, what all this will end in; Ambition & faction feared: ...

24 The King passes into France, whither the queen & child wer gon a few days before ...

26 The Peeres & such Commons as were members of the Parliament at Oxford, being the last of Charles the first: meeting, desire the Pr: of Orange to take on him the Government, & dispose of the publique Revenue 'til a Convention of Lords & Commons should meete in full body, appointed by his Circulary Letters to the Shires & Borrowghs 22. Jan:

I had now quartered on me a Lieutenant Coll: & 8 horses:

30 Our Lecturer on 122. Psal: 6: Pomerid: a Stranger on 6. Eccles: This day Prayers for the Prince of Wales were first left off in our Church pew & pulpet.

Greate preparations of all the Princes of Europ, against the French &c: the Emp: making peace with the Turke:

1689

January 15 I went to visite my Lord Archbish of Cant: where I found the Bishops of St. Asaph, Ely, Bath & Wells, Peterborow & Chichester; The Earle of Alesbery & Clarendon, Sir Geo: Mackenzy Lord Advocate of Scotland, & then came in a Scotch Archbishop: &c. After prayers & dinner, were discoursed divers serious matters concerning the present state of the publique: & sorry I was to find, there was as yet no accord in the judgements of those who both of the Lords & Commons were to convene: Some would have the princesse made Queene without any more dispute, others were for a Regency, There was a Torie part (as then called so) who were for <inviting> his Majestie againe upon Conditions, & there were Republicarians, who would make the Prince of Orange like a State-holder: The Romanists were also buisy among all these severall parties to bring them into Confusion: most for Ambition, or other Interest, few for Conscience and moderate resolutions: I found nothing of all this in this Assembly of Bishops, who were pleas'd to admitt me into their Discourses: They were all for a Regency, thereby to salve their Oathes, & so all publique matters to proceede in his Majesties name, thereby to facilitate the calling of a Parliament according to the Laws in being; this was the result of this meeting: My Lord of Cant: gave me greate thanks for the advertisement I sent his Grace in October, & assur'd me they tooke my counsel in that particular, & that it came very seasonable:

I found by the Lord Advocate of Scotland that the Bishops of Scotland, who were indeede very unworthy that Character & had don much mischiefe in that Church, were now coming about to the True Interest, more to save themselves in this conjuncture, which threatned the abolishing the whole Hierarchy in that Kingdome, than for Conscience: & therefore the Scotish Archbish: & Lord Advocate requested my L. of Cant: to use his best endeavors with the Prince, to maintaine the Church there in the same state as by Law at present settled: It now growing late: I after some private discourse, tooke my leave of his Grace, most of the Lords being gon: I beseech God of his infinite mercy to settle truth & peace amongst us againe: ...

23 I went to Lond, The greate Convention being assembled the day before, falling upon the greate Question about the Government, Resolved that K.Jam: 2d, having by the advise of Jesuites & other wicked persons, endeavored to subvert the Lawes of church & state, and Deserting the Kingdome [carrying away the Seales &c] without taking any care for the manegement of the Government, had by demise, abdicated himselfe, and wholy vacated his right: & They did therefore desire the Lords Concurrence to their Vote, to place the Crowne upon the next heires: The Prince of Orange for his life, then to the Princesse his wife, & if she died without Issue to the Princesse of Denmark, & she failing to the heires of the Pr: Excluding for ever all possibility of admitting any Ro: Cath:

27 ...I din'd at the Admiralty, where was brought, a young Child not 12 yeares old, the sonn of one Dr. Clench, of the most prodigious maturity of memorie, & knowledge, for I cannot call it altogether memory, but [something more] extraordinary; Mr. Pepys & my selfe examining him not in any method, but [by] promiscuously questions, which required judgement & wonderfull discernement, to answere things so readily & pertinently:

There was not any thing in Chronologie, Historie, Geographie, The several systemes of Astronomers, Courses of the starrs, Longitudes, Latitudes, doctrine of the Sphears, Sourses & courses of Rivers, Creekes, harbors,

Eminent Citties, staples, boundaries & bearings of Countries, not onely in Europe but any other part of the Earth, which he did not readily resolve & demonstrate his knowledge of, readily drawing out, with his pen any thing that he would describe:

He was able not onely to repeate the famous things which are left us in any of the Greeke or Roman histories, Monarchie, Repub, Warrs, Colonies, Exploits by sea & land; but readily, besides all the Sacred stories of the Old & New Test: the succession of all the Monarches, Babylonish, Persian, Gr: Roman, with all the lower Emperors, Popes, Heresiarches, & Councils; What they were cald about, what they determined, [&] in the Controversie of Easter, The Tenets of the Gnostics, Sabellius, Arius, Nestorius; The difference twixt St. Cyprian & Stephen about rebaptization; The Schismes, we leaped from that to other things totaly different: To Olympic yeares, & Synchronismes; we asked questions which could not be resolved without considerable meditation & judgement: nay, of some particulars of the Civil Lawes, of the Digest & Code:

He gave a stupendous account of both Natural, & Moral Philosophie, & even in Metaphysics: Having thus exhausted our selves, rather than this wonderfull Child, or Angel rather, for he was as beautifull & lovely in Countenance, as in knowledge; we concluded, with asking him, if in all he had read, or heard of, he had ever met with any thing which was like, this Expedition of the Pr: of Orange; with so small a force, to obtaine 3 greate <Kingdomes>, without any Contest: He after a little thought, told us, that he knew of nothing did more resemble it, Than the coming of Constantin the Greate out of Brittane, thro: France & Italy, so tedious a March, to meete Maxentius, whom he overthrew at ponte Milvij, with very little conflict, & at the very gates of Rome, which he entered & was received with Triumph, & obtained the Empire, not of 3 Kingdomes onely, but of all the then known World: He was perfect in the Latine Authors, spake french naturaly, & gave us a description of France, Italy, Savoy, Spaine, Antient & modernly divided; as also of the antient Greece, S<c>ythia, & Northern Countries & Tracts, in a word, we left questioning farther with astonishment:

This the child did without any set or formal repetition; as one who had learned things without booke, but, as if he minded other things going about the roome, & toying with a parat there, & as he was at dinner [(*tanquam aliud agens*[1] as it were)] seeming to be full of play, of a lively & spiritfull temper, allways smiling, & exceedingly pleasant without the least levity, rudenesse or childishnesse: His father assur'd us, he never imposed any thing to charge his memorie, by causing him to get things by heart, no, not the rules of Grammer; but his <Tutor> (who was a French-man) reading to him, in French first, & then in Latine: That he usualy plaied, amongst other boys 4 or 5 hours every day & that he was as earnest at play, as at his study: He was perfect in Arithmetic, & now newly entered into the Greek: In sum [(*Horesco referens*)][2] I had, read of divers, forward & præcoce, Youthes, & some I have known; but in my life, did never either heare or read of any like to this sweete Child, if it be lawfull to call him Child, who has more knowledge, than most men in the world: I counseled his father, not to set his heart too much upon this Jewell, *Immodicis brevis est ætas, et rara senectus,*[3] as I my selfe learn'd in my sad

---

[1] 'An effective [child] just like another.'

[2] 'I dread the reference.' Virgil, *Aeneid* II.204.

[3] 'Life is excessively short, and old age rare.' Martial, *Epigrams* VI.29.7.

experience in my most deare child Richard many yeares since, who dying before he was six yeares old, was both in shape & Countenance, & pregnancy of learning, next to prodigie even in that tender-age, as I have given ample account in my præface to that Golden book of St. Chrysostome, which I published on that sad occasion &c:

28 The Votes of the House of Comm: being Carried up, by their chaire-man Mr. Hamden, to the Lords, [29] I got a station by the Princes lodgings at the doore of the Lobby to the House, to heare much of the debate which held very long; The Lord Danby being in the chaire (for the Peres were resolved into a grand Committee of the whole house) after all had spoken, it comming to the question: It was carried out by 3 voices, again<s>t a Regency, which 51 of 54 were for, aledging the danger of dethroning Kings, & scrupuling many passages & expressions of the Commons Votes; too long to set downe particularly, some were for sending to his Majestie with Conditions, others, that the K. could do no wrong, & that the maladministration was chargeable on his Ministers. There were not above 8 or 9 Bish: & but two against the Regency; The Arch Bishop was absent: & the Cleargie now began a new to change their note, both in pulpet & discourse, upon their old passive Obedience: so as people began to talke of the Bishops being cast out of the House: In short, things tended to dissatisfaction on both sides, add to this the morose temper of the Pr: of Orange, who shewed so little Countenance to the Noblemen & others, expecting a more gracious & cherefull reception, when they made their Court: The English Army likewise, not so in order, & firme to his Interest, nor so weaken'd, but that it might, give interruption: Ireland in a very ill posture, as well as Scotland; nothing yet towards any settlement: God of his infinite mercy, Compose these <things>, that we may at last be a Nation & a church under some fixt and sober establishment: ...

February 6 The Kings Coronation day was ordred not to be observed, as hitherto it yearely had.

The Convention of L: & Comm: now declare the Pr: & princesse of Or: Q: & K of England, Fr: & Ireland (Scotland being an Independent Kingdome) The Pr & Princesse to enjoy it jointly during their lives, but the executive Authority to be vested in the Prince during life, though all proceedings to run in both names: & that it descend to the heires of both, & for want of such Issue to the Princesse Ann of Denmark, & in want of such to the heires of the body of the Pr: of Or: if he survive, & for defect, to devolved to the Parliament to choose as they think fit: These produc'd a Conference with the Lords, when also there was presented heads of such [new] laws as were to be enacted: & upon those Conditions they tis thought will be proclaim'd: there was much contest about the Kings abdication, & whether he had vacated the Government: E. of Notingham & about 20 Lords & many Bishops, entred their protests &c, but the Concurrence was greater against them – The Princesse hourely Expected: Forces sending to Ireland, that K<ing>dome being in greate danger, by the E. of Tyrconnells Armie, & expectations from France: which K. is buisy to invade Flanders, & encounter the German Princes comming now to their Assistance: so as this is likely to be one of the most remarkable summers for action, as has happed for many Ages: ...

22 I saw the new Queene & King, so proclaim'd, the very next day of her coming to White-hall, Wednesday 13. Feb. with wonderfull acclamation & general reception, Bonfires, bells, Gunns &c: It was believed that they both, especialy the Princesse, would have shewed some (seeming) reluctancy at least, of assuming her Fathers Crowne & made some Apologie, testifying her

regret, that he should by his misgovernment necessitat the Nation to so extraordinary a proceeding, which would have shewed very handsomly to the world, (and according to the Character give<n> of her piety &c) & consonant to her husbands first Declaration, that there was no intention of Deposing the King, but of Succoring the Nation; But, nothing of all this appeared; she came into W-hall as to a Wedding, riant & jolly, so as seeming to be quite Transported: rose early on the next morning of her arival, and in her undresse (as reported) before her women were up; went about from roome to roome, to see the Convenience of White-hall: Lay in the same bed & appartment where the late Queene lay: & within a night or two, sate down to play at Basset, as the Q. her predecessor us'd to do: smiled upon & talked to every body; so as no manner of change seem'd in Court, since his Majesties last going away, save that infinite crowds of people thronged to see her, & that she went to her prayers:

This carriage was censured by many: she seemes to be of a good nature, & that takes nothing to heart whilst the Pr: her husband has a thoughtfull Countenance, is wonderfull serious & silent, seemes to treate all persons alike gravely: & to be very intent on affaires, both Holland, & Ireland & France calling for his care: Divers Bishops, & Noble men are not at all satisfied with this so suddain Assumption of the Crown, without any previous, sending & offering some Conditions to the absent King: or, upon his not returning & assenting to those Conditions within such a day: to have proclaim'd him Regent &c. But the major part of both houses, prevailed to make them King & Q: immediately, and a Crowne was tempting &c – This was opposed & spoke against with such vehemency by my L. Clarendon (her owne Unkle) as putt him by all preferments, which must doubtless, <have> been as greate, as could have ben given him:

My L: of Rochester his bro: overshot himselfe by the same carriage & stiffnesse, which, their friends thought, they might have well spared, when they saw how it was like to be over-ruled, & that it had ben sufficient to have declared their dissent with lesse passion, acquiescing in due time: The AB of Cant, & some of the rest, upon scruple of Conscience, & to salve the Oathes they had taken, entred their protests, & hung off: Especially the Arch-Bishop, who had not all this while so much as appeared out of Lambeth: all which incurred the wonder of many, who observed with what zeale they contributed to the Princes Expedition, & all this while also, rejecting any proposals of sending againe <for> the absented King: That they should now boggle & raise scrupuls, & such as created much division among people, greatly rejoicing the old Courtiers, & Papist<s> especialy:

Another objection was the invalidity of what was don, by a Convention onely, & the as yet unabrogated Laws: which made them on the 22, make themselves a parliament, the new King passing the act with the Crowne on his head: This lawyers disputed; but necessity prevailed, the Government requiring a speedy settlement: And now innumerable were the Crowds who solicited for & expected Offices, most of the old ones turn'd out: Two or 3. White Staves were disposed of some days before, as L: Steward to the E. of Devonshire, Tress: of the Household to L: Newport, L. Cham: to the K, to my L: of Dorset &c: but there were yet none in Offices of the Civil government, save Pr: Seale to the Marq: of Halifax: A Council of 30 was chosen, L. Danby Presedent: but neither Chancellor, Tressurer, Judges &c not yet declared, A greate seale not yet finished: ...

March 8. Dr. Tillotson deane of Cant: an excellent discourse on 5. Matt: 44: exhorting to charity and forgiveness of Enemies; I suppose purposly, The new Parliament now being furiously about Impeaching those who were obnoxious: & as their custome has ever ben going on violently, without reserve or moderation: whilst wise men were of opinion that the most notorious Offenders being named & excepted, an Act of Amnesty were more seasonable, to paciffie the minds of men, in so generall a discontent of the nation, especialy of those who did not expect to see the Government assum'd without any reguard to the absent King, or proving a spontaneous abdication, or that the Pr: of Wales was an Imposture, &c: 5 of the Bishops also still refusing to take the new Oath: In the interim to gratifie & sweeten the people, The Hearth Tax was remitted for ever: but what intended to supply it, besids present greate Taxes on land: is not named: The King abroad furnished with mony & officers by the French King going now for Ireland, Their wonderfull neglect of more timely preventing that from hence, and disturbances in Scotland, gives men apprehension of greate difficulties before any settlement can be perfected here: [whilst] The Parliament dispose of the greate Offices amongst themselves: The Gr: Seale, Treasury, Admiralty put into commission, of many unexperienc'd persons to gratifie the more: So as, by the present prospect of things (unlesse God Almighty graciously interpose, & give successe in Ireland, & settle Scotland) more Trouble seemes to threaten this nation, than could be expected: In the Interim, the new K. referrs all to the Parliament in the most popular manner imaginable: but is very slow in providing against all these menaces, besides finding difficulties in raising men to send abroad, The former army (who had never don any service hitherto, but received pay, and passed the summers in an idle scene of a Camp at Hounslow) unwilling to engage, & many of them dissaffected, & scarce to be trusted: ...

29 ... The new King, much blamed for neglecting Ireland, now like to be ruined by the L. Tyrconnel, & his popish party; too strong for the Protestants; wonderfull uncertainty where King James was, whether in France or Ireland: The Scotts seeme as yet to favor King William, rejecting K James letter to them: yet declaring nothing positively: Souldiers in England, discontented: Parliament preparing the Coronation Oath: Presbyterians & Dissenters displeased at the vote to preserve the protestant Religion as established by Law; without mentioning what they were to have as to Indulgence: The Arch-Bishop of Cant, & the other 4: refusing to come to Parliament, it was deliberated whether they should incurr premunire: but this was thought fit to be left to fall, & connived at, for feare of the people, to w<h>om these prelates were very deare, for their opposing poper<y>: Court Offices, distributed among the Parliament men: no Considerable fleete as yet set forth: in summe: Things far from [the] settlement was expected by reason of the slothfull sickly temper of the new King: and unmindfullnesse of the Parliament, as to Ireland, which is like to prove a sad omission. The Confederats, beate the French out of the Palatinate, which they had most barbarously ruined: ...

April 11 I saw the procession both to, & from the Abby Church of Westminster, with the greate feast in Westminster Hall &c: at the Coronation of the new K William & Q. Mary: That which was different from former Coronations, was, something altered in the Coronation Oath, concerning maintaining the Prot: Religion: &c: Dr. Burnet (now made L.B. of Sarum) preached on with infinite applause: The parliament men had Scaffolds & places which tooke up one whole side of the Hall: & when the K & Q. had din'd. The Ceremonie of the Champion, & other services upon Tenures: The

Parliament men were also feasted in the Exchequer Chamber: and had each of them a Medaile of Gold given them worth five & fourty shill: the K. & Q. effigies inclining to one another, on one side, the Reverse Jupiter throwing a bolt at Phaeton, the Word which was but dull seing they might have had out of the poet something as apposite The sculpture also very meane: Much of the splendor of the proceeding was abated, by the absence of divers who should have made it up: There being as yet 5 Bish: 4. Judges, (no more at present, it seemes [as yet] sworn) & severall noblemen & greate Ladys wanting: But indeede the Feast was magnificent: The next day, went the H of Commons & kissed their new Majesties hands in the Banqueting house:

12 I went the next day afternoone [with the B: of St. Asaph] to visite my L. of Canterbery at Lambeth, who had excused himselfe from officiating at the Coronation, (which the Bishop of Lond: performed assisted by the A.B: of Yorke) we had much private & free discourse with his Grace, concerning severall things, relating to the Church, there being now a Bill of Comprehension to be brought to the Commons from the Lords: I urg'd that when they went about to reforme some particulars in the Liturgie, Church discipline, Canons &c: The Baptising in private Houses, without necessity, might be reformd: as likewise the Burying dead bodies so frequently in the Churches: The one proceeding merely from the pride of [the] Women, bringing that into Custome, which was onely indulged in case of iminent danger: & out of necessity, during the Rebellion and persecution of the Cleargy, in our late Civil Warres &c: The other from the Avarice of the Minister, who made in some opulent parishes, almost as much of permissions to bury in the chancels & churches, as of their livings, and were paid with considerable advantage & gifts, for baptising in Chambers:

To this the two Bishops, heartily assented: and promised their indeavors to get it reformed: utterly disliking both practice<s>, as novel, & undecent: We discoursed likewise concerning the greate disturbance & prejudice it might cause should the new oath (now upon the anvile) be imposed upon any, save such as were in [new] office; without any retrospect to such as either had no office; or had ben long in office, who likely had some scrupules about taking a new othe, having already sworn fidelity to the Government, as established by Law: and this we all knew to be the case of my L. Arch Bishop & some other worthy persons, who were not so fully satisfied with the Conventions abdicating the late K James, To whom they had sworn alegiance &c: So I went back to Whit hall, & thence home:

K. James now certainly in Ireland; with the Marshall d'Aveaux, whom he made a Pr: Counselor, who immediatly caused the King to remove the protestant Counselor<s> (some whereoff it seemes had continued to sit) telling him that his Master the K of France would never assist him, if he did not immediatly do it: by which tis apparent how this poore Prince is menag'd by the French:

Scotland declare for K. William & Q: Mary, with the Reasons of their laying K James aside [not as Abdicating but forfaiting his right by maladministrat<ion>, the particulars mentioned] which being published, I repeate not: proceeding with much more caution & prudence than we did; who precipitated all things to the great reproch of the Nation, but all that was plainly menaged by some crafty, ill principled men: The new Pr: Council having a Republican Spirit, & manifestly undermining all future Succession of the Crown, and prosperity of the Church of England: which yet, I hope, they will not be able to accomplish so soone as they hope: though they get into all places of Trust and profit: ...

26 ... There now came certaine newes of K: James's being not onely landed in Ireland, but that by surprizing London Derry, he was become absolute Master of all that Kingdome: to the greate shame of our new King & Assembly at Westminster, who had ben so often solicited to provide against it, by timely succors, & which so easily they might have don: This is a terrible beginning of more troubles, especialy should an Armie come thence into Scotland; People being so generaly dissafected here & every where else; so as scarse would sea, or Landmen serve without compulsion:

A new Oath was now fabricating, for all the Cleargy to take, of obedience to the present Government, in abrogation of the former Oathes of Alegeance: which it is forseene, many Bishops, & others of the Cleargy will not take, the penalty being the losse of their dignit<i>e & spiritual preferment: so as this is thought to have ben <driven> on by the Presbyters & Comm: welth party, who were now in much credite with our new Governors: God in mercy, send us help, & direct the Counsel to his glory, & good of his Church: ...

May 5 ... Matters publique went very ill in Ireland, Confusion & dissention amongst ourselves, stupidity, unconstancy, emulation, in the Governours, employing unskillfull in greatest offices: No person of publique spirit, & ability appearing &c: threaten us with a very sad prospect what may be the conclusion: without Gods Infinite mercy: A fight by Admiral Herbert with the French, imprudently setting on them in a Creeke as they were landing men &c in Ireland: by which we came off with greate slaughter, & little honor: so strangely negligent, & remisse in preparing a timely & sufficient fleete. The S<c>ots Commissioners offer the Crowne &c to the new King, & Queene, upon Condition. [Act of Pole mony came forth sparing none:] ...

June 6 I din'd with the L.Bish: of St. Asaph. Monsieur Capellus, the Learned son of the most learned Ludovicus, presented to him his Fathers workes, not til now published: ...

16 ... Our Fleete, not yet at sea, & thro some prodigious sloth, & mens minding onely their present Interest: The French riding master at Sea, taking many greate prises, to our wonderfull Reproch: No certaine newes from Ireland, various reports of Scotland, discontents at home:...The E. India Company like to be disolv'd by the Parliament for many arbitrarie actions:

Oates acquitted of perjurie to all honest mens admiration.

20 Dined with me the Countesse of Bristoll & Sunderland, Sir W: Godolphin, Dr. Tenison & Mrs. Penelope Godolphin: Brought newes of a plot discovered, upon which divers were sent to Tower & secured: ...

July 8 To Lond: [9] I sat for my Picture to Mr. Kneller,[1] for Mr. Pepys late Secretary of the Admiralty, holding my Sylva in my right hand: It was upon his long and earnest request; & is plac'd in his Library: nor did Kneller ever paint better & more masterly work:

---

[1] Godfrey Kneller (1646-1723), Dutch, came to England 1675; knighted 1691, principal court painter of the period and of dignitaries. This portrait survives, having been bought by E's grandson from Ann Jackson, wife of Pepys's nephew and heir John Jackson in 1724. A copy was presented to the Royal Society in 1707 by Mary Evelyn. E seems to have sat to Kneller earlier (see 8 October 1685) but this painting is lost.

11 I dind at my L: Clarendons, it being his Ladys Wedding day: when about 3 in the afternoone, so greate & unusual a storme of Thunder, raine and wind suddainly fell, as had not ben known in an age: many boates on the Thames were over wh<e>lmed, & such was the impetuosity, as carried up in the waves in pillars & spouts, most dreadfull to behold, rooting up Trees, ruining some houses, & was indeede no other than an Hurocan:

The Co: of Sutherland told me, that it extended as far as Althorp, that very moment, which is about 70 miles from Lond: But I blesse Almighty God it did us no harme at Deptford, but at Greenewich it did much mischiefe: ...

16 I went to Hampton Court, about buisinesse, the Council being there; A greate appartment, & spacious Garden with fountaines, was beginning in the Parke, at the head of the Canale: I return'd to Lond that evening:

19 I returned home: The Marishall de Scomberge, went now Generall towards Ireland, to the reliefe of Lond:Derry: Our Fleete lie before Brest: The Confederates, now passing the Rhyne, beseege Bonn, and Maence to obtaine a passage into France: A greate Victory gotten by the Muscovite, taking & burning Procop: A new Rebell against the Turks, unkle to Yegen Bassha threatens the destruction of that Tyrannie: All Europe in armes against France; & hardly in memory of an<y> Historie, so universal a face of Warr: The Convention (or Parliament as some called it) sitting, exempt the Duke of Hanover from the Succession to the Crowne, which they seeme to confine to the present new King, his Wife, & Princesse Ann of Denmark, who is so monstrously s<w>ollen, that its doubted, her being thought with child, may proove a Tympane[1] onely: so as the [unhappy] family of Steuarts, seemes to be extinguishing: and then what government is next, is likely to be set up, whether Regal & by Election, or otherwise, The Republicaries & Dissenters from the C. of England looking evidently that way: The Scots having now againe newly, voted downe Episcopacy there: Greate discontent still through the nation, at the slow proceedings of the King, & the incompetent Instruments & Officers he advances to the greatest & most necessary charges: ...

October 9 Came to visite us the [young] Marquis de Ru<v>ignie & one Monsieur le Coque a French Refugiè, who left greate Riches for his Religion, a very learned civill person: he married the sister of the Dutchesse de la Force.

31: My Birthday, being now 69 yeares old: Blessed Father who hast prolonged my years to this greate Age, & given me to see so greate & wonderfull Revolutions, preserved me amidst them, to this moment; accept I beseech thee the continuance of my Prayers & thankfull accknowledgements, and graunt to me the Grace to be working out my Salvation, & redeeme the Time, that thou mayst be glorified by me here, & my immortal Soule saved, when ever thou shall call for it, to perpetuate thy prayes to all eternity, in that heavenly Kingdome, where there is no more Changes, nor Vicissitudes, but rest & peace, & Joy & consummate felicity for ever: Grant this, ô heavenly Father, for the sake of the L. Jesus, thyne onely Sonn & our Saviour: Amen: ...

November 5 Bish: of St. Asaph Lord Almoner &c: preached before K. & Q: on 57: Psal: 7: the whole discourse being almost nothing save an historical narrative of the C. of Englands several Deliverances, especialy that of this Anniversary, signalized, by that of the P: of Oranges Birthday, & Marriage (which was on the 4th) & of his Landing at Tor-bay this day: which ended with a splendid Ball, & other festival rejoicings:

---

[1] A swelling or tumour.

In the Meane time, No, or not sufficient supplies, Ireland gives greate apprehension of the successe of our Army there, under the D: of Shomberg, K. James, being more powerfull in Horse: & the Weather exceedingly wet & stormy: [& we having lost all the past summer for want of prudent menagement of affaires: The Convention vote a Tax of 2 Million &c:] ...

27 I went to Lond [with my family] to Winter at Sohò in the greate Square.

30 I went to the R: Society, where I was chosen one of the Council, my Lord Penbrok president, we dined together:

December 11 To Deptford to see my Grandson falln ill of a scarlet feaver at the French Schoole at Greenewich, which, after blood letting so abated that by Gods mercy I left him in an hopefull way ...

16: I return'd to Lond: blessed be God, in good hopes of the Childs recovery.

[My Servant Jo: Brake a rib by a fall, but is I hope in good way also of recovery.] ...

1690

January 11 There was this night, so extraordinary a storme of win'd accompanied with snow & sharp weather, as had not ben known the like, in almost the memory of any man living: greate was the harm it did in many places, blowing downe houses, Trees &c, killing divers people: it began about 2 in the morning and lasted til 5: being a kind of Hurecan, which Mariners observe, begin of late yeares to come northward, What mischiefe it has don at sea, where many of our Best ships are attending to convey the Q: of Sp<a>ine, together with a thousand merchants laden for several ports abroad, I almost tremble to think of:

This Winter has ben hithertoo, extreamely wett, warme, & windy: Such as went before the death of the Usurper Cromwell, which was in a stormy day: The Death of the Queene of Bohemia, & what this portends, time will discover, God almighty avert the Judgements we deserve, if it be his blessed will: ...

24: The famous Infamous Tryal of my unworthy Nephew Montague at the Kings-bench, which indeede I heard with much regrett, that so vile and scandalous a Cause should have ben <published>, the dammages being 6500 pounds: The immense wrong this proflygate wretch did my Niepce, drawing justly on him this disgrace: so vile a Cause had never ben brought to so publique an example: ...

February 16 The Dutchesse of Monmoths Chaplain on 12: Heb: 12 at St. Martins, an excellent discourse exhorting to Peace & Sanctitie, it being now at the time of very greate division & dissention in the nation: first among the Churchmen, among which the moderate & sober part, were for a speedy Reformation of divers things, which were thought might be made in our Liturgie, for the inviting of Dissenters: Others of the more stiff & ridigid were for no Condescention at all, Bookes & pamphlets published every day pro & con: so as the Convocation Were for the present forc'd to suspend any farther progresse; There was likewise a fierce & greate Canvasing about being elected in the new Parliament to meet the next moneth ...

19 I dined with the Marqu<i>s of Caermarthen (late Lord Danby) where was Lieutenant Gen: Duglas, a very considerable & sober Commander, going for Ireland, & related to us the exceeding neglect of the English Souldiers, perishing for want of Clothing & necessarys this winter; & exceedingly magnifying their Courage & bravery during all their hardships: There dined also my Lord Lucas Lieutenant of The Towre, & The Bish: of St. Asaph &c:

The Privy Seale was now put againe into the hands of Commissioners, Mr. Cheny (who married my kindswoman, Mrs, Pierpoint) Sir John Knatchbull, & Sir William Poultny: I think I might have ben one of them, had I thought it seasonable, & would have ingaged my friends: ...

25 I went on foote to Kinsington, which K. Will: had bought of my Lord of Notingham, & new altered, but it was yet a patch'd building, yet with the Gardens a very sweete Villa, having to it the Parke, and the straite new way through the park: I din'd with the Bish: of St. Asaph, Dr. Tenison & Stradling ...

March 7: I din'd with Mr. Pepys, late Secretary of the Admiralty, where was that excellent Shipwright, & sea-man (for so he had ben, as also Commissioner of the navy) Sir Anthony Deane, who amongst other discourses, & deploring the sad condition of our Navy, as now Govern'd by unexperienc'd men &c since this Revolution: Related to us, what exceeding advantage we of this <nation> had, by being the first who built Fregats: the first that was ever made, being that Vessel, which was afterward called the Constant Warwick; which Pet: of Chattham built for a tryal of making a Vessel that would saile swiftly, it was built with low Decks, the gunns lying neere the water; & was so light & swift of sailing, that in a short time, he told us, she had ere the Dut<c>h-War was ended, taken as much mony from Privateers as would have laden her, & that more such being built, did in a yeare or two scoure our Channels, from being exceedingly infested by those of Dynkirk & others: And added that it were the best and onely infallible expedient, to be masters at sea, & able to destroy the greatest Navy of any enemy whatsoever, if instead of building huge greate ships, & 2d and 3d rates &c: they quite left off building them with such high decks, which he said was nothing but to gratifie Gentlemen Commanders who must have all their Effeminate accommodations, & for pomp, which would be the ruine of our Fleetes, if such persons were continued to command, they neither having Experience, nor [being] capable of learning, because they would not submitt to the fatigue & inconveniences, which bred seamen could do, in those so otherwise usefull swift fregats:

Which he made appeare, being to encounter the greatest ships, would be able to protect, set on, & bring off, those who should manege the Fire-ships, & that whatsoever [Prince] should first store himself with numbers of such (viz. Fireships) would thro the help and countenance of such Fregats, be certainly able to ruine, the greatest force, that, of never so vast ships, could be put to sea for fight, & that by reason of the dexterity of working those light & swift-sailing vessels, to guard the Fireships: & this he made so evident, that he concluded there would shortly be no other method of sea fight: & that our greate ships & Men of Warr, however stored with Gunns & men, must submitt to whosoever should encounter them with far lesse number: He thereupon represented to us, the dreadfullnesse of these Fireships; & that he continualy observed in our last maritime warr with the Dut<c>h, that when ever an Enemys fireship, approch'd, the most valiant both of Commanders & common Sea-men & sailers, were in such feare and Consternation, that, though of all times, there was then most neede of the Gunns, boomes, & other Instruments, to keepe the misch<ie>f off; they grew pale & astonish'd, & as if possessed with a quite other meane soule, slung about, forsooke their gunns & worke, as in dispaire, everyone looking about, which way they might get out of their ship, though sure to be drown'd if they did so, or to be burnt to death if they staied: This he said was likly to prove hereafter the method of sea fights & that whatever King, got provision of this before his Neighbour potentats, must demonstrably destroy the other, & did therefore wish, it might not be the misfortune of England; especialy, if they continued to put the Gentlemen Commanders over experienced sea-men, upon accounte of their ignorance, effeminancy & Insolencie: ...

11 I went againe to see Mr. Charletons Curiosities both of Art & nature; as also his full & rare collection of Medails: which taken alltogether in all kinds, is doubtlesse one of the most perfect assemblys of rarities that can be any where seene: I much admired the contorsions of the Thea roote, which was so perplext, large & intricate, (& with all hard as box) that it was wonderfull to consider: ...

30: ... This was the first time of my poore wifes going to church, after above a yeares Infirmity, for which God Almighty be praised:

June 4: K: William set forth upon his Irish Expedition, leaving his Queene Regent during his absence &c:...

10 I went to Lond: Mr. Pepys read to me his Remonstrance, shewed with what malice & <injustice> he was suspected, with Sir Ant: Deane, about the Timber of which the 30 ships were built by a late Act of Parliament: with the exceeding danger the present Fle<e>t would be shortly in by reason of the Ignorance & incompetency of those who now manag'd the Admiralty & affaires of the Navy, of which he gave an accurate state, & shewed his greate abilitie: I retur<n>ed in the Evening: ...

24 Dined with & Visited me Mr. Pepys, Mr. Stuart & other friends. Mr. P: sent the next day to the Gate-house, & severall greate persons to the Towre, on suspicion of being affected to K. James: amongst which was my Lord Earle of Clarendon, unkle to the Queene [Mr. Pepys was the next morning imprisoned &c:]

July 6 ... The whole Nation now exceedingly alarm'd by the French fleete braving our Coast even to the very Thames mouth: our Fleete commanded by debauched young men, & likewise inferior in force, giving way to the Enemy, to our exceeding reproch: God of his mercy defend this poore church & nation: [Hollanders fleete beaten at sea:] K: William in Ireland taking a passe, wounded in the shoulder with a Cannon bullet: greate expectations from thence:

13 ... King William having vanquished K James in Ireland, there was much publique rejoicing: It seemes K. J: army would not stand, namely the Irish, but the English Irish & French made greate resistance: Shomberg was slaine, and Dr. Wa<l>ker, who so bravely defended L.derry: K.W: received a slight wound by the grazing of a cannon bullet on his shouldier, which yet he endured with very little interruption of his pursuit: Hamilton, who brake his word, about Tyrconnells, was taken: K.J. is reported gon back to France: Droghedah & Dublin surrendered: and if K.W. be returning, one may say of him as Caesar, *Veni, vidi, vici*, for never was such a Kingdome won in so short an Expedition; But to alay much of this the French fleete having exceedingly

beaten the Dutch fleete, & ours not daring to interpose, ride at present in our Chanell, threatning to Land, which causes an extraordinary alarme &c: ...

17 I went to London to visite some friends in the Toure, where asking for my Lord Clarendon (now with divers other Noble persons imprisoned upon suspicion of a plot) by mistake they directed me to the E. of Torrington who about 3 days before had ben sent for from the Fleete, was put into the Toure for his Cowardize and not fighting the French Fleete, which having beaten a Squadron of the Hollanders (whilst Torrington did nothing) did now ride masters at sea with that power as gave terror to the whole nation, in daily expectation of a descent, which God Almighty avert: ...

30 I went to Lond: Dined with Mr. Pepys now suffered to returne to his house in reguard of his Indisposition: I return'd home calling in at the R. Society, where Mr. Hook read a discourse of the cause of most hills & mountaines to be from subterranean eruptions &c:

August 1 Came the Duke of Grafton to visite me, going now to his ship at the mouth of the River: [to transport him to Ireland where he was slaine.] ...

15 I was desired to be one of the Baile of the Earle of Clarendon for his Lordships release out of the Tower, with divers other noblemen: [Bishop of St. Asaph expounds his Prophesys to me & Mr. Pepys &c:] ...

October The 8th of this moneth my Lord Spencer writ me word from Althorp out of N.hampton-shire that there happened an Earthquake the day before in the morning, which, tho short, sensibly shook the house: The like, & at the very same moment, (which was betweene 7 & 8 in the morning, viz, halfe an houre after 7:) the Gazette of this week aquainted us it so happned at Barnstable, Holy-head, & Dublin in Ireland: we were not at all sensible of it at Lond: ...

26 ... KingSale at last surrendred; meane while K. James party burne all they have in their power of houses, & amongst them that stately palace of the Lord Orories which lately cost as reported 40000 pounds: By a disastrous accident a 3d rate ship (the Breda) firing blew up & destroied all the passengers in which wer 25 prisoner of War to set saile for England the very next day: Many excellent ships have we thus unfortunately lost this yeare beside aboundance taken by the Enemy:

November 3 Went to the Co: of Clancarty, to condole with her concerning her debauched & dissolut son, who had don so much mischef in Ireland, now taken & brought prisoner to the Toure: ...

23 ... Carried my Lord Godolphin (now resuming the Commission of the Treasury againe to all his friends wonder) Mr. Pepys Memoires:[1] ...

December 1 R: Society St. Bartholomews day, I having been chosen President, by 21 Voices, with much difficulty, by all meanes [resolved] to avoyd it in this ill Conjuncture of publique affaires, with greate difficulty, devolved the Election on Sir Rob: Southwell, <Secretary> of State to the King William in Ireland: ...

---

[1] Not of course his *Diary*, but his *Memoires relating to the Royal Navy*, published in 1690, an account of his second Secretaryship to the Admiralty from 1684-89.

1691

January 4: ... This weeke a plot discovered for a generall rising against the new Government, for which my Lord Clarendon, Lord Preston & others were sent to the Towre; I went to see my Lord Clar: the next day &c: The Bish: of Ely also searched for: Trial of Lord Preston (as no English Peer) hastened at the old Baily:

The Parliament adjourned, for the Kings Journy into Holland, but he is stayed by the exceding hard & now long frost ...

March 11 ... I went to visite Lo:Clarendon, prisoner in the Tower, but was not suffered to come to him any neerer than the windowe &c: ...

April 10 This night, a suddaine & terible Fire burnt downe all the buildings over the stone Gallery at W-hall, to the waterside, begining at the Appartments of the late Dut<c>hesse of Portsmouth (which had ben pulled down & rebuilt to please her [no lesse than] 3 times) & Consuming other Lodgings of such lewd Creatures, who debauched both K. Char: 2d & others & were his destr<u>ction: ...

16 I went to see Dr. Sloans Curiosities, being an universal Collection of the natural productions of Jamaica consisting of Plants, [fruits,] Corralls, Minerals, [stones,] Earth, shells, animals, Insects &c: collected by him with greate Judgement, several folios of Dried plants & one which had about 80: severall sorts of Fernes, & another of Grasses: &c: The Jamaica pepper in branch, leaves, flowers, fruits &c: [which] with his Journal, & other Philosophical & naturall discourses & observations is indeede very extraordinary & Copious, sufficient to furnish an excellent History of that Iland, to which I encouraged him, & exceedingly approved his Industry.

19 ... The Arch-Bishop of Canterbury, Ely, Bath & Wells, Peterborow, Glocester & the rest who would not take their Oathes to K William now displac'd, & in their roomes. Dr. Tillotson Deane of Paules made A.B. of Cant: Patric removed from Chichester to Ely, Comberland to Gloucester, <Beveridge>, Comberland ...

May [7 I visited the Earle of Clarindon prisoner in the Tower, kept there still about the late Plot, he told me he expected every day deliverance, and bespake me to stand with his Brother the E: of Rochester &c for security which I promised.] ...

12 I went to see the Hospital & Infirmarie for Emerited Souldiers lately built at Chelsey, which is indeede a very Magnificent, Compleat & excellent Foundation, the two Cutts from the Thames, Courts, and other accommodations wonderfull fine: The several wards for the souldiers, Infirmary for the sick, Dispensatory, Governors house & other officers, especialy the Refectory for 400 men, & Chapell; In the Refectory is a noble Picture of heroic argument in honor of Char: 2d painted by Virrio: also the Kings [James] Statue in Brasse, of the worke of Gibbons in the Court next the Cloister &c: ...

<21> This day died my Nephew John Evelyn of Wotton, onely son & heire of my Eldest Bro: Geo: who sent me word of it the next day: He had ben long, & so dangerously sick, a greate part of the Winter, that Physitians despaired of his Recovery; but on the suddaine he began so to mend, that though his limbs were weake, his Appetite, (before lost) Spirit, & cherefullnesse returned, so as

he was thought past danger, & went not onely down about the house, but tooke the aire abroad in the Coach, when unexpectedly, a Veine breaking carried him away, nothing being able to stop the flux, so greate was the sharpnesse of his blood, & weake the vessells, which inconveniences accompanied with a Palsy, was contracted by an habit of drinking much wine & strong waters to comply with other young intemperate men: He had else a very strong & robust body, and was a person of very good sense & parts: He died about 35 years of age, to the greate griefe of my Bro: & Joy (I believe) of his Wife, who never behaved herselfe so discreetely, as to give him any greate comfort, which made him at last, almost wish himselfe out of the World: He had had severall Children born, & lately a Son, a very pretty Child, & likely to live, but God was pleased to take them all to himselfe: So as now (there remaining onely Daughters, women grown, & of an Elder sons of my Bro:) according to the Intailement; I became the next heire to my Bro: & our Paternal Estate, exceeding far from my least expectation, or desert: The God render me & mine worthy of this Providence, & that I may be a comfort to my Bro: whose prosperity I did ever wish & pray for: ...

June 1. I went, together with my son, & Bro: in Law Glanvil & his son, to Wotton, to solemnize the Funeral of my Nephew, which was performed the next day, very decently, & ordered by the Herauld, in the Afternoone, a very greate appearance of the Country being there: I being the chiefe Mourner, the Pal was held up, by Sir Fr: Vincent, Sir Rich: Onslow, Mr. Tho: Howard, son to Sir Robert, Auditer of the Exchequer & Cap: of the Kings Guard, Mr. Hyldiard, Mr. James; Mr. Herbert, Nephew to my L:Herbert of Cherbery & Co: German to my deceased Nephew: He was layed in the Vault at Wotton Church, in the bur<y>ing-place of that Family: an innumerable Concourse of Coaches & people accompan<y>ing the solemnity:

July 11 ...Now also was possession given at Lambeth to Dr. Tillotson, by the Sherif, the Arch-Bishop Sancroft being gon, but leaving his Nephew to keepe possession, who refusing to do it upon the Queenes message, was dispossessed by the Sherif, & imprisoned: This stout demeanor of the few Bishops refusing to take the oaths to K:William &c: animated a greate party, to forsake the Churches, so as to threaten a Schisme: Though those who looked further into the antient practise, found, that when (as formerly) there were Bishops displac'd, upon secular accounts, the people never refused to acc<k>nowledge the new Bishops, provided they were not hereticks: The truth is, the whole Cleargy had till now stretched the duty of Passive Obedience, that their now proceedings against these Bishops, gave no little occasion of exceptions: But this not amounting to Heresy, there was a necessity of receiving the new Bishops, to prevent a failure of that Order in the Church: ...

I went to visite my L:Clarendon, in the Tower, whom I found gon into the Country [for aire], by the Queens permission, under the guard of his Warders: ...

19 ... The greate Victory of K: Williams Army in Ireland[1] was now fresh & looked upon as decisive of that Warr, for the total reduction of that Iland: The Irish foote had 'tis sayd, much advantage by being intrenched, over numbered us in horse, but they forsaking the foote, a total route, greate slaughter, & losse of all the Canon & baggage followed: The French Gen: St. Ruth, (who had ben so cruel a slaughter man to the poore protestants in France,) slaine with divers

---

[1] The Battle of Aughrim, 12 July 1691. William was currently in the Low Countries.

of the best Commanders: nor was it cheape to us, neere 1000 kild, but of them 4 or 5000: ...

November 5 ... This Festival was celebrated with Illuminations, that is, by setting up innumerable lights & candles in the windows towards the streete, in stead of Squibbs & Bonefires, much mischiefe having ben don by Squibbs: Illumination was the custome, long since in Italy, [& France:] & now introduced here: ...

December 6 ... Discourse of another plot, in which severall greate persons were named, but believed to be a foolish sham: ...

[18 A very pretty Act or exercise of the Schoole boys where was my Grandson: Speeches & Orations, Verses in Gr: Lat: French: ending with a consort of voices of the boys, & then exercises in Mathematics]: ...

25 Christmas day was my daughter in Law brought well to bed of a Daughter, exactly at 12 at noone: Blessed be God.

28 Dined at Lambeth with the new AB: farr politer than the old man: the Effect of my Greenhouse Furnace, first set in practise by the AB: son in law.[1]

1692

January 1 This last week died that pious admirable Christian, excellent Philosopher, & my worthy Friend Mr. Boyle, a greate losse to the publique, & to all that knew that vertuous person: aged about 65:

6 At the Funeral of Mr. Boile, [at St. Martins] preached Dr. Burnet Bishop of Salisbery on 2: Eccles: 26: To a man that is good God giveth Knowledge & Wisedome & Joy: on which he made a Philosophical Discourse, Concerning the Acquisitions of Mans knowledge, by the example of Salomon, who had made so many experiments of what this World, & the opportunities of his glorious Circumstances could attaine, and after all that there could be no Joy or true satisfaction in this knowledge, without its being applied to the Glory of God: Thence passed to Elogie due to Mr. Boyle, who made God & Religion the object and scope of all his excellent Tallents in the knowledge of Nature, who had arived to so high a degree in it, accompanied with such zeale and extraordinary piety, which he continualy shewed in the whole Course of his life: & particularly in his exemplary charity upon all occasions: That he gave 1000 pounds yearly to the distressed Refugies of France & Ireland, was at the Charge of Translating the Scripture into Irish, & Indian Tongues, & was promoting a Turkish Translation, as he had formerly of Grotius de Veritate R.C. into Arabic, which he caused to be dispersed in those Eastern Countries; That he had setled a funds for Preachers who should preach expressly against Atheists, Libertins, Socinians <&> Jewes: besids given 8000 pounds now in his Will to Charitable uses, but that his private Charitys which no man knew of save himselfe were Extraordinary:

He delated also of his greate learning in the Tongues, Heb: Greeke, his reading of the Fathers, & solid knowledge in Theologie, once deliberating

---

[1] Described and illustrated in *Kalendarium Hortense*, 8th edition and later (see my *Writings of John Evelyn*, 1995, 399 ff).

about taking holy Orders, & that at a time when he might have made a greate figure in the Nation as to secular honor & Title, namely at the restauration of his Majestie Char: 2d: his feare of not being able to discharge so weighty a duty as the first made him decline the first, and his humility the other: He spake of his wonderfull comity and Civility to strangers, the greate Good he did by his experience in Medicine, & Chymistry, & to what noble ends he applied himselfe to that his darling studies, The works both pious & Usefull which he published, the exact life he led, & the happy End which made: something was touched of his sister the Lady Ranelagh, who died but very few days before him: And truly all this was but his due, without any grain of flattery: It is certainly not onely England, but all the learned world suffred a publique losse in this greate & good man, & my particular worthy friend:

This Weeke was committed a most execrable Murder on Dr. Clench, by Villans, who under <pretence> of carrying him in a Coach to see a Patient strangled him in the Coach, & under pretence of sending the Coach-man a litle distance, left the poore man dead, & escaped themselves in the dusk of the Evening: This is that Doctor, father of that extraordinary learned Child, whom he brought me sometime to my house &c:[1]

12 Was my Grandaughter Christned Jane, by Dr. Tenison Bishop of Lincolne, being the first Infant, that was ever Christened in Trinity Church: Godfather & Mothers, Mr. Pepys, Mrs. Steward, Mrs. Wiseman: ...

24 ... The Lord of Marboro, L:Gen: of K Williams Army in England, Gent of Bedchamber, &c. dismissed from all his Charges Military & other; & given to divers others: for his excessive taking bribes & Covetousnesse & Extortion upon all occasions from his inferior officers: Note this was the Lord who being intirely advanced by K James, the merit of his father being the prostitution of his Daughter (this Lords sister) to that King: Is now disgraced; & by none pittied, being also the first who betrayed & forsooke his Master K: James, who advanced him from the son of Sir Wi<nston> Churchill, an officer of the Greene-Cloth.

29 Died my Sister Evelyn of Woodcot, who had made our family so unkind a returne of so neere Relation, by violating my Brothers Will, in causing her daughter my Niepce, to cut of an Intailement & give it to her husband Montague, a Vicious young man, who leaving no children, defrauded my Bro: George of Baynards an Estate worth neere 500 pounds per Ann: &c: I pray God forgive her:

February 13 Being by the late Mr. Boile, made one of the Trustees for his Charitable Bequests, I went this morning to a Meeting of the Bishop of Lincolne, Sir Robert Ashwood,[2] & Serjeant Roderith; to settle that Clause in Mr. Boyles will, which he had left for Charitable Uses, & Especialy for the Appointing & Electing a Minister to preach one sermon the first Sunday every month <except> [the] 4 summer moneths, June, July, Aug: <September>: expressly against Atheists, <Deists>, Libertins, Jewes &c, without descending to any other Controversy whatever; for which is a fund left of 50 pounds per annum to be paid the Preacher quarterly & at the end of 3 years, to proceede to a new Election of some other able Divine, or to continue the same, according as we shold judge convenient; so we made choice of one Mr. Bently, a Chaplain to the Bishop of Worcester: Dr. Stillingfleete for our first preacher;

---

[1] See above, 27 January 1689.
[2] E's error for Sir Henry Ashurst.

& that the first sermon should begin on the first Moneday of March, at St. Martins Church, Westminster, & the 2d <on the first> Monday of Aprill, at Bow-Church in the Citty & so *alternis vicibus*:

March 20 ... My son was made one of the Commissioners of the Revenue & Tressury of Ireland, to which Imployments he had a mind, farr from my wishes, had it consisted with his Circumstances: ...

May 29 ... I find that though this day, were set a part by a Law expresse for the celebrating the memorable Birth, Returne & Resta<u>ration of the late King Char: 2d: There was no manner of notice taken of it, or any part of the Office (annext to the Comm prayer booke) made use of which I think was ill don: In regard his Restauration not onely redeem'd us from Anarchy & confusion but restored the Church of England as it were miraculously:

June <1> Impatient expectation of hearing the event of an expected Battel at land for the raising the Siege of Namur, the Armys on both sides being so very Greate K. Will: Eighty foure tho<u>sand men, with 25000 horse: The French above 100000 &c: ...

9 I went to Windsor to carry my Grandson to Eaton Schoole, where I met with My Lady Stonehouse & other of my daughter in Laws relations, who came on purpose to see her before her Journey into Ireland: We went to see the Castle, which we found furnish'd, & very neately kept as formerly, onely the Armes in the Gard Chambers & Keepe were removed & carried away:
[16 My Bro: confirmed to me our paternal Estate without revocation &c.] ...

July 23 I went with my Wife, Son & Daughter &c: to Eaton to see my Grandson & thence to Cranburne my Lord Godolphins house, where we lay & were most honorably entertained ...

25 We went to Mr. Hewers's to Clappham, who has a very excellent, usefull & Capacious House upon the Common: built by Sir Den: Gauden, & by him sold to Mr. Ewers, who got a very Considerable Estate in the Navy, in which, (from being Mr.Pepys's Cleark) he came to be one of the principal Officers, but was put out of all Employment upon the Revolution, as were all the best Officers, upon suspicion of being no friends to the change: & such put in their place, as were most shamefully Ignorant: & unfit: Mr. Hewers lives very handsomly and friendly to every body &c.

August 11 Went my Son, Wife & litle daughter, towards Ireland; there to reside one of the Commissioners of the Revenue: The Lord Jesus, accompany & blesse him, if it be his blessed will, & prosper him, & grant that I may yet see him in prosperity againe: ...

September 15 Happn'd an Earthquake, which though not so greate as to do any harme in England, was yet universal in all these parts of Europe; It shoke the House at Wotton, but was not perceived by any save a servant or two, who were making my bed, & another in a Garret, but I & the rest being at dinner below in the Parlor was not sensible of it. There had ben one in Jamaica this summer, which destroyed a world of people & almost ruin'd the whole Iland: God of his mercy, avert these Judgements, & make them to incite us to Repentance: This, of Jamaica, being prophanely & Ludicrously represented in a puppet play or some such lewd pass-time in the Faire at Southwarke, caused the Queene to put-downe & abolish that idle & vicious mock-shew ...

25: ... I received Assurance of my Sons &c being safely landed at Dublin, for which God be blessed:

November 6 ... There was a Vestry called, about repairing or new-building of the Church, which I thought unseasonable in reguard of the heavy Taxes, & other improper Circumstances, which I there declared, as also spake my opinion against the ill custome of burying in Churches &c:[1]

1693

February Unheard of stories of the universal increase of Witches, men women Children devoting themselves to the Devil, in such numbers in New-England, That it threatened the subversion of the Government: ...
    19 ... [Proposals of a Marriage by Mr. Draper with my daughter Susanna, which I embraced:] ...

April 25 Writing sealed for setling my Daughter<s> Joyntur:
    27 This day my Daughter Susanna was Married to William Draper Esquire, in the Chapell of Ely-house by my Lord Bishop of Lincoln [Dr. Tenison, since Arch Bishop of Cant:] I gave her in portion 4000 pounds: Her Joynture is 500 pounds a yeare: Which Marriage I pray Almighty God to give his Blessing to: She is a good Child, religious, [discreete,] Ingenious, & qualified with all the ornaments of her sex: especialy has a peculiar talent in Designe & Painting both in oyle & Miniature, & a genious extraordinary, for whatever hands can pretend to do with the Needle: Has the French Toung, has read most of the Greek & Roman Authors, Poets, Using her talents with greate Modesty, Exquisitely shap'd, & of an agreable Countenance: This Character is due to her, though coming from her Father.
    Much of this Weeke spent in Ceremonie, receiving Visites and Entertainments of Relations ...

May 11 My Daughter we accompanied to her Husbands house, where with many of his & our Relations we were magnificently treated & there we left her in an Appartment very richly addorned and furnish'd, & I hope in as happy a Condition as could be wished: & with the greate satisfaction of all our friends for which God be praised: ...

June 21 I saw a greate Auction of Pictures exposed to be sold in the Banqueting house, White-hall; they had ben my Lord Melfords, now Ambassador of K. James at Rome, & ingaged to his Creditors here: My Lord Mulgrave & Sir Ed Seymor came to my house & desired me to go along with them to the Sale: Divers more of the greate Lords &c were there who bought pictures, deare enough: There were some very excellent Paintings of V:Dikes, Rubens, Bassan; My L:Godolphin bought the boyes of Morella the Spaniard for 80 ginnies, deare enough: my Nephew Glanvill the old Earle of Arundels head of Rubens for 20 pounds. I<t> growing late I did not stay till all was sold but went immediately home to Deptford:

---

[1] St. Nicholas, Deptford, E's parish church.

July 17 I saw the Queenes rare Cabinets & China Collection, which was wonderfull rich & plentifull, but especialy a huge Cabinet, looking Glasse frame & stands all of Amber much of it white, with historical Basrelie<vos> & statues with Medals carved in them, esteemed worth 4000 pounds, sent by the D. of Brandenburg, whose Country Prussia abounds with Amber, cast up by the sea &c: Divers other China, & Indian Cabinets, Schreens & Hangings: also her Library in which were many Bookes in English, French, Dutch, of all Sorts: also a Cuppord of Gold Plate, a Cabinet of silver Fillgrene which I think was our Q.Marys, & in my opinion with other Things, Cabinet pieces, should have ben generously sent her Majestie.

September 28 I went to Lond to finish the Conveyance & deeds of the sale of the land for my daughters portion & did receive 3000 pounds, which with 1000 before made up the summ of 4000: now paied to my Son Draper: & returned home this Saturday ...

October 31 An extraordinary & dangerous Indisposition, taken by a Cold, kept me within a full fortnight, so as I could not stir abroad without greate Danger; my Wife also suprized with her wonted winter Rheumatisme; but by Gods infinite Goodnesse both now much recovered; I am arived this day to the 73rd yeare of Age: The Lord Jesus make me thankfull for this & all his mercys, & so cause me to number the rest of my days, which by the Course of nature cannot be many, that I may apply them to that Wisdome which shall bring me to his Everlasting life in his heavenly kingdome: Amen ...

November 12 My Son Draper & Daughter, now with Child, came to see us; after their some moneths absence in Visiting their Relation<s> in divers places of the Country &c and returned on Tuesday: ...

1694

January 8 I went to London in order to Remove our Goods & furniture out of our House in Dover Streete in order to the letting of it:

March 28 I went to the Duke of Norfolck to desire him to make my Co: Evelyn of Nutfield one of the Dep: Lieutennants of Surrey, & intreate him to dismisse my old Bro, not now able by reason of age & Infirmity to serve: The Duke granted the one, but would not suffer my Brother to resigne his Commission; but keepe the honor of it during his life, though he could not act &c: professing very greate kindnesse to our Family &c ...

April A publique Bank of 140000 pounds set up by Act of Parliament among severall other Acts [& Lotteries] for mony to carry on the War:[1] ...

May 4th. I went this day, with my Wife & 3 Servants from Says-Court, & removing much furniture of all sorts, books, Pictures, Hangings, bedding &c: to furnish the Appartment my Brother assign'd me; & now after more than 40 yeares, to spend the rest of my dayes with him at Wotton, where I was borne;

---

[1] The Bank of England, see below, 8 July 1694.

leaving my House, & 3 servants at Deptford (full furnished) to my Son in Law Draper, to passe the summer in & what longer time he thought good to make use of it: I Pray God this solemn Remove may be to the Glory of his mercy, & the good of my family: ...

27 ... There was no offering, & very few Communicants, of both which I complained, & desired it might be reformed if possible; The truth is, The present Incumbent, put in by my good natured Brother, upon the importunity of Relations, was one who having another fat living, tooke very little care of this parish, putting it under an hireling, tho' I believe a good man, but one altogether without spirit or Vigour: The same did my Bro: to the next Parish in his Gift also, to a Relative of his Ladys, slothfull, & fitter to have ben any thing than a divine: The Lord pardon this fault & reforme it in his good time: ...

July 8 ... The first greate Banke for a fund of Mony, being now established by Acct of Parliament was now filled & compleated to the summ of 120000 pounds, & put under the government of the most able & wealthy Cittizens of Lond, by which all who adventured any summs had 4 per Centum, so long as it lay in the banke, & had power either to take it out againe at pleasure or Transferr it: ...

Many Executed at London &c: for Clipping mony, which was now don to that intollerable degree, that there was hardly any mony stiring that was intrinsi<c>aly worth above halfe the value, to such a strange exorbitance things were arived, beyond that any age can shew example: ...

August 4 I went to visite my Co: G:Evelyn of Nutfeild, where I found a Family of ten Children, five sonns, & as many daughters: all of them beautifull Virgins, women growne & extreamely well fashioned; all painted also in one piece very well by Mr. Lutterell in Crayon upon Copper and seeming to be as finely painted as the best Miniature: They are the Children of 2 most extraordinary beautifull Wives: The Boys were abroad at Schoole: After dinner I returned againe, where I found my poore Wife exceedingly afflicted with the stone, now of late very much increasing her paine; from which I pray God to deliver her ...

September 13 Hearing that my daughter Draper began to Complaine & be uneasy of her greate belly, we went on the 13th towards Deptford, hoping to get thither some competent time before there would be neede of a Midwife: But were met upon the way about Meecham,[1] with the good newes of her being delivered of a Boy the night before, about betweene 7 & 8 a clocke: & so found her, after it seemes, a very sharp Conflict, very well layd to all appearance, & so continualy without any unusual Accident for 2 or 3 days; but after that seized with a feavour, loosenesse, vapours & other evil symptoms which increased upon her to that degree, that on [<21>] the friday senight after, we had very little hopes of life: so as receiving the B:Sacrament, we recommended her condition to Almighty God, not expecting her to continue many hours after: But it pleased God (of his infinite mercy) that escaping that night, Sir Tho Melington & Dr. Cade (the physitians) gave us so<me> hopes & so from thence day to day, her feavor, & fits abating, tho' very slowly, exceeding thirst, & no sort of rest, put us into many doubts what would be the issue of it: She is now God be praised in some more ease, lesse thirsty, now &

---

[1] Mitcham, Surrey.

then sleepes; but still so exceeding Weake & low in Spirits, as puts us in feare: God of his infinite mercy restore her:

I never saw a finer or goodlier Child: The Baptisme is, against my will, deferr'd, expecting when Sir T: Draper (who is to be one of the Godfathers) can come downe, who it seemes is gon a journey, & returnes not til some days:

October 2 My Daughter visibly mending of her hitherto dangerous Condition & giving us greate hope of a perfect recovery, I went to Lond: about severall buisinesses:

5 I went to <St.> Paules to see the Choire now finished, as to the stone work & that part both without & within the scaffolds struck: some exceptions might yet perhaps be taken without <as> the placing Columns upon Pilasters, at the East Tribunal: As to the rest certainly a piece of Architecture without reproch: The pulling out of the Formes, like drawers from under the stalles, is very ingenious:

I went also to see the building beginning near St. Giles's where seaven streetes make a starr from a Doric Pillar plac'd in the middle of <a> Circular Area. Said to be built by Mr. Neale, Introducer of the late Lotteries in Imitation of those of Venice: now at this time set up here, for himselfe twise and now one of: 20000 for the state[1] ...

11 This day Mr. Holden our Viccar Christned my Grandchild by the name of Thomas, being the Name of Sir Thomas Draper of Sunning Hill in Barkshire Unkle to my Son-in-Law, My selfe being the other Godfather: The Godmother the Lady Temple his Aunt: The Infant (much against my desire) being thus long from Baptis<m>e; by reason of Sir Thomass Indisposition which hindred him from comming abroad; & that my daughter had [not] ben recovered of her so late dangerous sicknesse: ...

December 16 ... Mr. Wells Curate at Abinger had a letter from me to the A Bishop of Cant to procure him a living in Surrey neere Gildford, in place of one Mr. Gerey, who was unhappily killed, by reaching a Gun to his son in a Tree, watching to shoote some rabbets, the Cock being up as he delivered the but end of the piece to his son it went of & hitting the father in the forehead miserably slew him:

29 I went together with my Wife to Wotton, for the rest of the Winter; which with long frost & snow was I think the very sharpest I ever past: The small pox increasing & exceedingl<y> mortal: Queene Mary died thereoff, full of Spotts: Died the 28: & I think was buried 2 or 3 days after: What this unexpected Accident may produce as to the present Government, many are the discourses, & a little time may shew: The K. seemed mightily afflicted, as indeede it behoved him:

---

[1] Seven Dials, near Covent Garden, built by Thomas Neale (d.1699). The column is now at Webridge, Surrey.

1695

January ... The small pox still raging: Greate expressions in most parts of England, & in Holland exceeding, for the death of the late Queene: The King & Princesse Ann (til now displeased with the Court, upon some suggestions, which made the two sisters strang to one another) now so fully reconciled, that she is invited to keepe her Court at White-hall (till now living privately at Berkely-house) & desired to take into her family divers servants of the Queene, to maintain which the King had assign'd her 5000 a quarter: Greate preparation in the meane time for a most magnificent funeral: All people in Mourning; Addresse<s> of Condolence from all parts both at home, & from abroad:

February 17 Cald to Lond by Lord Godolphin one of the Lords of the Tress: offering me the Kings making me Treasurer of the Hospital designed to be for emerited sea-men &c: to be built at Greenewich, which I deliberated about ...

March 5 Was the Queens funeral infinitely expensive, never so universal a Mourning, all the Parliament men had Cloaks given them: 400 poore women, all the streets hung, & the middle of streets boarded & covered with black cloth: there was all the Nobility, Mayor & Aldermen, Judges, &c: ...
    8 ... supped at the B: of Lichfild & Co: who related me the pious behaviour of the Queene in all her sicknesse which was admirable & the noble designe she had in hand, her expensive Charity, never enquiring of the opinion of the partys if objects of charity: that a Cabinet <being> opened some time after her decease, a paper was found wherein she had desired her body might not be opned or any expense on her funerall extraordinary when ever she should happen to dye; both which were not perform'd, finding this paper too late after all was already prepared: Other excellent things under her owne hand to the very least of her debts, which were very small, & every thing in that exact method as seldom is found in any private persons: In summ such an admirable Creature (abating for her taking the Crown without a more due Apology) as dos if possible out do the Renowned Q:Eliz herselfe: ...
    Now was pub: the new Edition of Cambdens Brit: with greate Additions, those to Surrey mine: so as I had one presented to me: Dr. Gale shewed me a MS. of some parts of the New Test. in vulg: Lect: that had belonged to a Monastery in the north of Scotland, which he esteemed to be above 800 yeares old: some considerable various readings observable as in 1.John: & Genealogies of St. Luke, left out &c: query more: ...

May [9 went to Lond:] In order to the first meeting of the Commissioners for Erecting an Hospital for Sea-men at Greenewich: it was at the Gild-Hall; present L.Archbishop of Cant: L:Keeper, L. Privy Seale, Lord Godolphin, Duke of Shrewsbery, Duke of Leedes, E. of Dorset, Monmouth: Commissioners of the Admiralty & Navy, Sir Rob: Clayton, Sir Chr Wren, & severall more: ...
    24 To Lond: where we made report of the state of Gr: House, & how the standing part might for 6000 pounds be made servicable at present & what Ground would be requisit for the whole designe:
    My Lord Keeper ordered me to prepare a booke for Subscriptions, and a preamble to it. Went this Evening to Deptford: ...

June 9 ... Went afterwards to see Sir Jo: Mordens Charity or Hospital on Black-heath now building for the Reliefe of Merchands that have failed, a very worthy Charity & noble building:[1] ...

July 6 I din'd at Lambeth making my first Visit to my L A Bishop, where was much company & greate cheere: After Prayers in the Evening, my Lord, made me stay, to shew me his house, furniture & Garden, which was all very fine, & far beyond the usual A Bishops: not as affected by this A.B: but as being bought ready furnished of his predecessor: we discoursed of severall publique matters, particularly of the Princesse of Denmark, who made so little a figure, & now after greate expectation, not with child &c: so I returned to Lond: ...

23 Dyed my Grandson & Godson Tho: Draper of a Convulsion fit at Nurse, just as they were about to have weaned it: A very hopefull, strong and lovely Child; to the very greate Griefe & affliction to us all, & especialy to my poore daughter, now big with another: The Lord pardon what ever in us might provoke him to deale thus severely & grant us his mercy in the preservation of my daughter with the fruite she now gos with: Amen: ...

September 10 Tuesday a quarter of an hour before 11, was my daughter Draper brought to bed of a daughter: for which God be praised: ...

29 Very cold weather: little Grandaughter Christned Mary: Godfather Mr. Roger Draper, my sister Draper (Niece Glan: standing for [her]): Sir Purbeque Temple unkle to my son Draper died sudenly: a greate funeral at Adiscomb, his lady being owne Aunt to my Son in Law, who hopes for a good fortune, there being no heire &c: I had most comfortable newes from my son of his perfect health in Ireland, for which I immediatly blessed God: & beseech him to confirme & improve it to the health of his soule:

There had ben a new meeting of the Commissioners about the Hosp: at Greenewich upon the new Commission, where my L. Major, Lord of Cant: Lord Keeper, &c appeared, but by reason of some Indisposition I could not be there: ...

October 25 The A Bishop & my selfe went alone to Hammersmith to visit & see Sir Sam: Moreland who was start-blind & could not see at all: a very Mortified sight & person: shewed us his Invention of Writing which was very ingenious, also his wooden Kalendar, which instructed him all by feeling, & other pretty & usefull Inventions of Mills, pumps &c. & the Pump he has erected that serves water to his Garden & to passengers, with an Inscription, & brings from a filthy part of the Thames, neere it, a most perfect & pure water: He had newly buried 200 pounds worth of Music books as he sayd 6. foote under ground, as being love songs & vanity, but playes himselfe on his Theorb, psalms & religious hymns. &c

---

[1] Morden College, by Wren, and still extant. Built out of gratitude for the safe return of merchant ships from Turkey, a dangerous undertaking.

1696

February 2: Greate Indisposition by paine in my kidnies, thro gravell &c: kept me from church this day also, but we had the Office by Mr. Wye &c:

The R: Sovraigne burnt at Chattham, that ship, which built 1637 was perhaps the original Cause of all the after trouble to this day:[1] ...

26 There was this weeke a Conspiracy of about 30 Knights, Gent, Captaines, many of them Irish & English Papists & non Jurors or Jacobites (as calld) to murder K. William, upon the first opportunity of his going either from Kensington, to hunting, or the Chappell, & upon a signal of fire to be given from Dover C<l>iffe to Calis, an Invasion designed, where there were in order to it, a very greate Army in readinesse, Men-of Warr & transport ships innumerable to joyne with a general Insurrection here, The Duke of Barwick being seacretly come to London to head them, & K. James attending at Calis with the French Army: but it being discovered by I think the Duke of   & other of the Confederats, & by one of their owne party; & a 1000 pounds, to who soever could apprehend any of the 30 named: The whole designe was frustrated, most of the Ingaged taken & secur'd: The Parliament: Citty & all the nation congratulating the deliverance & Votings & Resolutions, that if ever K. William should be Assassinated, it should be revenged upon the Papists & Party throout the nation, an Act of Association drawing up to impower the Parliament to sit upon any such Accident, til the Crowne should be dispos'd of according to the late settlement at the Revolution; All Papists in the meane time to be banished 10 miles from London; which put this nation into an incredible disturbance & general Animosity against the Fr: King, & K. James: The Militia of the Nation raised, several Regiments sent for out of Flanders, & all things put into a posture to encounter a descent: which was so timed abroad, that, whilst we were already much confused, & discontented upon the greatnesse of the Taxes, and corruption of the mony &c, we had likely to have had very few Men of Warr neere our Coasts; but so it pleased God, the V Admiral Rooke wanting a Wind to pursue his Voyage to the Straites, That Squadron, with what other forces at Portsmouth & other places, were still in the Channell, & soone brought up to joyne with the rest of the Ships which could be gotten together: so as there is hope this Plot may be broken; It is certaine it had likely have ben very fatal to the [danger of the] whole Nation, had it taken Effect; so as I looke on it as a very greate deliverance & prevention by the Providence of God; for tho many did formerly pitty K. James's Condition, this designe of Assassination, & bringing over a French Army, did much alienate many of his Friends, & was like to produce a more perfect establishment of K. William, it likewise so much concerning the whole Confederacy: What it will yet end in, God onely knows, may he of his Infinite mercy to this sinfull & miserably divided Church & nation, put an end to this bloody unchristian Warr, & restore peace & quietnesse:

March 1 ... The wind northerly & Easterly all this Weeke brought so many of our men of Warr together, & before the french Coast, that tho most of the French finding their designe detected & prevented, made a shift to get into Calais & Dunkirk roode, we wanting fireships & bombs, to encounter & disturbe them; but they were yet so ingag'd among the sands & flatts that tis said they cutt their Masts, & slung over their greate Gunns to lighten their

---

[1] See above, 19 July 1641.

Vessels: we are yet upon them, & what the Event will be must be expected: This deliverance is due onely to God: The French preparation was at once not onely to invade England, but Scotland & Ireland also; most seacretly & solemn<l>y Concerted, by all the French Commanders & polititians, that making the seate of the Warr here, the Confederats might at once be so distressed, as to submitt to his Arme<s>: but this God has in greate mercy prevented: ...

15 ... Three of the unhappy wretches (whereoff one a Priest) executed this weeke for intending to assassinate the King; accknowledging their intention, but acquitting K. James, of instigating them to it in that manner, & dying very penetently: [Divers more in danger & some very Considerable persons:] ...

April 23 I went to Eaton, din'd with Dr. Godolphin the Provost. The Scholemaster assured me that there had not ben in 20 yeares a more pregnant youth in that Place than my Grandson: I return'd that evening with Lady Jane Leueson & her daughter &c, who went to place Sir William Windham at that Schole:

I went to see the Kings house at Kensington with some Ladys: The House is very noble, tho not greate; the Gallerys furnished with all the best Pictures of all the Houses, of Titian, Raphel, Corregio, Holben, Julio Romano, Bassan, V:Dyke: Tintoret, & others, with a world of Porcelain; a very pretty private Library; the Gardens about it very delicious: ...

28 ... Oates dedicated a most villanous reviling booke against K.James, which he presumed to present K.William, who certainly could not but abhorr it, speaking so infamously & untruely of his late beloved Queenes owne father: ...

June 1. I went to Deptford to dispose of our Goods, being [in order to] lett it for 3 years to V.Admiral Benbow, with Conditions to keepe the Garden &c.

4: A Comitty meeting at W-hall, about the Hospital at Greenewich at Sir Chr: Wrenn, his Majesties Surveyor Gen: We made the first agreement with divers Workemen & for Materials, & gave the first Order for the proceding on the foundations, ordering payments to be Weekly to the Workmen & a general Accompt to be monethly: ...

I let my House at Deptford to V:Admiral Benbow for 3 years &c ...

Want of current money to carry on not onely the smalest concernes, but for daily provisions in the Common Markets: Ginnys lowered to 22s: & greate summs daily transported into Holland, where it yeelds more, which with other Treasure sent thither to pay the Armies, nothing considerable coined of the new & now onely current stamp,[1] breeding such a scarsity, that tumults are every day feared; no body either paying or receiving any mony; so Imprudent was the late Parliament, to damne the old (tho clip't & corrupted) 'til they had provided supplies. To this add the fraud of the Bankers & Goldsmiths who having gotten immense riches by extortion, keepe up their Treasure, in Expectation of a necessity of advancing its Value. Duncumb not long since, a meane Goldsmith, having made a purchase of neere 90000 pounds of the late D. of Buckinghams Estate, & reputed to have neere as much in Cash &c: Banks & Lotteries every day set up, besides Taxes intollerable, & what is

---

[1] Hammered coinage, produced until 1662, now ceased to be legal tender. Only the new milled coinage was valid (see 10 January 1662).

worse & cause of all this, Want of Publique Spirite, in a Nation [daily] sinking under soe many Calamities ...

[20 I gave my Lord Cheny a Visite at Chelsey. I saw those ingenious Water works invented by Mr. Vinstanley wherein were some things very surprising & extraordinary.][1] ...

30 I went with a select committee of the Commissioners for the fabri<c>k of Greenewich Hospital, & with Sir Chr: Wren the Surveyor, where with him I laied the first stone of that intended foundation; precisely at 5 a clock in the Evening after we had dined together: Mr. Flamsted the Kings Astronomical Profes<s>or observing the punctual time by Instruments: Note that one of the workmen in helping to place the stone, being a Corner large stone, grating his fingers against the gravelly banke, some drops of blood fell upon it: We afterwards returned to Lond: ...

July 4. Note that my Lord Godolphin was the very first of the Subscriber<s> who payed any mony towards this noble fabric: ...

September 6 ... I went to Congratulate the Marriage of a Daughter of Mrs. Boscawen, to the son of Sir Phil: Meadows: she is niepce to my Lord Godolphin: They were Married at Lambeth 30 Aug: by the Archbishop: a most vertuous discreete young Vergin & as hopefull a young Gentleman ...

13 ... After confident discourses of the poysning the Q. of Spaine & cutting the Infant alive out of her belly when dead, & of the French Kings death, waigers layed of the truth, not one word was found true, so strangely was the nation given to lying: ...

1697

January 1 Beging Gods blessing the yeare entered into; we had news of my daughter Draper being brought to bed safely of a fine Boy, who was christened by my Bro: Evelyn by his name George, whom God Almighty blesse & preserve ...

September 9 My son, came in his melancholy Indisposition from Lond, hither, where his mother had ben to visite him:

October 3: It being a wet cold day, we went not to Church, officiating at home:

So greate were the stormes all this weeke, that there were nere 1000 poore men cast away going into the Texell,[2] & many other disasters: ...

17 ... My Daughter Draper husband & family awakned in the night by the noise of fire, Escaped being all burnt in their bed, in the dead time of sleepe; by timely extinguishing it, in their owne chamber: for which God be ever praised: ...

---

[1] This is Henry Winstanley (1644-1703), an engineer who subsequently designed the Eddystone lighthouse.

[2] The sea by Texell, at the mouth of the Zuyder Zee, Holland.

Peace was signed with France at Ryswick in early September

December 2 The Thanksgiving day for the peace, I went in the morning to W.Hall, where was the K. & a very greate Court: the Bishop of Salisbery preached, or rather made a florid Panegyric on 2.Chro:9.7.8. Shewing how neere <to Solomon> for successe & felicity this present K. was, & how God had chosen him, & by many signal providences reserved him to deliver this Church & nation, yea all Europ from the haughty & insulting Enemy, Established us in this nation in our Religion & propertys, & freed all our Neighbor nations from the ambition of France, broken the power of Insulting foes, & don such things by his Conduct & Courage that as the Q. of Sheba came far to admire him, so a greate Prince (meaning the Zar of Mus<c>ovy) came a farther, to see him who had don such wonders, concluded with that of the Text, that all this was that he might do Justice & Judgment & govern his people righteously, by encouraging the good, & rebuke the prophane & reform the nation which now needed it, & for which God had preserved & cald & set him up: This was the summ, but rather see the printed sermon:

The Evening concluded with fire-works & Illuminations, of [such] greate expence as would have erected <a> Triu<m>phal Arch of Marble & the fireworks in nothing answering expectation, but were the destruction of some spectators & of a person of quality a stranger: ...

5. Was the first Sonday, St. Paules had had any service in <it>, since it was Consumed at the Conflagration of the Citty; 1666: which I my selfe saw, & now <w>as likewise my selfe there, the Quire being compleatly finished, & the Organ esteemed the best in Europe of I thin<k> 40 stops; There were the Bishop of Lond, Lord Major & innumerable multitude, one Mr. Knight preaching (for Dr. Sherlock the Deane) on Epist Jude ver:3. exhorting to Contend for the Faith once delivered, to the Church; most of which he applied against the Socinian doctrine now so rife: & this he did most excellently & to the satisfaction & Conviction I believe of all that heard him: The H. Sacrament followed, the B. of Lond. & Residentarys distributing the Elements: I was invited & dined with Dr. Godolphin, a Resider & Provost of Eaton ...

1698

January ... I presented my Booke of Medals[1] &c to divers noblemen, before I suffered it to be exposed to sale ...

---

[1] *Numismata, A Discourse of Medals, Antient and Modern. Together with some Account of Heads and Effigies of Illustrious and Famous Persons, in Sculps, and Taille-Douce, of Whom we have no Medals extant; and Of the Use to be derived from them. To which is added A Digression concerning Physiognomy.* The book was something of a disaster for E. The subject matter was new to him and he had spent a great deal of time assembling the many engravings required. When printed the book was found to contain innumerable *errata* to E's shame and embarrassment. He blamed everyone and everything except himself, for example his remoteness from London out at Wotton, the problems involved with the wrangle over the Wotton estate (see 8 July 1698, and 26 June 1699), and the printer. The book is also weakened by its rambling

2: ... White-hall utterly burnt to the ground, nothing but the walls & ruines left:[1]

February 6 ... The Czar Emp: of Moscovy, having a mind to see the Building of Ships, hired my house at Says Court, & made it his Court & palace, lying & remaining in it, new furnish'd for him by the King: ...

May 8 My daugh<t>er Draper brought to bed of a fine Boy: ...
19 Was my Grandson Draper Christn'd William; they would faine have had it Evelyn (making me Godfather as I was) but for some reasons I desired it might be William: Sir Jo: Conniers stood for me; The Godmother was one Mrs. Brent, a Relation of my Son in Laws, a very fine prudent Lady: ...
30 I dined at Mr. Pepyss, where I heard that rare Voice, Mr. Pate, who was lately come from Italy, reputed the most excellent singer, ever England had: he sang indeede many rare Italian Recitatives, &c: & severall compositions of the last Mr. Pursal,[2] esteemed the best composer of any Englishman hitherto: ...

June 9 I went to Deptford to view how miserably the Tzar of Moscovy had left my house after 3 moneths making it his Court, having gotten Sir Cr: Wren his Majesties Surveyor & Mr. London his Gardener to go down & make an estimat of the repairs, for which they allowed 150 pounds in their Report to the L: of the Treasury:[3] Then I went to see the foundations of the Hall & Chapell, wharfe & other parts of the Greenwich Hospital: & so returned: ...

July 8 I came to passe the rest of the summer <at> [my sonns house] in Berkly-streete, during my Brothers (or rather, my Neipces & Dr. Fulhams) displeasure, because I could not assent to the alteration of a settlement of my Brothers gift freely to me: &c which I pray God to reconcile.

---

text, and digressions all of which show that E had seriously overreached himself.
[1] An exaggeration, the Banqueting House and Holbein Gate, for example, survived.
[2] Henry Purcell (c. 1658-95).
[3] Peter the Great's ruinous tenancy at Sayes Court was brought to E's attention by his servant John Strickland who wrote to him on 16 February 1698:

> There is a house full of people, and right nasty. The Tsar lies next your library, and dines in the parlour next your study. He dines at ten o'clock and six at night, is very seldom at home a whole day, very often in the King's yard, or by water, dressed in several dresses. The King is expected there this day, the best parlour is pretty clean for him to be entertained in. The King pays for all he has.

E recorded the damage in *Silva*, 1706, p.182:

> Is there under Heaven a more glorious and refreshing Object of the kind, than an impregnable Hedge of about four hundred foot in length, nine Foot high, and five in diameter; which I can shew in my now ruin'd Gardens at Say's-Court, (thanks to the Czar of Moscovy) at any time of the Year, glitt'ring with its arm'd and varnish'd Leaves? The taller Standards at orderly distances, blushing with their natural Coral: It mocks at the rudest assaults of the Weather, Beasts or Hedge-breakers ...

The Tsar had made a habit of being pushed through the hedge in a wheelbarrow.
Wren's report can be found in Dews, 1884 (and 1971), *History of Deptford*, 34-38.

1699

March 24 Friday [To my exceeding griefe & affliction:] after a tedious [languishing] sicknesse contracted in Ireland, & increased here, died my onely remaining son John: <who had> now ben [6 years] one of the Kings Commissioners of the Revenue of that Kingdom, & performed his Employment both with greate ability & reputation, aged 44 years & about 3 moneths: Leaving me one Grandson, now at Oxon, whom I beseech A. God to preserve, & be the remaining support of the Wotton family: Upon this Interruption I could not appeare at Church the following Sunday: ...

[30 My deceased Son, was according to his desire Carried (being put into lead) into Surry, & layd amongst our Relations, in the Vault belonging to that family, accompanied by severall.]

April 16 My Grandson sent me a latin Epist<le> from Oxon, giving me account of the progresse of his studys there, & of his preparation for the receiving of the H.Eucharist, the first time, on Easter Sonday: I beseech God to blesse him, that he may proceede as he has hithertoo:

June 26. 28, after a yeares tedious altercations caused by one Dr. Fullham who had married a Grandaughter of my Bros, against the full Consent of her Relations, a Crafty & intriguing person, he so insinuated into my good Bro, after a few moneths, as to perswade my Bro: to require me, to cut off an Intaile of the Estate he had given me, & that in Case, I should die without Issue Male, it might fall to the Grandaughter, which by the reiterated settlements the law would not give him: My Bro: having often professed, that he would have it descend to the name, & I by no meanes willing it should be otherwise, & that the Patrimony of my Ancestors should be dissipated, sold or scattered, among strangers, as it would soon have ben, & our name & family extinguished, as it almost was, by Sir Jo: Evelyn of God-stone, Sir Jo: of Wilts, Sir Ed of Ditton, who leaving nothing to their name, 3 considerable Estates went away to the female:

My Bro: likewise, having amply provided portions to his 3 Grandaughters; & so many years persisting to have his Estate Continue in the name: Was as I sayd, so wrought upon by the Crafty Doctor as upon my refusal to alter the settlement, to exhibit a Bill against me in Parliament now sitting, tho' I often promised not to alter the settlement, but let it passe with the Contingencys, offering in the meanetime, that provided the Mannor of Wotton & Abinger might be reserved, to comply as to the rest, that in Case I had no heir Male it should go to the Grandchildren: but when I found nothing would pacify the Doctor & the rest, but the swallowing it all; I so answered my Bro: Bill, shewing how absolutly it was conveyed to me; That the house of Commons was so convinct of my Case, that they durst not proceede, I having so very greate an Interest among them in favour of my right: So as hoping to fare better with the Lords, they attempted all they could to gaine a party among them; but, when they found I had not onely almost all the Bishops, & so very many of the secular Lords, as were the most eminent speakers, that they had no hope to prevaile there: My Bro: (who 'til now they would not suffer, to accept of any Composition) did at last, offer that if I would alowe him 6500 pounds, to inable him to discharge [some of] his owne debts, & give legacys to his Gr:-Children, he would make a new settlement, that should more expressly Convey the whole Estate by an indefeasable Inheritance, & being Tennant for life onely, oblige himself not to make any farther wast of the woods & other spoile he had begunn, & was in his power to do:

To this, in reguard of his free & original gift (tho most believed it had ben intended by my Father but which my Bro: deneyed) & to quiet his Mind, & indeede in Gratitude, I did consent to, The mony to be payd by 1000 pounds a year for 7 years to begin after his decease: Now my good Bro: being sufficiently Convinct, & declaring that what he settled on me, was not onely absolutly in his power, to give his Estate as he pleased, and peremptorily affirming to the Doctor himselfe, that he would do it again if what he had settled was not sufficiently valid: Yet so dextrous was this Insinuating faire tongued & crafty man, assisted with the perpetual solicitation of the Women; that then they set on my Bro: with a Case of Conscience, & that tho' he had power to give the Estate as he had don, yet in Conscience he ought not to have don it:

Upon this I sent my Case to the learned Bishop of Worcester Dr. Stillingflete, not more esteemed for his being an Excellent Lawyer, but a profound divine, who, as indeede did the A Bishop of Cant: Bishop of Ely, Chichester, Peterborough, Chester, Salisbery, Lichfield &c: who universaly affirm'd my Bro: was not obliged by Conscience to revoak what he had settled on me: And as to matter of Law, the other Lords, Dukes, Earles & Peers who were generaly for me, as were the Commons: I had so much the advantage, that, had I not ben tenderer of my Bro: reputation than some would have had me: I might have saved 6500 pounds: but I chose rather to incumber the Estate with it, than not to gratify my good Bro: notwithstanding the advantage I had, & least it should be said I was ungratefull; my designe & desire being nothing so much in all this Contest, but to preserve the patrimonial Estate to the famely: So as now, a settlement being made as strong as Law could do it, all was Reconciled: my Good Bro: having ben prevailed with, contrary to his own resolution, but suffers them to govern his as they pleased, & this in my absence, whilst I was cald to London about other affairs: to both our trouble & charge: The Writings were sealed 26. of June, & a Recovery suffered on 28:

After this finding my Occasions calling <me> so often to Lond: I tooke the remainder of the Time, my sonn, had in his lease of an house in Dover-streete, To which I now removed, finding my being at Wotton as yet Inconvenient: So as I resolved to continue at Lond: without removing my furniture at Wotton; having enough at Says Court, I furnished the house in Dover-streete, & came to it on Saturday, July 1. from Berkley streete, where I had ben ever since I came from Wotton, in reguard of my unhapy Sons Indisposition: I pray God of his infinit mercy, whose gracious providence has hitherto so wonderfully extricated me <out> of this, & other disturbances & afflictions, to sanctifie it to me, and to blesse the remainder of my life & now very old age with peace, & Charity, & assist me with his Grace to the End: ...

October 4 Wednesday night departed this life my worthy & dear Bro: Geo: Evelyn at his house at Wotton in Surrey in the 83d yeare of his Age, & of such Infirmitys as are usualy incident to so greate an Age, but in perfect memory & understanding: A most worthy, Gentleman, Religious, Sober & Temperate, & of so hospitable a nature as no family in the whole County maintained that antient Custome of keeping (as it were) open house the whole yeare, did the like, or gave nobler & freer Entertainement to the whole County upon all occasions: so as his house was never free, there being sometime 20 persons more than his family, & some that stayed there all the summer to his no small expense, which created him the universal love of the Country: To this add, his being one of the Deputy Lieutenants of the County; and living to be the most antient Member of Parliament living: He was Born at Wotton, Went to Oxford, Trinity Coll: from the Free Schole at Guilford, Thence to the Midle Temple, as gent: of the best quality did, tho' with no intention to study the Law as a Profession:

He married the Daughter of Colwall, [of] a worthy & antient family in Leicester-<s>hire, by whome he had One son; she dying in 1643, left George her son an Infant, who being educated liberaly, after Traveling abroad, returning home, married one Mrs. Goare; by whom he had severall Children but left onely 3 daughters: He was a Young man of a good understanding, but over Indulging to his Ease & pleasure, grew so very Corpulent, contrary to the constitution of the rest of his fathers relations, that he died: after my Bro: his Father had married a most noble & honourable Lady, relict of Sir Jo Cotton, she being an Offley, a worthy & antient Staffordshire family by whom he had severall Children of both sexes: This lady dying left onely 2 daughters & a son: the younger daughter dyed, before Mariage: The other lived long [as] a Virgin, & was afterward married to Sir Cyrill Wych, a noble learned Gent: sonne to Sir <Peter> Wych: he had ben Ambassador at Constantinople: Sir Cyrill was afterwards Made one of the Lords Justices of Ireland: Before this Mariage her onely Bro: John Maried the daughter of Aresfeild of Sussex [of] an honorable family, whom he left a Widdow, without any Child living: He dying about Anno 1691 & his wife not many yeares after, without any heire: My Bro: resettled the whole Estate on me: His sister who maried S<ir> C.Wych having had a portion of 6000 pounds to which what was added was worth above 300 pounds more: The 3 other Grandaughters, with what I added to theirs about 5000 pounds each:

<This> my Bro: having seene performed, died this 5t of Octob: in a good old Age, & greate Reputation: & making his beloved Daughter my Lady Wych sole executrix (leaving me onely his Library & some Pictures of my Father, Mother &c:) She indeede buried him with extraordinary solemnity, rather as a Noble man, Than a private Gent: There were I computed above 2000 people at the funerall, all the Gent of the County doing him the last honour: This performed [20th] I returned to Lond, where I came the day before, leaving my Concernes at Wotton, 'til my Lady should dispose of her selfe & family: & sending onely a servant thither to looke after my Concerns:

<22> ... I presented my *Acetaria*[1] dedicated to my Lord Chancelor, who returned me Thanks by a most extraordinary civil lett<er> shewing him to be a person of greate parts, & learning &c: I waited on his [22] Lordship who received me with greate humanity & familiar kindnesse:

November <5> ... There happned this Weeke so thick a Mist & fog; that people lost their way in the streetes, it being so exceedingly intense, as no light of Candle, Torches or Lanterns, yeilded any or very little direction: I was my selfe in it, and in extraordinary danger, robberys were committed betwene the very lights which were fixt between Lond: & K<e>nsington on both sides, and whilst Coaches & passengers were travelling: & what was strange, it beginning about 4 in the afternoone was quite gon by 8, without any wind to dissipate it. At the Thames they beate drumms, to direct the Watermen to make the shore, no light being bright enough to penetrat the fogg: ...

---

[1] *Acetaria, A Discourse of Sallets* [Salads].

1700

January 25 I went to Wotton, the first time, after my deare Brothers funerall, to settle my Interest & Concernes there, and furnish the house with necessarys, thro my Lady Wyche & Nephew [<Glanvill>] being Executors, having sold & disposed of what goods were left of my Brothers.

March 13 [I] was at the funerall of my Lady Temple, who was buried at Islington, brought from Adscomb neere Croydown: She left my son in Law Draper (her Nephew) the mansion house of Addscom, very nobly & compleatly furnished, with the Estate about it, which with the Jewells, money, plate &c, is computed to be worth neere 20000 pounds: She was a very prudent Lady: gave away many greate Legacys besids which 500 pounds to the poore of Islington, where her husband Sir P: Temple (both dying without Children) was buried ...

April 3. I went, with Sir Chr: Wren, Surveyor of his Majesties Workes & Buildings, to Kensington, to present the King with the Model & several drafts ingraved, of the Hospital now erecting at Greenewich for Sea-Men, The A: Bish: of Cant: introducing us; His Majestie receiving us with greate satisfaction, & incouraging the prosecution of the Work: ...

May 24 I went from Dover Streete to Wotton for the rest of summer, whither I removed the rest of the goods from Says Court, to the House at Wotton ...

16 ... Mr. Creech fellow of All-Soules in Oxon: an Excellent Poet & Philosopher who published Lucretius with notes in Latine, & an English translation, with many other pieces, & <seemed> to be of a grave & sollid temper, was found hanged, none knowing upon what occasion or apparent discontent or Cause, his Circumstances being so very easy, for besides one of the best fello<w>ships in the University, he had a living, I am told worth 200 pounds per ann: This disaster much astonished me, who knew him, By this, we find, how greatly it concernes us to implore Gods Almighty Preventing, & Assistant Graces all the days of our life ...

July <7>: ... I was now visited with an attaque of a Feaver, accompanyed with the strangury, which detain'd me in bed & house neere a moneth & much weakned me; But it pleased God, as to mittigate & allay my feavor, so to abate of my other Infirmity also; for which forever be praise ascribed to him by me, & that thereby he has againe so gratiously advertiz'd me of my duty, to prepare for my latter end which now cannot be far off, at this greate Age of mine:

The death of the Duke of Gloucester, dying of the smallpox, is very astonishing, a hopefull child of 12 or 13 years old, & the onely Child of the Princesse Ann by the Prince of Denmarke, she having had & ben with child of many sonns & daughters, but commonly none living, & often misscarying: So as now there is none to succeede to this Crowne, according as lately settled by the Parliament on the late Revolution, but <on> some Protestant Prince, the next I think being the Prince of Hanover,[1] Grandson, to the Q: of Bohemia, sister to K. Charles the first: otherwise, I think, descending (if the P: of Wales be utterly excluded) on the Dutchesse of Savoy, daughter to the princess

---

[1] George Louis (b. 1660), Elector of Hanover 1698, George I of England, 1714-27.

Henrietta, Sister to Charles the first: Wher the Crowne will now Settle, should the Princesse of Denmark breed no more to live, is matter of high speculation to the Politic: ...

August 18: ... This being the first and onely yeare & time, I was obliged to turne [to] Husbandry, plowing & sowing, it pleased God <t>o answer our hopes & labours by a most plentifull Harvest, which was brought home whilst the weather continued faire; for which God be blessed in the use of it: It turn'd to raine the next daye after: [My sonn <and> daughter<s> 2d sonn, an Infant, <died>, to our greate sorrow.] ...

September 13 A Considerable Estate in land, faire house, richly furnished, Plate, Mony &c being fallen to my Son in Law, Draper, at Adscome neere Croydon: I went with my Wife thither & stayed there till the 26, when I returned back to Wotton: ...

20: I went to see Bedington, the antient seate of the Carews formerly & in my remembrance, a noble old structure, capacious, & in forme of the buildings of the Age in Hen: 8 & Q. Eliz: <time> & proper for the old English hospitality, but now decaying with the house it selfe, heretofore adorned with ample Gardens, & the first Orange trees that ever were seene in England, planted in the open ground, & secured in winter onely by a Tabernacle of boards, & stoves, removable in summer; thus standing 120 yeares large & goodly Trees & laden with fruite, but now in decay as well as the Grotts & ther curiositys, Cabinets & fountaines in the house & abroade, thro the debauchery & negligence of the Heires, it being now fallen to a Child under age,[1] & onely kept by a servant or two from utter delapidation. The Estate & Parke about it also in decay: the negligence of a few years, ruining the Elegances of many: ...

23: I went visite Mr. Pepys at Clapham, who has there a very noble, & wonderfully well furnished house, especialy with all the Indys & Chineze Curiositys, almost any where to be mett with, the Offices & Gardens exceedingly well accomodated <for pleasure> & retirement: ...

November 5 Came the newes of my dear Grandsons (the onely male of my family remaining) being fall'n ill of the Small-pox at Oxford, which after the dire effects it had, taking a way two of my Children (Women grown) exceedingly Afflicted me: But so it pleased my most mercyfull God, that, being let-blood, at his first complaint of uneasinesse; and the extraordinary Care of Dr. Mander, head of the Coll: & now Vice-chancelor, (who caused him to be brought out of his owne Chamber, & lodg'd in his owne Appartement, Bed & Bed-Chamber) with the advise of his Physitian, & care of his Tutor: That as they came out kindly, separatly, and but few: and no evil symtom accompanying: There was all faire hopes of his doing well, to our infinite Comfort, & refreshment; as <appeared from> the account, which was se<n>t us by letter every day since their appearance, by letters either from the V: Chan: himselfe, or his Tutor, for which Almighty-God be forever praised & depended on: ...

---

[1] Nicholas Carew (1687-1727), cr. baronet 1715. He restored the house. See above, 1632 for E's visit to the house as a boy.

1701

February 27 By an Order of the house of Commons, I layed before the Speaker the State of the Accompt, what had ben received, & expended towards the building of the Marine Coll: at Greenwich of which I was Treasurer:

I had newes of the death of Mr. Wye, the Parson of Wotton, a very worthy, & good man, so the next presentation falling to me as Patron, I had some application to me very Early: But I had promised it, to Dr. Bohune, a learned person, & excellent preacher: He had ben my sones Tutor, and lived long in my family: To whom I now gave the presentation ...

March 18 I went to Greenewich, saw the progresse made of the new Hospital advancing: Thence to Says-Court, which I had now let to the Lord Ca<r>narvon sonn to the Duke of Leedes, but the Lease was in the name of another: ...

April 23d. I returned from Wotton by Greenwich, where my deare Wife being gon, thinking to have the benefit of the aire on the heath, for the recreation of her breath & lungs exceedingly still afflicted of the Cough, fell into a Feaver & Pleurisy, of which she was hardly relieved to my greate sorrow; but leaving her better the next day, businesse hastened me to Lond: ...

May 11 ... My daughter Draper was delivered of a Daughter safely, for which God be praised; & my Wife gathering strength apace ...

June 11 My Wife going into Surry, The Ax<l>etree of the Coach firing on Bansted downe, they endeavored to quench it, with the fat of the meate was caried with them and a bottle of sack, to refresh them on the way, no water neere them til they came to Letherhead.

22 I went now to congratulate the arival of that worthy & Excellent person my L. Galloway who <was> newly come out of Ireland, where he behaved himselfe so honestly, & to the exceeding satisfaction of the people; was yet removed thence, for being a Frenchman; tho they had not a more worth<y> valiant discre<e>t & trusty person in the 3 kingdoms on whom they could have relyed for his conduct & fitnesse, & one who had so deeply suffered, (as well as the Marquess his Father) by having their Estates confiscated & all they had, because Protestants: so this worthy Gent: design'd to go with his Majestie. − I also visit<ed> the Co: of Sunderland, Earle of Kent, [Lord Kingston] E. of Pembroke now precedent of the Counsel, & one of the Lords Justices during the Kings Absence: the B. of Norwich [Sir R Onslow] and some other friends being myself preparing for the Country in few days: ...

July 19 A poore [old] Labourer falling off from the Hay Cart, not any height, but pitching on his head, breaking his Collar-bone, & doubtlesse disordering his braine, tho neither quite speechlesse, & let blood but without effect, died, to my exceeding sorrow & trouble, it being in my Haying: ...

September ... The death of K. James hapning the 15 of this Moneth N. style after 2 or 3 days Indisposition, put an end to that unhapy Princes troubles, after a shorte & unprosperous Reigne, by his owne indiscreete attempting to bring in Popery, & make himselfe absolute, in imitation of the French, & impatience of the Jesuits & zeale of the Queene, to subduce the Kingdome & Religion to the Roman, which the nation would not indure: but thus was the Church of England againe preserved by Gods wonderfull providence:

14 ... The Prince of Wales was now proclaimed, K. of G.B. at Paris & so owned & visited by the F. King, Popes Nuntio & others: [Upon which the English Ambassador was called home without taking leave or giving any notice to the French King:] ...

29 *ad* **October** 4 Michaelmas day I kept Courts Leete & Barron every day this whole Weeke, in the Mannors & Lordships of Milton, Westgate, Abinger, padington & padington penbrokis &c. On the last on Saturday in Wotton; being the first courts I kept since I came to this Estate in Surry: The Steward was Mr. Hervey, a Counsellor, Justice of Peace, & Member of Parliament & neighbour: I gave him 6 ginnys which was a ginny per diem, & Mr. Martin his Cleark 3. ginnys. I have employed him upon many other occasions: ...

31 I was this day 81 yeares old Compleate in tollerable health considering my Great Age: God also delivered my Grandson sick at Oxford of the smalpox, for which and many other preservations, continuing my familys health, I rendred (as most bounden) my sincere Accknowledgements: ...

1702

March <8> The King having had a fall from his horse as he was hunting, which broke his coller bone, & being himselfe much Indisposed before & Aguish, with his former long Cough & other weaknesse, put into a Feaver, died at Kensington this Sonday morning about 8 a clock, to the extraordinary disturbance of the whole Citty, & I feare, to the Interests of the whole nation, in this dangerous Conjuncture, without Gods Infinite mercy: Matters both abroad, & at home being in so loose a posture, & all Europe ready to breake out into the most dangerous Warr that it ever suffered, & this Nation especially being so unprovided of persons of the Experience, Conduct & Courage, just as we were concluding this Confederacy so long concerted with the Emp: & other Princes, to resist the deluge of the French: How this may concerne the measures hitherto taking: God onely knows: The Parliament sate all this day &, I think all last night, & Queene Ann Proclaym'd at the usual places, & Ceremonys: These two days have ben warm & bright as Summer, all people else, especialy the Souldiers holding downe their heads: God has some greate thing to do, grant it may be to our good, & his Glory &c...

I carried to the Committe of the house of Comm: appointed to the Examination of the Accompt of what had ben received, & payed by me as Treasurer, for the Building of the new Hospital at Greenwich for Sea-men &c: which amounted to neere 100000 pounds:

11 ... There was orders published in print, after what manner the publique Mourning for the King was expected to be, as to the Clothes of persons of quality: In the meanetime, there seemed to be no sort of alteration, or Concerne in the people, upon the Kings death but all things pass't without any notice, as if he had still ben alive: Onely the Shopkeepers, who had provided store of Silke & other modish things, complained of the deadnesse of Trade they feared would insue: The Queene[1] was proclaymed with the usual

---

[1] Anne (1702-14), younger sister of Mary II and younger daughter of James II.

Ceremonies, the greate men, Lord Mayor & Aldermen &c: crouding to kisse the Q: hands & felicitate her Accession to the Crown: ...

April <9> I being surprized with a Vertiginous Indisposition; I tooke a Vomite & afterward letting Blood, found much reliefe, thro Gods greate mercy: ...

12 This night is buried the Body of the Late King William the IIId in Westminster Abbey.

This night died my B. in Law Glanvill after a tedious sicknesse: in the 84th yeare of his Age; & Willed his Body to be wrapt in Leade, and carried downe to Greenewich, where it was put on board in a yaght, and Buried in the Sea, between Dover & Calais about Godwin-Sands: which was don the Tuesday or Wednesday after, which made much discourse; he having no relation at all to the Sea. He was a Gent. of an Antient family in Devonshire, Married my Sister Jane, who left one Son: & by his prudent parcimony much improved his fortune: Was a greate friend when he tooke a fancy, & as greate an Enemy when he tooke displeasure: Subject to greate passions, positive: well spoken, of good natural parts; of a governing Spirit where he was intimate, Apt to take Exception, not easily reconciled, of greate authority with my Bro: In person handsome, very Temperat: In his Judgement inclining to Socinianisme, upon which point we differing, he who till of late had much obliged me, on a suddaine withdrew his kindnesse to my greate prejudice. He died one of the <commissioners?> of the Alienation Office, & might have ben an extraordinary man, had he cultivated his parts: ...

26 ... My Wife going to Wotton for a few days, to se<e> what the Workemen had don in repairing the house not yet finish'd: & my steward came up with his Accompt I adjusted all the particulars, finding them very faire: & his Trust honestly m<anaged>, amounting to 1900 pounds ...

May not having the benefit of natural evacuation for severall days, I was very ill, & feavorish, but by Gods mercy relieved, I began to be more at Ease, [3] so as I was able to go to Church this After noone ...

June 27 I went to Wotton with my Family for the rest of the Summer, whether came my Son-in law Draper with his family to stay with us, his house at Adscome being New Building, so as my famely was now above 30 ...

December 30 ... After: <th>e excesse of honors conferred by the Queene on the E. of Marborow, to make him a knight of the Garter, & Duke for the successe of but one Campagne, <that> he should desire 5000 pounds a yeare out of the Post-office to be settled on him was by the parliament thought a bold & unadvised request, who had besides his owne considerable Estate, above 30000 pounds per Ann in places & Employments, with 50000 pounds at Interest: His Wife also (whose originall & his every body knew, & by what merit become such favorite, for his sister was a Miss to K. James the 2d when Duke of York, his Father but a cleark of the Green-Cloth, ingrossing all that stirred & was profitable at Court: But thus they married their daughter 1 to the Sonn of my L.Tress: Godolphin, another to the E. of Sunderland, 3. to the E. of Bridge-Water:) Thus suddainly rising was taken notice of & displeased those who had him til now in greate esteeme: He is indeed a very handsom proper well spoken, & affable person, & supplys his want of acquired knowledge by keeping good Company: In the meane time Ambition & love of riches has no End:

1703

February 28 ... The duke of Marborow after all his prosperity riches & glory; lost his onely son, who died at Cambridge of the small pox, to the unexpressable sorrow of that family:[1]...

March The 8th of this moneth, going out to Brompton parke to take the aire after my late Indisposition In walking in one of the Alleys, I hapned to stumble on a short stake left in the ground, which breaking my shin, kept me <in> greate paine, as yet it dos, remaining unhealed: & denying me to go to church this [14] being the 5t Sonday in Lent, to my grate sorrow: I beseech God to be mercifull to & heale me: ...

April 11 I came downe out of my Confinement in my Bed & Chamber my leg being in a faire way of cure: It was still most gentle & seasonable weather: There was no Considerable news either from abroad [or at home.] ...

May 14 We came safe with our Family from Dover street to Wotton, ferying over by Lambeth, where I went to talke with my L. of Cant concerning suffrage for a Chaplaine of the Bishop of Norwich to be next Lecturer for Mr. Boyles sermons.

I call'd in also at Clappham to visite Mr. Pepys now <l>anguishing with small hope of recovery which much affected me ...

26 This <day> dyed Mr. Sam: Pepys, a very worthy, Industrious & curious person, none in England exceeding him in the Knowledge of the Navy, in which he had passed thro all the most Considerable Offices, Clerk of the Acts, & Secretary to the Admiralty, all which he performed with greate Integrity: when K: James the 2d went out of England he layed down his Office, & would serve no more: But withdrawing himselfe from all publique Affairs, lived at Clapham with his partner (formerly his Cleark) Mr. Hewer, in a very noble House & sweete place, where he injoyned the fruit of his labours in g<r>eate prosperity, was universaly beloved, Hospitable, Generous, Learned in many things, skill'd in Musick, a very great Cherisher of Learned men, of whom he had the Conversation. His Library & other Collections of Curiositys was one of the most Considerable; The models of Ships especialy &c. Beside what he boldly published of an Account of the Navy, as he found & left it, He had for divers years under his hand the *History of the Navy*, or, *Navalia* (as he call'd it) but how far advanced & what will follow of his, is left I suppose to his sisters son Mr. Jackson, a young Gent: whom his Unkle had educated in all sorts of usefull learning, Travell abroad, returning with extraordinary Accomplishments, & worth to be his Heire: Mr. Pepys had ben for neere 40 years, so my particular Friend, that he now sent me Compleat Mourning: desiring me to be one to hold up the Pall, at his magnificent Obsequies; but my present Indisposition, hindred me from doing him this last Office:...

July 11 I had this week a severe fit or two of a quartan Ague, the 2d so sharp, as I was neere Expiring, but it ended in greate sweats, & suddaine breaking-out of my face, with a sore Eye: <But> by Gods mercy, I was so well recovered, that a few days after, I adventured to go [in Coach] as far as Adscome, 16 miles from Wotton, to see my Son-in Laws new house, the

---

[1] The title passed to his daughter Henrietta, see above 3 September 1678.

Outsides to the Covering being so excellent Brickwork, Based with Portland stone with the Pillasters, Windows & Contrivement within, that I pronounce it, in all the good points of good & solid Architecture, to be one of the very best Gent: Houses in all Surry, when finished, to which God give a Blessing:[1] ...

18 My late severe Conflict, lasting me on Saturday the <10th> past, that I could not go to Church the next day: When the Doctor preached on 27 Pro.23 Concerning the pride & Luxury of Apparell, which could be applyed to none save my Wife & Daughter, there being none in all the parish else, but meane people, who [had no] more than sufficient to cloth them meanely enough &c upon which I told the Doctor that I conceived the sermon had ben more proper to St. James's or some other of the Theatrical Churches in Lond, where the Ladys & Women were so richly & wantonly dressed & full of Jewells: But this reproofe was taken so very ill of the Doctor, that falling into a very furious passion, he hardly spake to me of some days, but preach'd the very same Sermon this day: which was indeed very learned, & fit for a Gallant Congregation; but by no meanes with our poore Country people: Both my Wife & Children having no sort of habits <but> what was universaly worne by the ordinary persons of their Condition; besides the sobriety & regularity of my owne domestick<s>: He now began to make a shuffling apology for his vehement discourse, that he meant it as one of the national sinns, <we> were to aske God pardon for & reforme, predicting greate Judgements otherwise to succeede it: But all this while sayed not a Word of the pride of the Clergy, their long powdered Perruks, silke Casso<c>ks, Covetousnesse, suppression of those passions they themselves preach against: In the Afternoone he Catechized very well, concerning the duty of Parents &c ...

August 10 I let out 4 ounces of Blood, which was perhaps too much at my greate Age, to try if it would help me, hithertoo tormented with the Hæmerrhoids: it was very faulty blood, much serum, & I had that Evening no reliefe, but at night a kind of Aguish fit: The next day easier & on the next Sonday, I was able to go to Evening prayer: God be praised:

12 The new Commission for the proceeding in the R. Hospital at Greenwich was now sealed & open'd [at Windsor] at which was my Son Draper present, to whom I resign'd my office of Treasurer, During which from Anno 1696: was expended in Building &c: 89364:14:8:¼.

November 26 The dismall Effects of the Hurecan & Tempest of Wind,[2] raine & lightning thro all the nation, especial<y> London, many houses demolished, many people killed:

[27] & as to my owne losse, the subversion of Woods & Timber both left for Ornament, and Valuable materiall thro my whole Estate, & about my house, the Woods crowning the Garden Mount, & growing along the Park meadow; the damage to my owne dwelling, & Tennants farmes & Outhouses, is most Tragicall: not to be paralleled with any thing hapning in our Age <or> in any history almost, I am not able to describe, but submitt to the Almight<y> pleasure of God, with accknowledgement of his Justice for our National sinns, & my owne, who yet have not suffered as I deserved to: Every moment like Jobs Messengers, bring<s> the sad Tidings of this universal Judgement:..

---

[1] Sold to the East India Company in 1809, and demolished in 1863.

[2] 'The Losses and dreadful Stories of this Ruin were indeed great, but how much greater the Universal Devastation through the Kingdom!' *Silva*, 1706, 341.

28 The apprehension of catching cold that might stop the bleeding of my hæmeroids, til now exceedingly afflict me, I was advise<d> not to expose my selfe to the aire this Sonday being the first of Advent: ...

December 7 I remov'd with my family to Dover streete, saw the lamentable destruction of Houses & Trees thro all the Journey: & observed it had least injured those trees &c which grew in plaine exposed & perflatil grounds & places; but did most execution where it was pent in by the Villages & among the bottoms of hills:

I thank God I found all well at my house in Lond: But both house, Trees, Garden &c at Says-Court suffered very much: ...

1704

March The beginning of this moneth I was so Indisposed with Obstructions in my bowells, not having had the benefit of Evacuation for severall days, that in my life I never suffered more torment, till after some Remedys it was removed & I restored againe for which God be Eternaly praised: So as after a Weeke I was alowed to take the aire: ...

June 18 ... Dr. Bathurst Pres: of Trinity in Ox: (I think the oldest acquaintance now left me in all the wor<l>d), at 86 years age, both start blind, deafe, & memory lost, tho a person of admirable parts & learning no<w> dying, was a serious alarm to me; God of his mercy grant that I may profit by it: He builded a very handsom Chapell to that College & his owne Tomb. Gave a legacy of mony, & the 3d part of his library to Dr. Bohune, [his nephew] who now went hence to his funerall ...

September 7. This day was celebrated preached the Thanksgiving for the late great Victory[1] with the uttmost pomp & splendor by the Queene, Court, greate officers, Lord Major, Sheriffs, Companys &c the streets scaffolded from Temple-barr (where the L.M<a>yor presented her Majestie with the Sword, which she returned), every Company ranged under their Banners, & Citty Militia with out the rails, which were all hung with Cloth suitable to the Colour of the Banner, the L.Major, sherifs & Aldermen in their Scarlet roobs on their Caparisoned Horses: The knight Martiall & pensioners on horse, the Footguard: The Queene in a rich Coach with 8 Horse, none with her but the Dutchesse of Marlbrow, in a very plaine garment, The Q: full of Jewells, Musique & Trumpet<s>, at every Citty Company: The greate officers of the Crown & nobillity & Bishops all in Coach of 6. Horses, besides innumerable Spectators in this order went to S. Paules where the Deane preached &c after which the Queene went back in the same order to St. James: The Citty & Companys, feasting all the Nobillity & Bonfires and Illuminations at night: Note that there was Musick composed by the best Masters of that art, to accompany the Church musique & Anthems &c to all which (after a<n> exceeding wet & stormy day) succeeded one of the most serene & Calmest bright-day<s>, as had ben all the yeare:

---

[1] The Battle of Blenheim, 13 August 1704, also known as Hockstet (Höchstädt).

November 13 My Wife went from Wotton to Lond, to be at the Labour of our Daughter Draper ...

December 3. My little Grandaughter [at London] Christened Evelyn at the desire of the Father & mother: my Grandson being the Godfather:[1] ...

1705

February 9 I went to waite on my L.Tressurer where was the Victorious Duke of Marlborow, who came to me & tooke me by the hand with extraordinary familiarity & Civility, as formerly he was used to doe without any alteration of his good nature. He had a most rich George in a Sardonix set with Diamond of an inestimable Value: for the rest very plaine: I had not seene him in 2 yeares & believed he had forgotten me:

April 9 I went [with my Gr:Son] for a few days to Wotton, returned the 14th, found my Wife had ben very ill in my absence of her old Cough: I myselfe much in paine by the Gravell, yet on: ...

22 ... I after many moneth<s> indisposition, since I came to Towne: went to the meeting of the R.Society, where among other things there was a picture of one of the Electoral princes, Guards, a young fellow, who was 8 foote ½ in height, don by the person himselfe, in his livery-habite, with a huge broad-Sword by his side, studdied with gilt plate; sent to a Member of the Society out of Germany: – I also saw Sir Isaac Newtons (now made knight at the Queenes entertaining at Oxon) the burning Glasse which dos such wonders as that of the K. of France which cost so much, dos not come-neere, it penetrating Cast Iron of all Thicknesse, vitrifies Brick, mealts all sorts of mettals in a moment: That of the French kings, made I think at Lions, being all of one piece of Mettal, & of a vast circumference, this made of 6 Concave Glasses not above a foote diameter; so plac'd about the middle Concave, that they prict their illuminated points all at once into the middle Concave focus where the rays meete & produce this Effect ...

June 17 I went to the R:Society, where were Tryals with Sir E Newtons Burning-glasse: which did strange things as to mealting whatever was held to it in a moment: one of the most difficult was common Slate, which lasted longer than Iron, Gold, brasse, Silver, flint, brick &c which it immediatly mealted, calcined & Vitrified: The Glasse was composed of 7 round burning glasses of about a foote diameter, so placed in a frame, as to cause all their Sun-beams to meete in one focus onely: ...

---

[1] Evelyn (1704-54), later wife of Colonel Charles Clarke of Oakley, now Ockley, was the only one of the Drapers' seven (at least) children to produce descendants of the diarist. She and her sister Susannah (1701-72; see 11 May 1701), were buried at Wotton Church immediately outside the Evelyn chapel, adjacent to the diarist's tomb inside. Her epitaph reads: 'EVELYN, Wife of CHARLES CLARKE of OAKLEY in the County of SURREY Esq[r]. Daughter of WILLIAM DRAPER of ADSCOMB PLACE in the County of Surrey Esq[r] and SUSANNAH his Wife, Daughter & only surviving Child of JOHN EVELYN of WOOTTON PLACE. Died August 24th 1754.'

I went to Greenewich with my Wife, daughter, Gr Son, Mrs. Boscawen, & her daughter, then proposed as a Wife for him &c: To see the Hospital, which now began to take in wounded & emerited Sea-men, who were exceeding well provided for, the Buildings now going on very magnificent; dined at my servant, J. Strickland, & Returning visited Mr. Cresset my Tennant at Says Court: This by water: ...

July My L Treasurer made my Gr-son one of the Commissioners of the prizes, the sallary 500 pounds per Annum: Greate drowth – ...

8 ... My Gr:son went this morning with Sir Sim: Harcourt the Solicitor Gen to Windsor to waite <on> my L.Treasurer, to whom I wrote to excuse my not being able to waite on him my selfe <&c:>

There having for some time ben a proposal of Marying my Gr-Son to a daughter of Mrs. Bosca<wen> Sister of my Lord Treasurer now far advanced: ...

14 I had this night a very severe fitt of [cold] Trembling, & heate after, with very greate pa<ine in my> sides & backe & all over my Body, all symptoms of the stone: yet I crept to church ...

29 ... The Marriage Settlement of my Gr:son with a Daughter of Mrs. Boscawen, sister to my L.Treasurer, now finished, stays onely for the comming back of Sir Sym: Harcourt to examine the deeds & seale: he being yet in the Circuit:

August 23 Mr. Solicitor being returned from the Judges Circuit: was finished my Gr:sons marriage settlement, & given to be Ingrossed, giving him my Intire Estate, reserving onely the possession of it during my life, and the absolute disposure of the personal Estate, to be disposed of by my Will: &c: The lease of the House, & intire furniture of my house at London I give absolutely to my deare Wife: ...

September 2. I was in excessive paine, no remedys working with me, by reason of a stopping in my Bowels, by being 6 days without Evacuation, in which Torment I continued two days, but was the next so relieved, that I was able to go take the aire, as far as Kensington, where I saw that House, [furniture] & the plantation about it, to my great admiration and Refreshment: It is a very noble Villa, the Gardens & Contrivances the worke of Mr. Wise, who was ther on purpose to receive me, & so returned I blesse God with much Ease & Refreshment &c:

6: Were Sealed the Writings &c. by which I settled my Estate on my Grandson, in order to his Marriage with Ann, Daughter to Mrs. Boscawen, sister to my L:Godolphin, L.High Treasurer of England: ...

18 [Tuesday] my Gr:Son was Married by the Arch-Bishop of Cant: in Lambeth Chapell: to Ann, Daughter to Mrs. Boscawen, sister to the L.Godolphin, L.High Treasurer: – And, with aboundance of Relations on both sides, most magnificently Entertained with supper that night, by her Mother:

Most of the rest of this Weeke spent in receiving Visites of greate persons ...

26. We invited as many of the Re<l>ations of Mrs. Boscawen and of my L.Treasurer as were in Towne [&c.], to the number of 18 to Dinner, which was as greate as the solem<n>ity of Marriage of my Grandson &c required: ...

December 9 ... An extraordinary wett-season & darke, severall Coaches & Travellers drowned, Greate Innundations also in Italy &c: The small-pox tooke this Weeke away, Ed: Boscawen, a Brother of my Grandaughters, in the

prime of his youth, just as an Estate fell-to him: To the great griefe of his
Disconsolate Mother & Family, there being onely his Elder Bro: remaining, a
Gent of an Antient Family in Cornwall, & greate Estate: There also died the
Lady Stonehouse, my Daughter in Laws, Mother, She died of a malignant
feavor, at her son in Laws, Sir Simon Harcourt, Sollicitor Gen, <so> as all 3
familys were going into Mourning:

1706

January 1 Making up my Accompts for the past yeare, payed Wages, [Bills],
New years Gifts according to Custome, &c: Tho much Indisposed, & in so
advanced an Age I went to our Chapell to give God publique Thanks:
Beseeching Almighty God, to assist me with his Mercy & protection to me &
my Family the Ensuing yeare, if he should yet Continue my Pilgrimage here,
& bring me at last to a better life with him in his heavenly Kingdom.

Divers of our Friends & Relations dined with us this day.

6 Epiphany Exceedingly Indispos'd: I could not go to church, which I
believe in very many yeares I have not omitted: And this whole Weeke, I had
3 fits of a shaking-fit, and feavor, with greate paines in the Kidneys, which
much afflicted me: – Some Snow & sharp dayes:

13 I got to church in the Afternoone, but was exceeding drowsy: ...

House of Comm, settling the Regency, in Case of the Q. death; & about
<admit>ting no officers Members in the future Elections.

I was much Indisposed most of this weeke: ...

27 The Raine and a Thaw upon a deepe Snow, hindred me from going to
Church.

My Infirmitys increasing, I was exceeding ill this whole weeke ...

February 3. A stranger at our Chapell on 19 Levit: 17, the necessity of
warning a Brother or Christian, & method of Admonition, when we find any
go astray or do amisse, with the Rules to be observed, according to the danger
and natur of the fault &c.

Afternoon a Scotchman, on Let every one that names the L.Jesus depart
from Evill, & increase in love of that profession.[1]

---

[1] At this point the *Kalendarium* or *Diary* ends. With the weather so bad it seems that
E decided to leave Wotton and return to London for the rest of the winter. He died on
the 27 February 1706 at 14 Dover Street, London. Most of his friends and
contemporaries were already dead, as were seven of his eight children and the
majority of his grandchildren. He was interred in the Evelyn chapel at Wotton Church
on the 4 March following. Mary Evelyn followed him three years later. Both were
placed in lead coffins enclosed in stone sarcophagi on the floor of the chapel. On the
cover stone of each were carved their epitaphs (see page opposite). They remained
undisturbed until 1992 when for reasons and by people unknown their graves were
desecrated and their skulls stolen.

EVELYN FAMILY EPITAPHS

I. WOTTON CHURCH

John Evelyn (1620-1706)

Here lies the Body of JOHN EVELYN Esq of this place second Son of RICHARD EVELYN Esq who having serv'd ye Publick in several employments of which that of Comissioner of ye Privy Seal in ye Reign of K. James ye 2^d. was most Honourable: & perpetuated his fame by far more lasting Monuments than those of Stone, or Brass: his Learned & usefull works fell asleep ye 27th day of February 1705/6 being ye 86th Year of his age in full hope of a glorious resurrection thro faith in Jesus Christ. Living in an age of extraordinary events, & revolutions he learnt (as himself asserted) this truth which pursuant to his intention is here declared. That all is vanity wch is not honest & that there's no solid Wisdom but in real piety.

Of five Sons, & three Daughters borne to him from his most vertuous, & excellent Wife MARY sole daughter, & heiress of S^r. RICH^D. BROWNE of Sayes Court near Deptford in Kent onely one daughter SUSANNA married to WILL^M DRAPER Esq, of Adscomb in this County surviv'd him ye two others dying in ye flower of their age, & all ye Sons very young except one nam'd JOHN who deceas'd ye 24th of March 1698/9 in ye 45th. year of his age, leaving one son JOHN & one daughter ELIZABETH.

Mary Evelyn (c.1635-1709)

MARY EVELYN, the best Daughter, Wife, and Mother, the most accomplish'd of Women, belov'd, esteem'd, admir'd, and regrett'd by all who knew her, is deposited in this stone coffin, according to her own desire, as near as could be to her dear Husband JOHN EVELYN, with whom she lived almost Threescore years, and surviv'd not quite three, dying at London, ye 9 of Feb. 1708/9, in ye 74th year of her age.

2. ST. NICHOLAS, DEPTFORD

Richard Evelyn, the diarist's eldest son (1652-58)

R. EVELYN, I.F. Quiescit hoc sub marmore, una quiescit quicquid est amabile, patres quod optent, aut quod orbi lugeant. Genas decentes non, ut ante risus lepore condit amplius. Morum venustas, quanta paucis contigit desideratur omnibus. Linguae Latina, Gallica, quas imbibit cum lacte materno, tacent. Tentarat artes, artium principiis pietatis elementa hauserat. Libris inhaesit improbo labore, ut sola mors divelleret. Quid indoles, quid disciplina, *quid labor possint, ab uno disceres. Puer stupendus qualis hic esset senex, si fata vitae subministrassent iter! Sed aliter est visum Deo. Correptus ille febricula levi iacet: Iacent tot una spes parentum. Vixit ANN V. M .V. III super D. Eheu! delicias breves. Quicquid placet mortale non placet diu, quicquid placet mortale ne placeat nimis.* (by Christopher Wase, see 27 January 1658) *

*Translation, N. Dews, 1884 (reprinted 1971), *History of Deptford*, 83:

Richard Evelyn, son of John, rests under this stone, and with him rests everything that father's love can cherish, and lament when deprived of. The fair face no longer as of old, bright with the smile of intelligence; the unusual grace of manner which few can attain, which all who knew him will miss; the simple talk in French or Latin languages which he took in with his mother's milk - all silent now. He had begun the study of the arts, and with the principles of the arts had learnt those of piety as well; and was so fond of his books that only death could tear him from them. His example showed how much natural quickness, discipline and labour, when united, could achieve. Marvellous as a child, what would he have been when old, had fate allowed him length of life! But God decreed otherwise. A slight fever carried him off after he had lived five years, five months, and a little over three days. He was the only child of his parents, and alas! how brief was their enjoyment! What mortals love, let them beware never to love too well!

Mary Evelyn, the diarist's eldest daughter (1665-85)

MARY EVELYN Eldest daughter of JOHN EVELYN and MARY his Wife, Borne the last day of Sept[br] 1665 att Wootton in the County of Surrey. A Beautifull young Woman, endowed with shining qualities Both of Body & Mind infinitly pious, the delight of her Parents & Friends. She dyed the 17 March 1685 at the Age of 19 years, 5 months, 17 dayes, regretted by all persons of worth that knew her value.

The texts for Richard and Mary are inscribed on the same stone at Deptford.

CHRONOLOGY

YEAR		EVELYN	HISTORICAL EVENTS
1620	Oct	Birth at Wotton, Surrey	
1625	Mar	E sent to Lewes	Accession of CHARLES I
1633	Nov	E's father made last Sheriff of Surrey and Sussex	
1635	Sep	Death of E's mother	
1637	May	Up to Balliol, Oxford	
1640	Apr	To Middle Temple	Short Parliament
	Oct		Long Parliament begins
	Dec	Death of E's father	
1641	May		Execution of Strafford
	July	Visits Low Countries	
	Oct	Returns to England	
1642	Aug		Civil War begins
1643	Oct	Leaves for France	
1644	Oct	Reaches Italy	
1645	Jun	Arrives in Venice	
1646	Mar	Leaves Venice	
	May	Switzerland and smallpox	
	Oct	Reaches Paris	
1647	Jun	Marries Mary Browne	
	Oct	Returns to England	
1649	Jan	*Liberty and Servitude* published	CHARLES I executed
	Jul	Returns to Paris	
1651	Feb	*State of France* published	
	Oct		Battle of Worcester
1652	Feb	Returns to England	First Dutch War (1652-4)
	Jun	Mary follows	
	Aug	Birth of Richard (i)	
1653	Feb	Purchase of Sayes Court, garden laid out	
	Oct	Birth of John Standsfield	
1654	Jan	Death of John Standsfield	
	Jun	Tours England with Mary	
	Dec	Richard (i) nearly chokes to death	
1655	Jan	Birth of John (JE junior)	
1656	May	*Essay on Lucretius* published	
1657	Jun	Birth of George	
1658	Jan	Death of Richard (i)	
	Feb	Death of George	
	Jun	Whale beached at Greenwich	
	Sep		Death of Cromwell
	Nov		Cromwell's funeral

YEAR		EVELYN	HISTORICAL EVENTS
1659		*Character of England* published	
	May		Long Parliament restored
	Nov	*Apologie for the Royal Party*	
1660	Feb		Monck marches on England
	April	*Late News from Brussels Unmasked*	
	May		Restoration of CHARLES II
	Oct		Execution of regicides
1661	Jan	E made councillor of Royal Society	
	Mar	Pr. Rupert shows Mezzo-tinto to E	
	Apr		Coronation of CHARLES II
	May	*Fumifugium* published	
	Nov	*Library Instructions* published	
	Dec	*Tyrannus* published	
1662		*Sculptura* published	
	Aug	Henrietta Maria visits Sayes Court	
1663	Apr	Charles II visits Sayes Court	
1664	Jan	Birth of Richard (ii)	
	Feb	*Sylva* published	
	Mar	Death of Richard (ii)	
	Oct	Becomes Commissioner for Sick and Wounded Sea-men & Prisoners of War *Parallel of Architecture* published	
1665	Jan	*Mystery of Jesuitism* published	
	Feb		Second Dutch War (1664-7)
	Jul	Visits fleet at Chatham	The Plague spreads
	Aug	Sends family to Wotton to avoid Plague	
	Oct	Birth of Mary	
1666	Mar	*Pernicious Consequences* published	
	Aug	Surveys Old St Pauls	
	Sep		Great Fire of London
1667	Jan	JE junior up to Oxford	
	Feb	*Publick employment* published	
	Jun		Dutch attack Chatham
	Sep	Birth of Elizabeth	
1668	Aug	*Perfection of Painting* published	
	Sep	Entertains Venetian Ambassador	
1669	Feb	*History of Impostors* published	
	May	Birth of Susanna	
	Jun	Takes Pepys to show brother Richard his kidney stone	
	Jul	Sheldonian encænia at Oxford	
1670	Mar	Death of brother Richard	
1671	Jan	Discovery of Grinling Gibbons	
	May	Councillor for Foreign Plantations	

YEAR		EVELYN	HISTORICAL EVENTS
1672	Apr		Third Dutch War (1672-4)
	Oct	Pact of friendship with Margaret Blagge	
1674	Aug	Suppression of *Navigation and Commerce*	
1675		*Terra: a Philosophical Discourse of Earth* published	
1676	Apr	E discovers M Blagge's marriage to Sidney Godolphin	
1678	Sep	Death of Mrs Godolphin	
	Oct		The Popish Plot
1679	Nov	Visits Pepys in the Tower	
1680	Feb	JE junior marries Martha Spencer	
	Dec		Trial of Stafford
1682	Jan	Discusses Chelsea Hospital with Stephen Fox	
	Mar	Birth of E's grandson John	
1685	Feb		Accession of JAMES II
	Mar	Death of Mary	
	Jun		Monmouth Rebellion
	Jul	Marriage of Elizabeth	
	Aug	Death of Elizabeth	
	Sep	Becomes Commissioner of the Privy Seal; visits Portsmouth with James II.	
1688	Mar		Bishops Revolt
	Nov		William of Orange invades
	Dec		James II flees to France
1689	Feb		Accession of WILLIAM III and MARY II
	Apr		James II in Ireland
1690	Jul		Battle of the Boyne
1691	May	Chelsea Hospital finished	
1692	Mar	JE junior made Commissioner for the Revenue and Treasury in Ireland	
1693	Apr	Susanna marries Will Draper	
1694	May	Leaves Sayes Court for Wotton	
	Jul		Bank of England founded
	Oct	Visits new St Pauls	
	Dec		Death of Mary II
1696	Jun	Greenwich Hospital begun	
1698	Jan	*Numismata* published	
	Feb	Peter the Great at Sayes Court	
1699	Feb	E's grandson up to Oxford	
	Mar	Death of JE junior, E takes over lease of JE junior's house in Dover St, London.	
	Oct	Death of brother George. E inherits Wotton *Acetaria* published	

YEAR		EVELYN	HISTORICAL EVENTS
1700	May	Final removal of goods from Sayes Court to Wotton	
	Nov	E's grandson contracts and survives smallpox	
1701	Jun		Hanoverian succession passed in Parliament
1702	Mar		Accession of ANNE
1703	May		Death of Pepys
	Nov		Hurricane devastates southern England
1705	Sep	E's grandson, marries Anne Boscawen	
1706	Feb	Death at Dover Street, London	

*** POSTHUMOUS EVENTS OF NOTE ***

1709	Feb	Death of Mrs Mary Evelyn
1713		E's grandson created Sir John Evelyn, Bart., (i)
1763		Death of Sir John Evelyn, Bart., (i)
1767		Death of Sir John Evelyn, Bart., (ii) the diarist's great-grandson
1812		Death of Sir Frederick Evelyn, Bart., (iii) the diarist's great-great-grandson
1817		Death of Lady Mary Evelyn, widow of above; Wotton estate devolved to John Evelyn, descended from the diarist's grandfather's first marriage. The present Evelyn family is descended from this line.
1818		*Memoirs of John Evelyn* published by William Bray
1825		*Miscellaneous Writings of John Evelyn* published by William Upcott
1847		*Life of Mrs Godolphin* published
1955		Definitive *Diary* text edited by E.S. de Beer published
1977/8		John Evelyn's Library sold at auction
1992		John and Mary Evelyn's graves desecrated at Wotton
1995		First annotated editions of some of Evelyn's major works published
1995		*Diary* and other Evelyn manuscripts acquired by the British Library

PRINCIPAL PERSONALITIES

ARLINGTON, Henry Bennet (1616-85), cr. Lord Arlington, 1663; cr. 1st Earl of Arlington, 1672; Secretary of State 1662-74; member of Cabal ministry; served as Lord Chamberlain 1674-85.

2 Jul 67; 10 Oct 71; 1 Aug 72; 18 Aug 73; 10 Oct 77

BERKELEY, Sir John (1607-78), cr. Baron Berkeley of Stratton, 1658; Lord Lieutenant of Ireland, 1670-72; ambassador to France, 1675-77.

23 Oct 75; 9 Nov 75; 12 Jun 77

BOHUNE, Ralph (c.1640-1716), E's son's tutor, later Rector of Wotton, 1701-16.

29 Jan 67; 5 Nov 82; 18 Jul 03

BOYLE, The Honourable Robert (1627-91), younger son of Richard Boyle, 1st Earl of Cork; natural philosopher, scientist and founding member of the Royal Society.

1 Sep 59; 25 Apr 61; 10 Jun 62; 25 Oct 64; 6 Jan 92

BROUNCKER, William (c. 1620-84), succeeded as 2nd Viscount Brouncker 1645, President of the Royal Society 1662-77.

29 Aug 62; 30 Nov 77

BROWNE, Sir Richard (1605-83), cr. baronet, 1649; E's father-in-law, Charles II's envoy to the French Court during the Interregnum.

27 Jun 47; 14 Oct 47 (note); 4 Jun 60; 12 & 19 Feb 83

BUCKINGHAM, George Villiers (1628-87), succeeded as 2nd Duke of Buckingham, 1628; member of Cabal ministry.

14 Dec 71; 18 Sep 76; 23 Jul 79

BURNET, Dr Gilbert (1643-1715), Bishop of Salisbury, 1689-1715.

12 Apr 81; 11 Apr 89

CARMARTHEN, Sir Thomas Osborne (1631-1712), succeeded to baronetcy, 1647; cr. Earl of Danby, 1674; cr. Marquess of Carmarthen, 1689; cr. Duke of Leeds, 1694; Treasurer of the Navy, 1671; Lord High Treasurer, 1673-79.

19 Jun 73; 16 Dec 78; 12 Feb 84

CARTERET, Sir George (c.1610-80), Treasurer of the Navy, 1660-67; Vice-Chamberlain of the Household, 1660-70; Naval Commissioner, 1673-79.

4 Nov 62; 12 Nov 69; 26 May 71

CASTLEMAINE, see CLEVELAND

CHARDIN [Jardine], Sir John (1643-1713), explorer and writer.

30 Aug 80; 27 Dec 83; 23 Feb 84; 6 Oct 87

CHARLES I (1600-49), reigned 1625-49.

19 Jul 41; 12 Jul 43; 10 Oct 47; 30 Jan 49; 30 Jan 71

CHARLES II (1630-85), reigned 1660-85.

18 Aug 49; 29 May 60; 4 Jun 60; 5 Jul 60; 17 Oct 60; 22 Apr 61; 8 May 61; 11 May 61; 20 Aug 62; 28 Oct 64; 26 Jan 65; 2 Mar 65; 5 Jun 65; 1 Mar 66; 6 Jun 66; 4 Sep 66; 11 Sep 66; 18 Oct 66; 13 Feb 69; 22 Mar 70; 22 Jul 70; 18 Aug 74; 1 Aug 79; 4 Oct 83; 17 Dec 84; 25 Jan 85; 4 Feb 85; 14 Feb 85

CHESTERFIELD, Philip Stanhope (1633-1713), succeeded as 2nd Earl of, 1656; Lord Justice in Eyre, 1679-85.

7 May 50; 15 Jul 69; 13 Sep 80

CLARENDON, Sir Edward Hyde (1609-74), cr. Baron Hyde, 1660; cr. 1st Earl of Clarendon, 1661; Lord Chancellor, 1660-67; dismissed and banished, 1667.

30 Jun 69; 31 Jul 72; 11 Aug 72; 16 Oct 72; 17 Jun 73; 9 Aug 74; 22 Dec 74; 16 May 75; 29 Jun 75; 9 Nov 75; 26 Apr 76; 3 May 76; 9 Oct 76; 31 Mar 77; 16 May 78; 3, 5, & 8 Sep 78; 16 Sep 78

GODOLPHIN, Sidney (1645-1712), cr. 1st Baron Godolphin, 1684; cr. 1st Earl of Godolphin, 1706; husband of Margaret Godolphin, 1675; his flexible loyalty led to his holding numerous offices under James II, William III and Anne; E's patron.
16 May 75; 14 Jan 79; 26 Sep 84; 17 Feb 95; 16 Jan 04

GRAFTON, Henry Fitzroy (1663-90), 1st Duke of 1675, Charles II's illegitimate son by the Duchess of Cleveland; Arlington's son-in-law, 1679.
6 Nov 79; 15 Dec 81; 20 Feb 86; 1 Aug 90

GUNNING, Dr Peter (1614-84), Bishop of Chichester, 1669-75; of Ely, 1675-84.
29 Mar 73; 20 Feb 76

GWYN, Eleanor [Nellie] (1650-87), actress; mistress of Charles II but never ennobled; mother of his son, Charles Beauclerk, Duke of St Albans (1670-1726).
1 Mar 71; 30 Mar 84; 6 Feb 85; 19 Jan 86

HOLDEN, Dr Richard (c. 1627-1702), Vicar of St Nicholas, Deptford, 1673-1702.
19 Feb 83; 16 Mar 85; 28 Aug 85; 30 Sep 94

HOOKE, Robert (1635-1703), scientist and founding member of the Royal Society.
1 Jul 63; 18 Jan 65; 7 Aug 65; 29 Oct 69; 21 Dec 71; 11 May 76; 20 Jun 82; 30 Jul 90

HOWARD, Mrs Elizabeth (unknown dates), in charge of Maids of Honour including her daughters Dorothy, afterwards Mrs Graham, and Ann, afterwards Lady de Sylvius, and their friend Margaret Blagge, afterwards Mrs Godolphin.
30 Jun 69; 8 Jul 75; 15 Jul 75.

JAMES II (1633-1701), reigned 1685-88.
13 Sep 49; 4 Jun 60; 16 Jan 60; 20 Apr 65; 1 Jul 65; 6 Sep 66; 27 Apr 79; 6 Jul 79; 12 May 84; 6 Feb 85; 10 Feb 85; 19 Feb 85; 23 Apr 85; 22 May 85; 3 Sep 85; 15 Sep 85ff; 15 Oct 85; 14 Oct 86; 2 Jun 87; 18 May 88; 10 Jun 85; 14 Oct 88; 1 Nov 88; 11 Nov 88; 16 and 18 Dec 88; 12 Apr 89; 13 Jul 90; 17 Apr 92; 15 Sep 01

JEFFREYS, Sir George (1645-89), knighted, 1677; cr. 1st Baron Jeffreys of Wem, 1685; Lord Chief Justice, 1682; tried Oates, 1685; Lord Chancellor, 1685-88; Commissioner of the Privy Seale, 1685; Chief Ecclesiastical Commissioner, 1686.
22 May 85; 31 Oct 85; 24 Dec 85; 26 Nov 86

KEN, Dr Thomas (1637-1711), Bishop of Bath and Wells, 1685-91; one of the Seven Bishops, 1688; opposed William and Mary.
15 Jul 85; 16 Sep 85; 10 Mar 87; 18 May 88; 15 Jan 89

LLOYD, Dr William (1627-1717), Bishop of St Asaph, 1680-92; Bishop of Lichfield and Coventry, 1692-1700; Bishop of Worcester, 1700-17.
18 May 88; 15 Jan 89; 11 Apr 89; 8 Mar 95

MARLBOROUGH, John Churchill (1650-1722), cr. 1st Duke of Marlborough, 1702; served under Charles II, James II, William III, and Anne; greatest victory at Blenheim, 1704.
24 Jan 92; 30 Dec 02; 28 Feb 03; 7 Sep 04; 9 Feb 05

MONMOUTH, James Scott (1649-85), Duke of Monmouth and Buccleugh, Charles II's illegitmate son by Mrs Lucy Barlow, née Walter (d. 1658); served under his father; banished, 1679; plotted against Charles II, 1682, banished again; challenged James II for the crown, 1685; defeated at Sedgemoor, and executed, 1685.

26 Aug 70; 28 Nov 79; 28 Jun 83; 23 Nov 83; 5 Dec 83; 5 and 8 Jul 85; 15 Sep 85

MORDAUNT, Elizabeth, née Carey (d. 1679), Viscountess Mordaunt.

7 May 74; 3 Sep 83

MORDAUNT, John (1627-75), cr. Baron Mordaunt of Reigate, and 1st Viscount of Avalon in Somerset, 1659; his children became E's wards.

23 Nov 66; 7 May 74; 11 Oct 81

NEEDHAM, Dr Jasper (c.1623-79), E's family physician.

27 Jan 58; 4 Nov 79

NORFOLK, Henry Howard (1628-84), succeeded as 6th Duke of Norfolk, 1677; E's friend, 'Mr Howard'.

4 May 63; 14 Jul 64; 9 Jan 67; 19 Sep 67; 18 Mar 69; 23 Aug 78; 9 May 83

NORFOLK, Henry Howard (1655-1701), Earl of Arundel 1677-84, succeeded as 7th Duke of Norfolk, 1684; supported William III, 1688; Privy Councillor, 1689.

18 Dec 84; 28 Mar 94

NORTHUMBERLAND, George Fitzroy (1665-1716), cr. Duke of Northumberland, 1683; Charles II's illegitimate son by the Duchess of Cleveland.

30 Mar 84; 23 Oct 84; 18 Dec 84; 29 Mar 86

OATES, Titus (1648-1705), perjurer; an hysterical anti-Catholic who created terror of the Popish Plot, 1678-80; tried for perjury, 1685; freed, 1689.

1 Oct 78; 24 Nov 78; 18 Jul 79; 2 Dec 80; 7 May 85; 16 and 22 May 85; 28 Apr 96

ORMONDE, James Butler (1610-88), succeeded as 12th Earl of Ormonde, 1633; cr. 1st Duke of Ormonde, 1682; Royalist general; Lord Lieutenant of Ireland, 1661-69, and, 1677-82; supported James II.

6 and 16 Jan 62; 24 Mar 75

OSSORY, Thomas Butler (1634-80), styled Earl of Ossory, 1642-80; eldest son of 1st Duke of Ormonde, whom he predeceased; naval commander.

7 May 50; 31 May 75; 4 Jan 78; 4 Dec 79; 26 Jul 80

PEPYS, Samuel (1633-1703), diarist, naval administrator, and close personal friend of E's from the 1660s on; charged in association with Popish Plot and imprisoned, 1679; Secretary of the Admiralty, 1673-70, and 1684-89.

10 Jun 69; 22 May 76; 4 Jun 79; 3 Jul 79; 28 Jan 82; 15 Sep 85; 2 Oct 85; 19 Apr 87; 25 May 88; 17 Jul 88; 27 Jan 89; 8 Jul 89; 7 Mar 90; 24 Jun 90; 30 Jul 90; 30 May 98; 23 Sep 00; 26 May 03

PETTY, Sir William (1623-87), political economist and inventor.

22 Dec 64; 24 Mar 75

PORTSMOUTH, Louise Rénee de Kéroualle [Quiervill] (1649-1734), cr. Duchess of Portsmouth, 1673; accompanied Charles II's sister Henrietta, Duchess of Orléans, to England in 1670 and became his mistress, 1671; mother of Charles Lennox, Duke of Richmond.

4 Nov 70; 9 Oct 71; 4 Oct 83; 24 Jan 82; 23 Oct 84; 6 Feb 85

RICHMOND, Charles Lennox (1672-1723), cr. Duke of Richmond and Lennox, 1675; Charles II's illegitimate son by the Duchess of Portsmouth.

30 Mar 84; 23 Oct 84

RUPERT, Prince (1619-82), Count Palatine of Rhine and Duke of Bavaria, Duke of Cumberland and Earl of Holderness. Charles II's cousin and a principal player during the Civil and Dutch Wars.

12 Nov 42; 13 Mar 61; 7 May 62; 1 Jul 65; 8 May 66; 29 Aug 70

SANCROFT, Dr William (1617-93), Dean of St Paul's, 1664-68; Archbishop of Canterbury, 1678-91.

27 Aug 66; 9 Jan 84; 12 May 86; 8 Jun 88; 19 Oct 88; 15 Jan 89; 22 Feb 89; 11 Jul 91

SANDWICH, Edward Montagu (or Mountagu) (1625-72), cr. 1st Earl of Sandwich, 1660; Parliamentary naval commander; transferred to Charles II, 1660; arranged Charles II's wedding to Catherine of Braganza, 1661; President of Council of Trade and Plantations, 1670; killed during Dutch War, 1672.

1 Jul 65; 17 Sep 65; 6 Jun 66; 26 May 71; 31 May 72; 7 Jun 72

SLINGSBY, Henry (1621-90), Master of the Mint; E's friend.

18 Jul 70; 20 Nov 79

STAFFORD, William Howard (1614-80), cr. 1st Viscount Stafford, 1640; youngest son of Thomas Howard, Earl of Arundel; accused by Oates of plotting Charles II's death, and executed, 1680.

18 Jun 70; 2 Dec 80ff; 29 Dec 80

SUNDERLAND, Anne Spencer, née Digby (1646-1716), Countess of Sunderland.

8 Oct 72; 23 Dec 75; 18 Nov 79; 16 May 81; 22 Oct 86; 15 Aug 88; 29 Oct 88

SUNDERLAND, Robert Spencer (1640-1702), succeeded as 2nd Earl of Sunderland, 1643; diplomat, professional turncoat and political opportunist; enthusiastic supporter of both James II and William III; Lord Chamberlain, 1697.

14 Jul 75; 3 Jul 76; 27 Aug 87; 29 Oct 88; 1 Dec 95

TENISON, Dr Thomas (1636-1715), supported Seven Bishops, 1688; Archdeacon of London, 1689-91; Bishop of Lincoln, 1691-94; Archbishop of Canterbury, 1694-1715; philanthropist and friend of E's.

13 Feb 84; 23 Feb 84; 30 Mar 84; 15 Jul 85; 25 May 88; 9 Dec 94; 6 Jul 95; 25 Oct 95; 29 Apr 99; 18 Sep 05

TILLOTSON, Dr John (1630-94), major preacher; Canon of St Paul's, 1675; Dean of St Paul's, 1689; Archbishop of Canterbury, 1691-94.

5 Nov 78; 11 Jul 91; 22 Nov 94

TURNER, Dr Francis (c. 1637-1700), Bishop of Rochester, 1683-84; Bishop of Ely, 1684-90; joined Seven Bishops, 1688, but supported James II otherwise.

18 May 88; 8 Jun 88; 15 Jan 89

WALKER, Obadiah (1616-99), intellectual Catholic; suspected during Popish Plot, 1678-80; active supporter of James II's policies.

5 and 12 May 86

WILKINS, Dr John (1614-72), warden of Wadham College, Oxford, 1648-59; founding member of the Royal Society, 1662; Bishop of Chester, 1668-72.

13 Jul 54; 12 Apr 56; 14 Nov 68

WREN, Sir Christopher (1632-1723), mathematician, astronomer, architect, and founding member of the Royal Society; charged with rebuilding London after 1666; President of the Royal Society, 1680-82; long-standing friend of E's.

10 and 13 Jul 54; 29 Jan 62; 25 Oct 64; 27 Aug 66; 9 Jul 69; 19 Feb 71; 17 Jun 69; 30 Aug 80; 5 May 81; 25 May 82; 4 and 30 Jun 96; 9 Jun 98

RULERS

ENGLAND: James I, 1603-25; Charles I, 1625-49; Commonwealth, 1649-53 & 1659-

60 (Protectorate, 1653-59); Charles II, 1660-85; James II, 1685-88; William & Mary, 1689-94; William III, 1694-1702; Anne, 1702-14

FRANCE: Louis XIII, 1610-43; Louis XIV, 1643-1715

THE EMPIRE: Ferdinand II, 1619-37; Ferdinand III, 1637-57; Leopold I, 1658-1705; Joseph I, 1705-11

SPAIN: Philip IV, 1621-65; Charles II, 1665-1700; Philip V, 1700-46; Archduke Charles of the Empire as the pretender Charles III from 1703

OFFICERS OF STATE

LORD CHAMBERLAIN: Sir Henry Bennet, Earl of Arlington, 1674-85.

LORD CHANCELLOR: Edward Hyde, Earl of Clarendon, 1660-67; Sir Anthony Ashley Cooper, Earl of Shaftesbury, 1672-73; Sir George Jeffreys, Baron Jeffreys of Wem, 1685-88; Sir John Somers, Baron Somers of Evesham, 1697-1700

LORD HIGH TREASURER: Thomas Wriothesley, Earl of Southampton, 1660-67; Sir Thomas Clifford, Baron Clifford of Chudleigh, 1672-73; Sir Thomas Osborne, Earl of Danby, 1673-79; Lawrence Hyde, Earl of Rochester, 1685-87; Sidney Godolphin, Baron Godolphin of Rialton, 1702-10

LORD KEEPER: Sir Francis North, Baron Guildford, 1682-85; John Somers, Baron Somers of Evesham, 1693-97

LORD LIEUTENANT OF IRELAND: James Butler, Earl of Ormonde, 1661-69; 1677-82; Sir John Berkeley, 1670-72; Henry Hyde, 2nd Earl of Clarendon, 1685-87

LORD PRESIDENT OF THE COUNCIL: Robert Spencer, Earl of Sunderland, 1685-88

LORD PRIVY SEALE: Henry Hyde, 2nd Earl of Clarendon, 1685

TREASURER OF THE HOUSEHOLD: Sir Thomas Clifford, 1668-72

VICE-CHAMBERLAIN OF THE HOUSEHOLD: Sir George Carteret, 1660-80

CHURCHMEN

ARCHBISHOP OF CANTERBURY: Dr William Laud, 1633-45; Dr William Juxon, 1660-63; Dr Gilbert Sheldon, 1663-77; Dr William Sancroft, 1678-91; Dr John Tillotson, 1691-94; Dr Thomas Tenison, 1694-1715

ARCHBISHOP OF YORK: Dr John Dolben, 1683-86

BISHOP OF BATH & WELLS: Dr Thomas Ken, 1685-91

BISHOP OF CHICHESTER: Dr Peter Gunning, 1669-75

BISHOP OF DURHAM: Dr John Cosin, 1660-72

BISHOP OF ELY: Dr Peter Gunning, 1675-84

BISHOP OF LINCOLN: Dr Thomas Tenison, 1691-94

BISHOP OF LONDON: Dr William Juxon, 1633-60; Dr Gilbert Sheldon, 1660-63; Dr Humphrey Henchman, 1663-75; Dr Henry Compton, 1675-1713

BISHOP OF ROCHESTER: Dr John Dolben, 1666-83; Dr Thomas Sprat, 1684-1713

BISHOP OF SALISBURY: Dr Gilbert Burnet, 1689-1715

BISHOP OF WINCHESTER: Dr George Morley, 1662-84

DEAN OF PETERBOROUGH: Dr John Cosin, 1640-60

RECTOR OF WOTTON: George Higham, 1612-58; John Higham, 1660-84; William Duncombe, 1684-99; Roger Wye, 1699-1701; Ralph Bohune, 1701-16

VICAR OF DEPTFORD: Thomas Malory, 1644-59; Robert Littler, 1659-61; Robert Breton, 1662-72; Richard Holden, 1673-1702

GLOSSARY

ACCEND: to kindle, ignite

AGUE: fever

ALCORAN: The Koran

AMAINE: in full strength

ANGEL GOLD: A gold coin first issued by Edward IV (1461-70) weighing 80 grains, valued at 6s 8d (33 pence)

ANNUS MIRABILIS: a wonderful year

ARCH-BOUTTEFEW: a particular specialist in causing trouble

BIELANS: bye-lanes, side alleys

BOLE: fine clay containing iron oxide

BROCATELL: use of silk or wool to imitate brocade, usually on furniture

CHIRURGEONS : surgeons

CLIMACTERICAL: a major turning point in one's life

COLLATION: a light meal

CONFRAGOSE: rough, fragmented

CONGÉE: a bow in deference

CONTIGNATION: joining of wooden boards

CORAM REGE: in the royal presence

DENISON: citizen

DIASCORDIUM: medicine from dried leaves

DISSENTERS: objecters to the beliefs or practices of the established Church

DROPSY: sickness involving swelling through fluid retention

ENSIFORME: in the shape of a sword

FAINE: forced, or obliged

FIFTH-MONARCHY: believers in the imminent Second Coming of Christ - (fifth of the five empires prophesised in the Book of Daniel)

GEORGE: Jewel or decoration in the form of a St. George's cross, part of the Garter insignia

GRAFT: raised area made of dug earth

GRIPINGS: a tight pain in the belly

HOUSSE: material covering the back half of a horse

INDENIZATION: to make a citizen

LAQUEY: a footman

LIMMER: a scoundrel

LIVER-GROWNE: enlarged liver

MANAGE: horse-training

MASSY: substantial, solid

MECHANICKS: believers in a 'mechanical', i.e. scientific explanation for nature

MEZZO TINTO: engraving technique producing white areas and half-tones

MOUNTEBANKE: charlatan

MULCTS: fine, as in a charge or levy

MUND: hand/palm used as a measure

MURRAIN: disease afflicting cattle

NAUPOGEUS: a ship-builder

OYER AND TERMINER: to hear and determine an offence

PEARCH: unit of measure equal to 5 metres (5½ yards)

PERFLATIL: an area exposed to winds

POMERIDIANO: an afternoon church service (i.e. *post-meridian*)

PRAEMUNIRE: legal device to deal with those who denied the ecclesiastical supremacy of the monarch

QUARTAN: every third day, see ague

REMORA: hindrance

RE INFECTA: with the job unfinished

RIANT: smiling, happy

SCORBUT: Scurvy

STREITLY: tightly, in the sense of having been drawn tightly

TALLÉ DOUCÉS: engravings

TERTIAN: every other day, *see* ague

TESTER: bed canopy

THEORB[E]: double-necked lute

THROUGH-STITCH: thoroughness of action in the manner of a stitch running right through the cloth

TICKE: mattress-casing

TUNNAGE & POUNDAGE: duty levied per ton and pound of goods

FURTHER READING

I. DIARY TEXTS

de Beer, E.S., 1955, *The Diary of John Evelyn*, six volumes, Oxford.

de Beer, E.S., 1959, *The Diary of John Evelyn*, Standard Authors Edition, Oxford University Press, London.

Bray, W., Ed., 1850-52, *Diary and Correspondence of John Evelyn, F.R.S.* (4 volumes). Numerous editions, for example G. Bell & Sons, London 1878. Text revised by William Upcott, and further editing by John Forster; the fourth version of the original 1818 Bray text with various reissues, including a single volume reprint for Routledge in 1906. Mainly useful for the 237 letters from and to Evelyn, the diary text is inaccurate, the letters less so but there is no other useful comprehensive source of these.

2. BIOGRAPHIES, BIBLIOGRAPHIES, AND OTHER WORKS

Bowle, J., 1983, *John Evelyn and his World. A Biography*, Routledge and Kegan Paul, London.

de la Bédoyère, G., 1995, *The Writings of John Evelyn*, Boydell and Brewer, Woodbridge (complete annotated texts of *Golden Book of St John Chrysostom, A Character of England, An Apologie for the Royal Party, The Late News or Message from Bruxels Unmasked, Fumifugium, Tyrannus, Sylva, London Redivivum*, and *Kalendarium Hortense*).

Hiscock, W.G., 1951, *John Evelyn and Mrs Godolphin*, Macmillan, London.

Hiscock, W.G., 1955, *John Evelyn and his Family Circle*, Routledge and Kegan Paul, London.

Keynes, G.L., 1937, *John Evelyn: a study in bibliophily & a bibliography of his writings*, Cambridge. Second edition Oxford 1968.

Upcott, W., 1825, *The Miscellaneous Writings of John Evelyn, Esq., F.R.S.*, London: Henry Colburn, New Burlington Street (contains the bulk of Evelyn's published writings with the principal exceptions of *Sylva* and *Numismata*).

Woolf, V., 1925, 'Rambling Round Evelyn' in *The Common Reader*, London.

3. BACKGROUND

Barber, R., 1982, *John Aubrey: Brief Lives*, The Boydell Press, Woodbridge. Contemporary descriptions of many of Evelyn's friends and associates, for example Boyle, Brouncker, Digby, Petty, and Wren.

Barker, F., and Jackson, P., 1990, *The History of London in Maps*, Barrie and Jenkins, London (contains many maps including E's plan for the post-Fire City).

Dews, N., 1884, reprinted 1971, *The History of Deptford*, Conway Maritime Press, Thamesmead Histories Volume III, Greenwich, London.

Fraser, A., 1993, *Charles II – His Life and Times*, Weidenfield and Nicholson, London. Includes numerous excellent illustrations of people and places of the period, many of whom and which are described by Evelyn.

Latham, R., and Matthews, W., Eds., 1970-83, *The Diary of Samuel Pepys, a new and complete transcription*, Bell and Hyman, London (a condensed text is available as *The Shorter Pepys*, 1985).

INDEX

This is a select index which concentrates on a small number of major personalities, such as the diarist, Charles II and James II, and major themes or subjects which characterise the content of the *Diary* text. Entries under each heading are usually listed chronologically and where Evelyn's choice of wording is especially distinctive I have provided a brief quotation to indicate the nature of the passage. The entries under Evelyn, John, *opinions of*, are especially revealing about the diarist's personality. Brief biographical details of other major personalities are given by name, above pp. 365-69 together with details of the most significant entries, and by office, above pp. 369-70.